FOUNDATIONS OF CRIMINAL JUSTICE

REPORT ON THE PRISONS AND REFORMATORIES

OF THE UNITED STATES AND CANADA

BY

ENOCH C. WINES and THEODORE W. DWIGHT

with a new introduction by

Martha Yourth Bouranel

AMS PRESS INC.
NEW YORK
LONDON   TORONTO
1973

FOUNDATIONS OF CRIMINAL JUSTICE

REPORT

ON THE

PRISONS AND REFORMATORIES

OF THE

UNITED STATES AND CANADA,

MADE TO THE

Legislature of New York, January, 1867.

BY

E. C. WINES, D. D. LL. D.,

AND

THEODORE W. DWIGHT, LL. D.,

COMMISSIONERS OF THE PRISON ASSOCIATION OF NEW YORK.

ALBANY:

VAN BENTHUYSEN & SONS' STEAM PRINTING HOUSE.

1867.

Library of Congress Cataloging in Publication Data

Wines, Enoch Cobb, 1806-1879.
   Report on the prisons and reformatories of the
United States and Canada.

   1. Prisons--United States. 2. Prisons--Canada.
3. Reformatories--United States. 4. Reformatories--
Canada. I. Dwight, Theodore William, 1822-1892, joint
author. II. New York (State). Legislature.
III. Title.
HV9471.W56 1973   365'.97   71-156036
ISBN 0-404-09138-5

Original size of this volume was 5 5/16 X 8 7/8
AMS edition is 5 1/2 X 8 1/2
Text size of this edition reduced 90%

Foundations of Criminal Justice Series, General
Editors: Richard H. Ward and Austin Fowler, John Jay
College of Criminal Justice

Reprinted from an original copy in the
collections of the New York Public Library

From the edition of 1867, Albany

Manufactured in the United States of America

An Early Exposé of Prison Failure

A Preface to the New Edition of

REPORT ON THE PRISONS AND
REFORMATORIES OF THE
UNITED STATES AND CANADA

Report on the Prisons and Reformatories of the United States and Canada was presented to the legislature of New York in January, 1867, by Enoch Cobb Wines and Theodore William Dwight. Dr. Wines appears to be the guiding spirit behind the report's inception and presentation, for one finds him to be a man of unusual intensity and sensitivity amidst the crusaders for prison reform.

Enoch Cobb Wines, born February 17, 1806 in Hanover, New Jersey, spent his childhood on a farm in Shoreham, Vermont, where he prepared to attend Middlebury College. Upon his graduation in 1827, until the late 1840s, Wines traveled about as an experimental educator. He became schoolmaster of midshipmen aboard the U.S.S. *Constellation* in 1829, an experience that provided the material for his *Two Years And A Half In the Navy*. Several years later, Enoch purchased a seminary in Princeton, New Jersey, and for the next seven years conducted this school on the pattern of the German gymnasia. Financial stress befell him in 1839, and he was led to try an instructorship at People's College in Philadelphia. Several years later, however, Wines purchased another classical school in Burlington, New Jersey, and this, too, failed to flourish. He then turned to the study of theology, producing his *Commentaries On The Laws of the Ancient Hebrews* (1853), in which he attempted to expose the Biblical origin of the essential principles of civil liberty and popular government. He became pastor of Congregational churches in Cornwall, Vermont, and East Hampton, Long Island, while he simultaneously chaired the department of ancient languages at Washington College, Pennsylvania. In 1859, Wines was appointed President of the newly founded City University of St. Louis, and it was there that he remained until the Civil War closed its doors in 1861.

Returning east, having reached his fifty-seventh year, Wines encountered the true work of his life by accepting the secretaryship of the Prison Association of New York in 1862 and by giving himself totally to the study and work of prison reform. Wines undertook his position with the Prison Association with tremendous enthusiasm, appealing energetically to local churches and city and state authorities to contribute generously to the Association. Upon his initial investigation of New York's state prisons, Wines revealed deplorable overcrowding and other unsatisfactory conditions, consequence of a politically unstable administration. He proposed that the Association undertake an extensive and comprehensive study of the problem in order to prepare a realistic and reasoned program for presentation at the forthcoming state constitutional convention. Thus, his appeals, talent, and energy made way for a tremendous program of investigation and recommendation — a program that would promote reform in the administration of criminal law and in the conduct of penal institutions throughout the world.

Wines' proposal and his adamant contention that "the result of these examinations has been a conviction that our whole prison system needs careful and judicious revision," led the New York Prison Association to appoint Wines and Theodore William Dwight to visit and consider the present organization of prisons and to assemble a reasoned plan for their reorganization to improve the system of criminal justice. While Wines contributed his talents to organize and his untiring motivation to reform and humanize, Dwight added his skill as an authority on the law.

Theodore William Dwight was born in Catskill, New York, on July 18, 1822. As a child, Dwight was an omnivorous reader possessing an exceptionally retentive memory, and at the age of fifteen he entered Hamilton College, graduating three years later with honors. For the next year, he studied physics and taught classics at Utica Academy, whereupon he decided to enter Yale Law School. But shortly thereafter, in 1842, he was appointed tutor at Hamilton College, and opted to remain there, initiating and conducting an informal class for instruction in law, rather than complete Yale Law School. In 1845 he was admiteed to the New York Bar and the following year appointed to the Maynard Professorship of Law, History, Civil Polity, and Political Ecnoomy at Hamilton. During his twelve years' tenure, he systematized and extended the law instruction courses and obtained approval for a department of law. In 1855, Hamilton Law School became incorporated and he became its head. Three years later, Columbia College, recognizing the need for a law school in New York, established the Columbia Law School and appointed Dwight as the professor of municipal law. For the next fourteen years Dwight conducted unassisted lectures on all facets of private law, justifying the claim that "he was himself the Columbia Law School." It was during this time, in 1866, that Dwight was appointed along with Wines to inspect the prison systems of New York State.

Thus, in 1866, Wines and Dwight visited and corresponded with all the prisons of eighteen northern states (none beyond the Mississippi) and the province of Canada, devising a series of interrogations to supplement their examinations into state prisons, county jails, houses of correction, juvenile reformatories, and the administration of criminal justice. This monumental effort, *Report on the Prisons and Reformatories of the United States and Canada*, which follows on these pages, was presented to the New York Legislature in 1867 in the belief that such an investigation "had become a felt want of the country and that it promises results. . . . "

Report on the Prisons and Reformatories of the United States and Canada exposes, in depth, the inequities and failures of the prison system as they existed then and, all too unfortunately, as many of them flourish today: the radical defect of making prisons a part of the political machinery of the state; the incarceration of youth with hardened, more experienced criminals; the lack of positive rehabilitation and reward and the overabundance of punishment and negativism; the deplorable conditions of overcrowding and inadequate ventilation; the unjustifiable contract system of prison labor, etc. Feeling that none of the prisons visited sought the reformation of its charges as a primary object, the report interjects among its factual and statistical data innumerable proposals to affect meaningful change among the prisons. In its dealings with juveniles, the report recommends the establishment of public nurseries for "abandoned children" as the earliest agency "in the prevention of crime in youth and manhood," and industrial schools of a family character. The recommendation is made for the creation of a nonpartisan board of commissioners whose terms should be staggered over a period of years in order to secure a permanent program of prison development. And within these pages, as if written yesterday, are the recommendations for hygienic reform, the use of reward and kindness, the need for screening of prison personnel, and the urging for educational programs, to name a few.

Although the state failed to adopt the necessary constitutional changes recommended in the report, this document and succeeding annual reports written by Wines gave impetus to a widespread movement of prison reform. Working with Franklin Benjamin Sanborn, Wines introduced America to the Irish-Crofton system of graded prisons and ticket-of-leave discharge, a system which led to the American systems of parole, indeterminate sentence, and young men's reformatories. Having stimulated the need for prison reform, Wines became the moving spirit behind the first national prison convention in 1870 – and the "Declaration of Principles" adopted by the Cincinnati Congress provided an adequate program for prison reformers for the remainder of the century. Wines was chosen secretary of The National Prison Association and remained its guiding spirit until his death in 1879.

Spurred on by his successes with the National Prison Association, yet disturbed by the need for international penal reform, Wines secured a joint resolution from Congress creating a United States Commissioner empowered to invite the countries of the world to an international congress on prison reform. He was appointed by President Grant as the U. S. Commissioner and went abroad in late 1871, representing the United States and Mexico, to study the prison methods of Europe and to arrange an international penitentiary congress which finally met in London on July 4, 1872. Through his untiring efforts of organization and motivation, twenty-six countries were represented and he was appointed chairman of this permanent international commission, which called a second congress in 1877 at Stockholm. Wines was appointed honorary president of this second international congress, his last appointment prior to his death. The following year he completed his final and most moving work, *The State of Prisons and of Child-Saving Institutions in the Civilized World*, having corrected the last proofs of this effort only hours before death overtook him in Cambridge, Massachusetts, on December 10, 1879.

Enoch Cobb Wines' contributions to prison reform, aided by Theodore W. Dwight, rank with the labors of John Howard, characterized as they are by sentiment and optimism. Howard agitated and campaigned against the same abuses as Wines and Dwight one century later, and now, over one hundred years after the report was published, one can read through it and realize that many of the same defects continue. The reprinting of this report will, one hopes, call the people to further reformation and enlighten them as to how far we have yet to go toward meaningful rehabilitation. Wines and Dwight accent a humanistic approach to penal reform coupled with realistic solutions to our failures at rehabilitation. No one can read through these pages and come away thinking there is little to do within the prisons.

Martha Yourth Bouranel
Burlington, Vermont

OFFICERS OF THE PRISON ASSOCIATION OF NEW YORK, 1867.

———◆◆———

State of New York.

No. 35.

IN ASSEMBLY,

January 8, 1867.

SPECIAL REPORT

ON THE PRISONS AND REFORMATORIES OF THE UNITED STATES AND CANADA.

Hon. E. L. PITTS, *Speaker of the Asssembly :*

Sir—We herewith transmit to you a Special Report on the Prisons and Reformatories of the United States and Canada, with the request that you will lay the same before the Legislature.

We have the honor to be,

Very respectfully,

Your obedient servants,

E. C. WINES,
THEO. W. DWIGHT, } *Commissioners.*

OFFICE OF THE PRISON ASSOCIATION, }
38 Bible House, N. Y., Jan. 8, 1867. }

CONTENTS.

———◆◆———

CHAPTER I.

SECTION FIRST.

SECTION SECOND.

X   CONTENTS.

SECTION NINTH.

[A 2]

SECTION FOURTEENTH.

SECTION FIFTEENTH.

CHAPTER II.

CHAPTER III.

CHAPTER IV.

Appendix.

REPORT.

INTRODUCTION.

It was under a deep feeling of responsibility that the undersigned, commissioners of the Prison Association of New York, undertook the duty assigned them; and it is under a no less solemn sense of responsibility that they now enter upon the task of embodying, in a report to be submitted to the Legislature of the State, the results of their observations and inquiries. Our instructions were, to visit and inspect the penal and correctional institutions of the states of our Union; to examine their prison systems; and to inquire into their administration of criminal justice. To facilitate the objects of our mission, in addition to the commission received from the President of the Association, we we were furnished with a circular letter from Gov. Fenton to the governors of the several states; and for the aid thus rendered—for such we found it—our thanks are due and cordially given to his Excellency.

It will be proper here to state the occasion of our appointment. Among its other functions, the Prison Assocation of New York is charged by law with the duty of seeking to improve the government and discipline of our prisons. To this end, it is charged with the further duty of annually visiting, inspecting and examining these institutions, and reporting their state and condition to the Legislature. In obedience to this injunction of law, all the prisons of the State have been repeatedly visited and reported on. The result of these examinations has been a conviction that our whole prison system needs careful and judicious revision. Under this conviction, a committee was appointed by the Association to consider the present organization of our prisons and to report a plan for their re-organization; that is, to prepare a comprehensive scheme for an improved prison system. It was at the instance of this committee, and because they desired the best lights attainable to guide them in their work, that the present commission was ordained, and the undersigned designated to compose it. By the terms of our appointment, there was no restriction to the field of our inquiries, other than the territorial limits of the United States. There was, indeed, a practical limitation, resulting as well from considerations of time and expense, as from a prudent discretion. No state beyond the Mississippi, except Missouri, was visited, and none of those lately in rebellion. But while the commissioners did not exhaust their full powers within the United States, they overstepped the letter of their authority by extending their inquiries to the prison system and some of the prisons of the neighboring province of Canada.

The states actually visited by the commissioners were: Connecticut, Delaware, Illinois, Indiana, Kentucky, Maine, Maryland, Massachusetts, Michigan, Missouri, New Hampshire, New Jersey, Ohio, Pennsylvania, Rhode Island, Vermont, West Virginia, and Wisconsin. Of these eighteen states, two, Delaware and West Virginia, have no state prisons, but confine their criminals, convicted of state prison offences, the former in the jail at New Castle, and the latter in that of the city of Wheeling. Of the remaining sixteen, two, Pennsylvania and Indiana, have each two state prisons; the rest each one. Five of the above states, Delaware, Indiana, New Jersey, Vermont, and West Virginia, had no reformatories at the time of our visit; but Vermont has since established one, New Jersey is about to do likewise, and Delaware is making efforts in the same direction. Of the other thirteen states visited, all have at least one reform school, Ohio has two, Pennsylvania three, and Massachusetts three. We inspected, more or less thoroughly, all the state prisons in the states visited, almost all the correctional institutions, and as many of the common jails, municipal prisons, workhouses, and houses of correction, as our time would permit. Of course, it was not possible to make an exhaustive personal examination of so large a number of prisons. Years, instead of months, would have been required for such a labor. Therefore, to supplement our personal observations, we prepared five distinct series of interrogatories on as many different branches of the general inquiry with which we were charged, viz: I. State Prisons. II. County Jails. III. Houses of Correction. IV. Juvenile Reformatories. V. The Administration of Criminal Justice. These interrogatories were drawn up with care, and were as exhaustive of the subjects to which they relate as we could make them.

As in none of the states is there any central authority, having charge of the county jails, and in none, except Massachusetts, any general system of houses of correction, or other prisons intermediate between the state prison and the common jail, but little use could be made of the questions relating to these two classes of prisons. The other series were committed to prison officers and other competent persons in the several states visited. No replies have been received in regard to state prisons from Delaware, Illinois, Maryland, New Jersey, West Virginia, the Eastern penitentiary, Pa., or that of southern Indiana. From fourteen prisons of this class, replies have been obtained, most of which are full and satisfactory, and must have cost their authors no little time and labor in their preparation. Answers have also been received, prepared with much care, from fourteen reformatories. Gentlemen of high legal ability and standing, in nine states, have responded to our interrogatories on the administration of criminal justice, sending us papers of very great value thereupon. A few answers have likewise been received relating to county jails and houses of correction, and a considerable number of private letters, from ladies as well as gentlemen, conveying valuable information and offering no less valuable suggestions touching the matters, in which all the friends of prison reform feel so deep an interest. To all who have thus aided us, at the cost of so much time and toil, we tender our heartfelt thanks, trusting that they will find their reward in the consciousness of having helped forward a work which will not prove wholly fruitless of influences favorable to the progress of a just and enlightened prison discipline.

In all the states visited, the commissioners sought opportunity to converse with governors, judges, attorneys general, and private citizens of eminence, on the matters to which their mission related. Everywhere we were warmly welcomed. Everywhere a lively interest was expressed in our object. Everywhere the present labor was regarded as having a national scope and importance. All this was gratifying to the commissioners, as indicating that the investigation in which we were engaged had become a felt want of the court , and that it promises results not confined to the state in wh. it originated, though she claims to be an "empire" in herself, but extending far beyond her boundaries, and indeed embracing the territorial limits of the whole United States.

We deem it proper, at this point, to indicate, somewhat more in detail, the sources, beyond the notes and memoranda of our personal observations, from which we have drawn the matter of the ensuing report.

I. PRINTED DOCUMENTS.

Of these we collected a very large number, which, having been bound, form the following volumes:

Vols. I.–IV.

Documents published by the legislature of Connecticut during the years 1862, 1863, 1864, and 1865, containing, among others, the Annual Reports of the State Prison at Weathersfield for those years.

Vol. V.

Annual Reports of the State Reform School of Connecticut for the years 1853 and 1854, and also for those of 1856–1865, inclusive. These Reports include the Act establishing the State Reform School, the Rules and Regulations for the government of the same, the Laws relating to the school, and the form of an indenture adopted by the trustees.

Vol. VI.

Annual Reports of the Board of Inspectors on the Canada Prisons, Reformatories, &c., for the years 1860, 1861, and 1862.

Vol. VII.

1. Preliminary Report of the Board of Inspectors of the Prisons, &c., of Canada (which should have been bound with the documents in the preceding Vol).

2. The Annual Reports on the same for 1863 and 1864.

3. Rules and Regulations for Common Jails.

4. Rules and Regulations for the Provincial Penitentiary.

5. A Glance at the Present State of the Common Jails of Canada. By E. A. Meredith, LL. D.

Vol. VIII.

1. Biennial Report on the Illinois State Penitentiary for the years 1857 and 1858, said report containing "Guards' Duty" and Rules and Regulations for the Government of the Illinois State Penitentiary.

2. Report of the Superintendent of the Illinois State Penitentiary for 1858.

3. Annual Reports of the Commissioners to locate and build an additional Penitentiary for the years 1857 and 1858 (First and Second).

4. Annual Reports on the Illinois State Penitentiary by the Commissioners, for the years 1859 and 1860 (Third and Fourth).

5. Biennial Report of the Warden of the Illinois State Penitentiary for the years 1859 and 1860, including the Reports of the Chaplain and Physician.

6. Annual Reports on the Illinois State Penitentiary, by the Commissioners, for the years 1861 and 1862 (Fifth and Sixth), including Chaplain's and Physician's Reports.

7. Annual Reports on the Illinois State Penitentiary, by the Commissioners, for the years 1863 and 1864 (Seventh and Eighth), including Chaplain's and Physician's Reports.

8. Copy of the Commutation Law of Illinois, approved Feb. 20, 1863.

9. Messages of Governor Yates to the Legislatures of 1863 and 1864, containing sections devoted to the State Penitentiary.

Vol. IX.

1. Annual Reports of the Chicago Reform School, from 1859 to 1865, inclusive.

2. Appendix to Fourth Report, under the title of A Consideration of the Cause·and Cure of Juvenile Crime, pp. 41–58.

3. Amendments to the law establishing the Chicago Reform School, approved February 13, 1863, appended to Ninth Report, pp. 41–46.

Vol. X.

1. Fifth Annual Report of the Board of Control of the Northern Indiana State Prison for the year 1864.

2. Eighteenth Annual Report of the Officers of the Southern Indiana State Prison for the year 1864.

3. Laws, Rules and General Regulations for the Government of the Indiana State Prison at Jeffersonville.

Vol. XI.

1. A Report on the History and Management of the Kentucky Penitentiary, from its origin, in 1798, to March 1, 1860. By Wm. C. Sneed, M. D., one of the Surgeons to the Kentucky Penitentiary. [To this volume are appended]

2. Report of the Keeper and Lessee of the Kentucky Penitentiary for 1864.

3. Ditto for 1865.

Vol. XII.

1. Report on the Maine State Prison for 1854, to which is appended a Report of a Committee of the Council appointed by the Governor to visit the State Prisons of New England.

2. Report on the Maine State Prison for 1863.

3.   do   do   do   1864.

4.   do   do   do   1865.

5. Rules to be observed by the Convicts of the Maine State Prison.

6. Report on the System of Disbursements, Labor and Discipline of the Maine State Prison, by the Hon. James G. Blaine, Commissioner appointed under a Legislative Resolve, approved March 27, 1858.

7. Annual Reports of the State Reform School of Maine for the years 1854–1865 inclusive, except the years 1859 and 1862, not furnished.

8. By-Laws for the Government and Regulation of the Maine State Reform School, to which are added the State Laws relating to the same.

Vol. XIII.

1. Annual Reports of the Maryland Penitentiary for the years 1857–1864.

2. Annual Reports on the Baltimore City Jail for the years 1861–1865.

3. Rules and Regulations of the Maryland Penitentiary.

Vol. XIV.

1. Annual Reports of the Baltimore House of Refuge for the years 1851–1865, except for 1852, not furnished.

2. A Memorial to the Legislature of Maryland, by the Managers, appended to their First Report (1851).

3. A History of the Baltimore House of Refuge, appended to the Fifth Report.

4. A Memorandum on Houses of Refuge in the United States, appended to same report.

Vols. XV and XVI.

1. Annual Reports on the Massachusetts State Prison for the years 1839–1865, except for 1842, 1843, 1846 and 1852, not furnished.

2. Annual Reports of the Massachusetts State Agency for aiding Discharged Convicts, for the year 1859–1864.

3. Rules and Regulations for the Government of the Massachusetts State Prison, approved by the Governor and Council, 1862.

4. Special Report on Prisons and Prison Discipline, by the Secretary of the Massachusetts Board of State Charities.

5. Catalogue of Books in the Library of the Massachusetts State Prison.

Vol. XVII.

1. Annual Reports of the Massachusetts State Reform School at Westborough, for the years 1857–1865.

2. Annual Reports of the Nautical Branch of the S. R. School for the years 1860–1865.

3. Message of Gov. N. P. Banks to the Legislature on the Destruction by Fire of the Buildings of the S. R. School at Westborough.

4. Sundry Communications to Gov. Banks from the Trustees and others in relation to the same.

5. Report of a Legislative Committee on the same subject.

6. An Act establishing the Nautical Branch of the State Reform School, 1859.

7. Legislative Resolves relating to said Nautical Branch.

8.   do   do   S. R. School.

9. By-Laws for the Government and Regulation of the S. R. School.

Vol. XVIII.

1. Annual Report of the Board of Directors for Public Institutions in Boston for the years 1858–1864. [These Institutions are the House of Correction, House of Industry, House of Reformation and Boston Lunatic Hospital.]

2. Rules and Regulations for the several Institutions of the City of Boston [those, to wit, above named].

3. Report of a Committee of the Common Council of Boston on Alleged Abuses at the Houses of Reformation and Correction, 1864.

4. Report of a Committee of the Board of Directors on the subject of a Piggery for the use of the City Swill, 1861.

5. Report of a Committee of same Board on the Supply of Butter and Milk for the Institutions under their charge, 1861.

6. Eleventh Annual Report of Rainsford Island Hospital, Boston Harbor, 1864.

Vol. XIX.

1. Annual Reports of the Massachusetts State Industrial School for Girls for the years 1856–1865, except that for 1857, not furnished.

2. A Memorandum on the Economy of Reformatories, with a Comprehensive View of European Preventive Institutious, appended to the First Annual Report of the Superintendent.

3. A Consideration of the Advantages of the Separate and Family over the United and Penitentiary System in Juvenile Reformatories, appended to the Third Annual Report of the Superintendent.

4. By-Laws for the Government and Regulation of the State Industrial School for Girls.

5. Form of a Circular Letter addressed to a Person to whom one of the Girls has been apprenticed.

6. Form of a Letter addressed to a Girl who has been apprenticed.

7. Letter to the Judges of Probate and the Commissioners under the Act establishing the Industrial School for Girls, in regard to the Persons proper to be committed to the said Institution.

Vol. XX.

Annual Reports of the Michigan State Prison for the years 1863, 1864 and 1865.

Vol. XXI.

1. Annual Reports of the Michigan State Reform School for the years 1860–1864.

2. By-Laws for the Mich. S. R. School, 1863.

3. Annual Reports of the Detroit House of Correction (Michigan) for the years 1862–1865, except that for 1864, not furnished.

4. Rules and Regulations of the Detroit House of Correction.

5. Report of a Special Committee of the Common Council of Detroit, appointed to inquire into alleged Abuses in the Management of the House of Correction.

Vol. XXII.

1. Two Biennial Reports of the Missouri Penitentiary, covering the History of the Prison for the years 1861, 1862, 1863 and 1864.

2. Annual Reports of the St. Louis (Mo.) House of Refuge for the years 1856, 1857, 1858, 1864 and 1865.

3. Act of Incorporation and Ordinances for the Establishment of a House of Refuge in the county of St. Louis, and Rules, Regulations and By-Laws for its Government.

4. Five Messages of the Mayor of St. Louis to the Common Council of that city, during the years 1863, 1864, and 1865, containing Reports on City Workhouse for said years.

Vol. XXIII.

1. Reports on the State Prison of New Jersey for the years 1842–1864, except those for 1843, 1846, 1847, 1848, 1850, 1855, and 1860, not furnished.

2. Rules of the N. J. State Prison, embodied in the Inspectors' Report for 1863, pp. 37–41.

3. Memorandum on Discharged Convicts, and the Duty of Society towards them, in same Report, pp. 41–43.

4. Report of the Inspectors of the N. J. State Prison, relative to a Reduction of the Expenses of that Institution, 1858.

5. Report of a Joint Committee of the Legislature of New Jersey on State Prison Accounts, recommending a change from the Separate to the Congregate System, with the Reasons therefor.

Vol. XXIV.

1. Annual Reports on the New Hampshire State Prison for the years, 1841, 1847, 1850, 1854, 1857, 1859, 1860, 1861, 1862, 1863 and 1865.

2. Rules and Regulations of the N. H. S. Prison, 1850.

3. Reports of the Vermont State Prison for the years 1854, 1864, and 1865.

Vol. XXV.

1. Annual Reports on the New Hampshire House of Reformation for the years 1856–1865.

2. Exercises at the Dedication of the N. H. House of Reformation, May 12, 1858, appended to the Report for 1859.

Vol. XXVI.

1. Annual Reports on the Ohio Penitentiary for the years 1850, 1861–1864.

2. Rules and Regulations for the same, appended to Report for 1863, pp. 96–102.

Vol. XXVII.

1. Annual Reports on the Cincinnati House of Refuge for the years 1851–1865, except that for 1862, not furnished.

2. Laws, Rules and Regulations relating to the same, 1861.

Vol. XXVIII.

1. Annual Reports on State Reform School, Lancaster, Ohio, for years 1858–1865, except that for 1860, not furnished.

2. By-Laws, Rules and Regulations for same, appended to Report for 1864, pp. 37–47.

Vol. XXIX.

1. Annual Reports on the Eastern Penitentiary, Pa., for the years 1831–1844, except that for 1834, not furnished.

2. Report of a committee of the Senate of Pennsylvania, on the Eastern Penitentiary and House of Refuge of the County of Philadelphia, 1837.

3. Two of the Laws passed by the Legislature of Pennsylvania relating to the Management of the Eastern Penitentiary, together with Rules passed by the Board of Inspectors for the Internal Government of the same, 1843.

Vol. XXX.

Annual Reports on Eastern Penitentiary for the years 1845–1854.

Vol. XXXI.

Annual Reports on Eastern Penitentiary for years 1855–1862.

Vol. XXXII.

1. Annual Reports on Eastern Penitentiary for ·1863 and 1864.

2. A Report on Reconvictions to the Eastern Penitentiary from the Admission of the first convict, Oct. 25, 1829, to April 25, 1863, embracing a period of thirty-three years and six months.

3. Separate Report on Second Convictions.

4.   do   Third   do

5.   do   Fourth   do

6.   do   Fifth and Sixth Convictions.

7. Tabular Statement of the Reception of Convicts during a period of thirteen years into the Eastern Penitentiary, classified according to their Crimes, Color, Sex, Age, Sentence, Parental, Conjugal, Educational, Moral and Industrial Relations, for each successive year from 1850 to 1862 inclusive.

8. Annual Reports of the Western Penitentiary, Pa., for the years 1862–1865.

9. Some notice of the County Jails and Alms-houses of Pennsylvania, by the Philadelphia Society for the Alleviation of the Miseries of Public Prisons.   1864.

10. Statement of the Government and Discipline of the New York State Prison at Sing Sing, by Robert Wiltse, Agent. 1834. (Bound by mistake in this volume.)

11. Report of the Commissioners of the Metropolitan Police of New York. 1864. (Bound in this volume by mistake.)

Vol. XXXIII.

Annual Reports on the Philadelphia House of Refuge for the years 1831–1843, except those for 1834, 1840 and 1841, not furnished.

Vol. XXXIV.

Annual Reports on same for the years 1844–1855, except that for 1852, not furnished.

Vol. XXXV.

1. Annual Reports on same for years 1857–1865.

2. By-Laws, Rules and Regulations for same.

3. Design and Advantages of the House of Refuge, with Acts of Incorporation. 1859.

Vol. XXXVI.

Annual Reports on the State Prison of Rhode Island for the years 1838, 1839, 1842, 1844–1848, 1850, 1851, 1857–1865.

Vol. XXXVII.

Annual Reports on the Providence Reform School for the years 1854–1865.

Vol. XXXVIII.

Annual Reports on the State Prison of Vermont for the years 1843, 1844, 1847–1860, 1864 and 1865.

Vol. XXXIX.

1. Duties of Prisoners in the State Prison of Wisconsin.

2. An Act relating to the Discipline of Convicts in the same. (Commutation Law.)

3. Annual Reports on the State Prison of Wisconsin for the years 1857–1865.

4. Annual Reports on the State Reform School of Wisconsin for the years 1860–1865, except that for 1862, not furnished.

5. Rules and Regulations for Government of same, embodied in the First Annual Report (1860), pp. 16, 17.

6. An Act for the Government and Management of the State Reform School, appended to the Second Annual Report (1861), pp. 24–27.

Vol. XL.

Sundry Papers on the Prison System of Pennsylvania, viz:

1. An Inquiry into the alleged Tendency of Separation of Convicts to produce Disease and Derangement. By a Citizen of Pennsylvania. 1849.

2. Report on Punishments and Prison Discipline, by the Commissioners to revise the Penal Code of Pennsylvania. Commissioners: Judge Shaler, Judge King and T. J. Wharton. 1828.

3. Remarks on Cellular Separation. By William Parker Foulke. 1861.

4. Remarks on the Penal System of Pennsylvania, particularly with reference to County Prisons. By William P. Foulke. 1855.

5. Considerations respecting the Policy of some recent Legislation in Pennsylvania. By Wm. P. Foulke. 1861.

Vol. XLI.

Sundry Papers on Juvenile Reformatories, viz:

1. Proceedings of the First Convention of Managers and Superintendents of Houses of Refuge and Reform Schools in the United States, held in the City of New York. 1857.

2. Proceedings of the Second Convention of Managers and Superintendents of Reform Schools, Houses of Refuge, &c., held in the City of New York. 1859.

3. Reports on the State Reform School of Connecticut for 1857–1862.

4. By-Laws for the Government and Regulation of the State Reform School of Connecticut, embodied in the Tenth Annual Report. 1862.

5. Thirteenth Annual Report of the Providence Reform School. 1863.

Vol. XLII.

[Some Papers, not collected by the commissioners, and therefore not properly belonging here, have been bound up in this and the three following volumes.]

Sundry Papers on Juvenile Criminals and Reformatories, and on the Irish Prison System:

1. Juvenile Criminals and a Plan for Saving them. By Edwin Wright. Boston: 1865.

2. Reformatories and what we know of them. By Alfred Aspland, Esq., F. R. C. S., Manchester, Eng. 1863.

3. Report of the Joint Committee to the Common Council, on

Juvenile Vices, Exposures and Wants in the City of Hartford. 1863.

4. Remarks of the Hon. C. C. Leigh, of New York, on the Bill Relative to Young Criminals, delivered in Assembly, March, 1855.

5. Memorial to the Legislature of New York, by the Society for the Reformation of Juvenile Delinquents, with an Abstract of a Report of a Committee appointed by the Society for the Prevention of Pauperism in the said city, on the subject of erecting a House of Refuge for Vagrant and Depraved Young People. 1824. To which are appended the three following documents:

A. A List of 450 Cases of Juvenile Offences and their Punishments, in the City of New York, for 1822.

B. Twenty-six Cases, extracted from London Reports, of Temporary Refuge to Juvenile Offenders, with their Results.

C. An Act to Incorporate the Society for the Reformation of Juvenile Delinquents in the City of New York. 1824.

6. Société pour le Patronage des Jeunes Libérés du Departement de la Seine. Paris: 1842.

7. Suggestions on the Management of Reformatories and Industrial Schools. By Mary Carpenter. London: 1864.

8. Observations on a Pamphlet recently published by the Rev. John Burt on the Irish Convict System. By Sir Walter Crofton, C. B. London: 1863.

9. The Present Aspect of the Convict Question. By Sir Walter Crofton, C. B. London: 1864.

10. Convict Systems and Transportation. By Sir Walter Crofton, C. B. London: 1863.

11. Reflections and Observations on the Present Condition of the Irish Convict System. By Baron Franz Von Holtzendorf, Professor of Law in the University of Berlin. Dublin: 1863.

Vol. XLIII.

1. Report on the State Prison at Auburn, made to the Legislature Jan. 7, 1828. By Gershom Powers, Agent and Keeper.

2. De la Mortalité et de la Folie, dans le Regime Pénitentiaire. Par L. M. Moreau Christophe, Inspecteur Général des Prisons de France. Paris: 1839.

3. Communication to Stephen Allen, Esq., Mayor of New York, from Thomas Eddy, with a Report on Tread Mills, by the London Society for the Improvement of Prison Discipline. New York: 1823.

4. Reports on the Stepping or Discipline Mill, at the New York Penitentiary : together with several Letters on the Subject. By the Mayor. New York: 1823.

5. Review of the Report of the Clinton State Prison. (No date).

6. Our Present Jail System deeply Depraving to the Prisoner, and a Positive Injury to the Community. Some Remedies Proposed. By Joseph Adshead, 1847.

7. Report of a Joint Special Committee of the Common Council of New York, on the Management of the Prisons on Blackwell's Island, 1849.

Vol. XLIV.

1. Report on the Penitentiary System in the United States, prepared under a resolution of the Society for the Prevention of Pauperism, in the City of New York. By Charles G. Haines, chairman of the committee.

2. Appendix to the above; containing Extracts from the Constitutions of the United States, and the several states, securing fair and impartial Trials to Persons accused of Crime; together with Letters in reply to a Circular addressed to them by the Committee from numerous Eminent Persons in all parts of the United States ; a Memorandum on Capital Punishments in England; Mr. Roscoe's Views on Capital Punishments; and a Report to the Senate of New York, by a committee of the same, on the Criminal Laws and Penal Administration of the State, 1822.

3. Special Report on Prisons and Prison Discipline, made under authority of the Board of State Charities. By the Secretary of the Board. Boston: 1865.

4. Observations on the Separate System of Discipline. By Sir Joshua Jebb, Surveyor-General of Prisons in Great Britain. London: 1847.

5. Sketch of the Principal Transactions of the Philadelphia Society for Alleviating the Miseries of Public Prisons, from its Origin to the Present Time. Philadelphia: 1859.

Vol. XLV.

1. Papers on the Penal Servitude Acts. By M. D. Hill, Recorder of Birmingham. London: 1864.

2. Newgate in Connecticut: A History of the Prison, &c., &c. To which is appended a Description of the State Prison at Weathersfield. By Richard H. Phelps. Hartford: 1844.

3. Report on the Comparative Health, Mortality, Length of Sentences, &c., by a Committee of the Philadelphia Prison Society, 1849.

4. A Report on Food and Diet, &c., suited to Almshouses, Prisons and Hospitals. By Hon. John Stanton Gould. New York: 1852.

5. Rules and Regulations for the Government and Discipline of the State Prisons of New York, 1857.

6. Presentment of the Grand Jury, at a Court of Oyer and Terminer, holden for the City and County of New York, in 1849, under Instructions from Judge Edmonds to make an Examination of the Prisons and other Institutions in this County, which are under the Direction of the City Authorities, 1849.

7. Rules and Regulations of the Essex County Jail, at Newark, N. J., 1857.

8. An Act to transfer the Charge of keeping the Jails and the Custody of the Prisoners in the Counties of Essex and Hudson, from the Sheriffs to the Boards of chosen Freeholders, and for the Employment of the Prisoners, and to regulate their Term of Service therein.

9. The Petting and Fretting of Female Convicts, 1863.

10. Annual Message of the Mayor of Cincinnati, containing Notices of the City Prisons, 1864.

11. Annual Report of the Chief of Police to the Mayor of Cincinnati, 1864.

12. Inaugural Address at the opening of the session 1863–64, of the Manchester Statistical Society. By A. Aspland, Esq. Manchester, 1863.

13. On American Prisons. By Alfred Aspland. Read before the Manchester Statistical Society, Dec. 14, 1864.

14. Report of the Joint Committee on Prisons, relative to the Condition and Management of Jails, to the Legislature of Connecticut. Hartford, 1865.

15. An Act concerning Prisons, proposed to the Legislature of Connecticut, 1865.

Vol. XLVI.

1. Annual Reports of William J. Mullen, Prison Agent of the Philadelphia County Prison, for the years 1854–1864.

2. Annual Report of the Inspectors of the Philadelphia County Prison, for the year 1864.

Vols. XLVII and XLVIII.

Revised Statutes of Kentucky.

Vols. XLIX, L and LI.

Laws of Indiana for the years 1861, 1862 and 1863.

Vol. LII.

General Statutes of Massachusetts.

Vol. LIII.

Supplement to General Statutes of Massachusetts.

Vol. LIV.

Revised Statutes of New Hampshire.

Vol. LV.

Laws of New Hampshire for 1860, 1861, 1864 and 1865.

Vol. LVI.

Statutes of Connecticut.

Vols. LVII and LVIII.

Compiled Laws of Michigan.

Vols. LIX and LX.

Revised Statutes of Rhode Island, and Supplement to ditto.

Vol. LXI.

Laws of Pennsylvania for 1860.

Vols. LXII and LXIII.

Revised Statutes of Missouri.

Vols. LXIV and LXV.

Revised Statutes of Ohio.

Vols. LXVI and LXVII.

Revised Statutes of Illinois.

Vols. LXVIII, LXIX and LXX.

Laws of Illinois for the years 1859–1863.

II. MANUSCRIPT DOCUMENTS.

Interrogatories on State Prisons :

1. Answers by William Willard, Warden of Connecticut State Prison.

2. Answers by Thomas Wood, Warden State Prison Northern Indiana.

3. Answers by the Rev. J. S. Hays, one of the Inspectors of the Kentucky Penitentiary.

4. Answers by Warren W. Rice, Warden Maine State Prison.

5. Answers by Gideon Haynes, Warden Massachusetts State Prison.

6. Answers by W. L. Seaton, Ex-Warden Mich. State Prison.

7. Answers by P. T. Miller, Ex-Warden Missouri Penitentiary.

8. Answers by Rev. Samuel Cooke, Chaplain N. H. State Prison.

9. Answers by John A. Prentice, Warden Ohio Penitentiary.

10. Answers by H. Campbell, Warden Western Penitentiary, Pa.

11. Answers by R. W. Blaisdell, Warden R. I. State Prison.

12. Answers by Rev. Malcolm Douglas, Chaplain Vermont State Prison.

13. Answers by H. Cordier, Esq., Commissioner Wisconsin State Prison.

[No answers were received from the wardens of the State prisons of Illinois, Southern Indiana, Maryland, New Jersey, and the Eastern Penitentiary, Pa., nor from the keepers of the jails in Delaware and West Virginia, in which State prisoners are confined.]

Interrogatories on Houses of Correction in Mass. :

14. Answers by F. B. Sanborn, Sec. Board of State Charities.

Interrogatories on the Detroit House of Correction :

15. Answers by Z. R. Brockway, Superintendent.

[The above are all the answers received on Houses of Correction.]

Interrogatories on County Jails :

16. Answers by F. B. Sanborn, Mass.

17. Answers by W. P. Crafton, Sheriff of Sangamon Co., Ill.

18. Answers by the Warden of Baltimore City Jail, Md.

[The above are all the answers received on county jails.]

Interrogatories on Juvenile Reformatories :

19. Answers by E. W. Hatch, Superintendent of the State Reform School of Connecticut.

20. Answers by George W. Perkins, Superintendent Chicago Reform School.

21. Answers by George B. Barrows, Superintendent State Reform School of Maine.

22. Answers by W. R. Lincoln, Sup't Baltimore House of Refuge.

23. Answers by Jos. A. Allen, Superintendent State Reform School of Massachusetts.

24. Answers by Richard Matthews, Superintendent Nautical Branch of State Reform School, Mass.

25. Answers by Rev. Marcus Ames, Superintendent and Chaplain Mass. State Industrial School for Girls.

26. Answers by C. B. Robinson, Superintendent State Reform School of Michigan.

27. Answers by H. S. Gleason, Superintendent St. Louis House of Refuge.

28. Answers by Abijah Watson, Superintendent Cincinnati House of Refuge.

29. Answers by Jesse K. McKeever, Superintendent Philadelphia House of Refuge—white department.

30. Answers by J. Hood Laverty, Superintendent Philadelphia House of Refuge—colored department.

31. Answers by James M. Talcott, Superintendent Providence Reform School, R. I.

32. Answers by Moses Barrett, Superintendent State Reform School, Wisconsin.

[There are no reformatories in Delaware, Indiana, New Jersey Vermont, West Virginia. That in Kentucky, near Louisville, had but just gone into operation. The only institutions of this kind visited, from whose superintendents no answers were received, were the Pittsburgh House of Refuge and the State Ref. School of New Hampshire.]

Interrogatories on the Administration of Criminal Justice :

33. Answers by Walter Pitkin, Esq., of Connecticut.

34. Answers by Hon. Conrad Baker and A. Wilsbach, Esqs., of Indiana.

35. Answers by Hon. E. L. Van Winkle, of Kentucky.

36. Answers by A. Sterling, jr., Esq., of Maryland.

37. Answers by George W. Searle, Esq., of Massachusetts.

38. Answers by H. K. Clark and Henry A. Morrow, Esqs., of Michigan.

39. Answers by Cortlandt Parker, Esq., and Jno. F. Hegeman, Esq., of New Jersey.

40. Answers by Hon. S. D. Bell, of New Hampshire.

41. Answers by J. J. Barclay, Esq., of Pennsylvania.

[No answers were received from the gentlemen in the nine other States, in whose hands we placed our interrogatories, although from most of them we received assurances that our request should be complied with.]

42. Three Letters from Mrs. Sarah Peter, of Cincinnati, Ohio, relating to the Female Prison of that city and those European prisons, on whose model it is conducted.

43. A letter from the Hon. Cyrus Mendenhall, of Ohio, giving an outline of the Prison System of that State, with Suggestions as to needed Modifications therein.

44. A valuable Letter on several Points connected with the Organization and Management of Prisons and the Objects of Prison Discipline, from a Gentleman connected as Inspector with a State Prison, who prefers that his name should not be mentioned.

45. A Letter on the Manner of Changing Books in the Prison Library of the Massachusetts State Prison, from the Rev. G. J. Carleton, Chaplain of the Prison.

Previously to the appointment of the undersigned as commissioners to visit prisons out of the State, a special committee, of which Dr. Lieber was chairman, had been appointed to correspond with ex-Governors of the several States in regard to the pardoning power. Letters containing a set of interrogatories on this subject were addressed to all the ex-Governors of the loyal States, but answers were received only from the following gentlemen, viz: Hons. Salmon P. Chase, of Ohio; Israel Washburne, Maine; Samuel Wells, Maine; Henry Dutton, Connecticut; Wm. W. Ellsworth, Connecticut; A. H. Holley, Connecticut; Isaac Toucey, Connecticut; H. B. Anthony, Rhode Island; Elisha Dyer, Rhode Island; Washington Hunt, New York; John A. King, New York; E. T. Throop, New York; Wm. F. Johnston, Pennsylvania; Wm. F. Packer, Pennsylvania; Wm L. Greealy, Michigan.

The above communications were passed over to the undersigned, who were also members of the special committee, for incorporation, as far as they might judge expedient, in the present report.

We deem it proper to append, at this point, the several series of interrogatories, referred to in a former part of this introduction.

I. INTERROGATORIES RELATING TO STATE PRISONS.

I. *The Prison System.*

1. What classes of penal and correctional institutions compose the prison system of this State?

II. *General Administration.*

2. Is there any central authority, having the control and management of the whole system?

3. If yes, how is it constituted, and what are its powers and duties?

4. If not, what opinion is held as to the probable utility of such central authority?

5. If a central governing power is wanting, in whose hands is the controlling authority of the prisons lodged?—the State prison?—the county jails?—the penitentiaries, workhouses or houses of correction?—the various institutions for juvenile delinquents?—any other penal institutions, not falling under the above designations? (The object of this interrogatory is to get at the machinery of the prison system of the State.)

III. *The State Prison.*

6. What, if any, are the *peculiar* features of the State prison— that is, what gives it its *individuality?*

IV. *Prison Premises.*

7. How extensive are the prison premises?

8. How are they inclosed? What are the thickness and height of the wall?

9. What is the drainage?

10. Is there a garden? Any ornamental grounds?

V. *Prison Buildings.*

11. What are the prison buildings?

12. What are the dimensions, material, structure, arrangements, etc., of the prison proper?

13. What the number, size, and furniture of the cells?

14. What are the dimensions and arrangements of the chapel?

15. What of the hospital?

16. What of the dining-hall, if there is one.

17. What of the guard-room?

18. What of the workshops?

VI. *Government of the Prison.*

19. Who compose the staff of prison officers?

20. How are the superior officers of the staff appointed? How the inferior?

21. What salaries are paid to the several officers composing the staff?

22. Do party politics control, or in any degree influence, the appointment of officers and the administration of the prison?

23. What are deemed to be the proper qualifications of prison officers?

24. How far are the requisite qualifications possessed by the officers actually employed?

25. What general line of conduct is marked out for officers in their intercourse with the prisoners?

26. Are officers required to abstain from intoxicating drinks and the use of profane language?

27. What special duties belong to each officer or class of officers?

28. How many prisoners are given into the charge of one keeper?

29. How many guards are there in the prison?

30. What is the designation of the body having the general oversight and control of the prison?

31. How many members compose it?

32. How are they appointed to their places?

33. Do they receive salaries, or are their services gratuitous?

34. What are their powers and duties?

35. How often do they meet, and how much service do they render?

36. Are any officers charged with the daily inspection of the prison?

37. Are there special inspections by the Governor and by legislative committees, and if so, how often?

VII. *Discipline of the Prison.*

38. What are the rules and regulations of the prison, so far as they apply to the convicts?

39. Are the rules explained to the prisoners on entering, or in what way are they made acquainted with them?

40. Does the chaplain converse with each convict before he is set to work?

41. Are convicts kept any time, and if so, how long, in solitary confinement before being assigned to labor?

42. How far is kindness employed as a means of discipline?

43. If yes, in what ways?

44. With what effect?

45. Are rewards employed, and if so, to what extent, as a stimulus to good conduct?

46. What is the effect of the commutation law on convicts?

47. Is this law explained to convicts on entering?

48. Do they appear to understand it?

49. Does each convict keep an account with himself, so that he knows how much time he has earned by good conduct, and how much he has forfeited by subsequent bad conduct?

50. How much time may a convict earn by uniform good conduct?

51. What is the effect of bad conduct on time previously earned?

52. Is any gratuity, or any portion of the earnings of the convicts, allowed to them for good behavior?

53. Has there been introduced into the prison any system of badges, marks, or classification of prisoners on the basis of their conduct, intended to stimulate them to industry and virtue?

54. If yes, with what results?

55. If no, what, if any, is the objection to the introduction of such a system?

56. Might not the principle of rewards be more extensively introduced into our prison systems, with advantage to the discipline and benefit to the prisoners?

57. What system of rewards, if any, would be likely to be least objectionable and most effective?

58. Are any special privileges accorded to convicts on public holidays? If so, what are they, and with what results have they been attended?

59. What are the different kinds of punishment employed in the prison?

60. Is the lash ever used?

61. If not, is its use prohibited by law?

62. What punishments are found most effective?

63. What is the relative power of kindness and severity as means of discipline?

64. Would not a greater variety of punishments be advantageous, particularly of the minor kinds, as privation of correspondence with friends outside, privation of bedding, of particular kinds of food, etc. ?

65. Since there can be no privation without pre-existing privilege, might not an increase of privilege be accorded, with express reference to privation on misbehavior?

66. Would it not be well to supplement the Auburn or congregate system of imprisonment, with a number of solitary cells for exceptional cases?

67. Are punishments frequent or infrequent?

68. To what extent are they recorded?

69. For what offences are punishments chiefly inflicted?

70. In what shops are punishments most frequent?

71. Do the surgeon's books indicate a greater amount of disease in shops where there are most punishments?

72. In the shops where the larger number of punishments occur, do any physical causes exist calculated to produce irritation in the convicts, or which otherwise might account for it?

73. Are the keepers of these shops observed to be more indolent and less watchful than in others, where punishments are less frequent?

74. Among which class of prisoners is there the larger proportional amount of punishments—among those who have been in one year and under, or five years and over?

75. Has death or permanent injury resulted from any of the punishments used in the prison?

76. Must all punishments be inflicted under the direction of the

warden, or may under-keepers, in any case, administer punishment?

77. If under-keepers may inflict punishment, have any abuses arisen in consequence of their possessing this power?

78. If they may not, has the discipline suffered for the want of the power?

79. Are there any tests in the prison by which the ability of prisoners to resist temptation can be measured?

80. How comprehensive and thorough is the vigilance of the officers?

81. What is the effect of vigilance on the discipline?

82. Is all intercourse among prisoners forbidden?

83. How far can this law be enforced?

84. How far and in what ways is the rule of silence evaded?

85. Can this evasion proceed to such an extent that the communications of the prisoners become mutually corrupting?

86. Are complaints from prisoners of injustice on the part of keepers ever investigated?

87. Is the testimony of prisoners ever received?

88. Has the distinctive prison-dress been abolished? If so, on what grounds and for what reasons?

89. What, thus far, has been the effect of its discontinuance on the prisoners? Has the result answered to the expectation?

90. If the prison uniform has not been abolished, might it not be discontinued, not only without detriment but advantageously to the interests of the prison?

91. Is the lock-step in use in this prison?

92. What are the feelings of the convicts toward it? Does it, or does it not, wound their self-respect?

93. If yes, are there any such advantages arising from it as to require its retention?

94. Is there a telegraph from each shop to the guard-room?

95. What arrangements are there for the extinguishment of fires?

96. In case of a revolt or rebellion of the prisoners, what provision is there for subduing it?

VIII. *Religious and Moral Agencies.*

97. What are the duties of the chaplain?

98. What are his rights?

99. Has he an office in the prison?

100. What are the services of the Sabbath?

101. Is there a Sabbath-school?

102. If yes, do all attend, or only a part?

103. Who conduct the Sabbath-school?

104. Are the convicts interested in it?

105. What religious services, if any, are held on week-days?

106. Do the prisoners appear to like the religious services which they are required to attend?

107. What effect appears to be produced upon them by these services?

108. What religious offices are performed to the sick and the dying?

109. What disposition is made of the bodies of convicts after death?

110. Is there any burial-service, and if so, what?

111. Is every prisoner furnished with a Bible? with a hymn-book? with a prayer-book?

112. How much use do they make of their Bibles?

113. Is there a choir in the prison?

114. Is there a melodeon?

115. Do the prisoners generally join in the singing?

116. What good effects, if any, are observed to result from the use of sacred song in the religious services?

117. Do baptisms ever take place in the prison?

118. Is the Lord's Supper ever administered?

119. Are persons from outside ever admitted within the prison to make efforts for the moral and religious improvement of the prisoners?

120. If yes, to what extent and under what restrictions?

121. How extensively does the chaplain visit and converse privately with the prisoners?

122. How are such visits received?

123. Is there now, or has there ever been, a prayer-meeting among the convicts? If yes, how conducted and with what results?

124. Are religious tracts and papers distributed to the convicts?

125. Does the chaplain converse with the prisoners immediately before their discharge, and for what special purpose?

126. Does the chaplain ever serve as a medium of communication between prisoners and their friends outside? If yes, for what purposes and with what results?

127. What, in a general way, are the results of the religious influences brought to bear upon the prisoners?

128. Do genuine spiritual conversions ever, in the judgment of the chaplain, take place among the convicts? If yes, to what extent?

129. How far does the conduct of prisoners, after discharge, justify the hopes inspired by their conduct while in prison?

130. Might the religious element be introduced with advantage to a still greater extent than it is at present?

131. Who has charge of the correspondence of the prisoners?

132. How often and under what restrictions are convicts permitted to correspond with friends?

133. What is the general character of the letters written by them?

134. What is the general character of the letters received by them?

135. What influence is hereby (that is, by their correspondence) exerted upon them—is it beneficial or otherwise?

136. Does the chaplain, or whoever has charge of the correspondence, avail himself of letters written or received by convicts to awaken or deepen good impressions on their minds by salutary counsels and exhortations?

137. How often and under what restrictions are convicts allowed to receive the visits of their friends?

138. May they receive eatables from their friends at such times?

139. Do these visits have a good or a bad effect upon them?

140. How extensively and under what regulations, are general visitors admitted into the prison?

141. Is a fee required of them for the privilege?

142. What is the influence upon the convicts of admitting general visitors?

143. Has it been observed to increase masturbation?

144. What proportion of the visitors are females?

145. Are convicts allowed to bring their difficulties and burdens to the warden for the purpose of seeking relief?

146. If so, in what manner? Does the warden set apart a certain hour of the day in which he will give audience to such cases, or is some other method adopted?

147. What is found to be the influence of allowing this privilege to convicts?

IX. *Secular Instruction.*

148. Is secular instruction given to the prisoners?

149. If yes, who has the general direction of this department?

150. What proportion of the convicts cannot read when they are received?

151. Of those who can read, what proportion lack such a mastery of the art as to be unable to read the Bible and other books without spelling out more or less of the words, and therefore need further instruction?

152. Is there a school in the prison, where the prisoners assemble and receive instruction in classes? If yes, how are the hours of instruction arranged, and what is the system of lessons adopted?

153. If the convicts are taught separately in their cells, how many are assigned to one teacher, how often is each visited by the teacher, and how much instruction does he receive?

154. What branches of knowledge are taught?

155. How much interest is taken in their lessons, and what proficiency is made by the convicts?

156. If the convicts are assembled in classes for instruction, what advantages, if any, and what disadvantages, if any, are found to result from the arrangement?

157. If they are taught separately, are there supposed to be any special advantages in this method?

158. Would the establishment of a school, in which instruction should be given in classes, be preferable to the system of individual lessons; and, if so, wherein?

159. If such is the judgment of the authorities, what hinders the introduction of the improved system?

160. What compensation is given to the teachers?

161. Who has charge of the prison library?

162. How many volumes does the library contain?

163. What is the character of the books?

164. What kinds are most read?

165. What are the regulations of the library, as to giving out and returning books, care of books, &c., &c.?

166. Are books examined when returned?

167. What proportion of prisoners are in the habit of taking out books?

168. What evidence is there that the books taken out are really read to any great extent?

169. What time do the prisoners have for reading?

170. If task-work is in vogue, are the men who accomplish their tasks before the close of the day allowed to read in the shops?

171. Is there an annual appropriation by the Legislature for the increase of the library; and, if so, how much?

172. If there is no appropriation by the Legislature, how are funds for this purpose obtained?

173. By whom are the books selected?

174. Are the prisoners allowed to take or to read any secular newspaper?

175. Are they allowed to take magazines?

176. Are many of the convicts evidently *growing in knowledge?*

177. What, on the whole, is thought to be the influence of the library on the discipline of the prison, and the reformation of the prisoners?

X. *Physical and Hygienic Relations.*

178. What is the ventilation of the prison?

179. What is the method of heating?

180. At what temperature is the prison kept in winter?

181. What degree of heat is reached in summer?

182. How is the prison lighted by day? Do the prisoners have abundance of light for reading in a cloudy day?

183. How is it lighted at night?

184. Do the prisoners have light enough to read by without straining their eyes?

185. To what hour are the lights kept burning?

186. What is the daily bill of fare for the prisoners?

187. Where do the prisoners take their meals? Which is thought to be the preferable mode—to have the convicts eat in a common dining-hall, or in their cells, and on what grounds is the preference given to one method over the other?

188. How are the supplies procured—by contract, or by the warden at his discretion? If by contract, how long does the contract last?

189. Which of these systems is preferred, and for what reasons?

190. What effect, if any, has the dietary on the discipline?

191. What is the clothing of the prisoners in winter?

192. What in summer?

193. What clothes are furnished to the convicts on their discharge?

194. What bedsteads are used?

195. Of what are the beds made?

196. Are pillow-cases and sheets supplied?

197. Is the condition of the beds inspected daily, and if not, how often?

198. What bed-clothes are furnished in winter? What in summer?

199. In what manner and to what extent is the prison supplied with water?

200. How often, and where, are the prisoners required to wash their hands and face?

201. Are bath-tubs provided, and if so, how often are the prisoners required to bathe?

202. Is any use made of the flesh-brush?

203. How often are the convicts' under-clothes washed?

204. How often their bed-clothes?

205. How often are the beds aired in the halls? How often in the sun?

206. How often are the cells white-washed? How often the prison walls.

207. How often are the cells scrubbed?

208. Are vermin ever found in the cells?

209. If yes, what means are found most successful in exterminating them?

210. How often and by whom are the convicts shaved?

211. How often and by whom is their hair cut?

212. Are night tubs used?

213. Of what material made?

214. What arrangement is there for emptying and cleansing them?

215. What provisions for satisfying the calls of nature in the day time?

216. What are the prevailing diseases?

217. How far contracted before and how far after imprisonment?

218. What are the most active causes of disease? Have miasms been generated within the prison walls?

219. What trades are found to be most injurious to health?

220. Do the men on the ground tier of cells suffer more from ill-health than those on the upper tiers?

221. Is the ground floor found to be more productive of heart

disease and rheumatism, and the upper floors of pulmonary complaints?

222. Which class yield most easily to treatment, those who have been confined a long time or a short time?

223. Do convicts who work in the State shop, the kitchen and the hall, have better or worse health than those who work for contractors?

224. What is the average daily percentage of convicts in the hospital?

225. What is the average percentage of convicts for whom daily prescriptions are made?

226. What diseases are most frequently simulated, and what tests are employed to detect simulating?

227. What are the hospital accommodations?

228. Who constitute the hospital staff?

229. What diet is provided for the sick?

230. What percentage of prisoners died last year?

231. What precautions are taken to procure pure medicines?

232. What is the supply of surgical instruments?

233. Are any insane convicts received into the prison, and if any, what proportion?

234. Do any become insane after entering, and if any, what proportion?

235. What are the regulations for testing insanity?

236. Are there State commissions of insanity?

237. If so, how often do they visit the prison?

238. What disposition is made of insane criminals?

239. To what extent is self-abuse practised in the prison?

240. To what cause is it believed to be traceable?

241. What efforts, if any, have been made to diminish the evil, and with what results?

242. What remedial agencies can be suggested toward its cure?

243. What is the effect of long imprisonment on health?

XI. *The Industries of the Prison.*

244. On what principle is the labor of the prison organized— on what is called the contract system, or some other plan?

245. If on the contract system, in what manner is the labor of the prisoners let out?

246. How many and what contracts are there at present in the prison?

247. How many men on each, and what wages per day are paid on the contracts severally?

248. How many convicts are employed on account of the State, and in what departments of labor? Give the number in each?

249. What has been found to be the effect of different kinds of labor on health?

250. How many hours do the prisoners labor in winter?

251. How many in summer?

252. What are the average hours of labor throughout the year?

253. How many and what agents are employed in the prison by the contractors?

254. What, in general, is the character of these agents?

255. What is found to be their influence on the prisoners?

256. What is the aggregate amount of salaries paid by contractors to their agents?

257. May contractors bring citizens into the prison as *laborers?*

258. Are contractors allowed to supply prisoners with tobacco, fruits, candies, or other eatables?

259. If not allowed, do they or their agents, or both, in fact, supply these things to the convicts in an underhand way, and if so, to what extent?

260. Have the contractors any control of the prisoners, or any power of punishment?

261. What proportion of contract men are paid for as able-bodied?

262. Are the contractors allowed to select their own men, or must they take what are assigned them?

263. Are the prisoners consulted as to their preferences?

264. What trades, if any, are preferred by the men?

265. Is it, or not, stipulated that they shall learn all parts of the trade at which they work?

266. What proportion of the convicts enter the prison without having learned a trade?

267. What percentage of these actually learn a trade while in prison?

268. Is it made a distinct object of the prison arrangement to teach a full trade to those who had never learned one?

269. Would the reformation of the prisoners be likely to be advantageously affected by giving greater prominence to this object than is done at present?

270. What contracts are believed to realize the largest profits?

271. What are the (known or supposed) total annual profits realized by contractors through the labor of the convicts?

272. Do contractors ever suffer loss through their contracts?

273. If yes, what is the usual course of things consequent thereupon? Do the contractors pocket the loss, or do they seek and obtain relief and indemnity therefor from the state?

274. Might not a warden, of competent business abilities and experience, manage the industries of the prison so as to make as much out of the labor of the convicts as the contractors; thus securing the profits to the State, instead of to individuals?

275. If not, why not?

276. If yes, ought not the contract system to be abolished on this ground alone?

277. To what abuses is the contract system most liable, and what have been found to have crept in under it?

278. Is the contract system found to affect the discipline unfavorably?

279. Does it, or not, exert an influence unfavorable to the reformation of prisoners?

280. If the two foregoing interrogatories are answered in the affirmative, ought they not to be regarded as decisive against the continuance of the contract system, if even a diminished revenue accrue to the state from the labor of convicts in consequence of such discontinuance?

281. Is not *reformation* the *primary* object, and supposing that result attained at whatever *present* cost, would not ultimate *pecuniary* gain thereby accrue to the State?

282. Is overwork allowed?

283. If so, how is it regulated? Are *all* permitted to do it, or do the contractors select such men as they please for this service?

284. Do the contractors or the prison authorities fix the tariff of prices to be allowed for overwork?

285. What is the compensation actually paid for overwork?

286. Is the price of overwork paid to the prisoners, or to the officers on their account?

287. Do the prisoners receive any interest on their accumulations?

288. Are they allowed to draw out any of their surplus earnings while in the prison, or must they wait for them till their discharge?

289. Is overwork found to be, in any case, prejudicial to the health of those who do it?

290. What is thought, on the whole, to be the influence of the system of overwork, as at present managed?

XII. *Security of the Prison.*

291. Is the prison regarded as secure, or otherwise?

292. How many convicts have escaped during the last ten years?

293. In what ways?

294. Are any special causes for the desire to escape known to have existed?

295. Was anything observed in the prisoners prior to their escape which caused a suspicion that they meditated the attempt?

296. Had there been, in any case, a change in the treatment of the prisoner which may have stimulated him to escape?

297. Has there ever been any complicity, known or suspected, on the part of subordinate officers, with prisoners who have escaped?

XIII. *Reformatory Results.*

298. What are the several reformatory influences brought to bear upon the convicts during their imprisonment?

299. What means are used by the prison authorities, by the State, or by benevolent individuals, to procure situations for the convicts on their discharge?

300. How far have such efforts been successful?

301. Are any efforts made to trace convicts after their discharge?

302. If yes, with what success, and what are the results shown?

303. What has been the percentage of the re-convicted to the whole number of prisoners for the last ten years?

304. What evidences of reformation do the prisoners exhibit while still in confinement?

305. What proofs of reformation are exhibited by convicts after their discharge?

XIV. *Pardons.*

306. What is the whole number of convicts who have been in the prison during the last ten years?

307. The whole number pardoned?

308. The whole number sentenced for life?

309. The number of life-men pardoned?

310. Average imprisonment of life-men pardoned?

311. What is the whole number sentenced for five years and less than ten?

312. How many of these were pardoned?

313. Their average imprisonment?

314. Whole number sentenced for ten years and less than fifteen?

315. How many of this class were pardoned?

316. Their average imprisonment?

317. Whole number sentenced for fifteen years and less than twenty?

318. How many of these were pardoned?

319. Their average imprisonment?

320. Whole number sentenced for twenty years and over?

321. How many of these were pardoned?

322. Their average imprisonment?

323. How extensively is the hope of pardon entertained by convicts?

324. What is the effect of this hope on the prisoners? Does it tend to unsettle their minds, to render them restless, and to prevent or impede earnest efforts at reformation?

325. Has the pardoning power been heretofore too freely exercised?

326. Is it exercised less or more frequently now than formerly, or about the same? What do the statistics on this subject show?

327. Ought some limitations to be placed upon the pardoning power? If yes, what limitations would be practicable and expedient?

328. Would a Board of Pardon, to aid the Executive by examining applications for his clemency, be advisable, or is it better to leave the matter as it now is in most of our states?

329. Would it be expedient to enact a law that a new crime, after a pardon, should work a forfeiture of the pardon, and remand the prisoner back to his former punishment?

XV. *Nature of Criminality.*

330. What has been the percentage of convictions for crime against property for the last ten years?

331. What the percentage of convictions for crimes against person?

332. What the percentage of convictions for forgery?

333. How many executions have taken place in the last ten years?

XVI. *Length of Sentences.*

334. What has been the average length of sentences for crimes against property during the last ten years?

335. What for crimes against person?

336. Is there any great variation between the terms of sentence awarded for the same offence by different judges, or by the same judge at different times? If so, illustrate by cases.

337. What is observed to be the effect, generally, of an imprisonment of ten years or more upon the physical, mental, and moral condition of prisoners who have been confined for that length of time?

338. Which would be likely to be most beneficial to convicts, so far as their reformation is concerned—sentences of moderate length, with the *certainty* that they must be served out, or sentences of greater length, with the *hope* that they may be abridged by pardon?

XVII. *Discharges.*

339. What is the whole number of discharges for the last ten years?

340. How many have been discharged by expiration of sentence?

341. How many by death?

342. How many by pardon?

343. How many have been removed because of insanity?

344. How many have escaped?

345. How many have been discharged in other ways, and what are those ways, if known?

XVIII. *Ages of Convicts.*

346. What is the whole number imprisoned during the last ten years?

347. How many were under twenty years of age, when sentenced?

348. How many were twenty, and under thirty?

349. How many were thirty, and under forty?

350. How many were forty, and under fifty?

351. How many were fifty, and under sixty?

352. How many were sixty, and over?

XIX. *Recommittals.*

353. What is the whole number of prisoners who have been discharged within the last ten years?

354. Of these, how many returned as recommitted?

XX. *Race.*

355. Whole number imprisoned in the last ten years?
356. How many white?
357. How many colored?
358. How many Indian?
359. How many of other races?

XXI. *Nativity.*

360. How many of native birth have been imprisoned within the last ten years?
361. How many of foreign birth?

XXII. *Social Relations.*

362. How many of the convicts for the last ten years have been married?
363. How many unmarried?
364. How many widowed?
365. How many have had children?

XXIII. *Education.*

366. How many of the convicts for the last ten years could not read?
367. How many could read only?
368. How many could read and write?
369. How many had a superior education?

XXIV. *Moral Condition.*

370. How many convicts, for the last ten years, have claimed to be total abstinents?
371. How many have claimed to be temperate?
372. How many have acknowledged themselves intemperate?
373. What proportion of those claiming to be temperate might be fairly adjudged intemperate?
374. What proportion did not attend Sabbath school, or attended irregularly, in youth?
375. What proportion of female convicts were prostitutes?
376. What proportion of male convicts had associated with loose women?
377. What proportion were not in the habit of attending church?
378. What proportion had gambled, less or more?
379. What proportion had been theatre-goers?

XXV. *Orphanage.*

380. What proportion of convicts for the last ten years have been full orphans?
381. What proportion half orphans?

XXVI. *Sex.*

382. What is the whole number of men confined in the prison for the last ten years?

383. The whole number of women?

384. If women are not committed to this prison, and there is no Female State prison, what number, sentenced to other institutions, would have been sent to the State prison, had there been one?

XXVII. *Religious Relations.*

385. How many of the convicts, for the last ten years, have been Protestants?

386. How many Roman Catholics?

XXVIII. *Industrial Relations.*

387. How many of the convicts, for the last ten years, had not learned a trade?

388. How many had learned a trade?

389. What proportion of the latter class had acquired but an imperfect knowledge of their trade?

XXIX. *Finances.*

390. Is the prison self-sustaining?

392. If yes, how long has it been so?

391. If not self-sustaining now, has it ever been, and for how long a time?

393. Why, if such is the fact, has it ceased to be self-sustaining?

394. What have been the earnings, and what the expenditures, year by year, for the last ten years?

395. How long has the prison been in operation, and what have been the aggregate earnings and expenditures for the whole period?

396. What has been the average cost per prisoner (including salaries and all other expenses) for the last ten years?

397. What has been the total cost of ground and buildings belonging to the prison?

398. What is the present estimated value of the same?

399. What was the cost of the prison proper, what the number of cells, and what the cost of each?

XXX. *Effect of the War on Crime.*

400. Has the number of male convicts committed to the prison been less or greater during the war than before?

401. If less, what percentage has the diminution reached?

402. What are believed to be the causes of this (at least *apparent*) diminution of male crime?

403. Has the number of female convicts committed to the prison (or guilty of State prison offences, and committed to other institutions) been less or greater during the war than before?

404. If greater, what percentage has the increase reached?

405. What are believed to be the causes of this increase of female crime?

XXXI. *Miscellaneous Inquiries.*

406. Is this prison conducted on the congregate or separate system?

407. If on the congregate, has it ever had inmates who had previously been imprisoned under the other system?

408. If yes, have they been interrogated as to their preference and the reasons of it, and what answers have they given?

409. If the prison is conducted on the separate principle, has it ever had inmates who had before been imprisoned under the other system?

410. If yes, have they been interrogated as to their preference and the reasons of it, and what answers have they given?

411. What reasons do re-convicted prisoners assign for their relapses?

412. Do any such aver that greater severity while serving out their previous sentence would have been more effectual to deter them from crime?

413. What parts of the State send the largest proportional number of convicts?

414. What causes can be assigned for this?

415. What are believed to be the most active causes of crime?

416. What legislation is thought to be required in order to a more effective repression of crime?

417. By what officers are the convicts conveyed from the jails to the state prison?

418. On what principle is the cost of conveyance regulated— on that of a fee to the officer charged with the duty, or that of paying the actual cost and no more?

419. If on the principle of a fee, what, on an average, is the excess of the fee over the actual cost?

420. What is the whole number of convicts received into the prison during the last ten years, and what the aggregate cost of conveying them? (If the exact cost cannot be stated, let the proximate or estimated cost be given.)

421. Is it customary to weigh the prisoners every three months, or at other stated times?

422. If not, will the authorities agree to have this done in the future, and a record kept according to the subjoined programme? The columns to be ruled with the following headings: 1. Name. 2. Weight. 3. Length of time imprisoned. 4. Height. 5. Number of tier of cell. 6. Uses tobacco or not. 7. Whether he has any hereditary or chronic disease. 8. Employment in prison. 9. Age. 10. Color. (It is believed that the statistics thus obtained will form the basis of important deductions in penal science.)

423. What, if any, are regarded as the defects of this prison?
424. What crimes are most common?
425. What measures are used for the detection of crime?
426. What for its repression?
427. Is the administration of criminal justice prompt or tardy?
428. If the latter, what are the obstacles to speedy trials?
429. What is done with children born in the prison?
430. What general improvements in prison arrangements and prison discipline can be suggested?

II. Interrogatories relating to County Jails.

1. How many counties are there in your state?
2. What is the number of county jails?
3. Is it, in any case, desirable to have more than one jail in a county, or is one in all cases sufficient?
4. What are the grounds of your opinion?
5. Is there any central authority which has the general control of the whole system of county jails?
6. If yes, what is it, how constituted, and what results are reached through its agency?
7. If there is no central governing power, what local authorities have charge of the jails?
8. In this case, is there anything like uniformity in the management of the jails throughout the state?
9. Is a uniform system desirable, and what evils, if any, are believed to flow from the want of uniformity?
10. Are the statistics of the jails kept with any considerable degree of fullness and accuracy, including the commitments and their causes, the discharges and their methods, and the national, social, educational, industrial, moral, and religious relations of the prisoners?
11. Is it obligatory on the sheriffs and jailers to keep statistics of this kind?
12. Is there a set of books, having uniform headings and rulings, with which all the jails are furnished?
13. If the three foregoing interrogatories are answered in the negative, to what extent and in what manner are the statistics of the jails made matter of record?
14. Do the jail-books belong to the counties, or are they the property of the sheriffs?
15. Are returns of jail statistics required to be made to any state officer or state board?
16. What has been the annual number of commitments (omitting only desertions from the army) for the last ten years, or any less number of years, covered by the records, distinguishing between males and females, and, if possible, between white and colored?
17. What has been the average daily number in all the jails?

18. What has been the effect of the war on male crime—is the number of men committed greater or less since than before its commencement?

19. What has been the percentage of increase or diminution?

20. What has been the effect of the war on female crime—is the number of women committed greater or less since than before its commencement?

21. What has been the percentage of increase or diminution?

22. What proportion of prisoners are re-committals?

23. What proportion are foreigners?

24. What proportion were orphans or half-orphans before the age of fifteen?

25. What proportion could not read?

26. Of those recorded as able to read, are there, or not, many who have but an imperfect mastery of the art?

27. What proportion of the prisoners are intemperate?

28. What proportion have not learned a trade?

29. What proportion did not attend Sunday-school in youth?

30. What proportion of female prisoners are prostitues?

31. What proportion of male prisoners have associated with loose women?

32. What proportion have gambled?

33. What proportion have been theatre-goers?

34. What proportion are Sabbath-breakers?

35. What proportion of those committed to the county jails are brought to trial?

36. What proportion are convicted on trial?

37. What proportion are convicted on confession?

38. What proportion of the whole number of prisoners confined in the county jails are undergoing sentences of imprisonment?

39. What is the average length of sentences in the county jails?

40. Is the system of *separate* imprisonment adopted for the county jails?

41. If yes, how effectually is it enforced?

42. If not, is there any system of classification of the prisoners; and if so, on what principle and how effectually enforced?

43. If there is neither separate imprisonment nor classification, do the prisoners sleep in separate cells, or in common sleeping-rooms?

44. Is there any imprisonment for debt, and if so, under what circumstances?

45. Are there many cases of such imprisonment?

46. Are witnesses ever imprisoned to secure their testimony?

47. If yes, are they compensated for the time lost by their imprisonment?

48. Are prisoners of all classes and ages associated together during the daytime?

49. If so, is this thought to be a good or a bad plan?

50. If bad, what are the evils resulting from it?

51. Would separate imprisonment, or would it not, be expedient in common jails?

52. What are the grounds of your opinion?

53. Would it, or not, be a good plan to make the jails simply houses of detention for prisoners awaiting trial, and to have a system of prisons intermediate between the jails and the state prison, in which all persons convicted of minor offences should be sentenced to hard labor?

54. On what grounds is your opinion held?

55. In what way are the keepers of the jails remunerated—by fees on the reception of prisoners, or by salaries?

56. Which of these methods is believed to be best, and why?

57. How is food provided for the prisoners—do the counties pay the actual cost, or is a certain sum per week allowed the sheriff for boarding them, so that he is thereby enabled to make profit out of their board?

58. Which of the above plans is in itself the preferable one, and why?

59. Is clothing supplied to prisoners who may need it?

60. How is medical attendance paid for—by salaries or fees?

61. What is (about) the aggregate amount paid for medicines and medical attendance for the whole state?

62. What is the average annual cost (proximate, if not exact) of each prisoner to the counties, including all expenses other than the interest on the value of the real estate belonging to the jails?

63. What is the estimated aggregate value (proximate, if not exact) of the real estate belonging to all the jails of the state?

64. What is the annual cost of each prisoner, with the interest on the real estate added to the other expenses?

65. Are the prisoners provided with any remunerative employments, and if so, what?

66. If not, would it be desirable and practicable to provide employment for them?

67. Are libraries provided for the use of the prisoners in the jails?

68. If not, would it not be desirable that some provision of this kind should be made?

69. Is there any provision for imparting secular instruction to prisoners who need it?

70. Are the jails generally provided with chaplains?

71. If not, what provision, if any, is made to meet the moral and religious wants of the prisoners?

72. If no provision is made by the authorities, is the lack, thence arising, supplied, to any extent, by volunteer effort on the part of ministers and private christians; and if so, how far?

73. Are Bibles supplied to the jails; if so, at whose expense, and how extensively?

74. When the prisoners are supplied with Bibles and other books, how do they use them—carefully or otherwise ?

75. What as to the prison dietary—is there a uniform bill of fare throughout the counties, or does each jail-keeper provide according to his own fancy ?

76. If the latter, is it the practice for each to have a regular bill of fare for his own prison, or does he vary from day to day, *ad libitum ?*

77. What is the general character of the dietary provided for the prisoners ?

78. Are the jails, as a general thing, well or ill-constructed in respect to ventilation ?

79. How as to the admission of light—are they well-lighted or otherwise ?

80. What diseases are most prevalent in the jails ?

81. What percentage of the prisoners die ?

82. What is the condition of the jails generally as to cleanliness?

83. How often are they scrubbed ?

84. How often whitewashed ?

85. Are means of bathing provided for the prisoners ?

86. What punishments are employed to subdue refractory prisoners ?

87. Are punishments often necessary ?

88. How far are moral means used to secure good conduct ?

89. How effectually is the separation of the sexes secured ?

90. Are many insane prisoners received into the jails ?

91. What disposition is made of insane prisoners?

92. Are the jails generally regarded as secure or otherwise ?

93. What are believed to be the most active causes of crime in your state ?

94. Are the jails themselves, on the whole, thought to be repressive or promotive of crime ?

95. If the latter, what modifications of the system would be likely to work a reform in this respect ?

96. Are sheriffs appointed, or elected, in your state ?

97. If elected, are they reëligible to successive terms of office ?

98. If yes, are they, as a matter of fact, often reëlected ?

99. Are jail officers often changed in your state ?

100. If yes, what is found to be the effect, and is not greater permanence in the tenure of office desirable ?

101. Is there any provision of law for the stated inspection of jails?

102. If so, what is it, and is the said provision, in point of fact, generally complied with ?

III. INTERROGATORIES RELATING TO HOUSES OF CORRECTION, &c.

1. Is there in your state a system of prisons intermediate between the state prisons and the county jails ?

2. If so, what is their designation—penitentiaries, workhouses, houses of correction, or some other name?

3. Do these institutions constitute a system for the whole state, or are they local and exceptional?

4. If for the whole state, are they found in every county, and are they carried on in connection with the county jails, or are they separate organizations?

5. If each county has one of this class of prisons, and if they are managed in connection with the jails, is this thought to be the most desirable arrangement, or would it be better (and if yes, why?) to have one such institution common to several counties?

6. If there are penitentiaries or houses of correction in your state, which are merely local, and do not form part of any general system, would it not be expedient to have such prisons organized on a general plan, and formed into a general system under state authority and supervision? And if yes, upon what grounds?

7. What number of penitentiaries or houses of correction are there in the state?

8. Are they under any general administrative authority, or is each subject only to a local administration?

9. What and how constituted is the governing power?

10. What officers compose the prison staffs in these institutions?

11. What is the aggregate amount of salaries paid to these officers?

12. Do party politics enter as an element, and if so, how far, into the government of these prisons?

13. Is there any authority, outside of the immediate governing powers of the prisons, charged with the duty of inspection, for the purpose of holding these powers to their just responsibility?

14. What punishments are employed? Enumerate *all*. State particularly whether the *lash* or the *shower-bath* is ever used.

15. How far are moral agencies used as a means of discipline?

16. Which method, on the whole, is found most effective—severity or kindness?

17. Is there a commutation law in the state; and if so, does it apply to prisoners in these institutions?

18. If yes, what is found to be its operation—beneficial or otherwise?

19. What are the offences for which punishments are most frequently inflicted?

20. Has death or permanent injury ever been known to result from any punishment inflicted in these prisons?

21. Do the prisoners sleep in separate cells or in common sleeping rooms?

22. Is the law of silence imposed on them while at work?

23. If yes, how effectually is it enforced?

24. Is there a distinctive prison-dress?

25. Are chaplains provided for this class of prisons?

26. If so, what remuneration do they receive?

27. Do they give their whole time to the prisoners?

28. What are their duties?

29. Are Sabbath schools held in these prisons?

30. Are Bibles supplied to the prisoners; and, if so, to what extent?

31. Might the religious element be advantageously made more prominent than it is?

32. Is anything done—and if anything, what?—to procure places for discharged prisoners, and so to prevent their relapse?

33. Is secular instruction given to the prisoners?

34. If so, in what way, and to what extent?

35. What proportion of the prisoners cannot read when they are received?

36. Are these prisons provided with libraries?

37. If so, how extensive are these libraries? '

38. At whose cost provided?

39. What is the general character of the dietaries of these prisons?

40. Where do the prisoners take their meals—in their cells, or in a common dining hall?

41. How are supplies procured—by contract, or otherwise?

42. What clothes are furnished to the prisoners on their discharge?

43. Is any money given them on their discharge; and if so, how much?

44. What are the prevailing diseases?

45. What is the percentage of deaths?

46. Is the labor of these prisons organized upon the contract system?

47. If yes, what is believed to be its influence on the discipline?

48. What proportion of the prisoners had not learned a trade before their incarceration?

49. What percentage of these learn a trade while in prison?

50. Are the prisons of this class generally regarded as secure?

51. How many convicts escaped from them?

52. Is, or is not, the *reformation* of the prisoners made the prominent object?

53. What is the percentage of recommitted prisoners?

54. What is the average length of sentences of the prisoners confined in these institutions?

55. What proportion of the persons received into these prisons are intemperate?

56. What, so far as the statistics of these institutions show, has been the effect of the war on male and female crime—to increase or diminish either or both?

57. What proportion of the prisoners are foreigners?

58. How do the incomes and expenditures of these institutions compare with each other?

59. What is the average annual cost of each prisoner, including all expenses other than interest on real estate?

60. Are insane prisoners ever received?

61. How is the question of their insanity decided?

62. What disposition is made of insane prisoners?

63. What is the average number of prisoners in these institutions?

IV. Interrogatories Relating to Juvenile Reformatories.

1. When was this Institution founded?

2. Was it founded by the authorities of the state or city, or by private benevolence?

3. How are the funds for its support obtained?

4. What is the extent and arrangement of the grounds belonging to the Institution?

5. What are the several buildings, their uses and arrangements?

6. How many inmates will they accommodate?

7. What was the total cost of the grounds and buildings belonging to the Institution?

8. Is the Institution governed by a board of managers, and if so, how is the said board constituted?

9. What are the powers and duties of the board?

10. Who compose the staff of officers of the Institution?

11. Are children of both sexes received? If so, are they kept entirely separate?

12. Between what ages are they admissible?

13. For what causes may children be received?

14. What authorities have power to commit them?

15. Are they committed for a specific time, or indefinitely?

16. If indefinitely, when does the right of guardianship expire?

17. Who judges whether the child is fit to leave the place before the time has expired, to which the right of guardianship extends?

18. What are the different modes of release?

19. Is the Institution to be regarded in the light of a prison or a school, or something intermediate between the two?

20. What is the character of the discipline—is it that of a prison, or otherwise?

21. What are the rules and regulations of the place?

22. What are the proceedings of a day? Please state them successively and in detail?

23. What are the proceedings of a Sabbath?

24. Have the children committed to this Institution any right of protection against the decision of the functionaries who sent them here?

25. If so, what is that right—may they or their parents test the legality of their commitment or detention by the writ of *habeas corpus?*

26. Is this right, in point of fact, ever exercised?

27. Have the children separate sleeping rooms?

28. May they communicate with each other during the day, or is the law of silence enforced?

29. How much of their time do the children spend in school?

30. What branches of learning do they pursue?

31. What progress in general is made by them?

32. Is there a library, and if so, how extensive, and what is the general character of the books?

33. Are the children, as a general thing, fond of reading, and what time do they have for it?

34. Are they all taught a trade?

35. What are the different handicrafts carried on in the Institution.

36. Is the labor of the children let out on the contract principle, or do they work for the Institution?

37. Has the Institution a chaplain? If so, how much of his time is given to the inmates?

38. To what extent are efforts made to cultivate the hearts of the children, and to inculcate the principles of religion and morality?

39. How much importance is attached to efforts of this kind?

40. When a youth is received into the establishment, are any, and if any, what instructions given him as to his future conduct?

41. Are the inmates divided into classes according to their conduct; and if so, how many classes are there, and how are the details of the classification arranged?

42. How far are the antecedents of the inmates recorded?

43. How far their history while connected with the Institution?

44. To what extent and by what means is a knowledge of them kept up after they are indentured or discharged?

45. What proportion are reformed, and turn out well in after life? What do the statistics of the Institution show on this subject?

46. What proportion of those received are orphans by the loss of both parents?

47. What proportion are half-orphans?

48. What proportion have idle or vicious parents, by whose neglect or evil example they have been pushed on to crime?

49. What are the recreations of the children?

50. Are they under supervision while at play?

51. Do the persons who have charge of the children at such times ever take part in their games?

52. What is the dietary?

53. Are the inmates allowed any food or drink beyond what is provided by the Institution?

54. What attention is given to enforcing cleanliness upon the children?

55. How often are they required to bathe the whole person?

56. How as to the health of the inmates?

57. What percentage are, on on average, on the sick list?

58. What percentage die?

59. What are the diseases most prevalent?

60. How often does the physician attend?

61. What hospital accommodations are there?

62. What have been the aggregate annual earnings of the inmates for the last ten years?

63. What the aggregate annual expenses for the same period?

64. What has been the average annual cost of each inmate, including all expenses other than the interest on the real estate belonging to the Institution?

65. What has been the average annual cost, including the said interest?

66. What is the average period during which the children are retained in the Institution?

67. What is the average age at which they are received?

68. What is the average age at which they are discharged?

69. What punishments are employed?

70. What rewards, if any, are offered as a stimulus to good conduct?

71. Is it customary to present a Bible to each inmate on leaving?

72. If so, is the gift accompanied with counsels, written or oral, as to his future conduct?

73. What classes of boys are found most difficult of reformation? What of girls?

74. What does the percentage of children reformed who were fifteen and over when received, compare with the percentage of those who were less than fifteen when they became inmates?

75. Does the Institution reserve the right of a guardian over those who have been indentured?

76. If an indentured youth leave his master, must he again be brought back to the Institution?

77. If this power over the indentured belongs to the Institution, does a like power over those who have gone out in other ways belong to it also.

V. Interrogatories Relating to the Administration of Criminal Justice.

1. What is the *judicial system* of your State? What are the several classes of courts, their jurisdiction and powers?

2. Are the judges appointed or elected? If elected, how long has this system prevailed? What is found to be its operation—favorable or unfavorable to the integrity and independence of the judiciary?

3. What are the punishments annexed to the several crimes forbidden by the law? Please make your answer to this interrogatory full and complete, embracing *all* the violations of law recognized as crimes?

4. When there is a considerable range in the punishments allowed, is there found to be, in practice, a wide diversity in the administration of the law by different judges? Is there, or not,

in your judgment, too wide a range in the discretion allowed to judges ?

5. Are sheriffs appointed or elected, and for what term of office? Which, in your opinion, is the best system? Is there any limit to their re-eligibility, or may they be re-elected as often as their constituents choose?

6. How many justices of the peace are there in each township? How are they chosen, and for how long a term?

7. What proportion of persons indicted are, on the average, brought to trial?

8. Of the tried, what proportion is convicted and what acquitted? In what percentage of cases are juries unable to agree?

9. Of persons arraigned, what proportion plead guilty, and are convicted on confession?

10. Do those who plead guilty generally plead to the offences with which they stand charged, or to others of a lower grade? If of a lower grade, can you suggest any reason, connected with the prosecution of the charge?

11. Of persons charged with homicide, what proportion are convicted? What proportion executed?

12. In what classes of offences is the disproportion between the arrested and the convicted apt to be greatest—those a higher or lower grade?

13. What is about the average length of imprisonment previous to trial?

14. Is it found that in offenses of a higher grade, convictions, when obtained, are frequently so long after the commission of the offense, that their moral effect is in great measure nullified?

15. If such delays occur, what are conceived to be the causes? Is it customary to send causes back and forth between criminal courts of different grades, as, for example, the general sessions and the oyer and terminer?

16. Do the courts, or not, fail *very often* to convict in cases where prisoners are on trial for crimes of a higher order?

17. If yes, what is the effect of such failure on the criminal population; that is, those who follow crime as a means of obtaining a livelihood? Are the terrors of the law found to have much of a deterrent effect upon this class of persons, or not?

18. Are prosecuting attorneys appointed or elected?

19. Is their compensation by salaries or fees?

20. If by salaries, what effect, if any, is this found to have upon their fidelity?

21. To what extent, in general, are forfeited recognizances enforced, and bail money collected?

22. How as to justices' fines—is there a rigid system of accountability here, or are matters in this department left at loose ends? If the former, what *is* the system? If the latter, what remedy can you suggest?

23. Is any special direction given to moneys collected in this way, looking to some public object (as, for example, the increase of school libraries), or do they go into the treasury of the county for general purposes?

24. Are policemen and constables found to be guilty, to any considerable extent, of corruption in the administration of their offices?

25. Are witnesses, who are imprisoned to secure their testimony, confined with persons arrested for crime? Do they receive any compensation for their loss of time while thus imprisoned?

26. Has the death penalty been abolished? If not, for what offenses is it inflicted? If it has been abolished, for how long a period has the new system been in force, and what effect, if any, has it had in increasing or diminishing the crimes for which it was formerly inflicted?

27. Has the method of indictment by a grand jury been abolished in your state, and if so, what system has been substituted in its place, and what has been found to be the operation of the new system? Please state your opinion on this point, and the grounds of it. If not abolished, has any attempt in that direction been made?

28. Is there, or is there not, found to be any considerable variety in the instructions given to juries by different judges, when the question of insanity is at issue?

29. Does the exercise of the pardoning power unfavorably affect the administration of justice? Is this power so often exercised as, in your judgment, to constitute an abuse thereof? Would it be expedient to have this power in any way restricted by law, and if so, what limitations would, in your opinion, be likely to prove wise and effective?

30. Are persons sentenced for life more frequently pardoned than those imprisoned for a term of years? If yes, what is believed to be the cause of the difference?

31. Is there in your state a system of annual returns of criminal statistics? If so, what are the items of information embraced in it, and to what officer are the returns made?

32. Has any code of criminal procedure been adopted, or does the common law practice in the main prevail?

33. What, in your judgment, if any, are the defects in the existing system of criminal procedure, and what suggestions can you offer on the subject of improvements to be made therein?

Victor Cousin, the eminent French philosopher, having been, many years ago, commissioned by his government to examine the school system of Prussia, in submitting the report of his observations to the authority from which he received his commission, with a felicity of expression equal to the patriotism which inspired it, exclaimed : " It is of Prussia that I speak, but it is of France that

I think." In like manner, the undersigned, appointed to inquire into the present aspect of the prison question in the several states of our Union, while they unfold the prison systems of those states, and spread before the Legislature and the public the condition and working of their penal and correctional institutions, have chiefly in view, and aim chiefly to effect, the reforms so much needed in our own state.

To New York belongs the double honor of having given to the world a system of prison discipline—that known as the Auburn, congregate or silent system—and of having originated the class of institutions called indifferently houses of refuge, reform schools, &c., &c. She was the first to adopt, with efficiency, the penitentiary system of prison discipline, and the first to attempt the prevention of crime by seeking out the youthful and unprotected who are in the way of temptation, rescuing them from vice, and rendering them valuable members of society, through the agency of religious, moral and intellectual instruction, and by training them to industrious and orderly habits. In neither of these departments of criminal administration, however, has our state accomplished all that could have been desired. Our prison system, owing to the undue influence of party politics in its administration and other causes, has failed to attain that degree of perfection which might have been reasonably expected ; and the system of juvenile reformatories, though good and effective as far as it goes, lacks the breadth and compass, which our great extent of territory and our large population, especially in cities, render not only desirable but necessary.

It is to improve and perfect our penal and reformatory system, to impress upon it a character worthy of our civilization, to make it a model for other States, and to render it effective in accomplishing the great end of all just prison discipline,—the reformation of its subjects and their restoration to civil life as honest and industrious citizens,—that the Prison Association has so much at heart, and that the undersigned, their commissioners, have, at their bidding, devoted so much time and labor to the investigation, whose results are embodied in the report, which they have the honor to offer, in the ensuing pages, to the representatives and the people of the Empire State.

CHAPTER I.

STATE PRISONS.

Prison discipline ! What is it ? What are its principles, aims, methods, results ? What its connexion with the onward march of society, of civilization, of man ? What relation has it to the repression and prevention of crime ? What means does it propose for diminishing the number both of offences and offenders ? What apparatus, agency, machinery does it suggest as most likely to thin the ranks and lesson the activity of the criminal classes ? These are pregnant questions, which are to be considered, and a solution sought, in the ensuing pages.

In all the wide range of social science, in all the varied fields of inquiry which command the study of the friends of human happiness and progress, there is scarcely one more comprehensive, more important, more inviting, or more abundant in the fruits which a wise culture will yield, than that which will engage the reader's attention in the details and discussions, which are to fill up the pages of the present report.

The science of punishment, the philosophy which investigates the treatment of criminals, holding the just balance between coercion and reformation, must have a profound interest for all lovers of the human race. It goes down to the foundations of public order. It touches the stability and security of the public peace. It affects the sacredness of human life. It is concerned with the protection of property and the safety of our homes and persons. It has a vital relation to the material well-being of communities, and a yet more vital relation to the purity of public morals and the redemption of multitudes of human beings, our brothers and sisters, from sin and suffering. It addresses at once the head and the heart, the intellect and the feelings. It attracts alike the statistician and the philanthropist, the student of political economy and the laborer in the cause of social virtue and happiness. It engages equally the attention of the statesman, who deals with the interests of nations, and of the christian, whose thoughts are directed to the concerns of eternity.

It is thus seen how wide is the scope of this inquiry, and how important the results which it aims to accomplish.

[Assem. No. 35.]   4

We have spoken above of details and discussions. The expression indicates the method of the following essay. Although history is philosophy teaching by example, it is, nevertheless, the custom of the philosophical historian to draw out and set forth the lessons which his narrative conveys. In like manner, discussion will, throughout these pages, be mingled with statement; the exhibition of principles will be combined with the exhibition of facts. This, it seems to us, will be at once the most natural in itself and the most entertaining to the reader; the most natural, because principles grow out of facts, as the fruit grows from the blossom; the most entertaining, because the tedium of discussion will be relieved and enlivened by the more vivid detail of narrative.

SECTION FIRST.

PRISON SYSTEMS.

The subject of this section may be viewed under a two-fold aspect; the inquiry may relate to the internal discipline of the prisons; or it may regard the several classes of penal institutions, into which are received those who have violated, or been arrested on a suspicion of having violated, the laws.

Under the first of these relations, there are two systems of imprisonment in the United States, which have received from the places where they severally originated, the names of the Philadelphia and Auburn systems, and from the leading elements in their respective discipline, those of the separate and congregate or silent systems.

The separate system exists nowhere in the United States out of Pennsylvania; indeed, it may be almost said nowhere in Pennsylvania, except in the Eastern penitentiary, at Philadelphia; for we believe that the system is very imperfectly enforced in the few jails that profess to have adopted it; certainly this is so in those visited by the commissioners; and the same appeared to us to be the case in the Western penitentiary, at Pittsburgh. Communications between prisoners, in a variety of ways, even by loud talking from cell to cell, seemed to be abundant in that prison. We visited a considerable number of prisoners in their cells, in company with the warden, Dr. Hugh Campbell, in whose presence, without contradiction from him, they all declared that communication was constantly kept up among them. One man said that he would know every prisoner within a certain distance from his cell, if he were to meet him in the streets of London, and they should enter into conversation with each other. Our attention was attracted, in one of the cells of the female department, by a string hanging down from the little window of the apartment, and, on inquiring of the occupant the object of the arrangement, we received for answer that it was designed as a medium for conveying notes to the inmates of the adjoining rooms. We naturally expressed some surprise at this announcement, and the warden explained by saying that communicating in this way had become, by usage, a sort of prescriptive right, a kind of *lex loci*, which was usually winked at by the authorities. Whether the same privilege is extended to the male prisoners, we are not informed. We further noticed that the iron pipes for conveying away the night soil of the cells appeared to be patched in spots, with some metallic substance. On inquiry, we were told that this was solder, used for filling up holes that had been bored in the pipes to obtain the means of inter-communication. We were informed that a murder was planned, and all the details arranged between prisoners occupying cells on opposite sides of the passage, and after their discharge carried into effect, as previously arranged. The warden himself admits, in his communication to us, in answer to our printed questions, that the rule of non-intercourse is violated by prisoners in various ways, and even that their communications can be carried to such an extent as to be mutually corrupting. Dr. Campbell appeared to us an excellent and humane christian gentleman, and he is, we believe, eminent in his profession. But, at the advanced age of nearly or quite three score years and ten, and without any previous experience in the management of prisons or prisoners, he had been, very recently, called to be the head of this great community of convicted criminals. They evidently, as was natural, took advantage of his want of knowledge and of his gentle, kindly disposition, to treat him, if not with positive disrespect, at least with undue familiarity, and even with a pertness of manner, which was exceedingly unbecoming the relation existing between him and them. As an instance, we may mention that the occupant of one of the cells visited by us, in his presence and without rebuke from him, said, in loud and boisterous tones, that such a system of imprisonment could have been invented only by the devil, and that none but devils ought ever to be subjected to it.

It is the opinion of Mr. Frederick Hill, a most intelligent gentleman, who has had long experience as a prison inspector both in England and Scotland—an opinion in which we concur—that no person, unless under very peculiar circumstances, should be appointed a prison officer, who is more than forty years old ; and that a preference should be given, other things being equal, to persons considerably younger than this. The reason is plain. The science of punishment and the science of moral training, like all other sciences, require a close and special study of their principles. A mastery of these principles is of supreme importance to the formation of a good prison officer. But such a mastery is the work of time and patient application, and requires, to secure it, that flexibility and elasticity of mind, which belong to the earlier stages of man's existence. The rigidity of age is unfavorable to new acquisitions in paths before untrodden; more especially on a subject so complex, so subtle, so manifold in its relations, and so profoundly philosophical, as that of prison discipline.

The State prison of New Jersey, at Trenton, was organized and for many years conducted on the Philadelphia or separate plan ; but this has been replaced by the Auburn or congregate system. The change, as we gather from the prison reports, appears to have been made chiefly, though not wholly, on financial considerations. As early as 1840 the board of inspectors expressed their misgivings as to the reformatory power of the system, though at the same time they acknowledged a still greater distrust of that to which it is opposed. The same year the physician, Dr. James B. Coleman, attacked the system with much vigor, as prejudicial to the health of both body and mind ; as diminishing the force of the prisoner's organs generally, and particularly weakening the muscular fibre ; as obstructing the lymphatic glands and vitiating the nervous action ; as weakening the powers of the mind, and in some cases producing absolute derangement. He states that there were at that time, among one hundred and fifty-two prisoners, twelve deranged men, some of whom had become so "from the nature of the confinement." Dr. Coleman renewed these assaults on successive years, and in 1846 attacked it as deficient in the reformatory power claimed for it by its advocates. He says : "To shut a man up alone in a narrow, imperfectly ventilated and poorly lighted cell, with a view to reformation of mind, paramount to all other considerations, for him there to work a change of feeling in the gloom of solitude, embittered by recollections of the past and paralyzed by the prospect of the future, this condition is most effectual to drive him mad, or reduce him to imbecility, besides inducing organic diseases almost incurable." From time to time, during the following years, the financial aspect of the question was recalled, and the scanty returns from convict labor referred to as calling for the earnest consideration of the Legislature. Under these successive blows—these arguments drawn from the non-reformatory character of the discipline, the physical and mental health of the prisoners, and the material interests of the State—the system was gradually relaxed, until in 1859 a joint committee of the Legislature reported as follows: " The prison is now so full that the system of solitary confinement is, in practice, disregarded, many cells having two or more prisoners. * * * The mode of working the prisoners, as at present pursued, is, in the judgment of the committee, detrimental to the interests of the State. * * * The advantages of the workhouse system are so obvious that this committee does not consider it necessary to go into lengthy details. * * * With a well established system, it is the unanimous opinion of the committee that the State prison will afford an income sufficient to sustain itself, and in a few years reimburse the full amount now asked for ($20,000). * * * From this statement it will be perceived that the committee are justified in recommending the workhouse system for its pecuniary advantages. All experience proves that the health of the prisoner is materially affected by solitary confinement, and consequently the moral improvement so much desired is entirely prevented. Broken down in health, with all the better feelings of manhood crushed out, moral improvement is out of the question."

From this time the separate system was wholly, as it had before been partially, abandoned; and the congregate system was thenceforth substituted in its place. While moral considerations were not excluded, it is evident, both from the spirit and the letter of the foregoing report, as it is from other official documents not cited, that financial considerations were most potent in effecting the change.

The State prison of Rhode Island, at Providence, has had a similar history. It was commenced, like that of New Jersey, on the Philadelphia plan, having been opened for the reception of prisoners the first day of November, 1838. Dr. Thomas Cleaveland, a very intelligent gentleman, was appointed warden, and was instructed to visit the Eastern penitentiary of Pennsylvania and the Penitentiary of New Jersey, that he might possess himself, as far as possible, of the course pursued in other similar institutions, and so be enabled to profit by their experience in organizing and managing that of Rhode Island. Doubts very early sprang up as to the wisdom and efficiency of the separate system. Just four years subsequent to the opening of the institution, the inspectors, in their Annual Report, recommended to the Legislature that they "cause a full examination to be made of the State prison, with a view to deciding whether the present mode of separate confinement be not expensive to the State and injurious to the minds of the convicts." They add: "Of the thirty-seven convicts who have been committed to the prison, six have become insane. Several others have, at times, exhibited slight symptoms of derangement."

The recommendation of the inspectors was acted upon by the Legislature, and the result was that a change from the Philadelphia to the Auburn system was begun the following year, and fully carried into effect during the year next ensuing thereafter. In an able paper, submitted to the Legislature in October, 1844, by Dr. Cleaveland, warden of the prison, that officer sets forth, with much fullness of detail, the considerations which led to the change. He says that it resulted from "a careful observation, extending through a period of more than four years, of the injurious and alarming effects of solitary imprisonment upon the mental and physical condition of those who were the subjects of it." He describes the system as a "slow, corroding process, carrying its subjects to the derangement or destruction both of body and mind." He avers that "of the forty prisoners, committed while the strictly solitary system was in operation, ten, or one-fourth of the whole number, manifested decided symptoms of derangement." He further observes: "Without dwelling on the greater expensiveness of the solitary plan, its effects on general health, its failure to deter from crime, according to the promise held out, and various other objections, I would remark that the advantage claimed for it, of greater calmness of demeanor and easier submission to the rules of the place, on the part of the solitary prisoner, has not been realized here. On the contrary, solitude has been found to produce restless irritability and a peevishness of disposition, impatient of the unnatural restraint imposed on the reluctant body and mind, difficult to be dealt with; while, in the performance of social labor, in silence, the men have been better subject to control, and have required less frequent exertions of authority than before. When shut up in the cells, they exercised, under the cravings of the social instinct, which walls and chains cannot repress, every contrivance that ingenuity could suggest, by means of the window and the pipes passing through the cells, to hold some communication with each other, and they were more frequently successful than would have been supposed possible. While, on the other hand, when the strict seclusion of the cells was done away, and the senses of the prisoners were once more opened to a portion of their accustomed impressions, and the social nature had been partially relieved, by permitting company without conversation, a very marked change came over the prisoners, and they manifested most clearly to the observer by their greater cheerfulness, alacrity in labor, and prompter compliance with orders, that their condition was much improved, and that they were sensible of it."

The whole argument is thus summed up: "Upon a review of facts like those I have now detailed, it is impossible for me to hesitate in condemning the penal system of solitary confinement. Were it preferable in an economical point of view, (and the case is widely the reverse,) we could not hesitate in deciding the question between economy and humanity."

While the state prisons of Rhode Island and New Jersey have thus the same general history, the change of system in them is distinguished by two marked differences. In Rhode Island, the separate system was of shorter duration, and was given up chiefly on moral and humane considerations; in New Jersey, it continued much longer, and was replaced by the rival system mainly, as we have seen, for reasons connected with the pecuniary interests of the institution.

Thus it appears that, as already stated, the separate system of imprisonment in the United States is confined at present to the state of Pennsylvania, and exists in vigor only in the city of Philadelphia. Wherever else the experiment has been tried in our country, it has failed. Are we to conclude from this that separate imprisonment is worthless? In our judgment, by no means. On the contrary, we are of the opinion that, in its proper place, it has an immense value. We shall have occasion, before concluding this report, to state our views more at large on this point, and will now only remark, in passing, that, apart from houses of arrest, where no other sort of imprisonment should be tolerated, the utility of separate imprisonment lies, as we conceive, not in employing it as a complete system in itself, but as the initial part of a system which, beginning in a species of confinement intensely penal in its character, ends in a form of restriction so slightly penal, that it is but one remove from entire freedom.

Everywhere, then, beyond the limits of Pennsylvania, the system of imprisonment in the United States is that which is called, indifferently, the Auburn, congregate, or silent system. The last of these designations, however, has become, in some prisons, quite inapplicable. Some do not even claim to conduct their discipline upon the strictly silent system; in others, where the claim is made, the rule of silence has but a partial enforcement; while, in comparatively few is the rigidity of the old discipline of absolute non-intercourse maintained in full force.

The separate and silent systems have, notwithstanding their diversity, a common basis. Isolation and labor lie at the foundation of both. They are fundamental principles of both, according to the ideal on which they were formed. The difference is one of application; of mode, and not of principle. In one, the isolation is effected by an absolute bodily separation by day as well as by night, and the labor is performed in the cell of each individual convict. In the other, the labor is performed in common workshops, and the isolation at night is secured by the confinement of the prisoners in separate cells, but during the day is of a moral species, being effected by the enforcement, so far as such a thing is possible, of an absolute silence. The bodies of the prisoners are together, but their souls are apart; and, while there is a material society, there is a mental solitude. Such is the theory on which the respective systems are founded; but in neither do the facts ever fully correspond to the ideal.

We come now to the second aspect of this subject—that which relates to the series of penal and correctional institutions forming the prison systems of the several States and of Canada. In most of the States visited by us there are three classes of these institutions, viz : State prisons, county jails, and reform schools or refuges. Two, however—Delaware and West Virginia—have no State prisons, and four—Delaware, West Virginia, Indiana and New Jersey—no reformatories, though the last named of these States is likely to have one soon. Several States have one or two prisons of a grade intermediate between the State prison and the county jail, called by different names—house of correction, workhouse, bridewell, etc. No State has a complete system of such institutions except Massachusetts, although in Connecticut every county jail is at the same time a workhouse. New York has six prisons, called penitentiaries, intermediate between her state prisons and her county jails; but they are all local institutions, created by special statutes and managed by the authorities of the counties in which they are situated, though receiving, except those in the counties of New York and Kings, inmates from the adjoining counties, for whose board they receive a certain stipulated weekly compensation, besides the avails of their labor during their imprisoment. One of these—the Albany penitentiary, under the charge of Gen. Pilsbury—is, in effect, a United States prison, receiving by contract all persons sentenced for felonies in the District of Columbia, and during the late civil war a large number of prisoners of state.

Besides these, there is another class of prisons in all the states, and in some of them quite numerous, called indifferently station-houses, guard-houses and lock-ups. They are little noticed and little known, and yet very important. They stand in great need of reform, being, as a class, the most filthy, cramped, comfortless and ill-managed of all our penal establishments. They would be the most demoralizing, were it not for the fact that their inmates remain commonly only a few hours, and seldom more than a few days.

With these general remarks we offer a few brief details touching the prison systems of the individual states, regarded in the light in which we are now contemplating the subject:

Connecticut.—1. A state prison at Wethersfield. 2. A county jail, which is also a workhouse, in each county. 3. A state reform school at West Meriden, and the Watkinson Juvenile Asylum and Farm School at Hartford.

Delaware.—The only class of prisons in this state are county jails, of which there is one in each county. The principal jail is at New Castle, in which are confined prisoners convicted of state prison offences. An act has been passed by the Legislature to establish a reform school, but as yet it remains a dead letter in the statute book.

Illinois.—1. A state prison at Joliet. 2. A city prison in Chicago, called the bridewell. 3. County jails—the whole number of counties in the state being one hundred and two, and of jails about eighty. 4. A reform school at Chicago.

Indiana.—1. Two state prisons, one at Jeffersonville and the

other at Michigan City. 2. County jails. There are no prisons
of an intermediate grade and no juvenile reformatories. This and
West Virginia are the only states visited by the commissioners, in
which no movement has been made looking to the establishment
of this latter class of institutions.

Kentucky.—1. A state prison at Frankfort. 2. A workhouse
at Louisville (city prison). 3. County jails. 4. A house of refuge
at Louisville, opened for the reception of inmates in July, 1865.

Maine.—1. State prison at Thomaston. 2. Two houses of correction. 3. County jails, 4. State reform school at Cape Elizabeth.

Maryland.—1. State prison at Baltimore. 2. Baltimore city jail.
3. County jails, one in each of the twenty-one counties of the
state. 4. A house of refuge at Baltimore.

Massachusetts.—The prison system of this state is more complete, and the prisons themselves, in our judgment, better manned
and better managed, than in any other of the states visited by us.
The whole series of institutions, constituting or intimately connected with the prison system, are the following: 1. A state
prison, at Charlestown, into which male convicts only are received.
2. A jail in each county, in which are confined persons arrested
and awaiting trial, and those who are temporarily detained prior
to their transfer to some other prison in execution of sentence. 3.
A house of correction in each county, which receives only prisoners in execution of sentence, and where all the inmates are required to labor. All females, convicted of offences against the
laws, are sentenced to the houses of correction, or to another
class of prisons to be immediately named. The two classes of
county prisons, the house of correction and the jail, though quite
distinct in their functions, are generally in the same enclosure and
under the same management. 4. Houses of industry. These are
much the same thing as the houses of correction, only under another name. We are not quite sure whether there are any houses
of industry, other than that on Deer island, in Boston harbor. 5.
State reform schools. Of these there are three: one for boys, at
Westborough; a second for boys (nautical), kept on board two
ships, stationed one at Boston and the other at New Bedford; and
a third for girls, at Lancaster. 6. Female refuges. These are
" homes " for the reception of discharged or pardoned female prisoners. There are two of them; one at Springfield, the other at
Dedham. They are private establishments, but are aided by the

state. Such establishments are essential aids to society in its great work of reforming criminals, and the state does well to assist them with contributions from the public treasury. 7. A state agency for the encouragement and aid of discharged male prisoners. The aim is to procure employment for them, and to afford them subsistence while seeking it. The fund for this object is made up, in part, of contributions by the state, and, in part, of private benefactions. The state officer who has charge of this fund is called the "agent for discharged convicts." This agency, and the female refuges named under the last head, are important supplements to the prison system. 8. Truant schools, another class of reformatory, or more properly, perhaps, preventive institutions. The oldest of these is the Boston House of Reformation, established in 1827, and accommodating, on an average, about two hundred pupils. Other schools of this class exist in Roxbury, Cambridge, Worcester, Springfield, Lowell and New Bedford. These accommodate, altogether, some two hundred more truant and vagrant children. They are supported by the several towns and cities which send pupils to them, the practice being, sometimes, to send truants from towns which have no such schools. As a general rule they are sent by police authority. 9. Private reform schools. The largest of these is a Roman Catholic reformatory in Boston, under the care of the bishop of the diocese, having a capacity for three hundred to four hundred boys. The oldest is the Farm School, on Thompson's island, in Boston harbor. It contains, usually, a hundred boys, more or less. There is a similar school at West Newton, containing a family of about thirty boys; and another is incorporated, but not yet established, at Salem. These institutions have not, so far, been aided by the state, being all sustained by private charity; but the proposition has been made, and is gaining favor, to aid them from the public treasury. 10. Guard houses, or lock-ups. Each town of 3,000 inhabitants is required to maintain at least one. This law is, in many cases, disregarded; yet the number of prisons of this class is something over one hundred. Such, then, is the penal and correctional system of Massachusetts, and so many and multiform the institutions and classes of institutions which compose it. It is not perfect, especially in the machinery by which it is worked; but it makes a nearer approximation to that standard than is elsewhere to be met with in our country; and it will surely be acknow-

ledged that it indicates at once a broad reach of benevolence in
the citizens, and a wise and liberal policy in the Legislature.

Michigan.—1. State prison, at Jackson. 2. House of correction, at Detroit. 3. County jails. 4. State reform school, at Lansing.

Missouri.—1. State prison, at Jefferson City. 2. Workhouse,
at St. Louis. 3. County jails. 4. House of refuge, at St. Louis.

New Jersey.— 1. State prison, at Trenton. 2. County jails.
3. State reform school, not yet located. The movement is in good
hands, and vigorously prosecuted. The benevolent design of the
Legislature will, no doubt, be speedily carried into full effect.

New Hampshire.—1. State prison, at Concord. 2. County
jails. 3. State reform school at Manchester.

New York.—1. Three state prisons, viz: at Sing Sing, Auburn
and Dannemora. That at Sing Sing alone receives female prisoners. Indeed, the female prison at that place is, in effect, a distinct institution, having separate buildings and an administration
of its own, wholly by female officers, the supplies only being
procured by the authorities of the male prison. 2. Six penitentiaries, which are local prisons. 3. County jails, 4. Juvenile
reformatories. (1.) A house of refuge, with male and female departments, on Randall's island, county of New York, under the
care of an incorporated society, but receiving State aid. (2.) A
house of refuge for boys only, at Rochester, Monroe county: a
state institution. (3.) A juvenile asylum, in New York, similar
in its general scope to the two preceding, though not strictly
punitive, but rather preventive and reformatory. (4.) A like institution under the care of the society for the protection of destitute Roman Catholic children. (5.) A truant home, at Brook-
lyn, designed for very young transgressors; chiefly indeed, as the
name imports, truant and vagrant children. (6.) A truant home,
at Rochester, similar to the above. The juvenile asylum, mentioned above, is authorized, by a law recently passed, to receive
truant children. 7. A Children's Aid Society, at New York.
8. Guard houses, or lock-ups.

Ohio.—1. State prison, at Columbus. 2. City prison, at Cincinnati, with male and female branches, entirely distinct and separate from each other. 3. County jails. 4. Correctional institutions, viz: (1.) A house of refuge, at Cincinnati. (2.) A state
reform farm, near Lancaster.

Pennsylvania.—1. Two state prisons—the Eastern penitentiary, at Philadelphia; and the Western ditto, at Pittsburg. 2.

County jails. 3. Correctional institutions, viz: (1.) A house of refuge, at Philadelphia, for white boys and girls. (2.) A house of refuge, same place, for colored children, of both sexes. (3.) A house of refuge for both sexes, at Pittsburg.

Rhode Island.—1. State prison, at Providence. 2. County jails. 3. Reform school, at Providence.

Vermont.—1. State prison, at Windsor. 2. County jails. 3. A reform farm school for juvenile delinquents, which has gone into operation since the visit of the commissioners. Its location is not known by them.

West Virginia.—This young state, born amid the convulsions of civil war, has as yet but one class of prisons—the county jails. Persons convicted of felonies are imprisoned in the common jail of Wheeling, at present the capital of the state.

Wisconsin.—1. State prison, at Waupun. 2. A house of correction, at Milwaukee. 3. County jails. 4. A reform school, at Waukesha.

Canada.—1. Provincial penitentiary, at Kingston. 2. County jails in Upper Canada, and district jails in Lower Canada. 3. Two reformatory prisons; one in each of the provinces.

Notwithstanding the encomiums bestowed, in a former paragragh, on the comparative excellence of the prison system of Massachusetts, we have no hesitation in expressing the opinion that there is no approach to perfection in any of the systems which have fallen under our observation. The one supreme aim of all public punishment is the protection of society by the prevention of crime. A system of prison discipline, which, combined with other agencies to be hereafter indicated, would banish crime from society and secure a universal observance of the laws, would be fairly entitled to be regarded as perfect; and, in proportion as such system should approximate the result stated, would be its approach to the standard of perfection.

Now, whatever differences of opinion may exist among penologists on other questions embraced in the general science of prison discipline, there is one point on which there may be said to be an almost if not quite perfect unanimity, viz: that the moral cure of criminals, adult as well as juvenile, their restoration to virtue and "the spirit of a sound mind," is the best means of attaining the end in view,—the repression and extirpation of crime; and hence that reformation is the primary object to be aimed at in the administration of penal justice. We have only, then, to ask our selves the question, first, how far any given penal system aims at the reformation of its subjects, and secondly, with what degree of wisdom and efficiency it pursues that end, to have an infallible gauge wherewith to mark its approach to or recession from the standard of perfection.

There is not a prison system in the United States, which, tried by either of these tests, would not be found wanting. There is not one, we feel convinced—always excepting the department which has the care of juvenile delinquents—not one which seeks the reformation of its subjects as a primary object; and even if this were true of any of them, there is not one, with the exception above noted, which pursues the end named by the agencies most likely to accomplish it. They are all, so far as adult prisoners are concerned, lacking in a supreme devotion to the right aim; all lacking in the breadth and comprehensiveness of their scope; all lacking in the aptitude and efficiency of their instruments; and all lacking in the employment of a wise and effective machinery to keep the whole in healthy and vigorous action.

Having given in this section a bird's eye view of the prison systems of the United States and Canada, and having stated the opinion that they are all, to a greater or less extent, deficient in their principles and methods, it may be proper, at this point, briefly to sketch the system which, after the best thought we have been able to give to the subject, appears to us most wisely adapted to the ends of a just and true prison discipline.

As a preparatory step, we would have a law enacted, by which the education of all the children of the state should be made compulsory. Every child should be compelled, within a certain range of years, to attend regularly some school, either public or private; or, if parents desire a more select education for their offspring, they should be required to show that they are receiving, during the legal age, adequate instruction at home. No half-way measures, no patchwork legislation will meet the necessities of the case. It is far better to force education upon the people than to force them into prisons to expiate crimes, of which neglect or ignorance has been the occasion. Deep and broad foundations of moral and religious, no less than of intellectual character must be laid in our common schools, despite the obstacles that bigotry and sectarian jealousy may throw in the way; and the children of the state must be there, even by compulsion, if need be, to be so trained.

This essential preliminary aid being thus secured, the first in our series of establishments, looking to the repression of crime, should be institutions of a preventive character. Here, indeed, to our view, is the real field of promise. The problem is to stay the current of crime, to turn it back upon itself, and to dry up its fountain-heads. In studying this question, the mind turns instinctively to childhood as the true field of effort for the accomplishment of the desired end.

Two classes of institutions, it appears to us, are needed and are sufficient at this stage of the work — public nurseries and industrial schools.

Public nurseries for children of two or three to five or six years old, of pauper parents, and perhaps of some others, are the first link, the earliest agency in the prevention of crime in youth and manhood. The importance of this class of institutions will appear evident when it is considered that the first impressions made upon the mind, whether good or evil, are the most lasting and the most difficult to eradicate. All experience shows that such impressions received in early childhood, and the habits formed at that tender age, usually exercise a controling influence throughout the period of youth. Accordingly, it is from the class of children who receive their impressions and form their habits in the streets, from the age of four to ten years, that our reformatories, jails, houses of correction and state prisons are mainly peopled. Is it possible, then, to exaggerate the importance to society of institutions such as those here proposed? Ought not systematic and energetic measures to be directed by legislators, as well as philanthropists, to this department of prevention? Can any system of legislation which aims at the suppression and extinction of crime overlook so potent an agency to that end as the one here recommended, and yet lay claim to the attributes of sagacity and humanity? Here the serpent may be crushed in the egg, the hydra strangled in the birth, the harvest of evil nipped in its first sprouting. A fact bearing on this subject, at once instructive and encouraging, is mentioned in a Government Report on Prisons in France. It is worth repeating here. A vast number of abandoned children in that country are received, almost from birth, into foundling asylums, where they are cared for and educated, till they are of a suitable age to put out; yet the number of children reared in these asylums, who have subsequently found their way into prison, is quite insignificant—a striking proof of the almost omnipotent power of early (the very earliest) moral, religious, intellectual and industrial training, as a security against the commission of crime.

The industrial school, whether called by that name or some other—truant, ragged, or whatever it may be—is the next link, the second agency in the preventive part of the system. The children of parents who neglect their offspring, either because they are vicious or indifferent to their welfare—children who roam the streets and prowl about docks and wharves, and are almost sure in the end to take up crime as a trade—should be gathered into institutions of this class, where they would receive that mental, moral and industrial training which their own homes would never afford them, and from which they would at length be sent out to good situations in the country, or elsewhere, where they would grow into virtuous and useful citizens, adding to, instead of preying upon, the productive industry of the country. A few schools of this sort have been established with the best results; but nothing has been done by them in rescuing vagrant children and youth of both sexes from vice and crime, at all commensurate with the good that might be effected in this direction through their agency. These schools should be open to the voluntary resort of neglected children, whose parents, regardless of their future character and condition, leave them to do for themselves, battling with their hard lot as best they may be able.

The discipline in these industrial schools should be strictly of the family character. All the arrangements should be such as to cultivate industrious habits, and prepare their inmates for the stations they are afterwards to fill. The kitchen, the wash-tub, the sewing and knitting room, the work shop, the farm, and, above all, the school room, together with such recreations as may be suitable to their years, should occupy the time of those who find their home there; and this home should be, though tidy and attractive, yet of the plainest character, partaking as nearly as may be of the nature of the domestic departments of families in moderate circumstances. Criminal and vicious habits should be the only bar to reception here; and children, tainted with such practices, should in no case be permitted to come in contact with the destitute but yet unfallen street children, for whom alone the industrial school is designed. Should any such, by mistake, ever be admitted, when discovered, they should be at once transferred to institutions, whose distinctive character is reformatory rather than preventive.

It is confidently believed that if these two classes of institutions—public nurseries and industrial schools—were sufficiently multiplied and placed under judicious control and management, and proper care taken to keep them free from those who have reached the point of crime, thousands of young victims of parental indifference or vice would be kept from idle and vicious habits, and from the ruin they bring in their train; the most prolific fountain of crime would be cut off; and the numbers confined in reformatories and prisons would be materially diminished, perhaps brought down almost to zero.

We have spoken of the need of judicious management in these institutions. Probably a union of private and public effort would best secure the requisite wisdom and efficiency; but, in any case, liberal pecuniary aid must be supplied by municipal and legislative grants.

Is the expense of such institutions made a point of objection? Let it be considered—for of this we are fully persuaded—that a judicious and effective system of prevention in behalf of this class of juveniles would be an arrangement the most economical to the public, as well as the most merciful to themselves which could be made. To save them—and the plan we propose would no doubt be the salvation of almost the entire class—would be to cut off one of the most copious sources of adult crime, and of course to dry up an incessant and tremendous drain upon the wealth of the state, through their depredations, when arrived at manhood, on the property of the citizens.

The next class of institutions in a well organized penal system, is the juvenile reformatory. These already exist in most of our states, and New York is better supplied with them than any others, except Massachusetts, and possibly Pennsylvania. But in all the states, the system needs extension, and in all there are modifications by which its organization might be improved. In the first place, there should be everywhere an absolute separation of the sexes. Stone walls and iron gates are not sufficient; but so much space should intervene, that the excitement and uneasiness produced by proximity, missing its aliment, would disappear altogether. In the second place, the family principle should be everywhere adopted, either exclusively or in combination with the congregate. And, thirdly, subdivisions, now unknown, should be introduced into the arrangements for each of the sexes. Of boy criminals, there are three classes, viz: those who have just entered on a course of pilfering; those who have more confirmed habits of stealing and lying; and those who, having reached the ages of sixteen, seventeen or eighteen, have become habitual thieves, and have discarded all other means of obtaining a livelihood. These several classes of juvenile offenders require each a different discipline and training, and should never, if it can be avoided, be brought into contact with each other. Of female juvenile criminals, there are but two classes requiring different treatment, viz: those who have formed only habits of pilfering and idleness, and those who have addicted themselves to unchaste practices. The classifications named in both sexes require, in order to secure the best results, separate houses and yards, not to contain, if possible, over one hundred inmates, with subdivisions of (say) twenty to twenty-five, constituting so many distinct families, each with its own eating, sitting, reading and sleeping rooms.

There is a principle, applicable to the management of all the institutions thus far included in our proposed system, extensively employed in other countries, but nowhere in our own, so far as is known to us;—we mean the principle of holding the parent responsible for the conduct and maintenance of his child, till he arrive at years of discretion, and the enforcement of that responsibility by the strong arm of the law. And what can be more reasonable and just than this principle? Why should a parent, whose own indifference or vices have been the occasion of leading his child into crime, be freed from all expense on account of that child, the moment he turns thief, or when the state, acting in *loco parentis*, removes him to a preventive institution, where the evil influences of his natural home may be counteracted, and their disastrous consequences averted? It is our opinion that the parent whose child falls into crime should be compelled, except in peculiar cases, to pay the cost of its maintenance in a preventive or reformatory institution, or, in default, be deprived of his liberty and forced to toil to that end. Is it said that such a rule would press hard on parents? But the expense and loss must fall on somebody; and, surely, it is less hard that it should fall on the child's parent than on any one else. Two advantages would result from the enforcement of this principle. First, it would relieve the public, in part, of the burden of supporting its neglected and criminal children; but, secondly, and chiefly, the fear of compelled contribution to the support of their children in an industrial or reformatory school, would be a strong motive, in the absence of higer ones, to a greater care of their education and conduct, so that the burden thus entailed might be avoided.

This principle has worked well, wherever it has been tried. Even in Ireland, where, from the extreme poverty of the classes from which the occupants of juvenile reformatories are supplied, it was supposed, even by those who placed the highest value upon it, that it would be of little avail, within two years from the establishment of reformatories in that country, nearly $1,500 had been recovered from the parents of their inmates; and this, notwithstanding the fact that sixty per cent. of the children received were orphans, having lost one or both of their parents.

The next class in the series of institutions, composing what we would deem an effective prison system, is the county jail. These should be made, in our judgment, simply houses of detention, and their punitive character be entirely taken away. The great evil of our present jail system, as has been again and again urged in the reports of the Prison Association, is the promiscuous intercourse of the prisoners, there being, in general, no classification, except that which results from an imperfect separation of the sexes. From this unchecked association, it results that our county jails are but public schools, maintained at the expense of the community, for the encouragement of vice, and for providing an unbroken succession of thieves, burglars and profligates; institutions in which, as Sidney Smith observed forty years ago, "the petty larcenous stripling, being left destitute of every species of employment, and locked up with accomplished villains, as idle as himself, listens to their pleasant narrative of successful crime, and pants for the hour of freedom, that he may begin the same bold and interesting career." This evil, which is a blot on our civilization, can be cured only by a radical change of the system. Our existing jails, which, for the most part, require demolition on other grounds, must be pulled down, and reconstructed on principles, which will admit the enforcement (and this must be, in all cases, rigidly exacted,) of an absolute separation of the prisoners throughout the whole period of their incarceration. But on all these points, and others connected with the improvement of our common jails, we shall have occasion to express our views more at large, and to enforce them with such arguments as may seem suitable, in a subsequent part of this report.

Next in the ascending series would come a class of prisons intermediate between the county jail and the state prison proper.

Prisons of this sort have received different designations in different states. In Massachusetts, the only state where there is anything like a general system of such institutions, they are called houses of correction; in New York, where they are purely local institutions, created by special statutes for particular counties, they receive the name of penitentiaries or workhouses; and in Canada, where the Board of Prison Inspectors is pressing the Legislature for their creation, they are to be designated (at least such is the title proposed) central prisons, and are to form one of the links in the general prison system of the country. We venture to suggest the name of district prisons for New York, whenever (if ever) there shall be a reconstruction of the prison system of the state, in accordance with the general views submitted in the present paper. These district prisons should be dispersed through the state, at points as convenient as possible to the several counties for whose use each is intended to serve. The counties that have already been at the trouble and expense of erecting and organizing local penitentiaries need not change their existing system, unless they prefer to sell or lease their several establishments to the state, and so become incorporated into the general system.

It is clear that our common jails are not now, and never can be made, houses of correction in the proper sense—places for the reformation of criminals. The fact that they are mere places of detention to the majority of their inmates, the circumstance that the sentences of those confined in them for punishment are, and are likely ever to be, too short to admit of the application of reformatory processes, the constant flux in their populations, the difficulty of organizing and enforcing a system of labor, without which there can be no reformation, and, above all, the want of a proper staff of officers, especially of chaplains and teachers, render it certain that common jails can never be converted into reformatory institutions. If, therefore, there are to be any such, below the grade of the state prison, as part and parcel of a general prison system, it must be by the establishment of the institutions here proposed, or others of a like character.

The advantages to be expected from the establishment of district prisons are the following:

1. The organization of the prisons, each with a full staff of officers, and all other appointments necessary to their proper and effective working as true houses of correction.

2. The arrangement of buildings, cells, workshops, schoolrooms, chapels and premises generally, as to kind and construction, suitable to a complete penitentiary system.

3. The introduction of a comprehensive, well-adjusted system of labor, a result that can never be attained in our common jails, but rendered comparatively easy in the district prisons, in consequence of the larger staff of officers, the greater number of prisoners, and the increased length of their sentences.

4. Diminished cost of maintenance, despite the increase of officers, owing in part to the earnings of the convicts,and in part to greater economy in the administration. The county jails we believe to be at present the most costly of our prisons, from the enormous prices paid to sheriffs by the county authorities for the board of prisoners, being, in one case at least, as high as $6.16 per week, and in others approximating to that figure—almost hotel prices.

5. The relief of the common jails by the absence from them of a large proportion of their worst and most frequent inmates, which would make the separate imprisonment of the rest comparatively easy, and that at a moderate cost for the necessary buildings, especially when taken in connection with another reform, to be hereafter noticed, viz.: the more speedy trial of persons arrested for crime, and held in custody to that end.

6. The relief of the state prisons by the punishment in the district prisons of all convicts sentenced for terms not exceeding three years, and perhaps also first offenders and young criminals with even longer sentences, according to the circumstances attending their several cases. But

7. The crowning recommendation of the system of district prisons, here proposed, lies in the reformatory character to be impressed upon their administration. This, indeed, is the great point to be sought and secured in their establishment. We will not now stay to enter into a detail of the means—religious, moral, educational and industrial—through which this end is to be reached. But there is one point on which, in this connexion, we feel constrained to offer a few remarks. The absurd practice of short repeated imprisonments must be discontinued, or all thought of reformation abandoned. Reformatory processes can have no time to take effect under such a system. On no subject are the enlightened friends of prison reform, and especially the governors of our penitentiaries, more generally agreed than on the utter

worthlessness of these repeated short imprisonments; while the
indirect expense to society in arrests and prosecutions, and yet
more in the amount of property of which it is plundered in the
intervals between the imprisonments, is enormous. The object of
all reformatory prison treatment is to conquer, in the prisoner,
his habits of evil ; to train him in the ways of virtuous industry ;
to sunder the tie that binds him to his associates in crime ; to ex-
tinguish in him the desire and the tendency to herd with them
again, and so to discipline him that he may go back into the
world with some settled principle and some steady purpose of
virtue. To effect these changes time, and no inconsiderable
amount of it, is absolutely essential; and all, without exception,
who have given attention to the subject, concur in the belief that
short sentences, at least in the great majority of cases, are not
only useless but pernicious. Excessive leniency in the administration of criminal law is an evil scarcely less deplorable than
excessive harshness. To be sternly resolute in the infliction of
necessary pain is as much a duty as it is to decline the infliction of
any that is not necessary ; and especially where the object is not
to punish vindictively, but to redeem and save, no hesitation
should be felt in awarding a sentence adequate to the accomplishment of that great purpose. The sentence, whose brevity deprives
the criminal of the full advantage of reformatory influences, is to
him not a mercy, but a cruelty, while to society it is an injustice
and a wrong.

The proposed increased length of the sentences to be awarded
to misdemeanants, and especially those who, by the frequent repetition of minor offenses, evince a proclivity to crime, would involve
the necessity of some changes in the criminal laws of the state,
particularly as to what should constitute a habitual or inveterate
offender—a "recidivist" in technical phrase, in common parlance
a "revolver." But these changes could be easily made, and when
made would be, as already intimated, no less to the real interest
of the transgressor than to that of society, whose laws he had
violated.

Without intending to burden the present paper with needless
details, we would suggest, just here, that, if the proposition for
district prisons should ever be made the basis of legislation, it
would be desirable on moral, sanitary, economic and administrative grounds, that the prisons for women should be separate from

those for men, the two being in distinct buildings and at a distance from each other.

Such separation is desirable on moral grounds, because where the two sexes are confined in the same building or the same enclosure, the very fact of this contiguity has an exciting and bad effect, and leads to endless attempts to communicate, which are not unfrequently, against all probability, successful. Even when both sight and hearing are impossible the mind will still work where there is proximity, and evil consequences will many times be the result.

It is desirable on sanitary grounds, because where prisoners of different sexes are confined in the same building or enclosure it is often necessary to impede light and ventilation by half closing windows, and by putting doors across passages which would otherwise be left open, thus violating the laws of hygiene and obstructing an important condition of health.

It is desirable on economic grounds, because, first, prisons built at less expense would be sufficiently secure for females ; and secondly, the management would cost less, as female keepers would require less pay.

It is desirable on administrative grounds, because, in prisons where there are inmates of both sexes, there is always a difficulty in apportioning the responsibility of the warden and matron. A woman is at least as able to govern female prisoners as a man, and she will certainly govern better, abstractly considered, when the whole responsibility concerning them rests upon her. But in a prison occupied by both males and females, such undivided responsibility cannot be lodged in the matron without creating two separate and independent authorities in the same building, which is contrary to all sound principles of administration. In such cases, therefore, on the one hand, the matron is necessarily made subordinate to the warden, and, as a consequence, the warden is made responsible for a number of matters, of which he can know but little; and, on the other, the influence of the matron is impaired by her not possessing full authority either over her subordinate officers or over the prisoners.

Next and last in the series of establishments which we propose as fit to constitute one comprehensive prison system for our state—consisting of preventive, reformatory and punitive institutions—is the state prison proper, the receptacle of criminals convicted of the gravest offences against society and its laws which are punishable by imprisonment, and not by death. It is here, we conceive, that are needed reforms the most material and radical. Even supposing the buildings to be retained as they are, and the system in its substratum to continue unchanged, still important modifications are needed to bring our state prisons into harmony with the true design of a penitentiary system, considered as an agency for reforming and reclaiming fallen men and women. A complete separation of the government of these prisons from party politics; permanence in their executive administration, effected by a permanent tenure of official position therein; the employment of officers possessing a higher grade of qualifications; the investiture of the wardens with the power of appointing and removing all the officers who constitute the police force of the prisons; the total abolishment of the contract system, and the organization of the convict labor upon a principle which, in seeking to make the prisons self-supporting, will seek still more to make their industries an agency in reforming the prisoners and restoring them to society, masters of a business that will enable them to earn an honest livelihood; greater breadth and efficiency given both to religious and secular instruction; the introduction of a carefully devised system of rewards as an encouragement to good conduct and industry, so that the principle of hope shall act with even greater vigor than that of fear; and the making of the reformation of the prisoners the real, as it is admitted to be the proper, object of the discipline of the prisons and of the efforts of the officers in carrying it into effect;—such are the essential reforms needed in the system, supposing it to remain in other respects what it is at present.

But we are not satisfied with the system as it is; we think it deficient in some very important particulars, and we ardently desire to see it replaced with a better. Neither have we any hesitation in expressing the opinion that what is known and has become famous as the Irish system of convict prisons is, upon the whole, the best model of which we have any knowledge; and it has stood the test of experience in yielding the most abundant as well as the best fruits. We believe that in its broad, general principles—not certainly in all its details—it may be applied, with entire effect, in our own country and our own state. What, then, is the Irish system? In one word, it may be defined as an adult reformatory. where the object is to teach and train the prisoner in such a manner that, on his discharge, he may be able to resist temptation and inclined to lead an upright, worthy life. Reformation, in other words, is made the actual as well as the declared object. This is done by placing the prisoner's fate, as far as possible, in his own hands; by enabling him, through industry and good conduct, to raise himself, step by step, to a position of less restraint; while idleness and bad conduct, on the other hand, keep him in a state of coercion and restraint.

There are four distinct stages in the prisoner's progress, under this system—the first intensely penal ; the second less so, but still strongly partaking of that character ; the third but slightly penal ; and the fourth losing the penal aspect entirely, unless subjection for a time to police supervision may be so regarded in a degree. In the first stage, the prisoner is confined for eight months in a cellular prison; is completely isolated from all his fellow prisoners ; and, during the whole period, works in his own cell. This is the hardest and consequently the most deterrent part of his imprisonment ; yet even this period may be abridged by good conduct, as it may be lengthened by bad. In the second stage, he is employed on public works in associated labor by day, but is confined in a solitary cell at night, and the strictest surveillance is maintained over him. Nevertheless, he has here every advantage of religious training, of books of a miscellaneous though moral character, and of instruction in secular knowledge by the lessons and lectures of competent schoolmasters. On entering this department, the prisoner is placed in the third class; from which, by industry, application and good conduct, all carefully measured by a system of marks, he rises into the second class ; thence, by a like probation successfully passed, into the first ; and, finally, through the same process, into the exemplary class. At each advance, his condition is improved; his privileges are enlarged ; and, particularly, the percentage of his earnings, placed to his credit and designed ultimately for his own use, is increased. All along, however, misconduct is punished by putting the offender back one or more steps, and even, if need be, to the cellular prison itself, from which he has to work his way forward again by slow and toilsome efforts. The third stage is the intermediate prison, so called because its inmates are in a state intermediate between imprisonment, properly so called, and freedom. Here they have almost as much liberty as if they were not prisoners at all ; they work, some at mechanical and others at farm labor, without overseers ; they are trusted, constantly and without hesitation, to go of errands anywhere in the city of Dublin or the country ; the education, carried on previously, is continued and greatly extended, through daily lectures by an accomplished teacher on interesting moral and practical subjects, and a sort of competitive inter-examination weekly, conducted by the prisoners themselves ; and the gratuities from their own earnings are increased, out of which they are permitted, if such is their pleasure, to spend 6d a week (12 cents of our currency) in procuring additional comforts for themselves ; which sum, however, is generally saved, and added to their little capital, the result of their hoardings throughout their prison life. Indeed, the main design of this permission is to cultivate the habit of providence and thrift. It should be stated that the convicts in the intermediate prison hold their position there under very serious responsibities ; since, for any offence, however small, they are returned to their former cellular prison, whence they must win their way back, as before, by a course of exemplary conduct and diligent application to work and lessons. The fourth stage is that in which prisoners, the requisite portion of whose sentence has expired, having had their cases investigated and being found worthy, receive a conditional pardon, and are discharged on ticket-of-leave. As long as their tickets-of-leave continue in force, there is in Ireland, contrary to what happens in England,* a *bona fide* police supervision kept up over the prisoner, and, on his relapse, or even if found without visible means of support and associating with bad characters, his pardon is revoked, and he is remitted to prison to commence anew the course of reformation. While it may be doubtful whether, owing to the numerous separate jurisdictions existing in our country, the ticket-of-leave system can ever be fully adopted among us, it may be modified, or, if necessary, even abandoned altogether, without seriously affecting the general theory on which the Irish prisons are framed. In adopting this plan, the advocates of the separate

---

* On the general subject of the English convict prisons, the Hon. M. D. Hill, late Recorder of Birmingham, in a recent letter to the corresponding secretary of the prison association, holds this language : "Your remarks on the state of our convict prisons, as represented in Miss Carpenter's book ["Our Convicts"], are well founded, as showing a lamentable state of things ; but great improvements have been made since she wrote, and our English convict prisons are now assimilated, in a considerable degree, to those of Ireland, the conduct and results of which are admirable." We believe that Sir Walter Crofton, the father of the Irish system, is now at the head of the English prison system, being so employed by the government, with a view of organizing that system, as far as circumstances will permit, on the Irish plan.

and congregate systems of imprisonment may meet on common grounds. We may state in this connexion—and it is pertinent so to do—that the inspectors of the Massachusetts state prison, in their report for 1865, favor the introduction into the penal system of that commonwealth of a modified form of the ticket-of-leave system. After referring to the mistakes which they have themselves sometimes made in seeking the interposition of executive clemency in behalf of convicts, whose good behaviour and seeming penitence appeared to justify their application, and of the general risk of an unconditional pardon as being such as justly to deter the executive from using this function with great freedom, they add that the executive clemency may be more safely exercised in the form of a conditional pardon, which is the essence of the ticket-of-leave system, to be revoked whenever the conduct of the released prisoner is such as to show that he is unworthy of the liberty and privilege extended to him. They then promise to present the "many arguments in favor of such a measure," when the subject is brought to the notice of the Legislature, then " soon to convene."

The results of this system have been most extraordinary (we have not space for details) both as regards the reformation of criminals and relief from trouble in the disposal of discharged convicts. In respect to the latter of these points, the difficulty is no longer for released prisoners to obtain employment, but for employers to obtain the prisoners whom they want, the demand for their services being in advance of the supply.

Now, for our state prisons, we propose, not certainly the adoption of the Irish system in all its administrative details, but a system based upon its principles and conforming to its general methods. Neither would we have the system, even to this extent, adopted and put in force all at once, but cautiously and gradually, on a small scale at first, with opportunity to watch its operation and to correct errors by the results of experience, and only as public sentiment should lend its sanction and support to the change.

But the state has not discharged its whole duty to the crimininal, when it has punished him for his fault; no, nor even when it has reformed him. Its obligation towards him does not cease when it opens his prison door, and bids him walk forth in freedom. Having raised him up, it has the still further duty to aid in holding him up. Some systematic provision to this end is the essential complement to any effective plan of reformatory punishment. In vain shall we have given the convict an improved mind and heart, in vain shall we have given him capacity for continuous labor and the desire to advance himself by worthy means, if on his discharge he finds the world as it were, in conspiracy against him, with none to trust him, none to meet him kindly, none to give him the opportunity of earning honest bread. The willing laborer can get no work to do. The man who yearns to prove himself worthy of association with the virtuous and the good is repelled, as if contact with him were pestilential. His good purposes are defeated, and his hope of redemption vanishes. What can such a man do, if he live at all, but live as a criminal? What though his reformation be genuine, can it be permanent? Impossible! He will surely be clutched again by his old associates in crime, and drawn back to the abyss of sin, from which he had vainly hoped and labored to emerge. So it has been, too often and too generally; and so it is, still.

Under these circumstances, it is the clear duty of the state, as it is also no less clearly, her true policy, after discharging her convicts from her prisons, to institute some agency, by refuges or otherwise, whereby, after their release, they may be strengthened in their good resolutions, provided with situations, and, in all suitable ways, encouraged and aided in their efforts to reform. Massachusetts, we have seen, has a state agent to care for her male convicts on their discharge, and two refuges for females of the same class—these latter being private establishments, but receiving grants of money from the state in aid of their benevolent work. Ireland has a commissioner to look after her liberated male prisoners, and two well conducted, efficient refuges, one Catholic, the other Protestant, to receive, temporarily support, and provide places for, her discharged female prisoners. In France, the Association of St. Vincent de Paul counts this care for liberated prisoners, thousands of whom have received the benefits of its assistance, among its noblest functions, its most loved and cherished labors. But in Bavaria, we have an example of the broadest and most systematic provision to this end. There is, in that country, a complete national organization, having this object in view, including a society for every province, and a committee for every district. Six weeks before the discharge of a prisoner, notice of such discharge is given by the governor of the prison to the district committee, with a full account of his character and habits, the amount of money earned by him during his imprisonment, and the circumstances which warrant the extension of assistance to him; and the committee, using its discretion as to each individual case, supplies to those who are worthy of it productive occupation, and maintains a watchful supervision over them. The Prison Association of New York, whose servants we are in the present labor, within a limited sphere has done an important work in this department of benevolent effort; and at the very moment we are penning these paragraphs, some public-spirited ladies of Buffalo are engaged in the work of organizing a home for released female prisoners, with a view to their redemption from further bondage to criminal practices.

We repeat, therefore, that in any reorganization of the prison system of New York, an essential complement of it will be some provision for the assistance and security of released prisoners.

SECTION SECOND.

GENERAL ADMINISTRATION.

In none of the states of the American Union, visited by the undersigned, is there any central authority having a general power of control and direction over the entire prison system of the state. The nearest approach to such authority (which, indeed, is scarcely an approach to it at all) is in Massachusetts, where the Board of State Charities has, to a certain extent, an oversight over the whole system, but no power of government, properly so called. Except in the right conferred by law of exacting statistical returns from the prisons, according to forms prepared by the Board, this body has little more actual power than the Prison Association of New York; the main function of the former, like that of the latter, being inspection and recommendation. In Canada we found a central authority, having a sort of general control (but with powers too limited) over all the penal as well as other public institutions of the country, whose legal title is: "A board of inspectors of public asylums, hospitals, the provincial penitentiary, and of all county jails and other prisons." Further on, in this section, we shall have occasion to describe more fully the organization, powers and duties of the said board of inspectors.

The general supervision and control of the state prisons, in the states visited by the commissioners, is lodged in boards of inspectors—sometimes called directors—varying from two to five in number, the more common number being three. These inspectors are commonly appointed either by the legislatures or the governors; in New England by the governor and council; but in Pennsylvania they are appointed by the supreme court, a separate board of five_members for each of the two state penitentiaries, the eastern and western. In New York alone are they elected by popular vote—one board of three members for all three of the state prisons. Missouri has a peculiar arrangement, by which the auditor, treasurer and attorney general of the state constitute the board of inspectors, all *ex-officio* members—a bad plan. In New Hampshire there is no board of inspectors, the governor and council acting in that capacity. Neither is there any such authority in Wisconsin, the whole power of government being in the hands of an officer called the state prison commissioner. He is both warden and treasurer. He is elected by the people at the same time and in the same manner as the governor and other state officers, and holds his office for two years.

The legal powers of the inspectors differ somewhat in different states; practically they differ much more, ranging from almost nothing, as in Kentucky, to an almost absolute control, as in New York. These officers are not usually appointed all at the same time, but, for the most part, one each year. They have a foolish law in Massachusetts, if it is not worse than foolish, which interdicts the same inspector from serving two consecutive terms.

The mode of appointing the wardens or governors of the prisons varies a good deal in different states. In some, the appointment is made by the governor, or by the governor and council; in some by the legislature; in others by the inspectors; and in one, as we have seen—Wisconsin—by vote of the people in a general election. Everywhere the power that appoints the warden may remove him at pleasure. The chaplain, physician and clerk are usually, not always, appointed by the same power as the warden. The officers constituting the police of the prisons—called, in some, keepers, and in others, overseers—are, in the great majority of cases, appointed either absolutely by the wardens, or, which is the more common practice, by the inspectors on the nomination of the warden; but this comes substantially to the same thing. In New York the warden has neither the appointment nor nomination of his subordinates, nor any power of removal; all is in the hands of the inspectors. Yet he is held responsible by the inspectors and at the bar of public opinion for the government and discipline of the prison, and is thus much in the same condition as the Israelites under their Egyptian taskmasters, when they were required to make brick without straw.

The immediate administration of the prisons is everywhere entrusted to the superintendent, by whatever name called; nevertheless, the inspectors have, for the most part, the general direction of it. It belongs to them, in general, to make the regulations,—subject in some states to the approval of the Governor,—which the superintendent is charged with executing; and also to watch over this execution. The thoroughness with which this duty of supervision is discharged varies exceedingly. Thus in Kentucky, Missouri, Maine, and some other states, the superintendence of the inspectors, from all we could learn, seems to be superficial and ineffective; while, in the Eastern penitentiary, at Philadelphia, it is, manifestly, vigilant, active, thorough and pervading.

The most important position in the state prisons, beyond a doubt, is that of superintendent; for, though his written authority is not very great, though his prerogative, as defined by law, is less extensive than that of the inspectors, yet he is the centre and soul of the administration. It will be obvious, on the least reflection, that the gentlemen who fill these places should be men of probity, humanity, experience, a deep sense of duty, a strong religious feeling, large knowledge of men, and the highest executive and administrative ability. The frequent changes of these high officers, as well as those occupying subordinate positions, resulting from the working of a principle to be noticed further on in this report, operates adversely in two ways;—first, by repelling men of the right stamp from seeking the places, and secondly, by preventing all from acquiring that broad and varied experience, without which no man, however eminent in other respects, can achieve the least success in the government of a prison. Yet we are glad to record the fact that our American State penitentiaries can boast of some noble officers at the head of their affairs, men who would grace the position in any country; among whom we cannot forbear to name Mr. Haynes, of Massachesetts, Mr. Rice, of Maine, Mr. Halloway, of Pennsylvania, Mr. Prentice, of Ohio, and Mr. Cordier, of Wisconsin, now in office; and of those who have been "relieved," Messrs. Hubbell and Seymour, of New York, Mr. Miller, of Missouri, and Mr. Seaton, of Michigan.

We have already stated that in none of our American states is there any central authority, charged with the general supervision and control of the whole prison system of the state, but that in Canada such central power exists, in a Board of Inspectors of Prisons and other Public Institutions. That board was created by act of the Legislature in 1859. The act authorizes the Governor General to appoint five inspectors; to hold office during pleasure, that is, in effect, during good behavior. There is no displacement from office but for cause.

We do not, of course, propose to give an analysis of the entire act, but only of such parts of it as relate to prisons.

First, as it respects the provincial penitentiary—state prison—at Kingston.

The inspectors are charged with the government of the penitentiary, and are held responsible for its discipline and management, but have no executive power, except that of giving instructions to the warden and other executive officers. They are empowered (among other things) to have access to the prison and its books at all times; to investigate the conduct of the officers, and to compel their attendance and that of any other persons as witnesses; and to suspend any officers appointed by the Governor for misconduct, till the case is investigated by the Government.

It is the duty of the inspectors to visit the penitentiary jointly at least four times a year, and to devote not less than seven consecutive days at each visit to a rigid inspection of the whole affairs, management and condition of the institution, and of one of them to visit the prison at least once every month, and devote not fewer than two days to an inspection of its affairs; to frame a code of rules and regulations for the government of the penitentiary; to inspect every cell each month, and to examine monthly the cash and credit transactions; to determine the branches of labor to be introduced into the prison and the manner of prosecuting the same—whether by contract or otherwise; to prescribe the food and clothing of the prisoners; to determine the system of secular education; to fix the number of overseers, keepers and guards; to require an annual report from the warden, physician, chaplains and schoolmaster, and to make an annual report to the Governor General, giving a complete statement of the affairs of the institution; and to erect not exceeding fifty cells, with a workshop attached to each, adapted to carry out the separate or solitary system of discipline (a duty, by the way, not yet discharged).

Secondly, as regards common jails, houses of correction, and other prisons.

In this department of their work, it is the duty of the inspectors to visit and inspect every jail, &c., at least twice each year; to report to the Governor General the improvements required in jails, and to determine, subject to the approval of the Governor, the plan of all jails to be erected, and of all material alterations and improvements to be made in jails already built. In deciding on the plan of a jail, the inspectors are enjoined to take into consideration the following circumstances, viz: the nature and extent of the ground on which the said jail has been or is to be built; its situation in relation to any streets and buildings, and to any river or other water; the comparative elevation of the site and capability of being drained; the materials of which it is or is to be composed; the necessity of providing for ventilation and guarding against cold and damps; the proper classification of prisoners as to sex, age and cause of commitment; the best means of securing their safe custody, without resorting to severe treatment; the due accommodation of the keeper, so that he may have ready access to the prisoners, and may conveniently oversee them; the prevention of intercourse with the outside world; the prevention of nuisances; the reformation and employment of prisoners; provision for outdoor exercise; and the enclosure of the premises with a secure wall. It is further made the duty of the inspectors to frame a system of rules for the government of the jails, including the maintenance of prisoners as to diet, clothing, bedding, &c.; their employment; medical attendance; religious instruction; the conduct of the prisoners and the restraint and punishment to which they may be subjected; and the treatment and custody of the prisoners generally, and the whole internal economy and management of the jails.

The counties in Upper and districts in Lower Canada are required to provide the necessary funds for erecting new jails and securing requisite improvements in the old. It is left optional with these authorities to provide the funds or not, however important the improvements recommended by the inspectors, and however urgent these officers may be to have them made. The jail at Kingston, the seat of the provincial penitentiary, is an example in point. It is a wretched affair, and wholly unfit for the purposes of such an institution; but, despite the earnest and long-continued efforts of the inspectors, the authorities of the three counties to which that jail belongs in common have, as yet, taken no steps to replace it with a better. Just here, it seems to us, is the weak point in the law creating the present board of inspectors. As it regards improvements in old jails and the erection of new ones, they can recommend, and when plans are submitted to them, can pass upon the same, forbidding the use of such as fail to meet their approval. But here their power ends. However imperatively a new jail may be needed in any county or district, they have no authority to compel its erection, but the whole matter rests with the local authorities. This, we are free to say, strikes us as a serious defect in the law. Gentlemen competent to the duties of a position so important and responsible should be clothed with some discretion in the discharge of those duties; and when, after due argument and a reasonable delay in awaiting the effect of their exhortations, the county or district authorities utterly refused to listen to the voice of reason, to the manifest prejudice of the highest interests of the nation, then the inspectors should have power, under proper guards and limitations, to proceed with the erection of the jail, despite the indifference or opposition of the authorities, at the expense of the jurisdiction, within whose bounds it should be erected.*

But, however imperfectly this board may be constituted in respect to its want of adequate powers for good, however cramped and restricted its sphere of authoritative action, let us test its utility by inquiring what it has accomplished during the six years of its existence, in the face of prejudice, indifference, and even active hostility, for the improvement of the prisons of Canada. As the result of their first inspection of the jails, they found defects pervading them throughout; in their construction, superintendence, discipline, sanitary arrangements, and all other departments of administration. They describe them all as in a frightful condition; as, in effect, nurseries of vice; as breeding and educating criminals for the work of preying on society; and as robbing the community of the wealth that might have been earned by their inmates, could they but have been saved from becoming felons through the baneful education thus received. There was not a solitary jail in Canada, adapted to the proper

---

* Mr. E. A. Meredith, LL.D., President of the Board, in a lecture before a literary society, says: "The powers of the inspectors reach but a short way, while the evils to be remedied were of long growth, widely spread and deeply rooted."

ends, or answering the just purposes of such an institution. Since the creation of the board, thirteen new jails have been built, and ten old ones altered in Upper Canada, on plans approved by them; plans for rebuilding or altering six others have been submitted to them, and these improvements will soon be completed; while there are but six jails in the whole province, in reference to which nothing has been done. When the board came into existence, there was no uniform dietary in the jails, and the daily cost of the rations of each prisoner exceeded twenty-five cents; now there are very few jails in which the dietary prescribed by the rules is not observed, and the daily cost of rations is about nine cents per man; thus the annual cost of the food of each prisoner has been reduced from $89.25 to $32.85 cents a year—an immense saving. Again, at the organization of the board, there was no uniformity in the registers of the jails, and many kept none at all; now full registers, covering every material point, are kept in all; and criminal statistics, of great value, are annually collected and published to the world. Moreover, the board has, from the first, recommended two most important measures of criminal reform, and, from year to year, has repeated and, with cogent reasoning, urged its recommendations upon the Legislature, viz.: the adoption of the principle of separate imprisonment in all common jails, and the establishment of central or district prisons, intermediate between the provincial penitentiary and the jail, in which reformatory discipline could be introduced; and there is reason to think that these great reforms may soon become a part of the penal system of Canada. These are exceedingly gratifying results, not a tithe of which could have been secured, except through the existence and agency of this board; and others, no less important would, doubtless, ere this, have been effected, had the board been clothed with powers adequate to the work entrusted to it. The wonder is, that in so short a time and with a discretion so restrained, so much should have been done.

In any comprehensive reorganization of the prison system of our state, we consider the creation of a central authority, having general powers of direction and control, absolutely essential. At present that fundamental principle of all good government—a responsible but supreme authority—is wanting in relation to our prisons; hundreds of persons, and if we include county boards of supervisors, perhaps thousands, having a direct power in their

management. This single fact affords an ample explanation of the
slow progress which has been made in general improvement. The
select committee of 1850 on prison discipline, in the British Parliament, took no wiser action than that of adopting a resolution,
with a view to securing uniformity in prison construction and
management, to the effect that "it is desirable that the Legislature should entrust increased powers to some central authority,
and that such increased powers would be best exercised by a
board," etc. Without some such authority, ready at all times for
deliberation and action, there can be no consistent and homoge-
neous system of administration, no well directed experiments, no
careful deductions, no establishment of broad principles of prison
discipline, nor any skillfully devised plans for carrying such principles into effect. But if the construction and management of all
our prisons were entrusted to a central board or bureau, improvements of every kind could readily be introduced, and that, too, in
the safest manner, by first trying the plan proposed on a small
scale and under the best circumstances for insuring trustworthy
results, and then, if successful, gradually, under the guidance of
experience, extending the sphere of its operations. It is material
to remark, though the observation would naturally occur to reflecting minds, that a supreme authority, like that here proposed,
is quite compatible with local boards acting under its direction.
But, with or without local boards, a general board, properly constituted and empowered, could find little difficulty in the efficient
management and superintendence of the whole system. We
ardently hope yet to see all the departments of our preventive,
reformatory and punitive institutions—the nursery of the infant,
the school of the juvenile, the jail of the adult, the local penitentiary, and the state prison—moulded into one harmonious and
effective system; its parts mutually answering to and sustaining
each other; the whole animated by the same spirit, aiming at the
same objects and subject to the same central control, yet without
the loss of the advantages of voluntary aid and effort where they
are attainable.

Among the interrogatories framed by the undersigned in relation to state prisons, was one as to the opinion held on the
probable utility of a supreme power, such as that proposed above,
to be entrusted with the direction of the whole prison system. In
their responses, the intelligent and experienced wardens of the
state prisons of Massachusetts, Maine, Ohio and Wisconsin, and

the no less accomplished late warden of that of Missouri—Messrs. Haynes, Rice, Prentice, Cordier and Miller—expressed themselves as decidedly favorable to the creation of such central boards in our states, as likely to be productive of many important reforms in prison discipline. Mr. Miller added the suggestion that the members of the proposed boards be paid liberal salaries, first, to the end that men of intelligence, experience and enlarged views may be secured to serve on them ; and secondly, because persons who labor in such fields from motives of honor alone are never found very efficient, and rarely do more than take the opinions of prison officers and make up reports from them, without giving the subjects of their reports much thought or investigation themselves.

In this connection, as strongly corroborative of our views as to the utility and importance of a central administration, we venture to make a brief reference to the history of penal administration in France. Prior to 1856, the prisons of that country were subject, in great measure, to the control of the departments in which they were situated. At that time they were for the most part in a shameful condition, being destitute of furniture, clothing, bedding, and indeed of all materials necessary to the service. Grave abuses existed in the supplies and the regulation of the expenditures. In most of them, a promiscuous mingling of the prisoners confounded all classes and both sexes. On the first of January, 1856, the state took charge of these prisons; that is to say, they became subject to that central authority and control, for which we are pleading in our own state. The result has been, the correction of the monstrous abuses named above, the introduction of excellent and cheap supplies into the prisons, a great diminution of expenses, and an almost incredible augmentation of the product of prison labor. Under the old regime of separate jurisdictions, the expense of the service was one franc and thirteen centimes a day for each person, which, under a central administration, has been reduced to eighty centimes—about sixteen cents of our money—or nearly one-third. The annual product of prison labor, which, prior to the change, had been in all the departments (except Paris), 14,466 francs, had increased even in 1862, the date to which our information extends, to 900,000 francs, an increase of more than sixty hundred per cent.*

---

* Journal of Prison Discipline and Philanthropy for January, 1866.

SECTION THIRD.

PRISON PREMISES AND BUILDINGS.

The grounds belonging to the state prisons visited by us, including those of New York (not visited last year, but often before), vary exceedingly in extent, ranging from half an acre, as in New Hampshire, to two hundred acres, as in the case of Clinton prison in our own state.

In treating the subjects mentioned in the title of this section, we will first give briefly the details belonging to the several prisons, and then offer a few general remarks.

Connecticut.—This prison is in Wethersfield, and is beautifully situated on the south side of an extensive bay. The premises embrace fifteen acres, a portion of which is inclosed by a wall seventeen feet high and three feet thick. The drainage is reported by the warden as "not extensive," by which we presume is meant, that it is not perfect, or not very good. There are both vegetable and flower gardens, and a handsome lawn in front, of four acres, ornamented with shade trees. The entire premises are clean and neat, and are altogether the most attractive, in point of rural beauties, to be found in connection with any state prison in the United States, as far as seen by us.

The buildings are plain, substantial structures, economically built, without needless ornament, and also suited, in their whole appearance and air, to the object to which they are devoted. There is a dwelling house for the chaplain standing by itself, and a residence for the warden adjoining the prison proper, with office, guard room, dormitories for officers, &c., &c. The cell building is of stone, two hundred and eighty feet long by forty-seven feet wide, with two blocks of cells, built of brick, four stories high. The number of cells is two hundred and fifty; their dimensions seven feet long, three and a quarter wide and about seven feet high. There are eight workshops, seventy feet by forty, well arranged and commodious. The chapel is forty-eight feet by thirty feet, and the hospital eighteen feet square. The prison has a department for female convicts.

Delaware.—There is no state prison here, but the county jail at New Castle is used instead.

Illinois.—The premises here contain fifteen acres, and form an exact square, the encircling wall being eight hundred feet long on each side ,and six feet thick at the base, three feet at the top, and twenty-five feet high, coped with dressed stone five feet wide and eight inches thick, forming a broad walk for the sentinels. At the corners of this wall are four turrets, twenty feet in diameter and sixty feet high, for the use of the sentinels.

The style of architecture adopted for the main buildings and walls is a castellated gothic; but for the buildings within the inclosure, convenience, security and durability have been studied more than architectural beauty.

The two wings, east and west, are each two hundred and fifty feet long by fifty-four wide, and their walls forty feet high; one of them containing four tiers of cells, the other five, there being one hundred cells in each tier, or nine hundred in all. Each cell is four feet wide, seven feet long and seven feet high in the clear; and their floors, ceilings and partitions are each formed of one well dressed stone, eight inches thick. The doors are made of cylindrical bar iron, and therefore admit nearly as much light and air when closed as when open. Each door has its own lock, besides which there is a bar extending the entire length of the wing, which is operated by a lever at one end. This bolts every door in one tier at the same moment, and the two sets of locks constitute a double security.

The warden's dwelling, which is between the two wings, and to which they are attached, is ninety-eight feet by eighty-seven, and five stories high, including the basement. It will readily be believed that the entire façade, over six hundred feet in length, of massive hewn stone, presents a magnificent and imposing appearance, and looks more like the palace of some mighty prince than the home of felons, who are expiating their crimes within its walls.

We have not space to pursue the description, but the entire appointments of the place, when the whole is completed—chapel, hospital, mess-room, kitchen, &c., will be in keeping with what has been already described.

Within the great enclosure, and having an encircling wall of its own—a wall within a wall—is the female department of the prison, having 100 cells, with the necessary workshops, &c., &c.

The work shops of the men are of stone, one story high of fifteen feet, forty feet wide, and 1,295 in length, with cross walls at intervals, extending through the roof with a battlement or fire-wall. Ventilation is secured by windows on both sides every four-teen feet.

No building within the enclosure is nearer than forty feet to the outside walls.

In his report of 1860, the warden says: "If the plan of the prison and character of the work are maintained till it is com-pleted, the people of this state may rely upon having a prison, which, for durability and convenience (he might have added, also, expensiveness), will not be equalled in the United States, and pro-bably not excelled in the world."

Northern Indiana.—We are not able to state the extent of the premises here. The prison is in process of construction, and at present is in an inchoate state. There is no cell-house, and the only place for the confinement of prisoners is a single room, sixty-six by forty feet. In this all the prisoners, who are well, sleep and are confined at all times, when not engaged at labor in the shops. Four guards are employed to keep watch over them at night, one of whom is in the room with the convicts. There is no female department here.

Southern Indiana.—Here, too, we are unable to give the extent of the grounds belonging to the institution. The buildings are old and inconvenient, and the whole appearance of the place struck us as slovenly and repulsive. The warden, Col. Merri-weather, had been in office less than two months at the time of our visit. He impressed us favorably, but failed to reply to our inter-rogatories, though he promised to do so, and was several times written to on the subject. The prison has a female department.

Kentucky.—This prison is at Frankfort, the capital of the state. The premises contain about six acres, without garden or ornamen-tal grounds. They are enclosed by a stone wall, four feet thick and twenty-two feet high. The drainage is stated to be good. Everything here wore a confused and slovenly appearance. This was, in part, no doubt, owing to the erection of new buildings now going forward, an extensive conflagration having occurred in the prison some months ago.

The prison buildings are: 1. The cell house. This is two hun-dred and ten feet long by forty feet wide, containing two hundred and fifty cells, in three tiers, arched. Their dimensions are seven feet long, three and a half feet wide, and seven feet high to the centre of the arch. The odor of the cells was most offensive even

in the day time, showing an exceedingly imperfect ventilation.
2. A hemp factory, three hundred and seventy feet long, seventy
feet wide, and three stories high. 3. Another large factory, three
hundred and fifty feet long, fifty feet wide, and two stories high,
containing a chair shop, a cooper shop, a shoe shop, a tailor's shop,
a carpenter and wagon shop, a blacksmith's shop, an engine room
and large store room. 4. A building, containing a hospital, fifty
feet by forty feet, with iron bedsteads, a guard room, twenty feet
by forty, and a female department, which had, at the time of our
visit, but two inmates. 5. A kitchen, wash house, and smoke
house. 6. A building (the new one in process of erection, and
nearly completed, when we were there), containing, in the first
story, a dining hall, eighty feet by fifty feet, well lighted and ventilated, with good seats, and every way commodious and comfortable; and a chapel over the same, of the like dimensions, with a
pleasant pulpit, settees for the convicts; and, altogether, presenting an air of neatness and comfort.

Maine.—The prison is in Thomaston, eighty miles north east
from Portland, situated on an eminence, and a few rods from navigable water. The grounds contain about four and a half acres,
but even this small space is considerably abridged by an old lime
stone quarry embraced in them, formerly worked by the convicts,
but long since abandoned as unprofitable. This old quarry gives
to the grounds a rough, unsightly appearance, and, what is perhaps worse, diminishes them to a compass less than is required
for the proper purposes of the prison. The premises are enclosed
by a stone wall, four feet thick and fifteen high, with a picket
fence on the top. There is a garden and a few shade trees.

The residence of the warden is outside of the prison walls. It
is a commodious brick dwelling, with necessary out buildings.

Within the walls are the cell house, work shops, &c., &c. The
cell house is a stone structure, one hundred and fifteen feet in
length and fifty in breadth, with which are connected the guard
room and hospital. There are one hundred and eight cells, seven
feet long, four feet wide and seven feet high. There is a large
carriage factory (the manufacture of carriages being the principal
business carried on here); a blacksmith's shop, where the iron
work for the carriages is done; and a shoe shop. Under this latter,
on the first floor, is the chapel, thirty-eight feet by thirty-three
feet; a neat and commodious apartment, with pulpit and settees,

very different from the cramped and comfortless room, in the attic of the carriage shop, which it replaces.

Massachusetts.—This prison is in Charlestown, two and a half miles from the centre of Boston. The site on which it stands is a point of land, washed on two sides by the sea, and affording, therefore, the purest and most salubrious air; no position could be more favorable than this in a hygienic point of view.

There are some seven acres, five of which are enclosed by a quadrangular wall, of solid granite masonry, 25 feet high, 5 feet thick at the base, and 3 feet at the top, surmounted by a strong iron railing, with watch towers placed at intervals on the summit. In the centre of the prison yard there is an oblong plat of grass, with shrubbery, flowers, and a fountain.

The prison buildings are of massive Quincy granite. There is an octagonal central structure, with three wings, or cell-houses, radiating from it at right angles to each other, and opposite one of these a range of brick buildings, consisting of the various prison offices, and two handsome dwelling-houses, the residences of the warden and deputy warden.

The octagonal is 73 feet in diameter, and of the same height. In the basement is the cookery; and over it is a room, separated from the three wings by iron bars, which commands a view of all the corridors, and every cell in the prison. In the centre of this stands a large glass case filled with gold fish; on one side is a book case containing the prison library; and on the others, a number of lounges, chairs, and writing desks for the use of officers and visitors. This spacious apartment is lighted by four immense arched double windows, extending from the floor to the ceiling. Over this room, and of the same dimensions with it, is the chapel; a well-lighted and airy apartment, having a neat and appropriate desk, provided with comfortable seats, and altogether cheerful and attractive in its appearance. It will seat 600. Above the chapel is another room of the same size, intended for a hospital, but never, as yet, used for that purpose, because sick prisoners would be unable to climb so high, and no apparatus for raising them has been introduced. The present hospital is at the end of one of the wings, though not a part of it. It is spacious and commodious, having fourteen cells of large size, with dispensary, bath-room, and kitchen attached.

In each of the three wings used as cell-rooms, the external walls have, we think, ten large arched windows, five on each side, extending from the eaves almost to the floor. Each window is 9 feet wide, by 26 feet in height, and made secure against attempts at escape by strong, upright, cylindrical iron bars. The doors of the cells are made of round iron bars. By this arrangement of the windows and doors, air and light are admitted almost as freely as if the outer walls were taken away, and the doors of the cells were set wide open. The number of cells in the three wings is 554. They are $8\frac{1}{2}$ feet long, $4\frac{3}{4}$ feet wide, and $7\frac{2}{3}$ feet high. Their furniture is an iron bedstead, with curled palm leaf mattrass, a table with drawer in it, a stool, a shelf, a knife, fork and spoon, a pepper box, a salt cellar, a vinegar bottle, a water kid, and a night bucket, together with a Bible and a slate. There is no common mess-room, the convicts taking all their meals in their cells.

There is a spacious guard room and a sitting room for the use of the officers.

There are two long brick structures, two stories high, forming two sides of a hollow square. These are divided into ten workshops, each about one hundred feet long by forty feet wide—all well lighted and ventilated. Ice-water is kept in them in summer for the use of the prisoners. There is, besides, a foundry, one hundred and twenty-five feet by seventy feet.

As the prison system of Massachusetts is the most extended and complete to be found in any of the states of our Union, so the undersigned have no hesitation in pronouncing the state penitentiary at Charlestown, though certainly far behind our ideal, the banner prison of the country. In its construction, its ventilation, its staff of officers, its discipline (there are others where the discipline is more rigid, more military), and all its appointments, except the department of secular instruction, it seems to us fairly entitled to this preëminence.

It has no female department.

Maryland.—This prison is in Baltimore, about three-quarters of a mile northeast from the centre of the city. It stands on elevated ground, and the situation, except that it is in a city, where no prison other than those for the detention of persons arrested and held for trial ought ever to be placed, is pleasant and healthy.

The premises contain some four acres, which are inclosed with a stone wall, twenty feet high.

Of the prison buildings we are unable to give any description. We neglected to make the usual memoranda, as Mr. Thompson, the warden, promised to respond to our interrogatories, but, though several times addressed by letter on the subject, failed to fulfill his promise. Our visit to this prison was a hurried one, and there was little about it which impressed us very favorably. Reforms seemed needed in all departments.

A female department, well filled at the time of our visit, belongs to this penitentiary.

Michigan.—The state prison is at Jackson, a little out of the town. The grounds embrace some six acres, and are encircled by a stone wall, five feet thick at bottom and three feet at top, with a height of eighteen feet. There is a garden in front of the prison, not inclosed by the wall, which, with proper care and at small expense to the state, might ·be made highly ornamental. The drainage is good. The sewer is of brick and circular in form, with a diameter of four feet. There is a fall of twenty feet to the river in a distance of six hundred feet.

The prison buildings include main prison, female prison, and solitary prison.

The main prison consists of a centre building, sixty feet square, and four stories high, with an east and west wing, each two hundred and twenty feet long, containing the cells. Each wing has three hundred and twenty-eight cells, arranged in four tiers. The cells are·three and a half feet wide, six and a half feet long, and seven feet high. They are each furnished with a cot bedstead, covered with canvas, a strawbed in winter, two sheets, a pillow case, quilts, a pillow of hay, straw, shavings, or other like material, a stool, a night bucket, &c., &c.

The chapel is sixty feet by sixty-five, twenty-two to twenty-eight feet high, with seats for visitors in the rear of the convicts.

The hospital is in the third story of main building, sixty feet square, with ceiling twenty feet high, and well lighted and ventilated. · It is not regarded as secure, and, therefore, convicts must be quite sick or they are not allowed to remain in it.

The mess room is sixty by sixty-five feet, and is furnished with long tables about a foot wide, a stool for each convict, and knife, fork, spoon, tin plate, and tin basin.

The guard room is in the main building, and there are four guard houses on the top of the wall.

The whole aspect of the prison struck us unfavorably. Everything wore a slovenly air; the discipline appeared feeble; and, generally, the administration seemed lacking in vigor and efficiency.

Missouri.—The prison is at Jefferson City, the capital of the state, and is situated on a bluff of the Missouri river, commanding a fine view of the adjacent country. The prison premises embrace five acres, enclosed by a stone wall, twenty feet high, and of a thickness of four feet at the foundation and two at the top. The drainage is good, the descent to the river being rapid.

The prison buildings consist of: 1. A large stone cell-house. Neither the dimensions of this building nor the number of cells are stated by ex-Warden Miller in the paper communicated to us. The size of the cells is seven and a half feet by four feet, and it is claimed that they are well ventilated; which, if true, is a novelty in American prisons. Each is furnished with an iron bedstead and a straw bed, with blankets according to the season. 2. A hospital building, also of stone. 3. Two large brick blocks for workshops, in one of which is a dining hall, which is likewise used for a chapel, being large enough to seat comfortably all the prisoners. There is a female department in the prison.

Most of the buildings here are quite indifferent, and not well adapted to prison purposes. The premises are much too confined for the size of the prison; and the *tont-ensemble* presented a slovenly, uninviting, we might almost say, repulsive appearance. How much of this might have been owing to the absence of the warden, Mr. Horace Swift, we cannot say. As it was in contemplation to erect an additional cell building, Mr. S. had gone to visit prisons in the eastern states, and gather ideas on prison construction that might be made available in the proposed enlargement of the Missouri penitentiary. It is to be hoped that his mission proved successful, and that its fruits will appear in sundry reforms, where reform seems so much needed.

In the absence of Mr. Swift, we sought an interview with the late warden, P. T. Miller, Esq., with whose reports during his administration we had been familiar. He spent an entire evening with us at our hotel. Mr. M. had been at the head of the prison for nearly four years prior to March, 1865, when he was removed from the position by Governor Fletcher; for what cause we did not inquire, and do not know. However able and worthy his successor may be—and we trust that he is proving himself among the ablest and the worthiest—we could not but regret that, for any cause other than malfeasance in office, it should have been deemed necessary to displace a gentleman of so much intelligence, such large experience, and views so enlightened and liberal on the whole subject of prison discipline and prison management, as we found Mr. Miller to be.

New Hampshire.—The prison is in Concord, the capital of the State, on one of the principal streets, half a mile north of the State House.

The prison grounds embrace only half an acre, which is enclosed by a stone wall, eighteen feet high and four feet thick at the base.

The cell building is a substantial edifice, built of granite, and is two hundred and forty feet by fifty feet. It contains one hundred and twenty cells, whose dimensions are eight feet in length, four feet in width, and seven feet in heighth.

The chapel is a small but neat apartment, with capacity for seating one hundred and fifty.

The hospital has four rooms, each ten feet by twenty, thus giving altogether, for hospital purposes, a space of forty feet by twenty.

There is a building, two stories high, and one hundred and twenty feet long by fifty feet wide, which is divided into two workshops by a hall and stairway.

New Jersey.—The prison is at Trenton, the capital of the state. It was among the last visited by us, and our stay there was very brief. As Mr. Walker, the warden, failed to fulfill his promise to reply to our queries, we are not prepared to offer any satisfactory description of the grounds or buildings.

Ohio.—The prison of this state is at Columbus, the capital. The grounds consist of fifteen acres, thirteen of which are enclosed by a stone wall, having an average height of twenty-one feet and an average thickness of twenty-two inches. The drainage is good, by sewers to the adjacent river. That part of the grounds not included within the walls is devoted to the purposes of a garden. The yard in front of the main building is ornamented with shade trees, shrubbery and flowers. The yard within the walls—a kind of court formed by prison buildings which surround it on all sides—is two hundred and seventy-five feet by two hundred and sixty-eight feet. The "engine" and "bell" houses are in the centre of this yard. The yard is sodded, and walks paved with brick intersect it in every direction. A few sycamore trees are growing here and there in it, and there is one piece of plain stone statuary, the subject of which we do not now recall.

The prison buildings consist of 1. The warden's residence, including guard room and boarding house for officers. It is five stories high, including basement and attic, and is built of dressed lime stone. 2. Two prison halls, or cell houses. 3. A female prison and laundry. 4. A three story building, containing dining hall, hospital and chapel. 5. A prison for the insane. 6. A state shop. 7. State kitchen. 8. An engine house. 9. A bell house. 10. Nine workshops, where contract labor is performed.

The prison proper consists of two cell houses, designated as the east and west halls. These halls are built of stone, with outer walls three inches thick. West hall is one hundred and ninety feet in length by fifty feet in breadth, and contains one block of cells. East hall is three hundred and thirty-three feet by fifty feet, and has two blocks of cells. The cell blocks are of dressed stone, one hundred and sixty-five feet by twenty feet, five ranges high, and each range containing thirty-five cells. The corridors surrounding them are eleven feet in width. There are ten hundred and fifty cells. Their dimensions are seven feet long, three and a half feet wide, and seven feet high. They are furnished with bed, night tub, water bucket, and gas burner.

The chapel is L shaped. Its length, exclusive of the L, is one hundred and forty feet; length of L ninety feet. One half of this part is partitioned off for the use of the school and the library, which gives for the dimensions of the chapel a length of one hundred and eighty-five feet and a breadth of fifty feet. It is on the third floor of a building, running at right angles with and midway of the east hall, from which the stairs leading to it ascend.

The hospital is on the second floor of the same building, directly under the chapel, with which its dimensions and general contour correspond. It is a large, cheerful, well aired apartment, with all needful appliances for its special purposes. There is an entrance by steps, outside, from the prison yard; also by a door communicating with east hall by the chapel stairs.

The dining hall is also in the same building, underneath the hospital. Its whole length, including the L, is two hundred and thirty feet, and its breadth fifty feet. There are three doors by which it is entered from the yard, and one from east hall. There are fifty-two tables, each fifteen inches wide and thirty-six feet long, the prisoners sitting, as in all other prisons where they eat in a common mess room, face to back. Every prisoner is furnished with a stool, knife, fork, spoon, plate, and tin cup. The prison kitchen and bake house, connecting with the mess room, is one hundred feet by thirty feet.

The guard room is thirty-four feet by eighteen, and is on the first floor of front house. It separates the two cell houses, and commands a view of both, communicating with them and with the prison yard.

There are ten workshops, including that where work is done for the state; or, to speak more accurately, there are ten buildings, each containing several shops or apartments, where the same branch of business is carried on. All the buildings are of brick, —most of them two stories high, but a few one story. They vary a good deal in size, the largest being three hundred and fourteen feet by forty-five, and the smallest (state shop) sixty feet by forty.

Pennsylvania.—There are two state prisons in this state, called the eastern and western penitentiaries.

1. *Eastern Penitentiary.*—This is situated in the city of Philadelphia, on an elevated piece of ground, called Cherry Hill, from which it is sometimes named Cherry Hill prison.

The prison premises contain ten acres, enclosed by a massive wall of hewn stone, six feet thick at the base, three feet at the top, and thirty feet high. The building for the warden's and matron's residence and for prison offices forms a part of the south wall, on each side of the centre. The magnificence of this part of the prison may be inferred from the fact that the enclosing wall cost about $200,000. The architecture of the prison is a Norman Gothic, and the whole structure, but particularly the noble gateway, presents an imposing appearance.

In the exact centre of the yard is erected the observatory, an octagonal building, from the middle point of which the spectator has a perfect view of all the corridors, and also of the broad, graveled walk, which extends from the entrance to the said central building, and each side of which is laid out in parterres, and planted with flowers and shrubbery. The cell houses are built in seven blocks, radiating from this common centre. The spaces between the radiating blocks of cells are cultivated as a kitchen garden, and yield a large amount of vegetables, which are all furnished to the prisoners as a part of their rations. More than twenty gas lamps, distributed through the grounds, light up the premises at night, and increase the security of the prison. Four of the wings are two stories high, and three one story. They vary in length from three hundred and thirty feet to one hundred and eighty feet. There are five hundred and thirty-six cells in all. Most of them are eight by fifteen feet, and twelve feet high, though a few, because of the kind of work carried on in them (chair making), are double that size. In prisons conducted on the congregate plan, the cell blocks extend along the middle part of the building, with corridors all around, and the cells are placed back to back. Here, on the contrary, the cells in each of the seven wings are arranged in two rows, on opposite sides of seven central passages, extending from the observatory to the wall at the end of the block. All the cells in the three blocks of one story, and all in the lower stories of the others, have exercising yards attached to the rear, of the same dimensions with themselves. Many of these yards have borders planted by their occupants with flowers, or with lettuce, tomatoes, and other vegetables, or covered with strawberry vines. Many also have grape vines, peach trees, plum trees, or other kinds of fruit. The products of the yards belong to the occupants of the cells to which they are attached, and they are at liberty either to eat or to sell them. One prisoner informed us that he had sometimes gathered three bushels of grapes from his vines; another has a peach tree which yields several bushels of peaches annually, of the finest quality and commanding the highest price in market. Each cell has double doors opening into the central passage, one on each surface of the wall— a grated iron door on the inside, fastened with three bolts, and a close wooden door outside. The latter are set about one-third of the way open on Sunday to enable the prisoners to hear the preaching, and the same during the hot days of summer, to secure a freer circulation of air. They are never opened wide enough for prisoners in opposite cells to see each other. The cells that have exercising yards have the same arrangements of double doors for the egress of the occupants to their yards. They are lighted by small skylights in the roof, six inches wide by thirty inches long. The light is rather dim, and, in cloudy days, we should think, hardly sufficient for purposes of labor. Oil lamps are furnished to each prisoner at night till nine o'clock.

The cells are furnished as follows: Each has a pine bedstead, with bed of straw and pillow of the same. The bed clothes are two sheets, a pillow case, a comfortable, and one or two blankets, as may be required. Each is also provided with a Bible, a prayer book (if desired, which is usually the case), a slate and pencil, a stool, a table (which lets down when not in use), a closet containing two shelves, a looking glass, a comb, a hydrant, a water bucket, a knife, fork, spoon, plate, tin cup, oil lamp, piece of soap, bottle of vinegar, and molasses can, holding two quarts (the allowance for a month), together with such mechanical implements as may be required for the work to be performed.

Each cell has also a water closet. Each block of cells has an eight-inch water pipe passing along the whole length on either side in each story (where there are two), with valves at the ends. The valve at the upper end is connected with a reservoir of water, and that at the lower end with a sewer. Each cell has a branch from this main pipe. In the morning, after breakfast, the lower valve is thrown open, and the contents of the pipe are discharged into the sewer. Then a stream of water is let on to wash out the pipe, after which the lower valve is closed and the pipe filled with fresh water, which, rising some inches in the bowl of the water closet, remains till next morning. Once a fortnight, or thereabout, each prisoner is furnished with a tablespoonful of chloride of lime, which he dissolves in a bucket of water, and pours the solution into his privy pipe.

Women, as well as men, are imprisoned here.

2. *Western Penitentiary.*—This is commonly spoken of as situated at Pittsburgh, but it is in reality in the city of Allegheny, which is separated from Pittsburgh by the Allegheny river, and is in fact but an appendage of that city, though forming a different corporation.

The prison premises here are in the form of an octagon, four hundred feet in diameter, and contain about seven acres. They are enclosed by a stone wall twenty-five feet high, with an average thickness of two feet. The drainage is good,—by sewers, which carry off all the filth to the river. There is a vegetable garden within the enclosure, and a fine lawn with shade trees in front.

The buildings of the western penitentiary are, the residence of the warden, in front; three blocks of cells, two stories high, radiating from a semi-circular observatory, after the model of the Philadelphia prison; one of which is five hundred feet long, and the other two, each two hundred feet; an engine and dye house, and a gas house.

The hospital is quite unworthy of a prison of the first class, consisting of two badly arranged rooms. immediately over the kitchen.

There are three hundred cells, seven by sixteen feet, each provided with a table, hammock, straw bed, hydrant, gas burner, and necessary table furniture and mechanical implements for their handicrafts. There are no exercising yards attached to the cells here.

At the external angles of the front building are two large circular towers, which, together with the warden's residence, present a handsome elevation, being finished in the castellated style of gothic architecture. A circular tower is also placed at the angle of the boundary wall on each side, for the purpose of overlooking the prison yards. There is a female department in the prison.

The original plan of this prison was very different from that of its present construction. The cells, according to the former design, were built in a double range on the outer edge of the octagon, being placed back to back, as in prisons on the Auburn plan, but in the form of a circle, the diameter of which was three hundred and twenty feet; part of them facing the boundary wall, and the others fronting the large internal area, which was subdivided into nine yards or courts. These cells were intended for the purposes of constant solitary confinement, of absolute isolation and non-intercourse. No labor of any kind was provided; indeed, the cells were neither large enough nor light enough for any such purpose. The prison was opened for the reception of convicts in 1827. It was soon found, on experiment, that solitude, although intended to be perfect and absolute, was far from being so in fact. From the bad arrangement and construction of the building, the prisoners could easily communicate from cell to cell, and to such an extent could these communications be carried as to become a source of mutual contamination, just as in prisons where promiscuous association is allowed. Their health suffered to such a degree that it became necessary to let them out in successive groups into the open court yards, which was, of course, utterly destructive of the solitary principle. Again, the difficulties in the way of effective supervision were found to be insuperable. After an experiment of three years, the inspectors recommended a complete change in the plan of the building; and two years subsequently, in 1832, an act was passed by the Legislature, authorizing the demolition of these cells and the construction of others similar to those in the eastern penitentiary, in which the same system of discipline might be established. But we doubt whether the usages which came into vogue in the old prison were not propagated, to a greater or less extent, in the new, and whether the separate system was ever enforced at Pittsburgh, with any great degree of rigor. Certain it is that such is not the case at the present time.

Rhode Island.—The grounds of this prison, which is in the out-skirts of Providence, cover an area no more than three quarters of an acre, and are encircled by a stone wall twenty-five feet high, with an average thickness of two feet. The county jail is within the same enclosure, and under the same administration. The drainage is good. There is no garden of any kind ; only a few shade trees in front.

Vermont.—The prison is situated on an eminence west of the village of Windsor, and about half a mile from the Connecticut river. The premises embrace only an acre and a quarter. The drainage is good—into the adjoining valley. There is no garden ; only a small bed or border of flowers within the enclosure.

There are two cell buildings, one of stone, the other of brick. The former is the original prison, and is built on the old plan of large night rooms, arranged on opposite sides of a common hall. This is now used as a women's prison ; and of course no attempt is made to enforce the silent system by day or by night. An im-provement greatly needed here is the demolition of this old struc-ture and the erection of a new one, where the female prisoners as well as the male can be separately confined at night. The male prison, of brick, is built upon the usual Auburn plan, with a sep-arate night cell for every prisoner. The cells are of unusual size, but none too large, being eight feet long, six feet wide and seven feet high.

There is no mess-room, as the prisoners take all their meals in the cells.

There is no chapel. the religious services of the Sabbath being held in the corridor of the male prison.

The workshops are three in number, all of brick.

West Virginia.—There is no state prison in this state.

Wisconsin.—This prison is situated at Waupun, and may be pronounced, in all respects, one of the finest in the United States. The premises comprise an area of twenty acres, eight of which are enclosed by a stone wall, twenty feet high and three feet thick. The front wall is a series of stone pillars and arches, five hundred and seventy-five feet long, filled with an iron net-work. At the time of our visit, the drainage was very imperfect. All the filth that accumulated was emptied into sink-holes, dug for the purpose of receiving it. But in the winter of 1863–4, the commissioner of the prison, Henry Cordier, Esq., succeeded in procuring the neces-sary legislation for the construction of a sewer, of ample dimensions, with a fall of about forty feet, from the prison yard to Rock river, by which the drainage will be made perfect. There is a handsome garden, of nearly an acre in extent, in front of the prison buildings.

The prison buildings consist of a main building (used as a residence for the commissioner, officers' rooms, chapel and hospital), a cell room, a female prison, workshops, wash-house, barn and stables and wood shed.

The prison proper,—or cell room, is two hundred feet long, fifty feet wide, and thirty-two feet high. It is a structure of dressed lime-stone, with ten windows on each side, each window being sixteen feet by five feet. In the middle part of this room is a stone block containing the cells. A corridor fourteen feet wide runs all around it. The cell room for female convicts, surrounded by a separate stone wall, fifteen feet high and two thick, is seventy-three feet in length, thirty-four in width, and twenty in height.

The cell room for men contains four tiers, with two hundred and eighty cells in all. The size of the cells is seven feet long, four feet wide, and seven feet high. That of the women contains thirty-six cells in two tiers, each cell being ten feet long, six wide, and eight high. They are placed on each side of the room, with a hall fourteen feet wide between. Each cell in the female prison has a window. The furniture of the cells, both in the male and female departments, consists of the following articles : a cot, stand, stool, wash basin, knife, fork, spoon, salt box, pepper box, vinegar bottle, spittoon, lamp and night tub.

The chapel is in the second story of the main building, and is sixty-seven feet long, thirty-six wide, and eighteen high. It is connected by a stairway with the cell house, and the only furniture is a pulpit and the necessary seats for the convicts, with a few for citizens also.

The hospital, likewise in the main building, and connected with the cell room, is an apartment twenty-eight feet long, twenty-seven wide, and eighteen high. It contains only six beds; but this number, up to the present time, has been found sufficient.

There is no dining hall, as the prisoners take their meals in the cells.

The guard room is twenty-eight feet by twenty-six feet by eighteen feet. It is on the lower floor of the main building, communicating with and overlooking the cell room. In it are kept the arms of the prison and the keys of the several departments.

A row of buildings, of cut stone, three hundred and fifty feet in length by forty in width, and two stories high, contains the workshops, viz: stone, cooper, cabinet, shoe, and tailor shops. Each apartment in these shops is forty feet by eighteen, and twelve feet high.

The blacksmith's shop, also of cut stone, is eighty feet by forty, and sixteen high.

The wash house (same material) is forty feet, by twenty-five by sixteen.

It is thus seen that the Wisconsin state prison is of the most durable materials throughout, well built, well appointed, and substantial in all respects. It is also the most orderly and the most neatly kept of all the western prisons visited by us.

Canada.—The provincial penitentiary—state prison of Canada —is situated two miles west of the city of Kingston, on the north shore of Lake Ontario, near its outlet into the St. Lawrence river.

As we obtained no answers to our interrogatories from the officers of this institution—owing, probably, to the power of red tape—we are unable to state, with precision, the area embraced within the prison wall, but should judge it to be some ten acres, more or less. There is also a farm, of considerable extent, belonging to the prison, in the immediate neighborhood, which is worked, we believe to good advantage, by convict labor.

The encircling wall is a parallelogram in form, extending from the highway to the lake, and it is twenty feet in height, with a uniform thickness of three feet, from the base to the top. Within this enclosure stand the numerous buildings, of which the penitentiary is composed; all of which, as well as the wall itself, are of hewn stone, of a dark gray color, and very hard. The whole, with the exception of the first edifice erected, is the workmanship of the convicts themselves. The masonry is of the very best quality,—massive, solid, and enduring in a very high degree. A round tower graces each angle of the exterior wall; and the gateway in front, which is of the Doric order of architecture, is a beautiful and imposing structure.

The central building of the prison is a rotunda, of ample dimensions, surmounted by a handsome dome, from which radiate four wings, at right angles to each other. One of these wings contains the residence of the warden, the various offices of the prison, and the female ward; the other three contain the cells of the male convicts, eight hundred and forty in number. In each wing there are two ranges of cells, with five tiers, there being twenty-eight cells in each tier, or two hundred and eighty in all. The corridors are between the ranges of cells, instead of encircling them, as is usual in prisons of the congregate order. The doors of the cells are thus made to face each other, and there is a window in each looking out into the prison yard, in our judgment a bad arrangement. It would be a natural inference from the above that the prisoners can see each other from the grated doors of their cells. This, however, is not the case; there is an obstruction preventing it. A double wall rises in the centre of the corridor, with a passage between, just wide enough to admit a man. In this wall, on either side of the narrow passage and directly opposite the door of each cell, is a peep hole, from which a person may have a full view of the interior of the cell, without being himself exposed to the observation of the prisoner. This struck us as an arrangement calculated to contribute essentially to the maintenance of the discipline and good order of the prison. The cells here are the smallest we met with anywhere, being only six and two-third feet long, two and a half wide, and six high. This is entirely too diminutive a space in which to immure a man, however guilty, during full one half of his prison life. The prisoner's bed fills up the entire width of the cell, and he can have no use of his little abode, till he has hung his mattress on the wall.

The prison is well provided with spacious workshops; and the hospital is, in every sense, a model one, the only cause of complaint being that its accommodations are too limited for the needs of the institution, under the extensive and alarming prevalence of epidemic fevers, which has marked the sanitary condition of the prison for some years past.

This state of things is, no doubt, due to the exceedingly imperfect drainage of the prison. We quite concur with the very intelligent and able physician of the penitentiary, Dr. John R. Dickson, in the opinion that a grave mistake was made in erecting the buildings in their present position, while, on the penitentiary farm, within six hundred yards of the ground that was selected, there is a beautiful site, fully thirty feet above the level of that now occupied by the prison. By using that position, instead of the one actually chosen, the almost insuperable difficulties with which the prison authorities now have to contend about sewerage would have been obviated. But even this original mistake as to the best site is not the worst. Probably the site selected would have afforded sufficient fall for good drainage, had not another most unaccountable mistake been made. That site offered a natural basis of solid limestone for the prison buildings, yet, with wonderful fatuity, the rock was excavated to the depth of several feet before laying the foundations, and thus was thrown away the opportunity of securing an effective system of drainage. On this subject we cite the following remarks from Dr. Dickson, in his last annual report: "Wherever large numbers of people are crowded into a comparatively small space, thorough drainage, and the consequent construction of good sewers, is a matter of very great importance. The prison is provided with drains that may be styled excellent, as far as their size, depth from surface, and the workmanlike manner in which they were built are concerned; but, unfortunately, the depth to which the excavations for the basements and foundations of the buildings were carried, prevented the architect giving the bottom of the sewers such a declivity as would insure the discharge of their contents. The enormous quantity of human filth which was removed from the drains last year, and the regular periodical flushing and cleansing of them since, have been productive of a great deal of good; much, however, requires yet to be done."

New York.—The undersigned, as has been previously stated, were appointed commissioners to visit prisons beyond the limits of our own state. It is, therefore, perhaps, not properly within our province to report on the prisons of New York; yet, as this report is likely to find its way, to a considerable extent, into other states, and even into other countries, we have thought that it might be acceptable to readers beyond our own boundaries to find in its pages some notices of the prisons of this commonwealth, as well as those of other members of the American Union. We mention this as a reason, or apology, for statements heretofore made, and for others to be hereafter made, touching the said prisons.

There are three state prisons in New York—Auburn, Sing Sing and Clinton.

Auburn Prison.—This prison is at Auburn, Cayuga county, on the Owasco creek, a few rods from the depot of the N. Y. Central railroad, and within half a mile of the heart of the city. Its situation is elevated, pleasant, and healthy.

The prison premises embrace an area of ten acres, inclosed by a stone wall in the form of a parallelogram, one thousand feet in length and five hundred feet in breadth. This wall is graded from a thickness of six feet at the bottom to four feet at the top. Its upper surface is level ; but, owing to the irregularity of the ground, its height varies from twelve feet to twenty-five. "Unquestionably, the solid masonry of this massive inclosure is well calculated to frown down the hopes and ventures of would-be fugitives; but had common sense inspired and superintended the construction of the building inclosed, it is safe to say that a fair proportion of the $90,000, given as the cost of the wall alone, might have been saved to the state, and made more useful elsewhere." The drainage is described by the officers as "sufficient in amount, but not perfect in regulation." A large main sewer discharges its contents into the Owasco creek, into which smaller sewers conduct the filth from different parts of the premises.

The buildings consist of a large central structure, five stories in height, of grey limestone, used as a residence by the warden, and for various prison offices ; two wings—cell houses—of similar height and material, extending from the two sides ; and a number of brick, stone and frame buildings, used as workshops and for other purposes, in the interest of the prison; these latter being arranged without much regard to symmetry or order, diminishing, by the irregularity of their location, the facilities for observation, and compelling an increased force of keepers for this purpose.

The number of cells in this prison is nine hundred and ninety ; their dimensions six and a half feet long, four and a half wide, and six and a half or seven feet high. There are, besides these, seven dungeons, or dark cells, used for the punishment of refractory prisoners.

Sing Sing Prison.—There are, in fact, two prisons at Sing Sing, the male and the female ; each entirely distinct from the other, but in near proximity ; the former being placed immediately on the east bank of the Hudson river, and the other on the hill directly in the rear.

The prison grounds contain seventy-seven acres, including the prison farm, with a frontage of fourteen hundred and nineteen feet on the river. The boundary line is somewhat irregular, but the form is, in the main, quadrangular. There are seven or eight acres between the river and the railroad, which are occupied by the buildings, gardens, yards and docks belonging to the male prison. The remaining portion of the grounds lies along the slope and on the brow of the hill. The surface is broken, with marble rock cropping out at various points. It was chiefly on account of the inexhaustible quarries of marble found here, that this spot was selected as the site for this prison. For many years these quarries were worked by the convicts, on account of the state, to considerable profit ; but not much is done in this way at present. About thirty-seven acres are cultivated as a prison farm.

The drainage of the prison is not perfect, but by vigilance and care it is made tolerably effectual.

The buildings here are very numerous ; we cannot undertake a complete description.

The male prison is a vast structure, the material being marble, obtained from the quarries on the prison grounds.   It is four hundred and ninety-four feet in length by forty-four in width, and contains twelve hundred cells, the dimensions of which are seven feet long, four and a half wide and seven high.   There is a window, one foot by three, opposite each cell, an exceedingly small amount of window space for a structure of such huge proportions.   The corridor encircling the block of cells is only nine feet wide, which, again, is far too narrow for so large a building. The cells were originally arranged in four tiers.   When an enlargement was needed, a fifth story was added ; and subsequently, a like necessity arising, a sixth.   How much farther it is intended to build towards the empyrean, we know not ; but fondly hope that the limit has been reached.

The kitchen, mess-room, chapel and hospital are all in the same building, near the centre of the prison yard ; the first two being on the ground floor, the others in the second story.   They are all, with the exception perhaps of the kitchen, too small for the proper accommodation of the prisoners, with exceedingly low ceilings.

There are sixteen workshops, most of which are of stone, scattered about the prison yard without the slightest regard to symmetry or convenience. By this hap-hazard distribution, the trouble and cost of supervision are much increased.

There is no wall around the male prison, and the Hudson River railroad, a thoroughfare of immense business, passes directly through its grounds.   The want of a wall is imperfectly supplied by eighteen guard posts, at which sentinels are stationed at all times when the convicts are not locked in their cells.   There is a guard house, built of marble from the prison quarries, forty feet by twenty-two, standing on the slope of the hill between the male and female prisons.   Here the guards, who are off duty, remain during their intervals of duty, always ready for any sudden emergency that may arise. Here also are kept all the arms belonging ing to the institution, consisting of sixty-five carbines, forty-seven muskets, and eleven navy revolvers.

The female prison is a handsome marble building, two stories high, with a basement in the front part, entirely above ground. It has a front of fifty feet, with a Doric portico of imposing proportions, and a depth of one hundred and fifty feet. There is a stone wall around these premises. That part of the edifice which overlooks the Hudson river is appropriated as a dwelling for the matron and her household. The remainder is used for prison purposes, and consists of cell house, hospital, nursery, kitchen, workshops, &c., &c. The number of cells here is one hundred and eight. They are much too few for the number of prisoners, and many of them very often have to receive two occupants. There is no dining hall, other than one of the corridors of the prison, a great defect; and no chapel, other than one of the workshops, a still greater defect.

The situation of this prison is unsurpassed. It is on the brow of the hill, which rises pretty sharply from the front of the male prison. The view from the portico, mentioned in the preceding paragraph, is one of the highest magnificence and beauty. The Hudson river, rolling along between its romantic and picturesque banks,—the abode of elegance, taste, and refinement,—is visible for nearly fifty miles, and a hundred sail of vessels can sometimes be seen at the same moment.

Clinton Prison.—It is situated sixteen miles west of Plattsburgh, at the village of Dannemora, in the county of Clinton, and in a fine mountain region. No site, affording purer air or combining more of the conditions of health, could have been selected; but whether other essential conditions in the proper location of a prison have been equally well met is open to very grave doubt.

The drainage here is excellent, the nature of the ground being such as to afford every facility for carrying off the sewage readily and completely.

There are two hundred acres of land belonging to this prison, thirty-seven of which are enclosed by a stockade, twenty feet high, constructed of the trunks of young trees, which has proved to be a very fair defence against escapes.

Within this enclosure are the numerous buildings necessary for the prison purposes—residences of officers (three in number), prison offices, chapel (a neat and commodious one), hospital, mess-room, cell building and many workshops, all of which are scattered about the premises in a very hap-hazard manner, and without any regard to convenient inspection, or, as far as we have been able to judge, convenience of any other kind.

It would occupy too much space to enter into a full description of all these buildings, nor is such detailed statement at all necessary. The cell building is four hundred and ninety feet in length, and fifty in width, containing five hundred and thirty-eight cells, arranged in three tiers. The cells are eight feet long, four feet wide, and seven feet high, being, as will be seen, considerably larger than those in either of the other male prisons of the state.

From the foregoing detail, it will have been observed that, in respect to location, the greater part of the prisons described (there are certainly a few exceptions, our own in Clinton county, for example), combine, if not all the advantages that are desirable, at least all that could be expected to meet in any one spot. The great objects to be kept in view, in fixing on the site of a prison, are—ease of access, facility of transportation, the means of obtaining lucrative employment for the prisoners, cheapness of the articles required for their consumption, salubrity of situation, and capability of effective drainage. These paramount advantages are in the main, secured for the majority of the state prisons of the Union, visited by the undersigned, and also for that of Canada, with the exception of the one last mentioned; and this, indeed, was there originally, but was, with unaccountable thoughtlessness, wantonly flung away.

There appears to have been, of late years, a growing and, as we cannot but regard it, an unfortunate disposition to lavish expenditure in the erection of prisons, both as it respects the materials used and the degree of ornamentation given to them. Walls of hewn stone—granite, marble, or the like—with all the architectural adornments usual in the most costly public edifices, seem to be becoming the order of the day. When the late Senator Douglass visited, a few years ago, Augusta, Maine, on being driven through the city, the carriage was stopped in front of a superb granite building in the heart of the city. Glancing at the well proportioned and imposing structure, he remarked, inquiringly : " That, I presume, is your state house ?" " No," was the response, " it is our county jail." In point of fact, the prison is a handsomer and more costly structure than the capitol, which is less than half a mile distant, and, we think, in the same street. The common jail at Lowell, Massachusetts, which must have cost an immense sum, is open to the same criticism. So is the state prison of Illinois, at Joliet; of Wisconsin, at Waupun; and of Canada, at Kingston; although, possibly, in the case of the two last named, there may be less objection, from the fact that the labor was performed mostly by convicts. In his able work on crime, Mr. Frederick Hill, for many years inspector of prisons in Scotland, speaking on this subject, says: " On my first visit to Cupar, having arrived late at night, and taking a walk early the next morning, I came to a mansion with a large portico in front, which I concluded must be the residence of one of the most opulent inhabitants; but after breakfast, being conducted to the place where I was to make my official visit, I found that this building was the *prison!*" The italics and note of wonder are Mr. Hill's, who is a strenuous opponent of needless expense and ornament in the erection of prisons.

The chief points to be aimed at in prison construction are security, the best arrangements for carrying on the several branches of labor selected, adaptation in all their appointments to the great end of reformation, facility of supervision, and a rigid economy. Costly materials and high architectural adornments are not essential to any of these ends, and are directly subversive of the last.

We are quite willing and even desirous that prisons of every class should be decent, substantial, and tasteful structures; but to buildings of a highly ornamental and costly construction we are unalterably opposed, and that for several reasons.

In the first place, such buildings add not a little to the cost of crime; a burden already quite as heavy as the public finds it convenient to bear. Let us test this by a comparison between the prisons at Joliet and Wethersfield. The former, when completed, will have cost the state about a million of dollars, and will contain nine hundred cells. That will make the cost of accommodations for each convict $1,111. Money, we believe, readily commands in Illinois ten per cent. interest. This will give as the cost of housing each prisoner $111.10 a year, supposing every cell to be occupied; when this is not the case, the cost will be increased in proportion to the difference between the number of cells and the number of their occupants. On the other hand, in the Connecticut state prison, the number of cells is 250, and the cost of the buildings and grounds was about $42,000, which gives $168 as the investment of the state for the accommodation of each of her convicts during his imprisonment. Money in Connecticut is worth six per cent. a year, which entails an annual expense upon the state for house room to her prisoners of $10.00 each; a difference of over $100 yearly in the cost of every convict in these two states in the item of rent alone. Yet the prisoners are as well accommodated in Connecticut as in Illinois. The prison is of hewn stone, well built, substantial, secure, and far from disagreeable to the eye; while the grounds are much more extensive in proportion to the number of prisoners, and incomparably more ornamental and attractive than those of the Illinois prison are, or can ever be made.

In the second place, a prison with a stately and imposing exterior, however plain the internal arrangements may be, has a mischievous tendency, as suggested by Mr. Hill, to give importance to criminals and dignity to crime. We would, therefore, fain hope that the taste, or the ostentation, which has led to the erection of such prisons, as the common jails of Augusta and Lowell, and the state penitentiary at Joliet, will soon pass away; and that we shall rid ourselves of that strange vanity which leads us to make a parade of moral deformity, as the unfortunate victim of the goître sometimes invites attention to her physical malformation by hanging jewels and gold chains about her neck. But

In the third place, there is a still more weighty objection to such costly prisons as those that have been, and others that might be named. The science of prison discipline is even yet in its infancy. Able minds, both in Europe and America, are turned, with increased earnestness and vigor, to the study of this deep problem. New principles, or new applications of old ones, are continually evolved. One improvement suggests another, and it is not in the power of the most far-seeing sagacity to forecast the result of such ceaseless and energetic efforts. One thing, however, is certain—that public opinion is gradually changed by them; and society comes at length to look with disfavor upon prisons which are incapable of admitting the improvements suggested by experience. It is but little more than a quarter of a century ago that the progress of penal science, the advance of sound principles of prison discipline, compelled the demolition of nearly all the more important prisons in this country and Europe; and it looks as if another revolution, not less potent and far more beneficent, were within the possibilities, if not indeed the probabilities, of the not distant future. Whenever such an era arrives, the old prisons will no longer meet the ideas, and, therefore, not the wants, of the community, and will have to be abandoned. It is, therefore, highly important that these establishments should be built upon the least expensive plan consistent with their essential objects, since otherwise they become obstacles to improvement; obstacles, too, difficult to be overcome in proportion to the amount of money expended upon their construction. How much harder, for example, would it be to persuade Illinois to adopt a prison system which would compel the abandonment of buildings, on which had been expended a million of dollars, than it would Connecticut, whose whole outlay upon her state prison has been but a fraction over $42,000? Let us not imagine, then, that our prison edifices must be so constructed as to endure through all coming ages; but rather hope that the advance of sound principles will be so rapid and the consequent change of public opinion so great as to require radical alterations in our methods of prison construction, to meet the demand of a higher and juster philosophy of public punishment.

We would only add, in this connection, that, in all points of view, whether as regards the productiveness of the labor, the facility of supervision, the health of the prisoners, the security against escapes, or economy in building, it is desirable that the plan of a prison should be simple, with as few divisions, passages and stairways, and as few obstructions to the view in the yard, as possible. In respect to these matters, improvements of the greatest value may often be made merely by the removal of division walls and staircases.

There is but one separate state prison for women, as far as we know, in the United States—the one at Sing Sing, N. Y.; and even here, the relations between the male and female prisons, both in respect of proximity and otherwise, are too close to permit to the latter the enjoyment of anything like the full benefits of separation. There are no women in the state prison of Massachusetts, persons of that sex, convicted of felonies, being uniformly sent to the county houses of correction, even where the sentence is for life. All the other state prisons, visited by us, have female departments, except that of Northern Indiana, at Michigan City, which is in an inchoate state, and could not, at present, receive them.

We have already, in the brief outline heretofore sketched in this report of a prison system for New York, stated, at some length, our objections to the plan of having male and female prisoners confined within the same enclosure, and especially in the same building; and it would be worse than superfluous to repeat them here. We would simply remark, in passing, that complaint was almost everywhere made of the trouble arising from this source, and the conviction expressed of the extreme desirableness, if not absolute necessity, of a complete separation of the sexes by confining them in different prisons, and placing those prisons in different localities. The great difficulty of preventing communication, when the sexes are confined in the same prison, is well illustrated by an incident related in the second annual report of the Boston Prison Discipline Society, 1827. In the state prison of New Hampshire, a male and female prisoner occupied rooms in the extremities of the building, one in the lower story at the north end, and the other in the third story at the south end; and yet, though strangers to each other at the commencement of their imprisonment, they managed to form an acquaintance and carry on a courtship, which resulted in marriage, after their discharge. This is matched, if not overmatched, by some female prisoners in Preston jail, England, mentioned by the Rev. John Clay, late chaplain of that prison, who, he says, climbed over a *chevaux-de-frise*, which he would have thought utterly impassable, in order to get into the ward of the other sex.

A practical difficulty, of no little magnitude, encounters us at this point. In most of the states, there are not female convicts enough to warrant the erection and maintenance of prisons for them alone, and there are no other prisons, as in Massachusetts, to which they can be sent. This difficulty would be obviated by the establishment in the several states of district prisons, intermediate between the state prison and the common jail, each to serve as a house of correction for several counties; a class of prisons which we consider essential in a comprehensive and efficient system of penal institutions for any state or county; and in the establishment of which, as intimated in our sketch of a plan for New York, the sexes should be in distinct buildings, at a distance from each other.

We have stated the dimensions of the cells in all the prisons mentioned in the foregoing detail. In reference to nearly all of them, we have the same criticism to offer—that they are much too small for either sanitary or moral purposes; and in most of them the furniture is deficient, whether viewed in relation to comfort, order, or cleanliness. In both these respects, they are, in general, inferior to the cells which Howard found in the principal prison of the Netherlands, the *maison de force*, at Ghent, on his visit there in 1776. Each cell, occupied by a single prisoner at night, was six feet ten inches long, five feet four inches wide, and seven feet eight inches high. The furniture of each was a bedstead, a strawbed, a mattress, a pillow, a pair of sheets, two blankets, a small bench, a shutter to the lattice window in the door, (nineteen inches by fifteen) which, when let down, served as a table, and a cupboard in the wall, two feet by one, and ten inches deep. We do not recall any cells of equal size in our American prisons, except those in the female department of the state penitentiary of Wisconsin, which are ten feet long, six wide and eight high; while those in the provincial penitentiary of Canada are considerably smaller than any of ours, being brought down to the most diminutive proportions in which an ordinary-sized mortal could find accommodations for his outer man. We consider the small size of the cells in most American prisons, our own state included, little, if at all, short of positive cruelty. It gives no additional security, is at war with cleanliness, and proves a perpetual hindrance to the mental, moral, and physical welfare of their inmates. The argument in its favor—economy—is one which no state has a right to use, where such vital interests, her own as well as those of her prisoners, are at stake.

We have not often, in the foregoing detail, noticed the size of the windows in the prisons visited; but we have this general remark to make concerning them, that, with comparatively few exceptions, they are altogether too small, the dead wall being out of all proportion to the window space. In this, as in most other points of construction, the Massachusetts state prison stands without a peer among the prisons on this western continent, there being, in effect, little more masonry in the walls that enclose the blocks of cells than what is sufficient to make them perfectly solid and firm, all the remaining space being taken up with windows. In the descending scale, Sing Sing has the place of bad eminence, the proportion of window to wall being, we should think, less than half what it is in any other prison in the country. Dr. Pryne, the intelligent physician of the prison, has expressed the opinion, officially, that the deficiency of sunlight contributes, in a great degree, to the ill health of the prisoners. There can be no doubt that the small windows of prisons are bad in their effect on health, by diminishing the supply of light, just as cellars and other darkened situations affect injuriously the health of plants. But there is another way, in which small windows have an unfavorable effect upon the health of prisoners, viz.: by obstructing the entrance of pure air. The air brought into prisons by means of flues is not at all comparable to that which comes direct through an open window; and, other things being equal, those prisons will be found most conspicuous for the health of their inmates, in which there is the most abundant supply of pure fresh air straight from the heavens. Prison windows should, therefore, be large; and they may safely be made so, if guarded by wrought iron bars, as in Massachusetts. We would also have the glass of the ordinary kind, instead of half opaque. There may be, and doubtless are, some advantages in preventing prisoners from looking out of their cells; but they are more than counterbalanced by the loss of light, with its attendant gloom.

The size of the prisons in some of the states is a point in them, which cannot fail to have attracted the attention of the careful reader. They contain eight hundred, nine hundred, one thousand, and in one case—Sing Sing—one thousand two hundred cells. Now we desire, just here, to express our opposition to prisons of such magnitude, and to utter our solemn caveat against them. They are subversive of one of the most important principles of prison discipline, as evolved and established by recent experiments, particularly in Ireland, and which has been named *individualization;* by which we understand the thorough study of the character of each prisoner, and the adaptation of the discipline, as far as that can be done consistently with a due regard to general principles, to his personal peculiarities. It is obvious, on the least reflection, that the application of such a principle is practicable only in prisons of quite moderate size. In our judgment, three hundred prisoners are enough to form the population of a single prison; and, in no case, would we have the number exceed five hundred or six hundred. In this judgment we are confirmed by the opinion of the most intelligent prison officers, examined by the commission of the Prison Association of 1866, who, we believe, with entire unanimity, expressed a similar conviction.

The erection of prisons of moderate dimensions would facilitate the classification of prisoners on the only sound principle and through the only effective agency—the classification of prisons themselves; the various classes of offenders being committed to prisons designed specially for their reception and treatment. As far as practicable we would have,

1. Separate prisons for females. But on this subject we have already presented our views sufficiently at large.

2. Separate prisons for the young. We do not here refer to houses of refuge or reform schools, but to prisons in the strict sense. Two advantages, arising from the division of prisoners according to sex, economy in construction and simplicity of management, would be still further promoted by a division according to age. In such a division there would be the added advantage of withdrawing from such youthful transgressors the frequent spectacle of men and women who have been convicted of crimes, and who are undergoing punishment; a sight in itself demoralizing, and to which they would be exposed, even though the arrangements of the prison should be such as to guard against the greater evil of contamination through promiscuous intercourse. In prisons of the kind here proposed, greater attention could be given to education than would be proper in institutions designed for offenders of more advanced age. Indeed, the whole might properly be made to assume the character more of a well-conducted work-house school than of an ordinary prison.

3. Separate prisons for different occupations. After securing a classification according to sex and age, the most important principle of distribution is identity, or at least similarity, of employment. As far as may be, let the same occupation be pursued by all the inmates of any given prison, so that there shall be no necessity of having tools and machinery adapted to different employments and officers qualified to give instruction therein. The application of this principle would necessitate the establishment of both agricultural and manufacturing prisons, and would require that the latter should be constructed, some for one kind of work and some for another.

4. Separate prisons for the worst class of offenders. As in the world at large, so in a prison, it is found that the chief trouble is given by comparatively few persons. It would, therefore, be a great relief to withdraw these few from the prisons where they are found so troublesome and create nearly all the difficulty, and to place them in buildings expressly adapted for them, and under officers possessing peculiar qualifications for their management.

Such an arrangement would simplify the administration of the ordinary prisons, and greatly diminish the cost of their construction, while, at the same time, it would be the greatest benefit to the class thus segregated, since they would thereby be placed under circumstances, and subjected to a *régime* best adapted to their special treatment. If corrigible, their cure would be likely to be effected through this instrumentality; if incorrigible, they should be made comfortable, and detained for life. But on this subject more hereafter.

It occurs to us to remark, in passing, that, however great the advantages of such a classification of prisons and of prisoners as the necessary sequence, the adoption of the system is quite impossible under the present plan of separate local jurisdictions, which prevails in this and other states. It is a system which can neither be established nor worked otherwise than by combined action and a general administration. If the system has any merit, it is a fresh argument for the creation of that central authority for the control and management of our whole prison system, which has been recommended and urged on other grounds in a former part of this report.

SECTION FOURTH.

GOVERNMENT.

The government of our American prisons has already been considered, in the section on their general administration, so far as the duties of their several boards of inspectors are concerned. At least, this has been done in part. The title of inspectors, as applied to these officers, we consider rather a misnomer. Their function is one of government rather than of simple inspection. Managers, governors, or directors (this last indeed they are sometimes called), would have been more befitting their true position in our prison systems than that of inspectors, which is the one given them in nearly all the states.

Although the inspectors are nowhere the immediate agents in the administration of the prison government, yet everywhere (or if there be any exceptions, such are very few), they direct it. They make the regulations, as stated in the last section, which the wardens are charged to execute ; and they constantly watch over this execution. Their legal authority is substantially the same in the different states; but the manner and extent of its exercise varies greatly, the part taken in the affairs of the prison being much more active in some states than in others. In New York, for example, this authority is all-pervading, and makes itself felt in every department of the government. In their associated capacity as a board, the inspectors are obliged to hold a meeting once every three months at each of the state prisons. They remove and appoint all officers; superintend the letting of contracts; examine and pass upon all accounts; inquire into and give directions concerning matters of finance; investigate the sanitary condition of the prison, and also the quantity and quality of the food furnished to the convicts; receive and consider the quarterly reports of the physicians, store keeper, and superintendent of the kitchen; and, in a word, make a general, which ought also to be a searching survey of the prison, in all its industrial operations and all the departments of its administration.

Besides these general functions, exercised by the whole body of inspectors, each inspector has the care of one of the three state prisons for four consecutive months of each year, under the name and title of the inspector in charge. It is the duty of the inspector in charge to spend at least one week of every month at the prison under his care; to fill vacancies that may have occurred, subject to the approval of the board; to receive and examine the complaints of convicts, and take such action thereupon as, in his judgment, the several cases may require; to examine and approve the estimates of the ensuing month; to order the removal of insane convicts to the state lunatic asylum at Auburn; and, generally, to supervise and direct the affairs of the prison in its numerous and varied interests and operations. He is further, required to record, in the inspectors' book of minutes, all his official acts during his term of superintendence, which record is examined and passed upon by the board at its next quarterly meeting.

In Pennsylvania, the services of the inspectors, both at Philadelphia and Pittsburgh, are gratuitous, the only exception being that the treasurer, who is always a member of the board, receives a moderate salary, to compensate him for the responsibility assumed and the time expended in the duties of the office. In all the other states, some compensation is paid; but it is, in general, quite small, not exceeding, for the most part, $100 or $200 per annum. In Ohio, Vermont and Michigan, it is in the form of a per diem (three dollars) paid only for actual service, and in the last named state, the time during which any compensation is allowed, is limited to thirty days. In New York and Canada, the case is quite different, *bona fide* salaries being there paid, intended as a full remuneration for services rendered. In New York, the salary is $1500, and all necessary expenses ; in Canada, we believe the law to be exactly the same in respect to both particulars ; and, under both governments, there is a liberal interpretation of the phrase "necessary expenses," it being expected that an inspector will travel and live like a gentleman.

The staff of officers in the prisons visited by us, consists usually of a head (called warden, agent, keeper, commissioner, and in our own state, agent and warden), a deputy under him (called also by different titles), a clerk, a chaplain, a physician, keepers or overseers, and guards. Some have also one or more teachers, though here the usage is far from uniform. The number of officers composing the staff differs exceedingly in different prisons, even beyond what would be supposed from their variant populations, ranging from six, the number at Windsor, Vermont, to eighty-nine, the number at Sing Sing, New York. Next to Sing Sing comes the provincial penitentiary, Canada—seventy-five ; then Auburn, N. Y.—sixty-three ; and then, the Ohio state prison—fifty-four. There are no resident chaplains in the prisons of Illinois, Northern Indiana, Kentucky, Maine, Maryland, Missouri, Rhode Island or Vermont ; and none in the county jails of Delaware and West Virginia, in which the state prisoners are kept ;—a fact as startling as it is painful, and evincing either a lamentable lack of interest in the religious welfare of the convicts, or a very low appreciation of the value of religious agencies as a means of doing them good. We do not mean to say that in none of the prisons named are any religious exercises held, nor even that the stated services of ministers of the gospel are not called into requisition to a greater or less extent. We will not, however, enter into further detail upon the subject at this point, as the whole matter will be fully set forth under another division of our report.

It is hardly necessary to enter into a detail of the duties of the several officers and classes of officers composing our prison staffs. Beyond what has already been said, in a former section of this chapter, in regard to the important position and functions of the head of the prison, these duties are, perhaps, sufficiently indicated, in a general way, by the titles of those officers; and to descend to minute specifications would swell the size of this report and tax the patience of the reader without necessity.

American prisons do not pay what can, with any propriety, be termed liberal salaries to their officers. The gentlemen at the head of the prisons receive a larger compensation than any of their subordinates, relatively as well as absolutely, since, in addition to their stipend in money, they are all provided with residences, and many of them have other perquisites of more or less value. Massachusetts pays the warden of her state prison $2,500; Canada, $2,250; Pennsylvania, Maine and Missouri, each $2,000; while New York gives the wardens of her vast penal establishments but $1,800; the great state of Ohio repays the services of her chief prison officer with $1,400; Connecticut and Wisconsin give each $1,200; and Vermont and New Hampshire each $800. It is obvious that, with an exception or two, salaries like these would not command that high administrative and executive ability which is required in such positions, and that men, like some of those now and heretofore in office, whom we could name, would not be found at the head of our state penitentiaries, if they were not influenced by a nobler sentiment than that of mere pecuniary interest. A few of the higher officers of a subordinate grade— deputies, clerks, chaplains, and physicians—are respectably remunerated; but the most of these, and nearly the whole body of officers constituting the police force of the prisons, receive a compensation less than the average wages now paid to ordinary mechanics. It is idle to even dream of securing officers for our penitentiaries, possessing suitable qualifications, when every person, gifted with some capacity, can so readily find a more profitable career than that offered by the administration of prisons. Now, in fixing the scale of salaries for prison officers, it must be borne in mind that, in order to induce persons endowed with the requisite qualifications to undertake the laborious duties which they will have to perform, it is necessary to offer a higher remuneration than that by which services can be obtained for ordinary employments, where the moral qualities of the individual are but slightly scanned, and where he is free from many of the restrictions and annoyances to which a prison officer must, of necessity, be subjected.

We have spoken of "suitable qualifications" in prison officers. What sort of qualifications, then, are those which may be deemed "suitable?" This question is important, since, without doubt, the very first requisite for obtaining good prison officers is to have a clear and just conception of their necessary qualifications. As a general rule, the success of any scheme of discipline will depend far more on the persons employed to carry it out, than on the precise regulations laid down. It is the moral influence of the man, not the stringency of a rule, however wise, that will do most for the objects we have in view in prison discipline. To such an extent do we consider this the case, and so supremely important do we regard the appointment of good prison officers, that we should confidently expect better results in one of the worst built prisons, without any prescribed system of discipline, but where there was an able and earnest head, aided by competent subordinates, than in the best constructed building, and under the most carefully devised plans of management, but where there was an incompetent chief, with ill-qualified assistants.

Prison officers should be men of strict and uniform sobriety.— "Touch not, taste not," should be their rule in regard to all intoxicating liquors. It is bad to see red faces in a prison staff. Convicts say at once, "These men indulge in a vice, which shows itself in their faces. Perhaps we can tempt them to do other improper acts, such as furnishing us with contraband articles, granting indulgences, and the like."

They should be men of mild temper, quiet manners, and pure conversation.—If they are passionate and irascible, if they use harsh or petulant language, if they are profane or vulgar in their speech, if they revile religion or even speak disrespectfully of it, if they sympathize in taste and feeling with the convicts—what can be expected but that they will harm rather than benefit their wards? What, indeed, but a revolting union of keepers and prisoners in one corrupt mass?

They should be men of decision and energy.—Quick to discern and prompt to act are qualities equally indispensable with gentleness and equanimity.

They should be men of humane and benevolent feelings.—Thousands of bad men are constantly immured in our prisons, and, while there, they are placed under the care and government of some hundreds of officers. The opportunities of usefulness, enjoyed by these persons, may be seen by what was accomplished by Elizabeth Fry in Newgate, Sarah Martin in Yarmouth jail, and John Howard in many prisons. These distinguished philanthropists showed how much can be done with even the most depraved criminals, and that human nature, in its very worst state, is not wholly lost, but can, by kind and benevolent agencies, be wrought upon with success. They entered prison walls as ministers of love and mercy; and guilt, in its most repulsive forms, relinquished its hold upon its victims, and repentance became, as it were, a new birth of innocence.

They should be men having a sincere interest in those placed under their care.—Such interest it is, which constitutes the true key to a prisoner's heart; and if an officer possess this, superadded to the other qualifications necessary to command respect, his influence over his prisoners will be very great. It is often the case that, up to the time of his commitment, a criminal has had no one to give him counsel or sympathy; no virtuous parent or kind relative, to feel for him or guide him aright. In the heart of such an one, there must, of necessity, be a void, which is, perhaps, first filled by a kind prison officer. As the effect of this sympathy and kindly interest, an almost filial affection sometimes springs up in the minds of prisoners towards a good warden, keeper, chaplain or matron. It is related by Mr. Frederick Hill, that under the influence of this feeling, liberated prisoners, when attacked with mortal sickness, have sent for Mr. Smith, governor of the Edinburgh prison, as the only friend on whom they could rely; and that hundreds of his former prisoners followed to his grave Mr. Brebner, late governor of the prison at Glasgow, mourning the loss of one who had been to them a friend, protector and guardian, rather than a stern prison officer, and by whom many of them had been redeemed from a life of crime and misery.

They should be men of high moral principle, and distinguished by habits of industry, order and cleanliness.—The lowest officer in a prison, even the keeper of a lock-up, should be a person superior, in these respects, to the ordinary run of the working classes, that he may constantly present to the wrong-doers who come under his charge an example worthy of their imitation.

They should be men possessing a knowledge of human nature in its various aspects and relations.—Experience in the walks of life, an acquaintance with the springs of human conduct, and a capacity to discern the leading passions of individuals, and especially all their weak points, are included in that knowledge of men of which we speak, and which we deem an essential, or at least an important, quality in a good prison officer.

They should be men of sterling and incorruptible honesty.—As keepers of unusually sound and vigorous minds are sought for the improved lunatic asylums of our day, so those who have the care of criminals should be not only without taint, but, like Cæsar's wife, above suspicion. They should be absolutely free from all those little practices of deceit, which, in ordinary persons, might pass, perhaps, without much animadversion.

They should be men of experience.—This qualification, which is one of prime importance and value, necessitates two conditions, viz : an appointment to office before the meridian of life has been passed, and, secondly, permanence in the tenure of office. Time and observation are necessary to obtain sufficient experience to enable men to act with discretion and efficiency in the management of prisoners ; and these are advantages which cannot be had in the case either of those who are appointed to office late in life, or of those who are ejected from office a few months or even a few years after their appointment.

They must be men of a just and steadfast purpose, free from prejudice and partiality.—That eminent American divine, the late Dr. Mason, was accustomed to say that there were three principles, which, being wisely applied, were sufficient to govern an empire ; they are : "Be reasonable, be firm, be uniform." These maxims are no less applicable to the government of a prison than they are to that of a state.

They should be men of untiring vigilance.—Convicts are prone to idleness ; most of them have never been trained to habits of industry ; and, as a class, they are cunning and deceitful. Keepers must be vigilant, or prisons will be schools of vice.

They should have a liking for the occupation in which they are engaged.—Without this, there can be no heart, no enthusiasm, little interest even in their work ; and these conditions wanting, everything is wanting adapted to insure success, or likely to render their career as prison officers useful.

Finally, prison officers should be men duly impressed with religious principles; men who fear God, and are in the habit, as the expression of that reverence, of attending the services of some religious body.—What adequate security other than that of religious principle, can they have against the temptations incident to their situation? Few men have greater temptations to fraud. Few are more open to the assaults of bribery. Few have greater trials of temper. Few become abusive and injurious with greater impunity. All these are sore trials of strength, severe tests of character. This is particularly the case in regard of the temptation to resort to improper methods of money-making. To this many prison officers succumb,—some even of those who fill the higher positions. Many convicts either have money secreted on the prison premises or can command it outside, and they are willing to pay liberally for exemptions and privileges, which their officers have it in their power, in various ways, to accord. Is it strange that a willingness of this sort in the prisoners should be met by a willingness of another sort on the part of those who have the charge of them? There are officers—we could wish that the number were less—who receive more money in gratuities from convicts, than they receive in salary from the state. It is painful to us to be obliged to make such statements; but if there is a canker of this kind at work in our prisons,—and that there is, no one conversant with them can doubt or deny,—the public should know it. How else can they apply the proper corrective? This corrective we conceive to be fourfold—the liberation of prisons from the control of party politics, the payment of higher salaries, a more permanent tenure of official position, and, as the resultant of all this, the appointment of better men to office. But we anticipate, as these matters will fall more naturally elsewhere.

In regard to the qualifications of prison officers, we will add no more, except to say, in the words of Mr. F. Hill, that "the higher the officer's position, the more varied and numerous are the qualifications required. The governor of a large prison should be a person of strong native talent, of great decision of character, yet of kind and affable manners; he should possess great insight into human character, and into the various causes of crime and springs of action; and he should be influenced by a strong desire to promote the permanent welfare [i. e., the reformation] of the prisoners committed to his charge. He should be possessed of powers of command and of holding others to responsibility; and, in order to maintain these effectually, it is necessary to be able to determine what every one under his authority can reasonably be expected to perform, and to judge of the manner in which every duty is discharged.

And this in regard to female officers: "The qualifications of female officers are, in many respects, the same as those of males. It is especially important, however, that female officers should be distinguished for modesty of demeanor, and the exercise of domestic virtues, and that they should possess that intimate knowledge of household employment, which will enable them to

teach the ignorant and neglected female prisoner how to econo-
mise her means, so as to guard her from the temptations caused
by waste and extravagance."

The wardens of all the state prisons visited by the undersigned were asked for an expression of their views as to the
proper qualifications of prison officers. The answers, given with
various degrees of fullness, agree substantially with the views which
we have set forth in the foregoing paragraphs, on that important
subject.

The wardens were further interrogated as to how far the requisite qualifications are, in point of fact, possessed by the officers
serving under them. One replies: "It is *intended* that no officer
shall be employed about the prison, who does not possess these
qualifications." A few say that the qualifications required are
possessed by their under officers in a moderate or fair degree.
One says that the qualifications for holding office in his prison are
"good morals, general intelligence, *vote the ticket*, and *support
the party;*" and that, as a general thing, the officers are qualified
according to the standard, though sometimes mistakes occur."
Whether the mistakes referred to concern the political or moral
part of the requisition is not stated. In their answers generally,
the wardens are quite free in the expression of their conviction of
the want of fitness or adequate qualification in their subordinates.
One declares them " very deficient in these qualifications." Another says that "not one in twenty is qualified." A third gives
his answer in these words: "Very few of the officers whom I
employed possessed the qualifications mentioned. Some came
near possessing them; but the majority had but a dim idea of
their duties and responsibilities." These last answers strike the
key-note of the majority received by us.

Now, where are we to look for the causes of this almost universal lack of qualification in our prison officers ? One cause, and
that too of no little potency, is the very inadequate compensation
paid them for their services. But of this we have spoken
before, and it is unnecessary either to repeat or to enlarge upon
that point.

The supreme cause, however, of this deficiency, as lamentable
as it is wide-spread, is to be found, we apprehend, in the controlling power given to party politics over the management of the
prisons in most of the states. We know of but one state that has
escaped this malign influence; the fortunate exception is Pennsyl-

vania. The inspectors in this state are appointed by the supreme court, a body at once more permanent and less subject to political influences than the appointing power in the other states; and to this circumstance, probably, is due the happy exemption which we have mentioned. It is claimed, indeed, that in Vermont, politics does not influence the appointment of officers or the administration of the state prison; and yet the directors and even the warden are elected annually by the legislature, a body, *ex necessitate rei*, essentially political. How, then, are we to reconcile the claim with the fact? Quite readily, at least in the only sense in which the claim can be truly made. Owing to her steadfast adherence to one policy, Vermont has received the name of "the star that never sets;" and the memory of man runneth not to the contrary of the uniform ascendency in that commonwealth of the same political party. So that no political control over the management of the prison means, there, an all-powerful control— a control so constant and pervading that, like the atmosphere, it is unseen and unappreciated. The same claim is made for Massachusetts and Maine, and, no doubt, upon the same ground, since it is made in the face of the fact that, in both states, the inspectors and warden, and in the former, the chaplain and physician also, are appointed by the governor and council, a body as necessarily and completely political as the legislature itself. No doubt Messrs. Haynes and Rice, the excellent wardens in those states, in the appointment of their subordinates, have a prime regard to fitness; but let political parties waver there as they do in some other states—this year one party being in the ascendant and the next another—and, unless human nature is a different thing in Massachusetts and Maine from what it is elsewhere, the idea that politics has nothing to do with the management of the prisons will soon be a thing of the past.

In other states there is no claim of exemption from political influence over the government and administration of the prisons. In the answers given to our interrogatories, such expressions as the following are of frequent occurrence: "the warden is chosen by the legislature, and, of course, his appointment is controlled by party politics;" "party politics influence, to a great extent, the appointments of officers in this prison;" "party politics controls absolutely the appointment of the staff of prison officers here."

But nowhere else, probably, does political influence act so directly and powerfully, indeed with such an absolute and dominating effect, as in Wisconsin and New York. In the former of these states, the head of the state prison, called there commissioner, is elected at the same time and in the same manner as the Governor, that is to say, by direct popular vote, at the general election, every two years. The present commissioner, Mr. Cordier, in answering our question on that point, does not, therefore, hesitate to say: "Party politics controls the administration of the prison entirely. The commissioner owes his position to a political party, and he therefore appoints such men to office as belong to that party." In our state, it is much the same, only worse in one particular, as we will presently explain. Here the inspectors, the governing power in our prisons, are also chosen by the people, one each year, at the general election. They are nominated by party conventions and elected by party votes. What can they do, therefore, but obey party behests? So far Wisconsin and New York seem to stand on much the same ground in reference to their prison affairs. But, as already intimated, there is one respect in which the latter is worse off than the former. In Wisconsin, the commissioner is the direct agent of the administration, and responsible for it. Clothed with the unrestricted power of choosing his own agents, he has a strong personal interest in having good ones, and consequently, though his selection must be confined to his own party, within that limit he will be likely to scan the qualifications of candidates with some degree of keenness. In New York, on the contrary, though the inspectors direct the administration, they are not its immediate agents, and so not responsible for it. Though invested with an unlimited power of appointment, they have no personal interest in the character of the officers whom they are charged with selecting. It is not to be supposed, therefore, that they will scrutinize very closely the qualifications of their appointees, but will look rather to the political services rendered by them during the canvass.

And such, in effect, is the operation of the system. It is in evidence, in the sworn testimony of numerous witnesses taken by a commission of the Prison Association, in 1866, that, in appointing persons to office in our state prisons, very little attention is given to the qualifications of the candidates. Appointments are made almost wholly on political considerations, and sometimes without the inspectors having even so much as seen the applicant.

This state of things operates two ways to lower the standard of official qualification in our state prisons;—first, by inviting a crowd of inferior men—often mere loafers, idlers, or blatant politicians—to these places; and, secondly, by repelling men of character and competency from seeking or even accepting them, partly because of the inadequate compensation given for the service, but still more because of the uncertain tenure by which the positions are held.

Here, indeed, is the radical defect of the prison systems in most of the states of the American Union; it lies in political appointments and the inevitably resulting consequence, brevity and uncertainty in the tenure of official position in our state penitentiaries. When the political complexion of the governing authority of the prisons is changed by the transfer of power from one party to another, there is, for the most part, a general change in the *personnel* of the various prison staffs. The incumbents belonging to the defeated party must give place to the hungry swarm of office seekers of the victorious phalanx, most of whom have little to recommend them, as the major part of their predecessors had not when they belonged to the conquering host, except certain party services, often of the lowest and most disreputable character. If this condition of things cannot be changed, if the management of our prisons cannot be lifted out of the control of party politics, if a character of permanency cannot in some way be imparted to their administration, so that bad officers only shall be sifted out and good officers shall be retained during good behavior, then farewell to all hope of improvement, or at least to all expectation of thorough, radical, enduring prison reforms. The best prison system that human sagacity has devised, or is competent to devise, can never succeed, can never work out its normal results, under the everlasting fluctuations entailed by making our prisons a part of the political machinery of the state, and the everlasting official incompetency necessarily growing out of such a policy.

Men never conduct their private business on any such principles. How is it with our railroad, banking, insurance, express, manufacturing and steamship companies? Do they change all their *employeés*, from the president to the porter, with every turn in the political wheel, dismissing all who belong to one party, and calling in an entirely new set belonging to the other? How long could the richest of them escape bankruptcy and ruin under such a system of management? And can that be wisdom in the management of a prison—Sing Sing, Auburn, Clinton, or any other—which would be madness in the management of the Central railroad, Adams' express, or the Bank of New York? Impossible!

What, then, is the remedy? One word will express it—common sense! Restore the reign of that exiled but most wise and safe counsellor, and the work will soon be done. But a special suggestion or two may not be out of place here.

Let party politics be discarded utterly from the management of our prisons. It touches but to mar their administration.

Let fitness alone be considered in appointments to office. An erroneous idea seems to prevail as to what an office is. It is not a reward for political service, an honor due to active devotion to a political party. An office is a position of toil and duty. It has the same relation to the public service, that a business post has in a commercial house. No one has any claim to it, unless he is fitted for it; and surely no one should be appointed to it, unless he is fitted.

Let suitable and effective tests be applied to ascertain the qualications of applicants for office, prior to their appointment. No applicant should be employed at first otherwise than on probation; and his probation should cover a term of at least six months. A daily record should be kept, as is done in the English prisons, of the manner in which he discharges his duties; and his formal appointment should be made to depend on the result of this trial. Then only should he become an officer, when he ceases to be a probationer.

Let the tenure of all offices be made permanent, that is, during good behavior, so that there shall be no removals, except for cause. Both appointments and removals are now made on party considerations chiefly, if not solely. Men are inconsiderately placed in office without reference to their fitness; and they are remorselessly removed from it as soon as they have learned their duties. Can it be expected that we should have effective service on such conditions? Can it be expected that men will do their duty intelligently, promptly, efficiently, and honestly, who know that, despite their utmost diligence and fidelity, next week, or next month, or next year, their places will be taken from them, and given to others? Would mercantile houses, would the directors of banking and insurance companies, be willing to employ their agents and clerks on this plan? To ask such a question is to answer it. We complain of the inefficiency and corruption of our prison officials; yet we could not devise a scheme of administration better adapted to produce these evils than the one actually employed. Would not men be almost more than human who, under such circumstances, would do their duty faithfully and effectively?

Let the appointment of all subordinate officers, charged with police duties, be placed absolutely in the hands of the head. This officer is responsible for the administration, and should be held strictly to that responsibility. Such being the case, it is but reasonable that he should have the unrestricted selection of his agents.

Let none but persons in the prime of life (say within the limit of forty years) be appointed as prison officers, except it be in extraordinary cases and for special reasons, and then the reasons of the appointment should be made matter of formal record. Two advantages would result from the adoption of this rule. First, the full vigor of the officer, and, secondly, all the benefits of his long experience, would be enjoyed by the institution with which he might be connected.

Let there be a gradation of rank in the offices, and a graduation of salary corresponding thereto. All incumbents should commence at the bottom of the scale, and promotion should follow merit.

Let adequate salaries be paid for the service required. It is thus only that we can hope to secure capacity, integrity, fidelity, and experience. It is thus only that temptation to increase the stipend by fraud or the acceptance of bribes can be effectually removed. A just and even liberal compensation will be found in the end the best economy.

Let some provision be made for the superannuated and the disabled. Officers who have faithfully and honorably expended their energies and worn out their strength in this hard and self-denying service, when they become incapable of further duty by reason of advancing years or some calamitous visitation of Providence, should receive a moderate pension, that they may not be left utterly destitute and forlorn in their old age or other disability, but may have at least a little to support and solace their waning life.

The merit of some such system as that here recommended, consists, unless we are mistaken, 1. In the supreme regard paid to fitness in the appointment of prison officers, whereby a far higher grade of qualification would assuredly be obtained for this department of the public service. 2. In the perpetuity of the tenure of office, by virtue of which the state would profit by the ever accumulating skill and experience of its servants. 3. In its system of promotions, by which the most competent and faithful men would be secured for the higher and more responsible grades of service. 4. In this, that, as a general rule, it would take only young men into service, and so would secure the benefit of their devotion during the best years of their life, as well as the ripe fruits of an experience gained through a long career of public service. 5. In the further advantage, that it would guaranty to them a constantly increasing livelihood, as the fruit of their diligence and fidelity, the reward of a meritorious devotion to duty. And 6. In the constant and strong inducement held out to the incumbent to do his duty faithfully, in the moderate provision to be made for him amid the infirmities of age or under the visitation of some unexpected calamity.

As regards the mode of appointing the officers in the prisons of the different states, or, more accurately perhaps, the authorities by whom they are appointed, the usage varies considerably. In Kentucky, New Hampshire, and Vermont, the warden is appointed by the Legislature; in Maine, Massachusetts, Michigan, and Missouri, by the Governor; in Pennsylvania and Rhode Island by the inspectors. In the above named states, the chaplain, clerk, and physician are variously appointed by the Governor, inspectors or warden; and in all of them, the other subordinate officers—keepers, overseers, guards, &c.—are appointed by the warden, either absolutely or subject to the approval of the several boards of inspectors or directors,—generally the latter. In Wisconsin, the commissioner (warden), as before stated, is chosen by the direct vote of the people; and he has unlimited power over the appointment of all other officers. In Ohio, the clerk is appointed by the Governor, by and with the consent of the Senate; all the other officers by the board of directors. This is almost as bad as in New York, where every officer in the state prison, without exception, receives his appointment from the board of inspectors. We have already stated our opposition to this mode of appointing the under officers, with the reasons on which it is grounded. It would but encumber these pages to repeat the arguments on that head.

In all the prisons visited, the rules and regulations require, on the part of the officers, an abstinence from intoxicating liquors and from the use of profane language. In some prisons, this rule seems to be well enforced ; in that of Massachusetts, for example, the smell of liquor on an officer's breath is a sufficient cause for dismissal. In reference to one prison, the statement is made that "the requirement (abstinence from liquor and profanity) is not at present much regarded." There is reason to fear that what is confessed of one is true of many more. We were informed by a person who kept a large boarding house for prison officers, that of more than twenty inmates there was but one who did not swear, gamble, drink to intoxication, and commit other improprieties both of act and language. It gives us no pleasure to make statements of this kind ; but our duty is to offer, as far as we may be able, an honest and true picture of American prisons.

As regards inspection of the prisons, we have before stated that the principal function of the several boards of inspectors and directors is one of control, direction, government, rather than of inspection, properly so called. In some of the states, the governor is required by law to visit and inspect the state prisons at least once a year ; and even in states where no law makes it obligatory, it is quite customary for the executive, under the promptings of his own sense of duty or feeling of humanity, to perform the same labor. In nearly all the states, it is also the usage either for a joint committee of the two houses constituting the Legislature, or for a separate committee of each house, during their annual session, to examine the prison or prisons of their respective states. In some states—Wisconsin, for example—this work seems to be quite thoroughly done, and the reports submitted to the Legislatures often contain valuable suggestions and recommendations. But it appears to be more frequently the case, that the examinations made by legislative committees are of a rather perfunctory character, and either no reports are made, or those that are, contain little that is of much interest or value. There are but two states, Massachusetts and New York, where there is anything like an efficient inspection of all the prisons in the state, and full reports made of their results, with suggestions of modifications and improvements required in their respective prison systems. In Massachusetts, this is done by the board of state charities ; in New York, by the prison association. It is much to be desired that in these and all the other states, a more effective system of inspection should be established through the institution of central boards or bureaus, clothed with higher powers than those possessed by either of the bodies named, or even by the board of inspectors of

Canada, which last might, nevertheless, serve as the general model for such organizations. In all the prisons, we believe, the deputy warden is the officer charged with the daily inspection thereof. In concluding this section, we recur to a topic already considered in it at some length,—politics as an element in the government of American prisons,—for the purpose of introducing an instructive extract from the excellent paper furnished by Mr. P. T. Miller, late warden of the Missouri state penitentiary, of whose merits as a prison officer, we have already, more than once had occasion to speak. In his response to our interrogatories on state prisons, Mr. Miller uses this language : " Party politics controls absolutely the appointment of officers in this prison ; and to this cause is to be attributed the total neglect of the great question of prison reform, and the slow progress made by earnest christians and philanthropists in awakening a proper interest in the subject. The very fact that prison officers expect to relinquish their positions on every change of administration begets indifference and inattention; and they are usually contented to drag along in the mere mechanical discharge of their duties, looking no farther than the expiration of their term of office; leaving whoever may succeed as head to shape a policy of his own. Under such a state of facts, patent to every observing eye, how can we hope for any permanent fruits from the labors of the wise and good men, whose hearts are in their work? Hitherto, arguments, which, it would seem, should have forced conviction on the most unwilling minds, have produced absolutely no effect; and the commonest rules of prudence, which are applied to all the affairs of life ·and business, have, in this regard, been intentionally ignored, or willfully violated. If legislators desire to know the cost and practicability of some great public improvement, they are careful to consult the skilled engineer, and not the common laborer, who is skillful only in the use of the spade and pick. If an exploring expedition is to be sent out, they select a practical seaman, and not a railroad conductor, to direct it. Or, if precautions are to be taken against the approach of a death-fraught epidemic, they consult a board of physicians, and not of lawyers. How careful are men, in their private affairs, to adopt the same prudent course in the selection of agents, and to look at the peculiar fitness of the man for the position he is to fill, regardless of his knowledge or opinions on other matters. The commonest experience of every-day life declares to all men that a great lawyer is not, for that reason, a skillful financier, and that successful bankers are not necessarily successful merchants. The truth certainly should be confessed, it *is* confessed theoretically, and practically, too, in all things else, that men become great, distinguished, useful and efficient in that one thing to which they devote years of study and practice. Is it not equally true that the proper qualifications for prison disciplinarians are not mere natural gifts, but are acquired in the school of experience, where all things valuable are learned? Nor is the frequent change of officers and systems less demoralizing to the officials themselves, than injurious to the convicts whom they may have under their care. While one warden imposes a certain rule of action, during his term of office, for the government of the prisoners, he is succeeded by another, who sees nothing good or valuable in the policy of his predecessor. A third follows *him*, with plans and purposes differing from both; and the result of all is, that the convict concludes there is no settled policy in regard to him. The wholesome lessons, taught him by one master, are dissipated and their effect destroyed by the rashness or folly of another. Take a number of children, employ one teacher one month, another the next, and so on through the succeeding months of the year, each having a system of teaching, differing from his predecessor, and what progress will they make? Will they not rather retrograde than advance, and, from the confusion of systems adopted, fail utterly to get any correct impression of their aim? The same reasoning will apply, with equal force, to prison administration. Unless something can be done to arouse public attention to the matter, and, through the interest thus awakened, the control of our penal institutions can be snatched from the possession of unscrupulous partisans, the whole system will continue to grow worse and worse, until it becomes a disgusting spectacle to reflecting and patriotic men, and our prisons, instead of correcting evils and diminishing crime in the land, will be but colleges of wickedness, where men will be educated and graduated in every species of villainy."

SECTION FIFTH.

DISCIPLINE.

With certain modifications on minor points, the rules and regulations relating to the deportment of convicts are substantially the same in all the prisons on the congregate plan, that is, in all the prisons of the United States, outside of Pennsylvania. The rules for prisoners in prisons conducted on the Philadelphia system will, of course, differ materially from those constituted on the Auburn plan. The simplicity of the separate system will naturally impress itself upon the regulations made for the government of its subjects. Comparatively few breaches of order are possible in absolute solitude. The isolation of the prisoner secures, to a great degree, the observance of the few and simple rules that are necessary under that system. Each cell is a prison in itself, and the convict detained in it cannot render himself guilty of offences, which can be committed only in company with others. The organizations of prisons on the Auburn or congregate plan is far more complicated, and involves the necessity of a greater number of rules of order. The general duty of prisoners in all prisons of this class is to work diligently, to obey all orders, and to preserve unbroken silence, as well during the labors of the day, as in their solitary cells at night; although in some prisons, there is a relaxation of this last rule, in that part of it which requires absolute silence during the hours of work. But we will here offer to the reader an outline of the regulations of a few of the leading prisons, as far as the same relates to the duties and conduct of the convicts.

In the Massachusetts state prison, convicts are required to show respect to the officers, to be diligent at their work, to obey all orders promptly, and to be submissive to all the rules and regulations of the prison. In speaking to an officer, they must salute him by raising the hand to the forehead. They must not exhibit ill temper when reproved, nor hold unnecessary conversation with an officer, nor have any traffic or collusive proceedings with him. They must not speak or write to other convicts, nor look at, speak to, or answer any questions of, visitors, except by permission of the warden. They cannot have any writing materials without permission, nor carry food into the yard or shops, nor make any alteration whatever in their clothing. They are required to be prompt in taking their places in the division at bell-ringing, to march the lock step, at a rather brisk pace, with the head a little inclined towards the officer, body erect, and hands hanging by the side; to take the first dish the hand is put upon, in passing the tables at meals; and to be careful not to spill or drop any food while in the prison. On entering the cell, they are to place the food on the table; to return and stand just within the door, with the face to the opening; to close the door gently, thrust the hand through the opening in the bars, and keep it in that position till the officer returns; to draw the hand in as soon as the officer has passed the door; and to thrust it out again, in the same manner, if an extra count is ordered. They are required to be cleanly in person, clothing, and cell; to spit nowhere but in the spittoon; not to mark or in any way mar or disfigure their cells, or injure or misuse any book or utensil allowed them therein; not to work in the cell, or bring in or carry out any article contrary to regulations; to keep bed and bedding in good order; never to rap on the cell door, except in case of sickness or other imperious necessity; and to pass nothing from one to another but by permission. They are required, at the ringing of the first bell in the morning, to turn out, dress, make the bed, fasten up the same, and have the bucket, dishes, and coffee pot ready for marching out; to open the door, gently, to the wall, step outside, and march at the word of command; to hold the dishes in the right hand, with the coffee pot in one of the smaller dishes,—the whole elevated so as to be distinctly open to the view of the inspecting officer; and to place the dishes on the table, on passing through the passage. Each convict, in marching into the chapel, is to take the seat assigned to him, and, while there, to give his entire attention to the services; to suppress, as far as possible, all disposition to cough, and to abstain from shuffling with the feet, spitting on the floor, and all movements of the body calculated to disturb the order and quiet of the place. If two or more convicts are passing about the yard at the same time and in the same direction, they must walk in single file, never abreast; nor must any convict ever loiter in the yard without permission. If convicts are unwell, they must report to the officer of their department, immediately on entering the shop in the morning; if sent to the hospital, they must proceed directly thither; and if ordered to the yard for exercise and air, they must confine themselves to the limits designated for the purpose. When a convict wishes to speak to the warden, or have an interview with the chaplain, he must first obtain leave from his officer; and in case he desires to speak to the inspectors or either of them, he must ask and obtain permission from the warden.

The following is the daily routine at this prison: The convicts are mustered out of their rooms in the morning, at hours varying with the season of the year, but, as a general rule, as soon as it is broad daylight; earlier than this is not considered safe. On reaching their respective shops, the first business is to have a thorough wash, after which, in summer, they engage in work for about an hour. After this season of work, or, in winter, immediately after washing, they return to their cells with their breakfast. As soon as this is dispatched, they attend prayers in the chapel, and then return to their workshops to labor. They remain there in associated labor, but in strict silence, except when permitted by their officer to make such inquiries or remarks as their work may require, until 12 m. Then they wash, and go with their dinners to their cells, for which they are allowed one hour; at the expiration of which, they return to the workshops and continue their labor till six o'clock in summer, and, when the days become shorter, until just before the sunlight begins to fail. With their suppers, they then return to their cells for the night. On their way thither, they pass a certain point, where the warden or deputy warden and the overseers of the workshops take their stand. Such of the men as have committed any offence during the day are ordered to remain at this point, while the others file off to their cells. The offence of each is stated by his overseer to the warden or deputy, who examines the case, and, in his discretion, either reprimands the offender, or sends him into punishment, which consists in the deprivation of supper and bed, instead of which latter he has only a board and blanket. On Sunday morning, those of the convicts who wish to take part in the exercises of a Sunday school, assemble in the chapel for that purpose an hour before divine service. Attendance upon this exercise is voluntary, and (unfortunately, we think, in a prison where there is so much that is excellent in many respects) this is the only stated teaching of any kind which is given in the institution. Divine service follows immediately on the close of the

Sunday school, after which the prisoners return to their cells for the day.

During their visit to this prison, the undersigned were present at Sunday school and the Sabbath morning service, and were deeply interested in both. In the former, the convicts gave earnest heed to the instructions imparted, and showed much intelligence as well as promptness, in their answers to the questions put to them; and in the latter, we listened to a highly practical and appropriate discourse on the prevalence and danger of disbelief in religion from the worthy chaplain, Rev. Mr. Carleton, delivered with much unction, and heard with profound attention by his convict congregation.

In the Ohio state prison, the duties required of the convicts are, in substance, as follows: To labor diligently, obey all orders promptly, and observe unbroken silence: not to communicate with each other by word, look, or writing, nor make use of any signs, except to convey their wants to the waiters: to approach their keepers in a respectful manner, to address them only when it becomes necessary in relation to their work or wants, and then to be brief in their communication: not to speak, without leave, to any person who does not belong to the institution, nor to receive from such any letter, paper, tobacco, or anything whatever: not to leave the place where they are put to work or the work they are set to do, nor to suffer their attention to be taken from their work to look at visitors, or even permit themselves to gaze or look at them when unemployed: not willfully or carelessly to injure their work, tools, clothes, bedding, or anything belonging to the prison, nor to mark, injure, or in any way deface the walls or other part of their cells: not to execute their work badly, when they have the ability to do it well: not to receive or transmit any letter or paper, except under the inspection of the warden; on entering their respective cells, each to draw the door of his cell till it strikes the latch, and in this position to stand, holding his door, until the turnkey approaches and puts in the key, then instantly to close it; to go to bed immediately on the ringing of the bell (they may go before if they choose), and observe a profound silence from that time until the sound of the bugle in the morning, when they must instantly rise, dress themselves and prepare to march out; to march in military step (lock-step); not to sleep with their clothes on; and, on becoming sick or from any cause unable to work, to report themselves to the officer under whose charge they may be, for leave to visit the hospital and consult the physician.

The following are the daily routine of duties and the regulations relating to the prisoners in the state prison of Wisconsin:

In winter, the prisoners rise at 6 A. M., and without previous labor, breakfast at 6½; in summer, they rise at 5½, and breakfast at 6½, after a period of work. Breakfast is served in the cells by the assistants. On the ringing of the small bell in the morning, the prisoners rise, dress, put up their bedstead, bed and bedding, and wash themselves. On the ringing of the large bell, immediately after breakfast, they come out of their cells and march in single file, taking the lock step, to their usual places of labor, where they remain till 12 M., working diligently and in silence. Then, at a signal, they quit work, wash, and prepare for dinner. At a second signal, they form in close order as before, and, carrying their dinner with them, march to their cells, where they are locked up. At one o'clock, they return, in the same manner as before, to their work, which they continue till six, when they quit work for the day. Receiving their supper, they return with it to their cells, where all their meals are taken. They are forbidden to hold any communication with each other at any time, in any manner, or by any means, unless the most urgent necessity connected with their work compels them to do so. They are not to speak to any person, who does not belong to the institution, unless permission is granted by the commissioner or the deputy, and then only in the presence of one or other of these officers, or of some other officer detailed for the purpose. They may not leave their work without special permission from the officer in charge. They are forbidden to sleep with their clothes on. They are required to approach the officers in the most respectful manner; and the use of all insulting, profane and abusive language to officers, strangers, or each other, is strictly interdicted. All are required to attend divine service in the chapel at least once every Sunday.

The following is a brief summary of what is required of convicts in the state prisons of New York: To labor diligently, obey all orders, and preserve unbroken silence; to march to and from their work and meals, under the care of their several keepers, in single file and close order (lock step), each looking over the left shoulder of the one immediately in front of him and with his right hand resting on the right shoulder of the same; to march straight and turn square corners; in chapel to sit erect and with arms folded, and the same in the mess room, except while eating; in meeting officers and visitors in the yard, to give way in all cases, and to tip the cap to them; to do no fancy work and make no trinkets; never to engage in traffic with fellow prisoners, officers, or any other persons; not to willfully or carelessly injure their work, tools, clothes, bedding, or anything belonging to the prison; not to execute their work badly, when they have the ability to do it well; not, at any time or on any pretence, to speak to any person who does not belong to the institution, nor to receive from them any letter, paper, tobacco, or other article or thing whatsoever; and, in their whole demeanor, to act in a respectful, quiet, and orderly manner, and in strict conformity to the discipline of the prison.

The foregoing summary of the rules and regulations, governing the conduct of convicts, in the prisons of four of the leading states of the Union, and those in widely separated localities, from the extreme east, to what until lately at least was the extreme west, may serve as a specimen of the whole. They confirm the remark with which we started, that, with some minor differences, they are everywhere, in substance the same. Indeed, if we should give these regulations for all the state prisons, it would be seen that they are, to a great extent, transcripts the one from the other. Those of Massachusetts and New York are the ones most extensively followed. In some instances, the rules and regulations of these states are almost literally copied.

The usage varies in different prisons as it respects the place of taking the meals. We do not intend to speak with exactness, but our impression is that in about one-half of the prisons visited, all the meals are eaten in the cells; in the remaining portion, breakfast and dinner are eaten in a common hall, furnished with narrow tables, not exceeding twelve to fifteen inches in width, with the prisoners all facing one way. But even in prisons where the first two meals are taken in mess rooms, the suppers are carried to and eaten in the cells.

The mode of receiving the prisoners and initiating them into the mysteries of their new prison life is substantially the same in all prisons where the same general system of discipline, that is, the separate or the congregate, is maintained; and a description of one is, to all intents and purposes, a description of the whole. We will, therefore, describe the *modus operandi* in two representative prisons, one, that is, of each class—Sing Sing, in New York, and the eastern penitentiary, in Pennsylvania.

When a convict is brought to the Sing Sing prison, various interrogatories are put to him by the clerk, and the answers elicited are recorded in a book. Any papers, money, or valuables in his possession are taken from him, and deposited with the warden for safe keeping, against his discharge. He is then given into the charge of the keeper of the hospital. This officer takes him to the dressing room, and causes him to be denuded of all his clothes, thoroughly washed in his whole person, and dressed in his prison garb; after which he is weighed and measured, and the results fully recorded. He is next conducted to the hospital, where he is carefully examined as to the state of his health by the physician, and the facts thus ascertained, together with a full description of his person, are entered in a register kept for the purpose. The prisoner is then conveyed to the cell building, where he is given into the charge of the hall keeper, who instructs him in the rules to be observed by him as a prisoner, and particularly as to the duty of implicit and prompt obedience, after which he assigns him to some vacant cell till such time as he can be permanently placed among the gang, or members of the shop, with whom he may be required to work. Either on that or the following day, if able bodied, he is assigned to some branch of prison work, and that part of his sentence which condemns him to hard labor begins to take effect. Convicts in feeble health at the time of their reception are either placed in the hospital, or put upon some light work for the state; they are never assigned to contract labor.

When a prisoner is received into the eastern penitentiary, at Philadelphia, he is first conducted into an ante-room, where a minute description of his person is taken by the warden, and recorded in a book kept for the purpose. He is then hooded, (i. e. a mask is put on his face,) taken to the bath room, thoroughly cleansed, and furnished with his new convict suit; after which he is again hooded and led into the cell, whose four walls are to constitute the limit of his locomotion during his prison life, and from which he is not to emerge till the expiration of his sentence.

In many of the prisons of the country, perhaps in most, the rules and regulations, so far as they relate to convicts, are printed on large cards and hung up in the cells, and also, not unfrequently, on the walls of the workshops. In addition to this, or as a substitute for it, where the usage just referred to does not prevail, it

Is the custom in many of the prisons to furnish each prisoner with a printed copy of the rules. In all cases where prisoners cannot read, the regulations are explained to them on entering.

In none of the prisons visited by the undersigned out of New York and within the limits of the United States, except Massachusetts and New Hampshire, is it either prescribed by the rules, or the settled practice, that the chaplains converse with the prisoners on their entering the prison. Even in the prisons named, there is no rule to this effect; but it is stated to be the uniform practice of the chaplains to hold a conversation with each convict either before he is set to work, or as soon thereafter as possible. In New York we have three state prisons. The chaplain at Sing Sing is not in the habit of conversing with convicts on their reception into the prison, and assigns as a reason the impossibility of doing so on account of the number coming there. The Rev. Mr. Canfield, chaplain of Clinton prison, is accustomed to hold a special interview with each convict as soon after his entrance as possible. One object of these interviews is to make the prisoners acquainted with the rules and regulations of the prison, more particularly those relating to his own department, that they may know how to avail themselves of the privileges of the library, correspondence, Sabbath school, and evening lessons in their cells. Another is to learn something of their previous history, to study their character, and, on the knowledge thus gained, to found such exhortations as may seem suited to each. A third object is to give them the assurance that, if they ever desire advice or assistance during their incarceration, he is their friend, to whom they may feel free to come at any time, to seek the counsel or aid, of which they may stand in need. The chaplain of Auburn prison, Rev. Mr. Ives, says that he makes it a point, *whenever he can*, to converse with convicts when they first come into the prison; that he first seeks to convince them that it will be to their advantage to obey all prison rules; that he next tries to impress upon them that their time in prison need not be wholly lost, but may be turned to account in making both intellectual and moral improvement; and that, finally, he endeavors to encourage them with the assurance that, though disgraced, they are not utterly lost, that they are not so fallen as not to have friends to hold out to them a helping hand, if only they try to do well, and especially that Jesus is ready to forgive and save the vilest sinners, if, like the prodigal son, they come to him confessing and forsaking their sin.

Both from our personal observations and from reading the answers to our questions, we have been impressed with the idea that, when the criminal first enters his prison-house, too little care and pains, as a general thing, are taken to give his mind a right direction. Then, if ever, it seems to us this important work is to be done. He enters disgraced, disheartened, disconsolate. Here is the golden opportunity to appeal to his feelings, his judgment, his sense of responsibility, his manhood. He may now easily be converted into a demon, if he is not one already, by abuse, harshness, injustice, unkindness and oppression. But if on the other hand, the officers, being really his friends as well as his keepers, tell him so and labor to make him sensible of this fact, if they seek to convince him that they feel for him in his situation, sympathize with him, besire his well being, and would induce him to turn that into a blessing which he looks upon as the greatest of curses, they will readily win his confidence. That gained, an important conquest has been achieved. It will then become comparatively easy to inspire him with a determination to reform his life and become a better man. Let them, from the first moment he enters the prison, point out to him the path of rectitude, as well by example as by precept. Let them convince him that they feel with and for him. Let them assure him that, while it is made their duty, as the officers of the law, to keep him confined in prison, no law forbids their giving him their sympathy and laboring for his good. Let them show him that they do sympathize with him, while they urge upon him the importance of cheerfulness and hope, and especially of forming the noble resolution that he will reform his life, and turn from the error and folly of his ways. Impressions like these, made upon the convict at the very beginning of his prison life, could not fail to exert a benign and salutary effect; they would be a long step towards his reformation.

Due effort, we are convinced, is not generally made in this direction. More is done, in this way, in the Charlestown prison than in any other that came within the range of our observations. There, as we learn from Mr. Haynes' paper in response to our interrogatories, the prisoners are kept from one to twenty days in solitary confinement, before they are put to labor. Prior to their being placed at work, they are instructed by the deputy warden in regard to the rules. Every necessary explanation is mildly, carefully, and understandingly made to them; after which, they are taken to the work shop, and commence labor. In the course of a day or two, the convict is sent for by the warden, who has a full and friendly talk with him. He inquires into his past history, interrogates him as to his parents, home and family; counsels him as to his future course; assures him of good and kind treatment so long as he shall deserve it; and endeavors to cheer up his spirits and inspire him with courage and hope. This interview rarely ends without bringing tears into the eyes of the most hardened, and leading to the formation of resolutions which have a strong influence upon their future lives. The chaplain also takes an early opportunity of conversing with prisoners after their entrance, in which he seeks to impress on their minds the same ideas, with such other suggestions as he thinks necessary.

In our opinion, it would be well to place it among the stated duties of prison chaplains and make it a matter of fixed regulation, that they should hold interviews of this kind with prisoners as early as possible after their committal.

In Vermont, convicts are kept one day in solitary confinement previously to being put to work ; in Massachusetts, as already stated, from one to twenty days. In all the other prisons visited by us, those who are able to labor are set to work at once, except in Wisconsin ; and the same rule holds there also ; unless the judge, in his sentence, makes solitary imprisonment for a certain period obligatory. Whether such imprisonment is often made a part of the sentence, and if so, to what length of time it may be made to extend, we are not informed, and of course cannot inform our readers.

The progress of prison reform, the advance of sound principles of prison discipline, within a hundred years, and especially within the last half of that period, has been as gratifying, as it is remarkable. The horrors, cruelties, and manifold abominations of English and continental prisons, prior to the time of John Howard, are almost past belief. It would almost seem as if the terrific personification of punishment in the Hindoo code had become a living reality there : " Punishment is the inspirer of TERROR ; with a *black aspect and a red eye*, it terrifies the guilty." Of course, it does not lie within the province of the present paper to enter into any detail upon this subject. It is enough to say that no sentiment of humanity towards the prisoner seems ever to have entered the breast of his jailor, no look or tone of kindness ever to have saluted his senses, or cheered the misery of his incarceration. Merciless scourgings, ponderous irons of cruel tightness, thumbscrews, underground dungeons, and chainings to dead bodies were among the punishments inflicted for an infraction of prison rules. It was with reference to these abuses and their early assailants, particularly Gen. Oglethorpe, the illustrious founder of the colony of Georgia, that, in bringing out a new edition of the Seasons, in 1730, Thompson introduced the following lines :

> " Ye sons of mercy ! yet resume the search,
> Drag forth the legal monsters into light ;
> Wrench from their hands oppression's iron rod,
> And make the cruel feel the pangs they give."

These lines contain both an exhortation and a prophecy. Bambridge, Acton, Huggins and Barnes, among the worst of the "legal monsters" thus lampooned, were indeed made to "feel the pangs they gave ;" they were ejected from their offices as jailors, and subjected to legal prosecutions and penalties ; some of them having been imprisoned within the very walls, which had been the silent witnesses of their own cruelties.

How wonderful the change which has been wrought by the combined agencies of religion, education, and the zealous labors of christian philanthropists ! Certainly neither harshness nor cruelty has been wholly banished from the administration of prisons ; nevertheless, the law of force is gradually giving place to the law of love. Year by year, an increasing number of prison officers are yielding to the conviction that counsel, reproof, remonstrance, persuasion, and motives addressed to the spiritual nature of prisoners are more potent as a means of discipline, than mere brute energy ; and that moral agencies are to be substituted for this to the utmost extent that such substitution is practicable. It is, indeed, quite possible that there are convicts of so coarse a mould by nature, and so brutalized by habits of sin, that they can be controlled only by bodily suffering. But the number of such we believe to be comparatively small. There are few, even among criminals, so degraded as to be insensible to sympathy and affection. There is a chord in the heart of the most depraved and the most erring, from which the touch of kindness will evoke an unfailing response.

Among the interrogatories proposed by the undersigned to the superintendents of state prisons was the following: "How far is kindness employed in your prison as a means of discipline; in what ways, and with what effect?" The answers returned were, in the main, in harmony with the views expressed in the preceding paragraph. The best officers, those of the largest experience and whose administration has achieved the highest success, are unanimous in the testimony that the humane system, the system which relies upon moral agencies, is more effective in securing obedience to prison rules, cheerful industry and correct deportment on the part of convicts, and in promoting their reformation, than the system of harshness and severity.   A few dissent; but the dissentients are gentlemen who have either had little experience as prison officers or possess but slight aptitude for the duties of their position.   One says that kindness is employed in his prison as far as it will serve, evidently meaning that it goes but a little way; another, that it is used as far as practicable, with, doubtless, a like reserve; a third, that it has very little effect upon prisoners.

But this is far from being the voice of the majority of respondents.   The key-note is struck by the three from whose replies we offer the following extracts:

Mr. Haynes, of Massachusetts, with that brevity and directness which characterize his utterances, says: "Kindness is the principal means of discipline employed here; and it is used in every consistent way.   It is believed that this renders the prisoners more confiding and obedient, and that it is better adapted than a more strictly coercive discipline to promote their reformation.   I have never known an instance where I thought that a man would be made better by the infliction of blows; nor have I ever yet, as I think, met the person, however low and degraded, however hardened and steeped in crime, who had not a spot in his heart that could be touched by kindness."

Mr. Cordier, of Wisconsin, says: "Every convict in this prison is treated like a human being, and not as an outcast from society. We never allow any officer to speak to him harshly, or to allude in any manner, however remote, to the crime of which he stands convicted.   No prisoner is punished for his first offence against the prison rules, unless it is a very grave one; he receives, instead, an earnest but kind warning not to repeat it.   Punishment is never inflicted, till it has been explained to the offender that his own good, as well as that of the institution, requires it; and corporal punishment is, in no case, inflicted.   We never let prisoners suffer for want of comfortable clothes, or of good, wholesome food.   We take good care of them when sick.   We encourage them, at every opportunity, to cultivate their mental, moral and physical powers, and to make a solemn pledge to enter society again as better men.

We find that kindness, thus employed, always has the most salutary effect."

Mr. Miller, late warden of the Missouri state penitentiary, remarks: "Kindness is the great central idea in a true theory of prison discipline; kindness in tone, look, and utterance, as opposed to a coarse, rude, and stern manner of treatment. It was upon this theory that I endeavored to administer the government of the prison. A failure to impress on the prisoner the conviction that you have an interest in and sympathy for him has always an unfavorable effect. Kindness is a means of discipline which I have always found effective. If really felt in the heart and constantly maintained in the administration, it will, in the end, subdue the most hardened, and reclaim those who have been found incorrigible by any and all other agencies. In many instances, where different kinds of punishment had failed to make any lasting impression on the subject, I have known kindness to work a thorough revolution in the man. Indeed, its effect is never lost."

It has often occurred to us, in reflecting on this subject, that we might take a lesson, both pertinent and valuable, from God's moral government. We are a world of malefactors. The position we occupy is that of a criminal revolt against our rightful Lord. And what is the object, what the method, of his administration? *Reformation through kindness.* Punishment, then, with reformation for its end and kindness as the means, is an old relation, which comes down to us under the sanction of an authority that none may question. When the first great crime was committed, the punishment awarded to the criminal was one which included in it the idea of reformation. Man was driven from Eden, but the very sentence that announced his punishment opened to him the hope of a second paradise, more glorious than the one he had lost. The method of the recovery is expressed, with a beautiful terseness, by the prophet Jeremiah, in the third verse of his thirty-first chapter: "With loving-kindness have I drawn thee." This loving-kindness of God is that cord of a man, that band of love, with which he draws us to virtue and to heaven. Our recovery is to be effected through the influence of a demonstration of good will in the gift and mission of his Son. The problem was to win back man's love and obedience. Kindness was God's device to achieve this miracle. In no other way, it would seem, could a responding affection be awakened in the heart of man. Authority could not command, nor terror charm it into existence. The human heart remains shut, as with the force of a vice, against all applications of strength or intimidation. But God, who knew what was in man, since he gave him the nature which he possesses, knew that in his dark and guilty bosom there was one hold which he still had upon him. He knew that to reach his heart, all leprous as it was, he must just lavish upon him the treasures of his kindness.

Here, it seems to us, we have a divine pattern, which, in our humble measure, we are to imitate in our treatment of criminals. The convicts in our prisons are not beyond the influence of the same principle which the Divine Governor, in the reach of his infinite wisdom, has employed with such stupendous results in his moral administration of our fallen world. Howard, the world-renowned philanthropist, as the fruit of his wide observation, came to this conclusion. He tells us that convicts are not ungovernable; that there is a way of managing even the most desperate among them; and that that way is, without in the least relaxing the steadiness of a calm and resolute discipline, to treat them with tenderness and humanity. Such was the conviction of this sagacious observer after years of intercourse with criminals of all classes. It would appear, then, that genuine kindness is a principle which keeps a lingering hold of our nature, even in the last and lowest degrees of human wickedness. In offenders, the most hardened and inveterate, there still remains one soft part which will yield to the demonstrations of tenderness and love. This one ingredient, at least, of a better character—susceptibility to kindness—is found to survive the destruction of all the others. However fallen a man may be from the moralities which once adorned him, whatever abyss of crime he may have reached in his descent, the manifestation of good will, of heartfelt kindness, on the part of his fellow man, carries with it a softening, purifying, redeeming influence. There lies in such demonstrations a recuperative and restorative power, which no degree of depravity can utterly destroy; and through the skillful application of this power, the very worst of men can be converted into consenting and willing agents of their own reformation.

The good effect of kindness upon prisoners is well illustrated in the following lines, lately addressed by a convict incarcerated in Sing Sing prison, to Mr. Gaylord B. Hubbell. Mr. H. was a few years ago at the head of that prison, and it is well known that he impressed upon its administration a stamp of extraordinary humanity and gentleness, without, however, abating a particle of its vigor and efficiency.   There was one practice adopted by him quite peculiar, and wonderfully effective as an instrument of government.   He appropriated one hour each day exclusively to receiving the calls of such convicts as had any care, grief, or burden, in reference to which they desired counsel or redress. There is an allusion to these interviews in the subjoined lines. One of us has often been present on the occasions when the convicts thus confided their sorrows to their chief, and sought his interposition ; and the patience with which he listened to their tales, the wisdom he showed in resolving their several cases, and the child-like confidence and submission with which they received his decisons were beautiful to see.

THE CONVICT'S FRIEND.

To the Hon. G. B. Hubbell, formerly Agent and Warden of Sing Sing Prison.

BY A CONVICT.

The Convict's Friend! the Convict's Friend!
  The people muttered "shame"!
That one so good should condescend
  To bear so vile a name.
He heeded not their idle words,
  Felt not their harmless stings;
His master was the Lord of Lords,
  He served the King of Kings.
And when the jealous world complained,
  Or cared not to commend,
He only smiled, and still remained
  The friendless Convict's Friend.

Till angels from above shall deign
  To come at mercy's calls,
We ne'er shall see his like again
  Within these prison walls.
With firm but gentle hand he curbed
  Our wild and wayward wills,
And calmed the storm that once disturbed
  Mount Pleasant's* peaceful hills.
He would not break our stubborn hearts ;
  He only sought to bend
By gentle means and kindly arts,
  And be the Convict's Friend.

His Christian spirit sympathized
  As only Christians can;
And in each convict recognized
  A fallen brother man.
And we to him could always go,
  As to a father dear,

* Sing Sing was formerly called Mount Pleasant.

And pour our tales of grief and woe
  In his attentive ear;
And none who sought him failed to see,
  Or failed to comprehend
Why he alone of all should be
  The Convict's steadfast Friend.

He knew what others never knew,
  Felt what they never felt;
He did what others never do,
  Dealt as they never dealt.
Where others saw unmingled vice,
  And mental, moral dearth,
He saw, with sense more just and nice,
  The accidents of birth,
A thousand hidden things, on which
  Our very lives depend;
And justice, love and mercy teach
  The honest Convict's Friend.

He would not grind us down for pelf
  In this accursed den;
He rather chose to wrong himself
  Than wrong his fellow man.
And if for true or fancied wrong
  We sought and claimed redress,
He listened patiently and long
  And answered "no," or "yes."
But with his judgments, just and kind,
  We dared not to contend;
We recognized a master mind
  Within the Convict's Friend.

The hate by other men inspired
  Was turned to love by him,
And his great kindness never tired,
  While they were harsh and grim.
And when he made his last good-bye,
  To come again no more,
Oh! there were many weeping eyes
  That never wept before.
No more upon his gentle will
  Our hopes and fears depend;
We miss him here, but he is still
  The Convict's cherished Friend.

Mr. Hubbell will please accept this humble token of a convict's gratitude and affection.
November, 1866.

Although kindness as a principle of discipline is, as we have seen, to a considerable extent, adopted in theory and applied in the practical administration of our prisons, yet it lacks the steadiness and efficiency, which would be imparted by comprehensive and judicious organization; in other words, by a well devised system of rewards as an encouragement to good conduct. On this subject an intelligent and trusted convict, in a large and important prison, said: "As matters stand, and as I have seen them during my four years' sojourn here, I have come to the conclusion that whatever convict conducts himself ill will be punished, and that he who is reformed, proving this by his conduct, will not, or but slightly, be rewarded." Doubtless, there is much (shall we say too much?) truth in the last part of this statement. It appears to us a matter of great importance, that there should be given to the convict, while expiating his crime, that stimulus to exertion which actuates men in common life. All hope of reward being taken away, who among us would be willing to toil? The case of the prisoner, with no prospect of reward, is like that of the man in society who has lost hope. He becomes torpid, indifferent, reckless. But set the hope of personal benefit before him, and give him a fair chance of securing it, and you have placed in his view an object which, while it elevates his aims, will, at the same time, rouse his ambition and stimulate his efforts.

We are sorry to be obliged to state the conviction that there is not a prison in the United States or Canada, where anything like a well considered and comprehensive scheme has been introduced, with a view of inspiring the convicts with hope and stimulating them thereby to industry and good conduct. And we are still more sorry to be obliged to add that many, even of those who must be esteemed our best prison officers, appear to have but a low appreciation of the benefits of such a system. One remarks: "The principle of rewards ought not to be employed to too great an extent," evidently thinking that the point of excess would be very near the point of departure. Another says: "We are opposed to *any system* of rewards to convicts." A third: "It is doubtful whether a more extensive system of rewards could be introduced into our prisons with advantage." A fourth: "The expediency of extending the system of rewards in our prisons is regarded as doubtful." A fifth: "It is doubted whether rewards to convicts would be beneficial."

Most of the gentlemen, whose opinions are given in these extracts, are wardens of important prisons, and some of them have deservedly acquired distinction as prison officers. In giving expression to the judgments cited, they have assuredly laid themselves open to the charge of a degree of inconsistency; since, with but one exception, they have been liberal in their praise of what is known in our statute books as the commutation law; a law which remits a certain portion of the convict's sentence, in consideration of his diligence and obedience to prison rules; a law, therefore, which constitutes a part of the very system of rewards which they condemn under that name. This shows, we think, that little earnest consideration has been given to the subject, and that the opinions of these persons are more the result of prejudice than the dictate of a calm and enlightened judgment. It is a relief to find those humane and thoughtful officers, Messrs. Cordier and Miller, warmly espousing the side of this question which looks to progress, to improvement, to reform in our methods of prison administration, and which unites all suffrages among the wisest and most enlightened of the friends of a reformatory prison discipline in Europe. Of the Irish prison system, whose one great aim is the reformation of its subjects, and which has succeeded in that design beyond all others known in history, the fundamental principle, the warp and woof of the whole, its very sum and essence, is hope;—hope born and nourished of rewards earned by good conduct and given only to the deserving; rewards manifold in their character and operating as a constant force, from the time when the prisoner enters his solitary cell at Mountjoy, till he walks forth a free man, " redeemed, regenerated, and disenthralled," from the intermediate prisons of Lusk and Smithfield. So, too, of the mark system of Capt. Alexander Machonochie,— that extraordinary man who was a full century in advance of his contemporaries in his philosophy of public punishment,—the essential principle was, in like manner, rewards given in the shape of marks for industry in work, progress in religious and secular knowledge, and general good conduct; which marks had a money value in the prison, and served for the purchase of food, clothes, and other comforts and indulgences during their incarceration (for the prisoners were obliged in this way to pay for everthing they had); and the surplus of marks, after defraying all their prison expenses, went, according to the theory, towards their liberation; but the Captain was never able, either at Norfolk Island or Birmingham jail, to induce the authorities to allow him to carry his plan to that length. The system, therefore, cramped and restricted as it was in its operation, never had a full and fair trial. Nevertheless, despite the narrow range to which it was confined and the limited power given to the marks, it accomplished wonders. The penal colony on Norfolk Island contained

the scum and scrapings of all the other colonies, the most
depraved and brutalized of all England's transported convicts.
Yet at the end of his four years' administration, he could declare
with truth: "I found the Island a turbulent, brutal hell; I left it
a peaceful, well-ordered community. The most complete security
alike of person and property prevailed. Officers, women and
children traversed the Island everywhere without fear; and huts,
gardens, stock-yards, and growing crops, many of them, as of
fruit, most tempting, were scattered in every corner without
molestation." He expresses the opinion that "there was more
manly purpose and a higher quality of moral agency in any six
of his better men on Norfolk Island than in all the exclusively
coercive prisons that were ever invented." This testimony is
abundantly confirmed by disinterested witnesses, one of whom,
the author of "Recollections of Sixteen Years in Australia," says:
"Captain Machonochie did more for the reformation of these
unhappy wretches than the most sanguine practical mind could
beforehand have ventured even to hope." And how were such
extraordinary results achieved? By moral agencies almost
wholly. His prisoners were reasoned with, not bullied; they
were sought to be raised, not crushed; above all, they had an
interest, vital and profound, in their own good conduct. In other
words, they were softened, subdued, and reformed through a
comprehensive and judicious system of rewards, by which the
principle of hope was kept in constant and active play within
their breasts.

In the face of examples and results like these, how cold, dry,
hard, and utterly jejune do such expressions as the following
from the presiding officers of our prisons appear: "We are opposed to any system of rewards"—"it is doubtful whether any
rewards to convicts would be beneficial"—"the principle of rewards should not be carried too far"—"the expediency of extending the system of rewards to convicts is doubted." In effect,
little play is given to this principle in the very best of our American penitentiaries. The warden of the Maine state prison observes: "Rewards are employed in this prison, to some extent, as
a stimulus to good conduct." How far or in what ways is not
stated; it is not probable that the detail would be very extensive.
The warden of the Wisconsin state prison says: "We grant to the
deserving little favors which are denied to the undeserving." The
late warden of the Missouri state penitentiary remarks: "Rewards

are in use here, such as extra privileges; for example, the privilege of having access to the yard on Sundays and after working hours are over in the evenings, and the privilege of more frequent correspondence with their friends. The effect of such indulgences has been found most excellent. The convicts appreciate highly these recognitions of their worthiness, and manifest the most grateful feelings; and when it is understood that all who earn the privileges named are entitled to them and will certainly be permitted to enjoy them, it proves a wonderful incentive to good conduct." In Vermont, the chaplain reports that well-conducted prisoners have certain special privileges accorded to them in the way of writing, reading, &c.; but gives no specifications.

The above statement exhausts the detail, as far as known to us —certainly a most meagre exhibit—of the rewards held out to convicts in American prisons as an encouragement and incentive to good conduct, beyond what is to be immediately noticed.

In nine of the states of our Union—Connecticut, Illinois, Indiana, Maine, Massachusetts, Michigan, New York, Ohio, and Wisconsin—an excellent foundation for an effective system of rewards has been laid in the passage of acts, under the general title of commutation laws, the design of which is to encourage and stimulate prisoners to industry, obedience, and general good conduct, by allowing them to earn thereby a certain diminution of their terms of sentence. By these acts, as a general rule, convicts, by uniform good conduct, can earn a diminution of five days per month; but in New York, from the fourth to the tenth year of imprisonment, they can earn seven and a half days per month, and thenceforward ten days, so that a convict sentenced for ten years can shorten his term of imprisonment by two years and one month; a fraction over one-fifth of the whole term; and one sentenced for twenty years can shorten it by five years and five months, rather more than one-fourth of the entire period.

The principle of this law we regard as founded in reason and justice, and the policy established by it as wise and beneficent. The effect of this policy is to change, in some respects, the aspect and condition of prison life. In keeping before prisoners a permanent and ever present incentive to good conduct, it fortifies the resolutions of many a feeble mind, and counteracts, in others, the tendency to feelings of despondency, recklessness, and revenge, which their situation is apt to engender, and in which many of them are prone to indulge. In encouraging them to perform their work cheerfully, it has, so far, the good effect of converting coerced into voluntary labor; while, as a means of discipline, appealing to the better feelings of all in whom such feelings still have a place, and substituting rewards instead of punishments, moral instead of mere brute force, and hope in the place of fear, its operation cannot be otherwise than healthful and bracing to their moral nature. A law of which all this can be said with truth, and we belive it can be so said of the one now under consideration, needs no further vindication.

But further vindication, and that in abundance, is at hand, in the fruits which it has borne. Tested by its actual operation and effect, it is found to be a most salutary law. Mr. Haynes testifies: "The effect of this law in the Massachusetts state prison has been good. I think it the most important step in prison discipline that has been taken in this country in the last forty years." The warden of the Wisconsin state prison says : "I consider the commutation law a more powerful agency to promote good conduct among convicts than anything else that could have been devised for that end." The warden of the Ohio state prison says of it : "No law ever passed by the Legislature has been so marked in its influence for good since Ohio has been a state, as that which enables prisoners to earn the remission of part of their sentence by good conduct. It works admirably, and has done much towards keeping up the discipline of the institution." The authorities of the Connecticut state prison attest the excellence of this law in the following terms : "The law authorizing a deduction from the sentences of convicts for good behavior has been attended with beneficial results. It has been received with gratitude by almost every inmate of the prison. The discipline of the prison was never better, and it has been maintained with less punishment than formerly ; a result owing, in a great measure, to the commutation law. More than eighty per cent. of the prisoners in 1865 had a perfect record of good conduct throughout the year." The late warden of the Michigan state prison, Mr. Seaton, bears this testimony to the good effects of the law : "Very desirable results have followed from making a prisoner's confinement, to a certain degree, depend for its duration upon himself. The intense anxiety which all convicts manifest in relation to their 'good time,' and the earnestness which they exhibit to save every possible day of it, show that they place some estimate upon their life in society again, and have not lost all appreciation of public opinion. More work is done, it is performed more cheerfully, and better discipline is maintained now than formerly, as the result of our 'good time' law. Of prisoners discharged last year (1864), more than ninety per cent conducted themselves with such propriety as to secure the whole of their good time."

In all the states that have commutation laws, except Maine, time earned by good conduct may be forfeited, in whole or in part, by subsequent bad conduct. In some of them, this forfeiture is in the discretion of the warden ; in others, it is in that of the inspectors or directors. It rests with these officers to determine, first, whether there shall be any forfeiture at all in any given case, and, secondly, to what extent, if at all, such forfeiture shall take effect. Iu Maine, time once earned is placed beyond all contingency ; there is no power in the prison or the state that can exact its forfeiture.

In the prisons of all the states where these commutation acts have been passed, the law is fully explained to the prisoners on entering, and they are made to understand it. In Massachusetts, each convict is annually furnished with an almanac, in which he carefully notes down, month by month, the number of days earned by good conduct and the number forfeited by bad. This record he guards with the utmost care : the days to be remitted from his sentence are a treasure, which he hoards and counts as a miser does his gold. As the heap, so to speak, increases, he becomes more anxious to add to its bulk ; and of course he is proportionally careful to observe the strictest propriety in his conduct, and to avoid all infraction of prison rules. How much these days of anticipated freedom are prized by convicts will appear from the following statement. A prisoner, in a certain prison, had earned by good conduct a considerable reduction of sentence, and by overwork a considerable sum of money. The money had been paid to him, and he was upon the point of receiving his discharge so many days prior to the expiration of his sentence. Holding up the greenbacks to the view of the principal keeper, he said : "Mr. W., I would sooner part with the whole of these than give up one day of the number I have gained by observance of the prison rules."

In no prison, except that of Massachusetts, do convicts appear to be furnished with almanacs for recording time gained, and in no other is there so much system in the record. In some others they keep a record, and know how much they have gained so long as they are not reported for a violation of rules; but when so reported, they are not informed whether any, and if any, how much time has been adjudged to have been forfeited; and so they lose the exact state of the account, which cannot but have a disheartening effect. The Massachusetts plan we regard as much the most satisfactory, where convicts are informed both what they gain and what they lose, and are furnished with the means of keeping an exact account of the same.

In the commutation acts of Illinois and Wisconsin there is a provision which must commend itself to every just and humane mind, and to which we earnestly invite the attention of the legislators of other states. In Illinois, every convict who passes the whole time of his sentence without having had any infraction of the discipline recorded against him, is entitled to a certificate to that effect from the warden, and on presentation of such certificate to the Governor, he is, in like manner, entitled to a certificate from him of restoration to all the rights of citizenship forfeited by his conviction, which certificate is to be taken as evidence of the fact in all courts of record and elsewhere. The provision in the act of Wisconsin is the same, except as to the mode of certifying the fact of restoration. It is in these words: "Any convict who, at the expiration of the term of his sentence, shall obtain a certificate from the deputy commissioner, that, during his term of confinement, such convict has maintained a good character for obedience, industry, and integrity, such certificate, countersigned by the commissioner, shall restore such convict to citizenship."

We have cited the opinions of a number of wardens against the policy of extending the system of rewards in our prisons. A considerable number, on the contrary, declare, in general terms, that there can be no objection to such extension, but might be some advantage in it. Still, it is quite evident that their hearts are not in the matter, and that they have given rather an unthinking than a well considered assent to the proposition. Only two seem to be cordial and earnest, and at the same time intelligent, in their approval and advocacy of the plan.

Mr. H. Cordier says: " A system of rewards in convict prisons, which should be most judicious in its principles and its methods of applying them, would be the least objectionable and the most effective. As long as our convicts are merely white slaves, working for their masters without compensation, they must be excused for not having much confidence in the sincerity of their lawgivers. Although they have, to a certain extent, forfeited their liberty, yet they should not, for that reason, be prevented from performing the duty, even when imprisoned, of providing in some measure, for the wants of their families. I have seen much, very much misery in the families of convicts. While the father works faithfully from morning till night, his children are cold and hungry, and the wife and mother is too often dragged down into vice and dissipation; and so the punishment of one criminal makes another. This ought not so to be. Something effectual should be done to correct this evil. I would, therefore, recommend that a correct account of the earnings of each convict, during his imprisonment, be kept, and that a portion—say twenty to twenty-five per cent.—be placed to his credit for the benefit of his family, or of himself if he be single, provided always that he should show himself deserving. This would be a powerful stimulus to diligence and good conduct. It would, in effect, place it in the option of each convict to punish or reward himself. It would make him diligent; and a diligent convict is always—so at least I have found it—a well behaved one. I confess that this plan would not help much to make prisons self-sustaining; but do we not profess to be a Christian people?"

Mr. P. T. Miller holds the following language on this subject: "I am of the opinion that an extended system of rewards might with advantage be introduced into our prisons. First in importance, in such a system, would be permission to the convict to abridge his term of imprisonment by good conduct; that is, the commutation law, already enacted by the legislatures of a number of states. As a disciplinary measure, this law is worth all the shower-baths, dark cells, iron caps, lashes, bucks, crucifixes, and other refined methods of punishment, known to the science of penology. These latter may, indeed, break the spirit of the convict, and reduce him to that sort of obedience which is yielded by the unreasoning brute, the obedience of fear; but the former, appealing to his personal interest and operating on his better nature, furnishes that which is necessary to every man, whatever his condition in life, a motive to do right, an incentive to the faithful performance of his duty. Man's nature is not changed by confinement within prison walls; there, as elsewhere, he is influenced by the hope of good and the dread of evil; and the former, if equal play be given to it, will be found as much more powerful within as it is without the precincts of a prison. The hope of reward, of personal benefit, in one form or another, is the mainspring of all human effort, whether in regard to the interests of time or the destinies of eternity; and they only are not influenced by such considerations, whose rational powers are so far obliterated that they are not accounted responsible to either divine or human law. The provision in a system of rewards for prisons, which I should place second in its power of beneficial influence, would be that which grants to the industrious and well-behaved convict a certain share—be the same less or more—of his pecuniary earnings; and the third, such special privileges and indulgences as may, considering the end in view and their adaptation to promote it, be deemed wise and proper. Combine, in due proportion and under judicious limitations, these three elements— diminution of sentence, participation in earnings, and certain well-defined privileges—and you have inaugurated a system which will revolutionize both the theory and practice of prison discipline, and make prisons what they are sometimes claimed, and always ought, to be—moral hospitals, aiming at and, to an extent beyond what would now be credited, effecting the cure of their inmates.

"In administering the discipline of the Missouri state penitentiary (Mr. Miller proceeds to say), I discarded much of the old theory of prison discipline, and substituted in its place what I conceived to be the dictates of common sense, justice, and humanity. The tendency of prison life, even under the most favorable circumstances, is to foster feelings of sadness and despondency, and to break down the mental and physical energies of the prisoner. A short time suffices for this, if the harsh and unnatural system is adhered to, which imposes perfect and perpetual silence, forbids all social intercourse, and denies all recreation to the imprisoned. On entering the prison, the convict is clothed in a uniform which serves to remind him, at every turn, of his degradation. He is marched to the workshop in the morning, where he labors in silence till noon; then to the mess-room, where he partakes in silence of a coarse repast; then back to the workshop, where he continues his silent toil till night; and then to his prison-house, where he is locked up in a cheerless cell; to be called forth again in the morning to the same unvarying round of silent labor, silent marchings, and silent meals. There is no relaxation, no recreation, no variety in his occupations; and, in the long vista of the future, he sees nothing before him but the same interminable and oppressive monotony. Meanwhile, thoughts of home and friends and family, and the sense of his own disgrace, come to worry and oppress him; and he finds no peace of mind by day or by night. He unconsciously lapses into a state of melancholy, which he has neither the courage to resist nor the energy to overcome. In my administration of the prison, it was my constant aim to mitigate, as far as was consistent with good order and proper subordination, this terrible evil. To this end I permitted (to the deserving) conversation and social intercourse to a certain extent, and allowed the use of magazines and even newspapers. I uniformly gave them the privilege of the yard on the fourth of July, Thanksgiving, and Christmas. To the well behaved and worthy, the same privilege was frequently extended on the Sabbath day also, when the weather was such as to warrant it; and this in all seasons of the year. The Sabbath day they ever observed in the most becoming manner, sitting quietly and conversing in subdued tones, without boisterousness or disorder of any kind. On the other occasions named—the public holidays—they amused themselves with theatrical performances, dinner parties, and a variety of athletic diversions. Not a solitary breach of decorum, that I remember, ever occurred on these occasions, and I know the result was to make the men more contented and cheerful, as well as more industrious and obedient. They felt better, worked better, and behaved better in all respects. It was often remarked by intelligent strangers, who had visited prisons in other states, that the convicts in this prison were the most cheerful looking they had ever seen. And why was this ? Simply because they were treated like men; because they were taught to believe themselves men, and, as such, to cherish still a feeling of self-respect; because they were urged to regard themselves, despite their imprisonment as criminals, as a part of the great world, and to recognize the just demands of society upon them, not only while here, but after they should return to it. How far such teaching was successful may be inferred, in part, from the fact that they made, in their own time, fancy articles to the value of several hundred dollars, to be sold at a fair for the benefit of the poor of Jefferson city, and they made a like donation to a fair for the relief of sick and wounded soldiers in the Union armies. It may be inferred from an incident that occurred on a certain fourth of July, when the prisoners, while enjoying their holiday, as usual, in the prison yard, having learned from one of their number who had been at work outside the walls the case of a poor widow and her children, who had found shelter in a shed near the prison, immediately (leave having been first obtained) raised by contribution among themselves a considerable sum of money, and deputed one of the officers to deliver it to her in their name. It may be inferred from the fact that on many occasions they contributed small sums to enable fellow-prisoners, on their liberation, to reach their friends in distant states. It may be inferred still more strongly from the little history which I will immediately relate. On one occasion, five of the convicts were on the prison steamboat, being employed as firemen, engineer, and pilot. On the voyage the boat fell into the hands of bushwhackers, and the captain was killed. The convicts were offered arms and horses, if they would join the murderers. To a man they refused, remained at their posts, and brought back the boat, with the dead body of the murdered captain. Very properly, as I think, the governor rewarded their fidelity by pardoning the whole of them. I mention these things more to give an inside view of the prison and to vindicate my treatment of the prisoners, than from any desire to parade them before the public, although I think that it will do the public no harm to know them."

In our opinion, the importance of a skillfully devised system of rewards in prisons can scarcely be over estimated. These should be, as far as possible, natural rather than artificial,—the legitimate fruit of good actions. So arranged, they will be found, in the great majority of cases, to have a salutary and powerful effect; and they would, in all likelihood, under a just administration, render punishments almost unnecessary. It is of great importance to maintain, as far as may be, a spirit of cheerfulness among the inmates of a prison. Little improvement, mental or moral, can be looked for when a prisoner is in a dull and gloomy state, and there is even danger that, in such a frame, he will become more hardened and depraved. Much may, doubtless, be done towards promoting cheerfulness by furnishing prisoners with entertaining and useful books, by speaking to them in a friendly manner, and by general kind treatment. But all this falls short of what is necessary to the full realization of the end in view. Nothing will contribute so directly and strongly to the result aimed at as a judicious and natural system of rewards, wisely and faithfully administered. This will give to the prisoners, as nothing else will or can, the element of hope; and certainly unless a prisoner has hope for himself, no one can have hope for him.

We fully agree to the conclusion reached by the Committee of the British House of Commons on Prison Discipline in 1850, announced in these words: "The Committee concurs with some of the most experienced witnesses they have examined, in the opinion that the majority of convicted prisoners are open to the same good motives and good impulses, which influence other human beings; and therefore that a system of encouragement to good conduct, and endeavors to inspire feelings of self-respect, self-reliance, and hopefulness for the future, which have been tried in some of our largest establishments, ought to be adopted as far as is practicable without impairing the penal and deterring character essential to any system of imprisonment."

Among the questions addressed by the undersigned to the superintendents of state prisons is the following: "Are any special privileges accorded to convicts on public holidays, and if so, what are they, and with what results have they been attended?" In nearly all the prisons, the convicts have a better dinner than ordinary on the Fourth of July, Thanksgiving, and Christmas; and in some, even luxuries are provided, such as turkey, oysters, mince pies, cake, &c. Beyond this, in the great majority, no special privileges are accorded on the occasion of public holidays. In the three state prisons of New York, some little indulgence is granted on the Fourth in the way of hurrahing, singing, shouting to one another from cell to cell, and patriotic speech-making to invisible audiences. As to the effects: One warden says that he sees no bad results from this license; another, that his mind is not made up on that point; and the third, that the effect is good on the majority, but bad on others, in whose case an increased amount of punishment becomes necessary for some days. In addition to the license thus granted, in Clinton prison it is customary, on the 4th of July, to dress the chapel in green, to have the prisoners assembled there, and a patriotic address delivered to them. The same was done at Auburn last year, and on each annual thanksgiving in that prison, the prisoners meet in the chapel, and the chaplain delivers an address to them. A license, similar to that accorded in New York, is granted to the convicts in the state prison of Northern Indiana on the 4th of July and Christmas, viz: to talk, sing, shout, &c., the effect is considered good on the whole. In the Maine state prison, *on one occasion*, the warden says, a turkey dinner was given to the prisoners in a hall together, and after dinner they were allowed an hour for conversation and amusement in the prison yard. The effect upon the men is stated by him to have been very good. Why an indulgence, attended with such beneficial results, was not repeated, we are unable to say. There are but three state prisons in the United states, so far as we are informed, in which the *custom* prevails of uniformly granting special privileges on public holidays, viz: Michigan, Missouri, and Massachusetts. Mr. Seaton, the late warden of the first named of these prisons, says that for the last ten years the convicts there have been allowed half a day on the 4th of July and Christmas, for holiday, *with very beneficial results;* so that Michigan appears to have led the way in this usage. Mr. S. does not state the nature of the amusements in which the prisoners indulge on these occasions, nor where the indulgence is granted, whether in the prison yard or in the cells. His statement would have been more satisfactory, had it included these particulars, as well as the general fact. Full information in regard to all matters connected with these holiday indulgences and amusements in the Missouri state penitentiary has already been given in an extract from a paper by the late warden of the penitentiary, Mr. Miller, inserted in a previous paragraph. To the very interesting statement on that subject, therein contained, the reader is referred; a repetition is not deemed necessary.

But it is in Massachusetts that such holiday privileges have, of late, been most consistently employed. Here they have been reduced to something like a system. Since 1863, on every public holiday, including even the national thanksgivings and fasts appointed by the President of the United States during the late rebellion, Mr. Haynes has allowed to the convicts in the Charlestown prison an hour and a half of unrestricted intercourse and recreation in the prison yard. Since this custom was first introduced, the prisoners have enjoyed from fifteen to eighteen of these (to them) festive occasions. On visiting the prison in our capacity of commissioners of the Prison Association, in order to afford us an opportunity of witnessing for ourselves the conduct and recreations of the convicts, when thus let loose to enjoy an hour of unrestricted freedom together, Mr. Haynes gave them an extra indulgence of this kind. The exhibition was as gratifying as it was novel, and impressed itself indelibly upon our memory. Some five hundred convicted felons were turned out in the prison yard, with a score or two of unarmed prison officers present, less to guard than to superintend them, during their season of recreation. The prisoners, summoned from their workshops at five o'clock, P. M., came marching in their military step, each company under its own turnkey, and formed themselves in a hollow square, with the officers and visitors in the centre. After a brief address by the warden, the word was uttered, which gave back to them one short hour of liberty. That word was like an electric current let into their souls. Joy swelled every bosom; gladness was depicted on every countenance. Their first movement was to rush, as it were, into each others arms, friend embracing friend, hand clasping hand in the strong grasp of manly affection, and tongues and lips, long unused to speech, once again using their powers in accents of friendly greeting and mutual endearment. These recognitions were, in many cases, of men working in the same shop, and perhaps side by side, yet interdicted from all free intercourse (the furtive cannot be wholly prevented) by the law of perpetual silence, enjoined by the prison rules. After these greetings, apparently and no doubt really so warm and cordial, were over, the prisoners separated into groups,—some quietly engaging in conversation, some walking back and forth, some playing football, quoits and other athletic games, and some "tripping the light fantastic toe" to the sound of the violin ; but all brimfull of quiet or hilarious enjoyment. We mingled freely with the convicts and conversed, perhaps, with scores of them during the hour ; praise of their kind and excellent warden being uppermost on all lips. No equal company of gentlemen—we say it in the certainty of speaking within the strict limits of truth—could have behaved with more decorum and propriety than these (temporarily) liberated felons. On the signal being given at six o'clock, with ready promptness the conconvicts formed themselves into the same hollow square from which they had been dismissed, and marched to their cells, receiving their suppers by the way, made happy by the hour's enjoyment, so unexpectedly as well as kindly granted them. At the annual meeting of the American Association for the promotion of social science, held at New Haven, Conn., in October last, Mr. Haynes read a well written and most interesting paper on "Holidays in Prisons," in which he gave a detailed account of the introduction of the system into the Charlestown prison, and sketched its history there down to that time. He claimed for it very great advantages to the convicts everyway, physical, mental and moral.

He averred that it had been attended with the most happy and encouraging results. Fewer punishments, greater cheerfulness, better health, diminished tendency to insanity, increased alacrity in labor, and a more careful observance of prison rules, particularly that which enjoins silence and non-intercourse, were among the good effects claimed for it. He insisted that it might be made an effective instrument of discipline, by limiting the enjoyment of the privilege to those who should have deserved it by their good conduct, just as a reduction of sentence must be so earned. Thus far, as we understand the matter, it has not been so employed, but is extended indiscriminately to the whole body of prisoners. We agree with Mr. Haynes in the opinion that such seasons of indulgence and recreation might be utilized as a means of promoting order and obedience in prisons. But it is manifest that, to that end, they must be made much more frequent than they now are ; that they must recur at fixed and not very distant points of time ; and that they must be subjected to a complete code of rules and regulations, within whose wisely adjusted and well understood enclosures the whole system must be worked. Let these occasions of recreation and regulated intercourse occur weekly, and none be permitted to enjoy them but those who have fairly merited the indulgence by a conduct absolutely free from blameworthiness, and we believe that scarcely any agency could be devised more powerful both in its quickening and restraining influence upon the inmates of our prisons. We understood Mr. Haynes to say that even the contractors in his prison were so impressed with the spirit and vigor it had infused into the labor of the men, that they had expressed a willingness to give up an hour each week for the purpose, adding the conviction that they would find their account in it. Mr. Haynes is therefore clearly the man to try the experiment, and he is as clearly surrounded by the conditions for a fair trial. We have no doubt that the experiment in his hands would be attended with satisfactory results, and would bear precious fruit beyond the limits of his own institution.

The punishments employed in the prisons of the United States and Canada, in the enforcement of the rules of order, are various; most of which, but not all, are unobjectionable on the score of humanity. On this point, some detail will probable be acceptable to those of our readers who, whether law-makers or prison officers, will be likely to take the deepest interest in the matters embraced in this report. The punishments employed in Connecticut are the lash, dark cell and loss of commutation; in Indiana, the lash, shackles, loss of time earned and privation of the privilege of sending and receiving letters to and from friends; in Kentucky, the lash and dark cell; in Maine, the dark cell with bread and water, the lash never being used, though not prohibited by law; in Massachusetts, solitary confinement in dark cell, and substitution of bread and water for the ordinary ration; in·Michigan, the lash, dark cell with bread and water, and ball and chain; in Missouri, the lash, dark cell, and occasionally shaving the head on one side; in New Hampshire, solitary confinement in dark cell, the lash never being used, though not forbidden by law; in Ohio, dark cell without bed and a diet of bread and water; in Pennsylvania, the withholding of rations, stoppage of correspondence, forfeiture of the use of the library or exercising yard, deprivation of the visits of the teacher, and shutting up in dark cell with a ration of bread and water. once a day, without bedding other than a single blanket, and the addition of irons in cases of desperate refractoriness; in Rhode Island, solitary confinement in the dungeon; in Vermont, the dungeon, confinement in their own cells, iron jacket, ball and chain, stoppage of correspondence, privation of bed and particular kinds of food, and, in rare cases, the lash; in Wisconsin, solitary confinement in the convict's own cell or the dungeon, forfeiture of commutation, privation of food, light, books, papers, and correspondence with friends,—the lash, though not prohibited by law, being never used; in Canada, an extra amount of labor, privation of bed, a diet of bread and water, confinement in ordinary cell or dark cell, hampering with a chain, cropping the hair (a female punishment), the switch (used in punishing boys), and the "cat;" and in New York, the shower-bath, dark cell, ball and chain, shaving the head, iron cap, bucking, and the yoke or crucifix.

From the foregoing statement it appears that, of the states enumerated, six still employ the punishment of the lash in their state prisons; that Canada does the same; and that New York, discarding the lash, makes use of three other punishments, not elsewhere employed, viz: the shower bath, the crucifix, and bucking. Shaving the head, so common in former times, is still occasionally—we are glad to say not often—resorted to in the Missouri state penitentiary and in the Clinton and Sing Sing prisons of New York; in the latter, it is said, only in cases of revolt. This punishment is objectionable, not so much on the score of inhu-

manity, as because it wounds the self-respect of prisoners—de
grades them in their own estimation. It is felt as an ignominy,
and is intensely hated. Punishment by the crucifix and by bucking we regard as at once cruel and degrading, and would have
them banished from all prisons *in saecula saeculorum*. The
shower bath has been characterized as "a relic of barbarism, a
connecting link between the outrages of the inquisition and the
inhumanities of the slave-pen, a process of gradual strangulation
by drowning, whose existence is a blot upon the fair escutcheon
of our state." Let it go with the others to the tomb of the Capu-
lets. They are all unworthy of a christian people, unworthy of
the civilization of the nineteenth century. But the most objectionable of the modes of punishment enumerated is, in our judgment, the lash; especially when it takes the form, as in the provincial penitentiary of Canada, of that terrible instrument of tor-
ture and degradation, the "cat." This punishment, in the prison
named, is, moreover, administered at a time, in a place, and under
circumstances, which intensify our horror of it. It is inflicted in
the mess-room, immediately after dinner, and in the presence of
the whole body of convicts, the entire prison staff, and any
strangers who may happen to be present. Could any condition,
any set of circumstances, be contrived or imagined, more calculated to produce feelings at once of degradation, anger, revenge,
and especially of an obstinate and insane bravado? Not long
before our visit—so we were informed—a very bad convict, for
some offence of unusual gravity, received one of the severest
flagellations ever given in the prison. As the terrific instrument
came down in successive blows, at each stroke tearing and mang-
ling his flesh, he uttered no groan, moved no muscle, gave no
token of suffering, but stood calm, erect, and proudly defiant.
The prisoners watched the process with breathless interest, and
when the last stroke had fallen, an involuntary and audible
"bravo!" burst from the vast congregation of felons, in irrepres-
sible admiration of what they looked upon as an instance of heroic
fortitude. Can punishments like this produce any salutary effect?
It is, indeed, possible to subdue a man, to break his spirit, to produce prompt and unqualified submission, by flogging, but it is not
possible to improve him morally by such a punishment. It excites no healing emotions, and offers no motive adapted to amend
the character, or calculated to deter permanently from the commission of crime. The lash, by a fixed law, opposes itself to

the operation of those moral and religious agencies, which experience has shown to be most efficacious in the recovery of the fallen and the redemption of the lost. In many convicts, punishment by scourging excites an undying hate. It is an indignity offered to their manhood, which they can never overlook, never sink in oblivion. This fact receives confirmation and illustration from the remark once made by a convict to his chaplain, who was urging him to a better spirit. Said he: "Sir, six years ago, I was flogged in this prison; I have the marks of the lash still on my body; when those marks *wear out*, I shall forget and forgive it." We say, then, let the lash go, with the shower bath, the crucifix, the buck, and all other punishments that are either cruel or degrading, into utter and perpetual disuse as an instrument of discipline in our prisons. Are there superintendents of prisons who say, "How shall we govern our men without at least some of the sterner means of repression?" To such we would say, go to Massachusetts and learn. At Charlestown, you will see a prison under as thorough and efficient discipline as any on the American continent, a prison where the convicts do as much work as any equal number of men outside, with but one punishment, and that seldom resorted to,—simple confinement in a dark cell on a ration of bread and water. And what is the secret of a government so successful, with so little that is coercive in its discipline? Just that the manhood of the convicts is respected; that, and nothing more. In Massachusetts, the lash has not been employed for the last ten years. It is true that it is now prohibited by law; but its use was given up four years prior to the passage of the act forbidding it. There are four states besides Massachusetts—Maine, New Hampshire, Ohio, and Rhode Island—in which no other punishment is employed than solitary confinement in a dark cell. In all these states, the discipline of the prisons is quite as effective as it is in prisons where more severe and coercive measures are employed. There are three states—Maine, New Hampshire and Wisconsin— in which the lash is never used, though no statute forbids it.

The wardens of the several state prisons were interrogated as to the kinds of punishment which they found most effectual in subduing the refractory and securing the observance of the rules of order in their respective institutions. With two exceptions, they declare that the dark cell with a diet of bread and water is most efficacious as a means of discipline, especially when, as is the case in Wisconsin, this punishment carries with it the loss of five days of commutation, previously earned by good conduct, and of course lengthens to that extent the duration of their imprisonment. This unanimity is as gratifying as it is remarkable, and, of itself, ought to be decisive against the use of the more sternly coercive measures. The two exceptions referred to are Mr. Willard, of the Connecticut state prison, and Mr. Wood, of the state prison of Northern Indiana. Mr. Willard says: " Both these punishments [meaning the solitary cell and the lash, which are the only punishments used in his prison] are good, when properly used." Mr. Wood unhesitatingly and boldly affirms: " The lash is the most effective punishment, when used with judgment and discretion." He adds (and we cite the words because we do not wish to do him the slightest injustice): "A man is never sentenced here to receive a specified number of lashes, but is only punished till he is conquered or promises amendment."

We must put in our earnest caveat against the want of ventilation, which we found almost universal in the dark cells. This must be very prejudicial to the health of the persons confined in them, and can scarcely be regarded otherwise than as a cruel addition to their punishment.

We put the question, " What is the relative power of kindness and severity as instruments of discipline?" and we regret that we are unable to report an equal unanimity in the responses on this point as on that treated of in the last paragraph. Still, those wardens who have most systematically and intelligently employed, and most confided in, the method of kindness, to the exclusion, as far as possible, of that severity, bear ample and gratifying testimony in favor of the superior efficacy of the former over the latter method. Mr. Haynes, of Massachusetts, says: "Kindness is the principal means of discipline employed, and it is used in every consistent way. We think that the superior excellence of this method lies in this, that it renders the convicts more obedient, more confiding, more cheerful, more industrious, and more susceptible, every way, to reformatory influences. Severity is thought to subdue and brutalize, but kindness to soften and reform." Mr. Seaton, of Michigan, testifies: "With most convicts, kindness is by far the best discipline." Mr. Miller, of Missouri, says: " Kindness is more powerful by far, as a means of discipline, than severity ; and its effects are more enduring. Justice, tempered with mercy, will break down the most stubborn nature. While an officer should manifest no pleasure in the infliction of punishment, he should not shrink from it when clearly necessary; yet he should ever punish more " in sorrow than in anger;" and this should be so evident that the convict could not fail to perceive and acknowledge it." Mr. Cordier, of Wisconsin, affirms: " Kindness as a means of discipline is more effective than severity, which is apt to harden prisoners and render them worse than before."

In the state prison of Ohio the punishments are reported, in general terms, as "rather frequent;" but neither in the communication made to us by the warden nor in the annual reports of the institution is there any definite statement from which we learn the absolute number or the percentage of these inflictions. In reference to all the other prisons in the United States, from which we have received answers to our questions, the statement is that punishments are " infrequent," or " very infrequent." A few of the wardens give us more specific information. In Massachusetts, with about five hundred prisoners, " there are, perhaps, four cases a week requiring punishment;" that is, four-fifths of one per cent weekly, or a fraction over three per cent monthly. The late warden of the Missouri state penitentiary, under date of December, 1864, says in his annual report: " From the date of my commission as warden up to the date of my first report, a period of fifteen months, punishment was inflicted in one hundred and forty-six cases. From the date of my first report up to this time, a period of two years, only one hundred and two offenses, considered worthy of punishment, have been committed. This very gratifying decrease of bad conduct, or, more properly, increase of good conduct, cannot be attributed to any failure to punish offenses against good order when they occur, but rather to the fact that the convicts have had time to study and understand the system of government brought to bear upon them, and have availed themselves of its advantages." The average number of convicts during these two years was about four hundred, which is a little more than one per cent a month of punishments. In the Wisconsin state prison the average number of convicts in 1865 was one hundred and ten, and the number of punishments nineteen, just about one and a half per cent a month. It will be interesting to give the exact punishments awarded here, in the words of the commissioner, as showing the adaptation of each (so far as that could be) to the offense for which it was inflicted : " Seven were punished, for various offenses, by being put into the dungeon; three were deprived of the use of the library for injuring their books; two, of their lights for soiling the cell; one, of his correspondence for writing on improper subjects; two, of their food for leaving bread in the cells; and four more, for other small offences." The minimum of punishment in the penitentiaries of the United States appears to be found in the state prison of Maine, where, with an average of nearly one hundred prisoners, the punishments are less than one per month; yet the discipline there, though mild and depending almost wholly on moral forces, is sufficiently effective; and the able bodied convicts do an amount of work equal to what would be done by the same number of men in the outside world, many of them earning for the state, as the warden informed us, fully two dollars a day. The number of punishments inflicted on the convicts in the provincial penitentiary, Canada, far exceeds, proportionally, the amount given in any of the prisons in the United States. The following are the statistics on that head for 1865, in the male department of the prison: Forty-two were punished with the cat; six with ball and chain; three hundred and ninety-nine in dark cell; thirty-nine in solitary cells; forty-five by deprivation of bed; and one thousand three hundred and ninety-five by meals of bread and water, varying from one to ten. This would appear to give an aggregate of one thousand nine hundred and twenty-six punishments for the year. It would be an error, however, so to conceive or represent the matter. On this subject the warden says : " It may be well to explain that confinement to what is termed the dark cell is, generally, for one or two nights, with three or four meals of bread and water, and is on the same report of breach of discipline as a night or two without bed, and three or four meals of bread and water, as the case may be. I have thought it proper to make these explanations, otherwise these punishments would be considered as being very numerous." Now, if we even deduct one-half the punishments by meals of bread and water on account of these duplicated cases, it will still leave one thousand two hundred and twenty-nine as the whole number of different punishments for the year. The average number of male convicts in 1865 was about seven hundred; by combining these elements, we find that the punishments amounted to within a fraction of fifteen per cent monthly; that is to say, they were nearly five times as numerous, proportionally, as in Massachusetts, and more than fifteen per cent in excess of those in Maine.

There is no record of punishments kept in the state prisons of Kentucky or New Hampshire, a grave omission; in all the other prisons visited by us, according to the statements of the wardens, complete registers are kept on this head; except that in Michigan, we were informed, the minor punishments, as privation of bed, food, &c., are not made matter of record, but only those which are accounted severe, viz: by the lash, dark cell, and ball and chain.

In nearly all the prisons visited by us, whether in the United States or Canada, punishments are most frequently inflicted on convicts for talking or otherwise communicating with each other. Insolence, insubordination, disobedience, quarreling, and attempts to escape, furnish not unfrequent occasions for the exercise of coercive discipline.

Everywhere, in our visits, we sought to ascertain, first, whether punishments were observed to be more frequent in some shops than in others, and, secondly, whether, if so, any causes for the difference existed either in the occupations of the convicts, as being chiefly sedentary or otherwise, or in the physical condition of the shops, as to ventilation, &c.; and whether this increased proportion of punishment was due to a morbid state of the system and irritation produced by the aforementioned causes. That a greater proportional amount of punishment was, in point of fact, inflicted on the occupants of some shops than of others, was generally admitted; but that it was due to the causes suggested was quite as generally denied. Whether this denial was founded on an intelligent and careful observation of facts is, perhaps, open to some doubt. At any rate, the undersigned thought that, in some instances at least, they could themselves discover the existence of inherent and permanent causes of irritation in shops where the greater number of punishments occurred; as, for example, the hemp shop in the Kentucky penitentiary, in some departments of which the dust was so great and so incessant as seriously to impair the health of convicts working there. Still, with remarkable unanimity, the wardens traced the excess of punishments in some shops over others to another and altogether moral cause, viz: the want of care and efficiency in the keepers or overseers of those shops. With one voice they unite in declaring that vigilance is vital to order; that it is the soul of discipline; that, in short, without it, all things would rush to confusion and anarchy. And there can be no doubt that they are right in this view. The old maxim, *vigilantibus, non dormientibus servit lex*,—"the law is the servant of the watchful, not of the slumbering,"—is as true in respect to prison discipline, as it is of any other department of government. Convicts who know that the keeper's eye is ever on them seldom expose themselves to punishment. Sleepless vigilance on the part of officers is more effective than the utmost rigor of penal infliction. Watchfulness in the keeper begets self-watchfulness in the convict; and this especially, when it is combined with humanity, discretion, and manifest conscientiousness. All this is abundantly attested by what is taking place every day in our prisons. The degree of vigilance and tact in the keeper measures the relative amount of punishment inflicted on the men under him with almost as much certainty as the height of the mercury in the thermometer measures the temperature of the atmosphere.

The testimony of the wardens is uniform to the fact that punishments are oftener inflicted on short-term men than on those who are in on long sentences.

It is claimed by the superintendents of all the prisons visited, who returned answers to our questions, that, so far as they know, and certainly under their own administration, neither death nor permanent injury has ever resulted from any punishments inflicted in their respective institutions. We are bound, and certainly not indisposed, to take the word of these gentlemen in regard to their own administration ; but we have grave doubts whether the claim, which is doubtless true in their own case, can be made, with equal truth, to cover the entire history of the prisons over which they severally preside. Sure we are that such a claim cannot be truly set up in the state of New York ; and we do not suppose that our state, even as regards the character and conduct of her prison officers, is justly open to the charge of pre-eminent barbarity among her sister states.

In the earlier history of the penitentiary system of the United States, it was a common practice to entrust to subordinate officers the power of administering punishment to convicts. It was claimed that punishment should follow instantaneously on the commission of any offence against prison rules, or otherwise the discipline could not be maintained with the necessary vigor ; and, therefore, that it was absolutely essential to clothe all officers, charged with the maintenance of order, with the power of punishing. We are happy to be able to state that, so far as we know, in all the prisons of the United States and Canada, with a single exception, this power has been taken away from the under officers; the exception being in the state penitentiary of Kentucky. The power of punishing is now everywhere, except as above stated, confined to the warden and deputy ; and the uniform testimony is, that the discipline of the prisons has not suffered from the change. On this subject, Mr. Miller, of Missouri, observes : "All punishments in this prison must be inflicted under the direction of the warden ; under-keepers are not allowed, in any case, to administer discipline in this way. If they were permitted to exercise the power of punishing *ad libitum*, there would be no end of abuses and no limit to tyranny and oppression." We fully concur with Mr. M. in this statement ; and the sworn testimony taken by the Prison Association this year (1866), affords abundant confirmation of its truth.

On the subject of prison punishments, we have these general thoughts to offer. The opinion expressed by Mr. Hill, in his work on Crime, meets our hearty concurrence, viz: that, under good arrangements and good management, there is little necessity for punishment in a prison, and that wherever the number of punishments is large, it may be safely concluded that either the building is ill-constructed, or the system of discipline is bad, or the officers are neglectful or incompetent. Still, there will always be more or less need of punishment in prisons, especially among new-comers; and it is, therefore, important to determine the principles on which punishment should be regulated. We would say, then, of prison punishments, as of prison rewards, that they should be made, as far as may be, to arise naturally out of the offences committed. Thus, idleness in a prisoner might be punished by the diminution or even temporary withdrawment of his food; injury done to work, by the imposition of additional labor; abuse of books, by withholding the privilege of the library; injury done to any article he is permitted to use, by deprivation of the article for a time, or by requiring him to pay for it, in whole or in part, out of any earnings of his own by overwork or otherwise; and so on, to any extent which the ingenuity of officers might suggest. We have already given a specimen of these natural punishments in an extract from the communication made to us by Mr. Cordier, of Wisconsin. In the rules of the Scottish prisons, it is expressly enjoined that recourse be had to punishments of this kind on all occasions where they are available. In prisons where artificial offences are reduced to a minimum, and where the arrangements are simple and natural, this principle would, we believe, be applicable to the greater number of punishments; and it has this recommendation, that the prisoner himself will generally feel its justice, and it will not, therefore, be likely to excite in him those bitter and revengeful feelings which punishment is so apt to engender, and which oppose themselves so strongly to his own moral improvement.

There is not, we are sorry to say, a prison on the American continent, in which any tests exist, whereby the ability of the prisoners to resist temptation can be measured; none where decisive and reliable proofs can, ordinarily at least, be obtained of moral amendment. This we regard as a radical, almost a fatal defect in their organization; for we fully agree with Mr. Frederick Hill in the opinion that "that system of prison discipline must be very imperfect, which does not afford the opportunity for obtaining indisputable evidence on this point."

The opinion was very generally expressed to us by prison officers that it is, in all cases, desirable to supplement the congregate system with a number of solitary cells, sufficiently large, well-lighted, and well-aired to serve for workshops as well as sleeping rooms. The policy of such an arrangement cannot be doubted. The percentage of men who give nearly all the trouble and receive most of the severe punishments in all our prisons is very small. We have already seen that in some prisons from eighty to ninety per cent. of the convicts go through their prison life without a solitary violation of prison rules, and earn the entire commutation, or deduction of sentence, which the laws of their respective states allow. Now, it is well known that there are many things prohibited in prison, not because they are wrong in themselves, but because, if allowed, the privilege would be abused by bad men. The most irritating of these restraints might be removed with safety, if a few mischievous men were permanently separated from the body of the prisoners. The multiplication of offenses, which are merely *mala prohibita* and not *mala per se*, is injurious to good discipline and detrimental to the reformation of offenders. The erection of the proposed supplementary cells and the incarceration of the troublesome and especially the dangerous prisoners in them, might render it both safe and politic to abolish these conventional offenses, and would certainly diminish the number of punishments, increase the security and comfort of the officers, and promote all the higher objects of prison discipline. It is not a little curious that the only objection to this plan comes from the warden of the western penitentiary of Pennsylvania, a prison established and conducted wholly on the separate principle. One would think that the governor of such a prison would hail, with gratulation, any approach by other institutions to the principle which he must be presumed to regard as the wisest and best ever yet devised as the basis of a prison system. Yet Dr. Campbell thus expresses his opinion on this question: " It is considered very doubtful whether it would be expedient to supplement the Auburn system with any solitary cells for exceptional cases." The ground of this doubt is not stated; and we confess ourselves quite incompetent to divine the thought that lies at the bottom of it.

In our state prisons, without exception we believe, it is the right of a prisoner, if he thinks that injustice has been done him by a keeper, to lay his complaint before the head of the prison. Such complaints are always received and investigated. From a few prisons we have the statement that in cases of this kind the testimony of convicts is not admitted; in the great majority, however, their statements are received, and such weight given them as the circumstances seem to warrant.

In four at least of the state prisons of the United States, the rule of silence is relaxed, so far as to permit prisoners to speak to each other in reference to their work, without the necessity of asking special permission for that purpose. The prisons referred to are those of Maine, Kentucky, Missouri, and Clinton county, New York. In all the other state prisons of the United States and the provincial penitentiary of Canada, absolute and unbroken silence is the rule; but the degree of strictness with which this rule is enforced varies greatly in different institutions. In a few, all the rigor of the ancient discipline is maintained. For instance, the discipline of the Wethersfield prison is stern, rigid, and inflexible. It bends to no offender, however obstinate and indomitable his spirit. It allows no insubordination, yields to no compromise, relaxes no restraint. In a word, it contemplates and enforces unqualified submission and obedience. To test its efficiency for ourselves, the warden desired us to make the circuit of a large workshop, in which the men were burnishing silver ware, each facing the windows. We passed the entire company, pausing a moment at the back of each to inspect his work. With the exception of a negro lad, who stole one furtive glance at the strangers, (and the warden apologized for him by saying that this was his second day in prison) not a man turned an eye towards us; not one seemed conscious of our presence; not one suspended for an instant the work on which he was engaged. All that long line of human beings, forming three sides of a large hollow square, seemed like parts of some huge machine; with such regularity, precision, steadiness, and absolute self-abnegation were all their movements conducted. No doubt all this was very admirable, as showing the power of one human mind over multitudes of others; but the effect upon us, instead of being pleasing, was intensely painful. To our apprehension, it seemed a process adapted to crush out every noble aspiration, every manly sentiment, from the breasts of those who were subjected to its operation. On subsequently mentioning the scene and its impression to the Hon. Mr. Blaine, Member of Congress from Maine, who had a few years before been commissioned by his own state to visit prisons for the purpose of inquiring into their financial management, that gentleman remarked that he had witnessed the same scene with the same feelings, when at Wethersfield in fulfillment of his mission. The discipline of the New Hampshire state prison we found marked by the same general characteristics as that at Wethersfield. Every man there is required to labor with downcast look, and forbidden, on any occasion or under any pretext, to lift his eyes from his work. We found discipline enforced in other prisons with much strictness,—for example, in Massachusetts, Ohio, Wisconsin, and elsewhere; but there the men work as they do in other great manufactories. The prisons in these states are busy hives of industry; but there is no requisition to be ever looking down upon the ground; the convicts stand erect, and even if they should occasionally look up towards heaven, or glance at a passing visitor, it is not regarded as a grave offence.

The theory of the congregate system of imprisonment is a rigid prohibition of inter-communication between the prisoners. Two means are relied upon to secure this result,—a total separation of the prisoners by night and a sleepless vigilance of the officers by day. The question is, how far non-intercourse is actually secured, despite the strong temptation to the contrary in beings endowed by the Creator with sociability, who are compelled, day after day, month after month, and year after year, to work together, march together, eat together, attend church together ; in a word, to be in perpetual contact with each other.

We have already stated that there are many degrees of strictness in the enforcement of the rule of silence, the variation being from the extreme rigor, found at Wethersfield and Concord, to a laxity quite as extreme, existing in some other prisons. Indeed, in many workshops the noise of the machinery employed is so great, that convicts at only a moderate distance from the keeper can converse aloud, and even sing and shout, without being heard by him. This is, to a great extent, the case in Sing Sing and Auburn prisons, and must be so in many others. The general testimony of prison officers, even in prisons where discipline is maintained with the greatest strictness, is that there are many ways in which the rule of silence can be, and is, evaded continually. Many of the best officers affirm that it can be enforced only so far as to prevent general conversation, and may be evaded to such a degree that the intercourse between prisoners can become mutually corrupting. How far communication can be, and has been, carried at Sing Sing, appears from the extensive conspiracy entered into by the convicts in that prison last summer, in which large numbers were implicated, and which was carried to the point of an open and dangerous revolt, that was prevented from attaining complete success, and, was finally crushed, only by the cool and heroic bravery of the guards.

Communication, then, we must believe, takes place among convicts continually, and, in most prisons, to a very great extent. The workshop, mess-room, chapel, hospital, water closet, yard, corridors, marchings, and even the cells themselves afford ample means for it. One officer declared that, if a keeper were placed over every five men, communication could not be prevented. Another said that the result of an election was known all over the prison almost as speedily as it was outside. A third affirmed that any interesting item of news, introduced by a new comer, circulated with amazing rapidity among the prison population. A fourth told us that a certain keeper learned the news of the assassination of President Lincoln from the men belonging to the company of which he had the charge.

In view of facts like these, and as the result of experiments made by him during his administration of the state penitentiary of Missouri, Mr. Miller does not hesitate to recommend a modification of the rule, which imposes absolute and perpetual silence upon convicts during their entire term of imprisonment. His language is : "In the congregate plan, the rule of absolute silence can scarcely be literally enforced. It can be evaded in many ways, but chiefly on the ground that one ask another to help or instruct him at his work. And the keeper is obliged to wink at violations of the rule, and take excuses that he knows are untrue, or else spend his time in reporting cases. It is better, therefore, in my opinion, in all respects, to allow conversation to a limited extent, than to encourage a system of falsehood by taking false excuses. I have found no evil to result from granting this permission. Indeed, so highly is the privilege valued by all classes of convicts, that the better disposed and more influential among them co-operate with the keepers in preventing the abuse of it."

For ourselves we have no hesitation in expressing our opposition to the multiplication of mere artificial or conventional rules, whether in prisons or out of them. As in the great world, so in the little world comprised within the walls of a prison, every departure from the laws of nature must cause an increase of these artificial transgressions. The tendency of this state of things is to confound moral offenses with mere breaches of regulations, and to diminish the feeling both of self-condemnation and public opprobrium, which ought ever to attach to real turpitude. To punish a prisoner for speaking to his comrade in marching to meals, or for calling to him from his cell, in the same manner as for striking him or stealing from him, must tend to lessen his sense of the ill-desert of the crimes of assault and theft. This is to draw no proper distinction between moral and conventional offenses. In most prisons, the number of these latter is multiplied by minute regulations, and their importance greatly exaggerated. In this way, the spirit of obedience is exhausted by the demand for what most prisoners look upon as mere frivolities, and their conscience becomes seared through indulgence in petty transgression. The natural tendency of minute, and especially of unreasonable, regulations is to provoke the breach of them, and thus to morally injure their victims by familiarizing their minds with thoughts and acts of disobedience.

Considerations like these, and others connected with the question whether a prison system is not to be preferred which works with rather than against nature, have led thoughtful men in this and other countries to query whether the absolute prohibition of all intercourse between prisoners is, after all, the best plan, and whether a "more excellent way" may not be found. There can be no doubt, at least we have none, that such unbroken silence should be exacted of convicts whenever they are shut up in their solitary cells. But we more than doubt the wisdom or utility of such exaction at all other times. We are, indeed, clear in the conviction that, to a limited extent and under judicious restrictions, conversation should be permitted among prisoners in certain stages of their imprisonment.

We have already, in a former part of this report, expressed our approval of a period of separate imprisonment, to be made longer or shorter according to the conduct of the prisoner and the exigencies of his physical condition, as part of a comprehensive scheme of prison discipline. This should be gradually followed, according to circumstances, by regulated association; the amount of association increasing or diminishing according to the use or abuse of the privilege, and as it should be found to be beneficial or otherwise. The first stage of a criminal's imprisonment should be severely penal. This highly punitive stage should by degrees melt into probation, and probation, again, into entire freedom, as gradually as possible. Sociability is one of the strongest of human instincts, and the social principles and relations are the great springs of improvement. It is by these that the heart is kindled, and warmth and energy imparted to the character. Man droops and pines in solitude, whether that solitude be created by a physical or moral separation—by walls of granite or a wall of absolute and eternal silence. No sound excites him like the voice of his fellow-man. This imparts strength to dare, to do, and to suffer; and these three words express the sum of human duty.

We have said that the free play of our social nature is the great spring of human improvement; and this, we think, is as true of man imprisoned, as of man in society; for imprisonment does not obliterate the human soul, nor in any way alter its principles and operations. If, then, sociability is a fountain of moral strength in civil life, it will be, under proper guards and restrictions, equally a source of moral strength in prison life. When, therefore, prisoners are brought together, we are of the opinion that they should really associate as human beings, and not be doomed, as Mr. Hill has said, to eternal dumbness, with heads and eyes fixed like statues in the same direction. We are of the opinion that all attempts to carry out such a warfare upon nature must be productive of endless deception, and so far tend to corrupt and destroy what remains of virtue yet linger in the men and women who compose our prison populations. That this warfare on nature gives rise to a vast amount of irritation, and is the principal source of punishment in our prisons, is attested by the almost unanimous voice of our prison officers, as reported in a former paragraph. As the object of discipline in a prison, so far as relates to mere control, is, or ought to be, to curb only the bad passions and evil propensities, and not to destroy the social feelings or stifle impulses and desires in themselves innocent, we are of the opinion that, when prisoners are brought into association, although neither idleness nor disorder of any kind should be allowed, they should be permitted to conduct themselves, in all respects, as a similar company of men outside would, engaged in the same occupation.

But, it will be said, the intercourse of prisoners is corrupting; and this is now commonly regarded as an axiom, a self-evident proposition. But, in our judgment, the nature and circumstances of that intercourse must be considered, before we can pronounce categorically upon its tendency. Promiscuous intercourse of prisoners, such as it existed in all prisons prior to the introduction of what is called the penitentiary system, and still exists in most county jails, is no doubt demoralizing to the last degree. But this corrupting power of association may be counteracted; nay, such association may be converted into a means of improvement and reformation, by being subjected to virtuous direction and control. The rule of absolute, uninterrupted, eternal silence, introduced contemporaneously with the penitentiary system, was doubtless a reaction of the promiscuous association to which we have referred, with its brood of drinking, smoking, gambling, swearing, stealing, cheating, fighting, obscenity, and ribald blasphemy. But, as usually happens, the reaction went too far, and swung over to the other extreme. Has Mr. Haynes found the intercourse allowed on public holidays among his prisoners a source of mutual contamination? Did Mr. Miller find it so, though permitted to the deserving on Sabbath days as well as holidays? Both testify, as we have seen, positively and strongly, to an influence the direct reverse of this; an influence healthful, purifying, invigorating, reformatory to a high degree. Mr. Haynes says that it has diminished punishments fifty per cent., and has been the source of numerous other benefits to the convicts. If he will grant this privilege of regulated intercourse weekly, instead of three or four times a year, and make it *bona fide* the reward of good conduct and industry, he may possibly bring his punishments down to zero, with a proportional amount of other advantages. The truth is, what we want is to gain the will, the consent, the coöperation of these men, not to mould them into so many pieces of machinery. But in order to do this, nature must be followed, not crushed; wooed, not coerced. It is by persuasion, not compulsion, that men are to be turned away from crime, and won back to virtue. They are best *compelled* by a powerful and minutely arranged external apparatus; but they are best *led* without it.

A man who has been tried on a criminal charge, convicted, sentenced, and shut up in a state prison, cannot but feel a degree of degradation. If he has any vestige of manhood remaining in him—and we believe there are few convicts who have not—this must of necessity be so. It is proper that the convict should feel the disgrace of his crime and his sentence. This is a part of his punishment, inflicted by heaven itself. But we agree with the inspectors of the Massachusetts state prison in the opinion, that beyond this there should be no degradation, no disgrace inflicted on him, except what may be requisite to his safe custody, or as a punishment for the infraction of necessary rules. No wanton outrage should be offered to his manhood. As the reformation of convicts is, perhaps, the most difficult and certainly one of the most important of the problems, whose solution is demanded by the welfare of society, any means, however slight in itself, adapted to create and increase their feeling of self-respect, should be seized and turned to the best account. On entering their prison house, they should be taught to feel that they have a character to redeem; a future of virtuous and useful industry to create.

Deeply impressed with this view, and knowing how intensely many convicts dislike the prison uniform which they are obliged to wear, and how stubbornly their feelings, at least, rebel against it, we made special inquiry on this point, hoping to find that the parti-colored dress had been extensively discarded, or at least that there would be a general concurrence of sentiment among prison officers against its continuance. This hope was doomed to disappointment in both branches of it. The hated uniform, carrying with it a degrading badge and at war with that sentiment of self-respect adverted to as so important to create and preserve, is retained in all the prisons visited by us, except that of Massachusetts; and the majority of wardens express themselves as favoring its retention. A few, however—and they are those who are most in advance of the times in their views of prison discipline—favor, wisely, as we think, the abolishment of the parti-colored uniform. Says Mr. Seaton, of Michigan : "The prison garb has not been abolished in this state, but, in my opinion, it should be discontinued. It has only a degrading tendency, and no advantages to counterbalance this evil effect." To the same effect is the language of Mr. Cordier, of Wisconsin: "The prison dress has not been abolished; it should be discontinued. I do not know a single good reason for its retention." Mr. Miller, of Missouri, says : "The prison dress has not been abolished; but I am perfectly satisfied that it might and should be. There is no advantage in any costume that has the effect of constantly reminding the wearer of his disgrace."

We have already stated that the parti-colored dress has been discarded in Massachusetts. On this subject the inspectors, in their report of 1864, say: "In regard to the dress of the prisoners, we have long thought that a reform might be made. We are quite clear that the law does not demand it, and that humanity forbids it. The parti-colored dress, heretofore worn, we have regarded as degrading, and calculated to drive the convict's manhood from him; the very thing we most want him to retain. And as this dress is not deemed necessary for his safe-keeping (the fact being that no absconding prisoner was ever detected by his dress), we have changed the parti-colored garb for one of uniform color. We believe that this change is an important improvement, and will result in good to the discipline of the prison, and in no way operate against the public welfare." A year subsequent to the date of this report, the warden, Mr. Haynes, expressed himself to us well pleased with the effect of the change, declaring that it had more than met the expectations of the authorities. It had developed the manhood of the convicts, inspired self-respect, soothed their feelings, promoted cheerfulness and industry, and elevated the whole tone of their character and bearing. The present outfit of a convict in the Massachusetts state prison is as follows: A new suit of clothes made of blue satinet, such as any workingman might wear; a pair of stout shoes, two shirts, two undershirts, two pair of stockings, two pair of drawers, and a towel— all marked with his own name; so that he has a kind of property in his prison clothes, and, contrary to what happens in most prisons, always wears the same garments. This also has a tendency to cultivate the self-respect of the convicts, and so far becomes an agent in their reformation.

The discontinuance of the parti-colored clothing is no novelty in other countries, however much its abolishment is opposed by many of our American wardens. In some of the English and all the Scottish prisons, the distinctive prison garb has been discarded. In the prisons of Scotland, the clothing is free from anything that can serve to degrade their inmates in their own estimation. What is aimed at is to give the prisoner that neat, durable, and cheap kind of dress which a thrifty working man or woman would be likely to wear out of prison, and such as it is desirable that the prisoner himself should wear after his liberation. In the Scottish prisons, every convicted prisoner is supplied with a complete prison dress; and even untried prisoners who desire it are, in like manner, furnished with full suits of clothing. In point of fact, with rare exceptions, the untried prisoners wear the prison clothing.

There is less opposition on the part of prisoners generally to the lock-step than to the parti-colored dress; yet some regard it with extreme disgust. We have known convicts to be exceedingly irritated and annoyed by it. In the majority of state prisons, this quasi-military step is in use, and is regarded by the officers as a means of keeping prisoners under more perfect control, and as an important help in enforcing discipline. In quite a number, however, it is not employed. It is not in use in the provincial penitentiary of Canada, where the discipline is otherwise very strict; nor in the state prisons of Kentucky, Maine, Missouri, and Vermont. In these prisons, it is considered as of no conceivable benefit, and as tending only to irritate and disgust the prisoners. It is not used in any of the prisons of England. Certainly, it is far less objectionable than the parti-colored garb; perhaps, as used in Massachusetts, where the prisoners march in divisions, at a full, easy step, with their hands hanging at their sides, it can hardly be regarded as objectionable at all.

In most of the prisons, abundant provision is made for quelling a revolt or rebellion by the convicts, should an emergency of that kind arise. The guard-rooms are well supplied with arms of various descriptions,—rifles, carbines, &c., with bayonets attached; and the officers, but especially the guards, when on duty, go well armed. In some prisons, as that of Wisconsin, for example, an alarm is arranged, by which, in a case of this kind, the citizens may be summoned to the assistance of the prison authorities. The revolt at Sing Sing prison, last summer, was, as we have seen, speedily suppressed by the courage and sagacity of the guards.

SECTION SIXTH.

MORAL AND RELIGIOUS AGENCIES.

The importance of suitable and adequate provisions for the moral and religious instruction of prisoners, whether regard be had to public worship, Sunday school lessons, daily prayer and reading of the scriptures, or private visitation, can scarcely be exaggerated. If the design be to reform and restore them to virtue, religion is needed above everything,—religion, as in the life of the family; religion, in its unbroken integrity, and in all its living and saving energy. We have a profound conviction of the inefficacy of all measures for reformation, except such as are based on religion, impregnated with its spirit, and vivified by its power. In vain are all devices of repression, coercion, even of counsel, remonstrance and persuasion, if the heart and conscience, which are beyond all power of external restraint, are left untouched.

Although we are persuaded that the religious element should, as a general thing, have a higher development and be made more prominent than it is at present in the administration of American prisons, yet very great progress has been made in this direction, both at home and abroad, and far more attention is given to the subject now than heretofore. We propose to introduce the present section with a brief sketch of what has been done, and of the progress made, in this important department of prison discipline.

Prior to the time of John Howard, the physical condition of the inmates of English prisons was disgusting and horrible to the last degree; and their moral degradation, the coarseness and brutality of their minds, kept even pace with the disease and misery of their bodies. Chapels and chaplains constituted no part of the penal establishments of the country. Some loose parson, on the verge of insolvency, was sometimes hired, at a cheap rate, for the office of ordinary. On a week day, he was ready to crack a bottle of gin or shuffle a pack of cards with his flock; on a Sunday, he mumbled a service and sermon to them in a day room. His congregation was a thin one, for attendance was easily evaded. In effect, of what use could the best religious teaching have been, as prisons were then constituted and conducted? Little more than a mere casting of pearls before swine. The drunkenness and almost unbridled debauchery of the prisoners would have thwarted the labors of the most zealous chaplain. A prison was a hot-bed of sensuality, even at night time men and women being often huddled together in the same room. Latimer, in a sermon preached before Edward VI, lifted up his voice against the un-checked heathenism of the London prisons. "Oh, I would," (says he,) "ye would resort to prisons, a commendable thing in a christian realm. I would there were curates of prisons, that we might say, 'the curate of Newgate,' 'the curate of the Fleet;' and I would have them waged for their labor. It is holy-day work to visit the prisoners, for they be kept from sermons."

In the reign of Elizabeth, Bernard Gilpin regularly visited all the jails that fell within the range of his missionary circuits in the northern counties, and preached to their inmates. The minis-ters who were ejected from their pulpits and imprisoned for their violation of the Act of Conformity, preached abundantly to the prisoners in the jails; among whom Joseph Alleine particularly distinguished himself by his zeal and success. It is almost always recorded in the lives of the humble worthies of England in the sixteenth and seventeenth centuries, that they visited those who were "sick and in prison."

In accordance with these traditions of English piety, when the "Godly Club" was formed at Oxford, the Wesleys and its other members offered their first ministrations to the prisoners in the Castle. The good work, once begun, was not lightly abandoned. For some years, Whitfield, the Wesleys, and their most zealous followers prayed, preached, and distributed alms in all the jails, bridewells, and bedlams that came within their circuits; and it was only on compulsion that they at length gave up this part of their mission. In the storm and tempest of their unpopularity, the doors even of prisons and madhouses were shut against them. It was then that John Wesley said: "We are forbid to go to Newgate for fear of making them wicked, and to Bedlam for fear of making them mad." From that time, he and his brother Charles discontinued their prison visitations.

But one of the band was not to be deterred from these labors of love and mercy. Sarah Peters, a woman noted for the fervency of her prayers and charity, despite the jail-fever which was raging in the prison, taking her life in her hand, ministered, day after day, in the name of God, to all the poor wretches under sentence of death, until at length, when her work was done, she sickened and died. But her mantle fell upon, her spirit entered into, a warmhearted man, named Silas Told, by whom she had been accompanied in her visits to the jail. For 25 years, he devoted his energies to the spiritual welfare of condemned malefactors in every part of England.

In the year 1773, the same in which Howard became high sheriff of Bedfordshire, and entered upon his great work of reforming prisons, an act of Parliament was passed, authorizing "the justices at their quarter-sessions to appoint chaplains to their jails," at a salary not exceeding fifty pounds per annum. "This," observes the Rev. Walter L. Clay, in his Prison Chaplain, a work to which we are indebted for the foregoing outline, "this was the first official recognition of the fact that prisoners are within the pale of salvation." But, happily for the honor of humanity and the progress of civilization, it was not the last. The English prisons of all grades are now well supplied with chaplains; men of piety, character and worth; quite a number of whom have been distinguished by great and shining abilities.

In the first annual report of the Boston Prison Discipline Society, issued in 1826, there is an interesting survey of the then condition of moral and religious instruction in American prisons, from which we condense the following statement:

In New Hampshire, at that time only $25 a year were appropriated to supply the state prison with the means of grace, despite the fact that the prison had been, for some years previously, making for the state a clear profit of $1,000 to $5,000. It is worthy of remark, however, that the warden, Moses C. Pilsbury, caused the Scriptures to be read to the convicts twice a day, and himself conducted the regular service of the Sabbath, when no clergyman could be obtained for the purpose. In Vermont, whose state prison had for five years been almost self-supporting, only $100 were appropriated for religious instruction; the chapel had been turned into a weaver's shop; only an occasional service was held on the Sabbath; and there was no daily reading of the Scriptures. In Massachusetts, where the state prison had, for the 2 preceding years, yielded a clear revenue, over all expenses, of $13,000, $200 a year only were devoted to the religious instruction of more than 300 convicts. There was only one short service on the Sabbath, and no daily reading of the Scriptures to the prisoners; nor did the chaplain perform any official duty in the prison during the week. In Connecticut, though a more liberal provision, in proportion to the number of the convicts, was made for their religious instruction, the chaplain did not reside in or near the prison, and the moral influence exerted over the prisoners is said to have been far from what it should have been. In New York, the duties of the chaplain of the state prison in the metropolitan city were devolved upon Rev. Mr. Stanford, a man more than seventy years of age, who was also, at the same time, chaplain of the penitentiary, the bridewell, the debtors' jail, the city hospital, and the alms-house—four penal and two eleemosynary institutions, containing altogether from two thousand to three thousand inmates. This venerable man was in the habit of preaching regularly at least ten sermons a week; but "what were they among so many?" Neither in New Jersey, Pennsylvania, Maryland nor Virginia, was any provision whatever made by the state for the moral and religious instruction of her convicted felons. In two of these states—New Jersey and Virginia—month after month frequently passed without a religious service of any kind; and in the other two, whatever religious instruction the prisoners received was given by benevolent individuals or societies; was altogether gratuitous; and, as a matter of course, was scanty, irregular, and sometimes not of the most desirable character.

Thus it appears that in 1826, as far as this report gives information, there was not a resident chaplain in any state prison in the United States, and the religious instruction imparted was for the most part, reduced down to the merest modicum. Who can wonder that a penitentiary system, characterised by an omission so fundamental, a neglect of the means of success so signal and conspicuous, should have come, in the end, to disastrous and inglorious failure? Doubtless there were other elements in the system, tending strongly in the same direction; but none more potent or fatal than this.

This melancholy exposition, in the report of 1826, of the want of moral and religious instruction in the prisons of the country seems to have produced a strong impression on the public mind, to have turned the thoughts of practical men more intently to the study of the subject, and to have led to efforts, more or less extensive, towards improvement. The report of the following year contained an expression of opinion in favor of the adoption of a more comprehensive and thorough system of moral, religious and intellectual instruction for prisoners than had hitherto prevailed, on the part of the following gentlemen: Dr. Rose, superintendent of the state prison of Maine; Moses C. Pilsbury, warden of the New Hampshire state prison; Mr. Lynds, superintendent of Sing Sing prison; Mr. Powers, keeper of Auburn prison; Mr. McLean, keeper of the state penitentiary of Ohio, and Mr. Parsons, keeper of the Virginia penitentiary. Resident chaplains, through pecuniary aid furnished by the prison discipline society, were placed at Auburn and Sing Sing, whose labors proved in a high degree acceptable both to officers and men, and very profitable to the latter. In Auburn, under the superintendence of the chaplain and through the co-operation of the students in the theological seminary, a Sabbath school was instituted for young convicts, the privilege of attendance upon which was embraced with avidity and thankfulness. To show how much this privilege was prized, the case of a convict is mentioned, who, being about to to be punished for some violation of prison rules, entreated that any punishment might be inflicted on him other than that of removal from the Sunday school. To evince the excellent moral influence exerted upon the convicts through this agency, a statement is made of the case of a young Indian, naturally intelligent, but grossly ignorant, who, having asked leave of his keeper to speak to him, said that he had been a bad boy, would lie and steal, but had now learned that such things were wicked, and he wanted to go to the warden, confess his faults, and promise that he would never disobey God any more. At Sing Sing, as well as at Auburn, the chaplain not only conducted public worship in the chapel on the Lord's day, but read the Scriptures and offered prayer every evening, so that the last words heard by the convicts before retiring to bed were words of religious instruction and consolation.

In the report of the same society for 1828, still further and very decided progress is shown in the right direction. In the Maine prison, a chapel was erected, and a weekly Sabbath service instituted ; but no Sunday or evening school was organized, and no morning or evening prayers, with reading of the Scriptures, introduced. Vermont doubled her annual appropriation, making it two hundred instead of one hundred dollars, for the purpose of supplying her prison at Windsor, with more constant and systematic religious instruction. Massachusetts raised her appropriation to five hundred dollars, with the view of procuring a chaplain who should devote his whole time to official duty within her state prison. In Connecticut, provision was made for regular public service on the Sabbath, in addition to daily reading of the scriptures and prayer by the warden. In New York, the legislature appropriated three hundred dollars towards the salary of the chaplain at Sing Sing; and the venerable Mr. Stanford, now almost an octogenarian, continued, as aforetime, his numerous appointments in the humane and penal institutions in the city of New York. In New Jersey, a large room was fitted up in the prison for a chapel, and the members of the Prison Discipline Society in the theological seminary at Princeton, by their committee, conducted religious worship every Sabbath during the year, with one or two exceptions, always, at the same time, distributing tracts to the convicts, and visiting and conversing with them in their solitary cells. In the Walnut street prison, at Philadelphia, public worship was regularly kept up on the Sabbath, and a Bible class and Sunday school as regularly instructed, all by volunteer and unpaid laborers. In the Maryland penitentiary, the ministers of the Methodist Episcopal church sustained a religious service on the Lord's day, both among the male and female convicts, once a day in winter and twice in summer. In Ohio, the Synod of the Presbyterian church appointed and supported a preacher for the state prison at Columbus, the members of the Synod contributing personally the necessary means to this end, as they had no fund upon which they could draw for such a purpose. So much was done in 1828, and certainly it was a great advance on previous efforts, to provide for and communicate religious instruction in the prisons of the United States.

No further notice is taken of this subject in the reports of the society, till we come to that of 1833. From this report we learn that in almost, if not quite, all the state prisons of the country, every cell was supplied with a copy of the whole Bible or the New Testament, most commonly the former. It had become almost as much a matter of course to see this book of books lying on the little shelf of the solitary cell, as to see the fastening of the door which secured the convict's person. The Bibles were, in nearly every case, provided by the state. The uniform testimony of the wardens was that they were much used by the convicts, many of whom had learned to read in prison, and multitudes of inquiries were proposed to the chaplains concerning the meaning of the sacred page. In cases not a few, its pungent truths had proved like the fire and hammer, and what was begun to be read, perhaps, with the design of finding matter for cavil, had penetrated the conscience, as a nail in a sure place.

But the living teacher is as necessary in a prison as the inspired volume. It is by the foolishness of preaching that it has pleased God to save them that believe. It is, therefore, pleasing to notice that resident chaplaincies had been established in Vermont, Massachusetts, Connecticut, New York, and the District of Columbia, and that in the prisons of most of the other states, chaplains were employed to conduct religious services on the Sabbath for the benefit of their inmates. And highly beneficial the labors of the chaplains were found to be; and they were no less acceptable than useful. The prisoners generally conceived a strong affection for their chaplain, as their best friend and counsellor. Many— such is the testimony of the chief officers—were morally reformed through their faithful efforts ; and some, there is reason to believe, truly and savingly converted. It may be proper, and the information will be interesting to some, to state, in this connection, that the first resident chaplain in this country, the Rev. Jared Curtis, was employed in the Auburn prison, N. Y. When that office was instituted in the state prison at Charlestown, Mass., Mr. Curtis received and accepted an invitation to become the incumbent.

From the report of this year, 1833, we further learn that in not less than ten state prisons, Sabbath schools had been organized, which were represented as flourishing and exceedingly useful. So successful, indeed, had this agency proved, and so much was it prized by inspectors, officers and prisoners, that a Sabbath school in a prison had come to be looked upon as an essential element in a good system of prison discipline. The number of teachers employed in prison Sabbath schools was about one hundred, and the number of convicts receiving instruction, fifteen hundred. As to Auburn belongs the honor of having had the first resident chaplain in the prisons of the United States, so the first prison Sabbath school was organized in the state prison at that place. This was doubtless one of the good results of having had a resident chaplain; for it is not likely that any person, other than one of tried wisdom and prudence, would have been permitted by the authorities to introduce into the prison a system of Sabbath school instruction; but the chaplain was able to do it, to the satisfaction of all concerned, without violating any of the prison rules, and to the great advantage of the institution in all respects.

Morning and evening prayers in prisons were also first introduced at Auburn, by Mr. Curtis, while filling the office of resident chaplain there; and this excellent custom of a daily service of prayer was adopted in all the prisons to which full chaplains were appointed. The service was usually held in the corridor of the prison, in front of the cells, after the prisoners were locked up for the night. The voice of prayer, falling on the ear of the convict in his solitary cell, was the last sound of the human voice heard by him before closing his eyes in sleep; and what influence could have been more powerful to reclaim the wanderer, to beget genuine repentance in his soul, and to restore him to a better mind and a better life? The importance of having a resident chaplain is shown in the fact that this practice was introduced in but one prison where the services of such an officer were not enjoyed,—that at Wethersfield, Conn., presided over by the Pilsburys—father and son in succession.

The subject of religion in prisons is again adverted to in the report of 1836. Copious extracts are given from the annual reports of the inspectors of the eastern penitentiary in Philadelphia, the directors of the state penitentiary in Ohio, and the inspectors of the provincial penitentiary in Canada. These gentlemen, in strong and forcible language, urge upon their respective Legislatures the great importance of appointing resident chaplains in their several prisons, and point out the many signal advantages to be expected from their labors. They allege that, as personal reformation, to be permanent, must be founded on religion, so no system of prison discipline can be effectual, in which religious teaching does not form a prominent part; that the depravity and vice, found in every jail, has led to an impresssion, far too general, that most criminals are beyond the reach of reformation; that a fair trial of this question has been made in few, if any, prisons; that when the number of prisoners is considerable, the whole time and attention of a chaplain should be devoted to the duties of that office; that, valuable as are the public services of religion, their effect on prisoners is, in general, but partial and unsatisfactory; that the labors of the chaplain should not, therefore, be confined to the performance of social worship; that to this should be added personal instruction, in the retirement of the cell, or the conversation of the office; that, to this end, the chaplain should be authorized, at his discretion, to take a prisoner aside and confer with him in private, at any time during the hours of labor, as well as at the door of his cell, after the close of his daily task; and that, finally, to insure the undivided and cheerful application of his energies to the moral improvement of his charge, he should receive a salary liberal enough for the comfortable support of himself and family, without the necessity for recourse to other employment. These wise and earnest pleadings had the desired effect. Full chaplaincies were established in the penitentiaries named, and were attended with the same happy results as their institution in other prisons.

The progress of Sabbath schools in prisons, and their great utility and popularity among prisoners, are also noticed in the report of 1836. The formation of such a school in the penitentiary of the District of Columbia is recorded, and its flourishing state and beneficial results are set forth in glowing terms. Its success had far exceeded expectation. At least, twenty-five prisoners, among whom were some very unpromising subjects, had, during the two years of its existence, learned to read, and had acquired such a mastery of the art as to be able to peruse the Scriptures with comfort and advantage. In this school, a new feature was introduced, that of employing the convicts themselves in the work of teaching their fellow-convicts; and the experiment appears to have been attended with entire success. The chaplain remarks : "I have been materially aided in the school by some of the prisoners, who have been selected by the warden as monitors. They seem to find a pleasure in imparting knowledge, and I believe they have been themselves materially benefited by the exercises. From all my observation, since I have had the honor to serve the institution, I am convinced that Sabbath school instruction in our penitentaries, may be rendered one of the most efficient aids in the work of reformation." In all the other prison Sunday schools, large numbers of convicts were taught to read. In that of Auburn alone, four hundred had, in the course of ten years, gained a competent knowledge of this elementary, but important science, who were totally ignorant of it when committed to the prison.

We will not, however, pursue this history further; but will come at once to an exhibition of the present status of religious instruction in the prisons of the United States and Canada, as we gathered it from our personal observations and from the documents, manuscript and printed, which are mentioned in the introduction to this report.

We begin with Canada. Much attention is given to the religious instruction of the convicts in the provincial penitentiary at Kingston. The prison has two chaplains: a Roman catholic priest, to minister to the catholic population, and a protestant pastor, to care for the spiritual interests of the protestant convicts. We did not have the good fortune to meet the former, though we heard a good report of his labors; the latter we saw and became well acquainted with; and it is but justice to say that he appeared to us eminently qualified for his position. Of his untiring industry and the vast amount of work done by him, we can speak only in terms of commendation. Mr. Mulkins has been, for some fifteen years, discharging the duties of protestant chaplain in this prison. He holds, and we fully agree with him, that the great mission of penitentiaries is to improve the mental and moral condition of their inmates, to implant in them the seeds and the love of virtue, to supply them wi h motives to a better life, and to animate them with higher, purer, and more godly hopes. And, truly, for the state to take these children of many races—these outcasts of many nations—these delinquents of many creeds; often diseased in body and always disordered in their moral powers; ignorant in all things, but especially ignorant of religion; vitiated, depraved, fallen and stained with guilt—and to seek, by wise and patient efforts, to overcome their ignorance, to repress their evil nature, to impart habits of industry, to instil right principles, and to surround them continually with agencies and influences adapted to make them wiser and better men; this is a purpose and a labor, whose grandeur and nobility it would be difficult to exaggerate. An observation and experience, extending through fifteen years, have convinced Mr. Mulkins that this exalted design—the noblest that a state can entertain towards its fallen and offending children— may, in a great degree, be accomplished; but only as it is acknowledged to be the chief aim of imprisonment, and all other things are made subordinate and subservient to it.

The convicts attend a daily service in the chapel, where a portion of scripture is read, confession of sin made, and prayer offered to God for his favor and blessing. Two public religious services are held on the Lord's day, and one in the middle of the week, immediately after dinner, at each of which a sermon is preached. At none of these services is there any singing, which, in our opinion, is a great defect, and much abridges their utility. Every protestant prisoner is provided with a copy of the scriptures, and several religious tracts and one religious book are supplied to each, monthly. These are much read by the prisoners. Many have read the Bible through several times, others once, and some only portions of it. Some have committed to memory, of course of their own free choice, entire books of the Bible, others whole chapters. Some can repeat many of the psalms; some the entire litany and most of the morning prayers; and scores have learned by heart the whole catechism. The convicts are also taught short prayers, that they may offer them up, night and morning, privately in their cells.

There is no Sunday school. We think that one of the public services of the Sabbath might be profitably replaced by such a school.

Much attention is paid to the spiritual improvement of the convict women. They spend a part of each day in reading the Bible and religious books. They have religious worship twice a day. They attend the two religious services of the Sabbath, and once during the week are visited, exhorted and prayed with, by a volunteer female worker. No available means to reclaim and reform them seem neglected.

In giving personal religious instruction to the convicts, Mr. Mulkins is indefatigable. He sends for each convict under his care once a month; talks with him privately; teaches him his catechism; inquires into his religious state; gives him advice suited to his case; exhorts and encourages him to reform; explains to him his special duties as a convict, and his general duties as a man; seeks to remove irritation from his mind; studies the best mode of reaching his heart; and at the close of the interview makes a brief record of it in a book kept for the purpose. He also visits the sick to converse and pray with them, always weekly, often daily. We did not wonder, no one can wonder, at a remark made by him, that it is too much labor for one man. There is scarcely a convict, he says, who is not pleased with these interviews; and even those who may not be religiously improved by them, are yet softened in their temper, and made morally better.

It has ever been the opinion of Mr. Mulkins (so he avers) that a congregation in prison should be managed, as far as possible, in the same way as any other; and that, as religious improvement is the end in view, its members should have the same means of grace as those enjoyed by other congregations. Hence, since the year 1860, he has regularly administered the communion to such prisoners as desired it, gave evidence of true penitence, and appeared properly prepared by religious knowledge and experience.

A good idea may be obtained of the nature and extent of the chaplain's duties, as well as of the orderly manner in which he discharges them, from the following enumeration of the record books kept by him: 1. A daily journal of all items of duty done; 2. A register, containing the personal history of each convict; 3. A record of monthly religious conversations with prisoners; 4. A communicants' book, in which are recorded the monthly conversations with communicants and with others who desire to become such; 5. An index, in which are entered, in alphabetical order, the name and registered number of each protestant convict received, and of all removals as they occur; 6. A directory of the convict population, showing the cells in which each is kept, and all the changes of location which are made from time to time; 7. A hospital book, in which are entered the names of the sick and the visits made to them for religious conversation and prayer; 8. A register of the convict women, and of the monthly religious conversations held with them; 9. A catalogue of the religious library; 10. A register, in which is entered monthly, the name of any book which may have been given out to a convict, together with the fact of its return.

From the above statement may be seen at a glance the great amount and variety of work done by this devoted and faithful man; work as beneficent in its effects as it must be exhausting in its performance.

Upon the whole, the religious influence pervading this prison constitutes one of its most marked and pleasing characteristics. The undersigned have, also, noticed with pleasure the strongly religious tone running through the annual reports of the inspectors. These gentlemen hold the opinion, decidedly, that all measures for the reformation of criminals will prove unavailing, except such as are based upon religion, and go hand in hand with it. They believe it to be useless to multiply punishments and reformatory agencies, unless the heart is touched, and the conscience enlightened and invigorated. It is moral discipline, to which, above and before all other means, the inspectors direct their chief attention, and bend their most dilligent efforts. They gladly and cordially co-operate with the chaplains, and do all they can to aid them in their high and holy mission.

On an average, about two-thirds of the convicts attend upon

the ministry of the protestant chaplain, and the remaining third upon that of the catholic chaplain. Each of these officers has a chapel, appropriately fitted up in accordance with the usages of his own church, and having seats for the women apart from those of the men. The chaplains are expected to be present daily in their respective offices, that they may give attention to the spiritual wants of the convicts severally under their charge. They may summon any prisoner at any hour of the day from any part of the premises for the purpose of holding religious conversation with him. It is made their duty to give especial attention to the sick.

Of the state prisons in the United States visited by us, those of New Hampshire, Massachusetts, Connecticut, New York, New Jersey, Pennsylvania, Michigan, Ohio, Indiana and Wisconsin have resident chaplains, most of whom have offices in their respective prisons, and devote their whole time to their appropriate work; while Vermont, Maine, Rhode Island, Delaware, Maryland, West Virginia, Kentucky, Missouri and Illinois, are without this advantage. Two of these last named states—Delaware and West Virginia—as already stated, have no state penitentiaries, but imprison their felons in the county jails of New Castle and Wheeling. What their arrangements may be (if they have any) for the religious instruction of their prisoners, we are unable to say. In the Maryland state prison, an excellent and devoted layman, a volunteer worker—Mr. Wisong—holds a Sabbath school each Lord's day, and, we believe, a public service in connection with it, for the benefit of all the prisoners. In the state penitentiary at Joliet, Illinois, a worthy Methodist clergyman, who resides in another part of the state, is employed, at a moderate salary, to preach to the convicts on the Sabbath; but, as a matter of course, he can perform little pastoral labor, which, after all, is the most important and the most telling. The other five prisons named—to wit, Vermont, Maine, Rhode Island, Kentucky and Missouri—have stated preaching on the Sabbath, either from the several pastors in rotation, or from a single pastor, resident in their several localities; but not much service beyond this is or can be given by these partial chaplains in behalf the prisoners.

Sabbath-schools are found in the prisons of Connecticut, Northern Indiana, Maryland, Massachusetts, New Hampshire, Michigan, Ohio, Rhode Island and New York, with the exception of the male prison at Sing Sing ; and in Vermont, a Bible-class is held on a week day. In the prison of Northern Indiana and the female prison at Sing Sing, the Sabbath-school is attended by the whole body of convicts. In the other prisons named, the usage as to attendance varies. In some, all prisoners are admitted to the privileges of the school, who desire it; in others, a selection is made of the more worthy, particularly among those who most need and are most likely to be profited by such instruction. Wherever a prison has a resident chaplain, it is a uniform rule that he acts as superintendent; but in the female prison at Sing Sing, that duty is performed by the matron. In most of the Sunday-schools, the superintendent is aided by other officers of the institutions, even in some instances- by the wardens, who act as teachers of classes, and generally also by volunteer laborers from outside. Without having exact data for the statement, the best judgment we can form from facts within our knowledge is, that from 1,500 to 2,000 convicts in our various state penitentiaries are receiving instruction from some 200 teachers in the Sabbath-school. The unanimous testimony of the authorities is, that the prisoners, as a general thing, are much interested in the exercises of their school, and that not a few are making commendable progress in religious knowledge. The following statement of the Rev. Joseph A. Canfield, chaplain and superintendent of the Sunday-school in Clinton prison, N. Y., may serve as a specimen. He says : " Convicts who attend the Sunday-school manifest a good degree of interest therein. After prayer and singing, I first examine the prisoners on two general questions that have been given out the previous sabbath, to be answered from the Bible [such as, What is the Bible testimony concerning stealing, profane swearing, Sabbath observance, repentance, faith, &c., &c.?] So much interest is taken in this exercise that sometimes the whole time is taken up with scripture citations and discussions growing out of the questions proposed. After these questions are disposed of and the general exercise is thus closed, the convicts recite in classes to their respective teachers, using for this purpose Dr. Clark's Questions on the Heroes of the Bible. I have no doubt, in fact I feel the strongest conviction, that the school is highly beneficial to those who attend it. A growing knowledge of and interest in the scriptures is most evidently the result ; for proof of which I may state the fact that I not unfrequently receive calls from convicts during the week, who desire religious conversation, which desire has been excited by attendance on the Sabbath-school. I have known the interest of more than one convict in religious inquiries excited to such a degree that they have read through the whole of Dwight's Theology, an achievement not often, perhaps, accomplished by laymen outside of prison walls."

In the state prison of Massachusetts, a daily religious service is held in the chapel immediately after breakfast, consisting of reading the scriptures, singing, prayer, and brief comments or exhortations at the option of the chaplain. Similar services are held in the Connecticut state prison both morning and evening. In both these penitentiaries, the effect of this daily service of prayer and worship on the convicts was reported to us as tranquilizing and quieting in a high degree ; the beneficial influence of it being felt throughout the entire day. We are sorry to be obliged to state that these are the only prisons visited by us, and, as far as we know, the only ones in the United States, in which there are regular week, day services of a religious character.

In all the state prisons which we visited in the United States, one public service is held on the Lord's day, at which a sermon is preached. In some a second service is conducted for the benefit of the female prisoners, and a third for that of the sick in the hospital. On all occasions of this kind, the singing of hymns forms a part of the worship, and in this the convicts very generally unite. It happens, also, oftener than otherwise, that there is a regular prison choir composed of convicts, varying in number from a half dozen to sixteen, and a melodeon as well, which is usually played by a prisoner. There is a uniform testimony on the part of the prison chaplains to the softening, soothing, humanizing influence of sacred song on these fallen men and women. There can be no doubt that singing is a part of religious worship, which is eminently adapted to calm the passions and to awaken good feelings. It has been noticed that prisoners have often been deeply affected by it, owing doubtless to the fact that it has revived thoughts and emotions that had long been dormant. The Rev. Mr. England, formerly chaplain of the juvenile prison at Parkhurst, in the Isle of Wight, once remarked to Mr. F. Hill, that the first symptom of a boy's improvement was his beginning to join in the singing, which at that prison is said to be remarkably good.

The Lord's supper is never administered in any of our state prisons, but baptism is, occasionally, in a few ; as in those of Ohio,· Vermont, Wisconsin, and by the Rev. Mr. Luckey in Sing Sing, while he officiated there as chaplain ; how this may be under his successor, we are not informed.

A convicts' prayer meeting was established by the Rev. John Luckey, chaplain, in the male prison at Sing Sing, in September, 1862. At first, it was held once a fortnight, but has since been changed to a weekly service. A similar meeting was also organized in the female prison in 1862, which was attended weekly from the start. Both these meetings have continued to the present time, being held every Wednesday afternoon for one hour. In the female prison, all go who wish; but in that of the men, no convict can join the meeting as a member but by permission of the chaplain; nor can a member attend any particular meeting, unless he has completed his task for the day. One of your commissioners has, upon several different occasions, attended these meetings. After his first attendance, he published, in a religious newspaper, under date of October 4, 1862, some account of the service, from which we take the following extract: " The meeting last Monday, was the third of the kind ever held in the prison. So far, everything has gone on satisfactorily. I have rarely, if ever, attended a religious service more solemn, interesting or touching. Some thirty or more convicts gathered in the chapel, and spent an hour together in prayer and religious conference. The chaplain presided, and took the general direction of the meeting; but the prayers and addresses were made by the prisoners. Considering the character and culture, or rather want of culture, of the persons offering them, they were quite remarkable. A portion of scripture was read, and probably a half dozen short prayers were offered, and as many brief addresses made, interspersed with the singing of hymns. They were direct, simple, earnest, fervent. Some of them gave evidence of deep emotion. Several of the convicts who spoke mentioned that their attention had but recently been turned to the subject of personal religion. A marked peculiarity of the prayers was, that, in almost every instance, confession was made in the first person singular. A convict who was unable to be present, sent in a request for the prayers of his fellow-prisoners; and the petitions offered for him were singularly fervent and importunate. It is impossible, of course, for man to read the heart; but the whole tone and spirit of the meeting were significant of sincerity in those who took part in it. Religion, the interests of the soul and of immortality, seemed to be a reality with them; seemed, indeed, for the time at least, to be everything.

The hour spent in the convicts' prayer meeting, was truly an hour of most intense interest, and has left a record upon the memory that nothing can ever efface." The average attendance has greatly increased since the date of the above extract, and has often been as high as fifty or sixty. The chaplain submitted the minutes of these meetings to our inspection. One of the entries is in these words : "Only about one-third of those whom we have admitted to our prayer meetings are, in my opinion, thoroughly changed in heart. The remainder are seriously inclined *for the present*. If they fall out by the way, which, under their peculiar disadvantages, would not surprise us, the present *restraint*, which this connection imposes, improves the discipline, and is therefore a decided benefit." Another record is this : "The son of one of our ministers, who has been a great grief to his pious friends, was specially wrought upon." A subsequent minute, referring to the same case, is in the following words : "Poor ——— was most deeply affected with a sense of his sins. He is a son, the only son of a minister. May he soon find relief." At another time the chaplain makes this entry : "I am satisfied that, in the main, the object of those who attend this meeting is spiritual benefit. But, oh! how frail and ignorant they are! Consequently, we hope with much trembling." After the 25th meeting, he says ; "Neither on this or any former occasion was there an attempt made at private communication. In fact, I never attended any social meetings more silent, orderly, and apparently devout than these convict prayer meetings have been." Many letters have been received from convicts, who had been members of the meeting, since their discharge—some addressed to the chaplain, some to brother convicts, and others to the meeting itself. These letters were also placed in our hands for inspection. We could wish that our limits would permit extracts. The spirit of penitence, humility, faith, prayer, resolution, and apparent sincerity, which breathes through these effusions of the heart, could then be seen by all. The present chaplain, Rev. J. B. Smith, informs us that the "convicts' prayer meeting," according to the testimony of prisoners who have known it from the start, is more largely attended than ever before, and that there is more religious interest among the convicts than has heretofore been known.

Subsequently to our visit, a convicts' prayer meeting was also established in the Massachusetts state prison by the Rev. G. J. Carleton, chaplain; in reference to which, in his annual report, under date of October 1, 1866, he holds the following language: "For some time there were interesting prayer meetings among the convicts, which were carried on with much earnestness and zeal. Some outsiders, who occasionally were present, expressed not only much pleasure but astonishment at the manner in which the men would pray, exhort and sing. Indeed, the prayer meetings here have been as ably sustained as the chaplain or any one else would find outside the walls. Perhaps it may be deemed that this is stating the matter strongly, and too strongly. However, facts will prove the statement correct. Ministers who have been here will say that they have heard as appropriate exhortations, intelligent remarks, fluent prayers, animated singing, &c., as in any other place. These meetings were held on the Lord's day morning at nine o'clock, and were highly prized by those who attended them; but they had to be given up, though with much regret, because the officers could not, with any convenience, be present to let them out from their cells to go to the chapel. The officers are so confined through the week, that it is hard to ask any extra duty of them on the Lord's day. It would not be fair to urge it, and I could not in conscience do so; and the thanks of the chaplain and the men who attended the prayer meeting are here expressed to them for the twenty-five mornings they did give their services. But why not have prayer meetings on a week day? I should be very glad to have them, and perhaps the day will come when such will be the case; though the contractors, of course, feel that the time of the men through the week is theirs, and whatever time is taken for a prayer meeting is so much time taken from them, and might be considered as lost. It is doubted, however, whether time taken for such a purpose would be altogether lost, even as far as the contractors are concerned. Might not the good the men would receive more than compensate them? Might it not be made manifest in greater diligence and thoroughness in their work, and the more cheerful promptitude with which the work would be performed? Indeed, it would seem as if the chaplain should be privileged to have the men whenever he might want them for a prayer meeting or any other religious meeting, and that nothing should be allowed to stand in his way to prevent him from preaching and praying and laboring just as much as he pleases, to do them good." We quite concur in the view expressed in the closing sentences of the above extract, provided the chaplains are men of judgment and discretion; and certainly none others should be appointed, or if appointed, retained.

There appears to have been, many years ago, a convicts' prayer meeting in the state penitentiary of Ohio, but it has long since been given up. The present chaplain says: "I do not know with what results it was attended." Beyond what is related above, we know of no meetings of the kind organized, or of attempts to organize such, in any of the prisons of America. The results at Sing Sing and Charleston are certainly such as to encourage efforts in that direction; but they should be prudently made, and only when there is a manifest call for such meetings on the part of the convicts themselves.

With much uniformity, though not with entire unanimity, the officers attest the interest and pleasure manifested by the convicts in the religious services which they are required to attend, and the beneficial results attending these services. "Their influence is good, very good," is the general testimony. Dr. Campbell, however, of the Western penitentiary, Pa., says of the convicts in that prison : "They listen more for the sake of a change than because they feel interested." Mr. Buckmaster, of the Illinois state penitentiary, declared, unequivocally, that he had never known any beneficial results from the labors of a chaplain there, and seemed to think such an officer quite a useless and impertinent appendage to a penal institution.

The chaplain at Sing Sing prison, N. Y., holds a short service in the male hospital for the benefit of the sick every Sabbath morning, and occasionally in the female hospital; and both in Sing Sing and the other state prisons of New York, the sick and dying receive daily visits from their religious teachers, by whom they are instructed, warned, encouraged, prayed with and consoled, according to the exigencies of their several cases. Like services are rendered to the same class, though possibly not in all cases with equal frequency, by most if not all of the resident chaplains in the prisons of the other states. These ministrations are, for the most part, exceedingly acceptable and often highly useful to the persons who are made the subjects of them. As a specimen of the manner in which this class of duties is performed and received, we offer the following extract from the last report of the Rev. Mr. Carleton: "In visiting, conversing and praying with the sick in the hospital, the chaplain has been much encouraged. He has enjoyed some very delightful seasons with those who were drawing nigh unto the grave, and who went down into the valley of the shadow of death fearing no evil, dying in the faith of the gospel, and going home to glory. One man, who had been confined for a long season with pulmonary disease, exhibited the most meek and uncomplaining spirit. Indeed, he was so patient, resigned and pleasant withal, that no one could be with him for any length of time without a feeling of affection and sympathy for him. He did not desire to stay in this world. He was not only willing to die, but desirous of departing to be with Christ. But a few hours before he breathed his last, he said to me, with much animation and emphasis, 'I don't want to stay here any longer. I'd much rather go. I want to see Jesus. Chaplain, if I could live many years, and have the riches and the honors and the pleasures of this world, I'd rather go now and be with Jesus.' And so he fell asleep without a struggle or a groan, trusting in Jesus, and I belive has gone to be with Jesus in one of those mansions of which He said there were many in His Father's house. When this man was dying, death did not look to him as the grim king of terrors (which some people speak of) to frighten, to alarm; but rather as a friend, to lead him from a world of sorrow and sin to one of joy and holiness."

As regards the disposition made of the bodies of deceased prisoners, the general rule in all state prisons is to notify friends, whenever it is practicable, either of their death or its near approach; and the remains are always surrendered to them for removal, if they desire it. When not so reclaimed, they are usually interred in a burying ground within the prison premises, though sometimes the place of sepulture is in some cemetery outside. All this is as it should be. But we are pained to report, and we cannot but regard it as a scandal to our civilization, that in very many of the prisons visited by us, certainly not less than one-half, and probably more, no funeral service whatever is performed over the bodies of deceased convicts, but the burial of dogs is awarded to them. When a convict dies, and is to be buried in the prison of Massachusetts, the whole body of convicts are assembled in the chapel, and a regular funeral service is held, consisting of reading the scriptures, a suitable address and prayer. We believe the same is true in respect to the prisons of Maine, New Hampshire, Connecticut and Vermont, but we think nowhere else. In Clinton prison, New York, there is a burial service, attended by all the men belonging to the gang or company to which the deceased was attached. The chaplain reads a portion of scripture, makes a short address, offers an appropriate prayer, and attends the body to the grave. At Sing Sing, the chaplain conducts a burial service, which, however, is attended by only two guards and four convicts, with occasionally some of the other officers. At the public service of the following Sabbath, the fact of the death and the circumstances attending it are stated in the chapel, and the event is always made the occasion either of brief practical remarks or of a regular funeral sermon. These things are well as far as they go, but convicts are men, though fallen, and we are a christian people. Our conviction, therefore, is, that we should accord to them, when they die, the burial of other men, and that nothing short of this will meet the demand of a christian civilization. All their prison comrades should be assembled in the usual place of public religious worship, and instruction, warning and exhortation given them, suited to the occasion.

In all our state prisons, a copy of the Bible is supplied to every prisoner who is willing to receive it. In a few instances it is refused; but even in such cases it not unfrequently happens that prisoners who at first refused, afterwards change their minds and ask for what they had previously declined. In most of the prisons, hymn books are also furnished to all the inmates, and in very many, prayer books to such as desire them. In the case of two or three prisons, the answers given to our interrogotary were, "few read the Bible with interest;" "it is not much read for good,". and the like. As a general thing, however, the responses were of quite a different character. The common testimony is, that a large proportion of the prisoners—some say half, others more than half—read the scriptures with interest, attention and profit. There are convicts who are reported as reading the Bible through once, twice, and even thrice a year; and some, who say they never read it before their conviction, have become, since their imprisonment, diligent students of it, and often ask questions, which evince an intelligent as well as interested perusal of its pages.

We met with an exceedingly interesting case in Sing Sing. We were present, when the chaplain, the venerable John Luckey, performed the rite of baptism upon six converted convicts. After the administration of the ordinance was over, he invited us to converse, individually, with the prisoners who had received it; an opportunity which we gladly embraced, and we were much gratified with the modest, intelligent, and, all things considered, satisfactory answers given by them to the questions put in reference to their religious experience. Religious tracts and papers are distributed freely in most of our state prisons; in some, more sparingly; and in ·a few, seldom if ever. In several of them, convicts who have the means are permitted to take a religious newspaper ; but this is an exception and not the rule. In a majority of the state prisons, the inmates read these publications with no little interest; in some they are abused, and therefore withheld. Wherever this happens, the presumption is that there is a lack either of discipline or tact on the part of the authorities.

In prisons which enjoy the services of resident chaplains, a good deal of pastoral labor is done by the incumbents ; but this department of work does not appear to be as thoroughly organized or as systematically performed in any of the state prisons of the United States, as it is in the provincial penitentiary of Canada. The chaplain of the New Hampshire prison spends· three hours every Sunday in going from cell to cell, conversing with the prisoners, and imparting such lessons and counsels as to him seem adapted to the case of each. Other chaplains spend two and others one hour each Lord's day in the same work. Some are in the habit of spending more or less time every day in this personal visitation. Our own chaplains made to the commissioners the following statements in regard to pastoral work done by them. Mr. Ives, of Auburn prison, said : "I visit prisoners in their cells a good deal on the Sabbath, to converse with them on religious subjects—on an average, I should think, about fifteen. I also see and converse with a number every day in my office, either on my sending for them or on their coming to me of their own accord. On these occasions it is quite usual to offer prayer with them. These labors are well received by the convicts, who appear to be grateful for the sympathy and interest thus shown to them." Mr. Canfield, of Clinton prison, said : "On an average, I spend at least an hour and a half every Sabbath in visiting prisoners in their cells, seeing usually ten or upwards. I visit the hospital daily, conversing with the patients and occasionally offering prayer. The most effective pastoral service, I think, is performed in my casual meetings with the convicts, in my office, when they call on me in connection with their correspondence, and in other parts of the prison premises." Mr. Smith, of Sing Sing prison, said : "I visit the sick in the male hospital every day, and in the female hospital about once a week; but oftener, if necessary. I converse with convicts on writing and library days, and I send for them to my office, from time to time, as there may be occasion. These labors are received with interest by the prisoners." What is done by the chaplains in New York is done, substantially, by those in other states. We feel a special gratification in being able to report a unanimous testimony to the kindly, serious and grateful spirit in which the convicts meet their chaplains in the discharge of these pastoral offices. As affording a specimen of this spirit, we cite the following statement of Mr. Cordier, commissioner of the Wisconsin state prison: "The chaplain visits and converses privately with the prisoners nearly every evening. *These visits are eagerly looked for.*"

We willingly and gladly bear testimony to the fact that, as a class, the chaplains of our American prisons are earnest, godly, devoted, and faithful men; but we are sorry to be compelled to add, that they are, in various ways, almost everywhere, restricted and hampered in their work, so that they cannot labor with that freedom and efficiency which would be desirable. The restriction to which we refer arises chiefly from the operation of the contract system, and from a want of a due appreciation, on the part of prison authorities, of the supreme importance of their labors, as shown in the remark before cited, of Mr. Buckmaster, lessee of the Illinois state penitentiary, although that, we admit, is an extreme opinion, and we hope and believe, a unique one.

We made inquiry whether it is customary for the chaplains of our state prisons to hold special conversations with the convicts of their respective institutions on their admission and discharge. We regret our inability to offer a satisfactory report on this point. Nowhere—not, as far as we are informed and believe, in a solitary prison in the United States—is this duty made obligatory on the chaplain; and in very· few is it ever performed; or if ever, not with exactness and punctuality. We have already, in the section on discipline, stated the practice of the chaplains in our New York prisons. By the incumbents in New Hampshire, Massachusetts, and Ohio, the duty seems to be generally, if not invariably, performed; elsewhere, neglect of the duty appears to be the rule, the doing of it the exception. The usage in Ohio is thus stated by warden Prentice, in his communication to us: "The chaplain visits new prisoners in their cells, on the first Sabbath. after they are received. He also always, as opportunity offers, converses

with prisoners immediately before their discharge. Such interviews are had with a view, first, to ascertain the effect of imprisonment; secondly, to learn to what extent new purposes have been
formed; and, thirdly, to counsel and encourage efforts towards a
better life."

Impressed with the conviction that valuable aid in the moral
and religious instruction of prisoners may be obtained from judicious volunteer laborers, since, to the honor of humanity, numbers
are willing to labor gratuitously in this department of christian
effort, we put this question to the authorities : " Are persons from
outside ever admitted within the prison to make efforts for the moral
and religious improvement of the prisoners ?" While grieved to
say that from quite a number of prisons we received a negative
reply, we are, at the same time, happy .to report that a goodly
number answered affirmatively. We cite a few of these responses.
Mr. Willard, of Connecticut, responds : "Persons from outside,
desirous of improving the moral and religious condition of the
prisoners, are permitted to hold public intercourse with them at
times, but never private." Mr. Wood, of northern Indiana, says :
"Persons from outside are allowed to converse with the convicts
on moral and religious topics, if they make application to that
effect and are deemed sufficiently discreet." Mr. Haynes, of Massachusetts, replies : "Volunteer laborers, desiring to make efforts for
the moral and religious benefit of the prisoners, are admitted
within the prison to teach in the Sunday school, to address the
prisoners in the chapel, and to distribute tracts among them."
Mr. Seaton, of Michigan, says : "Persons outside may, if they
wish, come into the prison to converse with the convicts on
religious subjects." Mr. Prentice, of Ohio, answers : "Sunday
school teachers may visit their scholars, and tract distributors are
admitted under such restrictions as the warden may impose." Mr.
Cordier, of Wisconsin, says : " Christian people from outside are
allowed to converse with the prisoners on religious subjects, and
they make a liberal use of the privilege. They are placed under
no other restriction than they would be in any church." In the
eastern penitentiary, Pa., the members of the Philadelphia Prison
Society labor abundantly and effectively for the moral and spiritual
benefit of the inmates. In the state prisons of New York, persons
of discreet judgment and otherwise properly qualified, find no
difficulty in gaining admission to labor in the way and to the end
indicated.

Persons who object to such assistance should remember that John Howard himself, the greatest, if not the first, of prison reformers, and the excellent Mrs. Fry, of England, were volunteer workers. So were Louis Dwight and Miss Dix of America. And so, also, have been multitudes of other efficient laborers in both countries, who have worthily followed in the footsteps of these illustrious individuals. There is a consideration in favor of admitting this species of service in prisons, suggested by Mr. Frederick Hill, in his work on Crime, which strikes us as of no little force. It is this: The feeling is quite common with prisoners, that persons who, of their own accord, come to visit them and to labor for their improvement, must have their interest at heart, and cannot be discharging a mere duty for which they are paid. This feeling, on their part, adds much to the power of such instruction; a power which, if discreetly used, may be turned to the best account. Mr. Miller, of Missouri, informed us that persons from outside had never, at Jefferson City, offered their services to converse with convicts in the state penitentiary on moral and religious subjects. Happily, such indifference on the part of religious and philanthropic people, does not extensively prevail, and is, we would fain hope, limited to the capital of Missouri. In most communities, to the honor of humanity, the number of persons willing to render gratuitous service of the kind indicated is such as to admit of considerable choice in the selection of those who seem adapted to the work. Even selfish, or at least self-interested, motives may and do, sometimes, come into play here. The divine provision, by which he who dispenses good thereby benefits himself, is not without its power as an inducement to this good work. Mr. Hill speaks of a lady of high rank in Scotland, who applied for permission for herself and others to visit the female inmates of a small prison in that country. In making the application, she distinctly stated that she wished to come, not as a condescending patroness, but, as she herself expressed it, " as a woman to women;" with a conviction that she and those associated with her would derive more profit than even the prisoners themselves. The physician of the eastern penitentiary of Pennsylvania, in his annual report some years ago, after dilating on the importance and utility of these volunteer labors in prisons, thus states his opinion as to the classes of persons proper to be admitted: "Heretofore, the persons permitted to visit the prisoners for the purpose of moral instruction, &c., have been invariably confined to the more educated classes. I believe this to be an error. Among those of our citizens who have less pretensions to intellectual culture, many will be found who possess every qualification necessary to render their intercourse with convicts highly beneficial. I would, therefore, earnestly recommend that their services be immediately solicited." The ties which convicts in this way form with some of the purest and best of their species, of both sexes, feeble as they may appear, are often of inestimable value to them after their liberation. This is shown by the large number of offenders, who have become respectable and useful members of society through the instrumentality of such volunteer workers in our own and other countries.

As it respects the nature, extent, value and permanence of the results accomplished by the various religious influences, as detailed above, which are brought to bear upon the convicts in the prisons of our country, prison officers, and even the chaplains themselves, differ not a little in opinion. In general, the response to our inquiries on this point, from prisons not provided with resident chaplains, was to the effect that no very clear, marked or decisive results were visible. On the other hand, the prisons enjoying the services of full chaplains, gave answer, for the most part, that the results were "favorable," or "highly favorable." Most of the chaplains think that genuine conversions, involving a radical change in the religious state and character of the subjects, do occasionally take place, though for the most part they represent such changes as comparatively rare, and to be admitted with a cautious reserve. Mr. Cordier, of Wisconsin state prison, however, reports his chaplain as of the opinion "that genuine spiritual conversions take place in at least one-third of the convicts." The response in regard to the Ohio prison is in these words: "It is difficult to determine, in a general way, what are the results brought to bear upon the convicts. The field is not a fruitful one, and yet there are in it encouragements to cultivation. It is safe to say that usually the influences are morally healthful." Vermont answers thus: "The chaplain trusts that genuine spiritual conversions do sometimes take place. He does not look, certainly, for many strong evidences of awakening; but he *does* look for such an impression as will make a man a better citizen, disarm his prejudice against the administration of the law, and lead him to look with sympathy and reverence on religion, and to desire to practice its precepts and grow into its spirit." Mr. Carleton, of the Massachusetts prison, in his last annual report, says: "It is with feelings of devout and grateful appreciation, as he humbly trusts, that the chaplain is able to say, that during the year there has been more attention to religious concerns than usual, and many of the prisoners have, to a greater or less extent, been interested in the question of their personal salvation. Some, there is reason to hope, have been truly converted, and by the grace of God have become new creatures in Christ Jesus, old things having with them passed away, and all things having become new. Some give the most satisfactory and decisive evidence that this gracious change has passed upon them, by a quiet, resigned, yet genial and cheerful spirit— willing to suffer as malefactors, because they are sensible that they have done wrong, and not urging any plea for pardon, on the ground that they have become reformed men. They acknowledge that they have broken the laws of the land, and have been justly convicted and sentenced, and they are willing to serve out the time of their punishment, because they believe it is just and proper that they should. Such, the chaplain must say, he has confidence in, and prays that they may go on their way rejoicing, which he believes will be the fact, and that they will not only do good here by their example and faith, but when they have gone out from this place, do good in their day and generation, wherever their lot may be cast."

There is a general concurrence, on the part of the prison chaplains of the United States, in the opinion that the religious element might to advantage be much more extensively introduced into our prison administration, especially by the formation of Sabbath schools where they do not now exist, the establishment of a short daily service in the chapel, and a more pervading and elevated moral and religious tone among the officers. On this latter point, Mr. Canfield, of Clinton prison, well remarks: "The teaching of morality and religion, to produce their best and highest effect, need to be illustrated and enforced by the character and example of all who are allowed to associate with the convict officially or otherwise. The 'powers that be,' may, if possible, employ an angel's tongue to enforce every command in the decalogue and all the teachings of the gospel, and yet if the same powers require the convict to systematically trample upon these commands, the practice will do much more to form his character than the preaching. 'Thou, which teachest another, teachest not thyself?'" To the like effect are the following remarks of Mr. Hill: "Much as the hearts and minds of prisoners may be improved by precept, still this is not the sole, or even the chief means of attaining the desired end. Much more will depend on the practice of the prison; whereof every rule and the example of every officer will have an effect, for good or for evil, on the character of the inmates, as it harmonizes or clashes with the great laws of reason and justice." On the general subject of an increase of religious agencies in prisons, a pastor who officiates with others in conducting the Sabbath services of a large state penitentiary, says: "In regard to the efficacy of religious instruction in prisons, I am unable to say much from actual observation and experience. Our opportunities for imparting religious instruction are so limited under the present management as to make it impossible to say how much might be accomplished in this way. Still, I have seen enough to know that much, very much, may be done by a discreet and faithful chaplain. Not only have instances of apparent conversion taken place under my observation, but in some cases I have kept my eye on them for years after they left the prison, and they have given every evidence of being thoroughly and permanently reformed. A few days since, I received a letter from one who left the prison more than a year ago. He has written to me as frequently as once a month ever since his discharge, and I do not know that I have a correspondent, ministerial or otherwise, whose letters breath more of the spirit of Christ than his. My firm conviction is that, if more time was spent with the convicts in an effort to improve their morals, fewer of them would so soon find their way back to prison after their discharge, and many would be soundly converted to God. The great difficulty would be in getting the right sort of a chaplain, for, while I do not want to underrate my brethren, I do not think one minister in five, no, not in twenty, is fit to go inside of a prison. One-half of them will allow their sympathies to pervert their judgment, and almost the whole of the other half would be rendered so skeptical by the continual deceit of the convicts as to be unwilling to do justice to the sincere. But I am satisfied that *daily prayers*, a *bible class*, and repeated *public services* under the superintendence of a competent chaplain, who is untrameled by outside influences, would do more to reform the convicts than all the terrors of the law with which it is possible to threaten or punish them."

In the year 1839, the Boston Prison Discipline Society addressed to the wadens of the different state prisons a series of interrogatories, including, among others, the following: " What do you think of a prison without a chapel, or place of worship, where the convicts can be assembled on the Sabbath for public worship and Sabbath-school instruction, and [on week days for] morning and evening prayers?" To this Mr. Moses C. Pilsbury, one of the most eminent prison keepers of that day, gave the following pointed and excellent reply: "It is impossible for me, in the limits of this, to give my views in detail on so important a question; but, in my estimation, not much unlike (in regard to wisdom) to a man who would build and adorn a beautiful ship, lade her with the richest cargo of goods, and send her to sea without rudder, compass or chart. I think there would not be much preventive, in a prison without a chapel, against insanity, but it would be written upon the very walls." This puts the supreme importance of religion in prisons in a light as clear as it is striking, and it is for this reason that we have cited it.

It appears, from the foregoing detail, that a good deal of prominence is given by some at least of our American prison chaplains to the work of personal visitation and conference. We cannot too warmly commend this practice, nor too strongly press it upon these excellent gentlemen. We approve and urge the universal introduction into prisons of a daily service of prayer, like that which we have described as in use in the Massachusetts prison; but we would give the preëminence to personal interviews, as likely to have the greater permanent influence. The benefit to convicts is obvious and incalculable of frequent conversations with an earnest, kind, godly, sympathizing and judicious chaplain, when the prisoner can express his feelings, and the pastor can give his counsels and admonitions, with no one by to check the free outpourings of the heart on either side. One special reason for such visits and conversations is, that the chaplain is thereby enabled the better to direct his inquiries and instructions to each prisoner's particular case; and one highly important use to be made of them is, as Mr. Hill has suggested, to inquire into the convict's prospects on liberation, and so by correspondence with his friends or former employés, to obtain for him, when there is evidence of contrition and amendment, another trial. The friendly offices of the chaplain may often, in this way, be of essential service in effecting the prisoner's restoration to society.

To the question, " How far does the conduct of prisoners, after discharge, justify the hopes inspired by their conduct while in prison?" we did not, for the most part, receive very satisfactory replies. Quite commonly the answer was, "We cannot trace them to any great extent after liberation, and consequently know little of their subsequent career." In other cases the statement was, that the after life of convicts seldom justifies the hopes excited by their professions in prison. In one instance, the significant response was given, "*Ten* lepers were cleansed, but *one* only returned to give glory to God." A few answers of a more cheering character were received. Mr. Miller, of Missouri, says: "On the whole, an encouraging number seem to justify our hopes of them by their conduct after their release, and give promise of permanent reformation. Mr. Haynes, of Massachusetts testifies: "The majority of prisoners, by their conduct after their discharge, justify our hopes of their conduct." Mr. Cordier, of Wisconsin, returns an answer the most gratifying of all. His testimony is: "I must confess that my most sanguine hopes, inspired by the conduct of convicts while in prison, have been fully justified by their conduct after discharge. During the four years I have been connected with this prison, there have been 284 convicts discharged. While only nine of them have been returned for a second time, I have met with a goodly number of these men, having traveled extensively through the state, who are now respectable citizens. One is editor of an ably conducted monthly magazine; another is a public officer, in the employ of the government; and others are mechanics, farmers and laborers. All whom I have had the pleasure to meet (and they were not a few) were in comfortable circumstances, of sober habits and of exemplary character." Can the fact that the contract system has never had an existence in the Wisconsin state prison have anything to do with the extraordinary results here exhibited?

A moral agency in prisons, of no little power for good or evil, exists in the correspondence of the convicts with their friends and others of the outside world. In all the state prisons of New York, this department of the administration is in the sole charge of the chaplains. In New Hampshire, this officer has the "principal charge" of the correspondence. In Massachusetts and Wisconsin, the correspondence of the prisoners is committed to the clerk. In all the other state prisons to which our information extends, this duty is discharged by the warden. There are, we think, important reasons, which will be referred to by and by, why the oversight of the prisoners' correspondence should be intrusted to their religious teachers.

There is nowhere any restriction as to the number of letters that convicts may receive, provided they be of a proper character. As regards the frequency with which letters may be written by them, the usage varies in different prisons not a little. In New York, Kentucky, Massachusetts, Michigan, Vermont and Pennsylvania, convicts are permitted to write one letter in three months. In Connecticut, they may write every six weeks. In New Hampshire, Ohio and Wisconsin, they enjoy this privilege monthly. In northern Indiana, there is no restriction as to time on prisoners, whose conduct record is fair. In Maine, they are permitted to write to their friends " as often as they wish ;" and in Missouri " as often as is convenient." The general rule in Wisconsin is, as above stated, one letter a month ; but the privilege of correspondence is there, very wisely, made an instrument of discipline ; and convicts, as a reward for good conduct, are allowed to write twice or even four times a month. The careful reader will not fail to have noticed, as he has followed the thread of this report, that the methods of convict treatment pursued in the Wisconsin state prison, are, in general, more natural, more in harmony with that which men receive in free society, than perhaps those employed in any other American prison ; and to this circumstance, taken in connection with the exclusion of the contract system from the start, we cannot but attribute, in great measure, a percentage of reconvictions below, and a percentage of permanent reformations above, the general average of the penal institutions of this country. There are other circumstances, however, which may have contributed to the same result. There are no very large cities in Wisconsin. The habits of the people are simple. The demand for agricultural laborers is very great ; and it is to this class that Mr. Cordier's observation was, as he himself informed us, mainly confined. We think it right to mention these circumstances, as we desire to be just and fair to all.

It is proper to state, in this connection, that in all our prisons letters may be written more frequently than at the stated times named in the preceding paragraph, by permission obtained from the proper authority, whenever the occasion seems to demand a letter, and the conduct of the applicant has been such as to merit the indulgence.

It can hardly be necessary to mention, as it could not fail to be presumed, that the correspondence both ways is subject to inspection; all letters, written and received by convicts, being carefully read, and those which are deemed objectionable inexorably withheld; nevertheless, when letters contain matter, a part of which is contraband and a part not, while the letters themselves are withheld, the portions not contraband are read to the persons to whom they have been sent.

The character of the correspondence carried on between convicts and their friends, is a matter of no slight interest and importance. We may remark, in general, that far too large a proportion of the letters written by prisoners relate to the subject of obtaining a pardon, in many prisons not less than one-half of them being of this character, and in some fully two-thirds. Of course, this necessitates, or at least involves, to a great degree, a like quality or strain in the answers returned. Such a state of the case is bad in itself and bad in its influence, since, until prisoners abandon the expectation of pardon, and make up their mind to quietly serve out their terms of sentence, they will give little earnest thought or effort to the work of personal reformation, which, for themselves, as well as for society, is the most important end to be gained through their imprisonment. So far, then, their correspondence is little to their profit, and not a little to their disprofit. But, barring this feature, there is much in prison correspondence to commend, and much that is calculated to do good. From most prisons we received statements to the effect that, with the exception named, the letters written by convicts to family friends, parents, wives and children, are kind, affectionate, sympathetic, showing warm domestic feeling, abounding in expressions of tender regard and attachment, and giving utterance to a strong purpose to do better in the future. The letters written to them by their friends, are marked by the same general characteristics, with the addition of much friendly admonition, counsel and encouragement. So that, while a few wardens express the opinion that the correspondence of their prisoners either simply does no harm or is positively hurtful, the great majority of these officers concur in the judgment that it is highly beneficial, as tending to bind them to their homes, to assure them that there are still those who care for and sympathize with them, to keep alive in their breast the sentiment of domestic affection, and to impart hope, confidence and courage, when otherwise they would be likely to give way to despondent and even despairing emotions.

All this is well illustrated by the remark of a convict, recently made to the chaplain of Sing Sing prison. Mr. Smith handed him a letter just received. On glancing at the address, the man observed: "Chaplain, that letter is from my mother; and if I were offered the choice between it and a hundred dollar greenback, I would take the letter."

The proportion of convicts in American prisons, who either write letters or have them written, is very large. Our New York chaplains say that the exceptions to this rule are rare indeed.

Whether the chaplains, or whatever officers have charge of the correspondence, avail themselves of letters written or received by convicts, to produce good impressions on their minds, or to deepen and render permanent those already made, is one of the points connected with this subject, on which we sought to obtain information. The importance of the subject-matter to which the question relates will be apparent, when it is considered that in a prison of the size of Sing Sing, not less certainly than 8,000 letters will be the annual aggregate coming in and going out. All of these must pass through the hands of the officer who has charge of the correspondence, and in every instance he must come in contact with the convict from whom he receives or to whom he gives his letter. Here, then, he will have not fewer than 8,000 opportunities of uttering a brief word of counsel, encouragement or exhortation, and that too under circumstances in which, as will occur to every reflecting mind, such a word, fitly spoken, will often have an effect tenfold greater than at ordinary times. It is on this account, chiefly, that we said, a little while ago, that the chaplain appeared to us the most suitable officer to be entrusted with the prison correspondence. We ground this opinion on two considerations: first, because he is the person most competent to the service suggested; and, secondly, because he will be likely to have the most leisure for it. As a matter of fact, the service is now performed only to a very limited extent, except in the prisons in which the chaplains have charge of the correspondence. Mr. Peirce, the excellent clerk of the Massachusetts prison, makes use of his opportunity in the way indicated; but we were surprised to receive from Mr. Cordier, who has utilized so many agencies neglected by others for the moral benefit of his prisoners, the statement that "their correspondence has never yet been used as a means either of awaking or deepening good impressions." Most of the wardens who supervise the prison correspondence, rarely, if ever, employ this agency in the manner stated; although Mr. Miller, late warden of the penitentiary of Missouri, was in the habit of doing so, and was even accustomed frequently to append to letters sent to convicts a postcript of his own, calling their special attention to some particular item of advice or warning contained in them. But the four chaplains named as entrusted with the oversight of the correspondence, viz.: the three in New York and the one in New Hampshire, seem fully to comprehend the value of the opportunities for good thereby afforded, and faithfully to improve the same; and they report, we can readily believe truly, great and lasting benefits accomplished in this way.

Another moral agency in prisons, which may be either good or bad, according to circumstances, are the visits which convicts are allowed to receive, with greater or less frequency, from their friends. In perhaps the larger number of state prisons, prisoners are permitted to see their friends only once every three months; but in Connecticut, Michigan, Ohio and Wisconsin, they may receive visits monthly; and in Maine, Missouri, New Hampshire and Vermont, at any time when their friends may come. In Northern Indiana, also, visits may be received by convicts without restriction, if their conduct be good. In the western penitentiary, Pa., convicts are never allowed to see their friends, except in particular cases, as severe sickness, &c.; a stern and harsh rule, which, for that reason, we record in the very words in which it was stated to us by the warden. The practice is quite different in the eastern penitentiary. Prisoners there are permitted to receive visits from their friends once in three months. Here, as also in all prisons on the congregate plan, these interviews must be held in the presence of an officer. In this prison, the grated door of the cell is closed between the convict and his visitor. The only exception to the rule of exclusion from the cell is when mothers visit their imprisoned offspring. They are admitted to a more private interview within the narrow walls to which their children are confined—a touching tribute to the sanctity and tenderness of the maternal relation.

With very few exceptions, persons making friendly visits of the kind described above may bring little presents of fruits and other eatables to the prisoners whom they call to see. Mr. Miller, of Missouri, says: "I have encouraged such attentions from their friends, and have seen tears flow freely at the reception of such home and heart offerings."

As to the effect of these visits of friends on the convicts, one warden reports it as doubtful; another, as of no benefit; a third, as doing no harm; and a fourth as bad, making the prisoners sad, discontented, restless and morose for a number of days. As a general thing, however, prison officers concur in the testimony that the influence of these friendly visits is good and wholesome.

Another moral agency in prisons, of no little potency, is constituted by the visits, more or less numerous, of the general public, most of which are prompted by an impulse of curiosity.

In nearly or quite all the prisons of the United States, general visitors are admitted, daily, during business hours, and are conducted, with very few exceptions, over the entire premises, including the workshops. No restrictions are imposed, other than that they be under the escort of an officer, and abstain from speaking to the convicts or delivering any article whatever into their hands; and they are, besides, quite commonly admonished not to indulge in laughter, loud conversation, or boisterous conduct of any kind. With almost entire unanimity, though a few exceptions must be noted, prison officers declare the influence of this system of general visitation to be evil. Let Mr. Cordier speak for them all. This intelligent, humane, and able governor says: "The influence upon convicts of admitting general visitors cannot be otherwise than injurious. This being gazed upon again and again, as criminals, tends to destroy all sense of shame, if there be any left. It further tends to harden their feelings, and make them indifferent to public opinion. These visits have, also, a very bad effect upon the discipline. It cannot be prevented that visitors speak loud enough to be heard by prisoners, and this draws their attention from their work, subjecting them to admonition, and sometimes even to punishment. I consider the custom of making convicts a kind of public show, a nuisance and a disgrace, and one that should be abolished very speedily." To all which we respond with an emphatic and hearty amen, especially as, in the great majority of American prisons, an entrance fee of twenty-five cents is charged, which gives the custom still more the air of a public exhibition, and makes the state a showman for a few paltry coppers.

All this is derogatory to the dignity of government, and we have never seen the price of admission taken by prison authorities without a feeling, almost, of personal degradation, as being, in some sort, identified with the system. It pains us to add that more than a moiety of these visitors—one warden says five-sixths, and quite generally the response is two-thirds — are women. Under the system of general admission, without any responsible authorization, it often happens—and, in the nature of things, cannot be otherwise—that improper characters are introduced, which, as a matter of course, intensifies the evil influence of the practice. In one instance it was reported to us, that a woman, on successive visits to the prison, at each of which she had paid her quarter for the privilege of going in and through, adroitly dropped, in the right place and without discovery, piece by piece, for a certain convict acquaintance, a complete disguise, including false whiskers and moustache, intended to facilitate his escape, which would, no doubt, have been thereby readily effected, had not a fortunate accident revealed the intent by revealing the means of its accomplishment. In this case, the collusive attempt, through facilities afforded by the system of indiscriminate visitation, to aid a convict in his escape, was detected and foiled; but in how many cases such attempts have succeeded remains unknown and unwritten. It would not be surprising if more money, in the aggregate, should have been expended in efforts to recapture prisoners who have escaped in this way, than the entire amount of admission fees received in all the prisons of the land. A moral influence, of an exceedingly pernicious character, an influence which sets itself in deadly antagonism to all efforts at personal reformation, and which need not here be more specifically described, emanates from the presence of such a multitude of female visitors in our prisons. Numbers of wardens both spoke to us and wrote to us of this influence, in terms as emphatic as they were condemnatory.

It is an important question in the practical administration of a prison, whether or not its inmates are allowed to bring their cares, griefs, burdens and complaints to their chief for conference and counsel. The relation existing between the head of a penal institution and those incarcerated in it, considered in this view, constitutes of itself a moral agency, of high power and significance. We therefore instituted inquiries upon this point, the results of which we here briefly record. The answer to the main inquiry, given by every warden, was to the effect that convicts may bring their difficulties to him for solution and relief. The warden of the Connecticut state prison gives audience to such cases onece every two weeks, and oftener if desired. The warden of the prison of Northern Indiana hears complaints every evening. Mr. Haynes, of the

Massachusetts prison, informed us that he is in the habit of passing through all the workshops daily, thus giving to all who desire it an opportunity to speak to him and bring their troubles to his notice; or, if any so prefer, it is understood that they may come to his office at any hour of the day. The convicts in the Missouri penitentiary may, at any time, see the warden by asking permission of the keeper in charge. Mr. Miller expresses his preference for this plan over that which permits their visits at stated hours, because, as he conceives, only those who are urged by strong desire, and really have something to communicate, will make an occasion of coming; whereas, on the other plan, many would abuse the privilege of coming without any substantial cause. Mr. Cordier is accustomed to visit the cell room every evening after supper. As he passes along in front of the cells, any prisoner may speak to him on any subject he wishes. Mr. C. listens to their complaints, and disposes of them either immediately or on the following day, always, however, giving his reasons for deciding as he does, and not otherwise—a course which almost invariably carries the judgment of the convict along with him.

The testimony of all the wardens, with absolute unanimity, attests the excellent results flowing from this practice. It wins the confidence of the prisoners, attaches them to their chief, leads them to regard him as a friend, ever ready to shield and assist them, cheers many a sad heart, inspires the timid with hope, imparts courage to the despondent, and strengthens the resolution of the feeble and vacillating.*

---

* We have referred, in the last section, to Mr. G. B. Hubbell's practice in this regard, when he was at the head of the Sing Sing prison. We think it proper to make a more extended reference to that feature of his administration, by citing, in a note, the following extract from the annual report of the Prison Association for 1863: "Mr. Hubbell, within a month from the time of entering upon his duties as agent and warden, established a rule in this prison, quite unknown elsewhere, as far as the committee are informed, in this country or any other. It is that of setting apart, each day, the hour from three to four o'clock, P. M., for personal interviews with such convicts as may desire conversation with him. At that hour, any prisoner who has any burden, care, grief or anxiety on his mind, is at liberty to approach the chief officer of the institution, for the purpose of confiding to him his trouble and seeking from him such relief as it may be in his power and will to impart. On an average he receives some ten or twelve such visits every day. Members of this committee have sat by his side repeatedly during the hour appropriated to these interviews, listening to the multifarious complaints and requests presented, and marking his manner of meeting them, and they have been deeply impressed with the genuine kindness, the warm sympathy, the quiet self-possession, the calm wisdom, and the true christian courtesy displayed by this officer on these occasions. It was easy to see that the men confided implicitly in his judgment, acquiesced cheerfully in his decisions, and looked up to him and reverenced him as a father. It is scarcely too much to say, that

SECTION SEVENTH.

SECULAR INSTRUCTION.

A person, passing through a prison as a visitor on a certain occasion, was shocked at the profane speech of one of the convicts. " Why do you not have better thoughts ?" he inquired. " Better thoughts !" was the forlorn response, " where shall I get them ?"

In that startling question, coming to us from the dungeon, coming to us from a felon and an outcast, we have the whole philosophy of crime and reformation. " Better thoughts " are what society should have supplied to criminals before they became such, and so have prevented their fall. " Better thoughts," now that they have fallen and are suffering the punishment she has imposed for the breach of her laws, are what, by a double bond, she is required to supply them, to the end that, when released from the stern grasp of justice, they may " go and sin no more."

This is what is proposed in the intellectual instruction of prisoners, viz : to expel old thoughts from their minds, and to provide them with new and better materials for meditation. Far more active as well as extended efforts should be made to this end than has heretofore been the case. It is vain to talk of ignorant, inert and corrupt minds profiting by their own unaided reflections. They will either sleep over these, or do worse. No, they must be assailed from without. They must be plied with an external intellectual apparatus, in the form of lessons, lectures, dicussions, and books, by which the mind will be awakened, stimulated, and kept alive and alert ; and by which, also, it will be stored with " better thoughts " than the disgusting and corrupting images hitherto most familiar. By the mental stimulants here suggested, many a devil, as Captain Machonochie has expressed it, will be kept out, and, perhaps, some good angels be let in.

It appears from Mr. Hill's treatise on Crime, that in the Scottish prisons, and we believe the same is now true of English prisons, every prisoner, whether male or female, who is sentenced to three months' confinement or upwards, has an opportunity of learning

---

that hour, between three and four, governs Sing Sing to-day. At any rate, it spreads over the place an atmosphere, soft, mild, purifying and elevating. Nor are burdens and prayers the only things which it brings. Sometimes important information, disclosures vital to the interests of discipline, are brought to the chief by prisoners, who at that time find their way into his presence. Powerful is the hold which the influences emanating from this occasion give him upon the love and fidelity of the Sing Sing convicts, and they are not less beneficent than they are strong.

reading and writing, and frequently arithmetic also ; and in many of these prisons, this privilege is extended to all who desire it. But in our American prisons, unfortunately, the opportunity for such mental improvement is much narrower. Indeed, the history of school instruction in them is short and meagre.

The first notice we find of any instruction of this kind being imparted to convicts, during their incarceration, is contained in a report made to the New York Senate, in 1822, by a committee on the criminal law, in which, speaking of the state prison in Greenwich, now a part of the city of New York, they say: "Schools are established in the prison." Beyond this naked statement, no information is given. It is not likely that these schools amounted to much, as the committee immediately go on to say that the prison system had utterly failed as an agency for reformation; and not only so, but that it operated, with alarming efficacy, to increase and extend the love of vice, and a knowledge of the arts and practices of criminalty.

The next mention made of anything like scholastic instruction in prisons is in the report of Judge Gershom Powers to the Legislature of New York on the Auburn prison, in 1827. In that paper Mr. Powers states that early in 1826 it was found, on investigation, that fully one-eighth of the prisoners were either wholly unable to read, or could read only by spelling most of the words. Many more, it was ascertained, could not write, and were otherwise grossly ignorant. This suggested at once the connection between ignorance and crime. The duty of enlightening by education these ignorant and degraded transgressors, of giving them "better thoughts," and so making them better men, pressed heavily upon his mind. To this end, a Sunday-school was opened in May of that year, and fifty of the most ignorant, whose ages did not exceed twenty-five years, were placed in it. In November following, the number was increased to one hundred. The school met both morning and afternoon. The primary object appears to have been secular instruction, including writing and arithmetic as well as reading, combined with which were lessons of a religious character, designed to impress upon their minds the sense of moral and spiritual obligation. The privilege was embraced by the convicts with avidity and gratitude. Their application and industry were unremitting, and their progress in learning exceeded the most sanguine expectation. A report made by the superintendent in 1827 informs us that few could then be found in the school, with the exception of those recently admitted, who could not read the Bible with a good degree of readiness and fluency. The use to which some at least of the convicts put their new found ability may be seen in the answer of one of them to his teacher, who, having listened to his recitation of verses as long as he thought the time would allow, inquired how much more he had to recite. His reply was: "I believe I can say thirty or forty chapters." When this convict entered the school, he could scarcely spell out a single verse. An interesting feature of the school, to which we shall have occasion again to refer, was that the pupils who were put at writing and arithmetic were taught, a class in each branch, by convict teachers, who discharged the duty thus assigned them to the satisfaction of the authorities. Convicts learning to read were stimulated by the privilege held out to them of joining these classes, whenever they should have made sufficient proficiency.

We may mention, in passing, that in all the numerous Sabbath-schools noticed in the last section as having been organized in state prisons, teaching convicts to read was made a prime object; and before any provision of law had anywhere been made for giving secular instruction in prisons, not hundreds merely but thousands of prisoners had been taught this useful art.

In 1829, an act was passed by the Legislature of Kentucky, requiring the warden not only to procure, if possible, one sermon to be preached to the convicts on each Sabbath;" but also "to cause the convicts, who are unlearned in reading, writing and arithmetic, to be taught in one or other of these branches at least four hours every Sabbath day;" with a proviso annexed that the expenses should "not exceed $250 per annum." This was the first act ever passed in Kentucky, and, as far as we know, in any state of our union, providing means for the secular instruction of convicts. The act was enforced, and instruction given agreeably to its terms, during what remained of Mr. Joel Scott's wardenship, a period of five years. Mr. Scott informs us, in one of his reports, that the prisoners were taken from their cells on Sabbath morning, and were engaged throughout the day, meal times excepted, in religious instruction, or in learning to read, write and cypher. He further says, that at least one-third of those sent to the penitentiary are entirely illiterate, and that most of the others have a very imperfect knowledge of the rudiments imparted in common schools. The persons employed as teachers received two dollars a day for their services. The secular instruction required by the law was discontinued under Mr. Scott's immediate successor, Mr. Thomas S. Theobald. The practice was revived by Mr. Newton Craig, who succeeded Mr. Theobald, in all its original life and vigor. In his time, a new chapel and Sunday-school room, 60 by 40 feet, was built, which he pronounced the greatest improvement made in the prison for years. In this room the prisoners were assembled throughout the Lord's day, receiving lessons partly in religion and partly in the common school branches; the educated convicts teaching the illiterate, an arrangement reported as "working well." Two of the prison officers remained in the room to keep order, and see that the teachers did their duty. The prisoners are said to have taken a lively interest in the school, and their "profiting appeared unto all." The arrangement was regarded as a material aid in promoting morality and the reformation of the prisoners.

The same year, 1829, in which Kentucky enacted the law just noticed in regard to common school instruction in her penitentiary, a report, containing matter of interest on the same subject, was made to the Legislature of New York by commissioners Hopkins, Tibbetts and Allen. These gentlemen speak, in their report, of a suitable apartment as about being finished, at Sing Sing, for a "chapel and school room." Whether the school room here referred to was for a Sunday or a secular school does not appear; most probably the former; for, although no Sabbath school was then in existence, a year or two afterwards the chaplain speaks of such a school as in successful operation. Moreover, it is plain from his report that the instruction imparted was largely of a common school character. He says that the school consisted of sixty to eighty men, all of whom were unable to read on entering, and most of whom did not even know the alphabet; adding that they showed an intense desire to learn, and that their progress corresponded to their zeal.

The commissioners, in their report, state that the chaplain, Mr. Barrett, was making the greatest exertion to teach the ignorant to read, making use of the Bible as his only school book, and imparting his lessons at the grate of their cell doors. An interesting account is given of a convict whom he taught to read in five weeks, from the first chapter of Genesis. At the end of the fifth week, he read fluently and correctly the whole of the first chapter, and, of course, after that had no more difficulty. He had mastered the art, and held in his hand the key to all the treasures of wisdom.

To him the question had been solved, where and how he should get "better thoughts."

In the report of the Prison Discipline Society, for 1841, three items of interest are recorded, bearing on the subject of secular instruction in prisons, and showing a gratifying advance in public opinion in that direction. The first is a statement to the effect that, in the House of Correction in South Boston, a day school had been taught by the clerk, two hours each day, during several years, for a class of young convicts, in the common branches of knowledge, in a room carefully fitted up for that purpose, and that great good had resulted therefrom. The second is a declaration of the Governor of New York, Wm. H. Seward, in his annual message, in these words : " I would have the school room, in the prison, fitted as carefully as the solitary cell and the workshop ; and, although attendance there cannot be so frequent, I would have it quite as regular." The third is an urgent plea by the chaplain of the prison at Wethersfield, the Rev. Josiah Brewer, in his report for that year, for school instruction to convicts. On turning to the report referred to, we find that, after urging that attention to the elementary branches be exacted of the more illiterate, he says : " And why should not oral instruction, by familiar lectures on the practical concerns of life, and various topics of history, science and literature, be imparted to all ? The laws of the human mind undergo no change, surely, by the body's being deprived of its liberty ; and what has been found, on full experiment, to elevate the tone of society generally, holds out the promise of good in particular instances." Here we have Mr. Organ's lectures in the intermediate prisons of Ireland clearly foreshadowed.

These are the first intimations we have anywhere met with of giving regular secular instruction to convicts in schools and classes. The next year, 1842, the same idea was further urged by a committee of the Legislature, in reference to the Connecticut state prison. They say: " The opportunities for giving instruction on week days are not considerable. The committee would recommend that prisoners, in small divisions, should, in rotation, have time and opportunity of receiving instruction from the chaplain. If half of each day, or from three to four hours, were allowed among two or three such small divisions of prisoners, the whole number might have an hour and a half or two hours once a fortnight, which would not take much from the earnings of each prisoner. Better still, if each division could be tried faithfully with an hour and a half, or two hours once in each week, in addition to the opportunities now afforded to them." The same year, the directors of the prison, among whom we observe the name of the Hon. Henry Barnard, Commissioner of the new Bureau of Education in Washington, adopted a code of rules and regulations, relating to the duties of the chaplain, one of which is that "he shall use his utmost endeavors to instruct, through the grating of the cell doors, all those who are unable to read."

The chaplains of Auburn and Sing Sing, about the same time, were pleading hard, and piling argument upon argument, for an enlargement of the means of instruction in their respective prisons. They insist that it is equally the dictate of philanthropy and sound policy that larger and more suitable provision should be made for the education of the convicts, and that at least one or two hours each day should be devoted to their intellectual improvement, alleging that thus, and not otherwise, that is, by elevating their minds and giving them "better thoughts," can they be prepared to become better sons, better husbands, better fathers, better citizens. Mr. Luckey states that the Sunday-school at Sing Sing had increased, within the year, from 114 to 337, one-half of whom were learning to read; and of those who had been discharged during the same time, no less than twenty-five had learned the art in the prison. A pleasing circumstance here was that from the lack of other teachers, a number of the convicts were employed in that capacity, who discharged the duty with great acceptance, taking the greatest interest in it, and preparing themselves for it with the utmost care by the use of Bible dictionaries, sacred geographies, and such other help as they could obtain. One of these convict teachers, having received a pardon from the Governor on Friday morning, begged that he might remain in the prison till Monday, that he might meet his Sabbath class once more, a request which shows more clearly than perhaps anything else could, the interest taken in the work.

Mr. Francis C. Gray, in his "Prison Discipline in America," published in 1848, informs us that, at that time, there was, in the Massachusetts prison, a society for moral improvement and mutual aid—in effect, as we shall see, a debating society—of which the warden, chaplain and clerk were president, vice-president and secretary. All convicts, approved by the president, could become members, on signing the constitution, which contained a promise to lead an orderly, upright life, and never to taste intoxicating liquor after their discharge. About three-fourths of the prisoners were members. There was a committee of conference, consisting of the officers and six convicts, chosen by their fellow members and approved by the president, to prepare business and propose measures for promoting the objects in view. The society held its meetings once a fortnight, at which the chief business was the free discussion of some question proposed at the previous sitting. Here we have the weekly competitive examinations of Mr. Organ's intermediate prisoners at Smithfield foreshadowed, just as we saw the foreshadowing of his system of daily lectures in one of the reports of the chaplain of the Connecticut state prison. "The society was founded," Mr. Gray observes, "on the consideration that convicts are to return to the society of men, not so totally different from themselves, as some would represent, and on the belief that, though erring and criminal men, they are not such incarnate demons, that every word is infectious, and every touch contamination; but that, on the contrary, all such intercourse among them as does not tend to corrupt them, to produce disorder, or to interrupt their labor, *and takes place in the presence and within the hearing of the officers,* engaging the sympathies and occupying and interesting the minds of the prisoners, is not only harmless, but humanizing and beneficial." This is a view which we have endeavored to enforce in our section on discipline, and we are glad to find it embraced and supported by so calm and philosophical a thinker as Mr. Gray.

In 1847, a comprehensive prison act, prepared by a committee of the Prison Association, was passed by the Legislature of New York, one of the provisions of which was that common school teachers should be appointed for all the state prisons, proportionate in number to the size of each prison, and to the number likely to be found therein unable to read. We have seen that, as far back as 1829, Kentucky provided, by law, for four hours' instruction of her convicts in reading, writing and arithmetic, to be given on the Sabbath; but this was the first law ever enacted in the United States, creating a distinct class of officers, whose duty it should be to impart such instruction during the week. Hence the Prison Discipline Society, in their report of 1852, say: "To the state of New York belongs the honor of taking the lead in this branch of prison discipline, viz: common education in prisons." Unfortunately, the salary attached to the office was so small ($150) that teachers could be obtained for only one hour daily.

Other states have followed the example of New York. Generally this business is given into the charge of the chaplains, and not unfrequently they are required to do the teaching themselves ; sometimes in a school, but more commonly through the gratings of the cell doors. We append the provision of the prison act of Indiana relating to this subject : " The moral instructor shall, in addition to his other duties and services, teach such of the convicts as the' warden may send to him for the purpose, the art of reading, writing, arithmetic and geography, at such hours as may be found most conducive to the interests of the institution."*

Libraries in·prisons, now regarded as the right arm of discipline and an essential agent in reformation, sprang up, as a general thing, at a later date than efforts to educate the more ignorant class of prisoners, of which, indeed, they are but the natural outgrowth. The first notice we find, looking towards the creation of a prison library, is in a code of rules and regulations enacted by the inspectors of the Kentucky penitentiary, as far back as the year 1802. The following is the provision of the said code relating to this subject : " The convicts shall be encouraged to employ any leisure time in reading; and *donations of books* will be thankfully received ; and the keeper shall take care of them, and procure a list, with the names of the donors."

The first prison library in New York, and one of the earliest, if not the earliest, in the United States (except what may have resulted from the above recited action in Kentucky), was established in Sing Sing prison in 1840, under Mr. D. L. Seymour, as principal officer, and the Rev. Jno. Luckey, as chaplain. These gentlemen applied to Gov. Wm. H. Seward, who told them to get what books were wanted and send the bill to him. About three hundred dollars' worth were procured, and Mr. Seward paid the bill out of his private purse.

---

* While these sheets are going through the press, we have received a letter from Mr. Cordier, of Wisconsin, of which the following is an extract:

"I have succeeded in having a bill passed by our Legislature last winter, authorizing me to establish a school for the purpose of teaching our convicts in the common branches of education. Saturday and Sunday afternoons are now devoted to this object. It is really surprising to notice the zeal manifested, even by aged men, to learn to read and write. I am proud to say, that hereafter no convict will leave this prison without a knowledge of those two useful and important branches. And what an excellent means of discipline! Not to be deprived of the advantages this school affords. all the scholars behave themselves with the utmost decorum. About seventy visit the school now, and not one of them ever gave cause for complaint. I am convinced that secular instruction has been neglected to a great extent in our prisons. Ignorance, being the mother of nearly all crimes, must certainly be removed at first, if a thorough reformation shall be realized. As to this school, I wish only to say, that I have much faith in the success of our undertaking."

The following year, 1841, a hundred dollars were appropriated by the Legislature of New Jersey, to lay the foundation of a library in the state prison at Trenton.

In 1847, we find libraries existing in most of the state prisons of the country, one of which—that of Ohio—is reported as containing 3,000 volumes.

The testimony of prison officers was uniform as to the good effects of this agency. They say that the books were sought with eagerness and read with avidity by large numbers of convicts, and that as the fondness for reading increased, the occasion for punishment diminished. Many had evidently become interested in acquiring useful knowledge, and, as a consequence, they were far more contented and cheerful.

The foundation of one prison library is so unique, and withal so interesting, that we cannot withhold it. In the fall of 1846, a clergyman from Illinois, on invitation by the chaplain, conducted the usual evening service in the chapel of the Massachusetts state prison. He expressed his particular delight at seeing the prison library, and congratulated the prisoners that they were so much better off in this respect than the inmates of the state prison at Alton, who had no books at all. The above statement is condensed from the work on Prison Discipline in America by Mr. Gray, who proceeds to say: "The next day, as the chaplain was walking through one of the work shops, a prisoner having asked leave to quit his work and speak to him, told him that he had some books which he could spare, and should like to send to the prisoners at Alton, if permitted, and so had some of his shopmates. The chaplain, having conferred with the warden, stated in the chapel, after evening prayers, that such an application had been made to him, and added, that if any prisoner had books which he wished to send to the Alton prison, he might leave them in the adjoining room, on coming to prayers the next morning. He also sent word to his friend the clergyman, that if he would call at the prison the next day, he would find some books for Alton. The reverend gentleman went accordingly, and took with him a large silk handkerchief to carry off the books. What was his astonishment to find, in the room adjoining the chapel, more than four hundred bound volumes, besides tracts and pamphlets. The silk handkerchief would not do; and the prisoners requested permission to make boxes to pack the books in."

Having thus sketched, as far as the sources of information were open to us and the limits to which we are confined would permit, the origin and progress of secular instruction in prisons, we now proceed to exhibit the actual state and condition of this important agency in the prisons to which our observations extended.

The provision made for the instruction of the convicts in the provincial penitentiary of Canada, in the elementary branches of a common education, is worthy of a humane and enlightened government. A teacher is employed who gives his whole time to the work. He is aided by as many assistants as may be needed, who are selected from the best educated and best conducted of the convicts. The coöperation of these convict teachers in the work of instruction is found to be of essential service. Under the direction and superintendence of the school master, they teach the classes assigned them to the entire satisfaction of the prison authorities. The school is attended by all the inmates of the prison who need instruction in reading, writing or arithmetic, and who are not incapacitated from learning by defective sight, deafness, mental imbecility, or other infirmity. There are four distinct sections of prisoners, whose members come under instruction in the course of the day, as follows: A morning class, commencing at six o'clock in summer and seven and a half in winter, and closing at nine; a noon class, commencing at twelve and a half and closing at one; an afternoon class, commencing at one and closing at three; and an evening class, from six to seven and a half in summer, and from five to seven in winter. The noon class, which is the largest, numbering sixty or more members, is composed of convicts who are engaged on contract work, and who devote to lesson learning one-half of the time allotted to the mid-day meal. The evening class is made up of prisoners who labor on the Rockwood Asylum for Criminal Insane, at the quarry, and on farm and garden work. Between 200 and 300 convicts are in this manner brought under daily instruction for a period varying from half an hour to three hours. The gentleman who had officiated as schoolmaster for some fifteen years, had just retired, and his successor had not been appointed at the time of our visit, so that, much to our regret, we had no opportunity of seeing the prison schools in operation. From the printed reports of the late teacher, we learn that these ignorant, criminal and degraded beings—though he was ever alone and unarmed in the midst of them—observed, during school hours, the strictest order and decorum; that they highly prized the opportunities for improvement afforded them; that their thirst for knowledge increased in proportion as it was gratified; and that they applied themselves to study with a zeal worthy of all praise, and with a success equal to that attained by the generality of pupils in other schools.

There is no prison in the United States, we are sorry to say, in which so much time and toil are given to this department of reformatory agencies.

The proportion of prisoners in the state prisons, who are unable to read at the time of their committal, varies a good deal in the several states; the extremes, as reported, being from one-twentieth in Vermont, where the proportion of the wholly illiterate is smallest, to one-third in Wisconsin, where it is greatest. In other states, the proportion fluctuates between these extremes. In Maine, it is reported at one-fifteenth; in Massachusetts, at one-tenth; in Connecticut, at one-eighth; in New Hampshire and Pennsylvania, at one-seventh; in Indiana and Ohio, at one-fourth; in New York, one-tenth; at Auburn, one-fifth; at Clinton, and one-third at Sing Sing. Of convicts who give themselves in as able to read, from a fourth to a half cannot, as a general thing, do so without spelling out more or less of the words; and in most prisons, few really good readers are received.

In much the larger number of prisons, secular instruction is imparted; but in some, and in this category are included Kentucky, Massachusetts, Michigan, Missouri, Rhode Island, Vermont and Wisconsin, either none at all is given, or only such as is imparted in Sabbath-schools. In two states only, whose prisons were examined by us—Indiana and Ohio—is instruction given in classes. In both these states, the chaplains are the teachers.

In Indiana, the school is held from November 1st to March 1st, a period of only four months in the year. We presume it to be held in the evening, as the law which creates it requires that the convicts should be taught "at such hours as may be found most conducive to the interests of the institution;" which means, doubtless, "least prejudicial to its *financial* interests," as these, in American nomenclature, are *the* interests in all penal establishments. The convicts generally attend the school, and take much interest in its exercises.

In Ohio, school is held, as it should be, throughout the year, on five days of each week, being omitted on Saturday. The hours are from three o'clock, P. M., to the closing up of the prison at night. Many commence with the alphabet, and are taught separately till they begin to read, after which they are grouped into classes, and advanced by regular gradations in school readers (McGuffie's first, second, third and fourth). Penmanship, arithmetic, geography and grammar are also taught. Very general interest is taken in the school by the prisoners, and in some instances, we were told, remarkable proficiency is shown. The chaplain is aided by convicts in the work of instruction.

In Connecticut, New Hampshire, and the western penitentiary of Pennsylvania, secular instruction is given by the chaplains to each prisoner separately, at the door of his cell; and in Maine (for the present) by the wife of the warden, in the same way. In the western penitentiary, the warden informed us, very little interest is taken by the convicts in these exercises. In the other prisons named in this paragraph, most of the prisoners were reported as taking a lively interest and making good proficiency in their studies.

In the three state prisons of New York, and the eastern penitentiary of Pennsylvania, schoolmasters are employed to give lessons to the convicts. In both these states, the lessons are given to the prisoners in their cells. In New York this is done only at night, and through the gratings of the cell doors. In Pennsylvania, instruction is given throughout the day, and the teachers enter the cells for the purpose.

In Ohio and Connecticut alone, as far as we are informed, is instruction imparted in branches as high as geography and grammar; in the latter state, even rhetoric is taught to some. Elsewhere, only reading and writing are taught, and the rudiments of arithmetic; the progress in this latter branch not being ordinarily beyond the rule of three, if indeed it reach even to that point.

All the prisons visited by us have miscellaneous libraries for the use of the prisoners. The aggregate number of volumes in thirteen prisons is 20,413, being an average of 1,570 to each. The largest prison library in the country is that at Sing Sing, which contains 4,000 volumes, and the smallest reported is in the Wisconsin prison, containing 250 volumes.

In the major part of the prisons, the chaplains, either independently or in conjunction with the wardens, are charged with the duty of selecting the books for the libraries. In a few, this duty is devolved upon the wardens; and in a still smaller number, on the inspectors.

The character of the books composing the prison libraries is, as might be expected, quite miscellaneous. Works on religion, histories, biographies, travels, works on science and general literature, and standard novels (those of a sensational character being generally excluded) predominate.

In the prisons of Ohio and Wisconsin, prisoners are not allowed a choice as to the books to be read by them, but are furnished, in the former once in two weeks and in the latter once each week, with such as the officers may choose to give them—an arrangement which we cannot commend, and which we were surprised to find in institutions where there is so much, in other respects, to approve. In all the other prisons visited by us, the convicts are allowed to select such books as may suit their taste. It is not strange that the preference should be given, in the majority of cases, to story books, magazines, and the lighter literature. But the reading of convicts is by no means confined to works of this character. Histories, travels, biographies, and even treatises on science and philosophy, find many readers. This we found to be pre-eminently the case in the Massachusetts state prison, where Humboldt's Cosmos, and other works of a no less elevated and philosophical character have been read through by many of the convicts. Indeed, the testimony is quite uniform to the effect that numbers of the prisoners are most evidently growing in useful knowledge; and we think, from the evidence before us, that there is more reading, and that of a solid character, too, done by the convicts in our American state prisons, than by any equal number of working people taken promiscuously in free society. On this subject Mr. Cordier, of Wisconsin, says: "I really belive that no convict, unless he be a perfect idiot, leaves the prison without having his mind improved, and without having gained some knowledge."

The method of distributing the books to the prisoners varies in different prisons. In Massachusetts the following plan is adopted: The convicts are allowed to take out one book at a time, on Mondays and Saturdays, and they keep it a fortnight. If it is wanted for a longer period, permission must be obtained from the librarian. Each volume is numbered, and every prisoner has a catalogue and card, and puts down on the card the numbers of (say twenty to fifty) such books as he would like to read, so that he may be sure of securing some one. He lays his book, after he has read it, on the stool in his cell, with the card in the book, and the runner takes them and carries them to the assistant librarian, who changes the book and sends back another. As the book is read, the number is rubbed off the card, and another one placed in its stead.

A somewhat smilar method of distribution is pursued in the eastern penitentiary, Pa. The books are distributed every two weeks, and each applicant is allowed to take out one large volume or two of more moderate size. Every convict has in his cell a printed catalogue and a card slate, on which he marks eighteen numbers, out of which the librarian is able to obtain some book that will suit his taste, though not always the one that he would prefer.

A very different plan from either of the above is adopted in two of our New York prisons—those at Sing Sing and Clinton. There the prisoners come in squads or companies, once in three weeks, and each one selects one or two volumes for himself of those that may be upon the shelves at the time. No doubt a good deal of time is consumed in this way, and the work might be done, is done in other prisons, in a much shorter period. But it is at least doubtful whether it would be wise to change the method on this ground. There are obvious advantages, and those connected with the higher ends of prison discipline, in the mode of distribution practised in these prisons. The coming of several hundred prisoners every three weeks into the chaplain's office affords him the opportunity of becoming personally acquainted with them, and of dropping into their ear, perchance into their heart, many a wise counsel and exhortation. These opportunities, we have reason to think, are gladly embraced and faithfully used.

At Auburn, a plan is in use, differing from either of the above and, as it strikes us, inferior to both. Prisoners have the privilege of exchanging their books once a week. The chaplain sends a quantity of books to each shop, together with a list of the same, to the keeper; and thus the exchange is effected in the shop where they are at work. The objection to this is, first, that it limits the convict's selection to a very small part of the library, and, secondly, that it must be a source (so, at least, we should think) of more or less disorder in the workshops.

The rule in all prisons is to examine books on their return; but it is enforced, as indeed all rules are, with different degrees of stringency. In the Wisconsin prison, if books—and they are carefully scrutinized when returned—are found soiled, dog-eared or in any way marred or defaced, the offender is deprived of the privilege of the library for a certain time, which is longer or shorter according to the extent of the injury done to the book. All injuries to books are recorded for future reference.

In all our state prisons, the proportion of prisoners who take out books is very large ; indeed the general if not the universal rule is, that all draw books who are able to read. We were anxious to ascertain whether the books so taken out are really read by the persons receiving them. The answers to our inquiries on this point were unanimous to the effect that such was undoubtedly the fact in the great majority of cases. On calling for the proofs of this, they were stated to be, first, the appearance of the books when returned; secondly, observation of the prisoners in their cells; thirdly, their comments on the books; and fourthly, questioning them on the subject-matter of the volumes taken out. In reference to the second of the above named proofs, the Rev. Mr. Ives, of Auburn, remarked: "In passing through the galleries, I see the men almost all engaged in reading. I have often been through on purpose to see what proportion were thus engaged, and have found ninety-seven out of one hundred. In the shops it is the same; when their tasks are finished." Wardens and chaplains of other prisons made substantially the same statement.

Convicts in all the state prisons have considerable time which they can devote to reading, if they are so disposed. Everywhere they have the whole of Sunday, after deducting the portion spent in public worship and the Sabbath-school, where such exists. Besides this, they have for reading, during the day and evening, on an average, from two to four hours. In the New York state prisons, prisoners are allowed to take their library books to the workshops, and read in them after they have finished the task of the day; but nowhere else, as far as we could learn, even where task work is in vogue, except occasionally by special permission.

In far the greater number of state prisons, the convicts are not allowed to take or read secular newspapers, but the reverse of this is true as regards magazines. In Wisconsin, and we believe also in Missouri, both classes of publications may be taken by the prisoners. In Maine, Harpers' Weekly is permitted.

The legislatures of many of the states make a fixed annual appropriation for the increase of the prison libraries. New York appropriates for her three prisons, $950; Pennsylvania for her two, $450 ; Michigan, $300 ; Massachusetts, $200 ; Connecticut, $100; New Hampshire, $50 to $100; Vermont, $25. The legislatures of Ohio, Wisconsin and other states appropriate for this purpose only on application by the prison authorities, accompanied with a statement of the necessities, and the amount required to meet the same.

We made it a point of special inquiry to ascertain the opinions. of prison officers, both wardens and chaplains, as to the utility of libraries in prisons. With a solitary exception—that of Dr. Campbell, of the western penitentiary, Pa., who regards the library as " of doubtful influence "—we found a perfect agreement among these officers in thinking a prison library a most important instrument of good. With singular unanimity, they represent it as valuable in communicating useful knowledge to the prisoners; in elevating their minds; in beguiling many a tedious and weary hour; in making them cheerful and contented; in affording them good material for reflection, and so diverting their minds from brooding over past offences and meditating schemes of future mischief; in affording good topics of conversation with them; in improving the discipline of prison; and in constituting one of the best and most effective of reformatory agencies. We quite agree, too, with Mr. Hill, in thinking it important that a prison library should contain many books which, while free from anything immoral or irreligious, are both interesting and entertaining. This will tend to create a taste for reading, to inspire a liking for other than sensual pleasures, and to give the mind cheerful subjects of thought, in addition to those of a more serious cast. A due mixture of books of this cheerful type, so far from interfering with reading of a more solid and even religious character, adds fresh zest to such reading. A prisoner, much given to drinking, and never a reader prior to his incarceration, read Robinson Crusoe in prison. It was the first book of entertainment he had ever read, and it evidently awakened in him a thirst for reading, which, by affording him pleasant occupation at home, would naturally tend to wean him from his habit of drinking. This prisoner was found, on examination, to have fully appreciated the great moral of the book, viz., that, under whatever circumstances a person may be placed, he can, by effort and perseverance, improve his condition. It was quite manifest, too, that his reading of this book did not at all interfere with his reading of the Bible; and his chaplain declared himself highly satisfied with his answers on the part of the Bible read by him during the week he was reading Robinson Crusoe.

It would be a good plan to examine prisoners on the subject-matter of the books which they read. If a prisoner, on receiving a book, were told that in due time he would be questioned respecting its contents, and required to give his views of their character and merits, this notification would make him more careful in its perusal; would afford a useful exercise for his intellect and memory; would offer good topics for conversation with him; would help him to derive from books all the benefits they are capable of yielding; would lead to the selection of books by different prisoners better adapted to their respective mental development; and would qualify him by degrees better to understand their subjects and to appreciate both their merits and their demerits. We would not, however, have this plan forced upon convicts against their will, as in that case reading might become a task instead of an amusement, and, as a consequence, be less pursued than it is now. But with the prisoner's hearty assent, we are persuaded that the plan would be highly to his advantage.

It will have been observed that in none of the state prisons visited by us, except so far as secular instruction is imparted in Sabbath schools, are the prisoners taught in classes, save only in those of Ohio and northern Indiana. Everywhere else, lessons are given either in the cell or at the cell door, mostly by the chaplains, but in New York by special teachers, of whom there are employed some eight or ten. This method of instruction in the separate cells is liable to very serious objections. Either instruction must be imparted to a most limited extent, or, in prisons conducted on the Auburn plan, where lessons can be given only at night, teachers must be multiplied so that there shall be one to every half dozen convicts. Now, even those who are most sceptical on the subject of penitentiary reformation, still agree that every opportunity should be given for improvement, and every facility afforded for amendment; and that, at least, a foundation should be laid for moral knowledge by imparting the elements of literary education to those who are ignorant ; of whom, as we have seen, the number confined in our prisons is always considerable. We, indeed, go much farther than this. We think that a penal establishment—certainly in the later stages of imprisonment—should be, as it were, one vast school, in which almost everything is made subservient to instruction in some form or other—mental, moral, religious or industrial. Of course, we would have school rooms fitted up and classes formed, into which should be gathered numbers of those in similar stages of advancement. In addition to which, we would have libraries, lectures, competitive examinations, and even museums, and every other needful appliance liberally provided, calculated to excite, and, in a greater or less degree, to gratify the rational curiosity of each. In this conviction we are fortified by the opinion of Mr. F. B. Sanborn, the intelligent secretary of the Massachusetts Board of State Charities, who, in his evidence before the commission of 1866, said : "I doubt if the instruction of prisoners has ever been carried far enough anywhere ; even in Ireland, it would be possible to improve it. I would have *all* convicts taught something, and put in the way of teaching themselves. As a class, they are wretchedly ignorant, and have sinned through some form of ignorance, conjoined with vice. To educate them is the plain duty of the state ; and, when seriously undertaken, their education would show important results. A portion of each day, as well as the evening, should be given to this duty; and those not compelled to labor should be stimulated to some mental occupation, as a defence against bad habits and evil thoughts."

The better educated and better behaved prisoners might, with propriety and advantage, be employed to assist the schoolmaster in the instruction of his classes. We have seen that this service is very acceptably performed in the secular schools of the provincial penitentiary of Canada and the state prison of Ohio, and also in quite a number of prison Sabbath-schools. Not only, as suggested by Mr. Hill, might the prison funds be economized by making use of assistance of this kind, but much good might often be done to the prisoners who gave it, since it would bring into action one of the most improving tendencies, that arising from the consciousness of being useful to others. It would, of course, be necessary to use care in the selection of prisoners to be so employed ; but with intelligent superintendence, there would be little, if any, difficulty in that respect.

We are sorry to be obliged to report that in many state prisons, our own among the number, very inadequate provison is made for the prisoners' reading at night. In England, there is a gas burner in every cell; in America, such an arrangement, we believe, is quite unknown. Lights, whether from gas or oil, are placed in the corridors, and very often at such a distance from each other that scarcely one prisoner in ten can see to read. For about five months in the year, the convicts are locked in their cells from thirteen to fifteen hours a day. There are prisons—we wish the number were less—in which, during all these long and dreary hours, only those few prisoners whose cells happen to be near the lights, can make any use of their books; all the rest being condemned to intellectual starvation, with ample stores at hand, as Tantalus was to eternal thirst, with the water reaching to his chin. Thus is left to the darkness of his cell and the deeper, sadder darkness of an ignorant, benighted mind, many a young man, who, if opportunity were afforded him of acquiring useful knowledge, might, despite his fall and its forlorn consequences, be awakened to hope, to cheerfulness, to virtue. More than once have we heard bitter lamentations by convicts over their inability, from want of light, to occupy themselves in reading, while locked in their cells during the long winter evenings. We look upon such deprivation as a hardship and a wrong; and we have known it to be, in many ways, most hurtful in its consequences. We think it no more than right—and certainly it would be good policy—that prisoners should have at least two hours of light for reading every night during the winter months. Such opportunity, added to the other means of enlightenment recommended in this section, would go a long way towards the solution of the problem proposed by the wretched prisoner mentioned in its opening sentences, " Where shall I get better thoughts?"

SECTION EIGHTH.

PHYSICAL AND HYGIENIC RELATIONS.

In general, the ventilation of American state prisons is very imperfect; and the same is true of the provincial penitentiary of Canada. On entering them, one is met by an odor made up of animal secretions, damp walls, pent-up dormitories and musty clothing. Yet, with the exception of a few in the more newly settled states, our prisons, for the most part, appear to be kept thoroughly clean, and well whitewashed. Whence, then, this disagreeable odor? It can come only from the want of adequate ventilation. Many of the prisons, probably the most of them, have ventilating flues in the walls of the cells, but there is no heat in them to create a current, and on trial with a lighted match, while, in some, the flame was slightly drawn into the opening, in others there was no draft at all. The best ventilation we found was in the Massachusetts state prison and the Albany penitentiary.

The prisons are variously heated with steam, coal stoves, and wood stoves. Steam, where used, is found the most economical, and the warmth created by it is much more evenly diffused. The degree of heat introduced cannot, for the most part, be accurately measured, as few, if any of the prisons are provided with thermometers, an instrument which ought to be found in all. Generally the officers claim that the cell houses are kept comfortably warm even in the coldest weather; while some admit that this cannot be effected with their existing apparatus for the purpose.

In a considerable proportion of the state prisons, a sufficient amount of sunlight is admitted to enable all the prisoners to read with ease and comfort; but in many this is not the case. In some, none can well see to read, especially in books with fine print, in a very cloudy day; in others, only those whose cells happen to be directly opposite the windows.

At night, the major part of the prisons are lighted by gas in the corridors; the others by kerosene lamps. In none of our prisons are the cells provided with burners, as is almost, if not quite, universally the case in New England. In Maine, Wisconsin, and Pennsylvania, each prisoner is provided with a lamp in his cell; in Michigan, with a candle. The time of extinguishing the lights in different institutions, varies from seven and a half to nine. We have already stated that, while in some prisons there are burners enough to enable all to read without straining the eyes, yet in not a few there is such a deficiency of light that much the larger portion are denied this privilege; a policy as contrary to wisdom as it is to humanity, since long confinement in darkness is injurious to the physical, mental, and moral interests of the convict, weakening the intellect, inducing mental indolence, blunting the moral sensibilities, exciting the passions, quickening and feeding a licentious imagination, and, in a word, debasing and brutifying the man.

In regard to the rations of the convict prisons of the United States and Canada, our general remark is, that they are abundant and good; if anything, too much so for persons convicted of crime, and undergoing the penalty of their transgressions. We think there is not one, in which there is any weighing or measuring of the food supplied; all have as much as they want, be the same less or more. We subjoin the dietaries of a few, both to confirm our statement, and to serve as a specimen of the whole.

Maine.—The warden, in his communication to us, says: " The prisoners have to eat—plenty of nice fish, brown and white bread, and coffee for breakfast; for dinner, two or more of these dishes on different days—baked beans and pork, corned beef, potatoes, stewed peas, and (once a week) fresh beef soup; for supper, wheat, brown and hard bread, with coffee."

Massachusetts.—For breakfast, meat hash and fish hash on alternate days, with brown bread and coffee ; for dinner, baked beans and pork on Sunday and Friday, corned beef and potatoes Monday, beef soup with the meat in it Tuesday and Saturday, stewed peas and pork Wednesday, and fish chowder, with white bread on Sunday, and brown bread all the other days ; for supper, mush and molasses with coffee on Tuesday, and white bread and coffee all the other days.

Wisconsin.—For breakfast, beef and potatoes five days, and beef hash two days, with white bread and coffee every day ; for dinner, beef soup with rice Sunday and Thursday, beef and potatoes Monday, vegetable soup and beef Tuesday. baked beans and pork Wednesday, codfish and mashed potatoes Friday, corned beef and potatoes Saturday, with white bread every day ; for supper, ginger bread and molasses Sunday, white bread and butter Monday, Tuesday, Thursday and Friday, brown bread and molasses Wednesday, and mush and molasses Saturday.

Eastern Penitentiary, Pa.—For breakfast, bread and coffee throughout the week ; for dinner, beef (always fresh) three days, mutton three days, and salt or smoked pork one day, with soup made from the meat as a uniform accompaniment, to which vegetables, with rice or barley are added. Potatoes, beans, hominy, and cabbage are the standard vegetables, but lettuce, onions, and tomatoes are furnished in their season, fresh from the prison grounds. We have no memorandum of the evening meal, but believe it to be usually, if not invariably, mush and molasses.

Ohio.—The warden reports : "The prisoners' fare is—bread (corn meal and wheat flour mixed), fresh beef and salt pork (alternately), potatoes, beans, cabbages, onions, vegetable soup (three times a week), and butter (twice a week)."

New York.—The following is the dietary at Sing Sing : Breakfast is uniform throughout the week, consisting of beef hash, bread, and coffee. Supper is also uniform, and consists of either mush and molasses, or bread and molasses, at the option of the prisoner. Bread is made fresh every day of the common grades of wheat flour and corn meal combined. It is furnished without stint at every meal. The dinner ration varies from day to day. Monday— corned beef and beans or peas, usually made into soup. Vinegar, salt and pepper are supplied daily, so that each can season his food to his own liking. Tuesday—corned beef and boiled potatoes. Wednesday—fresh beef boiled, and soup made of the liquor, in which are boiled turnips, carrots, onions, rice and a little flour, making, when properly seasoned, a savory and palatable dish. Occasionally, instead of soup, a stew is given, made of pork, fresh beef, potatoes and onions, which is much relished. Thursday— corned beef and cabbage or beets, with potatoes. Friday—salt fish, with boiled potatoes. Corn bread is often given on Friday, and sometimes warm from the oven. Saturday—same as Wednes- day. Sunday—pork and potatoes, with white bread made of a better quality of flour, and occasionally pickles. For prison beef, it is quite usual to purchase only the rougher and cheaper parts of the animal; in Sing Sing, on the contrary, the entire carcass is bought and used for convicts' rations.

In all the New England state prisons, and in those of Pennsyl- vania, as a matter of course, convicts take their meals in the cells. Almost everywhere else, they eat together; in Wisconsin, all meals are taken in the cells, not because any preference is felt for that mode, but simply for the want of a common dining hall. As a general thing, a strong preference is felt for the method in actual use. Mr. Haynes, of Massachusetts, says: "The plan of taking the meals in the cells is here considered preferable, for the reason that it allows the prisoners to rest and read, and also because it affords the officers an opportunity to eat their meals at the same time." On the other hand, Mr. Prentice, of Ohio, states his opin- ion in these words: "The mode of giving the meals in a large hall is preferred, as it is infinitely less trouble."

There are two methods of procuring supplies; one by contracts running for a greater or less period (commonly a year), the other at the discretion of the warden. The first of these methods was most prevalent formerly, the latter is most common now, and, in our opinion, the better has superseded the worse. Contracts for furnishing provisions, as a matter of course, are given to the low- est bidder; and, equally as a matter of course, the cheapest article is supplied which the terms of the contract will permit. Besides, under the system of supplies by contract, the ration is fixed by an inflexible rule; whereas, when provisions are purchased in open market, it can be varied as considerations of health and discipline may require. But let us hear what the advocates of each system have to say in its favor. Mr. Cordier, of Wisconsin, says: "I do not believe in the contract system. As soon as a contract (say for flour or beef) is let—and contracts of that kind generally run for a year—the contractor tries to make just as much out of it as he can, and therefore needs constant watching—a very unpleasant business. Aside from this, opportunities are constantly arising for purchasing things at cheaper rates than those specified in the contract." Per contra, Mr. Seaton, of Michigan, gives his view thus: "Most supplies are procured by contract—contract lasting one year. This system is thought best, for the reason that the supplies can be procured just as good, just as cheap, and with far less trouble." On the last point, all must agree with Mr. Seaton; but, much as we commonly respect his judgment, we dissent from it on the other two. We think that supplies, as good in quality would be dearer; and that, if as cheap in price, they would be of an inferior grade.

Not only is a suitable prison dietary necessary to the health of the convicts, but its moral effect is also good. On this point there is entire unanimity in the testimony of prison officers. This influence shows itself in the better health of the prisoners, in the general improvement of their temper, in the greater cheerfulness with which they work, in the increased amount of work done, in the diminution of complaints and punishments, and in the augmented power of reformatory agencies over them.

The clothing furnished to convicts in our American state prisons, though coarse, is generally substantial and comfortable. The fabric used is composed wholly or chiefly of wool, and the suit is, for the most part, the same in summer as in winter, except that the under-clothing is less. It is quite common to supply woolen drawers and undershirts during the winter, which are left off in summer. In the provincial penitentiary, the summer suit is of cotton, and in the state penitentiary of Kentucky, of a light woolen fabric. In most of the prisons, the convicts interchange their clothing when it is washed, so that no one is sure of receiving back from the wash the suit that he put in. In the Massachusetts prison, a different and far preferable usage prevails. All the clothes worn by convicts are marked with their own names in full, even to their towels, sheets and pillow-cases. There is wisdom as well as kindness in this arrangement. It fosters in the prisoners a feeling of self-respect, moves them to take better care of their clothes, and strengthens the sentiment of personal responsibility. Every convict here is furnished with a pocket comb.

In all our state prisons, convicts, on their liberation, are provided with a suit of citizen's clothing; in some cases an extra shirt being supplied, and in others, as in Wisconsin, a flannel under-shirt and drawers, if the discharge takes place in winter. Each female convict in Sing Sing prison is provided, on her release, with the following outfit: Two dresses (one delaine and one calico); two skirts (one quilted and one muslin); two pairs of drawers; four chemises; two pair cotton hose; one pair calfskin shoes; one pocket handkerchief; a straw hat trimmed with ribbon, and a shawl, suited to the season of the year.

Iron bedsteads are provided in all the New England prisons, and in, perhaps, the major part of the others visited and inspected by us; although in quite a number the old wooden bunks are still in use, and among them, we are sorry to say, our own great prison of Sing Sing, the largest on the American continent.

Straw beds are in universal use, except in the Massachusetts prison, where mattresses, made of curled palm-leaf, are used. They are much superior to those made of straw, and, in the long run, cheaper. A bed of this sort, it is said, will last seven years, at the end of which time the material in two old ones will make a third one as good as new.

Sheets and pillow-cases are provided in the majority of American prisons; they should be in all, on considerations of cleanliness, health, comfort, and even economy.

Bed-clothes—blankets, comfortables and quilts—appear to be everywhere supplied in sufficient quantity; or if there be occasionally some lack in this department, such cases are quite exceptional.

The condition of the prison beds, as a general thing, is made a matter of daily inspection.

As regards airing the beds—a most necessary process both for cleanliness and health—there is a great diversity in point of frequency. In New Hampshire, we were informed, this is done every day; while in some prisons, it appears never to be done at all. In Kentucky and Wisconsin, it is done monthly; in Massachusetts, at no regular set times, but frequently; in Michigan, " not often; " in Vermont, " when necessary; " in Ohio, " no special rule."

Few prisons are free from vermin. The warden of the Maine prison reports that th**ey** are *never* found in the cells there, and the commissioner of the Wisconsin prison, that in half the cells in that institution they are not found *at all*. Nowhere else was any such statement made to us on this subject. The most common report was that they were sometimes troublesome; but it was not uncommon to be told that they were in "great abundance," or that there was "any quantity" of them. On the question how to get rid of them, various opinions were expressed. Several wardens gave judgment in favor of cleanliness and care, combined with perseverance, as the best remedial agents; no doubt an excellent prescription. One said, coal oil; another, kerosene oil and whitewash; a third, corrosive sublimate and alcohol; and one, in blank despair of any effectual remedy, exclaimed: "I wish some wise man would tell us how to get rid of them."

Water is abundantly supplied to most state prisons—to those of Charlestown, Sing Sing, Philadelphia, and perhaps some others, from city water-works; to that of Michigan, from an artesian well; to the greater part, from ordinary wells and cisterns.

The moral influence of a habit of personal cleanliness is neither slight nor unimportant. It has been said, and there is truth in the saying, that clean rogues are about as plenty as white blackberries. We were, therefore, glad to be informed that, in nearly all the prisons visited, the prisoners are required to wash their hands and faces three times a day, although in one or two, this requisition stops at a single ablution. We were no less pleased to learn that in very many prisons ample means are provided for bathing the whole person, and that this is exacted of prisoners monthly, fortnightly, or weekly, though not in all cases during the winter. In the Michigan state prison, it was stated to us by the late warden, Mr. Seaton, that the convicts are required to wash the entire body every morning in a trough provided for the purpose. Every token of improvement in the direction of personal cleanliness must be hailed with gratulation by the friends of prison reform. It is important, moreover, that the means of bathing should be available in winter as well as in summer. It is admitted that the bath is not so absolutely necessary in cold as in hot weather; yet it is, at all times, refreshing, invigorating, healthful. Many of the employments in prisons are of such a nature that the frequent use of the bath is demanded as well to

insure self-respect as to promote health; for who so degraded as
not to feel a deeper degradation from personal uncleanliness?

The flesh brush, as far as we could learn, has never been introduced into any of our prisons. This is to be regretted. Long
experience has shown that few things contribute more to health
than the free use of the brush upon the skin, in combination with
a liberal supply of water and soap ; and even without these
adjuncts, it is still useful. Nothing is more restorative, after a
day's dirty labor, than a good hard brushing. Cool water will
produce a feeling of *refreshment;* but water, moderately warm,
with soap and the brush, or even a rough towel, really *restores.*

In most prisons, the underclothing of the convicts is washed
weekly ; twice a week would not be too much ; but in Kentucky,
Maine and Ohio, even the shirts are washed but once in two weeks ;
and in New Hampshire only after a lapse of three weeks ! The
outer garments are washed less frequently. Many convicts are
employed on work which soils very quickly ; and, on looking at
the garments worn by them, we could not resist the impression
that a more frequent contact with the soap and other appliances
of the washtub would be every way desirable.

The sheets and pillow cases are washed weekly in the prisons
of Massachusetts and Michigan ; but in other prisons where they
are used, not oftener than once in two weeks, and in New Hampshire only every third week. The blankets and comfortables,
which must quickly become saturated with the effluvium of human
bodies heated by work (especially when, as is often the case, they
come into direct contact therewith), were, more frequently than
we could have desired, reported to us as being washed "as often
as required." We have no gauge to measure the diversity of
judgment which no doubt exists as to the proper length of periods
of time to be covered by that expression.

With few exceptions, chiefly in the western states, the prisons
under our inspection exhibited a remarkable degree of neatness.
In many, it would be difficult to find a speck of dirt on the floors
of the corridors or cells, or a soiled spot upon the walls or ceilings.
The whitewash brush knows little remission of its toils, except
during the hours of eating and sleeping, but exercises its purifying
and healthful influences constantly and thoroughly. Floors and
stairs are swept daily, and, in addition, undergo frequent scrub-
bings.

In the Massachusetts state prison, the men are shaved twice a week; in all others of the congregate order, weekly. In Maine and Wisconsin, this is done by each man for himself; elsewhere by convict barbers, who go round to the different work shops for the purpose. Hair-cutting is done in the same way; in some prisons, bi-monthly, in others quarterly.

In all the state prisons, except those of Pennsylvania, night tubs for the cells are in use, which are emptied and cleansed daily. They are invariably made of wood,—pine, oak, or red cedar. For meeting the calls of nature during the day, there are water-closets in all the workshops; and some are also provided on other parts of the premises.

The diseases most prevalent in American prisoners are rheumatism and those connected with the lungs, the bowels, the skin, and the digestive organs.

As regards the comparative readiness with which disease yields to medical treatment in convicts long in prison and those but recently imprisoned, the preponderance of testimony was in favor of the latter class; some stated that no difference had been observed; but the warden of the Wisconsin state prison observed that, as a general thing, the prisoners who had been confined for a number of years are in better health than those recently committed.

Of the numerous trades pursued in our prisons, none in particular seem to be more prejudicial to health than others, except certain departments of hemp manufacture, stone cutting and polishing steel and iron on emory wheels, grind-stones, or sand paper, as the men are thereby exposed to inhale particles of vegetable or metallic substances injurious to the lungs.

The daily percentage of prisoners in hospital varies from one, as in Maine and Massachusetts, to fifteen and a half, as in Ohio; and the percentage of persons for whom daily prescriptions are made, varies from one and a half, in Maine, to $31\frac{1}{2}$, in Ohio.

The diseases most frequently simulated are insanity, rheumatism, diarrhœa, cholic and headache. Feigned insanity is detected only by close and careful observations; the other complaints by various tests. Mr. Cordier, of Wisconsin, says: " We have two classes of convicts: one class works well and diligently, the other shirks work. If a convict of the first class complains, we take his word for it, and he is treated accordingly. If a convict of the other class complains of headache or rheumatism, we consider him for the time being as a sick man, and give him the food of a sick man. These short rations cure him in a wonderfully brief space of time. He is not apt to complain a second time."

The diet prescribed by the physician is everywhere given to the sick; and for the very sick such delicacies are for the most part provided as are usually given outside.

A few insane prisoners are received into most of the state prisons, and a few also become insane after their reception; the exact percentage we could not ascertain in either case. The disposition to be made of insane convicts is a question of grave importance. The best arrangement for their disposal is in our own state and Canada, where large and admirably arranged asylums for criminal insane are provided; in New York, at Auburn; in Canada, at Rockwood, a mile or two from the provincial penitentiary. In Massachusetts, they are sent to one of the state lunatic hospitals. In the majority of states, no provision is made for the removal of these unfortunates from their places of incarceration, but they are retained in prison to their own detriment and the sore inconvenience of the authorities.

The testimony of prison physicians is unanimous, or nearly so, to the effect that long imprisonments are prejudicial—some say decidedly so—to the health of the imprisoned.

SECTION NINTH.

PRISON INDUSTRIES.

Persons convicted of felonies (not capital) in the United States are uniformly sentenced to imprisonment with hard labor. The element of hard labor in the sentence is the dictate at once of justice and policy : of justice, because it is right that criminals, who have put the state to more or less expense, should do something towards defraying the public cost of their crimes ; of policy, because work is an essential condition of the prisoner's reformation ; and reformation, so far as this class of persons is concerned, is the great interest of the state.

Four systems of convict labor have prevailed, at different times and in different prisons, in the several states of our Union.

The first system is that of working the convicts on account of the state—the state supplying the capital and raw material, and undertaking, through its agents, the sale of the manufactured articles.

The second system consists in leasing the prison for a stipulated annual sum, to some individual or firm, the lessee having the entire control both of the discipline and labor of the convicts, procuring all supplies of food, clothing, medicines, &c., and conducting the whole business of the establishment; everything, in effect, being in his discretion and at his disposal.

The third system consists in working the prisoners on the joint account of the state and the warden; the latter agreeing to be at all the expense of conducting the prison, and receiving a certain percentage of the profits in lieu of salary.

The fourth is what is known as the contract system of convict labor. It consists in letting the labor of the convicts to certain parties, called contractors, who hire it for a stipulated period, commonly five years, at so much per day for each man. Generally the rates paid for this labor are low, ranging from thirty to forty-five cents a day. At present, owing to the great demand for skilled labor and the high price of all commodities in the market, the rates are considerably in advance of former times. Thus, the average daily rate of wages on all the contracts in the Massachusetts state prison is eighty cents; in that of Ohio, sixty-five cents; at Sing Sing, forty-eight cents; at Auburn, sixty-three cents, and in other prisons on the same general scale of advance. But now, as heretofore, these rates are not more than one-third or one-fourth of what is paid for the same kinds of labor outside; while, at the same time, the convict laborers perform, in some prisons (that of Massachusetts, for example), quite as much as the same number of citizen laborers would accomplish; and in none is the proportion less than three-fourths or two-thirds. Moreover, not only do contractors get the labor of the convicts at these cheap rates, but they are also furnished with all the necessary shop and yard room, without any charge for rent; a consideration worth, not unfrequently, several thousand dollars per annum.

We propose, in this section to go, at some length, into the exposition and illustration of the several systems of convict labor, more particularly the one last mentioned; previously to which, however, we will submit a few general facts connected with the industries of our prisons.

The average number of hours during which convicts are worked throughout the year, varies from nine to ten hours, the extremes being from eight hours in the winter to twelve in the summer.

It is surprising how small, comparatively, is the number of skilled mechanics found among the inmates of prisons. The great mass of prisoners is made up of day-laborers, domestic servants, boatmen, sailors, carmen, bar-tenders, &c., &c. Mr. Cordier, of Wisconsin, says: "Not ten per cent. of the convicts received during the last four years—the period covered by my administration—were good mechanics; about ten per cent. knew the first rudiments of a trade; and not less than eighty per cent., or four-fifths, were without a trade entirely." This is about the usual proportion, as given by the officers of other prisons. It is the same in other countries. The governor of the borough prison at Glasgow, Scotland, says in one of his reports: "The number of skilled workmen in the prison is always very small, not more than twenty out of the whole number of men, that is, twenty out of about one hundred and fifty, on an average. The great majority of our prisoners are from the worst-paid and poorest classes. There is a large class who have not been brought up to any regular occupation."

The fact in regard to the mechanical knowledge and skill of persons committed to prison being as stated above, it is much to be regretted that in our American prisons it is not made more of a distinct object to teach a full trade to all who had never learned one before their committal. Yet truth compels us to report that this, as a general thing, is not the case, although there are, happily, some exceptions. It is the case in respect to the eastern penitentiary at Philadelphia, where a complete trade, most commonly shoemaking, is taught to every convict. But in prisons conducted on the congregate plan, the general rule is to keep the men at work on some particular branch of business, and teach them nothing beyond that, so that they get, for the most part, only a little piece of a trade. Yet sometimes it is otherwise. In the prison of northern Indiana, a distinct stipulation (so the warden informed us) is incorporated into the contract letting the labor, to the effect that the men shall learn all the different parts of the trade at which they work; as a consequence of which, about sixty per cent. of those not knowing a trade when committed, learn one during their incarceration. In the Wisconsin prison, where the contract system of convict labor does not obtain, the commissioner informed us that he made it a point to teach every convict, having a term of two years and upwards to serve, a full trade, provided he had any mechanical aptitude; and here, also, sixty per cent. of those not having learned it before, acquire the complete knowledge of a trade during their imprisonment. In the Maine state prison, likewise, from whose industries the contract system is excluded, all who are sentenced for three years, and nearly all sentenced for two years, who were not previously mechanics, are taught a full trade while in prison. In New Hampshire, in like manner, a portion of the convicts employed on productive labor are worked not by contractors, but by the state; and in respect to these, it is made a distinct object to give to all of them the knowledge and mastery of a complete trade, if they had never learned one before their imprisonment.

The importance of imparting to prisoners the complete knowledge of a trade, as it lies in the minds of those most competent to form and pronounce an opinion, may be inferred from the fact that, with absolute unanimity, prison officers declare it to be their judgment that the reformation of the imprisoned would be promoted by giving greater prominence to this object than is done at present; and they further declare it as their opinion that reformation, genuine and permanent, whatever the first cost of it may be, is, in the long run, the cheapest and most profitable, and will prove the greatest ultimate pecuniary gain to the state.

There is a question of considerable interest and importance connected with the general subject of prison industries, which we investigated to some extent, and in reference to which it is proper that we report the result of our investigation—we mean over-work. In most American prisons, this is not allowed; but all prisoners are required to work from bell to bell, that is, the entire day, for the benefit of the contractor, or for that of the state, if they are engaged on state work. In other prisons, tasks are assigned to the men, which the majority of them can accomplish before the expiration of the working hours of the day, some even as early as eleven or twelve o'clock in the morning, and others at different hours of the afternoon. What they do, when they are permitted to do anything beyond their allotted tasks, is called over-work; and the avails of such labor belong to themselves.

This whole matter seems to be better managed in the state penitentiary of Ohio than in any other prison to which our inquiries were directed. It is here brought under subjection to the law, by which it is regulated in all its parts and ramifications. All prisoners, who finish their tasks before the close of the day, have the right secured to them of employing the hours that remain in doing over-work. The law regulates the prices to be paid for this extra labor, which are, in all cases, to be at the same rate per day as paid by contractors to the state for the same kind of work. The task to be exacted of the prison laborers is fixed by agreement of the prison authorities and contractors; it is at present equal to four-fifths of the ordinary day's work required of an average mechanic in the same department of labor. The wages for over-work are paid into the state treasury to the credit of the prisoners who earned the same; but no interest is allowed on their accumulations. Prisoners may draw money so deposited for the use of their families, or for the purchase of such books as may be approved by the authorities. It is stated to be " not *particularly* prejudicial to health; " and the influence of the system, regulated and managed as described above, is reported as " generally good."

The account given us of the organization and working of the system of over-stent in the state prison of northern Indiana agrees substantially with that which we have set forth in the preceding paragraph, as found in the state penitentiary of Ohio.

In most other prisons, where it is allowed, overwork has neither legal existence nor legal regulation. It has sprung up and grown, as it were, unconsciously, without plan or design, and is conducted in a loose and irresponsible manner. Mr. Seaton, late warden of the Michigan state prison, says of it: " It is of no benefit to either convict or discipline, as at present managed."

In the state prisons of New York, the system of overwork has had an existence for many years. The whole thing has there been mostly in the hands and under the control of the contractors— mere outsiders, having no interest in the discipline of the prison or the reformation of the prisoners, but only in making as much money out of them as possible. Some contractors granted and some refused permission to their men to do overwork. Some allowed perhaps half, and others not more than a fourth or an eighth, of their employes to engage in it. These discriminations were an endless source of discontent, jealousy, heart-burning and deception. They were the occasion of no small proportion of all the punishments inflicted in the prisons. The system in the end proved so demoralizing to the *morale* and discipline of the prisons that, as we have been informed, the inspectors have issued, or declared their intention to issue, an order abolishing it altogether. But while we approve of the abolishment of a system so partial, so irresponsible and so fruitful of mischief, we cannot approve of doing so without replacing it with a better. To deprive men, who for years have been permitted to earn something for themselves, of all opportunity of such self-help, from no fault of their own, is too violent a wrench to their feelings, and must react unfavorably in many ways. The bestowment of gratuities in money, the allowance of a certain percentage of their earnings, or some other equivalent, under proper regulations, should have been made at once to take the place of the forbidden and exploded system of overwork.

We come now to a consideration of the several labor systems, which either at present prevail, or have heretofore prevailed, in the different state prisons of our country.

The system noted in our enumeration as the third—that, namely, which consists in working the prisoners on the joint account of the state and the warden—no longer exists in practice in any prison of which we have any knowledge. It is the principle on which the industries of the penitentiary of Kentucky were formerly, for so many years, conducted; but it has long since been abandoned. It is a principle which we consider utterly unsound as a basis of prison management; but its financial results were remarkable. They will be exhibited under another division of this section.

The system noted as the second in our enumeration—that, to wit, which consists in leasing the prison for an annual consideration to some individual or firm for a specified number of years—is the one now adopted in Illinois and Kentucky. It was formerly practiced in Missouri, but has been disused there. Of the working of the system in the penitentiary of that state, Mr. Miller, late warden of the same, who knew it from personal observation, observes: "Bad as the contract system is in a reformatory view, even when checked and controlled by the state's appointed agent, it is, nevertheless, far better than the system of absolute leasing, as was once the case in this state, and is now practised in Illinois and Kentucky, and perhaps in some other states. For, while the leasing system is liable to all the abuses of the contract system, it is open to some peculiar to itself; or if not peculiar, at least in greater strength than in the other. As the lessee is unrestrained by any authority, and is in the position of absolute master, the temptation to excessive gains and to whatever abuses may be thought conducive to that end, will only cease when self-interest itself cries, "Hold, enough!" In this short exstract we have the very quintescence of the system. The same principle underlies it as that which generated all the horrible and disgusting abuses of the old English jail system, against which Howard lifted up his voice and arm. The great, central evil of that system was, that the keeper, free from supervision and restraint, was left to make his living out of the prison. A salary was seldom paid to him. Sometimes he paid a rent; sometimes he bought his place. Howard, in his "State of Prisons," mentions many examples. Thus, for the wardenship of a prison in Norwich, the keeper paid £40—equal to $200—a year. One Huggins purchased a lease of the wardenship of the Fleet, in London, for his own and his son's life, at £5,000. When he became old, as "his son did not care to take on him so troublesome an office," he sold out to one Bambridge what remained of his lease for the same sum, £5,000. These men enriched themselves and lived in luxury from the fees, rents parings from prison rations, garnish, prison taps, and other devices for squeezing money out of the poor prisoners; our lessees do the same thing through the use of their muscles and sinews, and by an undue stinting in their allowances of food and clothing.

The same persons in the penitentiaries of Illinois and Kentucky, contract for the food, clothing, labor, and sanitary care of the convicts ; a system, as DeToqueville has suggested, equally injurious to the interests of the convict and the discipline of the prison. It is injurious to the convict, because the lessee, seeing nothing but a money transaction in his lease, speculates on the food and clothing, as he does upon the labor ; if he loses on the clothing, he indemnifies himself on the food ; if the labor is not as productive as he calculated, he seeks to balance his loss in that direction by spending less on the supplies. The system is injurious to the prison, because the lessee, looking upon the convict simply as a laboring machine, thinks only how he can use him to the greatest pecuniary advantage ; and he cares little, if the gains are made to the prejudice of the discipline and good order of the institution.

Such is the *rationale* of the operation of this system. Do the facts tally with the theory ? We think so. During our visit to Frankfort, divers complaints or charges were related to us as having been made against different lessees of the prison, on the ground of their unjust and unfeeling treatment of the prisoners. One was charged with having greatly overtasked his men, so that they became broken down in health and constitution; another, with having kept them on rations so stinted in quantity and so inferior in quality, as to have induced a general epidemic of the scurvy ; and all, with treating them badly towards the end of their lease in respect to food, clothes, bedding, and other supplies, being naturally anxious to spend as little and make as much as possible, in anticipation of the winding up of the whole business. Thus, every interest of the prisoner, bodily and spiritual, and every interest of the state, material and moral, are lost sight of in the one, all-absorbing idea of making money. Every effort of chaplains or inspectors to improve the morals of the convicts, which will demand a moment of their time, is regarded with disfavor and trameled by the lessee in all conceivable ways. Food and clothing are brought down to the minimum point. The strength of the convicts is tasked beyond all bounds of reason or endurance. The property of the state is either abused or suffered to go to ruin. Convicts are regarded as so many machines or slaves, and are valued and cared for only for the work they are able to do. The idea of reforming them is ignored, and all the higher ends of penal discipline are held in abeyance. Such are the impressions which we received from what we saw and heard during a day's sojourn in the capital of Kentucky.

The present lessee is Captain H. I. Todd, who was absent at the time of our visit, but was spoken of to us as a just and humane man. The bonus which he pays the state for the use of the prison, and the labor of the convicts for four years, is $2,800; that is, $6,000 a year for the first two years, and $8,000 a year for the last two. By the terms of the lease, he is constituted warden or keeper of the prison; is invested with its government and discipline; is charged with the entire expenses of its support; and is to return the property to the state, at the expiration of the lease, in as good condition as it was received. The pecuniary results of this system will appear further on.

The system of prison labor, first in our enumeration that of working the convicts on account of the state—is adopted, as far as we are informed, in but three state prisons in the country, established on the Auburn plan, viz.: Clinton prison in New York, and those of Maine and Wisconsin; it is also in partial use in that of New Hampshire. All these establishments are more than self-supporting, except that of Wisconsin, which lacks little of having an income from the labor of its inmates equal to its expenditures.

The fourth system named—that known as the contract system—is the one commonly adopted in our American prisons. What the system is, has been already declared. It remains to inquire what effect it has on the finances and discipline of the prisons in which it exists; and what on the reformation of their prisoners and their preparation for a return to civil life and a re-absorption into free society?

The general influence of letting the labor of the convicts to a class of outside persons, called contractors, was, from the first, regarded with apprehension by those three early apostles of the Auburn system of prison discipline, Elam Lynds, Gershom Powers, and Moses C. Pilsbury, the two former connected with the system in New York, and the latter with the same system both in New Hampshire and Connecticut. The dread of it felt by Mr. Lynds, we learn from a remark of De Toqueville, in his Penitentiary System of the United States. He says: "Mr. Elam Lynds seems constantly to fear that the presence of the contractors in the prison will lead, sooner or later, to the total ruin of the discipline." Judge Powers' fears are thus expressed by himself in his report to the Legislature of New York, in 1828: "This mode of employing convicts is attended with considerable danger to the discipline of the prison, by bringing the convicts in contact with contractors and their agents, unless very strict rules are rigidly enforced." To the question, "How does your contract system work now?" Mr. Pilsbury replies. in 1839: "Destructive to everything which may be called good, both as it relates to the institution and the prisoners; and I am not sure, but I may add, to the contractor also." The question and answer refer to a contract system similar to that which now prevails in Illinois and Kentucky; a system by which one man contracts to support the institution and have all the proceeds. This must be understood in order to appreciate the keen sarcasm conveyed in the last part of Mr. Pilsbury's statement.

In what we say on this subject, we shall draw our facts in part from the results of our own inquiries, and in part from the evidence taken before a commission of the Prison Association in 1866.

How, then, does the contract system affect the pecuniary interests of the state ?

It would naturally be inferred from the essential character of the system, as above exhibited, that the state must be a loser by it. Taking the statements most favorable to the state, it appears that prison contractors obtain the labor of three convicts where they would get that of one citizen, and yet that each convict performs, on the average, three-fourths as much work as a citizen laborer. Putting these elements together, the case stands thus: The labor of twelve convicts will cost no more per day than that of four citizens; yet the convicts will do nine days' work, while the citizens will do but four. Thus every dollar paid for convict labor will produce as much as two dollars and a quarter expended on citizen labor. Is it possible that the state can be other than a loser by a system which sells the labor of its convicts at one hundred and fifty per cent. less than the same labor could be obtained elsewhere?

On its face, this statement appears as incredible as it is astounding. We will, therefore, explain how it is that the state sells, and indeed finds itself obliged to sell, its labor at such a discount. In the first place, the contract system amounts, in practice, to an almost absolute monopoly, arising from the fact that the contractors own the power, machinery and stock of the shops; they are established in the business, and knowing the profits, which, as far as possible, they keep in their own breast, they can, almost uniformly, so regulate their bids as to keep out all others who aspire to become contractors. In the second place, contractors sometimes combine to keep down the rates to be paid for convict labor to the lowest possible point. In the third place, when a new branch of business was to be introduced into a prison, similar combinations have been entered into by persons outside, who sought to become contractors, one party paying to the others certain stipulated sums of money, on condition that they would decline to put in bids, and thus obtaining the prisoners at a price much below that which would have been just and fair. And finally, they have been known to decry, in the strongest terms, the labor of the convicts, and to impugn the rigor of the ,regulations as affecting contractors, with a view both to discourage competition and reconcile the public to a low compensation for convict labor. All this appears in the evidence, but we have not space for citations. We will merely mention one fact, stated by Mr. Augsbury, warden of Auburn prison. He says that when the bids for a certain contract were made, a contractor who had taken pains to disseminate statements depreciating the value of convict labor, trusting to the effect of his misrepresentations, put in a bid at a very low rate, while he was, at the same time, interested in another contract at nearly double the rate of compensation offered by him.

There can be no doubt that the profits made by contractors out of convict labor, are very large. The testimony of all the witnesses is concurrent to this point. Mr. Haynes, of the Charlestown prison, says: "Our contractors have always become wealthy, if they have retained their contracts for any length of time." And this is a fair specimen of the general tone and tenor of the evidence. Nothing can more conclusively demonstrate the very large gains realized from convict labor than a fact mentioned by Mr. Augsbury. There was, he says, a contract given out at Auburn, in 1863, on which the men were let at forty cents a day. A water power, worth $1,500 a year, was charged to the contractors at $240; and yard and shop room, which would have rented outside for $2,000, was, as usual, thrown in without charge. This contract was to run five years. At the expiration of the second year, the balance of the contract was sold to another party for a bonus of $30,000. In this case, a considerable fortune was realized from a single contract in the brief space of two years.

The question arises here, whether the same or nearly the same profits might not be made for the state under a system, in which the industries of a prison should be managed by its head; it being pre-supposed that the said chief officer is a person of competent ability, of incorruptible integrity, and permanent in his position, so that the lights of experience may be added to the force of natural endowments. That this question may be answered in the affirmative is clear to our conviction from the proofs which we are about to submit. These proofs are of a two-fold form, that of opinion and that of experience or fact.

We will first summon to the stand a company of witnesses, whose competency is unquestionable. The first we offer is the veteran, Amos Pilsbury, the oldest and most experienced prison officer in America. General P. says in his testimony: "I have no doubt that more money might be made by managing the prison labor myself." Mr. G. B. Hubbell, ex-warden of Sing Sing prison, testifies: "I believe that a competent general officer can manage the industries of a prison much more to the interest of the state and the convicts, in all respects, than can be done under the contract system." Mr. D. L. Seymour, also an ex-warden of Sing Sing, says: "I have no doubt whatever that, if the contract system had been abolished and I could have managed the prison labor myself, I could have earned a considerable surplus revenue for the state." We will not encumber our pages with further citations. The same opinion is expressed by Mr. Rice, of Maine; Mr. Seaton and Mr. Brockway, of Michigan; Mr. Wood, of Indiana; Mr. Miller, of Missouri; and Mr. Cordier, of Wisconsin; all of them gentlemen of intelligence, and most of them of large experience as prison officers.

So much for authority. Now let us interrogate experience. What do facts say? Their voice is no less decisive.

We will begin, as before, with the veteran of Wethersfield and Albany. In his evidence before the commission of 1866, General Pilsbury states that, during a portion of the time when he was warden at Wethersfield, he managed the entire labor of the convicts himself, and that, during another portion, about one half of the labor was let to contractors. He adds: "In a financial point of view, the management of the labor by myself was most successful." In Clinton prison, N. Y., the contract system having been abolished, the labor was last year managed by the prison authorities. The result of this change is, that the institution, instead of being a drain upon the public treasury, as heretofore, to the amount of $30,000 or more a year, has become a source of revenue to the state, the income having exceeded the expenditure by some $3,000, and the inspectors anticipate a much larger surplus in future years. At the time of our visit to the state prison at Thomaston, Me., Mr. Rice had been warden for two and a half years, the prison labor being wholly managed by himself, on a capital of $10,000 furnished by the state. During that period, with an average of less than one hundred convicts, he had, despite the extraordinary cost of all prison supplies, paid the entire current expenses of the institution, including officers' salaries, and earned a clear profit of $7,000. Mr. Cordier, commissioner of the Wisconsin state prison, says: "Our average number of convicts last year was 110, only 63 of whom could be employed on productive labor. Their earnings amounted to $25,727.34, which shows that these 63 men earned each $1.36 per day. If the labor of the convicts had been let to contractors at (say) sixty cents a day (a high figure), they would have earned only $11,340, supposing them to have lost no time on account of sickness and from other causes, and the state would have sacrificed in one year $14,387.34."

A strong light is thrown on the matter of prison labor by the financial history of Illinois and Kentucky. In the former of these states, the plan of leasing the prison, at a bonus of so much per annum, has been practised from its foundation. During the greater part of this time, Mr. Samuel A. Buckmaster has been the lessee. This gentleman, as the result of such arrangement, has (so we are informed), amassed a very large fortune. We certainly do not commend, but, on the contrary, oppose as objectionable to the last degree, the principle of this arrangement; yet the fact just stated shows that the industries of a prison may be successfully managed by the same mind that presides over the discipline.

The history of the Kentucky penitentiary affords additional proof of the same thing. In 1825, the principle was adopted of allowing the keeper, in lieu of all other compensation, one half of the profits, after defraying the current expenses. Joel Scott was the first keeper under this system, and he served for nine years. The clear profits from convict labor during his administration were $81,136. Mr. Scott was succeeded by Thomas S. Theobald, who took the prison on the same terms. The aggregate profits of his administration of ten years, the average number of prisoners being less than one hundred and fifty, were $200,000; and one year they reached the extraordinary sum of $30,000. Every dollar of the state's share—$100,000—was paid into the public treasury. In 1855, Zebulon Ward leased the prison for four years, at an annual rent of $6,000; and at the end of his term, he retired with a fortune variously estimated at $50,000 to $75,000. Mr. Ward was succeeded by J. W. South, who leased the prison for a like period, though at the advanced rent of $12,000 a year. He also, at the end of his four years' service, is reported to have retired with an ample fortune, as the product of convict earnings. The above facts are derived from a History of the Kentucky Penitentiary, by William C. Sneed, M. D., long the medical officer of the prison, and a perfectly reliable authority.

The above argument, to prove the repugnance of the contract system to the pecuniary interest of the state,—resting on the essential nature of the system, on the authority of competent judges, and on the results of experience,—we cannot but regard as a three-fold cord, not to be easily broken.

But in New York there is a special argument of no little potency demonstrative of the same proposition. It is in evidence in the testimony taken by the commission of 1866, that the state has, through a long series of years, been mulcted in damages of colossal magnitude, paid to contractors; damages resting, for the most part, if not altogether, on no foundation of justice or reason. We will cite but one case out of many. Col. Wilkinson, of Auburn, in his sworn testimony, says: "A contractor who was allowed the valuable water power of this prison without charge, and yet

paid less for the labor of his men than other contractors who furnished their own power, has gone back on the state for heavy
damages, claimed to have accrued through a long series of years,
in consequence of some deficiencies, from time to time, in the supply of water. The damages claimed were, if I rightly remember,
some $200,000 ; and they were allowed to the amount of $125,000,
and I think more." The colonel puts it with epigrammatic aptness
and force, in the added remark, that "this sum was paid by the
state, in effect, for the privilege of making a present to the contractor of the use of the prison water power." After such Napo-
leonic achievements as this in the science of public plunder, it is
hardly worth while to mention a little item in the evidence of the
Rev. Mr. Ives, chaplain of the Auburn prison, who stated that
cases had occurred, wherein, in consequence of the absence of
some half dozen men from a shop for a fortnight (they being sick
or under discipline), the contractors have claimed damages equal
to the entire wages of all the men in the shop for a whole month,
and, what is more, have recovered a considerable part of it. Nor
is it worth while to state the variety of devices, the fact itself is
enough, whereby these gentlemen contrive to get numbers of their
men on half pay, who are yet made to do full work.

Our next inquiry is, how does the contract system affect the
discipline of the prison in which it may be found ?

The first effect of this system is to place, for the whole working day, all the prisoners contracted for, to a great extent, under
the control of men with no official responsibility; men independent, in a great degree, of the prison authorities; men who see in
the convicts only so much machinery for making money; men
whose only recommendation to the positions they hold in the prison is that they proved the highest bidders for the human beings
hired to them. The second effect of the system is to introduce
among the convicts, as superintendents of their labor, strangers
to the prison, who are employed by the contractors as agents,
foremen, instructors, and, in some instances, even as laborers;
men utterly irresponsible; men selected with little regard to their
moral character, and often without morals; men who do not hesitate to smuggle liquor and other contraband articles into the prison and sell them to convicts at 100 and 200 per cent., and even
more above their fair market value. A third effect of the system,
at least in New York, is to set up in the prisons, " a power behind the throne greater than the throne;" a power which, by the

almost unanimous testimony of present and former prison officers
in our state, is well nigh omnipotent, a power which coaxes, bribes,
or threatens, according to the exigency of the case, in pursuit of
its selfish ends; a power which makes and unmakes officers, imposes and remits punishments through agents it has bent to its
will, and even stoops to devices to get the poor prisoner who has
incurred its wrath into straits and difficulties, that its revenge may
be gratified by the sight of his punishment.   Surely, after such a
recital as this, it will not be regarded as matter of wonder that
numerous witnesses, and among them those model wardens, David
L. Seymour and Gaylord B. Hubbell, and that distinguished prison chaplain, the Rev. John Luckey, attest by their oath that the
contract system exerts a most demoralizing influence on the discipline, and that, in the New York State prisons, more than half of
all the irritation, discontent, insubordination and punishment is
due, directly or indirectly, to its baneful influence.   We do not
doubt that the influence of the system is worse in our state than
in any other; but it is felt elsewhere as a power for evil.   Thus,
Mr. Seaton, of Michigan, says in his communication to us: "The
contract system exerts an influence unfavorable to discipline; it is
the source of continual strife between the contractors and the
convicts."

Our only remaining inquiry as regards the contract system is,
how does it affect the reformation of prisoners and their successful reabsorption into free society?

Formerly, the thought of reforming the violator of law hardly
entered the mind of the philanthropist, much less that of the men
who were called to make and administer the laws of the states.
The ban of society was upon him. Thrust away from public view,
he was abandoned as irreclaimable, to the mercy of men often
more wicked than himself.   The logical issue of this theory, and
the true policy of states on the assumption of its correctness,
would be hanging for all offences.   Happily, this cold, repulsive,
cruel doctrine has been exploded.   Experience has demonstrated
the practicability of reformation even within the walls of a prison.
It has brought thinking men to the conviction that the proper
object of prison discipline is to cure the bad habits of criminals,
and make them peaceable and honest members of society; that is,
to reform them; and this, to gain the broader end of preventing
crime and insuring the safety of society.   Such is the present

theory, which we believe to rest upon a foundation of reason and truth.

But reformation does not follow, as a matter of course, upon imprisonment. It can be effected only through a system of agencies, wisely planned and patiently carried out. These reformatory agencies are, as we conceive, chiefly the following:

1. *Religion.*—This, undoubtedly, is the first in importance, and the most potent in its action. But we have sufficiently declared our conviction on this point in the sixth section of this chapter, and need not repeat views which were there fully set forth. We will but add, in this connection, that religion is the only power that is able to resist the irritation which saps the moral forces of those men of powerful impulses, whose neglect of it has been the occasion of their being immured within prison walls.

2. *Education.*—This, carried to the farthest extent consistent with the other purposes of a prison, is a vital element in the reformation of the fallen. Education quickens the intellect, gives new ideas, supplies food for thought, inspires self-respect, supports pride of character, excites ambition, opens new fields of labor, and offers opportunities for social and personal improvement. What argument, beyond this statement, can be needed to show the importance of education as an agent in the reformation of criminals?

3. *Habits of Industry.*—Labor, steady, active, honorable labor, is as much an auxiliary of virtue as it is a means of support. It was an aphorism of John Howard, one of his most favorite maxims, "make men diligent, and they will be honest." And therein the great philanthropist was unquestionably right. Or, if any doubt whether honesty is the necessary sequent of diligence, at least it will be conceded by all that the fallen cannot attain and retain this essential attribute, if they are not diligent. Hence work is the only sure basis of an effective system of prison discipline. "Unless prisoners acquire habits of industry, and a liking for some kind of labor," as Mr. F. Hill has observed, "little hope can be entertained of their conduct after liberation." What ought, therefore, to be aimed at as a matter of prime, not to say supreme, importance, is the formation of fixed, permanent habits of useful labor. Good resolutions are well, as far as they go; but as a dependence for the future, unsupported by the habit of honest, useful toil, they will prove entirely fallacious. It will turn out with them as with sick bed resolves, which usually vanish with returning health. In her efforts to reform Newgate, Mrs. Fry's first exertions were

directed to the introduction of useful labor. In like manner the society, of which she was the most distinguished and influential member, paid the salary of the first female officer engaged to teach the women needlework in the jail of Edinburgh. The reformed convict must support himself by work after his release. His labor will come into competition with that of the whole laboring community. If he would succeed as they do, he must toil as they do. He will have to be up as early, labor as unremittingly, continue as long at his work, and be in all respects as regular in his industry as they, or he will find himself without employment, while he sees them occupied. All this he will never do, unless the habit is formed during his imprisonment. It is in prison that he must be trained up in the way he should go. It is there that he must become accustomed to work steadily, diligently and strenuously from eight to ten hours a day, just as other laborers do, or he will never be able to live by the labor of his hands amid the sharp and active competitions that exist among the toiling millions of America.

4. *The acquisition of a trade.* Next to the habit of steady, unremitted, persevering labor, the most important acquisition of the convict, as an aid to self-support after his liberation, is skill in his occupation, a mastery of the business in which he is engaged, be it what it may. The ranks of criminals, as we have seen, are recruited chiefly from the class of persons who have no regular business, and especially from that class who have never learned a trade. To teach a convict a trade is to place him above want, that is, to remove from his path one of the greatest occasions of crime. Make a criminal a good mechanic, and you have gone far towards making him an honest man. The true doctrine is, that all people should learn to help themselves. If they do not know how, the best service we can do is to teach them. A convict learning a trade is mastering the art of self-help. He feels that he is doing something for himself. As a consequence, he is filled with hope; he is in better temper; his spirits are cheerful and buoyant. This state of mind is in itself a reformative agency, and the man in whom it is found is much more likely to be morally improved by his incarceration than another in whom hope, alacrity, and cheerfulness, have been extinguished. And unless a prisoner acquire both the habit of industry and the knowledge of some handicraft, that is, the power as well as the wish and purpose to live honestly, he will be sure, sooner or later, to go back to his old criminal practices.

Now, the pursuit of the prisoner's reformation, through the agencies above enumerated, is a work in which time, and no little amount of it, is an essential element. It is at this point that the contract system infringes, with a crushing force, upon the great work: and too often the collision proves fatal to it. Contractors have no interest, *per se*, in the reformation of prisoners. Their interest as contractors and the interest of the prison as a reformatory institution not only do not run in parallel lines, but they are repellant and antagonistic. Let any changes be suggested with a view to giving more time to the mental, moral and industrial improvement of the prisoners: for instance, that the number of religious services be increased; that the present fragmentary system of secular instruction be replaced by one more rational and effective, or that the convicts be taught a complete trade instead of such snatches thereof as are now commonly imparted. Suggestions of this sort would be sure to be met with the objection: "The contractors would not agree to such an arrangement; they would not consent to such an abridgement of the convict's labor."

Thus does this system of prison labor, by a necessary law, by an instinct of its very nature, oppose itself to all those great and vital forces of reformation, except the simple habit of industry, by which, if at all, the inmates of our prisons must be reclaimed, regenerated, and re-absorbed into the mass of upright, industrious and honorable citizens.

Upon the whole, it is our settled conviction that the contract system of convict labor, added to the system of political appointments, which necessarily involves a low grade of official qualification and constant changes in the prison staff, renders nugatory, to a great extent, the whole theory of our penitentiary system. Inspection may correct isolated abuses; philanthropy may relieve isolated cases of distress; and religion may effect isolated moral cures; but genuine, radical, comprehensive, systematic improvement is impossible.

SECTION TENTH.

FINANCES.

It is the occasion of no little regret to the commissioners, that we are unable to give much reliable information on this important subject, beyond what is contained in the preceding section relating to the prison industries. This inability is due to two causes. In the first place, the wardens of nearly all the prisons who responded to our printed interrogatories, were entirely silent on the department of finance ; and, in the second place, the matter is presented, in the annual reports, in a manner so complex, confused and obscure, that we find it, in the majority of cases, quite impossible to arrive at clear and satisfactory results. For instance, the warden of the western penitentiary, Pa., says : "For the last five years, the prison has been self-sustaining, with a surplus, at the beginning of 1865, of about $19,000." On turning to the prison reports for the three last of those years, which are all in our possession, the balance, as far as we can understand the financial exhibit contained in them, seemed to be on the other side. For one of said years (1862), we have an explicit statement of the inspectors, confirming this view. A committee of the State Senate was appointed in 1863 to inquire into the condition and management of the prison. They prepared a series of questions, to which they required answers from the authorities. One of their questions and its answer were as follows : " QUESTION 13TH. *What has been the amount of your expenditures in the last year, and the amount realized from different sources ?* ANSWER. In our last annual report, the item of subsistence of prisoners (for 1862) was $17,-153.64. In same period there was realized by convict labor the sum of $14,622.73." This, of course, would leave a deficit of $2,530.91. It must be remembered, too, that, as in Pennsylvania, the subsistence of the prisons is a charge upon the counties, the salaries of the officers, which are paid by the state, are not included in the above statement. This item for 1862 was $13,330.00, which gives a total of expenditures for that year of $30,483.64, and leaves a total deficit of $15,861.51

The manner in which the officers are apt to strain a point in order to place their finances before the public in as favorable a light as possible, is more than intimated in the communication made to us by Mr. Prentice, warden of the Ohio state penitentiary. To our question, "Is your prison self-sustaining?" he replies, "It is not." Q. "Has it ever been ?" A. "The *annual reports* show that, at times, it has been fully and beyond self-sustaining." Q. "If such is the fact, why has it ceased to be self-sustaining ?" A. "The *fact* is not clear that it has *ever* been *really* so." It is to this over-anxious desire of prison officers to make the best possible financial exhibit, that we attribute the involved and obscure methods so generally adopted in keeping the prison accounts.

The comparative earnings and expenditures in the Ohio prison, as shown by the reports, for ten years, are as follows;

Year.	Earnings.	Expenditures.
1855	$67,935 34	$64,017 95
1856	64,324 45	73,421 40
1857	70,667 85	73,774 43
1858	62,700 76	79,850 90
1859	83,456 28	77,516 36
1860	97,905 60	97,610 26
1861	92,823 11	100,125 28
1862	73,071 21	93,443 72
1863	83,260 73	98,177 10
1864	85,264 96	103,309 17
Total	$781,410 27	$861,246 57

The aggregate deficit for these ten years; it thus appears, was $79,836.30, or an average of $7,983.63 per annum. The average annual cost per prisoner for these ten years is stated at the enormous figure of $319.94, which seems almost incredible. The present building has been occupied since 1835. The aggregate earnings during thirty years, according to the reports, amounted to $1,586,863.07, and the aggregate expenditures $1,500,639.07; being an excess of income over expenses of $86,224

The earnings and expenditures of the Charlestown prison for the last twelve years, omitting fractions of dollars, are as follows:

Year.	Earnings.	Expenditures.
1855	$53,801	$67,759
1856	55,077	62,749
1857	53,599	68,297
1858	51,425	69,533
1859	55,242	64,359
1860	60,317	57,706
1861	62,992	65,410
1862	43,951	64,656
1863	61,426	71,261
1864	56,206	83,709
1865	62,799	84,960
1866	81,709	80,868
Total	$698,544	$841,267

The aggregate deficit for these twelve years is seen to be $142,723 ; the average annual deficit, $11,893.   In only two years was there a surplus of earnings.   The tide turned first in 1860, only to recede again in 1861.   Again, it changed in 1866, and this time the change is likely to be permanent, new contracts at greatly increased rates having recently been made.   Mr. Haynes estimates that the expenses of the prison for 1867 will be $100,000, and the earnings $120,000; giving a clear profit of $20,000.

The state prison of Connecticut, during the forty years of its existence at Wethersfield, has been more than self-supporting, with the exception of three years.   The exception occurred during the progress of the late civil war, and was due to two causes; first, to the very high price of every article consumed, and secondly, to the fact that the labor of the convicts had been let for a term of years, prior to the general advance in prices, including, of course, labor as well as merchandise.   During the first twenty years of its history, under the administration of Moses C. and Amos Pilsbury, the prison realized a clear profit, in round numbers, of $100,000.   What the surplus earnings have been since the younger Pilsbury retired, we are not informed.

The financial management of the New Hampshire state prison has been, for a long series of years, eminently successful.   In nine years preceding and including 1866, with an average number of prisoners rather under than over one hundred, the aggregate net gain to the institution from the labor of the convicts has been about $20,000, or $2,325 a year.   Only one year was there a deficit, and then it was only to the trifling amount of $471.68.   It is probable that deficiencies would have occurred much more frequently, but for the fact that a portion of the prisoners are not let to contractors, but labor directly for the prison, in the manufacture of shoes and other articles, which are sold and thus increase its income.   It is estimated by Mr. Mayo, the warden, that the profits of the penitentiary, during the financial year ending May 1st, 1866, had the contract system been discontinued, would have been from $12,000 to $20,000, whereas the actual gain was less than $1,000.

The admirable financial results attained in the Maine state prison, since the abolishment of the contract system, have been stated in the immediately preceding section.   Many of the convicts in that prison are earning for it not less than two dollars a day, so we were assured by the warden.

The prosperous condition, in a pecuniary view, of the Wisconsin penitentiary, has also been exhibited in the same section. Of the finances of this institution, Mr Commissioner Cordier holds this language: " The prison of the state of Wisconsin has been in operation since 1851. My predecessors in office kept no account of the earnings of the prisoners. I am, therefore, not able to say what the average annual cost per prisoner for the last ten years, or for the whole period, has been. By considering the following figures, however, we may judge whether or not the management of this prison, under its present system of labor, has been economical and profitable, and conducted to the best interest of the state. The Legislature has appropriated in all, for prison construction, improvements and current expenses, the sum of $525,826. The present estimated value of grounds and buildings is $436,000; consequently, the actual cost to the state for the support of her convicts for fourteen years, would be only $89,826, or a trifle more than $6,400 per year. It should be taken into consideration that the average number of convicts employed on productive labor amounted to only eighty per year; that we have been all the time without machinery in our workshops, and that, in short, this institution is yet in its infancy. Under these circumstances, the results obtained are, I think, highly satisfactory."

The average number of convicts in the eastern penitentiary, Pennsylvania, which is conducted on the separate plan, from 1855 to 1864 inclusive, did not vary materially from 375. Their earnings during those ten years, including the work done for the prison, which is always omitted in estimating the earnings in congregate prisons, amounted to $201,331. The expenditures, in the same period, on account of subsistence, were 273,289, and for salaries, $178,705, making an aggregate of $451,994, and showing an excess of expenses over income of $247,663.

SECTION ELEVENTH.

SENTENCES.

The just and proper duration of imprisonment for a violation of the laws of society, is one of the most complex, difficult and perplexing questions in jurisprudence. The law usually fixes a minimum and maximum for the period of incarceration; but there is for the most part, a broad interval between the two extremes, so that a wide discretion—perhaps, upon the whole, too wide—is left to the courts in determining the length of each individual sentence. We have been informed by an eminent member of the bar of Baltimore, now deceased, that he had known a man to be sentenced to the Maryland penitentiary ten years for stealing a piece of calico, not worth more than ten dollars, and another man to be sentenced for only ten years to the same prison, who had committed an atrocious murder. Surely, *such* inequalities are beyond all bounds of reason; and they suggest the necessity, or at least the propriety, of confining judicial discretion within narrower limits in affixing the penalties to different offences.

Both on our tour of inspection, and in their written communications, not a few of the wardens complained to us of these inequalities, as tending to exasperate and dishearten prisoners, and thus to affect injuriously the discipline and reformatory power of the prisons.

Mr. Rice, of Maine, observes on this subject. " There is very great variation between the terms of sentence, awarded for the same offence by different judges, and even by the same judge at different times. Thus, two brothers, convicted of larceny under circumstances of about equal aggravation, were sentenced by different judges—one of them for one year, and the other for six. Again, of four persons convicted of manslaughter, one has ten years, another five, another two, and the fourth only one; and yet the last is the worst case of the four."

Mr. Cordier, of Wisconsin, says: " There is a great difference in the length of sentences awarded by different judges for the same offence. For instance, three men were convicted of forgery. One of them forged a check for some $3,000; was found guilty; and, though this was his third offence, was sentenced to but four years' imprisonment. The second forged a note for eleven dollars (his first offence), and was also sent for four years. The third forged a check for several thousand dollars on a bank in Milwaukie, and was only sentenced to one year's imprisonment. Another illustration: Two men were convicted of larceny. One stole some clothes (his third offence), and was sentenced to six months' imprisonment in the state prison. The other who had, up to the time of his arrest, borne a good character, attempted, in a drunken fit, to sell a saddle belonging to his employer; for which attempt, on conviction thereof, he was sentenced to two years' hard labor in the same prison."

Mr. Haynes, of Massachusetts, on this question, holds the following language: " One of the most perplexing matters is the inequality of sentences; each of our judges appears to have a standard of his own by which he is guided, and a great diversity of opinion seems to exist among them upon this subject. I know it is impossible so to regulate sentences that equal and exact justice will be administered in each individual case, as crimes of the same class vary so much in the aggravation attending them. I do not wish to be understood as favoring either of the extremes, but simply to point out the fact, and the influence it has upon the discipline of the prison. To illustrate this point, I would refer to the sentences for passing counterfeit money, the aggravation in such cases being only in the amount passed, or in the reputation of the one passing it.

"Of those in the prison at the present time for passing one counterfeit bill, the sentences vary from one to five years; for the passing of two bills, from two to ten years. We have one man here who plead guilty to passing three counterfeit five dollar bills, who was sentenced to fifteen years; another who plead guilty to passing four twenty dollar bills, who was sentenced to but four years; one man, for having in his possession ten counterfeit bank bills, was sentenced to one year; another, for the same offence, to twelve years. These men may work near each other, and, of course, learn the facts, and it can be easily imagined that great dissatisfaction would be engendered, and our discipline suffer in consequence. No logic can convince a man that justice requires him to serve fifteen years here for passing fifteen dollars in bad money, when his neighbor serves but four for passing eighty, everything else being equal. Scarcely a week passes that I am not appealed to in regard to such cases. It is in vain for me to say that I am not responsible for it. Many of these men are friendless, and naturally look to me for advice and assistance."

Dr. Campbell, of Pennsylvania (western penitentiary), remarks: " To the officers of the prison, who are unacquainted with the commission of the particular crimes, the length of the sentences seems very unequal. For example : " It is not long since that a prisoner was discharged after serving his full sentence of one year for horse-stealing ; while to-day (Sept. 12th), three men were brought in under sentence of five years each for the same offence."

The average length of sentences in different state prisons varies considerably ; the shortest average being in Wisconsin, where it is about two years, and the longest in Vermont, where it is nearly or quite seven years. In Massachusetts, the average duration of imprisonment approaches six years ; in New York and Ohio, it does not vary much from three and a half years.

The testimony of the officers of our American state prisons—so far as we have any expression of opinion from them at all—is unanimous to the effect, that an imprisonment of ten years and upwards breaks down, physically and mentally, the greater part of those who are subjected to it. Mr. Prentice goes so far as to say that nearly all such become monomaniacs.

Among others, we put the following question : "Which would be likely to be most beneficial to convicts, so far as their reformation is concerned—sentences of moderate length, with the *certainty* that they must be served out, or sentences of greater length, with the *hope* that they may be abridged by pardon?" We append a few of the answers.

Mr. Rice, of Maine : "Sentences of moderate length, with the certainty that they must be carried out, are much better than any others. Give a young man a ten years' sentence for a crime, committed most probably under the influence of liquor, and it takes all heart out of him ; whereas he would accept a five years' imprisonment philosophically, and make the best of his term. The chances of his reformation are, I think, much better in the latter case."

Mr. Haynes : "Moderate sentences, with *certainty*, are the best."

Mr. Prentice : "Short sentences, and no *pardon*, are better than long sentences, and *hopes*."

The Rev. Mr. Douglass, of Vermont : "Short sentences, and no pardon, are much better than the other plan."

Mr. Miller, of Missouri : "I think that short sentences, with the certainty that the term must be served out, would be more beneficial, especially to young convicts, than the other plan. But I am not in favor of a system that shuts out all hope of pardon, as implied in the former of the two alternatives propounded.. I have found the hope of pardon to have a powerful influence for good in making prisoners do well and continue to do so, hoping thereby to make friends, who may speak a word in their favor at some future time. My own opinion is, that the only restraint necessary (if there be any necessary), to be placed on the pardoning power, is to require the governor to refuse a pardon to all who cannot procure a certificate of good conduct from the warden. I found this plan, voluntarily adopted by Gov. Gamble and Gov. Hall, to be of great service."

It will have been observed that, in the judgment of state prison officers, moderate sentences, carried out with certainty, are preferable, as an agency in reformation, to longer sentences, with the hope of pardon constantly agitating the breast of the convict, and exhausting those energies which ought to be given to the work of his own amendment. The great majority of state prison sentences are as long as it would be desirable to make them; probably not a few are quite too long. Thus, of the 518 convicts received into the Massachusetts state prison in 1866, no less than 293, or nearly four-fifths, were sentenced for five years and upwards; 135, or nearly one-fourth, for ten years and over; and the astounding number of 42, equal to one-fifth of the whole, were sentenced for life ! Of the 1,456 admitted into the male state prisons of New York for the same period, 376, nearly one-fourth, were sentenced for five years and over; while 119, about one-twelfth, were imprisoned for ten years and upwards.

But there are other classes of prisons—the houses of correction or penitentiaries and county jails—in which the major part of the sentences are far too short either for the good of the prisoner or the welfare of society. The undue brevity of sentences is matter of complaint in other countries. Thus, we learn from Mr. F. Hill's work on Crime, that the average period of imprisonment in England, in other than the penal servitude prisons, is about fifty days, and in Scotland about forty; while in the prison of Edinburgh, the greater part of the prisoners remain less than 14 days ! Even this last statement is almost paralleled by what happens in the Erie county penitentiary of our own state, where last year, out of 1,768 persons committed, 1,149, nearly-two-thirds, were sent under sentences of thirty days or less. In the Monroe county penitentiary, and probably also that of Albany, if the convicts sent from the District of Columbia are excepted, the average length of sentences is about four months. In the county jails, the average does not exceed much, if at all, two months; and in the majority of cases, the sentences are for only a few days. The class of prisoners known as "revolvers," that is, who are returned to prison almost as soon as they are discharged, is very numerous. There are criminals, or, more properly perhaps, misdemeanants, who are committed to the penitentiaries and common jails of New York, ten, fifteen, twenty times a year. On our visit to the jail in Kingston, Canada, we asked an old woman whom we saw there, how many times she had been in jail? "Oh," said she, "the times are uncountable,"

The insufficiency of these short terms of imprisonment, however often repeated, to produce any permanent good effect upon the character of the imprisoned, must be apparent on the least reflection. On no subject are the superintendents of prisons more generally agreed, or more earnest in their convictions, than on the utter futility and worthlessness of such imprisonments. And with good reason do they so believe and hold. For 1. These short periods of confinement have the effect to demoralize the prisoners and make them reckless of punishment. Indeed, the chief tendency is, through the temporary check put on their passions and the vigor received from wholesome diet, to stimulate their criminal propensities and impart increased power to do mischief on their discharge. 2. They have, and in the nature of things cannot but have, a discouraging influence on the officers. Their effect is to weary out the very heart, from utter despair of doing the prisoners any good, making them callous and indifferent to their condition, and exhausting, on a round of petty and useless services, the strength and spirits which are required for more important duties. 3. The indirect expense to society, occasioned by these continual re-arrests, prosecutions and convictions, and still more in the amount of property stolen in the intervals between the imprisonments, is enormous, and may well plead for a change in the system. 4. The practice of short imprisonments is fatal to anything like reformatory treatment. It is impossible even fairly to initiate a reformation during a detention of a few weeks or months, to say nothing of carrying it out to its normal results. The first thing necessary to change the modes of thought and feeling in a criminal, to improve his habits, to elevate his character, and to make him an honest man, is, that he be certain that he is cut off for a considerable length of time from his former associations and practices. If he be sentenced to an imprisonment of but a month or six weeks, or indeed anything short of six months or a year, he will not give a thought to any change in the plan and habit of his life; he will think only of the number of days that must pass away before he can be restored to his old liberty of action. We are, therefore, of the opinion that such a reform in our criminal laws is necessary as will, on subsequent convictions, raise the maximum of punishment, and that by great advances. When a person, by repeated petty offenses, evinces a proclivity to crime, his term of imprisonment should be made so long that idle and vagrant habits may be broken up, and replaced by habits of industrious and steady labor. We look upon sentences of considerable length as absolutely essential to the reformation of prisoners, while short ones we regard as not useless merely, but as having a decidedly mischievous tendency in many ways.

But this whole question of prison sentences is, in our judgment, one which requires careful revision. Not a few of the best minds in Europe and America have, by their investigations and reflections, reached the conclusion that time sentences are wrong in principle; that they should be abandoned; and that reformation sentences should be substituted in their place. Among the advocates of this view, abroad, we may mention Mr. Commissioner Matthew Davenport Hill, for nearly thirty years recorder of Birmingham, and one of the ablest criminal judges of Great Britain; and his brother Frederick Hill, for many years inspector of prisons in England and Scotland, and the author of a judicious and valuable treatise under the title of " Crime: its Amount, Causes, and Remedies."

Mr. Commissioner Hill thus delivers himself on this subject, in a charge to the grand jury of Birmingham, in 1855: "Gentlemen, if you desire, as I most earnestly do, to see this principle [that of allowing convicts to earn a diminution of sentence by good conduct] universally adopted, you must be prepared to strengthen the hands of government, by advocating such a change in the law as will enable those who administer the criminal justice of the country to ·retain in custody all such as are convicted of crime, until they have, by reliable tests, demonstrated that they have the will and the power to gain an honest livelihood at large. You must be content that they shall be retained until habits of industry are formed—until moderate skill in some useful occupation is acquired—until the great lesson of self-control is mastered—in short, until the convict ceases to be a criminal, resolves to fulfill his duties both to God and to man, and has surmounted all obstacles against carrying such resolutions into successful action. But as no training, however enlightened and vigilant, will produce its intended effects on every individual subjected to its discipline, what are we to do with the incurable? Gentlemen, we must face this question; we must not flinch from answering, that we propose to detain them in prison until they are released by death. You keep the maniac in a prison (which you call an asylum) under similar conditions; you guard against his escape until he is taken from you, either because he is restored to sanity, or has departed to another world. If, gentlemen, innocent misfortune may and must be so treated, why not thus deal with incorrigible depravity? This is a question which I have asked times out of number, without ever being so fortunate as to extract a reply. It is always tacitly assumed that imprisonment must not be perpetual; but whether that assumption is founded on any reason supposed to arise out of the nature of things, or whether it only rests on the present state of public feeling, I know not. If the former ground is taken, I would give much to learn what the argument is; when disclosed, I must either answer it or yield to it; but while I am kept in the dark, each alternative is barred against me. If, however, this assumed inadmissibility of perpetual imprisonment is rested on the present state of public sentiment, I have seen too often the change from wrong to right in that mighty power, to despair of its becoming an ally instead of an opponent. It is my belief that if long terms of imprisonment, even to perpetuity, were placed before the public mind as indissolubly connected with the privilege to the convict of working out his own redemption from thraldom, by proving himself fit for liberty, it would require no great lapse of time to produce the change in opinion which I contemplate. Alarm on the score of expense ought not to be entertained, for two reasons. First, because no unreformed inmates of a prison, however extravagant its expenditure may be, cost the community so much as they would do, if at large. This fact has been so often proved that I must be allowed to assume it as undeniable. But the second reason is that prisons may be made either altogether, or to a very great extent, self-supporting."

The charge, from which the above extract is taken, provoked a very general discussion in the public press of Great Britain. Most of the prominent papers of the realm had leading articles on the subject. The London Times thus expresses its judgment: " We believe it will be found the cheapest and most politic course, as well as the most humane, to leave no stone unturned to bring about the reformation of the criminals, *and not to discharge them upon society until they are reformed.* In desperate cases, we must even acquiesce in the conclusion of imprisonment for life." The Spectator, one of the ablest and most influential journals in England, emphatically indorses the view of Mr. Hill and the Times.

"Their detention," it observes (that is, the detention of criminals till their cure), "would be justified upon the same grounds that justify the detention of the insane. As long as they are criminally disposed, they are (morally) insane, and should be in safe custody. As soon as they have ceased to be criminally disposed, and become disposed, like ordinary people, to earn their livelihood in an honest way, they are cured of their insanity, and may safely go at large." The same paper goes on to say: "The conclusions which we are enforcing have been conceded, weighed, set aside for after-thought, re-examined, sifted, reduced to their best working form, and at last consistently advocated by some of the most influential men of all parties, in this country as well as in France. We have had meetings on the continent and in England; and within the last fortnight, besides the conference of the friends of reformatory discipline at Birmingham, we have had Mr. Demetz, of Mettray, addressing friends at Bristol on the subject, and an admirable address by Mr. M. D. Hill to the grand jury at Birmingham. By degrees, no doubt, these earnest, consistent and laborious reform-ers are gaining ground; they have established their case clearly on the grounds of logic and practical experience; they are obstructed by nothing but that inherent laziness, which continues the influence of bad laws in keeping up the numbers and force of the criminal part of the population. It is thus shown as clearly as it is possible to establish any social fact, that, monsters and acci-dents excepted, we might cut off the larger part of the supply of criminals, and remove the large portion of permanent criminals from society; but society, too lazy to go into the detail, unwilling to take the responsibility which a conviction thus worked out could alone justify, again compromises the question with adult as well as juvenile offenders, and in lieu of detaining the culprit until he has proved his cure, determines that he shall be sentenced to an imprisonment for a definite period, as if we said to a man laboring under insanity, or under any infectious disease, you shall go to the doctor's for two months, then to be driven forth upon society, cured or uncured."

The following extracts from Mr. F. Hill's work on Crime will show the views entertained by him on this important question: "The leading principle of the criminal law of Britain," he observes, "like that of most other countries, as I understand it, is to deter from crime by awarding punishment for different offences, in pro-portion to their magnitude. The objections to this principle appear to be insurmountable. It is impossible to carry it out with anything like accuracy, owing to the infinite variety of circumstances which increase or diminish the guilt appertaining even to the very same act, or which, indeed, make the commission of a comparatively small offence really more culpable, sometimes, than that of a great offence. * * * But even if it were possible to draw up a list of offences according to their real turpitude and their injury to society, and to prepare a corresponding scale of punishment, it appears to me that it would not be wise to act on such a system. The object of punishment being the prevention of crime, that punishment cannot be well fitted for its purpose which, after its infliction has terminated, allows an offender to be let loose again on society without regard to the cause of his offence, or the fact whether such cause has been been removed. * * * * I maintain that the natural consequence of crime, in the withdrawal of the offender from the privilege of mixing with society, which he has abused, and his confinement until he be safely restored, more fully carries out this principle of punishment than almost any other plan that could be proposed, for in proportion to the length of the habit of crime and heinousness of the offences committed, would, in general, be the period necessary for effecting a cure, and consequently the duration and amount of the punishment.

"Whether, therefore, we try to suppress crime by the mere infliction of punishment according to the number and magnitude of the offences committed, or whether we try to stop it by curing the criminal, or, where complete cure is impossible, by improving him to the greatest possible extent, the natural and self-regulating punishments which God has instituted and pointed out appear to be the best and most accurately adapted for securing that the amount of punishment shall be in proportion to the offence committed.

" But who is to determine the fact of cure, and who the precise means by which a cure is to be effected? I would submit that those only are fully qualified to do this who are entrusted with the charge of the offender ; who have time to study his character and to watch the effect of the different influences brought to bear upon him in the formation of new habits ; and who have opportunities of gradually relaxing the system of discipline and of trying the new powers of their moral patient to resist those temptations to which he would be exposed on his return to society.

" No one thinks of sending a madman to a lunatic asylum for a certain number of days, weeks or months. We content ourselves with carefully ascertaining that he is unfit to be at large, and that those in whose hands we are about to place him act under due inspection, and have the knowledge and skill which afford the best hope for his cure ; that they will be kind to him, and inflict no more pain than is necessary for his secure custody and the removal of his malady ; and we leave it for them to determine when he can safely be liberated.

"Perhaps it may ultimately be found, by cautious experiment, that a somewhat similar process may be safe and expedient in the treatment of criminals ; and that while it is still left to the courts of justice to determine on the guilt or innocence of the accused, and on the necessity of their withdrawal from society, it may be assigned to those entrusted more or less directly with the reformatory treatment to determine the time of release ; subject, however, to a most competent, well-appointed, careful and responsible supervision and control, such as ought to be invariably exercised in the case of mad-houses, and subject to the proviso, that no amount of subsequent good conduct should be considered sufficient to warrant the liberation of a person who had once been guilty of deliberate murder.

"Such a mode of proceeding, however, even if attainable, must be approached by slow degrees ; partly because it is the spirit of English improvement (and happy for the country that it is so !) to proceed cautiously and deliberately, ascertaining the consequences of each step before venturing on the next ; and partly because it seems essential to the successful operation of a law, especially in this country, that it should not only be wise and just, but that it should be approved of by the great body of the intelligent and well informed among the people ; who, however, with a sufficient allowance of time for inquiry and reflection, never fail to give their sanction to what is really good."

Our own convictions are well and forcibly expressed by the several writers, from whom we have taken the foregoing extracts. When a man has been convicted of a crime—burglary, arson, forgery, or any other—we would have the judge address him somewhat after this manner : John Doe, you have wickedly broken one of the just and necessary laws of society. You have shown yourself to be a dangerous man, unfit to go at large. You must be separated from your fellows. You must suffer the penalty which the law has righteously annexed to transgression. You must be made to feel that the way of the transgressor is hard. You must be shut up in prison, and remain there until you give evidence that you are a changed man and can be safely permitted again to enjoy your freedom. In thus dealing with you, society has no resentments to gratify, no vengeance to inflict. It is for your good, as well as for her safety, that she so afflicts you. You must be punished for what you have done ; but while you are in prison, we will give you every chance to recover yourself. Nay, more ; we will help you in that work. If you are ignorant, we will teach you ; we will give you an opportunity of learning in the prison school what you ought to have learned in the common school. If you never learned a trade, we will put you in possession of one. If religious truth was withheld from you in childhood, you shall be made acquainted with it in your adult age. We will, through these various agencies, impart to you the power, and we would fain hope the disposition, to earn and to eat honest bread. But you must work with us. Your will must be in accord with ours ; your efforts must tend in the same direction. There must be, on your part, a real and a hearty co-operation with us. On this condition alone can you attain that radical reformation of character, to which we wish to bring you, and the attainment of which is indispensable to your liberation. Until you show, to our satisfaction, that you can be restored to freedom with safety to the community, your imprisonment must continue ; and if you *never* give us such satisfaction, then you *never* can be discharged ; your imprisonment will be for life. We do not set the madman free, till he is cured of his madness ; neither can we safely, or even justly, set the criminal free, till he is cured of his propensity to crime. As the security of society and the good of the lunatic require that his confinement should be regulated upon this principle ; so, equally, do the security of society and the good of the criminal demand that his incarceration should be adjusted upon the same principle. We put your fate into your own hands ; and it is for you to determine the period, within certain necessary limits, during which the restraint upon your liberty shall continue. You may either prolong it to the close of your life, or restrict it to a duration which you yourself will allow to be but reasonable and just.

Towards the main conclusion here announced, thinking men, devoted to the great work of prison reform, have been struggling through years of careful study and patient reflection. In the fourth edition of his Lectures on Political Economy, published in 1855, Archbishop Whately remarks : " With respect to every sentence of confinement to hard labor, whether at the treadwheel, or of any other kind, we would venture to suggest what we cannot consider as a most important improvement, viz., that instead of a certain period of *time*, a convict should be sentenced to a certain quantity of *work*. * * * * The great advantage resulting would be, that criminals whose habits probably had previously been idle, would thus be habituated not only to labor, but to form some *agreeable association* (i. e., the thought of their liberation) with the idea of labor. Every step a man took on the treadwheel, he would be walking out of prison; every stroke of the spade would be cutting a passage for restoration to society."

Captain Machonchie, the great pioneer in our day in the introduction of new and better, because more rational, *principles* in prison discipline, also recommends the adoption of task sentences instead of time sentences. By his system, the offender is required to accumulate a certain number of marks, to be given as a reward for work, which marks may be forfeited by misconduct, or may be expended, if the prisoner so choose, up to a certain point, in procuring extra indulgences. But first of all, his very living must be paid for by these marks, for in prison they have a certain money value; and it is only the balance which remains, after deducting the sum of the marks forfeited and expended, that can go towards his liberation. The same principle underlies this system and that which we here recommend, viz., that the duration of sentences is to be measured, not by time but by conduct. This, indeed, is distinctly recognized by the captain in his General Views on Convict Management, where he adds, as an argument in favor of the principle, the following consideration: "The object of this is to make good conduct a steady object of pursuit to all prisoners, if only in the beginning, as an indispensable means to recover their freedom; and the habit of thus considering it as a valuable means will gradually give it value, in their estimation, as in itself a desirable end."

SECTION TWELFTH.

REFORMATION.

Diligent inquiry was made by the undersigned, both when visiting the prisons and through their printed interrogatories, in regard to the reformatory results reached by the discipline of our American prisons as at present administered ; but, despite our diligence, the information obtained was rather meagre than otherwise.

The reformatory influences brought to bear on the convicts, are the usual religious services of the Sabbath ; Sunday-school instruction in some prisons ; a certain amount of pastoral labor, where resident chaplains are employed ; the prison libraries ; a certain degree—amounting in general to a mere modicum—of secular instruction by teachers ; the influence of hope, so far as that element is supplied by the commutation laws of such states as have them ; in a few prisons, the philanthropic labors of volunteer workers from outside ; the distribution of religious tracts and papers ; the Bible furnished to every convict, who is willing to receive it ; regular labor ; the trade taught, alas, to but very few ; and, in the majority of prisons, kind and humane treatment, especially by the higher officers.

The following is all the statement we are prepared to make on the subject of reconvictions. In Massachusetts, the percentage of reconvictions, as reported to us, is about thirteen ; in New Hampshire, five ; in Ohio, six and an eighth ; in Pennsylvania, western penitentiary, fourteen ; and in Wisconsin, five and a tenth. We have no information on this point from other prisons. But little reliance, for practical conclusions, we apprehend, is to be placed on the statistics here exhibited. Criminals in the United States are continually changing their jurisdiction, so that of the number of inmates in a given prison at any given time, it is impossible to know how many who are first comers there, may have been imprisoned elsewhere one, two, or more times. Add to this, that just in proportion as we are distant from the period of the first crime, it becomes difficult to prove the recommittal ; and the difficulty is increased where men change their abodes incessantly, where no records are kept, and especially where one prison administration is so frequently replaced by another as is the case in many of our prisons. There are, therefore, many sources of fallacious inference from statistics of reconvictions in American prisons, however the case may be in other countries. Still, there can be no doubt that the proportion of recommittals is less in the United States than it is in most European countries. On this subject, Mr. Commissioner Hill, in a letter to the secretary of the Prison Association, says : "We cannot boast of so small a proportion of relapses as in your prisons ; the difference is, indeed, enormous ; but you will permit me to doubt whether your superiority is due to your prison discipline. I may be mistaken, but I cannot attribute it to such a cause. To me it appears that you owe it to the unspeakable advantage you have over us in the high value of labor, skilled and unskilled, in the United States. Your prisoners, after discharge, can maintain themselves by honest means, with far less difficulty than is encountered by ours ; who, when they go forth from the prison gates, have to encounter a severe struggle, first to obtain employment, and then to keep it. These difficulties are, I trust, diminishing ; but they are still such as to make the disposal of our prisoners a work of trouble and anxiety."

As regards the evidences of reformation shown by convicts, we have but little testimony; and that little is not particularly satisfactory. Mr. Willard, of Connecticut, says: " Some convicts, when discharged, exhibit good proofs of reformation; but the majority give none." Mr. Seaton, of Michigan, remarks: "The cases of reformation are few and far between." Dr. Campbell, of Pennsylvania (western penitentiary), observes: "Very little evidence of reformation is given by convicts either before or after discharge." Mr. Prentice, of Ohio, testifies: "Many"—the proportion, however, is not stated, and therefore we cannot judge of the value of the testimony—"many, when discharged, return to their homes, and engage in the pursuits of honest industry. Their conduct is generally good." Mr. Cordier, of Wisconsin, gives an attestation of much interest. He says: " Those of our discharged convicts whom I have met"—and it will be remembered that, in his travels through the state, he fell in with numbers of them—"were working at their respective trades; they were sober, honest, industrious men, and had the full confidence of their employers." This testimony is highly gratifying. We are the less surprised at it and the more ready to put faith in it, since we know that, besides the use of other important reformatory agencies, it is made a special point in the discipline of the Wisconsin prison to impart the full knowledge of a trade to every convict who remains long enough to acquire it. From Vermont, we have no general statement concerning the reformation of prisoners; but an isolated fact has been communicated to us, at once so interesting and so honorable to the actor, that we are constrained to transcribe it. A prisoner, on his discharge, enlisted in the army and received five hundred dollars bounty money, the whole of which he used to pay the principal and six years' interest of losses sustained by three or four persons through his criminal acts. This man certainly gave the highest possible evidence that the work of reformation in him had been thorough and complete.

As regards the important matter of aiding convicts, on their liberation, to procure situations at work and so helping them to stand firmly to any resolutions they may have formed to lead a better life, we have little to report that is encouraging. "No efforts are made to procure situations for discharged convicts;" "there is no system employed to obtain places for liberated prisoners " — "no efforts of any importance have been made toward procuring situations for released convicts "—" I have done *something* towards procuring situations for discharged convicts "— " no special person is appointed to aid discharged convicts in obtaining work; officers sometimes interest themselves to this end"—such is the tenor and such the form of nearly all the answers received on this point. They show that, in the case of most of the state prisons visited, either nothing at all is done, or nothing on system, nothing effective, to extend to prisoners, after their release, the help most essential in their struggles towards an honest life. In only four states is such aid given systematically and to purpose. These are Pennsylvania, New York, Massachusetts and California.

In the first named of these states, this duty is performed by the Philadelphia Prison Society, the oldest and most venerable organization in America, looking to the relief and reformation of prisoners. The *modus operandi* of their work we learned from their secretary, Mr. John J. Lytle. The society has a committee on discharged convicts, whose duty it is to visit every convict in the eastern penitentiary previous to his discharge, and to ascertain from him his necessities, the state of his clothing, where he proposes to go when liberated, what are his wishes, prospects, plans, &c., &c. Having thus gained the needed information, the committee proceed to another part of their duty, that of action. They furnish the prisoner, when necessary, with suitable clothing; procure railroad tickets to send him to his friends, if he so desire; obtain employment for him, if he wishes it, and it is practicable; and, in general, give such counsel and assistance, as seem suited to his need. Every convict in the prison, on the eve of his liberation, had been, during the year preceding our visit, thus interrogated, advised and aided, according to the exigencies of his individual case.

The Prison Association of New York performs a similar service for discharged convicts in this state. The general agent of the society, under the instructions of the committee on discharged convicts, receives such prisoners on their liberation as need and desire his kind offices; furnishes needful clothing to the deserving; procures temporary board in respectable families for such as require it, taking numbers of females to his own house, to whom his wife performs the office of matron; obtains situations for them; purchases tickets or gets free passes on railroads for those who desire to return to their friends at a distance, or go to work in the country; provides tools for such as are comptent to start in business for themselves, and can be trusted to that extent; and performs other offices innumerable of kindness and philanthropy to this and other classes of the fallen and unfortunate, particularly those arrested and held for trial, for whose benefit the Association was organized. In this way the society has, during the twenty-two years of its existence, provided permanent places for 3,677 liberated prisoners, being an annual average of $167\frac{1}{7}$ persons. So far as these persons could be traced, after coming under the care of the Association— and correspondence has been kept up with a large proportion of them, sometimes running through a series of years—they have, almost to a man, done well. We cannot learn that more than three per cent. of the released prisoners so cared for and so aided, have ever relapsed into crime. Some of them have risen to eminence and acquired wealth as merchants, manufacturers, master mechanics, members of the learned professions, &c.; while the mass, with growing families around them, have been and are earning an honest competence in the humbler walks of life.

Of all the states of the American Union, Massachusetts alone has established a "state agency for discharged convicts," and employs a public officer, whose duty it is made by law "to counsel such discharged convicts as may seek his aid, and to take such measures as he may deem proper and expedient to procure employment for such of them as may desire it, by corresponding with persons engaged in agricultural and mechanical pursuits, and with benevolent individuals and associations." His general method of procedure is as follows: Being officially informed when such and such convicts are to be liberated, he visits them in prison some time previous to their discharge. In the interviews thus sought and obtained, he learns something of the history of the men, their condition in the past, whether or not they have homes, and if so, where, and what are their wants and wishes, whereby he is the better able to devise fit means for their relief and assistance. He inquires whether they desire him to find situations for them, or to aid them in any other way, and if they want places, in what part of the country and at what business. He directs every one who wishes his help to call at his office, in the city of Boston, on leaving the prison. In the meantime he exerts himself, by correspondence and otherwise, to meet their desires and provide for their necessities. The warden of the Charlestown prison, in one of his annual reports, states that the agent has never failed to find, for every one who asked it, employment at the work he wished. A cabinet maker of Boston declared that he had employed from forty to fifty discharged convicts, whom he knew to have learned their trade in the prison, and that he had never found it necessary to dismiss one of them for bad conduct. The results of this agency for discharged convicts are most encouraging. They show that most of the prisoners, when discharged, are enabled, through the offer of employment provided by the agent, to resist the temptations to idleness and crime, by which they are assailed, and so to become industrious and good citizens. Surely, in this view, they offer an example well worthy to be studied and imitated by other states. The legislation which provided such an agency to aid in the recovery and restoration to virtue of fallen men and women cannot be regarded otherwise than as both considerate and merciful, and as no less wise than it is beneficial.

Although California, for obvious reasons, was not included in our visitation, it may not be improper to mention, in this connection, that a society has been formed in that state on the model of the New York Prison Association, under the name and title of the "California Prison Commission." A like attention to the interests of discharged prisoners is given by the younger as by the elder of these organizations. The secretary and agent of the commission, the Rev. James Woodworth, in his first annual report, mentions several interesting cases of discharged convicts, who were relieved by the society. He adds, in a general way, that forty-nine persons of this class had been sent by him from San Francisco to various points in the interior, where they had a prospect of work, and fourteen provided with places through personal effort by himself. This officer further says: I am confident that many have seen great cause for thankfulness in our efforts in their behalf, and I feel very sure that the moral power exerted over many by the

Commission, through its agents, in the counsel he has given them and the kindness he has endeavored to show them, has been great, and will be lasting in its effects upon them."

It is much to be regretted that so little interest is felt, and so little effort made by the community in general, in behalf of convicts who, having served out their terms of imprisonment, have been restored to freedom. It seems to us that there are few obligations bearing more heavily on society than that of making systematic and adequate provision for the encouragement of discharged convicts. Very few of these men, when they leave prison, have any means of support, except the ability to labor. Going forth into the world, in the majority of cases with a mere pittance of funds, and in all with a tainted name, objects everywhere of distrust and aversion, however good their resolutions (and not a few have formed such), they find it exceedingly difficult, when no helping hand is extended to them, to obtain honest employment. Enforced idleness will, in the natural course of things, lead to bad company. In such company, all the inducements to crime will again be spread before them, when they have no virtuous friends whose advice and example may shield them from temptation. Will it be matter of wonder, is it not rather within the compass of reasonable expectation, that they yield to such temptation? If, then, society would complete the cure of its criminals, which has been begun in prison, it must not refuse its sympathy and aid on their liberation. Everywhere, meet assistance should be rendered either directly by the government, as in Massachusetts, or indirectly by voluntary organizations, as in New York, Pennsylvania and California. The citizens of any state, who refuse the needed aid, are false to themselves, as well as derelict to a high social duty. They betray an important interest of society, and may be called to answer for a brother's blood.

As to tracing convicts after their liberation, with a view to ascertain the effect of the discipline to which they have been subjected, this appears, scarcely anywhere, to be regarded as a duty. The general report is : "No effort is made to keep trace of prisoners after their discharge."

Upon the whole, as the result of our observations, and with a sincere desire to do injustice to none, we are constrained to avow the opinion, that there is not a state prison in America in which the reformation of the convicts is the one supreme object of the discipline, to which everything else is made to bend, and which the whole administration, in all its arrangements, is intended to advance. The eastern penitentiary, at Philadelphia, probably, comes the nearest to that design, considering not only what is done by the prison authorities themselves, but also the official connection of the Philadelphia Prison Society with the institution and its systematic and earnest labors for the moral amendment of the prisoners. Massachusetts and Wisconsin, we think, would come next. But neither of the three, in our judgment, makes the reformation of its inmates the primary and leading aim. In the first named, the deterrent element is, as we conceive, designedly made the prominent one ; and in regard to the other two, to prove that reformation is not their one great and controlling end, it is enough to refer to the common report received from them and others, and just cited, to the effect that no efforts are made to keep track of their convicts after they have left them ; for, surely, some little exertion would be put forth to ascertain how far their chief design, the supreme object of all their plans and toils, had taken effect ; and this could only be learned from the conduct of their wards after they should have been set at liberty.

Among the witnesses examined by the Prison Association commission of 1866, was Mr. Benjamin Leggett. This gentleman, by a rare good fortune, has served as an under-officer in Sing Sing prison from 1831 to the present time, with intervals not amounting in the aggregate to more than six or seven years. Of the thirteen administrations, numbered in the history of the prison, he has been connected with ten; and his unprecedented retention in the service is due to his rare merit as an officer. He has seen much, observed closely, and formed his judgments with calmness and candor on the facts which have fallen under his notice. The following questions and answers occur in his examination: " What do you conceive to be the primary object of prison discipline?" "The reformation of prisoners." "Do you think that our state prisons in New York are conducted with a prime regard to reformation?" "I do not." "What is, practically, the end in view?" "I should think the view was to make the prison pay its way." This is a mild statement of the case, and shows the caution of the witness. In reality, the view is, not only " to make the prison pay its way," but to show as large a surplus revenue as possible. In the execution of the duty whose results we are now reporting, we have had occasion to read hundreds of prison reports and other documents relating to prisons; and there are few of them whose perusal has not caused us pain. One string is harped upon, *ad nauseam*—money, money, money. This crops out everywhere, in executive messages and the reports of wardens, boards of inspectors, legislative committees and special commissions. To bring the prisons to the point of self-support, to secure net profits from convict labor, to make financial exhibits that will gratify the public craving for such profits—this seems to be the supreme object of all (except the chaplains and physicians) connected with their administration and sharing its responsibility. The directors of a bank or a railroad could hardly be more anxious for large dividends than these gentlemen are for good round incomes from the labor of their prisoners. Where one word is spoken for reformation, hundreds are spoken for revenue. Do we blame these officers for their anxiety? Far from it. It is but natural that agents should wish to please their principals. It is the public that is to be blamed. It is the public that demands such financial exhibits from those whom they have put in charge of their penal institutions. It is the public that exacts balance sheets, in which the credits shall exceed the debits to the greatest possible extent. General Pilsbury has presided over two prisons in succession for a period of nearly 40 years; and during that time his clear profits from convict earnings, with but a moderate number of prisoners, have amounted to nearly or quite a quarter million dollars. The General has mani. fold merits as a prison superintendent, but with the public his balance sheet crowns all the rest. Ninety per cent of his prisoners reformed and restored to society honest men, with the quarter million in the other column, would have made him less of a hero with the multitude than he is to-day. And yet his actual record leaves that very multitude poorer by many millions than would the record we have supposed. Can we wonder that prison officers should be so eager to show striking financial results, or blame them for their eagerness? They are human, like the rest of us; but they would be more or less than human, were it otherwise.

When Howard was on his tour of prison inspection on the continent of Europe, he found at Rome, as a part of the great hospital of San Michele, a prison for boys and young men, which equally surprised and interested him. Over the door of this prison was placed the following inscription: "Clemens XI, Pont. Max. Perditis

Adolescentibus corrigendis instituendisque, ut qui inertes oberant, instructi, Reipublicæ serviant.   An. Sal. MDCCIV, Pon. IV." In English: "Pope Clement XI.   For the conviction and instruction of profligate youth; that they who, when idle, were injurious, may, when instructed, be useful to the state. 1704."   And within the prison, in the principal apartment, he found this (as he says) "admirable sentence:"   "Parum est coercere improbos pœna, nisi probos efficias disciplina."   In English: "It is of little use to restrain the bad by punishment, unless you render them good [reform them] by discipline."   "In which" [sentence], says the illustrious philanthropist, "the grand purpose of all civil policy relative to criminals is expressed."   In the centre of the room was hung up the inscription, "Silentium;" so that, as would appear, the silent system of associated labor, combined with a reformatory discipline, was fully inaugurated in Rome, in the very beginning of the eighteenth century; that is, more than 150 years ago.   One of the main agencies relied upon to effect the desired reform of the young prisoners was steady, productive labor, and imparting to them the knowledge of a trade; for various handicrafts were taught in the establishment, such as printing, book-binding, designing, smithery, carpentery, tailoring, shoemaking, weaving, dyeing, and the like.   Surely, Pope Clement XI must be allowed a place among the most enlightened rulers and reformers that adorn the annals of our race.   On some points, the world might still go to school to him with advantage.

Howard's opinion as to the importance of making the reformation of criminals the special and primary object of prison discipline, is clearly enough indicated in his remark, above cited, on the inscription in the prison of San Michele.   But he has declared his conviction on this point more fully, if not more explicitly, in numerous passages of his published writings.   We transcribe one or two such passages from his works.   On the reformatory character of penitentiaries, he remarks :   "Many have been reclaimed and made useful members of society in foreign houses of correction, and have thanked God for their confinement in them.   These houses are called in Holland *verbeter huizen*, that is, bettering houses ; and the settled object, in all such houses, should be to make men better, at least more useful subjects."   On the comparative value of reformation and pecuniary gain in a prison, he has this observation : "Their earnings constitute, in my opinion, but a secondary consideration ; for surely it is impossible to place any degree of *profit* in competition with the prospect of meliorating the minds of our fellow-creatures." In another place, he assigns as a reason for "embarking in the scheme of erecting penitentiary houses," "the pleasing *hope*, that such a plan might be the means of promoting the salvation of some individuals ; of which (he adds) every instance is, according to the unerring word of truth, a more important object than the *gaining of the whole world*." On the significance of the word "penitentiary," as indicating the design of government in founding such institutions, he has the following remark : "The term *penitentiary* clearly shows that parliament had chiefly in view the *reformation* and *amendment* of those to be committed to such places of confinement." The italics in the above extracts are the author's; not ours.

In the prison laws of most of the states of the American Union, there is a distinct recognition of the principle that the reformation of criminals is to be accounted as one and, indeed, a main object of imprisonment. The earliest mention of this which we have seen (there may have been earlier) is in an act passed by the Legislature of Kentucky in 1797, in which it is declared that "the reformation of offenders is an object highly meriting the attention of the laws."

The commission of 1866, put this question to nearly every witness whom they examined : "What do you conceive to be the primary object of prison discipline ?" Without a dissenting voice, their answer was, "the reformation of the imprisoned." This, then, is at once the theory of our laws and the opinion of those who have thought most and are best able to form a correct judgment on the question. Alas, that there should be so wide a chasm between our theory and our practice.

Another question put by the commission of 1866 related to the opinion of the witnesses whether convicts could be reformed. All agreed that much the larger portion could be reformed and returned to society honest men, while some thought that this result might be attained with nearly all. Mr. Haynes stated his judgment to be that eighty per cent. (four-fifths) might be reclaimed; and without stopping to examine all the answers, our impression is that something like this is about the proportion believed to be reformable by most of the witnesses.

Captain Machonochie went much beyond this. He believed that convicts could be "gained, *to a man*, by a system which would *study their natural feelings and seek their own improvement* (advantage), together with that of their country, in their treatment." Again he says (Norfolk Island, pp. 14 and 15): "I fear neither bad habits nor any other difficulties. I believe that while life and sanity are spared, recovery is always possible, if properly sought. There is indefinite elasticity in the human mind, if its faculties are placed in healthful action, and not either diseased by mal-treatment, or locked up in the torpor of a living grave. These latter causes may intimidate outside, but they must, even in their best form, injure the sufferer himself. And the christian morality seems more than doubtful that would sacrifice the known for the unknown, the actual patient for the supposed looker-on. Every difficulty would, I feel assured, be removed from the administration of penal law, if we but recognize the principle that to seek well and wisely the reform of our criminals, we *must* inflict on them all the suffering that is really necessary for example, and that *we are not entitled to do more.* We may not do evil that good may come. There is no qualification to this precept."

The reformatory principle of prison discipline was wholly unknown to the ancient world. Indeed, its discovery and application are of a comparatively recent date even in modern times. It rests upon a foundation made up of four subordinate principles, viz: 1. That, for the practical purposes of society, human law should deal with crime not to avenge, but to prevent it. 2. That punishment, which is merely vindictive and repressive, defeats its own purpose, and does but increase the mischief which it would avert. 3. That severity, out of proportion to the offence and pressed beyond the point at which it may suffice to restrain the culprit from repetition and the looker-on from imitation, is both unnecessary and injurious. 4. That the justice of human punishment is measured by its necessity; and while the wise legislator should labor to make it fall with certainty on guilt, he should, at the same time, as far as may be, reconcile the claims of society to protection against crime with the reformation of the transgressor, and should make such reformation, where he can, an instrument in securing that protection. These four principles form a broad and solid basis on which to rest the necessity and duty of a reformatory discipline in prisons.

Happily for the interest of society, the reformatory principle of prison discipline, since its introduction as an element into modern civilization, has made remarkable progress. Indeed, its history

affords one of the most signal illustrations of social advancement
in our day.   The age is full of material wonders.   Each year
brings forth something more startling than the last, and imagination is less swift than reality.   Physical science has annihilated
space and time.   Thought travels, on the wings of the lightning,
from continent to continent; and the morning paper brings us,
from distant nations, the events of yesterday.   We know what
took place last night in London and Paris, just as we know what
took place in Washington and New York.   But amid all these
prodigious changes, as bewildering in their rapidity as they are
astounding by their grandeur, it may well be doubted whether
there is anything more novel, anything fuller of interest and true
joy to the genuine lover of his kind, than this quiet movement,
which embraces the outcasts of earth, and wins its noiseless vic-
tories within prison walls.   This movement has, indeed, borne
precious fruit, which has developed itself in institutions most excellent and beneficent—reformatories for the young, intermediate
prisons for adults, refuges and homes for liberated female convicts, and aid societies for the relief and encouragement of prisoners of both sexes, who are disposed to amend their lives; the
whole constituting what may be called The Modern Reformatory
System of Prison Discipline.   This system has found its most perfect development in what is now known throughout the civilized
world as the Irish plan of convict treatment, devised and carried
into execution by Sir Walter Crofton, who therein gave effect to
principles, with important modifications of his own, first distinctly
announced by Captain Machonochie.   This system was prompted
by and finds its support in an inspiring faith in the capability of
human beings, though stained with crime, to be won back to virtue.   Moreover, the founders of the Irish system had the further
faith that the fallen are reformable through the action of the same
motives of hope and fear which control the conduct of the unfallen.   Its great aim has been, acting on that faith, firmly but
kindly to apply those motives to convicts, dealing with them, not
as a chaotic mass, but as men having idiosyncrasies like other men,
and to be swayed and moulded, like them, by personal influence,
by individual care, and by wise adaptations to particular cases,
though without sacrificing important and necessary general rules.
Before our day, the faith of which we speak found little acceptance among statesmen and legislators, and it is still repudiated by
numbers both among the leaders of opinion and in social life.

And no doubt it has its limits and qualifications; for there are moral incurables—we speak ethically, not theologically—just as there are men and women who are placed by physical disease outside the resources of the healing art. What the proportion of incorrigibles may be, we know not; but, with the institution of a prison discipline truly and thoroughly reformatory, we are persuaded that it will turn out to be but insignificant.*

The question whether a reformatory discipline can be made also self-supporting, is one which has its importance; but that importance is by no means paramount. In the first place, we think that the salaries of prison officers should be a charge upon the government, not upon the industries; and that a prison ought to be accounted self-supporting, which meets all other necessary expenses; of which, under the discipline which we propose, the moral and intellectual machinery would form a much larger proportion than it does under that which now prevails. In the Pennsylvania state prisons, this is even now the method of computation; the government paying the salaries, and the counties making up any deficit in the cost of subsistence, &c., accruing in the earnings of the convicts. In the second place, we entertain not the slightest doubt that, under an apportionment of expenses according to the principle here suggested, reformatory prisons could readily be made self-sustaining, and even to yield a surplus revenue to be applied in the accumulation of gratuities to convicts as a reward for industry and good conduct, as in the Irish and other foreign systems; said gratuities either to be paid to their families during their incarceration, or to themselves, in instalments, after their discharge, on the condition of forfeiting whatever may still remain unpaid by any further offence committed by them.

But even if the improved system should fail to accomplish what is here supposed, it would, nevertheless, in the end, be less burdensome to society, if it should, as we believe, show itself really endowed with the power of reforming the wicked; for, in truth, reformation is the cheapest, whatever it may cost. A prison system, however economical it may be in appearance, will be found, in practice, very expensive, if it does not correct the majority of the prisoners; for the reason, as Mr. Livingston well said in his letter to Roberts Vaux, that " discharging an unreformed

---

* See paper read before the British Social Science Association, in 1861, by the Right Honorable Thomas O'Hagan, her Majesty's Attorney-General for Ireland.

thief is tantamount to authorizing a tax of an unlimited amount to be raised on individuals."

We have spoken of gratuities to be paid to convicts out of their prison earnings, as a stimulus to good behavior. In this regard, there is a broad distinction between American and European convict prisons. In none of the former, so far as we are informed, is any such allowance made; in few, if any, of the latter, is it withheld. The only way in which convicts in our prisons can earn anything for themselves is by doing over-work. But in many American prisons, over-work is not allowed; in few is it subjected to legal regulation; in prisons where it is allowed, but a moderate percentage usually have the privilege of doing it; and in none is the permission to do it made the reward of good conduct. In European convict prisons, on the other hand, gratuities or a percentage of earnings are the common, if not the universal, rule. In Ireland, they are given, *bona fide*, as a reward, and are designed to stimulate, first, to general good conduct; secondly, to industry; and, thirdly, to fidelity and attention in lesson-learning. In England, the theory is the same; but the application of the principle, if Miss Carpenter's book " Our Convicts " is to be taken as authority, not quite so faithful. When Howard visited the celebrated penitentiary at Ghent, in 1778, he found the prison " a well regulated manufactory," and says that " the prisoners were allowed one-fifth of their earnings for themselves." Buxton visited the same institution in 1817, at which time it was as busy a hive of industry as he had ever seen, the prisoners receiving the whole of their earnings—which he justly characterizes as a " bad arrangement." In 1823, according to the report of the London society for the improvement of prison discipline, one-third of their earnings was then allowed to the prisoners; and this, we believe, is about the proportion of to-day. It was made a special object there to impart to all comers the knowledge of a trade, and the consequence was that not more than five per cent ever returned a second time. Many instances are on record, in which convicts, on leaving prison, have set up the business which they learned during their imprisonment, have acquired the means of doing so by the capital they saved at the same time, and have prospered by those habits of industry, which they formed while undergoing the hard discipline of penal servitude. In France, also, a considerable part of the convict's prison earnings goes to himself; in De Tocqueville's time, it was two-thirds, which he rightly regarded as out of all proportion to reason and fitness; but, at the same time, he remarks, that "the expenses, by means of which the wicked are reformed, are investments, of which society reaps the fruits at a later period;" and adds that, if the gratuities allowed to prisoners do but have a tendency to improve them, however considerable they might be, he would be far from censuring the allowance. We may add, in this connection, that most of the witnesses before the commission of 1866, who were interrogated upon this point, expressed their preference for a percentage of earnings over a permission to do over-work.

SECTION THIRTEENTH.

PARDONS.

On the subject of pardons, the undersigned inquired diligently in reference to the following points: The proportion of convicts, under different terms of imprisonment, pardoned during a term of ten years; how extensively the hope of pardon is entertained by the inmates of state prisons; the effect of this hope on prisoners, particularly as regards their reformation; whether the pardoning power has been heretofore, or is now, too freely exercised; whether any limitation should be placed on the pardoning power; whether a board of pardon, to aid the Executive in examining applications for clemency, would be good policy; and whether it would be expedient to enact that a fresh crime, after pardon, should work a forfeiture thereof, and remand the prisoner back to his original punishment unabridged.

We were not as successful in obtaining information on these points as we could have wished to be. Indeed, there is, in most American prisons, too little system in keeping criminal statistics, and the prison registers are restricted to too narrow a range of topics. There are various points, not included in the records, on which it would be desirable to have information; and as it respects the points actually embraced in the registers, too little care, at least in some prisons, is used to have the registers kept with regularity and exactness.

As regards the first point named above—"the proportion of convicts, under different terms of imprisonment, pardoned during a term of ten years,"—we are able to give the statistics of only four prisons, those, to wit, of Massachusetts, Ohio, Wisconsin, and the eastern penitentiary of Pennsylvania.

The statistics of the Charlestown prison, Massachusetts, cover

the whole period of its history, from October 3d, 1828, to Octo-
1st, 1866. They are as follows:

Whole number of commitments		5,207
Different persons committed		4,607
Discharged by expiration of sentence	3,754	
Pardoned	659	
Died	178	
Committed suicide	5	
Discharged by order of the courts	36	
Sent to insane hospital	34	
Escaped	23	
Convicted for the second time		475
do third time		97
do fourth time		23
do fifth time		4
do sixth time		1
Now in prison		518
Sentenced less than two years		1,182
Served their time out		1,116
Pardoned	20	
Died	15	
Sentenced from two to three years		1,253
Served their time out	1,078	
Pardoned	86	
Died	26	
Sentenced from three to five years		1,394
Served their time out	1,034	
Pardoned	160	
Died	36	
Sentenced from five to ten years		919
Served their time out	481	
Pardoned	216	
Died	40	
Sentenced to ten years and upwards		*274
Served their time out	45	
Pardoned	83	
Died	31	

* Not including life sentences.

Sentenced for life	185

Pardoned	96
Died	29
Escaped	2
Discharged by order of the courts	12
Sent to insane hospital	5
Now in prison for life	41

Whole number received last year 247

Average sentence received last
    year .... 5 years, 3 months, 5 days.*
Aggregate amount of sentences, 18,911 years, 4 months.
Average sentence of all received, 3 years, 9 months, 5 days.
The longest time served by any
    one now in prison, on one
    sentence .... 18 years, 8 months.
The next longest .... 14 years.

The statistics of pardon for ten years in Ohio are as follows :

Whole number of prisoners during last ten
    years 2,843
Whole number of pardons during last 10 yrs. 535
Whole number of prisoners sentenced for life
    during last 10 years..................... 59
Whole number of prisoners sentenced for life,
    pardoned last 10 years.................. 21
Average imprisonment of life-men pardoned
    last 10 years......................... 6 yrs. 7 mos. 5 dys.
Whole number sentenced five years and less
    than 10 during last 10 years............. 513
Whole number sentenced five years and less
    than 10, pardoned...................... 109
Average imprisonment of the pardoned .... 2 yrs. 8 mos. 5 dys.
Whole number sentenced 10 years and less
    than 15 years........................ 81
Whole number sentenced 10 years and less
    than 15 years, pardoned............... 23
Average imprisonment of this class......... 4 years 26 days.
Whole number sentenced for 15 years and less
    than 20 years........................ 16

---

* Not including life sentences.

Whole number sentenced for 15 years and less
than 20 years, who were pardoned_____ 3
Average imprisonment of the pardoned ____ 5 yrs. 4 mos. 8 dys.
Whole number sentenced for 20 years and
over _____ 7
Whole number sentenced for 20 years and
over, pardoned_____ 1
He was in prison_____ 5 yrs. 8 mos. 10 dys.

The following are the pardon statistics of Wisconsin for ten years :

Whole number of prisoners confined during
last 10 years_____ 919
Whole number of prisoners pardoned during
last 10 years_____ 187
Whole number of life-men in prison during
last 10 years_____ 36
Whole number of life-men pardoned during
last 10 years, (6 convicted before '56)____ 12
Average imprisonment of life-men pardoned 6 years.
Whole number sentenced for five years and
less than 10_____ 49
Whole number sentenced for five years and
less than 10, pardoned_____ 25
Average imprisonment of this class_____ 3 years.
Whole number sentenced for 10 years and less
than 15_____ 17
Whole number sentenced for 10 years and less
than 15, pardoned_____ 10
Average imprisonment of this class_____ 3 years 5 months.
Whole number sentenced for 15 years and less
than 20_____ 2
Whole number sentenced for 15 years and less
than 20, pardoned_____ 1
Average imprisonment of this class_____ 3 years 8 months
None sentenced for over 20 years.

The following statistics of the eastern penitentiary, not exclusively, however, relating to pardons, like those of the Charlestown prison, cover the entire period of its history from October 1, 1828, to January 1, 1865. We give the entire table, as its information, as well that not relating as that relating to pardons, will be found both interesting and valuable :

Whole number received	5,063
Discharged by expiration of sentence	3,715 or 73 per ct.
Pardoned	671 or 13⅓ per cent.
Average time served or pardoned	1 yr. 10 mos. 5 dys.
Pardoned and subsequently re-convicted	6 per cent.
Died	279 or 5½ per cent.
Average time served	2 years 4 days
Committed suicide	11
Escaped and removed in various ways	62
Second comers	413 or 8⅞ per cent.
Sentenced less than two years	1,878 or 37 per ct.
Served their time out	1,608 or 85 per ct.
Pardoned	146 or 7 per cent.
Average time served	7 months 9 days.
Died	27 or 1⅔ per cent.
Average time served	8 months 29 days.
Now in prison	80 or 24½ per cent.
Sentenced from two to three years	1,307 or 26 per ct.
Served their time out	1,003 or 76 per ct.
Pardoned	169 or 13 per cent.
Average time served	1 year 19 days.
Died	58 or 4½ per cent.
Average time served	1 yr. 2 mos. 7 dys.
Now in prison	65 or 20 per cent.
Sentenced from three to five years	1,240 or 24¼ per ct.
Served their time out	861 or 69 per cent.
Pardoned	173 or 14 per cent.
Average time served	1 yr. 8 mos. 26 dys.
Died	102 or 8⅕ per cent.
Average time served	1 yr. 8 mos. 22 dys.
Now in prison	77 or 23⅔ per cent.
Sentenced from five to ten years	491 or 9¾ per cent.
Served their time out	213 or 43 per cent.
Pardoned	133 or 27 per cent.
Average time served	3 years.
Died	69 or 14 per cent.
Average time served	2 yrs. 8 mos. 1 day.
Now in prison	66 or 13½ per cent.
Sentenced to ten years and upwards	147 or 3 per cent.
Served their time out	30 or 20 per cent.
Pardoned	50 or 34 per cent.

Average time served................. .... 5 yrs. 5 mos. 18 dys.
Died.. 23 or 15 per cent.
Average time served .... 4 yrs. 10 mos. 4 dys.
Now in prison............................... 37 or 11⅓ per cent.
Average time served...................... 4 yrs. 1 mos. 7 dys.
Sentenced for life......................... None.
Pardoned..................................... None.
Average time served .... None.
Died... None.
Average time served...................... None.
Now in prison............................... None.
Average time served...................... None.
Sentenced to five years and upwards........ 638 or 12½ per cent.
Served their time out...................... 243 or 38 per cent.
Average time served...................... 6 yrs. 5 mos. 10 dys.
Pardoned..................................... 183 or 29 per cent.
Average time served...................... 4 yrs. 5 mos. 28 dys.
Died... 92 or 14½ per cent.
Average time served...................... 3 yrs. 2 mos. 12 dys.
Now in prison for five years and upwards.... 103 or 31¾ per cent.
Average time served...................... 3 yrs. 8 mos. 15 dys.
Served ten years and upwards of all received 30 or ½ of 1 per ct.
Whole number now in prison............... 325
Average time served...................... 3 yrs. 2 mos. 5 dys.
The longest time served on one sentence.... 17 years 3 months.
Received last year.......................... 150
Average sentence........................... 2 yrs. 5 mos. 15 dys.
Aggregate amount of sentences............. 13,690 years.
Average sentence........................... 2 yrs. 8 mos. 13 dys.

The foregoing statistics yield some curious results, which are in part exhibited in the following table. There are no life sentences in Pennsylvania.

	Percentage of convicts pardoned, whose sentences were life.	Average time served by life-men.	Percentage pardoned of whole number imprisoned.	Percentage pardoned, whose sentences were for five years and less than ten.	Average time served by the foregoing class.	Percentage pardoned, whose sentences were for ten years and over.	Average time served by the foregoing class.
		Years.			Years.		Years.
Massachusetts _____	50	7¾	12¾	20½	4	32	7
Pennsylvania _____	____	____	13½	27	5	34	5½
Ohio _____	40	6½	18¾	21½	2⅔	25	5
Wisconsin _____	33	6	20	50	3	53	3½

In Massachusetts the life men have formed one twenty-fifth of all the committals, and yet these have constituted a full seventh of the pardoned. In Ohio, the disproportion is not so great, and yet it is very considerable ; the men sentenced for life constituting one-forty-eighth of the imprisoned, and one-twenty-fifth of the pardoned. In Wisconsin, the life men are one-twenty-ninth of the prison population, and one-fifteenth of the pardoned. Thus, the convicts for life would seem to form, in some respects, a privileged class, and the chances are that they will have a shorter imprisonment than men sentenced for twenty or even fifteen years. The pardoning power much more frequently chooses these men, in proportion to their number, as the objects of its clemency, than it does the general mass of prisoners ; and it would hence seem to be the interest of the criminal to have meted out to him the heaviest punishment which the law accords to his offence.

The gross average of pardons on all convicts confined in American prisons will be from fifteen to twenty per cent.; the average on convicts sentenced for five years and less than ten, will be from twenty to twenty-five per cent.; the average on convicts sentenced for limited periods of ten or more than ten years, will be from twenty-five to thirty per cent.; while that on convicts sentenced for life reaches the enormous proportion or forty to fifty per cent.

The eminent French commissioners, De Beaumont and De

Toqueville, who visited this country some thirty years ago, to examine the penitentiary system of the United States, have thus philosophized on the causes of this free, not to say extravagant, use of the pardoning power by American executives : " Without examining the question whether it is absolutely necessary for society that some authority should have the right to suspend punishment, it may be said that the less this authority is elevated above the rest of society and the less independent it is, the greater will be the abuse of pardoning. In the United States, the governor of each state, alone, has, generally, the dangerous privilege of pardoning. * * * In spite of the extent of his prerogative in special matters [that of an unrestricted right of pardon, for example], the governor of a state occupies a social position by no means elevated. Every one may approach him at any time ; may press upon him anywhere and at any moment. Thus given up, without an intermediate person, to urgent solicitations, can he always refuse ? He feels himself the slave of public caprice ; he depends upon the chances of a re-election ; and he is obliged to treat his partizans with extreme care. Would he dissatisfy his political friends by refusing a slight favor? Moreover, being invested with but little power, he loves to make as much use of it as possible."

There can be no doubt that the accessibility of American executives—all citizens, even the humblest, feeling at liberty to approach them and demand an audience—is a great, probably the greatest, occasion of the extraordinary number of pardons dispensed by them. We have heard Dr. Francis Lieber mention that, on a certain occasion, when he happened to be the guest of the late Gov. Marcy, of New York, on emerging from the breakfast table one morning, they encountered not less than a dozen women in the hall; whereupon the governor remarked, that those women were probably all in pursuit of pardons for rascally husbands, who would, in all likelihood, beat them as soon as liberated.

After the statements made above, showing the enormous percentage of pardons actually granted, it will excite nobody's wonder to be told that, according to the unanimous testimony of the wardens of state prisons, the hope of pardon is well nigh universal among convicts. This occupies their thoughts by day, and fills their dreams at night; and to the attainment of it their best energies are given, as well as the greater part of the money they earn by over-work, or can otherwise command; for the race of pardon brokers—men who make a regular business of procuring pardons for convicts—long since noticed and denounced by Matthew Carey, is not yet extinct. What this eminent philanthropist says in his Thoughts on Penitentiaries and Prison Discipline, is as true now as it was then, that the grant of pardon does not so much depend on the degree of guilt, as on the pecuniary means of the convict to hire this corps. A person convicted of murder in the second degree, attended with the most aggravating circumstances, who has powerful friends, or is plentifully supplied with money, has tenfold more chance of a pardon, than a poor wretch found guilty of petit larceny.

The wardens are also nearly, though not quite, unanimous in the conviction, that the hope of pardon, so generally entertained by convicts, has a bad effect upon them in many ways. It unsettles their minds, makes them uneasy, indisposes them to labor, and impedes their efforts at reformation by directing their thoughts and energies to another and inferior end. The wardens who dissent from this view are either in charge of prisons which are very small, as Mr. Rice, of Maine, or of prisons in which the concurrence of the head is made an essential condition to the attainment of a pardon. This is the case in the Wisconsin prison, whose chief officer, Mr. Cordier, says : "Knowing that no pardon can be obtained without the commissioner's certificate of good conduct, the convicts are careful not to render themselves liable to any complaint. The hope of pardon stimulates them to please their officers by obedience, diligence, and general good behavior." This, in effect, lodges, at least to a degree, the ultimate power of pardon in the head of the prison, and puts the fate of the convict measurably into his own hands. So far, it assimilates itself, though under conditions which greatly mar its completeness and impair its efficiency, to the Irish system of prison discipline, and to that which we have recommended in our section on " Sentences;" the essence of which consists in the substitution of reformation sentences in place of those which limit the imprisonment to a fixed period of time.

It is further the general opinion of the superintendents of the prisons that the power of dispensing pardons has been, in former years, too freely exercised ; and while some say that, at present, it is less, quite as many affirm that it is more freely used than formerly; while others, still, represent the proportion of the pardoned now to be about the same that it has ever been. The following statement of Mr. Cordier gives the annual pardons in Wisconsin for ten years, showing a moderate diminution during the last four:

"There have been 187 convicts pardoned within the last ten years, as follows:

By Gov. Parkford, in	1856		12
do	do	1857	9
By Gov. Randall, in	1858		16
do	do	1859	31
do	do	1860	27
do	do	1861	31
By Gov. Salmons, in	1862		10
do	do	1863	20
By Gov. Lewis, in	1864		11
do	do	1865	20

"It will be seen that our Governors are generally more careful in granting pardons during their first year of office than subsequent, and I think the increase is due to political considerations."

Again, the wardens of our state prisons, with almost entire unanimity, concur in the judgment that some limitations should be placed on the prerogative of pardon; and a goodly number express themselves in favor of the creation of a board of pardon to aid the executive by examining and giving judgment on applications for his clemency.

Quite a number of the more judicious of these officers favor the enactment of a law to the effect that a new crime, after a pardon, should work a forfeiture of the pardon, and remand the prisoner back to his original punishment, to which of course the new punishment should be superadded.

A few opinions of prison officers in reference to the foregoing points are here appended: Mr. Rice, of Maine, says: "I think the pardoning power should never be used except with the approval of the warden." He would have the power limited by this restriction, imposed by law. Mr. Seaton, of Michigan, remarks: "I think an application for pardon should be noticed in some paper published in or near the place where the offence may have been committed, for a certain length of time, so that the governor may be placed in possession of all the facts, should those who would be most likely to know feel disposed to communicate them to him." Mr. Haynes, of Massachusetts, observes: "We have a

board of pardon* to aid the Executive by examination cf applications for his clemency. It would be expedient to enact a law that
a new crime, after a pardon, should work a revocation of the pardon, and that the prisoner should be remanded to his former punishment." Mr. Cordier, of Wisconsin, says: " A board of pardon
to aid the Executive by examining applications for his clemency
would be advisable, and I should prefer the judges of the highest
court of each state as such a board. A law working the forfeiture
of a pardon for a new offence, and remanding the offender to serve
out his original sentence, would be not only expedient but also
just."

We have already mentioned, in the introduction to this report,
that in reply to a number of printed interrogatories sent, in 1865,
by a special committee to all the ex-governors of the loyal states,
then living, letters had been received from fifteen of those officers,
whose names are there given (p. 19), and that those letters had
been placed in our hands, to make such use of them as we might
deem proper. As they contain the matured opinions of gentlemen
of large experience and high ability on topics of grave importance
connected with the general subject of pardon, we have judged it,
on the whole, fairest to the authors and best for the public to print
them in full, and they will accordingly be found so printed in the
appendix.

What will most strike the reader, in the foregoing detail of fact
and opinion, will no doubt be the extraordinary percentage of
pardons dispensed by executive clemency. Pardon, which is
either a total or partial remission of the penalty incurred by
transgression, is an act which vacates and nullifies legal justice,
although, since all human laws are imperfect, it may, in doing so,
give effect to essential justice. A power of pardon has existed in
all states. It is a wise and necessary power. Injustice is sometimes inflicted through the forms of law; and to correct wrongs so
done, the interposition of the pardoning power is sometimes required. Beyond this, its exercise is perilous. When it assumes
the province of review, and sits in judgment on the proceedings
of the courts, it becomes a usurpation, and, by invading the province of the judiciary, tends to bring its power into popular contempt.

We object to the frequent exercise of the pardoning power on
several grounds.

* Meaning, we presume, the Governor's Council.

1. It nullifies the certainty of punishment. This quality of certainty is the most potent element in the whole punitory system. This was the favorite maxim of Beccaria. Sir Samuel Romily, one of the most eminent of British lawyers and reformers, laid down the doctrine that, if punishment could be reduced to absolute certainty, a very slight penalty would prevent every crime that is the result of premeditation. What grave offence was ever deliberately committed, except under the expectation, in the mind of the perpetrator, that he would escape the grasp of justice? The felon does not weigh the gain of his misdeed with the penalty annexed to it, and strike the balance; but in his mind, the gain and the belief that he will somehow elude the penalty, are joined together. Would any man pass a five dollar counterfeit note if he were sure that five years' imprisonment would be the consequence? Would the boldest robber rifle the mail if he knew that death would be the certain doom entailed by that act?

But what is the effect of granting frequent pardons? Is not its direct tendency to diminish the certainty of punishment and multiply the chances of escape? The practice, therefore, holds out a positive encouragement to transgressors, and contravenes that vital requisite of every criminal code, on which Beccaria, Romily, and all succeeding writers have so strenuously insisted. So strongly did the late Sir James McIntosh feel on this subject, that, in a debate in the British House of Commons, in 1819, he declared that one pardon contributed more to excite the hope of escape than twenty executions to produce the fear of punishment, and expressed concurrence in the opinion of a magistrate, whom he pronounced peculiarly competent to judge, that pardons contribute to the increase of crime.

2. It increases the hope of pardon, already too strong in the criminally disposed. But this follows as a necessary corollary from the argument under the last head, and we therefore need not enlarge on the subject.

3. It impedes the reformation of criminals, which we have seen to be a leading object of all wise human punishments. On this subject the warden of the Western penitentiary, Pa., in his report for 1865, has the following remarks: "Nothing so much hinders the proper management and reformation of the prisoner, as his restless anxiety to obtain a pardon. Almost every man enters the prison with the hope of pardon, and that hope is based principally upon the fact that so many of his fellow prisoners have been

released." The frequent exercise of the pardoning power is undoubtedly an anchor of hope to the incarcerated criminal; and there is very little likelihood of penitence or reformation so long as there is hope of escaping punishment. Until the convict has given up the expectation of pardon, and made up his mind to submit cheerfully and patiently to the award of justice as rendered in the sentence of the court, he will put forth no vigorous, sustained and persevering effort in the direction of personal reformation.

We will only add that should the principle of reformation sentences, or even task sentences, agreeably to Capt. Machonochie's plan, be practically adopted, all difficulty on the matter of pardons and all peril thence arising, will be done away with, as the prisoner's fate will then be put in his own power ; that is, within certain limits, for under that and every other effective system, there must, of necessity, be a minimum of punishment.

SECTION FOURTEENTH.

CRIMINAL STATISTICS.

In the preceeding section, we have spoken of the defective and imperfect manner in which the statistics of American prisons are, for the most part, kept. In an able paper on Punishment and Reformation, by Thomas Chambers, Q. C., Common Sergeant of London, published in the Transactions of the British Social Science Association for 1862, there are some paragraphs of much interest on the utility and value of statistics, from which we shall take the liberty to draw, to some extent, in the remarks which we propose to offer on this subject.

The whole science of statistics, so far especially as it relates to crime and criminal justice, is too little appreciated and, therefore, too much neglected in the United States. The laws of social phenomena can only be ascertained by the accumulation and analysis of statistical facts. Returns of such facts, carefully gathered from a wide field of observation and skilfully digested, are indispensable to enable us to judge of the real effect of any law or system which we may have put in operation. What we want to know is the facts ; but a knowledge of the facts relating to so complex a subject as that of crime and criminal administration implies a mass of figures, collected from all quarters, and arranged and tabulated with reference to some definite object. The local and the special are to little purpose here ; it is the general only that has value ; that is, returns so numerous, so manifold, and drawn from so wide a field and amid such diversified circumstances, as to give a significance to the results. It is such returns alone that will yield inferences of practical value. We want to get an average ; and in order to this, we must have scope enough and variety enorgh, both in the range and character of the returns, to be enabled to eliminate whatever is local and accidental. Only on this condition can our conclusion upon what constitutes the essence of the matter be sound and safe. Only on this condition shall we be able to feel that our inferences rest, not upon mere incidents of the phenomena, which may be partial, casual and immaterial, but on the phenomena themselves, apart from variations which are only temporary or adventitious.

We wish to know, for example, whether the stern severity of the old system of prison discipline, or the benign pressure of the new, is the more successful in repressing crime. How are we to decide this question? Obviously, our conclusion will have little force, unless our facts shall have been collected from a wide territory, and under the greatest diversity of conditions and incidents; so that every phase and relation of the phenomena shall have been included in our returns, and all that is special and exceptional shall have been corrected, and a result reached not neutralized or vitiated by any circumstances which have not been noted, and due allowance made for them in the analysis. But the materials for a generalization, having the breadth and reliability here supposed, are criminal statistics. A reformatory prison in one place may signally succeed, and in another as signally fail; yet the success of the one and the failure of the other may have little if any value as an argument; both the triumph and the defeat may have been the result of accidental causes—as, for example, the competency or incompetency of the head—and they will, therefore, afford no ground for any general conclusion. But if the experiment of the new and mild discipline has been tried in a score of different places and under conditions widely variant, and yet has always succeeded in securing a larger proportion of reformations than the old and rigid system, except in a few cases where the failure can be clearly traced to adventitious causes, such an induction will afford a solid basis for our inferences, and we shall feel that we stand upon the rock in affirming the proposition, that kindness is more effective than severity in reforming prisoners and leading them back to virtue.

In proportion, therefore, as our facts are gathered from narrow districts and confined to brief periods of time, our generalizations will be unsafe as a basis of argument; for we can never be sure that the mere accidents of the experiment may not have determined the character of the result. A practice, founded on conclusions arrived at in this way, though scientific in form, would be empirical in fact; dogmatism would be mistaken for induction. Nor can we correct this false reasoning otherwise than by returns, which, if not universal, are at least general; that is, broadly comprehensive both of space and time. As we know crime to be occasionally local and epidemic; so, under a certain conjunction of circumstances, may reformation be; for what else than this are those mighty revivals of religion, which have marked the history of the church in all ages? Results may be secured in one place and by one agency, which we may in vain seek to parallel in another place and by a different agency. If, therefore, we would test the general or average results of a reformatory prison discipline, we must collect our facts from all quarters, even from distant states and nations; returns from one or two localities will be without value; nay, they may prove deceptive and misleading. If we would know what a curative agency can accomplish on the whole, we must know what it is effecting in the manufacturing towns and in the rural villages; what in the seaports and in the mountains and valleys of the interior; and what in the coal beds and in the gold mines. We must learn its results, not in selected spots and under particular circumstances, but over broad regions and amid conditions endlessly varied. The essential, inwrought power of our philanthropic machinery then comes out and makes itself manifest, when it is seen in conflict with the special obstacles it has to encounter in the agricultural, commercial, manufacturing and mining populations of a country. The result of its struggle with all opposing difficulties is the result which alone is of any worth to us. And this can be known only as the facts are gathered from all these fields, and are collated, digested, and reduced to tabulated forms upon some uniform system, or at least in a way that will admit of practical comparison.

We want such statistics—uniform, full, and collected with regularity from all the prisons and reformatories of our state. Their systematic collection would be a great step in advance; and yet it would go but a short way towards supplying what, as a nation, we really need. New York is but a unit in a great system of states, constituting one vast nation. What do the American people know about American prisons? Something they know of the prisons of Charlestown, Sing Sing, Auburn and Philadelphia; but what information have they of the state and progress of prison discipline in Oregon, Minnesota, New Jersey, and other members of the American Union? How many know the principle on which convict labor is conducted in the penitentiaries of Illinois and Kentucky? Yet prison discipline is a mighty interest, touching profoundly the nation's well-being, and involving, by its success or failure, its material interests to the extent of scores, if not hundreds, of millions every year. Is not prison discipline, then, a subject on which the people everywhere ought to be interested, and on which they need information, full, systematic, trustworthy and regular? It is not in reference to a prison here, a reformatory there, and a truant home somewhere else, that they require to be informed; but they should have such information touching all the penal and correctional institutions of all the states, and then they would be able to judge whether the work of reforming criminals is really accomplished, or whether our penitentiary system is a mistake and a sham.

The direction in which these remarks point, it is easy to discover. The national government has recently instituted a bureau of education, a step in legislation which we have long regarded as highly important to the great interest of popular enlightenment. Is not a prison bureau equally desirable, if not, perchance, equally necessary? We know of no other way of effecting the object than by the agency of the general government, which is alone competent to the task of collecting, collating, digesting and issuing such returns as we have indicated. Among the functions of such a bureau would be to devise and promulgate the best forms for prison registers; the best method of recording judicial proceedings, with the view of supplying statistical information on legal subjects; the best modes of tabulating criminal and judicial statistics, and the best means of securing the preparation of comprehensive, scientific and accurate prison returns. A prison bureau, like that here proposed, would, it it is true, cost its annual thousands; but it would, indirectly, as we think, beyond a peradventure, save to the nation its annual millions. Let it be remembered that crime is the foe against which we war, a mischief great and multiform; and it is to lead the battle and suggest the best methods of assault, that this bureau is needed. The conflict must be bold, skillful, untiring, hopeful, and with weapons of love rather than of vengeance. So assailed, the evil will yield, slowly, no doubt, but surely, to the attack. The principle of all true and effective prison discipline, cetainly of all that is is intended to be curative as well as deterrent, is enunciated in one terse dictum of inspiration: " Overcome evil with good."

SECTION FIFTEENTH.

MISCELLANEOUS ITEMS.

The cost of conveying prisoners from the place of conviction to prison and the principle on which the said cost is regulated, are matters of considerable importance, as will appear from statements about to be submitted. In most of the states, the officer charged with the conveyance of convicted criminals, is the sheriff, and the principle on which the charges thereon are regulated is that of a fee or mileage. In other states, as Massachusetts, Maine, and Connecticut, the actual cost of conveyance is paid, and the officers who attend to the business are the wardens or other officials of the prisons deputed by them, and for whose fidelity they are held responsible. The other principle named is the one adopted in New York. Now for the comparison of expenses: During the year 1866, 1,527 convicts were conveyed to the three state prisons of New York, at a cost to the state of $30,000 (it was a little over, but we cannot give the fraction); or, $19 per man. During the same year, there were conveyed to the state prison of Massachusetts, 247 convicts, at a gross cost of $240.22, or ninety-seven cents per man. Had the convicts in our state been conveyed at the same rate (and considering we have three state prisons, it should not have been much more), their conveyance would have cost $1,381, and there would have been a saving to the public exchequer of $28,619. We cannot hesitate to recommend, can the Legislature hesitate to adopt, the Massachusetts plan?

During the late tremendous civil war, there was a diminution of male prisoners in all the state prisons, of ten to fifty per cent. This, by no means, indicates a diminution of crime. Criminals were as numerous, perhaps more numerous, than ever; but convictions were fewer. This was due to several causes. One of these causes was tersely expressed by a sheriff, who observed to one of us during the progress of the strife, that the penalty of crime now-a-days was to enlist in the army, and get a large bounty.

This was, perhaps, "putting too fine a point upon it;" but there was an element of truth in the remark. Mr. Prentice, of the Ohio penitentiary, thus explains the matter : "Local committees have secured young men from punishment for minor offences, on condition that they would enlist. Others have fled for refuge to the army, and have thus avoided arrest. Old criminals have sought the army not only for refuge, but as a field for fresh depredations." The number of female convictions increased during the war ; though this increase was less marked in the state prisons, than in prisons of an inferior grade, where minor offences receive their punishment.

In most states, the wardens reported the administration of criminal justice as tardy and proportionally lax. Mr. Prentice has this remark on the subject : "A man of wealth or influence, or an expert criminal, may retard trials, when the postponement is likely to aid a release or mitigation ; but a poor or friendless wretch is disposed of summarily." This is so in other states than Ohio, and other countries than America.

On an average, nearly or quite one half of the inmates of our state prisons are under thirty years of age.

The percentage of convicts of foreign birth varies from a third to a half of the entire prison populations, which is out of all proportion to the populations of the several states. The proportion would be larger, if the children of foreigners were also taken into the account.

The reasons assigned by reconvicted criminals for their relapses are, in the main, liquor, old associates, bad company, and the prejudice existing in the community against them on account of their having before been in prison.

CHAPTER II.

COUNTY JAILS.

The several European commissions, which visited the United States some thirty odd years ago to examine our penitentiary system, while commending American state prisons as at that time far in advance of the same class of institutions in Europe, both in their organization and working, speak of our county jails as among the worst prisons they had ever anywhere seen. From the observations we have made in our own and other states, we fear that there has been little improvement in this class of prisons within the last generation.

A distinguished member of the bar of New Jersey writes to us in the following strain about the jails of that state: "You ask me to add a paragraph concerning our county jails. This I can hardly do without feeling my indignation to rise. I regard the outrages which are committed through these institutions as disgraceful and oppressive. They are not constructed properly. I have never been able to see by what right a person is deprived of the light and air of heaven, when he is committed only for trial; especially when, in nearly one-half of the cases of such commitment, there is not even an indictment found, and when, even if the accused is indicted, there is no conviction. Such persons are confined only to answer, and not as a punishment. There is no law justifying the privation of air and light, a comfortable bed, books to read, and other like reasonable comforts. Persons who have never before been charged with crime, and only now with a small offence, not able at present to give bail, are thrust into jail; subjected to dirt, vermin, offensive air and darkness; without a chair or table in the room; fed like a felon behind the bars; associated with the depraved and disgusting criminal; eating, sleeping and living with the wicked and profane: the whole suffering and degradation far heavier to bear than the penalty of the offence charged, which would only be a small fine, if convicted at all, which may not be the case. Oh! what a burning shame! There is no law for such treatment. Inexperienced youth, male and female, and respectable men and women, are sometimes obliged to be put into the sheriff's custody for a day or two, or longer, and they suffer such outrages as those described above, without any redress.

"There should be more variety in the cells. There should be comfortable rooms, made secure, but not dark cells only. There should be more discrimination in the treatment of persons in jail. There should be an eye to the prevention of crime in the jailor. The jail, which generally is only preliminary as it were to the state prison, is a far greater punishment than confinement in the prison. Mercer county jail is notoriously bad. Several grand juries have presented it."

Mr. Cyrus Mendendall, the foremost man in Ohio on the subject of prisons and prison discipline, in a letter to the undersigned, thus speaks of the county jails of his state: "Our jails are left almost entirely to the charge of the county sheriffs, without any control as to internal regulation by the state. The judges of the courts, at long periods, give their 'instructions' to the sheriffs; but little further attention is paid to the matter, and those instructions are seldom obeyed. I had occasion, recently, to visit St. Clairsville, our county seat, and was kindly shown through our jail by the sheriff. I found it to contain three cells and two upper rooms. (The population of the county is about 40,000.) The cells were on a level with the ground; were poorly ventilated, or rather not ventilated at all; were damp, and not occupied. The rooms over them were about fifteen by eighteen feet, with two small windows on one side, and a small hole in the door, opening into a hall on the other. One of these rooms was unoccupied, and in the other were four men, and a boy twelve years of age. The men had just been sentenced to the penitentiary for terms of one to five years, and the boy was to go to the reform school. They had all, boy included, been confined in this manner several months, or during a long vacation of the court. No other care had been extended to them than to prevent their escape, and to feed and keep them tolerably clean. * * * * It is the practice for prisoners of the same sex to associate promiscuously in our county jails, except such as are confined, for greater security, in cells. As to the influence of such associations, my own observation at home, and a somewhat extensive inquiry of prisoners in the Ohio penitentiary as to their experience, would pronounce it decidedly bad; and our jails, in many cases, are crime-producers instead of crime-repressers. So fully am I convinced of this, that I have often to rejoice when I see a young man, and especially a boy, escape a confinement there, even though he was clearly liable to it by law."*

A few years ago, Mr. Wm. J. Mullen, agent of the inspectors of

* The whole Mr. Mendendall's valuable letter will be found in the Appendix.

the Philadelphia county prison, and also of the Philadelphia Prison Society, was commissioned by the governor of Pennsylvania to visit the principal prisons of the state, and instructed to make a report thereupon. We cite a brief passage from his description of the Allegheny county jail:*

"I found confined therein 120 prisoners in a most deplorable state; many of them were almost starving. The untried prisoners are allowed by the authorities fifteen cents per day for their food, and the vagrants ten cents; but it seems nine cents of the fifteen and four of the ten cents are retained by the sheriff as a perquisite. And the sum used for the prisoners is expended on bread, with an addition on Tuesdays and Fridays of about a cent's worth of beef broth. It appears that five days in the week the prisoners get no other food than bread and water; and it is said that out of the sum allowed for their support, the sheriff makes about $4,000 a year. This large amount is accumulated at the expense of the comfort and health of the poor prisoners, who are unable to procure relief from friends outside. * * * * I found this prison, besides being ill ventilated and filthy, to be in an extremely disorderly and confused condition. Every cell door was open, and the prisoners had free access to each other, with the opportunity of unrestrained intercourse. I refer to the males. The women were not, indeed, actually permitted to intermingle with the men, but they were allowed everything short of that. They might, at pleasure, walk round the corridor in front of their cells, from which they could look down upon and talk with the men. With such facilities for corruption, both parties must become debased. Apart from this objectionable feature of the administration, it was most distressing to see convicts, burglars, murderers, young and old, guilty and innocent, black and white, all having unrestricted access to each other's cells, many of whom were amusing themselves by playing cards, smoking cigars, and doing whatever else they chose for passing away the time. For, be it noted, the prisoners have no regular employment whatever; a fact much to be regretted, since, leaving economical considerations out of the question, the beneficial effects of steady occupation in some useful labor must be obvious, it being the best preservative both of moral and bodily health."

We found this prison and other county jails in Pennsylvania in much the same state as that above described. The principal difference was, that the men were let out into the corridor one part of the day and the women the other; but the evils of association were

---

* This county contains the important city of Pittsburgh.

as rife as ever; for, in addition to mingling in the corridors, there were, in some cases, as many as four or five in a cell.

In 1864, the Philadelphia Prison Society made a thorough examination of the county jails throughout the state, most of which they found in a deplorable condition. They complain, among other things, of the general neglect to provide for a proper separation of the sexes. "In some cases," they remark, "there was found to be no attempt to separate them during the day. * * * In regard to the association of male and female prisoners, there is no rule, and the practice varies. Whether they shall be separated, or together, depends on the will of the sheriff. It is a usually recognized principle that the sexes shall not associate at night. Yet even this principle is infringed occasionally. But, however strictly it may be observed, the grossest immorality may exist without the sexes being permitted to spend the night together. * * * * It is doubtful, when male and female prisoners spend the day together, whether much evil is prevented by their separation for the night only."

Other deficiencies are pointed out, particularly the general and almost total neglect of any moral, mental or industrial training of the prisoners. There is no labor in the jails, except in a few conducted on the separate plan; religious instruction is scant, and the ignorant remain in ignorance, except that their faculties are sharpened to wrong by mutual instruction in the arts of crime. Upon the whole, the opinion of this excellent and humane society is, that the mass of Pennsylvania jails promote crime instead of repressing it. They say: "Social confinement of the guilty without moral instruction, without proper books, without steady employment, must be productive of more evils to society at large than would flow from the entire neglect of justice toward the criminal. Prisons badly constructed and badly conducted must, in the nature of things, be schools of vice, weaning the young offender from the taste and use of the little good that is left in him, and making the bad worse."

We visited the jails in the great western and southern cities of Detroit, Chicago, Indianapolis, St. Louis, Louisville, and Cincinnati, and found them all quite unfit for the purpose to which they are devoted.

In the jail at Chicago, Illinois, the cells were dark, without ventilation, and swarming with vermin. Some were so foul that, after a few minutes stay in them, we felt a sickening sensation. Yet in these close and filthy abodes human beings, crowded together, are confined for days, weeks, months even, many of whom are afterwards adjudged to be innocent. It is a crime against humanity to deprive any one, however depraved, of the light and air of heaven, since, apart from its essential injustice, such physical punishment invaria bly induces moral deterioration, and the individual subjected to it re-enters society a worse man than he left it. How great, then, must be the crime of such deprivation, when inflicted on the innocent.

The county jail in St. Louis, Missouri, is in even a worse condition than that at Chicago, as described in the foregoing paragraph. It has been, as we learn from the Rev. Dr. Elliott, regularly presented as a nuisance, once every two months, by the grand jury of St. Louis, for the last ten years. Not one solitary redeeming feature is found in it; and such are its situation, construction, and arrangements that the moral improvement of the prisoners and even any systematic attempt at such improvement are rendered well nigh impossible. The cells are eight feet square and ten high; and furnished with a bunk and one stool or chair. At the time of our visit, each of these cells contained from three to six inmates; the average number, we were informed, is about four. All the light and air, admitted for the use of the human beings packed into these apartments, come through a slit in the wall, three and a half inches wide by about five feet high. The bunk may hold three persons, if they are well crowded together; all beyond that number must sleep on the floor. There is no sewerage; everything must be carried out, as well as brought in, by hand. There is no water-closet for the prisoners; and only once a day is the slop bucket removed, whatever sickness may prevail; the rest of the time it remains in the cell, covered with a filthy cloth. Two meals a day are handed in in tin pans, to be eaten in the cells, the men sitting on the bed or floor. "In short," observes Dr. Elliott, "the whole monotonous routine of their dreary lives, day and night, in sickness and health, in summer and winter, sometimes for twelve consecutive months, is passed in that little stone box, containing six hundred and forty cubic feet of air. Try to realize the situation for a moment, if you can. By the sanitary regulations of military hospitals *twelve hundred* cubic feet of air is allowed to every patient in a well ventilated room. In these cells, with four prisoners, without ventilation, six hundred and forty feet is allowed, giving only *one hundred and sixty feet* to each man, that is to say, four feet square on the floor, by ten feet high. A box to hold a grand piano, set up on end, would not be far from the required dimensions. If six should be confined in a cell, which sometimes happens, and at the rate crime is now increasing is sure to happen, a large sugar hogshead would fill about the space allowed to each of them." How pestilential must be the moral atmosphere of these crowded cells, where employment is impossible ; where reading is almost equally so, as well from want of light as because of the noise and tumult that must prevail ; and where the professional burglar and thief and the young transgressor, or perchance the wholly innocent boy, are shut up together, with nothing to do, with nothing even practicable, but to impart and to receive lessons in crime. Well does the venerable doctor add to what is cited from him above : "Religious or moral influence is out of the question ; and to preach the gospel of Christ there, in that dismal place, to those kenneled human beings, seems like a mockery before high heaven. I have tried it more than once, and felt it to be so ; and I have no doubt the prisoners felt the same. Religious tracts are received with a grim smile, and perhaps some try to read them ; but the majority must regard such gifts as no better, under the circumstances, than a practical insult. * * * * Alas, our practice exhorts to blasphemy, while our words exhort to praise."

Such is the county jail in the great commercial metropolis of the west, with a population of more than 200,000 souls. Now, what do we find to be the condition of the same institution in Jefferson city, the capital of Missouri ? We visited it in August, 1865, with mingled feelings of horror and disgust. It has but two rooms for prisoners. The largest is only fifteen feet by fourteen, with a ceiling not, we think, exceeding eight feet in height ; which gives 1,680 cubic feet. This apartment has four windows, each about one foot square, with a double set of immovable slats, one at the outer and the other at the inner surface of the stone wall, which fill up more than half the space afforded for the admission of light and air. It is so dark that it is quite impossible to read, without a lamp, even close to a window, and on the lightest summer day. Into this kennel, this dungeon, whenever there happen to be female prisoners, are thrust all the men and boys who are in the jail, to the number, sometimes, of ten or fifteen. When the latter of these numbers are in confinement, each one has just 112 cubic feet of air for his use, and a space on the floor at night two feet wide by seven feet long. And this in a land which claims to be christian! Fifteen human beings crammed into such a space, with absolutely no ventilation! Think of their passing a night there, with the thermometer at 90 deg., as it was at the time of our visit. It is the "black hole of Calcutta," repeated with aggravations! No words could paint such barbarism in darker colors than the simple statement of the facts, as just given. The other room is rather smaller, but it has one large window, that is, large comparatively; which gives more air and light. When there are no women in jail, the men occupy both rooms, and are a little better accommodated. This jail at Jefferson city, we were told, is a fair specimen of the county prisons throughout Missouri. It was a relief to be informed that there are many counties in the state, which have no jails. It would be a blessing if what there are could be utterly demolished.

We paid a hasty visit—though quite long enough—to the county jail in Indianapolis, the seat of government of the great state of Indiana. It is the old story—promiscuous association, mutual contamination, cramped and crowded cells, no work, no books, no healthful moral influences—everything, in a word, disgusting, repellant, and demoralizing.

We found things in much the same condition in the jail in Louisville, the chief city, though not the capital, of Kentucky. We saw one group of prisoners busy at a game of cards, which did not appear to be forbidden, as it was done openly and before the eyes of the officers. But we have no heart for extended details.

The government of the jails, in the several counties of Kentucky, is in the hands of the county court, a board of three county officers, corresponding in many of their functions, though with material differences to our boards of supervisors. In Kentucky the sheriffs are not, as they are in most of our states, the keepers of the jails and custodians of their inmates; but the jailors are special officers, chosen by popular vote, in the same manner and for a like term of office as the sheriffs. The state pays the board of all prisoners confined in the jails, at the rate of seventy-five cents a day, or five dollars and twenty-five cents per week. Other expenses, such as fuel, bedding, clothing, medical attendance, &c., &c., are met by the counties. The same system, substantially obtains in Missouri. We cannot affirm positively, but our impression is, that the jailors get no remuneration for their services, other than the profits made on the board of the prisoners. We know that such is the fact as regards the jail in St. Louis, where the keeper receives eighty cents a day, equal to $5.60 a week, for each inmate. But, in a prison averaging perhaps a hundred or more inmates, this compensation is not only ample, but munificent; for we cannot suppose that, at the outside, it will cost more than ten to fifteen cents a day to feed men the way they are fed in jail.

The common jail in the city of Cincinnati, is an imposing and costly structure, built of hewn stone, with interior arrangements of a very complicated and unique, but to us, unpleasing character. Discipline, however, we found utterly wanting there. Though the prisoners were confined in separate cells, it was the noisiest and most disorderly prison we ever visited. They talked and shouted to one another without restraint. As far as appeared, the keeper had no control over them whatever; and the jail must be, as administered at the time of our visit, anything but a school of reform, or even of decency.

The common jails in our own state are in a deplorable condition; utterly unworthy of our civilization, and of the renown and fame we have acquired among our sister states and the nations of the world. Their general characteristics (happily some exceptions exist to a part of the counts) are: insecurity, bad ventilation, overcrowding, too great facility for communication with the outside world, promiscuous association of all ages and grades of criminals of the same sex, and consequent mutual contamination, abundance of vermin, absence of employment, want of libraries and neglect of intellectual and moral culture. We will not go into detail here, as these things are spread out, *ad nauseam*, in the annual reports of the Prison Association..

It will have been seen, from a statement in the introduction, that the undersigned prepared an extended series of interrogatorise on county jails. These were extensively distributed; but we received only three responses, viz., from sheriff William P. Crafton, of Illinois; warden Thomas C. James, of Maryland; and secretary F. B. Sanborn, of Massachusetts. We submit a *résumé* of the information furnished in these papers.

Mr. Crafton is, or at least in 1865 was, sheriff of Sangamon county, Illinois, and, as such, keeper of the jail in Springfield. From his communication we learn the following facts: There are 102 counties in the state, but not more than about eighty jails. There is no central authority, having a general charge and superintendence of these prisons. The sheriff of each county has control of the jail, and it is made the duty of the grand jury, at every term of the circuit court of the county, to examine the jail and report its condition to the court; the consequence of which is that the system lacks unity, and there is no uniformity in its management. No statistics are kept, except a simple record of commitments and discharges; and even the books in which these items are registered, are the property of the sheriffs and not of the counties. No returns of jail statistics are required by law to be made to any board or officer of the state. The number of commitments of males to the Springfield jail increased largely during the war, a remarkable fact, if there is no mistake about it, since it is different from the state of things as reported to us everywhere else. Sheriff Crafton states that the increase in female commitments is not so perceptible in the county jail, adding: "You should consult the records of the city calaboose for an answer to this question, as the demoralizing effect of war is developed by licentiousness in the female, and leads her into offences which the city government has made special provision to punish; and as the judicial machinery of the city is running all the time, it swallows up all the petty crimes which show the pernicious influence of war." He adds a statement of a most painful and astounding character, in these words: "Perhaps the question is fully answered by citing the fact that more divorces were applied for and granted at the last term of court than during the whole period of the county's history since 1821." About one-third of the prisoners received are of foreign birth. Intemperance, Sabbath-breach, licentiousness and gambling characterize nearly all who are committed. Something like seventy per cent of those committed are brought to trial, of whom about ten per cent plead guilty, and fifty per cent are convicted by juries. Not more than two per cent of the prisoners in Springfield jail are undergoing sentences of imprisonment; all the rest are awaiting trial. The average length of sentences in jail is about six months. Imprisonment for debt is legal in Illinois, but is seldom resorted to, when the the plaintiff has the board to pay. The defendant can always release himself from confinement by scheduling the amount of his property; if it be more than the law exempts from execution, the excess is proceeded against; if less, he is discharged. Witnesses are not imprisoned to secure their attendance; all the security required is their personal recognizance. Jailors are remunerated by fees, and not by salaries. The sheriff boards the prisoners at so much per week, but the sum allowed is not stated. Clothing is supplied to prisoners, when necessary, at the expense of the counties. The compensation of the medical officers of the jails is by salaries, and not by fees. No employment is provided for the prisoners, nor are there any libraries furnished at the public expense; whatever books the prisoners have to read are loaned by the sheriff, or provided by their friends or themselves. There are no chaplains or schoolmasters; nor is the lack of religious and secular instruction, consequent on the neglect of the authorities, supplied, to any great extent, by volunteer workers. Bibles, however, are provided; but to what extent is not stated. They are not extensively read, newspapers and yellow-covered novels being generally preferred. There is no fixed dietary; each sheriff supplies rations at his own discretion. As a general thing, little attention is paid to ventilation in the construction of jails. Drink, gambling and licentiousness are regarded as the most active causes of crime in the state. Sheriffs are chosen by popular suffrage, and are not immediately re-eligible. Prison officers are usually changed as often as once in two years, the effect of which is found to be every way bad.

Sheriff Crafton has appended to his paper a presentment of the grand jury, in which the jail of Sangamon county is denounced as "totally inadequate" to its purposes; as "insecure and unsafe," it being "necessary to employ a special guard to prevent escapes;" and as having "cells so small and so badly ventilated that confinement in them during the summer is cruel and inhuman."

From the communication of Mr. Thomas C. James, warden of the Baltimore city jail, we glean the following information concerning the county jails of Maryland: There are twenty-one counties in the state, each of which has a jail, in addition to which the city of Baltimore has one of its own. There is no central authority having a supervision and control over the whole system of county prisons. In place of such a board, the sheriff of each county has control of the jail in said county, and in Baltimore city the warden of the city jail has charge, under the direction of a board of visitors, composed of five gentlemen appointed annually by the mayor and city council. There is, consequently, no uniformity in the management of the jails throughout the state. In Baltimore city jail, the commitments and their causes, as well as the discharges and their methods, are kept with fullness and accuracy; but the social, national, educational, industrial, moral and religious relations of the prisoners are not recorded. The jails throughout the state are required to keep statistics of all committals to their custody and the causes thereof, together with all discharges therefrom. In the counties, the jail-books belong to the sheriffs, but in the jail of Baltimore they are the property of the city. In the latter prison, full returns of jail statistics are required to be made annually to the mayor and city council, but such returns are not exacted of the several county jails. The number of men committed to the Baltimore city jail during the war, charged with a violation of the civil laws, was less than it had been before the war, or has been since its close. There was a moderate increase of female commitments during the war, but the percentage was not large. About three-fourths of the prisoners committed to Baltimore city jail have been previously inmates of the same. The proportion of foreigners committed is not far from one-fifth. Not less than four-fifths of the prisoners in this jail are of intemperate habits. Three-fifths of the prisoners committed to all the county jails are, on an average, brought to trial. The length of sentence in Baltimore city jail extends, generally, from one week to six months, and in some cases it is prolonged to one and even two years. The system of separate imprisonment is adopted in Baltimore city and Baltimore county jails, but not in the others. Only one prisoner in these two jails is confined in each cell, except when the number of prisoners exceeds the number of cells, of which there are three hundred for solitary confinement, besides some rooms of larger size. The women are confined in a separate part of the building from the men, and parties committed for breach of the peace, court cases, sentenced prisoners, &c., are each confined in different parts of the prison, according to the nature of the charges against them. There is no imprisonment for debt in the state of Maryland; but witnesses are frequently imprisoned to secure their testi-mony. Persons imprisoned as witnesses are usually compensated for the time lost by their imprisonment. The officers of Baltimore city jail are remunerated by fixed salaries ; but in the counties the sheriffs receive a *per diem* for all prisoners confined, and out of the sum so received, furnish food and other supplies. Necessary clothing is provided for the inmates of the jails. The cost of Baltimore city jail, including the lot on which it stands, was (say) $350,000. The average annual cost of each prisoner therein including all expenses other than the interest on the jail property, was, for 1861, $116.80 ; for 1862, $105.85 ; for 1863, $93.07 ; for 1864, $153.30; and for 1865, 155.12. For the same years, the average cost per prisoner, including interest as aforesaid, was $193.45; $195.27; $155.12; $240.90; and $242.72. In Baltimore city jail, sentenced prisoners are hired out by contract, and are employed in the workshop of the prison ; other prisoners are employed in cleaning, white-washing, and in various other ways. A library is provided therein for the use of the inmates. Religious services are held in the prison chapel every Sabbath afternoon, under the direction of a committee of the American Tract Society, by G. S. Griffith, Esq., chairman, assisted by clergymen of various denominations ; and much valuable religious reading matter is distributed to the prisoners on those occasions. The jails are extensively supplied with Bibles by the liberality of the Maryland Bible Society. As a general thing, the prisoners use their copies carefully, but in some cases it is otherwise. In Baltimore city jail, there is a weekly bill of fare, varied daily, but in the county jails, each sheriff provides rations according to his own judgment. The former is admirably ventilated ; the others but poorly. Ample bathing facilities are provided here, but not elsewhere. Almost the only punishment in this jail is confinement in dark cells ; and this even is infrequent, considering the large number of prisoners confined. Moral means are in all cases employed, until they are found to be unavailing, and other measures become indispensable. Drunkenness and prostitution are regarded as the most active causes of crime. Sheriffs are elected, not appointed, in Maryland ; and they are not re-eligible for two years from the expiration of their term of office. It very seldom happens that they are re-elected afterward. In Baltimore city jail, the officers are not often changed; elsewhere, changes are more frequent. This jail is inspected by the board of visitors, at their pleasure. They constitute a standing committee for that purpose, as also for controling all matters connected with the government of the jail. The prison is likewise inspected by the several grand juries of the criminal court. Both classes of inspection are provided for by law ; and the examinations, so required, are faithfully and thoroughly performed.

From the answers of Mr. Sanborn, secretary of the Massachusetts board of state charities, we gather the following concerning the common jails of that state : There are but fourteen counties in the state, yet there are twenty jails; that is, there are six counties that have two jails each.   On this subject, Mr. Sanborn says : " I think one jail in each county quite sufficient.   The grounds of my opinion are these : 1. The supposed necessity for several jails arises from the fact that courts are held in several places, in each of which a jail has been thought necessary. But the railroad facilities are now so great, that prisoners can be brought with ease from any part of the county to the court, as they are wanted for trial.   Moreover, there are town prisons now required by law, so that there is less need of county prisons for temporary detention.   2. The great number of our jails interferes, seriously, with any attempt to reform the prisoners, who are scattered in small prisons through the state, and deprived, in consequence, of systematic treatment and instruction. 3. The inspection of jails by the state, which I believe desirable, would be much facilitated by having fewer jails."

There is no central authority in Massachusetts having a general control of the jail system, but each jail is in charge of the county commissioners for the county in which it is situated ; the consequence of which is, that there is nothing like uniformity in the management of the jails throughout the state.   Mr. Sanborn regards such an organization as highly objectionable, and in regard to it remarks : " The evils which flow from a want of uniformity are the same here as elsewhere.   Whatever is managed regularly, and according to a knowledge of principles, is more likely to be well managed than what is left to local custom or the whim of those in authority at any given time and place.   Greater uniformity would economize time and money, and would make the labor of the prisoners of greater account and their reformation more attainable."

The statistics of the jails in Massachusetts are kept with a good degree of fullness and accuracy.   They include commitments and their causes, discharges and their methods, and the national, social, educatianal, industrial, moral and religious relations of the prisoners.   It is made by law obligatory on the sheriffs to keep full registers, embracing the items above stated.   The books in which these registers are kept belong to the counties, and not to the sheriffs.   Full returns of jail statistics must be made periodically to the board of state charities.   Mr. Sanborn furnishes the following table, showing the number of male and female prisoners committed to the county prisons—both jails and houses of correction— for eleven years, viz : 1854—1864 inclusive :

YEARS.	JAILS.			HOUSES OF CORRECTION.			TOTALS.		
	Whole No. committed.	Males.	Females.	Whole No. committed.	Males.	Females.	Whole No. committed.	Males.	Females.
1854	11,526	9,819	1,652	4,734	3,735	999	16,260	13,604	2,651
1855	12,858	10,819	2,026	4,599	3,550	1,048	17,457	14,369	3,074
1856	9,419	8,775	626	4,936	3,840	1,090	14,355	12,615	1,716
1857	7,903	6,675	1,228	5,169	3,974	1,195	13,072	10,649	2,423
1858	8,603	7,390	1,213	5,996	4,660	1,336	14,599	12,050	2,549
1859	8.286	6,716	1,579	5,180	4,113	1,089	13,466	10,829	2,668
1860	6,752	5,756.	1,031	5,012	4,000	1,012	11,764	9,756	2,043
1861	5,693	4,689	1,013	5,424	4,322	1,154	11,117	9,011	2,167
1862	5,211	3,967	1,244	4,494	3,139	1,355	9,705	7,106	2,599
1863	5,568	3,768	1,797	3,823	2,374	1,449	9,391	6,142	3,246
1864	4,932	3,180	1,752	3,184	1,917	1,267	8,116	5,097	3,019

It appears from the foregoing table that the number of men committed to the county prisons during the years covered by the late war, was considerably less than it had been prior to that time, while the number of women committed was greater, absolutely, than before, and very far in excess relatively. In 1854, the females were only one in seven of the whole number of inmates of the jails, while in 1863, they were very nearly one in three ; a a startling increase in female criminality. The average daily number in the jails, for the last ten years, has been from 300 to 500; for the last two or three years, but little more than 300. Nearly one-half of the prisoners in jail are recommittals, and seventy per cent. are foreigners. A full third of those committed are unable to read at all, and of those registered as possessing that ability, many have but a very imperfect mastery of the art. Three-fourths, at least, are intemperate. Eight per cent. are undergoing sentences pursuant to conviction, the average length of their sentences being about four months. Promiscuous association of prisoners, with all its corrupting influences, exists to a great extent ; there being, in general, no classification other than the separation of the sexes. Imprisonment for debt is confined to cases of fraud or an intention to evade payment by leaving the state. But few cases of such imprisonment occur. Witnesses are frequently imprisoned to secure their testimony, and are only in part compensated for the time thus lost. The officers of the jails receive compensation in the form of fixed salaries. The custom of remunerating officers by fees, which formerly existed, was found to lead to the imprisonment of persons merely for the sake of the fees. Besides doing away with this evil, the method of payment

by salaries is thought to be more economical. The rations of the
prisoners are supplied at actual cost, so that sheriffs make no
profit out of their board. Mr. Sanborn thinks this method much
the preferable one, and that it should be continued "until angels
are jailors." Clothing is supplied to prisoners when needed.
Medical service is paid for in some jails by salary, and in others
by fees. The aggregate annual cost of medicines and medical
attendance in all the jails of the state is $3,000. The average
annual cost of each prisoner, including all expenses other than the
interest on the value of the real estate belonging to the jails, is
about $180. The actual cost of the real estate aforesaid was (say)
$1,000,000; the estimated value now is about $500,000. Jail
prisoners are seldom provided with remunerative employment,
though this, it is thought, would be entirely practicable. Libraries are generally provided for the use of the prisoners, and about
one-half of the jails have chaplains. In the jails without chaplains, no provision is made to meet the moral and religious wants
of the inmates, except in some cases by Sunday schools. Bibles
are supplied to the jails at the expense of the counties, frequently
one in every cell. By about one-half the prisoners they are used
carefully; by the others they are apt to be abused. There is no
uniform dietary in the jails, though, usually, each jail has its own
bill of fare, regulated by the sheriff and county commissioners.
Good rations are provided; there is no fault to be found on that
score. The jails recently built are well constructed, both for
ventilation and the admission of light ; some of the old ones are
objectionable in these respects, particularly as to ventilation. The
jails are in a good condition as to cleanliness, being often thoroughly scrubbed, and whitewashed once a month. The means of
bathing are every where provided. The only punishment used is
the dark cell, and this is not often found necessary. The separation of the sexes is not so perfect as to prevent all communication.
Insane prisoners are not often received into the jails, but when
this happens, they are sent to the state hospitals. The jails of
Massachusetts are regarded as generally secure. Idleness and
the various forms of self-indulgence are believed to be the most
active causes of crime. Mr. Sanborn's individual opinion is that,
upon the whole, the jails of Massachusetts are promotive rather
than repressive of crime. The reform he proposes is "a thorough
classification of the prisoners, with a system of marks which would
enable each prisoner to promote his own comforts and secure an

early discharge by good conduct," and "a change in the spirit of prison officers who generally do not believe in the practicability of reforming their prisoners." Sheriffs are elected by popular vote; they are re-eligible; and, as a matter of fact, they are almost always re-elected. Prison officers are not often changed. Inspection of the jails is provided for by law. On this subject Mr. Sanborn remarks : "The county commissioners are inspectors, except in Suffolk, where our largest jail is. The Suffolk jail, since May, 1864, has been, by law, exempt from inspection, except as the board of state charities have that duty, in connexion with others. The inspection by the commissioners is probably formal in most cases. The board of charities has a general power of inspection, which has been chiefly exercised by its secretary."

The common jail system of Connecticut is, in some respects, peculiar ; and it has in it points of interest which will repay a careful study. Connecticut is a thrifty little commonwealth, and its thrift appears conspicuously in the management of its jails. Every jail in this state is also a workhouse. All sentenced prisoners are *required* to work "according to their strength and ability;" and all others are *provided* with work if they desire it, which more commonly than otherwise is the case. This feature marks a broad distinction between the jail system of Connecticut and those of the other states. The financial results of this system, in counties where it is skillfully and vigorously carried out, are remarkable. It should be stated that Connecticut pays, out of the public treasury, to the several counties, the board of all their jail prisoners, at the rate of $3.00 each a week, except in the case of a few, which refuse to receive more than $2.50, the amount allowed prior to 1863. The payments thus received from the state treasury, added to the avails of the prisoners' labor, together constitute a sum sufficient, in several of the eight counties of the state, to defray not merely the entire expenses of the jails, but all the ordinary and extraordinary expenditures of the counties themselves, so that, in one case at least, not a dollar has been exacted of the citizens for county purposes, during a period of more than twenty years.

This statement, on its face, will appear so incredible, that we are glad to be able to fortify it by official authority. A joint committee of the legislature made a report, in May, 1865, on "the condition and management of jails." Of the jail in New Haven county they say : "This jail has not only paid its own expenses and all the ordinary expenses of the county, but has, since 1858, paid the sum of $10,660.99 into the treasury of the county, which has been applied to the payment of extra expenses, and leaving in the treasury, at the close of the last fiscal year, a balance of $3,132.19." This marvellous result has been achieved, with an average of prisoners not much, if at all, exceeding fifty in number.

Of Windham county the committee remark : "The result, in this county, of the prudent management of its [the jail's] affairs, the manner of working prisoners, and the reasonable and honest charges of its officials is, that all the ordinary and the greater part of the extraordinary expenses of the county, including extensive repairs and additions to the court house and jail, and the erection of new buildings, have been paid, and that too without calling upon the towns in the county for either tax, contribution or assessment, for more than twenty years."

But as there is no central authority in the state, having the general charge and superintendence of the jails, different systems prevail in different counties. In two of them, at least, the leasing system obtains, which we found practised in Illinois and Kentucky in reference to the state prison. As regards this plan, we are not surprised to find the committee using the following language : "The practice of farming out the prisons and prisoners, your committee regards as most objectionable. It places the jails entirely in the hands of the jailors, and is liable to many abuses. It is wrong in principle and pernicious in practice, and has ever proved unprofitable in those counties where it has been adopted."

The joint committee accompanied their report with "an act concerning prisons," the main purpose of which was to take the charge and custody of the jails" out of the hands of the sheriffs, and to place it in the hands of special keepers appointed by the county commissioners. In advocacy of the proposed change, the committee say :

"The time was when by far the larger number of commitments to our jails were debtors, and the sheriffs were held responsible for the sufficiency of the jails, and the safe keeping of the prisoners. But that time has passed. Imprisonment for debt has ceased. The commitments on civil process are very rare. The counties are held responsible for the sufficiency of their jails, and for the escape of prisoners through their insufficiency; and the reason for sheriffs being keepers of jails and having power to appoint deputy keepers having ceased to exist, this power of theirs should also cease, and should be held solely by the county commissioners."

The principle of the bill proposed by the committee has been incorporated into the legislation of New Jersey, so far as the counties of Essex and Hudson, in that state, are concerned. An act was passed in 1867, transferring "the custody, rule, keeping and charge of the jails in said counties" from the sheriffs of the same to the boards of chosen freeholders therein, and authorizing those boards to appoint keepers of the jails, to continue in office five years, unless sooner removed for cause. The same act constitutes the jails of the two counties named, workhouses, and requires "hard labor" of certain classes of their inmates. It further authorizes the boards of chosen freeholders of the other counties to adopt all its provisions and fully to carry them out in their respective counties, whenever a majority shall, at a regular meeting, vote so to do, and file a certificate to that effect in the office of the secretary of state.

The Philadelphia Prison Society strongly urge that this principle be made practical in the legislation of Pennsylvania, in a letter addressed to the governor of that state, under date of December, 1864. We cite the following passage from their communication, in which the view entertained by them is expressed with clearness and force: "Many of the evils of the county prisons (they say) spring from the fact that the sheriff of the county is, *ex officio*, the keeper of the prison. It is not believed that men are selected for that important office who are not humane and just. But men do not seek the office of sheriff for the sake of being the jailor; and if there is any business for the sheriff to do beyond the walls of the prison, so much of the time of that functionary is taken from the discharge of a duty which he assumes, but which has no affinity with the other more desirable parts of his official labors. Besides, the office of a sheriff is not a permanency, while that of a prison keeper ought to be. The duties of his place as sheriff must, if discharged, prevent the personal supervision of the prison and the prisoners which a jailor ought to give. And he must be often tempted to enlarge his small income by such efforts at economy as must tell hard upon the prisoners, often hard upon the county." The society has touched the kernel of the question in what it says on the necessity of permanence in the office of prison keeper.

The tenure of office in this department of the public service should be during good behavior, since prison keepers, supposing them to possess an original aptitude for their special duties, become valuable in proportion as their experience is enlarged.

In the states of Kentucky and Missouri, as we have seen, the care of the common jails and the custody of their inmates are no longer in the hands of the sheriffs of the several counties, but are committed to a distinct class of officers, specially chosen to that service. It is true that they are elected by popular vote, and are consequently political officers, which is a most objectionable feature; but at least the fact stated shows that there is no natural, and especially no necessary, connection between the office of sheriff and the custody of persons arrested on a charge of crime and detained in jail for trial.

Upon the whole, the result of such inquiries as we were able to make into the condition and administration of the common jails of the United States is exceedingly unsatisfactory. There are a few model prisons of this class scattered here and there, like oases is a wide desert, among which may be named the Suffolk county jail in Boston and the Baltimore city jail; but the mass of these prisons throughout the country are in a deplorable state. Another Howard is needed to go from jail to jail through the length and breadth of the land, as the great prison reformer of the last century traversed not only the British Islands, but almost the entire continent of Europe, exploring the prisons of many lands, and dragging their manifold and countless abuses to the light of day. A new "State of Prisons" is wanted, in which every jail in the United States should be minutely described, after the manner in which Howard, in *his* "State of Prisons," dealt with the jails and bridewells of his day.

Our state prisons need many and great reforms, as we have pointed out in a former part of this report; but the reforms needed in our jails and jail systems are, literally, legion. In most common jails the old system prevails in full force; the crowding of prisoners, confusion of crimes, ages, and sometimes sexes; the mixture of indicted and convicted persons, of criminals, debtors, and witnesses; frequent escapes; an almost total absence of what may properly be called discipline; no silence leading the inmates to reflection; no labor accustoming them to industry; enforced idleness that depraves; few books; little religious and no secular instruction; in a word, the assemblage of all vices and all immoralities. In hundreds upon hundreds of these congregations of prisoners, the livelong day is spent in talk; and what sort of talk?

Alas! too well do we know the character of the conversation carried on among criminals in a prison. It relates, almost wholly, to the crimes they perpetrated before their committal, or to those which they meditate after their liberation. In such conversations, each one boasts of his misdeeds; all dispute for the priority in infamy; and, in the end, an equilibrium in vice and crime is reached by the whole, or nearly the whole, company. The less advanced in crime listen eagerly to the greater villians; and the blackest individual among them becomes a type of depravity for the others.

Such is the painful and revolting picture, which truth compels us to draw of the great majority of the common jails of America; and we grieve to say that most of those in our own state form no exception. Here is a work for the friends of prison reform. The whole system of common jails, both in respect of organization and administration, needs revolutionizing. It is a herculean labor which we propose, but we feel confident that it can be done. Truth, patience, zeal, activity, and co-operative effort are essential elements in the problem; but, these elements being given, the solution of the problem, the success of the undertaking, is certain. The system as now existing must be approached prudently, no doubt, and in meekness of wisdom; but, nevertheless, it must be approached, assailed, and battered with the weapons of truth, of reason, of argument, and of godlike love, till it is swept away by the force of the assault, and a new and better system adopted in its place.

And what shall that better system be? We will not undertake to draw out a plan in detail, but will content ourselves with a few general hints.

1. We must see to it that, at least, the prisoners in our county jails are not made worse by a residence in them, and that, if possible, they leave them improved in principles and character. In locking them up in jail now, nobody thinks of making them better; the whole thought is that of securing their persons and repressing their malice. Restraint, coercion, the putting of fetters on the will, if not on the body—this expresses the whole policy; and the effect is, that, instead of being corrected, they are rendered more depraved and brutal than before. But this is all wrong. These arrested persons are precisely those for whom well constructed and well governed prisons are most needed. Surely, he who has not yet been pronounced guilty, and he who has

committed but a slight offense against the laws, ought to be surrounded by a greater moral protection than he who is sunk to a lower depth in crime, and whose guilt is acknowledged. Persons under arrest are often innocent, and are so proved on their trial. Is it right to let them find in the prison a corruption which they did not bring to it? But even if they are guilty, why place them first in a detention prison, which can hardly fail to corrupt them still more? Is it that, on their conviction, they may be sent to a state prison to be reformed? It has been well remarked by De Tocqueville that "to neglect the less vicious, in order to labor only for the reform of great and hardened criminals, is the same as if only the most infirm were attended to in a hospital; and, in order to take care of patients, perhaps incurable, those who might be easily restored to health were left without any attention." Surely, there must be a screw loose, there must be something out of joint, there must, in short, be a radical deficiency, in a prison system which offers anomalies and self-contradictions like these.

2. County jails should be made simply houses of detention for persons under arrest and awaiting trial. Their punitive character should be abrogated, and a class of prisons established, corresponding to the houses of correction in Massachusetts, intermediate between the state prison and the common jail, in which all persons convicted of minor offenses should be confined, under sentence of "hard labor." Detention for trial and punishment on conviction are essentially different processes, and the "fitness of things" requires, in each, a special method, in harmony with its nature and adapted to the end in view. The two systems have points widely variant and even incompatible with each other, and cannot be as successfully managed in conjunction as they can separately. Besides, officers who have the custody of prisoners awaiting trial, and who convey them to and from court, lack the requisite opportunity to enforce discipline among sentenced prisoners, of whom hard labor is exacted, as it should be in the case of all who are undergoing punishment on conviction.

3. Separate imprisonment should be enforced in all common jails. If association, as we firmly believe, is the seminal evil of our jail system, then its remedy must lie in individual imprisonment. The Prison Association has held this view from the start, and maintained it throughout. It is certainly our own, and we are happy to have it fortified by the judgment of so judicious a writer as Mr. F. Hill, who says: "The separation of prisoners is peculiarly

proper immediately after arrest, in police prisons, while under examination or waiting for trial. At such time, comparatively little can be known of the prisoner's character, or of the character of those with whom he may be placed in association; and at such periods, therefore, it is generally desirable to enforce a strict separation, not to speak of considerations arising from the danger of the defeat of justice."

4. Provision should be made for imparting religious instruction to all, and secular instruction to such as may need it. Our views on these points have been fully set forth in former parts of this paper, as they stand related to state prisons; and the arguments there adduced are equally applicable here. Possibly they will apply, in the present case, with added force, since medicines may be administered to the slightly sick with greater hope of advantage than to those in whom disease is approaching the point of incurable malignity.

5. The reform which would crown, and give efficiency to, all the others is a central authority of some kind, having the general oversight and control of the entire prison system of the state. The shocking anomalies and contradictions, noticed in a preceding paragraph, spring chiefly out of the want of unity in the government and administrations of the prisons. The state prisons are controlled and governed by state authority; the common jails and the houses of correction, where such exist, by whatever name called, are directed by the counties; while the city prison is superintended and managed by the city itself. These various departments of administration in the several states being almost as independent of each other as the states themselves, it results that they hardly ever act either uniformly or simultaneously. One may originate a useful reform within the sphere of its powers; but the others, clinging to ancient abuses, remain inactive, and make no progress. This is a sore evil. While it continues, though there may be improvement in isolated localities, there can be little general advance in prison discipline. Something may be effected here and there by spasmodic efforts, but there can be no combined, comprehensive, systematic agencies at work throughout the whole field, accomplishing reforms, commensurate with its territorial limits, and adequate to the demands of an enlightened statesmanship and a progressive civilization. May our noble state, whose example (for evil, we fear, as well as for good) is so potent with her sister states, soon apply the appropriate remedy in the estab-

lishment of a central authority, invested with the necessary powers, and animated with the zeal and ardor, which alone can insure broad and solid results. How much can be accomplished by such an authority, even with restricted and inadequate powers, has been seen in the exhibition, embodied in the previous chapter, of the remarkable improvements in jail construction and jail administration, achieved in Canada, within the last half dozen years, through the agency of the board of inspectors, so wisely created by the legislature of that province.

CHAPTER III.

PRISONS INTERMEDIATE BETWEEN THE COMMON JAIL AND THE STATE PRISON.

Prisons of the grade mentioned in the heading to this chapter, receive different designations in the different states—house of correction, penitentiary, workhouse, bridewell and city prison. Massachusetts is the only state in the Union which has a general system of this class of penal institutions, called there houses of correction. Even in Massachusetts, these prisons are not managed by the state, but are county institutions. Each county has one of them. New York has six penitentiaries, all of them created by special statutes, and directed by the counties in which they are severally situated. Michigan has a house of correction, erected and governed by the city of Detroit. Illinois has a bridewell in the city of Chicago, managed by the common council of the same. Missouri and Kentucky have each a workhouse, situated, the one at St. Louis, the other at Louisville, and both city institutions. Cincinnati, Ohio, has a city prison. Wisconsin has a house of correction at Milwaukie, which was in process of construction at the time of our visit to the state, and has since, we presume, gone into operation. It has been reported to us that there are two houses of correction in Maine; but we did not hear of them at the time of our visit to that state, and we conclude that they are either of little account, or belong to the class of establishments which exist only on paper. We visited about one-third of the houses of correction in Massachusetts, and all the other institutions named in the foregoing enumeration, except those of our own state, which we have often inspected at other times. We left our printed interrogatories in the hands of their superintendents, but we have received only two responses—one from Mr. Secretary Sanborn, of Massachusetts, and the other from Mr. Z. R. Brockway, superintendent of the Detroit house of correction, Michigan. As our observations extended to Canada, we ought, perhaps, in this connection, to state that there are in that province no prisons of the kind under consideration; but the board of inspection is urging upon the Legislature, with much zeal and force of reasoning, the necessity of such institutions, to which they propose to give the name of "central prisons."

The number of houses of correction in Massachusetts is nominally seventeen, but actually thirteen. In some cases they are wholly distinct establishments; more commonly, they are carried on in connection with the county jails. Each is under a local administration, there being no common bond of union among them. The governing power is vested in the county commissioners and the sheriff, except in Suffolk, where a body of city officers, called the "board of directors," manages the house of correction, as it does the other penal and reformatory institutions belonging to the city of Boston, with the exception of the common jail. Party politics enters but slightly, if at all, into the adminstration. The aggregate of salaries paid to the officers of these institutions is $50,000, being an average to each slightly under $4,000. The average number of prisoners confined in them is about 1,000. Almost the only punishment is the dark cell; the lash is never used. The commutation law is applied in the houses of correction, and its operation is found beneficial. The prisoners work in association during the day, and, with few exceptions, sleep in separate cells at night. The law of silence is imposed on prisoners while at work, but it is rather nominal than otherwise; in some cases it is scarcely enforced at all. Chaplains are provided for some of these prisons, but not for all. None of them give their whole time; their labors are commonly restricted to a Sunday service. In a few only of these "houses" are Sabbath schools held; in most, there is a full supply of Bibles. About thirty-five per cent. of the prisoners cannot read when received; and yet no provision whatever is made for teaching them. Libraries are provided, at the cost of the counties, for the greater part of these prisons. The aggregate number of volumes in all is about 3,000, the largest being 650. The dietaries are everywhere good. The meals are usually taken in the cells. A suit of clothes is furnished to each prisoner on his discharge, if he has not a decent one of his own, and money enough to pay his expenses home. Scarcely anything is done to prevent relapses, by aiding liberated prisoners to procure places where they may eat honest bread. There are no statistics showing either what proportion of the prisoners had learned a trade prior to their reception, or what during their imprisonment. The contract system of labor generally prevails, and works badly, both for the discipline and the finances. The expenses are greatly in excess of the revenues. The average length of sentences is from three to four months. The reformation of the prisoners is scarcely considered at all. Is it not a pregnant commentary on the foregoing exhibition that from thirty to ninety per cent. of the inmates are recommitted? At least three-fourths of the prisoners are of intemperate habits, and just the same proportion are foreigners. The effect of the war has been to diminish, during its continuance, the number of men committed, and greatly to increase that of women. The astounding and alarming fact is stated by the secretary that, while in 1854 the females constituted only one-fifth of the inmates of the house of correction, in 1864 they were almost one-half. Admitting that "this startling increase in female criminality is not wholly intelligible," he finds the solution, in part, at least, in the "distribution of state aid and bounty money." He remarks: "The possession of more money than usual makes the poor women idle, and, as I have said, exposes them to temptation; they drink, and from this they are led on to worse offences, while the absent sons, husbands and fathers leave them without restraint or protection." No doubt there is much force in this view; but it does not, in our opinion, afford a complete solution. Causes quite opposite in their nature have been at work to produce the result which we so much deplore. While some have sinned through the abundance of money, others have been led into crime from the want of it; for not all the women left at home had their resources increased by the absence of those on whom woman naturally leans for support. Both perils are alluded to in the prayer of Agur, the son of Jakeh, a prayer dictated by the highest wisdom: "Give me neither poverty nor riches, lest I be full, and deny thee, or lest I be poor, and steal."

As we have not hesitated to avow the conviction that the Massachusetts state prison is, all things considered, the best which it has been our fortune to visit, so we have as little hesitation in expressing the opinion that, so far as our own knowledge goes, the Detroit house of correction holds a like preëminence among the prisons of its class. This establishment is under the care and direction of Mr. Z. R. Brockway. There are few prison officers in this country, or probably in any other, who combine, in an equal degree, the varied qualifications reqisite for the successful management of a penal institution. Mr. Brockway began his career under the famous Amos Pilsbury, of the Albany penitentiary, with whom he served, so to speak, an apprenticeship of several years. From

Albany he was called, such was the distinction he had achieved there, to be the first superintendent of the Monroe county penitentiary, at Rochester. This position involved a work of organization, as well as administration, in both which he justified the confidence of those who called him to it. He continued at the head of that institution for a period of five or six years, and would, no doubt, have remained there to the present time, had he not, at the urgent invitation of the authorities of Detroit, accepted the position which he now holds. In organizing the new prison at Detroit and in subsequently administering its government and discipline, he displayed an ability no less signal and achieved a success no less conspicuous, than he had previously done at Rochester. A gentleman of endowments so marked and an experience so extended, while his work would naturally claim attention and study, may well be permitted to declare it himself; and, certainly, his utterances are entitled to a most respectful consideration. We therefore give place, without abridgement or alteration, to a communication of Mr. Brockway, in which he favors us with an account of the institution under his care. The following is the paper to which we refer :

DETROIT HOUSE OF CORRECTION, }
29th November, 1865. }

Rev. E. C. WINES, D. D. :

My Dear Sir—Events over which I had no control, have rendered it impossible for me to fulfill my partial promise to answer the four hundred and thirty questions touching the prison system, or to write at length upon the subject of convict employment. I should have advised you of this before, but had not relinquished the purpose until to-day. Trusting to your benevolence to overlook what may reasonably seem to you to be a want of regard for yourself and lack of interest in your work; assuring you of my deep interest in the proposed reorganization of our prison system and of my profound respect for yourself, I will append some facts of interest about this institution, which, together with the set of our annual reports some time since forwarded to you, will comprise the whole of my communication at this time

The House of Correction is managed by the superintendent, appointed for three years by the common council of the city, on the nomination of the mayor and board of inspectors, consisting of five persons, viz., the mayor of the city of Detroit, and the chairman of the Board of Inspectors of the State Prison, ex-officio, and three citizens appointed in the same way as the superintendent, one being appointed annually

The buildings were erected in 1861, at a cost of $80,000, exclusive of its site, and are arranged in the form of a Latin Cross. and are in their general aspect, quite similar to the Albany county penitentiary. In the rear of the wings containing the cells, are two yards; one for males and the other for females; the former about 175 feet square, containing workshops; the latter, about the same size, contains the fuel building, and is used chiefly for domestic purposes. These yards are surrounded by a brick wall sixteen feet high, surmounted with sentinel towers, and are neatly laid out, graded, graveled and sodded, and are separated by a wing two stories in height, used for kitchens, hospitals, chapel, &c. Immediately in front of the building and outside of the enclosure, are ornamental grounds, 100 by 600 feet, aud an additional space of 600 feet square is being subdued, and is soon to be added.

There is also a fine garden of about ten acres in the rear.

The staff of prison officers is composed of the superintendent, clerk, chaplain, four overseers, two guards and four matrons—all appointed by the superintendent, subject to the approval of the inspectors, and removable by him at his pleasure.

The salaries are as follows :

The superintendent	$2,500.	per annum and perquisites.	
assistant do	650	do	and board.
clerk	400	do	do
chaplain (equal to),	500	do	do
overseers	300	do	do
guards	240	do	do
matrons	200 to 250 do		do

Appointments are not affected by party politics, except in the appointment of inspectors; and the influence of this does, in no degree, affect the administration of the prison.

In the administration of the discipline, kindness is employed, and is esteemed a very important means. Prompt attention to the reasonable requests of prisoners, considerate treatment and the maintaining of a kind, benevolent demeanor in the intercourse of officers and prisoners, produces the most gratifying effect. Rewards are also employed as a stimulus to good conduct, viz.: commutation of sentence three days per month; the allowance of overwork (paid only at the expiration of the sentence) ; and, in the female prison, the division of the prisoners into two grades.

The lowest grade are kept in separate cells when not at work; live upon the coarse prison diet, without tea or coffee, and non-intercourse is always enforced among them. They are, however, admitted to the privileges of the library, attend upon the daily and weekly devotions, and receive visits from the chaplain at the cell door.

The higher grade sleep and spend their business hours in a room together, are allowed to converse with each other, under the restraint imposed by the proximity of the matron, who can hear the conversation, though she is not present in their room. They are allowed some privileges of diet, a distinction is made in their clothing, and they are supplied with greater variety of reading matter. The chaplain, superintendent, and other friends, frequently visit their room after work hours, for the purpose of reading, or speaking, or studying the scripture with them, and usually engage in family devotions before leaving.

I am unable to state definitely as to results, the grade having been so recently established. I have great confidence, however, that a similar system may be successfully introduced into the male prison, and that I shall be able next year to furnish you with interesting facts in relation to it in both prisons.

The commutation law is most salutary in its effect upon the conduct of prisoners, and in every instance, save two, during the three years of its operation, prisoners have gained the whole time allowed by law.

The allowance of overwork, as before stated, is not as a pecuniary reward for good conduct, but as a stimulus to industry and the cultivation of habits of application that shall be of service to the prisoner on his release from confinement.

Religious services are held in the chapel every morning, at which *all* the prisoners and officers are present; and, on Sunday, there is a preaching service at 9 o'clock, A. M. The remainder of the day is spent by the prisoners in their cells, and by the chaplain in visiting them for personal conversation and the distribution of books and papers.

No Sabbath school is maintained. It is believed that the sermon in the morning, the opportunity for reading afforded by a good library, and the personal intercourse with the chaplain, are of more value to prisoners sentenced for such short periods as these are, than would be a Sabbath school.

The subject of punishments naturally comes in here, and I regret that I have not time to write out my views as they stand after an experience and observation of many years. Many of the punishments used in the prisons of our country are barbarous and worse than useless, while some which have been abrogated are most valuable, if properly administered.

I doubt if the wisdom of man can devise any *system* of punishment that can be universally applied with uniform results. Very great power *must* be vested in the governing officer of a prison, and when abused, the officer should be removed. There has been a tendency to so legislate on this subject that a bad or incompetent officer *could not* commit an error or an outrage, and the effect has been injurious to the discipline of our prisons and to the prisoners themselves.

I trust, however, that as Christ's new dispensation of love submerged and practically annulled the old dispensation of law, so the new era of "rewards," in the management of prisoners, will render the discussion of the subject of punishments compartively unimportant.

The prisoners in this institution are employed at the manufacture of chairs, the wood work of which is made by the males, and the females are engaged in braiding the seats.

There are no contractors in this prison. The superintendent purchases material, directs the labor, and sells the goods. The prison, under this system, is entirely self-sustaining, as will be subsequently shown, and funds sufficient to test the value of "rewards" and other modifying appliances are supplied, without an appeal to the treasury of the state. I have no doubt that so soon as the number of males in confinement reaches the maximum capacity of the prison, we shall be able to adopt the *eight hour system*, and still be "self-sustaining."

The institution was opened in August, 1861. The average number of prisoners in confinement up to December 31, 1862, was $96\frac{3}{10}$, more than one-half of whom were females. The whole expenditure for that period was $16,036.85 and the income, $6,794.51, leaving a deficit of $9,242.34.

The average number of prisoners in confinement for the year ending December 31, 1863, was 126 and a fraction, not quite one-half of whom were females. The expenditure for this year was $16,231.20, and the income $13,231.20, leaving a deficit of $3,000.

The average number of prisoners in confinement for 1864, was 142 and a fraction, one-third of whom were females.

The expenditure for the year was $24,305.08; and the income, $26,316.88, leaving a surplus of $2,011.80.

The year 1865 is not yet closed, and my statements are not ready. I estimate, however, that the average number of prisoners will be about 175 (one-half females); that the expenditure will be $25,000, and the earnings $30,000, or in that ratio; and that I shall be able to report a surplus of $5,000.

The contract system meets with very general denunciation in these days, and I confidently expect will soon be superseded throughout the prisons of the land, though much of the evil attributed to it more justly belongs to its mal-administration.

I have refused all offers for the employment of the prisoners here, and intend to test by actual experiment the value of the system now in operation.

I feel that there are very gross defects in the prison system of the land, and that, as a whole, it does not accomplish its design; and that the time has come for *reconstruction*. There are, doubtless, in operation in the prisons of this country, religious and moral agencies, physical and hygienic regulations, and a system of employment for prisoners, which, if combined in the management of one institution, would produce a *model prison* indeed. To find them, combine them, and apply them, is to my view the great desideratum. When this shall have been accomplished, and every state is supplied with a graduated system of graded prisons, controlled by an independent central authority; and when the criminal code shall have been made to correspond with the new state of things, then, and not till then, may we *rest*.

This is an age of *demonstration*, and the practicability of the proposed improvements must be demonstrated at every step to insure their adoption.

In my quiet corner here, I am at work at this, and trust that by next year the practical operation of our system of labor and partial operation of prisoners will add at least a mite to the progress of prison reform.

I am, my dear sir, with very great respect,
Your obedient servant,
Z. R. BROCKWAY.

From this noble institution, worthy in many respects to be regarded as a " model prison," we pass to one most opposite in its character, the "bridewell," of the city of Chicago, Illinois. With a single exception, soon to be noticed, this, we think, is the worst prison of its class we have ever seen. Several reporters of the city presses accompanied us on our visit to it. On the following morning the Chicago Times and Tribune had extended notices of the inspection, from each of which we take a brief extract.

The Times said: " The commissioners paid a visit to the bride-well, and the sights which there met their eyes seemed to astonish them a little. They were not prepared, indeed, to see a model institution, but they certainly never expected to see in a great city, like Chicago, a penal establishment which is scarcely fit for a dog kennel. The keeper of the bridewell, who showed the party through the place, seemed himself to be ashamed of it, and, by way of apologizing for the wretched condition in which they found it, complained of the want of means at his disposal for rendering it a fit habitation for human beings. In the first ward are a succession of narrow little dungeons, where a man can barely stand erect, and where he can stretch forth his hand and touch the walls all around. Each cell is provided with a bed, which occupies nearly the whole space, so that when a prisoner is seated on the bed his knees touch the opposite wall. The bed linen was not over clean, because, as the keeper said, the supply of bedding was insufficient, so that he could not possibly change it. In each of these deplorable dungeons two men were confined together. How they manage to sleep at night it is impossible to guess, for the bed itself is quite narrow for one man. The wretched inmates glowered at the visitors as they passed, like wild beasts in a cage. By far the greater proportion of the prisoners in the bridewell at the present time are women, and the accommodations being insufficient, a large number of these are obliged to be transferred to the men's quarters. One thing seemed to suprise the commissioners, and that was, that quite a number of the cells were entirely unfurnished. The city cannot afford a few wretched pallets, and the consequence is that, while the bridewell is over-crowded, a considerable portion is absolutely lying empty—hungry for tenants. It is no wonder that the commissioners said that our prisons are a disgrace to the city."

The Tribune speaks in a similar strain, adding some facts not contained in the article of the Times. It remarks: "The buildings are of wood, old, rotten and rickety, affording nests for innumerable vermin, which all the efforts of the people in charge cannot make effectual fight against. They will be destroyed only when the building is burnt down; and it is terrible to think of the consequences that would ensue, should that building take fire. No power on earth could save it from total destruction. Its walls and partitions are of the most rotten kind of wood, into any part of which one may run a knife almost to the hilt, and it would burn like tinder. * * * * The match of the incendiary or the careeslsness of an attendant might, at any moment, envelope the building in flames, when nothing short of a miracle could save those confined there. The next crying sin is the lack of proper provision for cleanliness and seclusion. The little cells, each intended for one person, and furnished with a single cot of boards and a tick filled with straw, are made, in many cases, to hold two persons, who, in this hot weather (August), are obliged to lie as closely packed as herring in a barrel; this, too, while several of the cells are unoccupied, and for the shameful reason that there is not enough of that bedding to supply one tick to each cell. Of course, this leaves no material for changing, and many of the ticks and covers are in a dreadfully dirty condition—they cannot be spared for washing. The privies were in a wretchedly filthy condition, and as for washing, the prisoners use one long trough, without soap. Another radical wrong of the place is the lack of any employment for the prisoners. The men are set to stone-breaking and wood-sawing, but there is not enough of these kinds of labor to keep them all busy. The women are much worse provided for in this respect. They had rag picking last winter, but that ran out long ago; and now they have nothing to do, except some little domestic labor. The maintenance of the prisoners is almost wholly a charge upon the city, whereas their labor should be a source of profit."

The city workhouse at St. Louis, Missouri, though very far from being what such an institution ought to be, is yet many degrees in advance of the city bridewell at Chicago. We spent part of a day in the institution, and were courteously shown through its several departments, by the gentlemanly superintendent, Mr. James Ludington. It was on a Saturday that we paid our visit and made our inspection ; and we had the good fortune to find there the mayor cf the city, the Hon. James S. Thomas, on an errand of mercy. It appears that all the sentences to this prison are alternative ones, that is, such an amount of fine or so many days' confinement. Every dollar of fine unpaid requires two days' imprisonment ; but the maximum of imprisonment is one hundred days. Now, as the inmates of the workhouse cannot appear personally before the mayor, and as few of them have friends to interpose in their behalf, the mayor is accustomed to spend one Saturday each month at the prison, which he devotes to hearing the statements of such as may be deserving of executive clemency. The result is, that some of the most worthy have their fines remitted, either wholly or in part. Several, after a hearing of their case, were released on the day of our visit. Such are required to report once a week to the mayor, giving the name of their employer and place of occupation. In case of a failure to pay a portion of the fine imposed from the earnings of each week, they are remanded back to prison to serve out the unexpired part of their sentence ; and, in case of a new arraignment and conviction, the fresh penalty is added to, not substituted for, the old. Several were thus conditionally discharged on the day of our visit; and, while expressing the most grateful sense of his honor's kindness, they made strong promises of amendment and an honest course of life for the future. Mr. Thomas informed us that quite a number were in this way reclamined and saved.

We find in our note book sundry memoranda made in connection with this inspection ; but soon after our return east, we received from the author, the venerable Dr. Elliot, for more than thirty years pastor of a church in St. Louis, a " Statement of the Actual Condition of the Prisons in the City and County of St. Louis, prepared after Careful Inspection, and respectfully addressed to his Fellow-Citizens." We do not hesitate to substitute his account for any we might frame from our own notes. He says :

"This institution is situated on Caron delet road, three miles below the city, on high and pleasant ground, including about ten acres, and might be made everything desired. I was there the other day, when a half a dozen of the calaboose graduates were received. One of them was an old man entirely blind, an habitual drunkard, who spends a great part of his time there, being out only long enough to commit some new outrage to send him back again. There were three degraded women, who looked as if they could not be made worse, and probably no attempt was ever proposed to make them better.

"Two of the men were hand-cuffed, evidently hardened offenders who had been there before, one of them a discharged soldier. They were required to sit down on the ground while shackles were riveted upon their ankles, with a chain just long enough to move with a shambling walk. During this process they were full of blasphemy and curses, and one, a young man, whose face was marked by the deep lines of dissipation, three score and ten years old in iniquity, was so insulting in his behavior that he was punished by a severe blow on the spot. They were then prepared, their hand-cuffs having been removed, to take their places with one of the work-house gangs, employed under the direction armed guards in the quarry or upon the streets in that vicinity, to work out their fines ; the publicity of their punishment lessening what poor hope there might be of their reformation.

"I went carefully through the whole building and grounds, and into many of the cells. The buildings are unskillfully arranged, and although kept with considerable care, some of the cells, in which some of the sick or insane were confined, were insufferably offensive. The cells are twelve by eighteen feet large, with tolerable ventilation, and each of them contains at night eight persons, with little or no regard to classification. There were forty-three insane persons in keeping, a few of them in close confinement, but the most of them at comparative liberty, several being regularly employed in different kinds of mental labor. The whole number of prisoners was about one hundred and fifty, nearly half of whom were women.

"The men were away at their different places of work, as I have said, but the women, to the number of forty or fifty, I found employed in breaking stone for macadamizing the streets. It was a sad sight. Nearly all of them are young, some only sixteen or seventeen years old. A few retained some little remaining modesty of appearance, but their faces, and manner generally showed, plainly enough, the absence of all shame. They were working lazily, but talking busily, and it was easy to see that whatever sparks of virtue might be left were in the way of rapid extinguishment.

"Throughout the institution I saw no evidence of severe physical hardship nor of habitual cruelty of treatment, although the law of force was evidently that which alone governed everything. It was equally evident that no moral or religious influence of any kind is at work there. The place is unvisited by ministers of the gospel, catholic or protestant, except perhaps upon some urgent occasion, and no instruction of any kind, week days or Sundays is given. Three-fourths of the inmates, taking ten years together, have belonged, as I was informed, nominally, to the Roman catholic communion, and formerly were often visited by their priests, but not at all during the last four or five years. They must have found it a most discouraging field of work, but it ought not to be neglected. Many of the prisoners were on sentence for the second or third time, and the officer said that some whom he found there ten years ago, are in confinement now, having been discharged and recommitted perhaps a dozen times. Financially, the institution is nearly self-supporting ; and taking the system as it is, I should say it is not unskillfully managed. But it is *the system* of which we complain. It is one of continual demoralization, to make the bad worse instead of better, to degrade instead of elevating, to ruin instead of saving, to increase the sum of iniquity by which the community is cursed, instead of lessening it. Take that calaboose and workhouse together, they train and graduate in wickedness more than any school or church in the city can educate in virtue. You may say that the material is worthless at any rate, and not worth saving, but Jesus Christ did not teach us so. No human being is worthless, and he died to save the vilest sinner from death. The ruin of these outcasts will be required at the hands of christendom. "Sick, and in prison and ye visited me not," is a sentence which christian churches and legislators may be compelled to hear to their confusion. Or, if humanity and christian love cannot enforce wiser systems of punishment, the self-protection of society should do so. It is the most expensive system and the most ruinous that could be devised. I am not so tender hearted as to screen the guilty from the punishment due to their crimes, nor do I believe in petting the criminal so as to change his punishment into a reward. But I believe that christi-anity and social science equally require that punishment should be so conducted as to prevent the criminal from being made worse, and to give him favorable opportunities for reform. Our present system is the exact reverse of this, and the baneful result is everywhere seen."

Of all the prisons of the class under consideration, the city work house at Louisville, Kentucky, is the vilest den we have ever seen used for the abode of human beings. The number of inmates at the time of our visit, was seventy, one-third of whom were women. The only employment here is crushing stone for roads; and men and women work together at the business. There is no restraint upon their conversation, which may well be judged the most foul and corrupting imaginable; and such, in point of fact, we were informed, it is. The same is true, when the two sexes are in their several yards within the prison enclosure. Though separated by a stone wall, they talk through it with ease, and without restriction. The cells are certainly not more than eight feet square; and yet five men sleep on a platform raised a little above the rest of the floor, without beds of any sort, and with no bedding but blankets; shuck beds being, however, as we were told, furnished in winter. All the ventilation these cells have is through a slit in the wall, some two or three feet long, and about six inches wide. The air, even in the daytime, with the doors open and no occupants inside, was the foulest we ever breathed. What must it be when five men have been locked in a cell for twelve or fourteen consecutive hours, and used it, more-over, for all the calls of nature; for, be it known, there is not a privy on the prison premises! Thirty years ago, the French com-missioners, De Beaumont and De Tocqueville, "found (so they report) in the prison of New Orleans, men together with hogs, in the midst of all odors and nuisances." They add: "It cannot be called a prison; it is a horrid sink, in which they are crowded together, and which is fit only for those dirty animals found here together with the prisoners, who were not slaves, but persons free in the ordinary course of life." We did not, indeed, find pigs associated in the Louisville work house with men, in the occupancy of these cells; but, at all events, their presence could scarcely have made them worse than they were.

The city prison at Cincinnati, Ohio, consists of two departments, one for males and the other for females, accommodated in different buildings, which are situated in parts of the city quite distant from each other. We do not remember ever to have seen, nor could we easily conceive of, two branches of one and the same institution in sharper contrast the one with the other.

The male prison is an old livery stable, which has been converted into a place for the confinement of criminals. It is indeed a horrid establishment—insecure, unventilated, filthy, most offensive in its smells, with no discipline, and without work for its inmates, or the first thought or effort towards their reformation. There is not, or at least there was not at the time of our visit, a single bed in the prison. The prisoners slept on boards, arranged tier above tier, in rows of iron crates or cages, running the entire length of the building. They had much of the aspect of the cages in a menagerie of wild beasts. In short, the whole appearance and tone of the establishment we found repulsive in the extreme, and the impression left upon the mind was deeply painful. We could not look upon it otherwise than as a discredit to the great city of which it forms one of the prominent penal institutions.

We felt it as a great relief when, after a ride of a mile or two in a street car, we found ourselves in the female department of the same prison. The contrast could scarcely be more complete than it is in all respects. The institution is under the superintendence of " Mother Mary Stanislaus, Religious of the Good Shepherd," assisted by sisters of the same order. The prison is an old school house, quite unfit for the purposes to which it is now devoted; but it is one of the best regulated and best conducted institutions we met with in all our travels. Every part was as clean as water, soap and brushes could make it, and as sweet as any private house. The women were tidily dressed in plain calico, each with a clean white apron. They wore a subdued and cheerful air, very different from the glum and sullen looks so often seen in persons of their class in other prisons. They were busy at work making garments, and seemed to ply the needle with a will. During the late war, they did a great deal of work, at remunerative prices, for the government; but since then, greater difficulty has been experienced in procuring profitable employment. As an encouragement to industry and good conduct, the prisoners are allowed, for their own use, from twenty to twenty-five per cent of their earnings. Those who remain six months, if they have been uniformly industrious and obedient, are presented with a neat calico dress and shaker bonnet, and sometimes, for extra good conduct, with a pair of shoes as well. Mother Stanis-laus informed us that these little rewards operated like a charm, and were found more effective in maintaining discipline than all the harshness and severity that could be employed. The number of inmates at the time of our inspection was seventy-five, and their average continuance in the prison was stated to us at about four months.

This admirable prison owes its present organization and man-agement to Mrs. Sarah Peter, a widow lady of great intelligence and philanthropy. To our regret, Mrs. Peter was absent from Cincinnati when we were there. We subsequently entered into correspondence with her, in the course of which we received three letters, which contain statements and views of so much interest and value, that we have deemed it proper to publish extended extracts from them in the appendix. These are commended to the reader as well worthy of his attention. Mrs. Peter, being an earnest Catholic, is rather warm in her praises of the sisterhood who have charge of the prison; a matter upon which, commis-sioned as we were simply to examine into the condition and man-agement of prisons and to report the facts concerning them, we do not feel called upon to express any opinion.

The county penitentiaries of our own state are, without doubt, the best penal institutions we have, owing, as we conceive, to the fact that their administration in some of the counties is entirely, and in the others measurably, free from the blighting effect of political influence. The penitentiaries in the counties of Albany, Monroe and Erie may, according to the theory of prison discipline heretofore and now prevalent in this country, be justly pronounced model institutions, except that, even under the prevalence of that theory, greater prominence might be and ought to be given to the departments of religion and education. But the prisons named, and others of their class, have been, both in their organic and administrative relations, so often and so fully set before the legis-lature and the people of this state, in the reports of the Prison Association, that we may well forbear to encumber these pages with what must already be familiar to all who take an interest in subjects and discussions of this nature.

We have thus completed the circle of prisons included in the designation placed at the head of this chapter. The houses of correction in Boston and Detroit, the female branch of the city prison of Cincinnati, and the three penitentiaries in New York, mentioned in the last paragraph, are undoubtedly the best organized and the best administered of their class in the country. Beyond them, the catalogue is limited and the results meagre. Massachusetts leads here, as she does in other classes of penal and correctional institutions ; but in this, as well as those, she is as yet far from having "attained." The number of these institutions in that state is too great both for economic and moral results. Her board of state charities is urging a reduction of the number to four ; and we quite concur in their views. New York needs from ten to fifteen; or, possibly, one in each of the eight judicial districts might be sufficient. On their importance and, indeed, necessity to complete an adequate prison system for our state, we will not now enlarge, as we have said all we deem needful on that subject in the first chapter of the present report; and to the treatment which the topic there receives (pp. 67–71) we refer the reader for what might fitly be said here, if it had not been said elsewhere before.

CHAPTER IV.

JUVENILE REFORMATORIES.

The undersigned, in the progress of their visitation, gave much attention to institutions devoted to the reformation of juvenile delinquents. We failed, indeed, from causes with which it is hardly necessary to trouble the legislature, to see either of the reformatories of Canada, the state reform school of Michigan, the state reform farm of Ohio, and the juvenile farm school on Thompson's Island, Massachusetts. With these exceptions, we visited and examined all the correctional institutions of much note, in the states constituting the field of our inquiries, viz : The Chicago Reform School, Illinois ; the State Reform School at Waukesha, Wisconsin ; the St. Louis House of Refuge, Missouri ; the Louisville House of Refuge, Kentucky ; the Cincinnati House of Refuge, Ohio ; the Western House of Refuge, Pittsburgh, and the Eastern House of Refuge (colored and white departments), Philadelphia, Pennsylvania ; the Baltimore House of Refuge, Maryland ; State Reform School at Meriden, Connecticut ; Providence Reform School, Rhode Island ; State Reform School, near Portland, Maine ; State Reform School, at Concord, New Hampshire ; and State Reform School at Westborough ; State Industrial School for Girls, at Lancaster ; Nautical Branch of State Reform School, on board School-Ships, and Boston House of Reformation, Deer Island, all in Massachusetts.

From the superintendents of all the correctional institutions visited by us we received answers to our printed interrogatories, except the State Reform School of New Hampshire, the Boston House of Reformation, the Pittsburgh House of Refuge, and the House of Refuge at Louisville. From the last named none were expected, as it had been in operation less than two months. We also received replies from one institution not visited—the State Reform School of Michigan.

The fourteen papers, embodying the answers to our questions, are published *in extenso* in the appendix. This will obviate the necessity of preparing any extended account of this class of institutions, thus saving both our own and our readers' time, and presenting the information communicated in a more authentic and, probably, more acceptable form. We desire, however, to make, and indeed feel it our duty to make, this general remark : That there is no class of institutions in our country, connected with the repression and prevention of crime, that will bear a moment's comparison with that which forms the subject of the present chapter. Indeed, almost every one of them might be pronounced a model institution of its kind. Many of the superintendents are not only eminently but pre-eminently qualified for their positions. Together with their assistants, male and female, they form, we feel quite sure, as noble a band of workers in the cause of humanity as are to be found in any quarter of the globe. If we might venture, among so many excellent institutions, to single out any that seem to us to possess an excellence superior to the others, we could not hestitate to name the reform schools of Massachusetts; and of these we should feel as little hesitation in pronouncing *first among its peers* the Industrial School for Girls at Lancaster. At the same time, truth compels us to state that there is one reformatory in the old Bay State, more open to criticism than any we met with elsewhere in the whole course of our visitation—we refer to the House of Reformation on Deer Island. We append a brief extract from our note book, being a memorandum made at the time of our visit: " September 28.—Visited the city institutions on Deer Island. Here we found, under the same roof, a city almshouse; a house of industry, which is a city prison for persons convicted of minor offenses, not unlike, in its general features, the county houses of correction; and the boys' department of the house of reformation, which was for a long time a general reformatory for juvenile delinquents, but has become, of late years, a mere receptacle for truant children from the Boston schools. The girls' department is in a separate building near at hand. All these different institutions are under one superintendent, who happened, unfortunately, to be away from the island at the time of our visit. The whole establishment is clean and orderly, but in other respects is much inferior to the reform schools at Westborough and Lancaster. It has, to our minds, a number of objectionable features. 1. The mixing up, in one concern, of criminals, paupers and truant children, is more than an incongruity; it is a monstrosity. 2. Meals are served to the prisoners in the kitchen, where all the food is prepared; and males and females eat at the same time, simply occupying different sides of the apartment, and sitting with their backs to each other. 3. The male criminals and the boys of the reformatory, work on the same farm (180 acres); not indeed, we were told, in company, but they must, necessarily, often meet each other and hold more or less intercourse, which can hardly fail to be corrupting to the boys."

Massachusetts boasts one institution for youthful offenders quite unique in its character—the Nautical Branch of the State Reform School. The inmates of this institution, to the number of 160, were accommodated, when we visited it, in the ship Massachusetts, of 650 tons burthen, then lying in Boston harbor. Another ship, considerably larger and capable of receiving 200 pupils with their officers, was then fitting up, and nearly ready for occupancy. It has been now, for a year or more, fulfilling the noble purpose to which it is destined so long as it shall be fit for use at all. These two ships, it will be seen, are capable of affording accommodations for 360 juvenile delinquents, who may have been committed to them by the proper authorities. One of them is stationed in Boston harbor, and the other in the harbor of New Bedford; but both spend a good part of the summer in cruising about the waters of Massachusetts, and visiting its various seaport towns.

The limit of age at which boys are excluded from the reform school at Westborough is 14; but they can be received into the school-ships up to the age of 18. The superintendent of the Massachusetts, when we visited her, was Capt. Richard Matthews, and the teacher, Mr. Martin L. Eldridge. Both of these gentlemen seemed to us eminently adapted to their work, and they were zealously devoted to it, even to enthusiasm. The boys were divided into equal sections. The members of each section were in school every other day. For our gratification, Mr. Eldridge put them through various exercises, the subjects of examination being arithmetic, geography, history, and especially navigation, on which latter branch the instruction seemed to have been particularly thorough. All the questions put were answered with the utmost alacrity, and with a promptness and accuracy which were surprising. They also sang a number of sailors' songs with a spirit and fervor, which showed that their soul was in the exercise. The section not engaged in lesson learning were on duty in cleansing the ship, cooking the meals, setting and clearing the tables, and other domestic employments; in repairing sails and rigging; in going through every variety of nautical evolution; in gaining a knowledge of sheet and halyard, brace and clewline, and the technical language of sailors; in short, in becoming practical seamen. A ready comprehension and rapid execution of orders, the dextrous handling of rope and oar, and the ability to climb the rigging with ease and rapidity, are thus acquired. The summer cruises are anticipated with eagerness, and enjoyed with a keen relish by the boys; and they serve at once to develop and to test their seamanship.

To the education of the mind and body, as declared above, is added a careful culture of the heart, the sedulous inculcation of moral and religious truth.

And what is the result of all this benevolent labor, which, receiving from the criminal courts these neglected, vicious and degraded boys, extends to them the hand of christian sympathy, shields them for a season from the rough blasts of temptation, teaches them their duty to God and man, imparts to them the principles of a noble science, trains them to skill in the application of those principles, and finally, opening to them a path of honorable usefulness, bids them go forth and walk therein, to the honor of their God and the benefit of their fellow-men? We answer, unhesitatingly, that the result is most cheering. The very qualities of sagacity and daring, of earnestness and enthusiasm, which, under their former evil training, were rendering them a terror as well as a pest to the community, have, in numerous instances, by the radical change wrought in their principles and habits through the wise and kindly efforts of their teachers, constituted a vigorous impulse to push them forward and to give them success in their new career of virtue, honor and usefulness.

We cannot better give an idea, first, of the vicious character of the boys received and the consequent criminal and pestilent lives they threatened to lead, and secondly, of the benefits resulting from the institution to themselves and to the community, than by offering a few brief extracts from late reports of the superintendent and teacher of the ship Massachusetts.

One hundred and seventy-two boys were sentenced to the ship in 1865. As showing the character of these youths, Capt. Matthews reports that of this number there were committed for assault and battery, two; assault with intent to rob, two; breaking and entering to steal, 32; idle and disorderly, one; incendiary, two; larceny, 70; malicious mischief, two; stubbornness, 44; vagrancy, two; returned from probation, seven; transferred from state reform school, eight. It is a sad view of the case of these boys that nearly two-thirds of them had lost one or both of their parents. Fifty-five had been arrested once previously; twenty-four, twice; eight, three times; two, four times; and two, five or six times. Thirty-one were habitual drinkers of ardent spirits, and ninety-five were in the constant use of tobacco. Their ages were as follows: Seven were 12 years old; seven, 13; thirty-eight, 14; fifty-three, 15; twenty-seven, 16; and forty, 17—the average of their ages being about 15 years. Of the 172 received, two did not know the alphabet; seven could not read at all; 34 could read a little in the first reader; 75 could read in the second reader; 40 could read in the third reader, and only 16 in the fourth; 23 could not write; 41 had not studied arithmetic; 65 had studied mental arithmetic, and 66 had studied written arithmetic more or less. The average length of time during which the boys had not attended school prior to their commitment, exceeded twenty months. Of course, they had forgotten much which they had previously learned.

Captain Matthews makes the following interesting statements in his report:

" We have spent as much time in cruising during the past year as formerly, having visited all the principal ports in the state. The boys have been active and handy, and have made a good degree of advancement in seamanship.

" The health of the boys has been very good indeed, and it gives me great pleasure to state that inflammation of the eyes, which has troubled us considerably, as it has almost all public institutions, has very much decreased.

" No death has occurred among our number during the year.

" The graduates from this institution, so far as heard from, have generally done well ; some, as might be expected, have lapsed into the pursuit of evil courses, but a great majority are doing well, and giving evidence of thorough reform. The fidelity and devotion of those who have served their country during the war, in the navy and army, is very gratifying, and will ever be a source of just pride in the institution which in part, at least, prepared their hearts to love and hands to defend the land of their birth.

" Many interesting letters have been received from boys who have been in the navy and army, giving very clear and truthful accounts of engagements by sea and land.

" Two boys have served three years in the navy, and then

enlisted two years in the army. One writes : 'Say to the captain that the boys, in the future, will thank him for all he is doing for them now.' The other boy says : ' If the boys are obedient and follow the advice given them by the officers of the ship, they will come out all right.' Scarcely a day passes now in which the ship is not visited by some of the former pupils of the school, returning from voyages at sea, giving good evidence that they are leading honorable and useful lives. Another boy writes : ' Give the officers and trustees of the school-ship my thanks, for all they have done for me.'

" The close of the war, and the consequent discharge of so many seamen from the navy, has so increased the number of men seeking voyages, and so reduced the rates of wages as to make the demand for boys much less than during the three years previous. You will observe by reference to Table 1, that fewer boys have been sent on voyages at sea this past year, than for two or three years before.

" This, however, I do not consider a misfortune, by any means, as the length of time which the boys have heretofore spent in the institution has been too short for thoroughness either in reform or instruction.

" With the increased facilities for the accommodation of boys, we shall not only be able to give instruction upon a broader system, but by having a greater range of selection, shall be prepared to give better satisfaction than ever before, by offering only boys whose characters and capabilities have been tested by a long residence in the school.

" Religious exercises have been regularly attended on the Sabbath, when the boys have been addressed by gentlemen representing the different religious denominations and the various callings in life. By this means the interest of the boys has been kept up, and doubtless many good resolutions have been formed and kept."

Mr. Eldridge makes statements of no less interest, as follows :

" The conduct of the boys in school has been very good, and they have shown as ready and prompt obedience, and as much application to study, as we could reasonably expect from their antecedents. The school has been as easily managed as in any year since it was organized, and the progress made in the several branches pursued as great as heretofore, while in some, especially in navigation, the advancement is certainly more marked than in any former year.

"This is very gratifying; for any one at all acquainted with our maratime population can point to many men of enterprise and correct habits, who have been checked in their aspirations for positions of command and trust, because their limited education did not embrace a knowledge of the theory of navigation.

"Penmanship receives special attention, since the acquisition of a good hand-writing is considered one of the best qualifications for a young man seeking employment, opening as it does to him many avenues of useful occupation, which otherwise were closed.

"It gives me pleasure to acknowledge the valuable service rendered by the assistant teacher, Patrick Murphy, who was promoted from the ranks during the year. Allow me to suggest whether a system of promotions to minor positions might not be adopted, and conducted in such a manner as to cultivate the self-respect of the boys and excite among them a worthy emulation.

"I cannot close my report without some allusion to those who were so recently my pupils, but who now sleep in southern graves or beneath the waves of the ocean. Eight are known to have fallen, by land or sea, in their country's defence. In the sudden shock of battle, or after days of suffering from wounds or disease, they have gone to their long rest in unknown graves, or 'in the bosom of the deep sea buried.' How great was the sacrifice they made for so good a cause. With them the morning of life was clouded by misfortune and chilled by neglect; and just as the beams of hope gave to life a meaning and a joy—in the opening years of manhood, they bade adieu to all the brightness of the future, and, faithful to duty, went down into 'the valley and shadow of death.' They were obscure and humble, but a nation's grateful remembrance shall be their monument. They were poor, but they have left a rich and imperishable legacy in their heroic example of devotion to country and to duty."

The sentences to the school ships are for no definite periods, but during minority. The trustees have the legal right to pardon in all cases where they see fit; and they have likewise the power to send a boy on a voyage to sea, which has the effect of a full discharge. They may also discharge boys on probation, and often do so. A discharge on probation allows a boy to go home or elsewhere on shore; but leaves him liable to re-arrest and re-committal, without a new crime, if his conduct is otherwise such as to render his return expedient. Probation is thus a conditional pardon, similar to that granted for good behavior, on ticket-of-leave, in English and Irish prisons, and is revocable, at pleasure, for adequate cause.

The experiment of school-ships has been an eminent success in Massachusetts, in respect both of its primary purpose of reforming juvenile offenders, and of its secondary purpose of rearing a more intelligent and better class of seamen. Numbers of the graduates (at one time no less than 165) have served in the navy, some of them with distinction. The school-ships have become highly popular with shipmasters and owners, especially of the better class. *One ship has taken six boys on each of five successive voyages to India.*

Since the addition of the second ship to this service, Mr. Eldridge, who has undoubtedly been the most efficient promoter of the success of this nautical institution for the reform of youthful transgressors, has been fitly promoted to the mastership of the original vessel, the Massachusetts.

We have been thus full in our account of the working of reform school-ships, because we regard it as of the highest importance that a similar reformatory agency should be instituted in New York; and to that end we are anxious to enlighten the public mind as to its importance and utility, and to awaken an interest in the subject in the legislature and people of the state, and particularly in the breast of gentlemen engaged in commercial pursuits.

There is reason to think—and it is certainly a painful subject of reflection to an American—that English ships are navigated with greater skill and freedom from disaster than our own. Such at least is the opinion of the conductors of the New York Shipping and Commercial List, who must, we suppose, be regarded as an authority upon the subject. In an article published in their paper last autumn, they remark: "The British Board of Trade Returns for 1865, recently published, afford many interesting details, with regard to marine disasters in British waters. It appears that the number of vessels which last year entered inward and cleared outward at the different ports of the United Kingdom (not counting vessels employed solely as passenger ships) was 409,255; they represented 65,231,034 tons, and the value of their cargoes has been estimated at five hundred millions sterling. Of this vast traffic, it appears that disasters occurred on the coasts of Great Britain to less than one per centum of the number of vessels employed in it; and the losses of the year 1865, too, are reported to have been considerably above the annual average for the previous ten years.

It would appear, from a perusal of the details, that the disasters, especially to steamers, might, in a large majority of instances, have been averted by the exercise of proper precaution. But, the fact that less than one per centum of British commerce is destroyed, and that only about five per centum of the damage occurs to vessels of more than 600 tons capacity, in the intricate and hazardous navigation of British waters, is proof conclusive, *we think, that British vessels, as a rule, are better equipped, and navigated with more skill than American vessels are.*"

The above list of disasters to English vessels looks light indeed, when placed beside the terrible register of calamities to American shipping; and the comparison proves, conclusively, the necessity of establishing some system which will furnish to our mercantile marine a better class of sailors.

On this subject, Lieutenant Commander S. B. Luce, commandant of midshipmen at Annapolis, an officer of high scientific and general culture, thus expresses himself in the Army and Navy Journal:

"It is risking little to assert that the frequency of marine disasters on our coast is due, in no little measure, to a want of seamanship in somebody.

"No special charge is brought against masters or owners, those who rig and equip, or those who command our steamers; but the broad assertion is made that many of the fearful disasters to our ocean steamers are owing, in a large measure, to the want of knowledge of seamanship.

"Seamanship is an element as essential to the making of a first-rate commander of an ocean steamer, as it is to that of a commander of one of the famous ' Black Ball Line.'

"Of late years steam has so largely taken the place of sails, that popular error ignores sailors, forgetting that whenever the field of operation lies on the sea, seamanship cannot be dispensed with with impunity. It is not our purpose to enter into a dissertation on the management of steamers in bad weather, or to expose the miserable apologies for spars and sails our steamers carry, and their consequent inability to ' lie to,' or to show how ships might have been saved by a resort to the well known expedients of drags, sea anchors, &c., but we will pass on at once to note the somewhat singular fact that our far-seeing, shrewd and practical insurance men have never seriously undertaken to remedy this evil of ignorance.

" The sure and only way of doing this is, of course, to begin at the beginning, and educate our young people for this special business of commanding steamers, just as boys are educated to be pilots, or anything else where proficiency is required in a certain branch.

" New York would do well to follow the example of Massachusetts. Why should not her correctional institutions have a nautical branch, to which might be sent those committed for stubborness, idleness, vagrancy and petty larceny, having due regard, of course, to their individual fitness for a nautical life? It is officially stated that in 1863, one hundred and thirty-eight of the elder boys in the House of Refuge, on Randall's Island (East river), were permitted to enlist in the army, and have acquitted themselves well. Why should they not pass through a reformatory school-ship, and thence into the merchant service, or, indeed, into the navy, and acquit themselves well?"

General Edward L. Molineux, some time since, wrote and published a series of articles of the same purport, in the New York Daily Times. In the course of his essays, referring to the paper of Commander Luce, he pertinently and forcibly remarks:

" This able officer has struck the key-note. It is only by bringing up an improved class of seamen that we shall succeed in this matter. Simply in a money point, setting aside the benevolent and nobler view of the case, a disaster to a vessel of average value and cargo, saved as it may be by superior skill, would pay double-fold the cost of school-ships for New York for years; while, if the saving of human life is taken into the scale, the benefit would be incalculable.

" It is not intended in this to be unnecessarily severe or unjust, in not giving credit to the skill, the bravery and correct habits of a great many of the officers and sailors of our merchant service; but it is only common sense to assert that by educating and reforming boys of our seaport towns, by giving them some knowledge of seamanship, habits of discipline and sobriety, it will tend to give our ships a better class of officers and crew, and, in consequence, we shall have fewer disasters from mismanagement, carelessness and ignorance."

We quite agree with these two intelligent representatives of the army and navy of the United States, in the views thus expressed. We think that New York should lose no time in organizing a school-ship, after the example of Massachusetts, and that, having done this, she should add others, as occasion might require. There would be true economy, as well as philanthropy, in the legislation which should give effect to this idea.

We have expressed the conviction, very sincerely felt, that our juvenile reformatories are the best managed and most effective institutions we have for the prevention of crime. But they are far, very far, too few in number, and need to be increased manyfold. They bear no proportion to the same class of institutions in the various countries of Europe. In the eighteen states visited, the whole number will scarcely exceed twenty-five to thirty, on the most· liberal allowance ; whereas, in Europe, there are from 800 to 1,000, not counting industrial and ragged schools, of which the number, in some European countries is very considerable. There are, in Great Britain, at the present time, about 120 reformatories proper; in Prussia, 225 ; in Bavaria, 122; in Wurtemburg, 23 ; in Saxony, 23 ; in Hanover, 11 ; in Baden, 21 ; in Switzerland, 51; in Sweden and Norway, 15; and so on of other states.

By far the larger number of European reformatories are established on the family principle, while the great majority of ours are conducted on the congregate system. We confess our decided preference for the first named of these methods, but will not now stay to marshal the arguments in support of that view.

We heartily approve of the principle of parental responsibility and its legal enforcement; but enough, probably, has been said on that head in a former part of this report, pp. 66 and 67.

MEMORANDUM ON THE ADMINISTRATION OF CRIMINAL JUSTICE.

The commissioners regret that, notwithstanding the most diligent efforts to that end, they were unable to procure answers to their interrogatories from more than nine states of the eighteen visited. The following are the gentlemen who responded : Hon. Conrad Baker, Lieutenant-Governor of Indiana, and A. Wilsbach, Esq., of the same state ; Walter Pitkin, Esq., of Connecticut ; Hon. E. L. Van Winkle, of Kentucky, since deceased ; A. Sterling, Jr., Esq., of Maryland ; Geo. W. Searle, Esq., of Massachusetts ; Hovey K. Clarke and Henry A. Morrow, Esqs., of Michigan ; Cortlandt Parker and John F. Hegeman, Esqs., of New Jersey ; Hon. S. D. Bell, of New Hampshire ; and J. J. Barclay, Esq., of Pennsylvania. These gentlemen are all distinguished members of the legal profession in their respective states, and the greater part of them have occupied high official position as judges, attorneys-general, &c., &c. Of their great ability we need not speak, as this is made abundantly manifest in the papers severally furnished by them, and which will be found published in the appendix. As we have an extended paper on the criminal administration of Indiana, from Lieutenant-Governor Baker, and as the replies of Mr. Wilsbach, of the same state, are mostly monosyllables, we have not thought it neceesary to give the latter, though equally grateful to him for his courtesy, as we are to the other gentlemen, who have so kindly expended time and thought on their interesting and able communications.

All of which is respectfully submitted to the Legislature by

E. C. WINES,
THEO. W. DWIGHT, } *Commissioners.*

ROOMS OF THE PRISON ASSOCIATION OF NEW YORK,
No. 38 BIBLE HOUSE, NEW YORK, *January 1st*, 1867.

APPENDIX.

I. REPLIES OF EX-GOVERNORS OF STATES TO INTER-ROGATORIES ON THE PARDONING POWER.

The following are the answers of ex-Governors of states on the exercise of the pardoning power, referred to in the introduction, page 19, chapter I, section 13. All the gentlemen named have replied categorically to the questions proposed, except Governors Hunt and Throop of New York, who have furnished extended papers upon the general subject, and Governors Dutton and Toucey of Connecticut, Packer of Pennsylvania, and Anthony and Dyer of Rhode Island, who have written brief letters relating thereto. The essays of Governors Hunt and Throop and the letters of the other gentlemen, will be published as prepared by them. The communications of those who have answered seriatim, will not be printed continuously; but all the replies to each question will be given in immediate connection with the same, each writer being credited with his own reply.

Question I.

When you were Governor of the State of ——, and had the privilege of pardon, did you consider it a desirable attribute of the executive power, or, on the contrary, a burden, and generally a painful moral responsibility? Do you think this unlimited authority of pardoning necessary in our political system; or is it, on the contrary, in your opinion, repugnant to our theory of government, which discountenances irresponsible and arbitrary power? Has the privilege of pardon, as it now exists, grown out of the polity, peculiarly our own, or does it exist because we found it when our own governments were established?

Answers.

Chief Justice Chase, of Ohio : I did not regard the power to reprieve or pardon as a privilege, but a constitutional power to be exercised like any other power, under the responsibilities, moral and political, which peculiarly belonged to it. The power, in all systems of government, must be somewhere; and I am not prepared to say that its exercise would be more wise or more beneficial in other hands, than in those of the state and national executives. In Ohio, the law requires the Governor, at each session of the Legislature, to report the pardons granted by him, and the reasons of his action. This requirement seems to me wise. Perhaps it would be well also to require the approval or consent of a board of council. The want of such a board, however, has not been attended with ill consequences, so far as I am advised, in Ohio.

Hon. WM. W. ELLSWORTH, of Connecticut : In Connecticut, the legislature has the exclusive power to pardon criminals. I have at no time heard an objection or intimation adverse to the wisdom and safety of this course.

The above is, I think, substantially, an answer to the various interrogatories put to me, so far as I may be supposed to possess official or peculiar means of knowledge on the subject. Having, however, been honored, for many years, with a seat on the bench, I will further state, in reply to the fourth interrogatory, that, as it is the jury which convicts of crime, the propriety of a pardon in a particular case, may, and do what we please, will have a bearing on the question of conviction. What influence such a recommendation, coming from either the jury or the judge, should have on the pardoning power is a different question, and one depending on the circumstances of the case.

Hon. A. H. HOLLY, of Connecticut : In this state, the governor does not possess the prerogative of pardon, and I do not consider it a desirable attribute of the executive power.

Nor do I think the authority to pardon by the executive necessary in our political system. This power should *never* be confided to any one man, in my opinion, and if it is practicable, it should be made impossible to pardon in certain aggravated cases of crime.

In this state, the pardoning power, as you are doubtless aware, resides in the Legislature.

Hon. ISRAEL WASHBURN, of Maine : I regarded it as an unavoidable or necessary attribute, and yet as a burden and grave responsibility.

I am not certain that I understand precisely what is meant by "unlimited authority ;" if that the authority should be lodged in the chief executive alone, I should say it was not necessary, but I believe the full power to pardon must exist somewhere—the privilege, as it is called, I suppose is in full harmony with our polity.

Hon. SAMUEL WELLS, of Maine : I do not know as I considered the power of granting pardons a burden. I considered it a duty to examine the applications made for pardon as thoroughly as my time would admit. It is the practice in Maine for a committee of the council to examine and report the facts to the governor and council for their action. The power of granting pardons ought to be lodged in some branch of the government, and I do not think it would be wise to limit it to any particular class of offences. The higher the grade of the crime, the more reluctant would any reasonable executive be to pardon. I do not think an unlimited authority is, by any means, absolutely necessary, but I do think that good policy and the power of exercising clemency in proper cases require it. It does not appear to me to be an irresponsible or arbitrary power, any more than what exists in numerous other cases, where the action of the executive is final. I presume we followed the English practice and laws in establishing it. But the power of pardoning seems to be incident to all well regulated governments.

Hon. W. L. GREENLY, of Michigan : When I was governor of the state of Michigan, the prerogative of pardon was vested in the executive fully, without any restriction and without any provision of law compelling him to give any reasons for his action. I had very many applications for the exercise of the pardoning power, and in nine cases out of ten without any previous knowledge of the character or habits of the convict ; and I always regarded it as a very undesirable attribute of the executive power and a burden, and in every instance calling for the exercise of a painful and responsible moral duty. I think this unlimited authority of pardoning not only unnecessary in our political system, but repugnant to our theory of government, and oftentimes subversive of the true ends of justice. This privilege of pardon undoubtedly grew out of the polity of old monarchical governments.

Hon. JOHN A. KING, of New York : It is not a desirable, but it is a necessary and proper moral attribute of the executive power—and, as that attribute is conferred by the constitution of the state, it is not repugnant to our theory of government. The power of pardon, as it now exists in this state, belonged to the colonial governors, and has, since, been wisely continued in the hands of the executive of the state. It is a power which must be lodged somewhere, and can, in my judgment, be best administered by a single person.

Hon. WILLIAM F. JOHNSON, of Pennsylvania : By the resignation of governor Shunk, the duties of the executive office devolved upon me, being, at the time, "speaker of the senate." This occurred in July, 1848. In October, 1848, I was elected governor of Pennsylvania, and served one term of three years. The exercise of executive duties was vested in me from July, 1848, till January, 1852. The power of pardon, by the state constitution, was vested in the governor unrestricted, and was frequently exercised as *well prior* to as after conviction for criminal offences. The proper exercise of this power or prerogative demands great caution and much investigation and labor with firmness of mind and goodness of heart, and withal moral and political courage enough to do what is right, regardless of consequences. I do not consider the possession of the power a *privilege*, but, contrariwise, a heavy burden and painful moral, religious and political responsibility. I believe that an unlimited and unrestricted authority to pardon ought to rest somewhere in all well regulated governments. Courts and juries, witnesses and prosecutors, however honestly intentioned, will commit errors. Partialities, prejudices, sudden excitements, very good or very bad character, and other causes will frequently enter the most cautious and best guarded court room and form its decrees. When unjust, there ought to be an appeal for purposes of revision and correction, and suspension of its erroneous and hasty judgments. It is preferable that the multitude of the guilty should escape, rather than that one innocent person should suffer, however august and learned the tribunal which tried, or the judges who pronounced his doom. With these views, I could not consider the power to pardon as repugnant to our theory of government ; although its abuse, in its exercise from selfish or partizan or dishonest motives, may be well considered a violation of the spirit of our glorious institutions.

We have adopted so many of the customs, habits and terms, both good and evil, from governments existing in the "old world" before and since the establishment of our nationality, that I hesitate to say what we have originated, what adopted, what made a good or bad imitation of ; or, indeed, to say what is our own peculiar polity on the subject. That we have endeavored to mitigate the severity of punishments and attempted the *amendment* instead of the *life* of offenders furnishes cause of self-gratification.

But I think we have learned the lesson of "forgiveness and mercy" to the trespasser and wrong-doer, "after his repentance," from "higher laws" than those of human enactment.

QUESTION II.

Is it, in your opinion, possible that, easily accessible as our chief magistrates necessarily are, the privilge of pardoning can be guarded against frequent abuse and serious mistakes? Does, or does not, the privilege of pardoning, as it now exists, lead, in many cases, to results wholly unconnected with the degree of guilt or the comparative innocence of the convicts, and does not the obtaining of a pardon very frequently depend upon the influence which can be brought to bear on the petition for the pardon, rather than on the merits of the case itself?

ANSWERS.

Chief Justice CHASE, of Ohio:—I can only answer for Ohio. I do not think the power has been abused in that state. Mistakes in its exercise have doubtless been made, but mistake is inseparable from human administration. I know of no case in Ohio in which the merits of the case have had less weight than the influence of applicants or their friends. Errors are usually on the best side—that of mercy.

Hon. A. H. HOLLEY, of Connecticut:—I have very little doubt that the power to pardon, when exercised by a chief magistrate, is liable to abuse, even when such chief magistrate acts from the purest motives, and with the fullest purpose of meeting the ends of justice; chiefly for the reason that there is, ordinarily, but one active party under such application. Hence it differs but little, if at all, from an ex parte examination. Hence, too, pardons are frequently procured under the influences brought to bear on the petition for pardon, rather than on the merits of the case itself.

Hon. ISRAEL WASHBURN, of Maine: It will be exceedingly difficult to guard it against some abuses and many mistakes. Undoubtedly these questions must be answered affirmatively.

Hon. SAMUEL WELLS, of Missouri: No doubt some pardons are granted when they ought not to be, and some are not granted when they ought to be, and there is frequently a want of proper regard to the degree of guilt or comparative innocence of the convicts, and pardons are sometimes granted through the influence of the petitioners, rather than on the merits of the case.

But the remedy for these evils can be found in the choice by the people of proper executives. Perfection cannot be expected, and errors are constantly arising in every branch of the government. It depends on the people whether they shall be corrected or perpetuated. It is hardly to be expected that a man devoid of common judgment and practical ability will be elected to the office of governor. Although he may act wisely, those who are unacquainted with the facts and circumstances may think otherwise, and place a false estimate upon his conduct.

Hon. W. L. GREENLY, of Michigan: In my opinion, the privilege of pardoning cannot be guarded against frequent abuse and serious mistakes, for the reason that the executive cannot, except in one or two cases, have any knowledge of the circumstances attending the individual case, nor of the habits or moral character of the convict, except such as he may derive from the petition drawn up and presented by the friends and relatives of the convict, and, in too many instances, backed up by the names of responsible, influential and respectable citizens, who are as ignorant of the circumstances under which the crime may have been committed, or of the principles of the convicts, as the executive himself. Such petitions are usually circulated by the wife, mother, sister or daughter of the convict, or by some influential person, and, when presented, are usually signed without any other thought or reflection than that simply of getting rid of the importunities of the persons presenting the petition, utterly regardless of the demands of justice or the well-being of the community. Again, powerful friends, political or otherwise, too often exercise an undue influence, and often procure a pardon, which, if resting on the merits of the case alone, would have been refused.

Hon. Jno. A. King, of New York : While the chief magistrate of this state is accessible to all, I know of no instance where a pardon has been obtained by corrupt or improper influence. He has the privilege of asking the opinion of any judge of the supreme court in any case, in respect to which his mind is in doubt, thus bringing to his aid the calm and deliberate judgment of an experienced and cultivated mind.

Hon. Wm. F. Johnston, of Pennsylvania : The authority to pardon, existing with our governors, will be abused, and frequent and grievous mistakes will occur. There is no doubt pardons are frequently granted without reference to the guilt, innocence or repentance of the convict. In such cases the pardon is the result of other influences than an honest investigation of the merits of the case. It cannot be otherwise under the system. The *knowledge* of the circumstances of each criminal case could not be possessed by the executive, unless the same is presented to him by persons claiming to be *disinterested*, and in whose statements and fair dealing, from personal knowledge or general reputation, the executive is properly entitled to place faith and credit. It is a peculiarity of our people, that they are easily persuaded to sign and endorse any application that appeals to them in behalf of mercy and freedom—hence ponderous petitions, groaning with names of the best citizens, are frequently presented to induce the pardon of bad and undeserving convicts. Your petitioner has permitted his heart, not his judgment, to lead him. To this cause many objectionable pardons may be attributed. Many persons, and many of them of the bar, get up and aid pardons for money. I *never* pardoned a man if I had reason to believe the *lawyer* was paid for his services. I considered that he violated his high calling by all such applications.

Question III.

Is it your conviction that the power of pardoning, as it now exists, leads more frequently to a defeat of the ends of justice than to the furtherance of a wise and even-handed administration of the same ?

Answers.

Chief Justice Chase : It is not.

Hon. A. H. HOLLEY, of Connecticut : When the pardoning power is confined to the executive alone, I have very little doubt that its exercise tends more frequently to defeat the ends of justice than to the furtherance of a wise and even-handed administration of the same.

Hon. ISRAEL WASHBURN, of Maine : I am not prepared to say that it is.

Hon. SAMUEL WELLS, of Maine : So far as my knowledge extends, I should answer this question in the negative. The practice of pardoning, where the conviction was proper and there is not full evidence of an entire reformation in the convict, is, in my opinion, very pernicious. It is the letting loose of a dangerous man to prey upon society. A similar objection exists to a sentence for a short period, when no reformation can be expected. As soon as the offender is liberated, he at once assumes his criminal course, and continues it until he is again arrested. But we cannot take from the judges the power of passing sentence upon convicted criminals. The only remedy that exists for such cases is the appointment of wise and considerate judges, who, while they look with a merciful eye upon the prisoner, will also look with a merciful eye upon the community.

Hon. W. L. GREENLY, of Michigan : It is.

Hon. JOHN A. KING, of New York : The power of pardoning, as it now exists in this state, has, upon the whole, served the ends of justice.

Hon. WM. F. JOHNSTON, of Pennsylvania : I have not sufficient facts within my reach to answer this inquiry. While I know the pardoning power has frequently defeated the ends of justice, I do not think its exercise has been more detrimental than beneficial to society. This opinion is scarcely worth your regard, as I have, as stated, no data to form it correctly.

Permit me to relate an incident. I had been in the habit, by way of caution, of consulting the warden of the Eastern penitentiary, upon almost every application for pardon of persons in the institution under his charge. I had pardoned a man, convicted of some slight offence and sentenced for a short time. Shortly after, I met in the streets of Philadelphia, the warden, who, after the usual salutations, remarked—" Governor, thee did a great wrong in pardoning 'Billy Blink.'" I had no recollection of the man or case. The warden then informed me that he was a very bad man, that Billy Blink was a flash name, and that he had been either once or twice before in his custody as an offender, and had been pardoned on former occasions. Being resolved to investigate the matter, I procured, to forward to the worthy warden, the names of the parties and influences they had brought to bear to procure the pardon. Within ten days or two weeks after this conversation, I met the warden at the seat of government. In our conversation he said, "I told thee, Governor, a few days ago, that thou hadst done a great wrong in pardoning 'Billy Blink.' I now wish to withdraw that declaration. He has been convicted, two days ago, of a much greater crime, and, indeed, of two. He has been sentenced to *seven* years in the penitentiary. He is now under my care. So thee may see that thee has not done so great a wrong as I supposed." Mr. Blink certainly remained during the balance of my official life.

Yet this man had secured, by some means, the active exertions of an eminent and worthy citizen, whose position commanded respect, and whose high character for truth and honor forbade suspicion of improper motives.

QUESTION IV.

Do you, or do you not, think that a recommendation for pardon by the jury, who pronounce the culprit guilty, ought to be excluded as incompatible with that verdict, and that the recommendation to a merciful consideration should be restricted to the judge or judges who tried the case ?

ANSWERS.

Chief Justice CHASE, of Ohio : I would not exclude from consideration the recommendation of juries who, being selected for trial of the facts, are, in general, most competent to pronounce on their value ; nor am I prepared to say that I would give them less weight than the recommendation of judges.

Hon. A. H. HOLLEY, of Connecticut : I think the only proper action of a jury is to determine whether a culprit is guilty or not guilty. Any mitigating circumstances that may have been developed on the trial are quite as likely to meet with proper consideration from a judge, in making his charge, as from a jury.

Hon ISRAEL WASHBURN, of Maine : There are many objections to receiving the recommendation of the jury, though it may not always be incompatible with the verdict. On the whole I think it would be better to restrict these recommendations to the judges.

Hon. SAMUEL WELLS, of Maine : A recommendation for pardon generally grows out of some mitigating circumstances apparent to the jury. It is merely the expression of their individual opinions, has no binding force in law, and not much in practice. It is not easy to exclude it, for if refused when the verdict is rendered, the jury can present it afterwards. It is not incompatible with the verdict, for when a jury feel bound to convict, by the law and by the evidence at the same time, they might desire that the offender should be pardoned. Their action is equivalent to saying, as honest men we are bound to convict you, but from favorable circumstances in the case, we would pardon you, if we had the power. A sensible executive would judge for himself whether a convict ought to be pardoned, and not substitute a mere recommendation of a jury for his own judgment. I think it is best to let the matter remain as it is.

Hon. W. L. GREENLY, of Michigan : The recommendation of the jury who pronounced the convict guilty would have a tendency to show that, although, under the law and the testimony, they might have felt bound to convict, still that in their minds there were some extenuating circumstances in the case. However, in my opinion, the recommendation of such jury should always be accompanied by the recommendation of the judge who tried the cause, with that of the district attorney who prosecuted the case.

Hon. JOHN A. KING, of New York : A recommendation for pardon by the jury should not be forbidden, for while the stern requirments of the law are satisfied by its verdict, the merciful feelings of the heart should never be wholly stifled. The jury and not the judge should recommend to mercy. It is the province of the jury to weigh the testimony and to agree upon a verdict, and of the judge to pronounce the sentence of the law.

Hon WM. F. JOHNSTON, of Pennsylvania : I would not regard the petition or recommendation of a jury for the pardon of a criminal whom it had found guilty, unless based upon after discovered testimony. It is simply asking us to be guided by their "word," instead of their oath. I consider it a weakness and infirmity of purpose for a juror to ask or unite in such applications. I know no reason why a judge who has tried a cause should not be heard in an application for mercy. Law may demand conviction and sentence, and yet the "end and purpose" of all punishment and penalties being the reformation of the offender, a conscientious judge, thus knowing *all* the circumstances and minutiæ of the case, may be regarded as a very safe adviser. Within my experience, I found judges very seldom interfered in such matters.

QUESTION V.

Is it your opinion that the ends of justice and the real interests of the convicts themselves would be better promoted, if the power of pardoning in the executive were modified and circumscribed by a wisely organized council board of pardon, as is the case in some states in this country and in some European governments; or do you regard the power of pardoning as an inherent, absolute and essential attribute of the executive, so that it ought to continue in the same form in which it now exists in nearly all the states?

ANSWERS.

Chief Justice CHASE, of Ohio: "In the multitude of counsellors there is safety," though not always for the counselled. As governor, I should certainly like the aid to counsel conclusions and the diminution of responsibility which a wisely organized council or pardon board would afford. I by no means think that the power of pardon is an inherent, absolute and essential attribute of the executive. On the contrary, it is in my judgment neither inherent, nor absolute, nor essential. It must be somewhere, however, or gross wrongs would remain without correctives; but it is for the people of each state to say where it shall be lodged.

Hon. WM. W. ELLSWORTH, of Connecticut: The course pursued in Connecticut is quite satisfactory to me.

Hon. A. H. HOLLEY, of Connecticut: I do not regard the pardoning power as an inherent right, or as an essential attribute of the executive; nor should it exist in any state in that form.

Let it be thoroughly understood that certain and speedy punishment will follow the conviction of crime, and in my judgment, the number of criminals will soon be greatly diminished.

Hon. ISRAEL WASHBURN, of Maine: I think the pardoning power should not be vested in the chief magistrate alone.

In Maine, the governor may pardon only upon the advice of the executive council, a body of seven members, elected annually by the Legislature. No doubt the power would be more wisely and judiciously exercised if vested in a governor or chief executive, upon the advice of a special board of pardon, such as is mentioned in the question.

Hon. SAMUEL WELLS, of Maine: It might be difficult to obtain " a wisely organized council or board of pardon," and such council or board would be liable to the same influences as now operate upon the executives.

It is not perceived that there could be any material difference in the examination of a case of pardon, and the decision in reference to it between a governor and council and a board of pardon. If they were sensible men, their views would be similar. A "council or board of pardon" would be full as likely to yield to popular clamor or tender sensibilities as the executive. They would be constantly assailed and soon become unpopular, and their usefulness impaired. They would be a sort of collateral power in the government, unsupported by either branch of it.

I think the pardoning power should remain with the executive.

The people can determine by their constitutions whether it shall be an attribute of executive power or not. It is certainly not an essential attribute to the existence of the executive power, but, in my judgment, properly appertains to it.

Hon. W. L. GREENLY, of Michigan: There are cases constantly arising, in reference to which after conviction may be had, some evidence has come to light, or some circumstances have arisen, showing that the convict was illegally or unjustly convicted; and of course, in such cases, the law should invest in some individual or some board the power to pardon, and I think that a wisely organized board of pardon would be the proper pardoning power.

Hon. JOHN A. KING, of New York: I think the ends of justice are best promoted by giving the power of pardoning to the executive alone, as one of its essential attributes. The responsibility is then perfect. An organized council or board of pardon divides the responsibility among several, which should, in my judgment, belong to one. I therefore regard the power of pardoning as an inherent, absolute and essential attribute of the executive, which should be continued in the same form in which it now exists in nearly all the states.

Hon. WM. F. JOHNSTON, of Pennsylvania: I don't know to what extent an advisory committee might be beneficial in aiding an executive in the exercise of this responsible power. Divided responsibilities do not work well in most matters, whether public or private. If an organized council of *wise* and *honest* men, beyond the reach of personal or partizan influences, would advise with an executive, it might occasionally prevent errors. If such council is wise to advise, it is well enough to let it act. I would not advocate the adoption of a system that would enable the executive to charge the council, or, *vice versa*—with any great injury that might arise from an injudicious pardon. In the formation of laws and institutions, there may be safety in a multitude of counsellors; in the execution of laws and duties, I think it is otherwise. Let us have no divided or shifting responsibility.

I consider that the proper and best depository of the pardoning power, is where it will be most faithfully exercised. I do not regard it as an inherent, absolute and essential attribute of the chief magistrate of any people.

QUESTION VI.

If you think that there should be a council or board of pardon, is it your opinion that, whenever state constitutions are changed, authority ought to be conferred upon the legislature to establish such councils or boards?

ANSWERS.

Chief Justice CHASE, of Ohio: I see no objection to legislative authority to establish such a council or board. It would, doubtless, be exercised or not, and if exercised, exercised wisely, with reference to the circumstances of each state.

Hon. A. H. HOLLEY, of Connecticut: The pardoning power should be restricted to the legislature of the state. A council or board of pardon being in existence perpetually, is accessible at all times, and if its decision were final, there would probably be less searching investigation than there would be before a legislature, acting, as is the custom in these days, upon the report of a committee. Such a committee would be an appropriate council, and its report would be subject to investigation by the body appointing it.

Hon. ISRAEL WASHBURN, of Maine: Unquestionably—aye.

Hon. SAMUEL WELLS, of Maine: The answer to the fifth question is an answer to this.

Hon. WM. L. GREENLY, of Michigan: I do think that the constitution of each state should confer upon the legislature the authority to establish such board, and in justice to the governor and to the people, should divest the governor of the pardoning power.

Hon. JOHN A. KING, of New York: For the reason assigned in my answer to the preceding question, I think that there should not be a council or board of pardon; and that authority should not be conferred by state convention on the legislature to establish such council or board.

Hon. WM. F. JOHNSTON, of Pennsylvania: Believing that a council or board of pardon, whether acting with or without the executive, would not lessen the evils arising from an abuse of the pardoning power, I could not recommend its creation by legislative authority. If, indeed, it should be the best depository of the power, let the authority be conferred by the organic laws or constitutional provision. These boards may become the instruments of party hatred or partialities, or may be condemned unjustly by such influences. They, at least, ought to be permanent enough to secure them from sudden changes. Our legislatures change frequently, and *never* fail to sacrifice those whom they cannot control. Freshly conferred power is always gently tried, and frequently without regard to ulterior results.

Question VII.

Is there any other mode besides that indicated in questions V and VI, whereby the power of pardon can be properly limited or regulated?

Answers.

Chief Justice Chase, of Ohio : It might be properly limited by constitutional provisions operating directly; and I am inclined to think that its restriction (except perhaps under special circumstances) to offences and crimes *after* conviction, would be wise.

Hon. A. H. Holley, of Connecticut : There may be other and wiser methods of regulating the pardoning power, but I have not the vanity nor the wisdom to indicate what they should be.

Hon. Israel Washburn, of Maine : No other so good has occurred to me.

Hon. Samuel Wells, of Maine : If the power of pardon should be taken from the executive, a council or board of pardon might be the next best depository of the power. But it is my opinion that the power ought to remain with the executive.

Hon. Wm. L. Greenly, of Michigan : None that occurs to me.

Hon. Jno. A. King, of New York : I know of no mode by which the power of pardon can be properly limited or regulated.

Hon. Wm. F. Johnston, of Pennsylvania: I believe the power would be more safely lodged with the officers of our prisons than anywhere else. They are necessarily well acquainted with the character and conduct of the convict. His submission to law and order, his repentance, his reformation or contumacy, are all within their knowledge. They are supposed to feel no sickly sentimentality. They would learn from their records the persons who were usually engaged in pardon "brokerage," or whose names were indiscriminately found to all applications, and whose influence was constantly presented for such indiscriminate pardons. They would soon understand and appreciate accurately the *quality* and *quantity* of brains and hearts possessed by the judges of criminal courts in different districts. With this knowledge or means of correct information, a mistake would seldom occur in the exercise of the power of pardon. I make this suggestion for your consideration, hoping that in your extended investigation some better mode may be adopted.

LETTER FROM THE HON. WASHINGTON HUNT OF NEW YORK.

LOCKPORT, N. Y., *August* 10, 1865.

GENTLEMEN :—I have received your circular letter, requesting me to answer some questions in relation to the pardoning power. My engagements make it inconvenient for me, at the present moment, to enter upon a full discussion of this important subject; but I will endeavor to give my views briefly on some of the principle points, presented by your interrogatories.

Our present system, which clothes the executive, with an unlimited power of pardon, is liable to many and grave objections. The strongest argument that can be urged in its favor is that it renders a single functionary directly responsible for the honest and enlightened exercise of the power. It must be conceded that this consideration is entitled to some force. But when you reflect upon the nature of this prerogative, the arduous labors and painful responsibilities inseparable from it, I believe it might be more wisely delegated to a board or council, composed of persons thoroughly qualified by study and experience, and enabled to devote their minds to the subject, free from the weight of other official avocations. There are other functions of his office, which demand from the executive his constant care, and his highest energies. It is not enough that the Governor may possess all the desired qualifications for the judicious use of the power of pardon, such as thorough knowledge of criminal jurisprudence and practice, combined with clearness of judgment and firmness of will. In a large and populous state like our own, the applications are so numerous and the labor of investigating them so arduous and perplexing, that no mind, however rapid or comprehensive, can do full justice to the subject, without neglecting, in some degree, those legitimate executive duties, which concern the whole people and perhaps involve the most vital public interests.

This is more especially the case during the session of the Legislature. I consider it desirable in every point of view, that the Governor should be relieved from daily appeals and importunities for the exercise of clemency. Our system was derived from the mother country, where the power of pardon is an attribute of the crown. The framers of our constitution were naturally influenced by precedent and analogy, and at that early period, perhaps it was reasonable to assume that the Chief Magistrate, chosen by the people, would prove to be the safest depository of this delicate power. In a monarchy there is much to be said in favor of vesting in the ruling prince, the prerogative of mercy. But this theory is inapplicable in a republic, where the executive is elected by the people for a limited term of office.

I assume, however, that the pardoning power will always be retained in some department of the government. My official experience confirmed my previous opinion that such a power is necessary, and that any system of justice which excluded it, would prove defective. In offences coming under the same general classification and subject to the same penalty, there are many shades and degrees of guilt. It frequently happens that there are mitigating circumstances, which ought to reduce the penalty imposed by the strict letter of the law; and sometimes youthful offenders furnish such proofs of reformation, that both justice and mercy demand a reduction of the sentence. From the very nature of the power of pardon, it must be largely discretionary. To limit and restrain, would virtually destroy it. I do not think it admits of material abridgement; but wheresoever it may be placed, its exercise should be subject to the most direct responsibility to the state and to public opinion. In addition to the present requirement, the annual list submitted to the Legislature should state concisely the ground of pardon, in each case.

That the power in question is liable to abuse, cannot be disputed. But all human institutions are imperfect, and the same objection applies, with more or less force, to other functions of government, especially in those branches of the administration where much is left to the discretion of official agents. The appointing power, the veto power, the legislative power, may be improperly exercised and perverted from their original ends; but for these evils, when they occur, our system of frequent elections affords the most effective remedy. Our aim should be to establish every fit and practicable safeguard to insure fidelity in the exercise of public authority. I am not prepared to adopt the conclusion that the pardoning power has been abused to any such extent as is sometimes assumed. In the exercise of the power, a man of sound principles must feel that he is executing a very sacred trust, and he will deem it a point of honor and conscience to discharge the duty independently, unmoved by personal or political influences. I have never known such influences to have any weight in respect to applications for pardons; but the governor is always in danger of being misled by partial statements and imperfect information. He is also liable to err in judgment when possessed of all the facts in the case. He is subjected to a continual struggle between his sympathies and his convictions of duty. The greatest danger of all is that in some cases he may yield to feelings of kindness and compassion, so far as to impair the supremacy of law and defeat the ends of justice. But if the power is exercised with reasonable discrimination and firmness, I do not conceive that it is calculated to promote crime or weaken the administration of justice. In the outset, most offenders indulge the belief that they will escape detection or conviction. The hope of pardon arises after the trial and sentence, and stimulates an appeal to executive clemency. I consider the practice, which is often adopted by juries, of annexing to their verdict a recommendation for pardon, highly objectionable. It ought to be strongly discountenanced, if not prohibited. If there are special circumstances calling for executive interference, the duty of presenting them should be left to the judges and public prosecutors.

In reply to your sixth interrogatory, I must say, that in my opinion "the ends of justice and the interests of the convicts themselves would be better promoted, if the power of pardoning in the executive were modified and circumscribed by a wisely organized council or board of pardon, as is the case in some states in this country, and in some European governments." It would invigorate and greatly improve the administration of the executive department, by releasing the incumbent from one of his most laborious and embarrassing responsibilities. I hope to see this change of system established in the next revision of our state constitution. It is only by an organic amendment that the object can be reached. Such a council as I have indicated should be composed mainly of judges who have retired from service, and whose weight of character, no less than their judicial and professional experience, would inspire public confidence and insure a wise and intelligent exercise of this delicate prerogative. I have thus expressed my views in a desultory manner, without following strictly the order of your interrogatories. You are at liberty to use my answer in any mode which you may deem advisable.

Very respectfully,
Your obedient servant,
WASHINGTON HUNT.
Messrs. FRANCIS LIEBER, LL.D., THEODORE W. DWIGHT, LL.D., E. C. WINES, D. D., &c., &c,

LETTER FROM THE HON. E. T. THROOP, OF NEW YORK.

To the Honorable FRANCIS LIEBER, *Vice-President N. Y. Prison Association ;* THEODORE W. DWIGHT, *Chairman Ex. Committee ;* E. C. WINES, *Corresponding Secretary :*

GENTLEMEN—Responding to the questions in your circular, propounded to the former chief magistrates, respecting the pardoning power, a copy of which I have had the honor to receive, I deem it not inappropriate to premise, that up to the time that I entered upon the duties of the executive of this state, I had been familiar with the working of the system of imprisonment for crimes at the state prison at Auburn, as it was in my immediate neighborhood, and its management had been in the hands of my friends. And further, that during the five years immediately preceding, I had been the presiding judge of courts, having jurisdiction of crimes of every degree.

In my message to the legislature in 1830, I thus expressed myself on the subject of pardons :

"I have pardoned from the state prison, twenty-eight convicts. Nearly all of those pardons were granted in cases where, first, great doubts of guilt were certified to me by the courts before whom the convictions took place, and those doubts appeared to me well founded, on examining a full statement of the cases ; secondly, on personal examination and inquiry of the keepers of the prison and the presiding judges as to certain convicts for whom petitions had *not* been presented, and whom I deemed fit objects of mercy ; and thirdly, from want of sufficient latitude of discretion in the courts, sentences too severe were necessarily imposed."

In my message of 1831, I say: "I have pardoned from the state prison, during the past year, seventy-six convicts. A great portion of them are persons to whom my attention was called by the officers of the respective prisons, and who were recommended to executive clemency by their youth or long sentences, particularly for life, on account of trifling burglaries. I found them enduring punishment incompatible with the mitigated severity of our laws."

In my message of 1832, I thus say: "I have pardoned out of the state prison during the last year, seventy-three convicts. A great proportion of these cases were brought to my notice without the intervention of friends, for many of them had none; and their claim to pardon, in some cases, became equitable on account of the mitigated punishments for similar crimes, prescribed by the revision of the laws."

In the above abstracts, you have my views of the propriety of pardoning in cases, which inevitably will occur, deserving it, and consequently, of the necessity of a pardoning power. Neither reflection nor experience since has changed my opinion. In the exercise of this power, a sensitive nature will be severely tried, and pained to reject the prayers, and resist the earnest, pathetic, passionate and persevering appeals of wives, children, sisters and parents, for mercy to a supposed repentant relative; but if the executive has clear views of his duty, he will discharge it without remorse, and be comforted by an approving conscience. Thus, although burdened, in the language of your question, with a "painful moral responsibility," it seems to me he has no occasion to regret it.

To the questions whether the pardoning power is judiciously vested in the executive, or whether it would not be more discreetly exercised by an "organized board of pardon," I must say that I do not see where that power can be so safely lodged as with the executive. The search for a perfect depository of the power is vain, and will be fruitless—all experience gives us a mortifying view of humanity. An executive, perfect in his intellectual or moral nature, is not to be found, however superior he may be to other men; nor are the people, although swayed by honest purposes, always right in their choice of persons to fill public offices. But where can power be more wisely lodged than with a person chosen to exercise the highest functions of government by a constituency too broad for corruption to cover? He may be unworthy, but chosen from the most conspicuous class of citizens with a well known character, it is not too much charity to suppose that moral unfitness for his high trust will be an exception. And should such a one ever receive from the people that proof of confidence, the public have a security in his interest and his pride; for, conscious of his responsibility to a jealous and scrutinizing public, he would be prompted to a just and unexceptionable discharge of his duties. On the other hand, a board of divided responsibility is much more accessible to corruption; every member is an avenue through which the wily advocate may approach his object.

The framers of our state constitution deemed it wise to surround the executive with a council, without whose assent no appointment to office could be made, and another to check him in the exercise of his function in assenting to or vetoing a law; but, after sufficient experience, these councils were abolished, on the ground that a divided responsibilty was inexpedient, and that it was more safe to leave the executive alone to the discharge of those duties. The council for the revision of the laws, composed of the chancellor and judges of the supreme court (men, up to that time of eminent character), and the council of appointment, selected by the house of representatives and of the senate, were abolished by the amended constitution, and the responsibility of nominating to office was imposed upon the governor with the only restraint, that nominations to office should not take effect without the assent of the senate.

Then, again, what power should create this board of pardon? If the governor—is it not better that he should do the thing himself and be accountable for it, than to do it by indirection, and throw the responsibility upon a board? If the legislature—we have too many and painful proofs of the little reliance to be placed upon the action of that body, when political or private or personal interests are in question before them. If the people at large, by popular vote—they do it when they elect a governor, and there is no reason to believe that they would act with more caution, or even as much, when voting for a board, than when voting for their governor.

The tribunal of mercy should be accessible, and the meanest meet no obstruction in his approach to it, yet it may be wise to encumber the exercise of its powers with many prudential rules. While I express the opinion that there should reside, somewhere, an unlimited power of pardoning to mitigate the severity and modify the unequal operation of laws (necessarily general, regarding classes and not individual cases), and also to consider matters, which would not come under consideration at the trial, perhaps occurring subsequently, I think it the duty of the legislature to surround the exercise of that power by every practicable precaution. The pardoning power should be conferred, subject to the right of the legislature to prescribe rules for its exercise. I made it a rule in all cases, to call upon the judge for a statement of the case, and his opinion, and to demand of the keeper of the prison an account of the convict's conduct and what he knew of his history. I omitted this precaution in only one case. While in the city of New York, the counsel for a convict called upon me and stated the case of a youth under age, of respectable parentage in Boston, who had the misfortune to commit a first offence, and was very penitent, and his parents were anxious to have him in charge that they might regulate his morals. I called upon the judge for a statement, and he appeared before me with his book of minutes and confirmed the relation of the counsel. It seemed to me so clear a case that I issued the pardon at once without asking advice from the keeper of the prison. The next day I received a letter from the keeper of the Sing Sing prison, saying, "I have let out of prison, on your pardon, a person convicted by a false name, who has been several times convicted, and whom you knew by his true name, a desperate malefactor in the Auburn state prison."

To the precautions above mentioned others might be added, such as a notice of the application for pardon, to elicit information of the case and of the character of the individual. This notice should be published and a copy served upon the keeper of the prison. After pardon granted, a brief statement of the case and the grounds for the pardon might be recorded and published, and a copy be sent with the pardon to be placed upon the prison records. Such precautions would operate not only to detect frauds, but to detect fraudulent applicants, and also as a caution to the pardoning power.

To one of the questions I reply, that I can see no good reason why the jury who try a cause should not recommend the convict's case to the lenient consideration of the court, or where there is discretion there, to the clemency of the executive. A jury, called upon to judge a case, will sometimes find themselves constrained, by rigid rules of law, to do what may seem to them injustice. This is one of the cases in which the pardoning power may interpose in aid of the just administration of the law—and the opinion expressed of an impartial jury, selected by lot, and not allowed to hear anything of the case except through the evidence, that they were compelled to give a verdict in conformity with law, designed for cases of greater turpitude than the one before them, is deserving of respectful consideration. I see nothing in it incompatible with their verdict.

I cheerfully comply with your request to contribute my mite to this momentous subject, and place the foregoing remarks at your disposal.

I have the honor to be, with respectful consideration,

Your obedient servant,

E. T. THROOP.

LETTER FROM HON. WM. F. PACKER.

WILLIAMSPORT, PA., *Aug.* 3, 1865.

FRANCIS LEIBER, LL.D. :

Dear Sir—The circular of the Prison Association of New York, propounding certain questions to the ex-governors of the several states, relative to the pardoning power, is before me, and I reply with great pleasure.

That the pardoning power should be conferred on some department of each state government, is, in my opinion, unquestionably true. That, occasionally, the privilege of pardoning will be abused or unwisely exercised is equally true. But after the experience of three years as governor of Pennsylvania, and after carefully examining hundreds of cases which came before me during that period, I am satisfied that nothing would be gained by taking away the pardoning power from the chief magistrate of a state and his cabinet, and conferring it on a " council or board of pardon," or on any other tribunal. While you have human agents to discharge public official duties, you cannot, in the performance of those duties, expect entire freedom from the errors, the passions, the prejudices, and the frailties of humanity. You will look in vain for perfection, no matter where you may confide the pardoning power. For myself, I would trust the chief executive of a state, in view of his great responsibility, aided by the counsel of his legal advisers, with quite as much confidence as I would any " council or board of pardon " that could possibly be selected.

Believing, therefore, that the power of pardoning should exist somewhere, in every state, and believing also that there is no safer nor better depository for that power than the chief magistrate of the commonwealth, I would not disturb the present system, as it exists in Pennsylvania. The founders of our institutions and the framers of our constitutions were, in my judgment, quite as wise, as moral and as patriotic, as those governmental innovators of the present day, who seek to disturb settled opinions and established systems and customs, by experiments of more than doubtful propriety.

Entertaining these views, I have not thought it necessary to answer your queries in detail. Substantially they are all answered.

I have no objection to the publication of this letter.

With great respect,

I am yours, truly,

WM. F. PACKER.

LETTER FROM HON. HENRY DUTTON.

·NEW HAVEN, CONN., *Feb.* 9, 1866.

REV. E. C. WINES, D. D.:

Dear Sir—I do not deem it important to reply fully to your circular letter, since in this state the sole pardoning power is vested in the legislature. Hence the execution of all criminals, convicted of capital offences, is required by law to be postponed, until after the session of the general assembly next after the conviction. I believe the general sentiment of the friends of justice in this state is in favor of our system. The legislature sometimes acts injudiciously, but it is very rare that the convict of a high crime escapes punishment altogether. The sentence is frequently shortened, and death commuted to imprisonment for life. Favor is shown to the inmates of the state prison somewhat in proportion to their penitence and good behaviour. This has a very favorable effect on the rest.

Your obedient servant,

HENRY DUTTON.

LETTER FROM HON. ISAAC TOUCEY, OF CONNECTICUT.

Gentlemen—I have received your circular letter to former chief magistrates of the several states, proposing certain questions on the subject of the pardoning power, and requesting an early answer to them. The first question is " When you were governor of Connecticut and possessed the prerogative of pardon, did you consider " &c. &c., and then follow the other questions.

Under the constitution of Connecticut, the prerogative of pardon is not conferred upon the governor, but is left with the legislature. I have, therefore, no official experience upon the subject, and could answer your qestions only by expressing my own private speculative opinions, which I presume you do not desire. I will, therefore, only say—the usual course is for the party convicted to apply to the legislature for a pardon by petition, which is referred to a joint standing committee, is investigated and reported upon to both branches, when a pardon is granted or denied upon a full public consideration of the case. The bill must receive the usual sanction of a law. This system, to which we have long been accustomed, has always worked well. I have heard no objection to it.

I am, very respectfully,

Your obed't servant,

ISAAC TOUCEY.

DR. FRANCIS LIEBER, AND OTHERS,

Committee, &c. &c.

HARTFORD, *May* 5, 1866.

LETTER FROM HON. ELISHA DYER, OF RHODE ISLAND.

PROVIDENCE, *Feb.* 13, 1866.

Gentlemen—Your "circular letter," of June, 1865, is this morning at hand. The constitution of this state wisely provides that "the governor, by and with the advice and consent of the senate, shall hereafter exclusively exercise the pardoning power, except in cases of impeachment, &c." This is as it should be. When occupying the executive chair of this state, many petitions for executive clemency were presented. Each application was made the subject of most careful, conscientious investigations. The prisoner was personally and privately conferred with. The circumstances attending the commission of crime ascertained, the antecedents and surroundings of his social position investigated, his *honest* contrition and probable reformation estimated; and if these investigations resulted satisfactorily, clemency was recommended. If not, the petition was not brought to the notice of the senate. Sometimes, *injudiciously,* if not wrongfully, personal influence was attempted to secure the desired results. These were promptly discarded, and created an adverse sentiment against the application.

If executive clemency is only exercised after a most patient, candid, responsible, and *conscientious* consideration, there can be no question of the propriety of its existence. And it is when abused from motives of personal favor or policy, or as the result of misplaced sympathy or careless indifference, that the continuance of its authority becomes, with propriety, a subject of anxiety and doubt.

The recommendation of a convicting jury always seemed singular, except in the acquisition of evidence and facts with which the public might not be familiar. I have hastily responded, as my many duties would allow.

Very respectfully yours,
ELISHA DYER.

Messrs. Francis Lieber, }
Theo. W. Dwight, } *Committee.*
E. C. Wines, }

LETTER FROM HON. H. B. ANTHONY, OF RHODE ISLAND.

WASHINGTON, *Feb.* 22, 1866.

Dear Sir—I have your circular making certain inquiries touching the most judicious depository of the pardoning power and the results of my experience as governor of Rhode Island.

When I held that office, the pardoning power was vested in the general assembly. An amendment to the constitution has since placed it in the senate on the recommendation of the governor. My views, therefore, derive no value from my having held the office of governor, and I have never given special attention to the subject. I regard a legislative body as a very unfit depository of the pardoning power. There are serious objections to placing it in the hands of a single officer, especially of one who is burdened with other grave cares and responsibilities. I think the present system in Rhode Island a good one. A board of pardon would probably be still better; the initiative being with the governor.

I have made this brief reply on account of my respect for your association; not because I have had the opportunity from experience or study to form any views that are worthy of your consideration.

Very respectfully,
Your obed't servant,
H. B. ANTHONY.

Rev. E. C. Wines, D. D.

II. A LETTER FROM THE HON. CYRUS MENDENHALL, OF OHIO, ON SUNDRY TOPICS CONNECTED WITH THE GENERAL SUBJECT OF PRISON DISCIPLINE.

MARTIN'S FERRY, OHIO, *December* 6, 1866.

Rev. E. C. WINES, D. D., NEW YORK—

Dear Friend: Your letter of the 21st ult., is received, and also the Report, previously, for which I did not know whom to thank; it is, indeed, truly interesting and acceptable. I rejoice that such attention is being turned to the improvement of prison discipline as will probably have a good practical result in your state, and ultimately in all the states. It is a work worthy the best efforts of the commission, and I should be happy could I be the means of any aid or encouragement to you in it. It is a subject in which I have, for many years past felt a deep interest, but in which, single-handed, it seemed impossible to effect much change in our own state, from the old, and in many respects, exceedingly defective character of our system. Yet, something has been done for the penitentiary at Columbus, and much more might have been, if the management could have been effectually separated from the evil influences of party politics; and the services of men of pure motives, and as well adapted to their position as John A. Prentice, could always be secured for warden, deputy warden and chaplain.

I feel assured that no system of prison government can be devised which will accomplish the object which all prison discipline should aim at,—the reformation of the criminal,—as fully as might otherwise be expected, unless entrusted for its execution to men of sound minds, controlled by the genial influences of the christian religion, and deeply impressed with the value, as immortal beings, of those so unfortunate as to have become subjects for the operation of criminal justice.

In reply to your inquiries:

First. "What is the prison system of Ohio?"

The prison system of Ohio embraces the reform school, the penitentiary at Columbus and the county jails. The latter are almost solely left to the charge of the county sheriffs, without any control as to internal regulation by the state. The judges of the court, at long periods, give their "instructions" to the sheriffs, and but little further attention is paid to the matter, and those instructions are seldon obeyed. The jails are in their general character, well described on page 15 of the report you sent me, in speaking of your own county jails. Since the receipt of your letter, I had occasion to visit St. Clairsville, our county seat, and was kindly shown through our jail by the sheriff. I found it to contain three cells and two upper rooms. (The population of the county is about 40,000). The cells were on a level with the ground—were poorly ventilated, or rather not ventilated at all—were damp, and not occupied. The rooms over them were about 15 by 18 feet, with two small windows on one side, and a small hole in the door opening into a hall, on the other—one of these rooms was unoccupied, and in the other were four men and a boy twelve years of age—the men had just been sentenced to the penitentiary for terms of from one to five years, and the boy was to go to the reform school. They had all, boy included, been confined in this manner for several months! or during a long vacation of the court. No other care had been extended to them than to prevent their escape, and to feed and keep them tolerably clean.

The reform school is under the control of three commissioners appointed by the Governor. It has, I am happy to state, been almost wholly preserved from the influence of party politics, and is doubtless accomplishing, if not all its originators and friends hoped from it, at least a great amount of good. The house of refuge, near Cincinnati, is under the exclusive control of the county. The Ohio penitentiary you know of.

Second. " Is there any central authority in charge of the whole system?"

There is no " central authority" having supervision or control of the system, unless the governor of the state may be so regarded; and he is certainly not the authority you enquire after. Such an officer or board, having a supervision of the whole system, including the county jails—in character somewhat corresponding to that of commissioner of public instruction—or, of our common school system, would, I think, be a wise and expedient provision. Before this officer or board, who would have opportunities of investigation of each case much superior to the governor, all applications for pardons might be made to pass, with a recommendation to the governor for final action.

Third. "Is it your opinion that you have sufficient number of juvenile reformatories, or should the number in your judgment be increased?"

I think we should have at least one other institution similar to those at Cincinnati and Lancaster, making large provision for females, which should be *entirely* separated from the other sex; and if the public mind could be brought to sustain the plan, these institutions should be multiplied, and be made to include the class you refer to as in danger of falling into crime, which, in my opinion, includes nearly all who are not sedulously cared for, and not engaged regularly in some employment. But I fear the idea is so much in advance of public sentiment on the subject, as to be regarded as chimerical, and an invasion of the license of manners so generally esteemed as inalienable liberty. But I am sure that a more strict and severe supervision and control of the habits of early youth, would exert a wholesome influence upon the character of American morals; and that there are unmistakable indications that such control is imperatively demanded.

Fourth. " Is promiscuous association of prisoners allowed in your common jails, and if so, what is the effect?"

It is the practice for prisoners of the same sex to associate promiscuously in our county jails, except such as are confined, for greater security, in cells. As to the influence of such associations, my own observation at home, and a somewhat extensive enquiry of prisoners in the Ohio penitentiary, as to their experience, would pronounce it decidedly bad, and our jails, in many cases, as crime producers instead of crime repressers. So fully and convinced of this, that I have often to rejoice when I see a young man, and especially a boy, escape a confinement there when he was clearly liable to it by law.

Fifth. " What changes do you conceive to be needed in your prison system ?"

The whole system in Ohio is wrong, and it cannot be remedied without the erection of a new prison or an entire reconstruction of the existing one; and this fact has thus far prevented any attempt at reforms, except such as are applicable to the present arrangement. Your Sing Sing and Auburn prisons are, I believe, nearly similar. The solitary or exclusive system of Pennsylvania is, in my opinion, greatly preferable as a reformitory means. I do not think the objection, so long and so persistently charged against that system, of increased liability to insanity, is justly chargeable to it. I am not in possession of any statistics of your prisons touching this subject, but I know that in times past, from two to two and a half per cent. of the prisoners in our state prison became fit subjects for a lunatic asylum after entering the prison, and that under what must be regarded as the most favorable operation of the congregate system.

There might, however, be changes from our present practices, which would, I think, be important improvements. I would remove everything having any tendency to degrade or destroy the manhood of the prisoner, so far as would be consistent with his safe keeping. I regard the parti-colored dress as decidedly of this character. The only sensible plea that I have heard for it is, that it increased the difficulty of escape. For this purpose, with a properly constructed prison, and due vigilance, it is unnecessary; and I would, on no consideration, expose him to public gaze. I would place evidences of good conduct upon his clothing, when deserved, after the manner of the markings on the sleeves of non-commissioned officers in the army. I saw this practised in the Canadian penitentiary at Kingston, and was informed that it was of marked utility in stimulating manhood and self-control; and whatever has this tendency—whatever awakens ambition to become what characterizes a good citizen, is certainly 'desirable. Men *in* a penitentiary are not materially changed from men *outside;* the motives and influences which operate to make and preserve men good citizens in the outside world, will have the same effect inside; consequently every practice or arrangement in a prison having a contrary tendency, is deleterious, and should be removed. I am convinced that no influence can be brought to bear upon man, of greater power or more blessed tendency than the christian religion put in practice towards him, and earnestly and perseveringly placed before him. In a prison properly regulated, these influences ought to be brought to bear upon him with peculiar power, for all others should be excluded. The prisoner should daily and hourly be made to feel that he is in the hands of those who have only his highest good at heart; that no vindictive or selfish motives operated to place him where he is, or regulate the conduct of his keepers toward him. The small difference in profit (if any) arising from his labor is too dearly paid for, if at the expense of character, when he comes out, to say nothing of his own eternal interests.

But the question arises, where are we to find just the right kind of men to place in charge of our prisoners? It can only be done, in my opinion, by an officer or board of officers in charge of the system, who possess qualifications of the highest and purest character that can be found in the state—whose whole time is devoted to the business, as any other state officer's time is to his; and who will find out the right men for the necessary places, and then be empowered to give them such compensation as will secure their services. The number of officers acting inside the prison should be reduced as low as possible ; under the congregate system they are necessarily numerous.

The stimulus of rewards for good conduct by shortening the term of sentence, has been eminently successful with us; and I believe the principle might be advantageously extended; and also permit the power of granting special rewards to be exercised at discretion of some officer in whom such power may safely reside.

Sixth. " What is found to be the influence of the contract system of convict labor in your state ?"

The contract system, as practised in our state prisons, I regard as decidedly deleterious in its influence. Under the solitary system, and properly regulated, I do not see that it is necessarily so; especially if such business was carried on as required but little contract with contractor or his foreman.

I have endeavored to give such replies to your queries as very pressing engagements permitted, and shall be happy to render you such further service, in your important and interesting investigations, as it is in my power to do, and should be pleased to have the benefit of the labors of the association through your valuable reports.

There is another branch of this subject to which I should, were

I a member of the legislature, turn my attention—that is, a revision of our penal code. I am satisfied that in very many cases the sentences are too long ; men without dangerous character are frequently found in prison long after all beneficial effect of confinement is at an end.

I would gladly also see all *life* sentences abolished. A large number of the insane and imbecile are to be found amongst the life prisoners; evidently the effect of taking away all hope. Every term of prison confinement should, I think, have an end, let that end be ever so distant; and then let it be in the power of the prisoner to shorten it by good conduct and unmistakable evidences of improvement of character.

Very truly your friend,
CYRUS MENDENHALL.

III. THREE LETTERS FROM MRS. SARAH PETER, ON THE FEMALE BRANCH OF THE CITY PRISON OF CINCINNATI.

CINCINNATI, Oct. 25, '65.

SIR—With great pleasure I hasten to reply to your letter, which has just reached me.

You ask me to give you "a full and true history of the origin and progress of our female prison."

Since it originated, so far as this country is concerned, with myself alone, its tale is brief. But as the ideas are all borrowed from foreign lands, you will perhaps desire from me some preliminary observations respecting the prisons abroad, and the motives which led me to adopt a system which has already proved a blessing to this city.

Guided by the precept of our divine Lord, I have for many years been a regular visitor of prisons; first in Philadelphia, and, after my removal to Cincinnati. I also passed some years in European travels, and employed much time in examining the modes of administering the various charities on the continent, desirous to familiarize myself with such as might seem best adapted to our own country. How much is thus to be learned, on many important subjects, I forbear to relate, and confine myself, with all due brevity, to female prisoners, who, poor things! are often merely victims to adverse circumstances, which they are unable to control or resist.

As soon as the reconstruction of society began, after the tornado of the French revolution, the Sisters of the Good Shepherd (whose order dates from some two hundred and fifty years since, and whose special object is the reformation of abandoned women and neglected little girls) recommenced their labors among female convicts. Their mother house, which I have visited, is at Angers, France, and contains usually some 700 or 800 subjects of both classes. One or two other orders are also employed in this work, but the "Good Shepherds" are pre-eminent. They have some twelve or fifteen houses in this country for penitents—which they manage entirely themselves—and thus, when I sought for an order of sisters to take charge of our prison, their work had already prepared them for it.

Wherever sisters can be had, in Prussia, Belgium, France, Austria, Italy and the British Islands (I speak from personal observation), sisters are employed by the respective states or municipalities to govern the female prisoners; and every where, without any exception that I ever heard of, their administration has been marked with undisputed success and approbation. In most places, as in ours, these prisons are under the sole direction and management of the sisters, who are, nevertheless, *always, in every point, subject to the laws and usages of the locality;* and it is well established that no "officers" can be found who are more carefully observant than they of laws and regulations. No change whatever was made in the regulations of our prison ; they remain precisely as formerly. Women, in Europe, convicted of hideous crimes, and sentenced to imprisonment for life, yield entire submission to the firm but gentle rule of the sisters, and become devotedly attached to them. The only punishment I ever knew inflicted was solitary confinement in a small but comfortable room, with work, and a book and bed. The sisters, on these occasions, serve them with their meals, and scarcely with an exception, the culprit, within a few hours, melts into tears, ceases to be angry or obstinate, and begs to be restored to favor. Trades are introduced into these prisons, which are not commonly practised in the neighborhood, so as to avoid competition with regular dealers. In Italy, for example, the finer French laces are unknown as a manufacture, until introduced into the prisons ; and now Flanders produces nothing more beautiful than the Valenciennes and point d'appliqué, produced by women whose long sentences give time for the perfection of their art. Embroideries of the finest kinds are made. Gloves are sometimes the staple of a prison ; others have saddle housings, &c., &c., &c. ; and in some places, the products of these suffice to meet all expenses. Thus, these poor convicts become valuable producers to the industry of the country, and new manufactures enhance its wealth ; while in the higher view of the subject, which perhaps you and myself would consider the most important, the careful instructions imparted, and the good examples always before them, together with the habits of regular employment, rescue many from lives of crime and immorality, who afterwards become good members of society, though always leading a life of retirement. *All these facts are fully established and unquestioned.*

Deeply impressed by what I had witnessed, I resolved, on my last return home in 1858, to make a strong effort on behalf of the hapless creatures in the wretched prison of this city, and addressed myself to the mayor and members of the council individually, endeavoring to persuade them of the great advantages to be gained by the reformation of their then apparently incorrigible delinquents, and also of the financial economy to result from the measures proposed. But these gentlemen, guided by their own bounded experiences, were incredulous of the capacity of any women to control the fierce and turbulent cases, who, they thought, could be subdued by brute force alone. I admitted that the class who usually are employed as "matrons," and who are attracted only by the salary, without pretending to any capacity or peculiar adaptation to such a charge, ought not to be expected to perform duties for which they had no qualifications; but assured them that the sisters were *devoted for life*—with long and severe preparatory discipline—with no ulterior views," &c., &c. Confident of the justice of my position, a refusal was not a discouragement. At length a more enlightened mayor, Mr. G. W. Hatch, and a city solicitor, Mr. Ware, warmly seconded the proposed reform. The sisters were forthwith installed, and entered the house which you have seen as the abode of neatness, order and lucrative industry. Only three years since, it was a scene of indescribable filth, intemperance and obscenity, where the wretched, half naked inmates roamed over the dilapidated place, engaged only in the brutal quarrels of inebriety. With the good sisters, a few days only were required to change the complexion of affairs. The nearly *inhumanized* creatures were washed and clothed, and work was put into their hands, which they undertook without difficulty. The mayor at first feared to leave the sisters without a police officer, in spite of their declarations that it was an unnecessary expense; but at the end of a few weeks the officer was dismissed as supernumerary. The prisoners are, of course, brought from the court room and delivered at the prison by an officer. They speedily become attached to the sisters, and it would be scarcely possible for a revolt to occur. They sometimes grow angry with each other, or are idle, but a little restraint, such as I have described, proves to them the folly of displeasing those who devote their lives to them. Most of these unfortunate women have fallen through intemperance, the most difficult to cure of all vices. Many of them would be good servants but for this vice, and on the expiration of their sentences, they find places in families—but alas, the fatal thirst returns! One of the most touching circumstances connected with the prison, is the *very frequent voluntary return* of the poor women, who, earnestly desirous not to mortify the sisters by being arrested, knock at the door and beg to be admitted until their thirst is again cooled. Of course they are never refused, and they go to work as if in their mother's house. As I must be very often at the prison, the recurrence of this fact has frequently brought tears into my eyes. A few hours more of exposure, and they would be lying, perhaps, in a gutter, and the city would again be charged with the expenses of arrest, trial, &c. We *must* regard the economical side also.

The result of all this is, that the large class who were once reduced to a state of brutal degradation by intemperance, neglect, and ill-treatment, *exist here no longer*. Though they are not always entirely reformed, a certain degree of self-respect is restored, which maintains decency. The police reports prove this. * * * * * * The building now occupied is merely an old school house, entirely unfitted for its present purposes, for there is no room for separate trades, &c.; but the municipality are preparing to erect a suitable work-house as soon as practicable.

The stipend of the sisters, fixed by myself, is $100 cash per annum, a sum only sufficient to furnish them plain clothing. Their food is prepared in the common kitchen. Of course the produce of their work, as well as that of the prisoners, is placed in the prison fund, and an account is rendered every month. It is hardly necessary to add that the prison is freely open to religious instructors of any denomination who may wish to impart their lessons and counsels to the prisoners. As I have already remarked, the regulations of the prison are precisely the same as under the old régime. * * * * * * I regret that my poor note is so long, but I have risked being prolix, rather than omit any fact which might be useful to you. Of course the details of the European prisons might be greatly extended, but all would tend only to prove the excellence of the system, and you have perhaps enough for your purpose.

One word as to myself. Having a profound dislike for *notoriety*, *I beg you will not mention any name needlessly.* I have referred to my own acts in this communication, only to be the more concise, and because there is really no one else on whom I could fix the reign of our prison under its present administration. My hastily written note is entirely at your disposal, so far as it may be useful. And let me add, that I shall be most happy to lend my poor assistance in any enterprise that you may undertake in this direction.

I am, sir, with great respect, truly yours,

Rev. E. C. Wines, D. D. SARAH PETER.

Cincinnati, *Dec.* 10, 1865.

Dear Sir—Unwilling to deprive you of the pleasure of a letter from our excellent sister Stanislaus, I have delayed replying to yours of the 11th ult. The good sister has wished and intended to respond to your enquiries, but at length she confesses that it seems impossible to find a leisure hour to collect her thoughts so as to place them in such order as may be useful to you. She therefore begs me to take her place.

And now, it is so long since I last wrote to you, that intervening interuptions have nearly effaced from my memory what I wrote—for I did not attempt to keep a copy—I only remember giving you a rapid sketch of what seemed most important. I do not know whether I added my conviction that none but "sisterhoods" could effect the results which are everywhere apparent in their work. The religious principle lies at the bottom of everything they do, and their training, based upon their faith, and built by prayer, entire self-abnegation, and long experience, enables them to accomplish what they undertake through love for God and their neighbor. * * * * * * * *

It would be hardly possible to explain to you the system of management of our sisters. A mother may be a model of order, yet, as among half a dozen children, no two may be of the same character, she modifies or changes her treatment accordingly, and all love her alike, for they know she loves them all *best.* "Men do not gather grapes of thorns, nor figs of thistles." *Their system is shown in its fruits.* We have, perhaps, both lived long enough to know that paper laws and constitutions are easily violated, when the moral sense of a people is depraved ; and, that after all, it is the *wise administration* of laws which makes them a blessing. *The men's prison which you saw here, has the identical set of laws which govern the sisters prison.* It would be rather presumptuous in me "to suggest modifications or improvements in our penal systems," as you propose. My thought would be to accept them as they are, and *place them under a better administration.* I could not ask a better illustration of this idea than that which you witnessed here. The men's prison* is elaborately and expensively built, and maintained at a great cost. It is idle, noisy dirty, &c., &c. The women's prison is a sort of old barrack, ill constructed for the purpose in all respects, and in a half ruinous condition ; yet it is the abode of order, cleanliness, cheerfulness, and productive industry, at the smallest possible expense.   *   *   *   *   *   *   *

I am really desirous to forward the work of making our prisons better, and would gladly second your views so far as I am able. If you would take the trouble to ask me such questions as may reach the point you aim at, I will endeavor to reply more clearly than in the "hit or miss" manner of this present note. Sister Stanislaus desires to present you her compliments.

I am, with great respect, yours,   SARAH PETER.

To Dr. Wines: CINCINNATI, *Jan. 8th,* 1866.

Dear Sir—It affords me much pleasure to reply to your interrogatories, and *I beg you will have no scruples in asking me any question by which our common object,* viz: the reformation of a class of unfortunates, who, by neglecting the grace of God, the only hope of our fallen race, have become violators of the laws may be aided. You now "desire specifically to learn respecting the management of the admirable prison of Sister Stanislaus," "the system of rewards and encouragements held out to the prisoners to secure good behaviour," &c.

Will you allow me to repeat, in the first place, what I think I mentioned in my last, i. e., that the same system, if pursued by *paid* matrons or stewards, however worthy, would be nearly or quite inoperative for moral reformation, as also experience has proven? Pardon me for another observation, which I trust may not grate harshly on your ear. *The reason of this difference is readily comprehended by any intelligent papist,* but it is misunderstood by protestants, and I therefore fear you may not enter into it. It is not a question of intellect, but of psychology, and I will merely state the fact as it exists. This being the case, a system which among sisterhoods or brotherhoods can hardly fail to attain its object (moral reformation), must not be expected to succeed under a different administration. Nevertheless, I will endeavor to

---

*Mrs. Peter undoubtedly refers to the jail here, and not to the male department of that prison.

reply to your questions. A great point, probably the most important in the successful treatment of transgressors, is, as you know, to become possessed of their entire confidence. They seldom consider themselves as being worse than other people, and fancy they are *victims*. The character, the proud self abnegation of the sisters, who have given up every worldly gratification to devote themselves to the unfortunates, and their gentle ways gain at once a spontaneous confidence, often gratitude, and these induce good will. Though each prisoner is entirely free in her religion, motives of religious duty are always held forth, and the living examples of piety before them are perhaps the most influential of their instructions. Sister Stanislaus has read your last letter, and with her kind regards, she desires me to say that you are right in regard to her giving nearly or quite 25 per cent. of earnings, together with a good substantial calico dress, and perhaps shoes, after a long sentence attended with good behavior. These and lesser rewards are distributed at the discretion of sister S. There is no rule beyond her judgment, which, you may be persuaded, is always kind. She also endeavors to secure work, or situations in families on their leaving the prison. *This is the entire sum of material rewards.* You are of course aware of the system practiced in the Eastern Penitentiary at Philadelphia, and elsewhere. But excellent as are the motives of the venerable men who compose the controlling authorities in these prisons, they fall very far short of the influence for good, which can be wrought under such an administration as ours. Experience proves that human laws and regulations are but fragile barriers against the torrent of human passions. Allow me to repeat, the *administration* of laws is of more force than the laws themselves. Besides in the sum of human action, the *heart* is far more powerfully effective than the *head*. This lesson is taught by our Divine Lord. If a power can be found capable of coping with human passions, it must exist in *purified affections*, not by appeals to self-interest, or even to the reasoning or intellectual faculties. We all *know* this, but law-makers seem to forget it—pardon my *prosing*. You will be glad to hear that a work house is to be erected immediately, and our worthy Mayor, in giving this information to sister S., added, "and I beg you, to consider yourself and band engaged to take charge of the female department, for if *you* cannot reform these people, no power on earth can do it."

With great respect yours, SARAH PETER.

P. S.—In a former note, I mentioned the result of our work so far, is, that by the statement of the police, the class of hidecus intemperate women, who formerly disgraced the streets, has *disappeared*. If they drink, they are more decent, and many are leading good lives in respectable families, &c. We have no published statistics. S. P.

IV. JUVENILE REFORMATORIES.

E. W. Hatch responds for the state reform school of Connecticut; Geo. W. Perkins, for the Chicago reform school, Illinois; Geo. B. Barrows, for the state reform school of Maine; W. R. Lincoln, for the Baltimore house of refuge, Maryland; Joseph A. Allen, for the state reform school of Massachusetts; Richard Matthews, for the nautical branch of the same; Rev. Marcus Ames, for the state industrial school for girls, of Massachusetts; C. B. Robinson, for the state reform school of Michigan; H. S. Gleason, for the St. Louis house of refuge, Missouri; Abijah Watson, for the Cincinnati house of refuge, Ohio; Jesse K. McKeever, for the eastern house of refuge (white department), Pennsylvania; J. Hood Laverty, for the colored department of same; James M. Talcott, for the Providence reform school, Rhode Island; and Moses Barrett, for the state reform school of Wisconsin. Having once stated the fact, it can hardly be necessary to repeat the names of these gentlemen in connection with each answer, and they are accordingly omitted.

QUESTION I.

When was your institution established?

ANSWERS.

Connecticut—In 1854.
Illinois—In 1855.
Maine—In 1850.
Maryland—Incorporated in 1849; opened in 1855.
Massachusetts—State reform school opened Nov. 1, 1848; nautical branch established in 1859; state industrial school for girls, founded Aug. 27, 1856.
Michigan—Opened September 2, 1856.
Missouri—Founded in 1854; incorporated in 1856.
Ohio—Opened in 1850.
Pennsylvania—Eastern house of refuge (white), in 1826; colored, 1850.
Rhode Island—In 1850.
Wisconsin—Incorporated in 1857 and completed in 1860.

QUESTION II.

Was the institution founded by the authorities of the state or city, or by private benevolence?

ANSWERS.

Connecticut — Partly by private benevolence ($10,000), but mostly by state funds.

Illinois—By the city authorities of Chicago,

Maine—By the state authorities.

Maryland—By private benevolence and city of Baltimore.

Massachusetts—State reform school, by the authorities of the state, aided by gifts from Hon. Theo. Lyman, to the amount of $72,500; nautical branch by the state; state industrial school for girls, $20,000 furnished by private benevolence, and $20,000 by the state, for the original buildings; two additional buildings have since been erected by state appropriation.

Michigan—By the authorities of the state.

Missouri—The act of incorporation provides that the board of managers shall be appointed in the following manner: The mayor of the city is a member *ex officio;* the city council elect *four* from their own body; the mayor appoints *two* from the citizens at large; the county court of St. Louis appoints *two*—total 9.

Ohio—It was founded under the authority of the state, by the city of Cincinnati, and by private subscription.

Pennsylvania—White department, private benevolence and appropriations from the state legislature and city councils, were the means relied upon for its establishment. Colored department was founded by private benevolence, legacy, and small appropriations by the city and state.

Rhode Island—By the city authorities of Providence.

Wisconsin—By the state authorities.

QUESTION III.

How are the funds for its support obtained ?

ANSWERS.

Connecticut.—From the state, from the earnings of inmates, from use of the farm, and from boarding pupils.

Illinois.—By city tax.

Maine.—The funds are obtained by annual appropriations by the state ; from taxes levied upon cities and towns for subsistence and clothing ; from the products of the farm, and from the earnings of the boys.

Maryland.—They are obtained chiefly from the city and state, and from the labor of inmates.

Massachusetts.—For State Reform School, they are obtained from the state, interest on the Lyman and Mary Lamb funds, and from earnings. For the Nautical Branch and the Girls' Industrial School, from appropriations by the Legislature.

Michigan.—It is sustained by an appropriation from the state treasury, and by the labor of the boys.

Missouri.—The expenses of the institution are paid by the *city*, with the exception of a comparatively small amount paid by the county for board of subjects committed by courts of St. Louis county.

Ohio.—This institution is sustained by taxation upon the property of the city, and incidental receipts for the labor of inmates, and for the board of inmates not otherwise entitled to admission to the Refuge.

Pennsylvania.—Both departments, from appropriations of money by the city and state, together with the earnings of the inmates.

Rhode Island.—The funds are derived from the city authorities.

Wisconsin.—By legislative appropriation, and a tax of one dollar per week for "incorrigibles" and "vagrants," imposed on the several counties from whence sent.

Question IV.

What are the extent and arrangements of the grounds belonging to the Institution?

Answers.

Connecticut.—The grounds consist of 160 acres.

Illinois.—Twenty-seven acres in extent.

Maine.—One hundred and sixty acres.

Maryland.—A farm of fifty acres.

Massachusetts.—State Reform School, a farm consisting of about 275 acres of ordinary farm lands, divided into wood land, pasturage, orchards and garden. Nautical Branch, one ship of 650 tons (another fitting). The Girls' School has 140 acres, including wood land, pasturage and tillage, 20 acres of which are connected immediately with the buildings.

Michigan.—There are 134 acres of land belonging to the school, nearly one hundred of which are covered with timber; the other thirty-four acres arranged as per report, which please see.

Missouri.—There are about twenty acres, three of which are enclosed and occupied by the buildings and play grounds for the female department; six acres are used for the buildings and play grounds of the male department, and the remaining eleven acres are cultivated as a garden for fruit and vegetables.

Ohio.—There are some ten acres of ground, about half of which is surrounded by a stone wall, twenty feet high, enclosing all the buildings except the stable and carriage sheds; the balance, in two lots, lies in front of the Refuge, with the main avenue between them.

Pennsylvania.—The lot of ground actually occupied by the buildings of the House of Refuge (white), is bounded on the north by Poplar street, on the east by Twenty-second street, on the south by Parish street, and on the west by Twenty-fourth street. The outer walls form a parallelogram of 685 feet by 400 feet. The wall of the colored department encloses an area of nearly two acres, on which are erected the buildings. There are moderate sized play grounds and flower and vegetable gardens.

Rhode Island.—There are two and a half acres belonging to the institution.

Wisconsin.—There are about seventy acres, of which only thirty-five acres are suitable for cultivation, the remainder consisting of river, meadow and woods.

QUESTION V.

What are the several buildings, their uses and arrangements?

ANSWERS.

Connecticut.—The main building is 175 feet long, and used for culinary purposes, for the school, for dormitories, for the residence of the superintendent and employés, and for the chapel; and a wing, containing the shops, drying room, &c., &c.

Illinois.—There are attached to this institution the following buildings: 1. A main building, containing a reception room, library, office, dining rooms, clothing room, and school room, laundry, &c. 2. Four family buildings. 3. A dwelling for superintendent and family. 4. Two buildings for workshops. 5. A building for bakery, kitchen, and officers' dining room and sleeping rooms. 6. A building for store-room.

Maine.—The buildings consist of a main building of brick, octagonal in form, 74 feet in diameter, including, in basement, boys' kitchen, laundry and bathing room; in first story, school rooms; in second story, dormitories, and in third story chapel and hospital. Three wings extend from the main building, cne of which contains the officers' apartments; the others, the dining room, workshops, playhouse and dormitories.

Maryland.—Main building for boys. The Baltimore House of Refuge is built of gneiss from quarries on the ground, with granite door and window dressing, coping and cornice, and roof of slate. Its architectural plan is simple, but extremely striking in its proportions, and wholly devoid of anything gloomy or prison-like in its character. The whole front is 446 feet, eight inches; but this great length is agreeably broken by the projections of the ground plan and the greater elevations of the central and terminating buildings. From the front gateway to the main entrance is 108 feet—the ground ascending so rapidly in that distance as to require to be broken by three terraces, each of which is reached by a flight of granite steps. This elevation affords, even from the windows of the first or principal story, a fine view, overlooking the entire height of the wall of enclosure, and extending over the city and surrounding country, with the river in the distance.

The main or front central building, occupied by the superintendent, with apartments for the accommodation of visitors and the managers, is 94 feet in length, by 33 feet in depth; to this is attached the nave, 111 feet in length by 44 feet in breadth. The basement or ground floor of the nave is entirely occupied by refectories for the inmates. The first or principal story is traversed by a wide passage way, on which open the superintendent's office, ware-rooms, and rooms for the apothecary and principal assistants. The passage terminates in a large room, with doors opening upon the wings, and windows in the circular end, thus giving a perfect oversight of the dormitories, as well as of the play grounds and exterior offices.

The second story has bed-rooms for the officials on each side of a passage shorter than that in the principal story, and leading directly into the chapel. This is a fine, spacious hall, 78 feet long, 44 feet wide and 20 feet high, and lighted by nine large pointed windows.

From the nave proceeds, on each side, a connecting passage, 30 feet in length, with narrow stairways to each gallery. These are only for the use of the officers. From these passages the wings commence; the dormitories separated by central corridor, 18 feet wide. The dormitories are each nine feet long, nine feet high, and six feet six inches wide, and each is lighted by a window four feet by two feet four inches, with iron frame and sash, with small diamond shaped glass. These apartments are fire-proof, having no wood in their construction, except the door, which is of double yellow pine, with a grated opening for oversight and ventilation.

The public kitchens and bakery are in a separate frame building, 70 feet in the rear of the refuge building proper, and 70 feet long by 26 wide. There is a separate building for girls, 71 feet wide by 110 feet long, three stories high.

Massachusetts.—The buildings belonging to the State Reform School are a farm barn, piggery, carriage house, farmer's house, farm house for family of thirty boys, Peter's house for family of twenty-four boys, ice-house, garden-tool house, cottage house, steam mill, gas house, boiler house; main building for the officers and congregate department, institution barn, sheds, &c., &c. The Nautical Branch accommodates its inmates in two ships. The industrial school for girls has four houses, accommodating thirty girls each, and containing school room, sewing room, dining room, kitchen and laundry; also, single sleeping rooms for all except ten of the smaller girls, who occupy a common dormitory, the whole having a home aspect and family arrangements, every house being entirely distinct and separate from the others. It has also a chapel, sufficiently commodious for all, a superintendent's house and a farmer's house.

Michigan.—The Michigan State Reform School is pleasantly situated on a slight elevation, at the east end of Shiawassee street, about one mile north of east from Capitol Square, City of Lansing.

A farm of thirty acres belongs to the Institution, four acres of which are enclosed by a high board fence, and the building in front. Within the enclosure are located the shops, and other buildings belonging to the Institution, except the barn and toolhouse. Ten acres are under constant cultivation, on a portion of which is planted an orchard of two hundred and ninety-two thrifty young fruit trees, apple, pear, plum and cherry. The remaining sixteen acres are used as pasturage and lawn.

The yard in front of the building, containing five acres, is surrounded by a neat picket fence. and laid out in drives and walks, and ornamented with trees and shrubs.

The grounds enclosed by the high fence, are devoted to the pleasure and comfort of the boys, on a portion of which a gymnasium is erected, which adds materially to their health and enjoyment.

The center building of the house proper fronts west, and is forty-eight feet wide, fifty-six feet deep, and four stories high. There are two wings, extending north and south, each ninety-five feet long, thirty-three feet deep, and three stories high, excepting the towers at the extremities, which are four stories high. On the first or ground floor of the center building are a kitchen and dining room for the Superintendent, a state-room and laundry. On the second floor are a reception room, parlor, Superintendent's office and private room. On the third floor are rooms for the officers and employés. On the fourth floor is the chapel, suitably arranged and furnished for seating four hundred persons.

On the first floor of the north wing are the dining-hall and wash room for the boys. Adjoining the dining-hall, in a small addition, are the kitchen, bakery and boiler-room, the latter being also used as a laundry for the boys.

On the second floor of the north wing are the hospital, medicine room, a dormitory, arranged for sleeping 42 of the smallest boys, and bedrooms for officers and employés. On the first floor of the south wing are a school-room, seated for forty-two boys, an ironing-room, and a tailor's shop. On the second floor are a large school-room, capable of seating one hundred and sixty boys, two recitation rooms and a library. The upper floors of the two wings are arranged with dormitories, and furnish separate sleeping apartments for one hundred and fifty-two boys. All the rooms in the building are warmed by means of stoves.

A brick shop, twenty-five by eighty feet, two stories high, containing four rooms, has just been erected in the north-east corner of the yard, affording abundant room for the employment of eighty boys; adjoining which is an engine room, twenty by twenty-five feet.

Missouri.—The buildings are as follows: Male department— One wing only remains, the other wing and central building were destroyed by fire, Feb. 14th, 1865. The remaining wing is three stories above the basement, which contains kitchen, family dining room, inmates' dining room, store-rooms, &c. First story contains Superintendent's office, family room and bed room, manager's room, family parlour, visitors' room, knitting room, and school room for small boys, and tailor's shop. Second story contains two large school rooms and one bed-room for teachers. Third story has a dormitory for boys, room for the night watchman in the dormitory, and assistant superintendent's bed-room.

One two-story frame building, of temporary character, contains, on first floor, assistant superintendent's office, small bath room for new comers, stove room, bed-room for foreman of shoe shop, stock room, boys' clothes room, and four cells for confinement of refractory inmates. Second story is used for a shoe shop, and is large enough to work conveniently 40 boys.

Two other one-story buildings serve the purpose of laundry, bed-rooms for assistants, &c.

The female department is distant from male department about 50 rods. It consists of five buildings, arranged in two groups, distant from each other about four rods. The largest building was erected in 1856, and is the only one that was erected for the house of refuge, the other buildings having been used many years as a county poor house.

Ohio.—The entire structure is 278 feet front, five stories high, and built of stone. The main building is for the use of the officers. There is a dormitory in the north end for boys, with 112 separate sleeping apartments, in which the inmates are locked up for the night. In the basement of this end is the bath room, 58 by $9\frac{1}{3}$ feet, with small side rooms for undressing. The water for bathing is warmed by steam to any desired temperature. The bath will accommodate at one time 140 boys. The dormitory on the south side is used for female inmates. It has seventy-two separate sleeping apartments; one school room; two sewing rooms; one hospital; bath room; a laundry; drying and ironing rooms.

The main building is two stories, has three public offices, two reception rooms, two officers' dining rooms, and one store room. The upper stories are used for the accommodation of the officers. The hospital accommodates fifty-two patients, and connected with it are four bath rooms and a dispensary.

In the rear of main building, and connected with it by a covered way, is a stone building, three stories high, containing a chapel, sixty feet by sixty-four feet; three school rooms; one dormitory for boys, four dining rooms, kitchen, bakery, and bread room. There is a cellar under the whole building.

In the rear of chapel building, and connected with it by a covered way, built of stone, is the engine room, one story high, built of stone, with four boilers of fourteen horse power, in which is generated steam sufficient to warm the entire buildings.

Attached to the engine room, on the south, is a three story stone building, containing a storage room for coal and wood, a carpenter's and blacksmith's shop, three shops for the manufacture of shoes, one shop for making shoes and clothing for inmates, one school room, one dormitory for boys, containing forty-two sleeping rooms, and four cells, one covered play ground, water closet, and accommodations for washing.

On the south side of these dormitories is a one story brick building for the manufacture of gas for the institution, with two retorts; on the north side is the gasometer, and on the southeast corner of the grounds is the ice house, 30 by 35 feet.

Pennsylvania—White Department.—The buildings contain the school rooms, dining rooms, kitchens, dormitories, chapel, reading rooms, officers' apartments, reception rooms, offices, work shops, bathing rooms, &c., &c. Colored Department—In the main building there are separate dining rooms for boys and girls; kitchen, laundry, drying room; girls' sewing room; *matrons'* parlor, officers' dining room; superintendents' parlor, dining room, kitchen, &c. ; and superintendent's and assistant superintendent's offices ; chapel; infirmaries for boys and girls ; girls' school room; eleven bed-chambers for officers and superintendent's family; superintendent's sitting room ; store rooms, closets, pantries, &c.

In the north wing, there are separate sleeping rooms for eighty girls; ten separate bath rooms, and separate wash rooms for each (A. & B.) division.

In the south wing, there are separate sleeping rooms for 120 boys. The boys' school room is a detached building, of three stories, in which there are accommodations for 120 pupils. In the basement is a fine pool for bathing, and all necessary conveniences for washing. The work shop is a three and a half storied building, having sufficient room for 159 boys.

Rhode Island.—A main building, with two wings, one for boys and the other for girls, used for all the purposes of the family and school, except a work shop, for which there is a separate building.

Wisconsin.—The *congregated plan* was the original one, and a large building was erected as one of *three,* connected by corridor extensions. This building is about one hundred feet by sixty—three stories besides a basement. Another building on the family plan was erected in 1864, about thirty rods from the former, for the small boys, with dormitories and school room for about forty. A small building about sixty by twenty-two, two stories, with three rooms for shops, with the under part for wood shed.

QUESTION VI.

How many inmates will the institution accommodate ?

ANSWERS.

Connecticut.—Two hundred inmates can be accommodated.

Illinois.—This institution can receive two hundred and fifty inmates.

Maine.—Can accommodate two hundred and forty pupils.

Maryland.—The boys' building is calculated for three hundred and fifty—girls, seventy five.

Massachusetts.—State Reform School—from three hundred to three hundred and twenty-five; Nautical Branch, three hundred and fifty boys, (two ships); Girls' Industrial School—the five buildings, each containing thirty, accommodate one hundred and fifty.

Michigan..—The institution was originally designed to accommodate one hundred and fifty-two boys, but there are in the house two hundred and sixty-two.

Missouri.—The buildings of the female department will accommodate well about one hundred inmates; those of the male department about one hundred and seventy.

Ohio.—The buildings will accommodate 350 inmates.

Pennsylvania.—There are separate rooms in the white department for 432 children—304 boys and 128 girls; in the colored department, for 198 children—122 boys and 76 girls; 630 children, in all, can be comfortably accommodated.

Rhode Island.—200 inmates can be accommodated.

Wisconsin.—The large building has 78 rooms for boys, and about 20 for girls. The family building will accommodate forty boys.

Question VII.

What was the total cost of the ground and buildings belonging to the institution?

Answers.

Connecticut.—The cost of grounds and buildings was $60,000.

Illinois.—The grounds are worth $27,000 and are owned by the county; the buildings are worth $46,000 and are owned by the city.

Maine.—$82,000.

Maryland.—About $200,000.

Massachusetts.—As a large portion of the main building was burned in 1859, and since rebuilt only in part, this question cannot be answered. As appraised last year, it stands $89,640. Nautical branch: Ship Massachusetts, $25,000; one fitting, $40,000. State industrial school for girls.—About $62,000.

Michigan:—About $70,000.

Missouri.—The ground was city common, and twenty acres were valued at $40,000. Total expense for buildings and permanent improvements, including fencing, $78,384.

Ohio.—The original cost was $150,000, to which large additions have been since made.

Pennsylvania.—The total cost of site, buildings and furniture of this institution, including both white and colored departments, now used as a house of refuge, was $348,000.

Rhode Island.—The original cost was $13,000. More than twice that sum has since been expended in alterations, additions, &c., &c.; making the entire cost not less than $40,000.

Wisconsin.—About $60,000.

QUESTION VIII.

Is the institution governed by a board of managers, and if so, how is the said board constituted?

ANSWERS.

Connecticut.—This school is governed by a board of trustees, consisting of eight persons, one from each county, chosen by the senate.

Illinois.—This institution is governed by a board of managers, consisting of seven members, the city comptroller being one; two of the remaining six are appointed each year, by the common council.

Maine.—This school is controlled by a board of trustees, consisting of five members, appointed by the governor.

Maryland.—This institution is governed by a board of managers, of whom ten are chosen by the corporation, ten appointed by the city government, and four by the governor of the state.

Massachusetts—State Reform School.—Is managed by a board of seven trustees, appointed by the governor and council. Nautical branch is under the control of seven trustees, five appointed by the governor and council, one by the marine society, and one by the Boston board of trade. Industrial School for Girls is governed by a board of seven trustees, appointed by the governor and council.

Michigan.—The school is governed by a board of control, consisting of three members, who are appointed by the governor and confirmed by the senate, and who hold their offices six years. One member is appointed every two years.

Missouri.—By a board of managers consisting of nine members, the mayor of the city, *ex-officio*, four elected by the city council from their own number, two chosen by the mayor from the citizens at large, and two by the county court of St. Louis county.

Ohio.—It is governed by nine directors, who are appointed as follows: Three by the city council, two by the Court of Common Pleas, two by the Superior Court of Hamilton county, and two by subscribers to a fund for the benefit of the refuge; but should the subscribers fail to elect them, the other seven are duly qualified to fill the places.

Pennsylvania.—The institution (both departments) is governed by a board of managers, 26 of whom are elected annually by the contributors, three appointed the judges of the Court of Common Pleas, and two by the mayor of the city.

Rhode Island.—This school is governed by a board of trustees, appointed annually by the city council, which consists of seven members, one of whom is the mayor, *ex-officio*.

Wisconsin.—Governed by a board of managers, consisting of five members appointed by the governor, divided in three classes and holding their office three years.

QUESTION IX.

What are the Powers and Duties of the Board?

ANSWERS.

Connecticut.—They have power to appoint all necessary officers to have the immediate care of the institution, and prescribe by-laws for the government and regulation of the same; and also to discharge any inmate by indenture, parole of honor or otherwise.

Illinois.—The board have full power to govern the school and hold and discharge inmates.

Maryland.—They exercise general supervision, authorize indentures, discharges, contracts, &c.

Massachusetts.—They have the general charge of the interests of the institution. They appoint the officers, subject to the approval of the governor and council.

Missouri.—The powers of the board are:

1st. To make all needful contracts for said house of refuge. 2d. To make, alter and enforce all needful regulations for the government and control of said house of refuge, its officers and inmates. 3d. To issue a writ directed to any sheriff, marshal or constable of the State of Missouri, for the reception of any fugitive from said house of refuge. 4th. To make all necessary by-laws for its government. 5th. To employ and appoint such officers as may be needful, and to fix their salaries. 6th. To apprentice any inmate of the house of refuge until the time when such inmates shall reach the age of 21 years, if a male, and 18 years if a female. 7th. To discharge any inmate of said house of refuge.

Ohio.—Under the laws of the state, the board have the exclusive control and management of the business of the institution.

Rhode Island.—The board have general charge of the institution and see that its affairs are conducted according to the requirements of the city council, and of such·laws as have been or shall be made from time to time for its management.

Wisconsin.—The duty of the board is to make rules and regulations, ordinances and by-laws for the management of the school. They have power to bind out the children at discretion with their consent or that of parents or guardians, and to appoint a superintendent and other officers.

QUESTION X.

Who compose the staff of officers of the Institution?

ANSWERS.

Connecticut—The officers of the Institution are a superintendent, assistant superintendent, treasurer, physician and chaplain, assisted by various clergymen in Meriden.

Illinois.—The officers are superintendent, assistant superintendent, clerk, four teachers, yard keeper, matron and the necessary officers for work department.

Maine.—Superintendent, assistant superintendent, physician, matron, two teachers, overseer of sewing room, laundress, cook, nurse, overseer of chair shop, overseer of shoe shop, two farmers, carpenter, overseer of brick and tile yard, and a man of all work—17.

Maryland.—Superintendent, four male teachers, three female teachers, with baker, shoemaker, tailor and contractors.

Massachusetts.—State Reform School.—Superintendent, assistant superintendent, teachers, matron, overseers of the work rooms, physician, farmer, engineer, carpenter, &c. Nautical Branch.—Superintendent, teacher, and first, second and third officers. Girls' Industrial School.— Superintendent and chaplain, five head matrons, five assistant matrons, and five housekeepers.

Missouri.—President, secretary, superintendent, matron, assistant superintendent, principal teacher, two assistant teachers, overseer of tailoring shop, overseer of shoe shop, housekeeper, laundress, day patrolman and night watchman. The *Female Department* is under the direction of the matron, assisted by two teachers, housekeeper, seamstress, cook, etc. A night watchman is on duty all night in this department also.

Ohio.—Superintendent, secretary, assistant superintendent, matron, assistant matrons, teachers, engineer, gas maker, tailor, shoemaker, care-takers, housekeeper and assistant, laundry maid and night watchman.

Pennsylvania.—White Department.—Superintendent, assistant superintendent, four male teachers, three female teachers, engineer, assistant engineer, gate-keeper, coachman, gardener and watchman, carpenter, baker, matron, assistant matron, housekeeper, cook and janitor. Colored Department.—Superintendent, assistant superintendent and teacher, gate-keeper, watchman, matron, assistant matron and female teacher, cook, nurse and overseer—in all, ten officers.

Wisconsin.—The superintendent appoints all his subordinates, who consist of matron, assistant superintendent, and such number of employés as are necessary.

QUESTION XI.

Are children of both sexes received?   If so, are they kept entirely separate?

ANSWERS.

Connecticut.—Only males are received.

Illinois.—Only males at present.   Are about ready to take girls, who will have separate apartments.

Maine.—Only males are received.

Maryland.—Both sexes are received and kept separate?

Massachusetts.—Only boys are received into the State Reform School and Nautical Branch of same; only girls in the State Industrial School for Girls.

Missouri.—Several small boys are kept in the female department.   With that exception, the sexes are kept about forty rods apart.

Michigan.—Only boys.

Ohio.—Both sexes.   Kept entirely separate.

Pennsylvania.—Both sexes are received and are kept entirely separate, both in white and colored departments.

Rhode Island.—Both sexes are received and kept separate.

Wisconsin.—Both sexes received and kept separate, except in school houses.

QUESTION XII.

Between what ages are they admissible?

ANSWERS.

Connecticut.—Between the ages of 10 and 16 years.

Illinois.—From 12 to 16 years of age.

Maine.—Between 3 and 16 years of age.

Maryland.—Boys from 9 to 16; girls from 8 to 12.

Massachusetts.—State Reform School—between 7 and 14 years of age.   Nautical Branch—between 12 and 18.   Girls' Industrial, —from 7 to 16.

Michigan.—Between 7 and 16.

Missouri.—From 2 or 3 to 16.

Ohio.—Boys under 16 years, and girls under 14.

Pennsylvania.—White department.   The law specified no limit as to age.   At present inmates range from 8 to 19 years of age. Colored department—between 9 and 16 years.   A special resolution of the board is necessary to admit any over 16, and under 21, sent from Philadelphia county.   If sent from other counties by the courts, they are received.

Rhode Island.—Children received from 7 years old to 18.

Wisconsin.—Boys received between 8 and 15; girls heretofore between 7 and 10.   The ages of girls was changed from 10 to 14 last winter, owing to want of sufficient accommodations.

Question XIII.

For what causes may children be received?

Answers.

Connecticut.—Children may be committed for any crime known to the law, and for which punishment may be jail or state prison.

Illinois.—In this institution, the only commitment is for want of parental care. Every child deemed a fit subject for the school, is sent before a commissioner appointed by the city for the purpose, who thoroughly examines the case, has power to call witnesses, &c., &c. Whatever may be the offence of the boy, he is only committed for want of proper parental care.

Maine.—Children may be received for any offence, punishable by imprisonment not for life.

Maryland.—Children may be received for criminal offences, incorrigible and vicious conduct and vagrancy, and as boarders.

Massachusetts.—State Reform School and Nautical Branch—for " any offence which may be punished by imprisonment, other than imprisonment for life." Girls' Industrial School—for committing any offence known to the laws of this commonwealth, punishable by fine or imprisonment, other than such as may be punished by imprisonment for life; also for leading an idle, vagrant, or vicious life, or being found in any street, highway or public place, within this commonwealth, in circumstances of want and suffering, or of neglect, exposure, abandonment, or beggary.

Michigan.—For all prison offences, except those of which the punishment according to law, is imprisonment for life.

Wisconsin.—For violations of state laws; for crimes such as larceny, arson, burglary, &c., and for being found abandoned, or dangerously exposed, or in lewd houses, or for incorrigibility.

Ohio.—Vagrancy, incorrigibility, and such crimes as are punishable by imprisonment in the county jail or the state prison.

Pennsylvania.—Received for incorrigible or vicious conduct, for vagrancy, and on complaint of parent, guardian, or nearest friend.

Rhode Island.—For vagrancy and being disorderly or criminal.

Wisconsin.—For vagrancy, incorrigibility, and any crime or misdemeanor.

Question XIV.

What authorities have power to commit?

Answers.

Connecticut.—All the various courts in the state have power to convict children to this institution.

Illinois.—Justices of the peace have power; but only on the commissioner's certificate.

Maine.—Supreme, police and municipal courts, trial justices and justices of the peace.

Maryland.—They may be committed by courts of the state and by magistrates, and, when admitted as boarders, by contract with parents or next friend.

Massachusetts.—State Reform School and Nautical Branch—Justices of superior courts and judges of probate courts. Girls' Industrial School—Judges of probate, and commissioners expressly appointed by the governor for this purpose.

Michigan.—All courts of record, having criminal jurisdiction and police courts and justices' courts in the exercise of their proper criminal jurisdiction, provided the commitments are approved by the probate judge.

Missouri.—The criminal court of St. Louis county, the recorder of the city of St. Louis, the mayor of St. Louis, any two justices of the peace, any two aldermen, and the board of managers, upon the petition of parents or legal guardians, may commit to this refuge.

Ohio.—Justices of the peace within the county, mayor of the city, judge of the probate court, judge of the police court, court of common pleas, and superior court.

Pennsylvania.—Magistrates and courts of the city and county of Philadelphia, the mayor and recorder of the same, judges of courts of common pleas of other counties, and quarter sessions.

Rhode Island.—Any court of justice—or the trustees, where parents or guardians pay the board.

Wisconsin.—Courts and magistrates may commit them.

QUESTION XV.

Are they committed for a specific time, or indefinitely ?

ANSWERS.

Connecticut.—They are committed for a definite period of time.

Illinois.—They are committed till 21 years of age, or till they become good boys.

Maine.—They are committed during minority.

Maryland.—For an indefinite period ; but in case of boarders, never less than six months.

Massachusetts.—During minority in all.

Michigan.—During minority.

Missouri.—During minority.

Ohio.—They are committed, subject to the laws and rules governing the institution, till of legal age.

Pennsylvania.—Both departments, the law with respect to boys, contemplates their commitment during minority, with power to bind. Girls under 16, are committed until 18, and those 16 and upward, till 21, with power to indenture.

Rhode Island.—For not less than two years, nor beyond minority.

Wisconsin.—In all cases during minority.

QUESTION XVI.

If indefinitely, when does the right of guardianship expire?

ANSWER.

The uniform reply to this question is in substance : " It expires with minority, unless the governing board sooner grant an absolute discharge."

QUESTION XVII.

Who judges whether the child is fit to leave the place before the time has expired, to which the right of guardianship extends?

ANSWER.

The general response is: The governing board, on the recommendation of the superintendent.

QUESTION XVIII.

What are the different modes of release?

ANSWERS.

Connecticut.—The modes of release are : 1st, expiration of sentence; 2d, discharge to friends; and 3d, discharge on parole of honor.

Illinois.—On good conduct; being 21 years old; and sometimes discharged to the care of parents.

Maine.—Unconditional discharge; and discharge upon trial; and on indenture.

Maryland.—By discharge to parents or friends, and by indenture.

Massachusetts.—State Reformed School and Nautical Branch.— Pardoned by governor; by order of the court, and by trustees. Girls' Industrial School.—Indentured till 18; or unconditionally discharged at 18; or discharged for good reason prior to that age.

Michigan.—By discharge; by leave of absence, and by indenture.

Missouri.—The power of discharging inmates who have been legally admitted, resides *only* in the board of managers. The following courts of St. Louis county have exclusive jurisdiction of all writs of habeas corpus for the discharge of any minor confined in the house of refuge, to wit: Circuit court, court of common pleas, land court, county court, and the criminal court of St. Louis county, or the judges of any of the said courts in vacation.

Ohio.—Discharged by indenture ; to the care of friends, and to their own care, mostly upon the evidence of reform indicated by a system of merits and demerits.

Pennsylvania.—By indenture; return to friends, and by order of court and examining judges.

Rhode Island.—By placing out at trades, with or without indentures; by discharge as reformed; or upon expiration of sentence.

Wisconsin.—1, On trial, with "ticket-of-leave," subject to be recalled for misbehavior; 2, full discharge to the care of parents or guardians. None have ever been indentured.

QUESTION XIX.

Is the institution to be regarded in the light of a prison or a school, or something intermediate between the two?

ANSWERS.

Connecticut.—It is to be regarded as a school, not as a prison.

Illinois.—As a reformatory *home*, where boys who have been neglected may be comfortably cared for, sent to school, and taught in some useful department of labor.

Maine.—It should be considered as intermediate, between a school and a prison.

Maryland.—As a reformatory, combining labor and instruction.

Massachusetts.—State Reformed School and Nautical Branch.— As a school for reformation, and not as a place of punishment. State Industrial School for Girls.—As a disciplinary family school.

Michigan.—As a school.

Missouri.—As *a manual labor school*, where youth are detained against their will by authority of *law*.

Ohio.—As a place of restraint and reformation, or a "reform school."

Pennsylvania.—The institution is to be simply regarded as a school for the cultivation of the moral and intellectual nature of the pupils. The fact is impressively conveyed to the mind of each inmate, when received, that *reformation*, not *punishment*, is the *one object* of the institution.

Rhode Island.—Prison is lost sight of as far as possible, and the *school* feature is kept prominent.

Wisconsin.—Most decidedly as a school.

QUESTION XX.

What is the character of the discipline—is it that of a prison or otherwise?

ANSWERS.

Connecticut.—Not like a prison.

Illinois.—It is that of a *home*—firm, sympathizing, kind.

Maine.—The discipline has some features like that adopted in prisons; but it is as far removed from it as the character of the inmates will allow.

Maryland.—The discipline is mild, but firm; differing, as far as possible, from that of a prison.

Massachusetts.—State Reform School.—It is intended to be like that of a family school, not that of a prison. Nautical Branch.— The discipline is that of a school. Girls' Industrial School.—The discipline is that of a family, except that they are confined to the grounds of the institution.

Michigan.—It is nearly like that of the common schools of the state.

Wisconsin.—Essentially the same as any well ordered school.

Ohio.—The discipline is that of a reform school.

Pennsylvania.—The discipline is of a parental character, no punishment being inflicted but such as might be imposed by a wise and judicious father upon his own offspring.

Rhode Island.—Not that of a prison.

Wisconsin.—The discipline is that of a well regulated school and family combined.

QUESTION XXI.

What are the rules and regulations of the place?

ANSWERS.

The almost uniform reply to this interrogatory is a reference to the by-laws of the several institutions, which are too voluminous for insertion. The general requirement in all is obedience, industry, and attention to study.

QUESTION XXII.

What are the proceedings of a day ?

ANSWERS.

Connecticut.—Rise at 5.30 A. M.; make beds; go to the yard ; then to wash-room ; school-room ; singing, reading the scriptures and prayer ; breakfast ; yard ; school till 9 A. M.; then yard again; work till noon ; dinner and play till 1 P. M.; work till 4.30 ; play and supper till 5.30 P. M.; school till 8 P. M.; then bed.

Illinois.—The first bell rings at 5.45 A. M., in order that the officers may be on hand to receive their different families at the ringing of the second bell at 6. The boys file out of their dormitories, and proceed to their respective bath-rooms, where fifteen minutes are occupied in attending to the toilet. At 6.15 the bell rings for breakfast, for which they have half an hour. Then the next bell rings for school at 6.45, when twenty minutes are occupied at the commencement for devotional exercises, at which every officer and inmate is required to attend. The boys remain two hours in school, when the bell rings for dismissal at 8.55. Fifteen minutes are allowed for the different families to wash and comb. Bell rings at 9.10 A. M., for work. All the boys in school, form in their respective lines, when a short time is occupied in inspecting the different families; they then march off to their work-shops, keeping time to the beat of the drum, in which they remain till the bell rings to close work at 12.10 ; fifteen minutes to wash and comb for dinner. The dinner bell rings at 12.25, when again the different families form together in the main yard parade ground, and file off to their respective dining halls. From the dining hall the boys pass to the play ground, and amuse themselves till 1.30 P. M., when the bell rings to wash up for work. The bell for work-shops rings at 1.40, when the boys again form in line and march off to work, occupying three hours, till the bell rings for their dismissal at 4.40. Then they prepare for supper, for which the bell rings at 4.55. From supper they file into school room as the bell rings at 5.20, and continue their studies for two hours, until the bell rings for prayers, when all persons connected with the institution assemble in school room. From there the different families proceed to their respective dormitories for the night

Maine.—Rise at 5.30 A. M. Boys make their beds and attend to their ablutions; then all assemble in the school room, where devotional exercises are conducted by superintendent; breakfast at 6.30 ; school from 7 to 9 ; 9 to 12, work ; 12 to 1 P. M., dinner and play ; 1 to 4, work ; 4 to 5, supper and play ; 5 to 7, school ; at 7, devotional exercises ; recess ; miscellaneous exercises ; at 8, retire to bed. In the warm months rise at 5 A. M. School in middle of the day.

Maryland.—Rise at 5 A. M. in summer ; in school from 5.30 to 7.30 ; from 7.30 to 8, breakfast ; from 8 to 12, labor ; dinner and play, 12 to 1 ; labor, 1 to 3 or 3.30 ; play, 3 or 3.30 to 4 ; school, 4 to 6 ; supper and play, from 6 to 8 or 8.30 ; after which retire.

Massachusetts.— State Reform School—These vary with the season. At present (Oct. 1, 1865), as follows : From 5.30 to 6, rise, wash, &c.; 6 to 6.45, school ; 6.45 to 7, recreation ; 7 to 7.30, breakfast ; 7.30 to 11.30, work, excepting recess ; 11.30 to 12 M., recreation ; 12 to 12.30, dinner ; 12.30 to 2.30, work ; 2.30 to 3, recreation ; 3 to 4.45, school ; 4.45 to 5, recreation ; 5 to 5.30, supper ; 5.30 to 5.45 recreation ; 5.45 to 7.15, school ; 7.15 to 7.30, recess ; 7.30 to 8, devotional exercises, and then retire. Nautical Branch—Piped up at 5.30 A. M.; wash ; breakfast at 6 ; one-half go into school at 9 A. M., and remain there three hours in the morning, and the same have three hours' schooling in the afternoon, the others performing ship's duties. Dinner at 12. Supper, 5 P. M. Piped to hammocks half an hour after sunset. State Industrial Girls' School—Rise at a quarter before 6 ; breakfast ; attend prayers in chapel at half past 6 (in summer); work (sewing, knitting, braiding and housework) ; recess at 10 A. M.; work till dinner ; recess of an hour and a half ; school from

2 to 5 ; supper; recess; work in sewing room and housework ; retire at 8.

Michigan—The proceedings of the day begin with the ringing of the yard bell by the watchman, at 5:30, A. M., to awaken the boys, officers and employés. Fifteen minutes is given for the boys to dress and make their beds, when the bell is again rung, summoning the officers who have charge of the boys' washing and morning meal to duty, and the boys to the yard.

Each boy is furnished with a tin vessel, which he brings down with him every morning and places bottom upward on a shelf numbered to correspond with that of his vessel and room. After a few moments necessary delay, they fall in line at the beating of the drum and march in military order to the bath-room. This is a room 35 by 59 feet, fitted up with water-pipes, so that the boys can wash under running water only. When they have washed and combed, they form in line again, and march to the dining-hall, where they are seated at tables, each large enough for four-teen boys. Two of these act as chiefs or captains; and are chosen from the highest grade of boys, *morally*, in the school. They are held responsible for the good conduct of those placed under their care. When all are quietly seated, each chief reports to the officer present the number of boys at his table, the number and names of the absentees, if any, and their whereabouts if known. Immedi-ately following this, a brief prayer is recited by the boys, after which all commence eating. Twenty minutes are allowed, when the whistle calls to *order*, which means folded arms. Another sound of the whistle notifies the chiefs that the time has arrived for the boys to be in school. Each chief raps his boys to a stand-ing position, and successively marches them to the school-room, where they remain for one hour, busy with their books. At 8 A. M., the bell rings the boys to the yard, for 15 minutes' recrea-tion, after which they go to their work, some to the shops, others to the house and farm. They are employed until 12, M., having a recess at 10:30. At 12 they go to the yard, form in line and pre-pare for dinner, which occupies the time until 1, P. M., as for the morning meal. At 1, the boys go to the shops and remain till 4, having a recess of ten minutes at 2:30. They assemble in the yard at four and play for half an hour, when they prepare for supper. At 5, they go to the school-room, where the large boys remain till 8, the small boys until seven o'clock. Devotions are held in the school-room both morning and evening; and after evening devotions they go to their dormitories.

The exercises of the day are varied a little, according to the season, as may be seen by the time table in the by-laws.

MISSOURI.—*Time Table for Months of May, June, July and August.*

	H. M.	H. M.	H. M.

Night watchman will call overseer of kitchen and dining rooms_____ 4:30

Night watchman will call superintendent and assistants _____ 4:45

Night watchman will have bell rung for at least three minutes_____ 5:00

Boys rise, dress, make beds, wash and prepare for breakfast____ _____ 5:00 to 5:40 = 0:40

Clothing and general appearance of boys inspected by ass't superintendent and principal teacher _____ _____ 5:40 to 5:50 = 0:10

Breakfast _____ 5:50 to 6:15 = 0:25

Recreation _____ 6:15 to 6:30 = 0:15

Morning prayers_____ 6:30 to 6:45 = 0:15

School (recess from 7:45 to 8:00)_____ 6:45 to 9:00 = 2:15

Labor_____ 9:00 to 12:00 = 3:00

(Small boys in pleasant weather on play ground, under eye of female teacher, from 9:00 to 9:30. In wet weather go into knitting room.)

Recess and boys counted on line_____ 10:30 to 10:40 = 0:10

School for classes of boys not necessarily employed at industrial pursuits_____ 11:00 to 12:00 = 1:00

Preparation for dinner, dinner and recreation 12:00 to 1:00 = 1:00

(Writing classes for small boys and those not employed in tailor shop, laundry, or on the farm, and also for backward ones employed in those departments, 1:00 to to 1:35, P. M.: recess of 15 minutes for small boys.)

Labor (recess of 10 minutes at 3 o'clock, small boys remain in yard 25 minutes, or 'till 3:25)_____ 1:00 to 4:30 = 3:30

Preparation for school_____ 4:30 to 4:45 = 0:15

School _____ 4:45 to 5:45 = 1:00

Supper and recreation_____ 5:45 to 6:15 = 0:30

(The boys should be seated in the dining-room at 10 minutes to 6, and should be seated again in the school-room at 20 minutes past 6.)

School _____ 6:20 to 7:20 = 1:00

(Singing school Monday and Thursday evenings, between 4:45 and 5:45. The ass't sup't when on the premises, will lead in this exercise.)

Evening prayers_____ 7:20 to 7:40 = 0:20

Retire to bed_____ 7:40 to 7:50 = 0:10

420

Ohio.—At 5.15, A. M., first bell; at 5.30, A. M., unlock dormitories; from 5.45 to 6, A. M., recess; from 6 to 7, school; from 7 to 7.30, breakfast; from 7.30 to 8, recess; from 8 to 10, work in shop and elsewhere; from 10 to 10.10, recess; from 10.10 to 12, M., work; from 12 to 12.30, P. M., dinner; from 12.30 to 1, recess; from 1 to 4, work; from 4 to 5. recess; from 5 to 5.30, supper; from 5.30 to 7.30, school, closing with devotions; at 7.30, retire to water-closets, followed by a parade and march to sleeping rooms, where they are locked in for the night. At 9, P. M., lights turned down—all quiet.

Pennsylvania.—The inmates rise at 5 o'clock; after washing and combing their hair, repair to the school rooms, where devotional exercises are held. Afterwards, a school session of two hours commences. Have a recess of 15 minutes in the yard, and breakfast at 7½. At 8 go to the work-shops; have 10 minutes during the forenoon for recreation. At 12, M., prepare for dinner; after dinner they spend 30 minutes in the yards. At 1, P. M., go to work again; have 10 minutes in the yards during the afternoon. At 5 prepare for supper; 15 minutes in the yards after supper. At a quarter to 6, school session for the evening commences. At 15 minutes of eight, after devotional exercises, they are dismissed to their dormitories for the night.

Boys employed in the shops are generally tasked, and if done before the time for general dismissal, they can go to the yards or do overwork for which they are paid. The smallest boys, not employed in the shops, have two additional school sessions, of an hour and a half each, both forenoon and afternoon. Books from the library are furnished every day. The girls are employed in household duties, and have two daily school sessions of two hours each, with sufficient time for recreation.

Rhode Island.—5, A. M., teachers, overseers and matrons, called; 5 to 5.10, inmates rise, and arrange their beds; 5.10 to 5.15, pass from halls; 5. 15 to 5.25, washrooms; 5.25 to 7, school; 7 to 7.15, recess; 7.15 to 7.35, breakfast; 7.35 to 7.50, morning devotions; 7.50 to 8, recess: 8 to 10, workshops; 10 to 10.10, recess; 10.10 to 12, work; 12 to 12.15, P. M., wash-room; 12.15 to 12.40, dinner; 12.40 to 1, recess; 1 to 2.30, work; 2.30 to 2.40, recess; 2.40 to 4, work; 4 to 4.15, wash-rooms; 4.15 to 4.35, supper; 4.35 to 4.45, recess; 4.45 to 6.30, school; 6.30 to 6.45, recess; 6.45 to 7, evening devotions; 7, retire to bed.

This arrangement of time has continued the same or nearly so, from the opening of the institution, a little more time being, for the past few years, allowed for play and school; a little less for work and sleep.

Wisconsin.—Rise at 5.30, A. M. ; breakfast at 6.30; devotional exercises at 6.50; school at 7; labor at 9; dinner at 12.30, P. M. ; recreation; school at 1.30; labor at 3.30; supper at 6.30; devotional exercises at 7; recreation; retire from 8 to 9; all officers and employés retire before 10.

The bell rings at 12 M. and 6, P. M., to close work and prepare for meals. From October 1st to April 1st, we rise at 6, A. M., and close work at 5.30

QUESTION XXIII.

What are the proceedings of a Sabbath?

ANSWERS.

Connecticut.—The inmates attend Sabbath-school from half past eight till half past nine. Religious service by superintendent at half past ten. Preaching at four, P. M.

Illinois,—At 7.15, the boys rise; at 7.30, the boys breakfast; at 8.00, the boys attend prayers; at 8.20 to 9.00, change shoes and put on collars, having bathed and changed clothing Saturday afternoon; 10.30 to 12 M., public worship; 12.15, P. M., dinner; 1.15 to 2.45, Sunday-school; 5.00 to 6.00, singing exercise; 6.00 to 6.30, prayers and good advice for closing duties of day; 7.00, retire.

Maine.—Religious services in the chapel in the morning; Sabbath school in the afternoon. After learning their Sabbath school lessons, the boys are permitted to read their library books and papers, and to converse with one another.

Maryland.—At 6, A. M., rise; at 7, breakfast; 7 to 9, dressing and preparing for chapel; $9\frac{1}{2}$ to $10\frac{1}{2}$. Sunday-school with teachers from the city; $10\frac{1}{2}$ to 11, exercise in the yard; 11 to 12, in school rooms preparing scriptural lessons; 12 to $1\frac{1}{2}$, dinner and exercise in play grounds; $1\frac{1}{2}$ to $2\frac{1}{2}$, in school rooms reading or studying scriptures; $2\frac{1}{2}$ to 3, washing and exercise in yard; 3 to $4\frac{1}{2}$, regular religious services in chapel; $5\frac{1}{2}$ to 7, supper and exercise in play ground; 7 to 8, vocal music in chapel; at 8, retire.

Massachusetts—State Reform School.—From 6 to 6.30, rise, wash, &c.; 6.30 to 7, breakfast; 7 to 8, yard and necessary house work; 8 to 9, school room, preparing Sunday school lesson, reading, &c.; 9 to 10, Sunday-school; 10 to 10.30, yard; 10.30 to 11.30, schoolroom, reading, singing, &c.; 11.30 to 12, yard; 12 to 12.30, dinner; 12.30 to 3, yard or school room; 3 to 4.30, chapel service; 4.30 to 5, yard; 5 to 5.30, supper; 5.30 to 6.30, necessary work and yard; 6.30 to 8, general exercises in chapel, singing and recitations, closing with devotional exercises. Nautical Branch.—Episcopal church service at half past 10, A. M., with addresses by gentlemen of different religious denominations; Sunday-school in the afternoon. Industrial School for Girls.—The inmates attend preaching in chapel at 9, A. M., and Sabbath school in chapel at 3, P. M. The Sabbath school exercises are conducted by the superintendent, the lessons having been prepared previously, with much care, under the supervision of the teachers. The exercises consist of a lesson in scripture biography, each family answering in concert, successively, and a simpler lesson in

Bible history, in which the superintendent calls upon any member of the school to answer separately; also, recitations of passages of scripture by ten girls every Sabbath, and general exercise from one family per Sabbath, consisting of sacred songs, recitations of poetry, and scripture texts, all the exercises being interspersed with singing. The remainder of the day is spent by each family according to the direction of its matron in reading, singing and religious instruction, varying from time to time as her judgment may dictate.

Michigan.—The Sabbath is like the week day, excepting there is no work, no play and no day school. A Sunday school is held from 9 to 10 A. M. The remainder of the forenoon is spent in singing, reading and walking in the yard. Chapel exercises are from half-past two until four P. M. The evening spent in reading, singing and talking until seven, when the boys retire.

Missouri.—Arrangement of time on Sundays: Morning prayers, 6:30 to 7 A. M.; boys with principal teacher, 7 to 8 A. M.; boys have recreation on play ground, 8 to 8:30 A. M.; boys with assistant superintendent in school room, 8:30 to 9:30 A. M.; boys walk in the play ground, 9:30 to 10 A. M.; Sunday-school for both sexes, under the instruction of the superintendent, 10 to 11:15 A. M.; boys on play ground, 11:15 to 12 A. M.; dinner and recreation, 12 to 1 P. M.; in school room with a teacher, 1 to 2 P. M.; recreation on the play ground, 2 to 3 P. M.; lecture, 3 to 4:15 P. M.; recreation on the play ground, 4:15 to 5 P. M.; supper and recreation, 5 to 5:30 P. M.; in school room with principal teacher, 5:30 to 6:30 P. M.; evening prayers, 6:30 to 7 P. M.; retire to bed at 7 P. M.

NOTE.—Between 7 and 8 A. M. the boys are taught in singing. Between 8:30 and 9:30 they listen to the reading of some appropriate book or paper. Between 10 and 11:15 they receive instruction from the Scriptures. Between 1 and 2 P. M. they listen to readers in their rooms.

The female Sunday-school at 10 o'clock is under the supervision of the matron in female department.

Ohio.—At 5:45 A. M., first bell; at 6 A. M., unlock dormitories; from 6:15 to 6:30 A. M., recess; from 6:30 to 7:15 A. M., devotions and Sunday-school exercises; from 7:15 to 7:45 A. M., breakfast; from 7:45 to 9 A. M., recess; from 9 to 10 A. M., exercises in chapel, consisting of singing, prayer, reading the Scriptures, a short, appropriate lecture, and oral instruction; from 10 to 10:45 A. M., recess, from 10:45 to 12 M., Sunday-school exercises in school rooms; from 12 to 12:30 P. M., dinner; from 12:30 to 1 P. M., recess; from 1 to 2 P. M., in school rooms—the exercises of this session are the reading of interesting books to the children, and oral instruction; from 2 to 2:30 P. M., recess; from 2:30 to 3:30 P. M., chapel exercises, consisting of usual devotional exercises, and a sermon by the chaplain; from 3:30 to 5 P. M., recess; from 5 to 5:30 P. M., supper; from 5:30 to 7 P. M., school exercises, same as 1 o'clock; at 7 o'clock, P. M., devotional exercises, a short recess and march to sleeping apartments and lock-up for the night; at 9 P. M., last bell.

Pennslyvania.—On the Sabbath the inmates rise an hour later, and after devotional exercises, breakfast. Sunday-school from 8:30 to 9:30; at 10, religious services in the chapel begin. From after dinner till 3 o'clock, the time is occupied in reading library books. At 3, religious services in the chapel. After supper the inmates are instructed in singing, and after devotional exercises, retire to their dormitories an hour earlier than during the week.

Wisconsin.—On the morning of the Sabbath, half an hour is usually spent in devotional exercises, after which, Sunday-school papers are distributed. A special monitor is chosen by the boys, whose duty it is to report any conduct improper for the day. The time is occupied in reading, washing and dressing till half past ten, when all assemble in the schoolroom, where the ordinary religious services are conducted. In the afternoon, at two o'clock, a Sunday-school is organized; most of the school being formed into classes of five or six, with teachers. About one hour and a half is thus occupied, the remainder of the time is filled up with reading and singing; the officers and teachers often collecting the children in groups, and reading Sunday-school books and papers to them. The whole time is appropriated.

QUESTION XXIV.

Have the children committed to this institution any right of protection against the decision of the functionaries who sent them here, and if so, what is it, and is it ever exercised?

ANSWERS.

Connecticut.—By writ of *habeas corpus*, any boy can be brought before a court for a rehearing. Only two cases of the kind have occurred in eleven years.

Illinois.—Only the right of *habeas corpus*. Recourse is not unfrequently had to it; about thirty boys have been discharged in this way within a year.

Maine.—We think they have the same right of protection against the functionaries who sentence them here, as criminals have against the magistrates who sentence them; but it has never been exercised.

Maryland.—Their cases can be brought before the courts by writ of *habeas corpus*, and this is sometimes done.

Massachusetts.—State Ref. School and Nautical Branch—Yes, such a right exists, and is sometimes exercised, but there never has been any trouble in this State. Industrial School for Girls—The following is an extract from the statute: "Any girl who shall be ordered to be committed to said school, under the provisions of this act, may appeal from such order, in the same manner and upon the same terms as is now provided in respect to appeals in criminal cases; and the appeal shall be entered, tried and finally determined in the court to which the same shall be made, in like manner as if it had been commenced there originally." There has never been any such appeal.

Michigan.—No doubt the legality of the commitment might be tested by *habeas corpus*, but I have never known an instance where it has been done.

Missouri.—Yes, either the children or their parents may test the legality of their commitment by *habeas corpus*. No inmate has ever made such a request, but the right is often exercised by parents and guardians.

Maryland.—They have such right, and it is sometimes used.

Pennsylvania.—Every commitment of a child sent here is carefully examined by a committee of the managers, specially appointed for this purpose ; their action is then reviewed by the entire board ; and even then, the commitment is not absolute in its character until examined by one of the judges of our courts. All this is done to see that the child is properly and legally commited. If after all this the parent is not satisfied, he can have the case reviewed by writ of habeas corpus. The right is occasionally exercised.

Rhode Island.—They have, by *habeas corpus*, but the right has been used in only one case.

Wisconsin.—The writ of *habeas corpus* could be granted upon proper application, but has never been asked for. The power to pardon rests with the Governor, but cannot be exercised without a certificate of good behavior from the superintendent. This power has been exercised two or three times, but *always to the injury of the inmate.*

QUESTION XXV.

Have the children separate sleeping rooms?

ANSWERS.

Connecticut.—The rooms are designed for one, but two boys are often put into one room.

Illinois.—They have not; they sleep in hammocks in common dormitories.

Maine.—They have separate rooms.

Maryland.—About two-thirds have separate rooms.

Massachusetts.—State Ref. School—Not all have separate sleeping rooms, but all have separate beds. Nautical Branch.—No, they have not. Industrial School for Girls.—One dormitory in each house accommodates 10; the remaining girls have separate rooms.

Michigan.—152 have separate rooms; the remainder sleep in dormitory halls, and a large room fitted up for the purpose.

Missouri.—They have not; they sleep in large dormitories.

Ohio.—They have separate rooms, except one division of small boys.

Pennsylvania.—They have separate sleeping rooms.

Rhode Island.—No, except about 30 of the larger girls. From two to four occupy each room, except the general sleeping room, for the smaller boys, occupied by some thirty-five boys. Each child is furnished with a separate bed.

Wisconsin.—The design was to provide separate sleeping rooms for all, but our crowded condition compels us, often, to put two into the same room, or rather into the same *bed*, in the larger rooms and halls.

QUESTION XXVI.

May they communicate with each other during the day, or is the law of silence enforced?

ANSWERS.

Connecticut.—The inmates are together in the yards, and, of course, communicate.

Illinois.—May communicate as much as they please, on the play ground.

Maine.—The boys have unrestricted communication on the play ground.

Maryland.—Free communication at play, is allowed.

Massachusetts.—State Reform School.—They can communicate, as in any family school. Nautical Branch.--They may communicate; there is no law of silence. Girl's Industrial School.—They communicate as members of a family.

Michigan.—We do not enforce silence as in prisons, but do not expect them to communicate during school or work hours.

Missouri.—They may communicate freely *during the time allotted to recreation*, with members of their own division. The boys are separated into two divisions, with reference to their ages; the younger being placed in one division, and the older in another, The law of silence is enforced, as far as it is deemed practicable, in work rooms, in which several (*say*) 10 to 30 are employed.

Ohio.—The inmates of each division may communicate with each other while on the play ground only; but one division is not allowed to communicate with another division.

Pennsylvania.—White—In the school rooms and workshops, conversation is not permitted, but in the yards, free scope is given them, subject to the supervision of the officer of the yard. Colored.—Proper communication is allowed at all times.

Rhode Island.—Free communication during the hours for recreation, always under the supervision of an officer.

Wisconsin.—Boys and girls are not allowed to communicate with each other, but each sex is permitted to communicate and play together, as in ordinary boarding-schools.

Question XXVII.

How much of their time do the children spend in school.

Answers.

Connecticut.—Four and a half hours per day.
Illinois.—Four hours.
Maine.—Four hours.
Maryland.—Four hours.
Massachusetts.—State Reform School—Four hours in school. Nautical Branch.—Six hours in school every other day. Industrial School for Girls.—Three hours a day in school.
Michigan.—They are in school five hours for six months of the year; four hours for three months, and three hours for three months.
Missouri.—About one-half of the boys are occupied *four hours and a half*, in school, the other half, *six hours and forty-five minutes*, per day. In the female department, the time occupied in school by the older girls, is about four hours daily; the small girls are in school about five hours daily.
Ohio.—They are in school on Sunday, five hours, on other days three.
Pennsylvania.—White—Four hours each day in school. Colored.—Two hours a day.
Rhode Island.—About four hours per day.
Wisconsin.—In school four hours daily

Question XXVIII.

What branches of learning do they pursue ?

Answers.

Connecticut.—The branches studied, are spelling, reading, writing, arithmetic, geography and grammar. A few study algebra and philosophy.
Illinois.—They study, reading, spelling, writing, arithmetic and geography.
Maine.—Reading, writing, geography and arithmetic.
Maryland.—They learn orthography, reading, penmanship, grammar, arithmetic, algebra, philosophy, music, both vocal and instrumental.
Massachusetts.—They are taught the common English braches, and in the Nautical Branch, navigation in addition. Industrial School for Girls.—The girls study reading, spelling, writing, arithmetic, geography, and general exercises of a miscellaneous character.
Michigan.—Reading, writing, arithmetic and geography.
Missouri.—They are taught the ordinary English branches.

Ohio.—Reading, writing, arithmetic, geography, grammar, &c.
Pennsylvania.—All the primary branches of an English education.
Rhode Island.—They learn the same as in our public schools, so far as the capacity of the children admits of it.
Wisconsin.—Spelling, reading, writing, arithmetic, geography, &c.

QUESTION XXIX.

What progres in general is made by them?

ANSWERS.

Connecticut.—They learn as rapidly as any class of boys.
Illinois.—Their progress equals that in the public schools.
Maine.—They advance about as far as the pupils of our grammar schools.
Maryland.—Variable; some make good progress, others very little.
Massachusetts.—Their progress will compare favorably with other schools. Industrial School for Girls.—Sufficient progress for ordinary intercourse with the world.
Michigan.—They are generally making very fair progress, nearly the same as in our common schools.
Missouri.—Taking into consideration the fact that they have no time out of the regular school hours to prepare their lessons, the improvement made is satisfactory.
Ohio.—Their progress is, generally, very fair.
Pennsylvania—White.—Progress, generally, very commendable. Colored.—With a few exceptions, they can read, write and cypher before leaving the institution.
Wisconsin.—Their progress will compare favorably with most common schools of the same grade.

QUESTION XXX.

Is there a library, and if so, how extensive, and what is the general character of the books?

ANSWERS.

Connecticut.—The library contains about 1,500 volumes, of a very miscellaneous description.
Illinois.—500 volumes, mostly Sunday-school books.
Maine—800 volumes, of miscellaneous character.
Maryland.—The library contains about 650 volumes, and is of miscellaneous character.
Massachusetts—State Reform School.—The library consists of 1,600 volumes, of miscellaneous character—biography, history and works of fiction, by such authors as Irving, Scott, Dickens, &c.; also, books usually found in Sunday-school libraries. Nautical

Branch.—Library contains 700 volumes, adapted to children, boys especially. Industrial School for Girls.—1,200 volumes, comprising juvenile, historical, moral and religious works.

Michigan—Library consists of historical, biographical and miscellaneous works. [Number of volumes not stated.]

Missouri.—The library is very small, not more than 150 volumes, which were donated several years ago. The books on hand are chiefly biographical.

Ohio.—There are 565 books in the library of the female department, and 585 in that of the male department. They are of a moral and instructive character.

Pennsylvania.—White—There is a library for both girls and boys, numbering about 2,500 volumes. The books are such as are adapted to their intellects—biographies, histories, and moral and instructive tales, &c. Colored—There is a library containing 1,200 volumes, of a moral and religious character.

Rhode Island.—About 1,200 volumes—history, biography, travels, &c., with miscellaneous works, selected with much care to meet the wants of our children.

Wisconsin.—Only a Sabbath school library of about 400 volumes.

QUESTION XXXI.

Are the children as a general thing fond of reading, and what time do they have for it?

ANSWERS.

Connecticut.—Those that can read well love to read; the others do not.

Illinois.—A portion of them are very fond of reading. They have their play-time and a part of Saturday and Sunday to devote to it.

Maine.—The boys manifest great interest in reading. Besides the time they have on the Sabbath, they have one hour every day that they can devote to that employment.

Maryland.—They are fond of reading. They have time for it during play hours and on the Sabbath.

Massachusetts.—State Reform School—They are very fond of reading, and much pains is taken to cultivate the habit. In some of the work rooms reading aloud by the overseer is a daily custom. The daily papers are regularly placed in the work-shops. A portion of Wednesday and Saturday is set apart for reading, in addition to the time they have on Sunday. Nautical Branch— They generally like reading; they have Sunday afternoons for it. Girls' School—Many of them are. Mornings and evenings it is customary to have some one read aloud in the sewing room, for the benefit of all. Those who wish to do so, spend a portion of their hours for recreation in reading, and several hours of the Sabbath are also devoted to it.

Michigan.—Many are fond of reading, and some time is given to it on Saturday and Sunday evenings.

Missouri.—They are. The time allotted to recreation affords an opportunity to those who are inclined to read. Lights are kept burning in the boys' bed-room all night, and those who are disposed to read for an hour, between 8 and 9 o'clock, may do so under the supervision of the night watchman, who remains in the room during the entire night.

Ohio.—They are generally very fond of reading, and have about two hours a day for it, which may be increased one-half hour by careful attention to their work.

Pennsylvania.—Many manifest a strong desire for reading. They have time every day to devote to it.

Rhode Island.—They are fond of reading, and have half an hour each day from the school hours, or more if lessons are thoroughly committed; also the school hour of Saturday, and about two hours on Sunday.

Wisconsin.—Some are fond of it, and spend their play-time in that way. Others read but little, except on the Sabbath.

QUESTION XXXII.

Are they all taught a trade?

ANSWERS.

The replies are all substantially the same. It is not an object to teach the children a trade; but they all have regular work, and are trained to habits of industry. The girls are instructed in household labor and in plain sewing. Some boys acquire a trade.

QUESTION XXXIII.

What are the different handicrafts carried on in the institution?

ANSWERS.

Connecticut.—Mostly on cane seat chairs; about 20 on the farm and 30 in the sewing shop.

Illinois.—Shoemaking, tailoring, basket-making, cane seating chairs and farming.

Maine.—Shoemaking, chair seating, sewing and knitting, farming, and brick and tile making.

*Maryland—*Shoemaking, combing and assorting bristles, tailoring, box making, farming and gardening.

Massachusetts.—State Reform School: Chair-seating, sewing and knitting, washing, domestic work, shoemaking, farming and gardening. They are taught to be industrious, and prepared to learn a trade. Nautical Branch—Practical seamanship. Girls' school—They are taught housework, knitting, braiding and plain sewing.

Michigan.—Tailoring, shoemaking, matting and weaving chair seats, farming, gardening, and braiding palm leaf hats.

Missouri.—At present shoemaking, to a limited extent tailoring, and knitting stockings for the use of the institution. The cooking, washing, ironing &c., are done by inmates. A limited number are also employed in gardening.

Ohio.—All the boys, not employed in performing the necessary work of the institution, are engaged in manufacturing shoes. The females are employed in the laundry, sewing room, kitchen, knitting room, hall and chamber work.

Pennsylvania.—Brushmaking, shoemaking, boxmaking, chairmaking, blacksmithing, the manufacture of umbrella wires, match boxes, and shoes for the inmates of both the white and colored departments.

Rhode Island.—Shoemaking.

Wisconsin.—Shoemaking and tailoring.

QUESTION XXXIV.

Is the labor of the children let out on the contract principle, or do they work for the institution?

ANSWERS.

Connecticut.—They work for the institution; none on contract.

Illinois.—They work for the institution.

Maine.—They work for the institution.

Maryland.—About one-half are let out on contract.

Massachusetts.—The officers of the institution have entire charge of the work and discipline of the boys. Girls' Industrial School: They work for the institution, a small portion of the profit being allowed the girls, to be spent at the discretion of the matron.

Michigan.—The children work for the institution or for others, by the piece, under the direction of the officers of the institution. We think contract labor pernicious to the best interests of the school.

Missouri.—They work for the institution. In the tailor shop work is done for the clothing stores by the piece.

Ohio.—All the boys, with the exception of those doing work for the institution, are contracted for by a Cincinnati firm, engaged in the manufacture of shoes.

Pennsylvania.—They are hired at so much a day to contractors. As $7\frac{1}{2}$ hours of the day are devoted to active labor in the shops, and this portion of the time constitutes about one-half of the days' exercises, it is important that the supervision of the boys should be entrusted only to those whose moral habits and kindly dispositions qualify them for so important a charge.

The system of labor, as at present administered, is radically defective. The children are hired to contractors at so much *per diem*, and it is reasonable to suppose that a pecuniary advantage to them is the only motive for the contract. Those immediately entrusted with the government of the boys are generally but illy qualified for so responsible a position. The amount of labor they exact is the *sine qua non* of their exertions. If the work be well done and a reasonable amount of it, they are satisfied. These seven and a half hours of labor are spent without one moral lesson taught the boys, at least so far as the workmen of the shops are concerned.

With respect to the enforcement of the discipline, as the overseers act merely in a monitorial capacity, and are not properly officers of the institution, frequent complaints on the part of the boys are heard, and in many cases it is difficult to determine which is the aggrieved party; but as it would be destructive to discipline, unless in a well attested case, to condemn the action of the overseers, it necessarily follows that their complaints must generally be received as truthful.

If the labor of the boys is profitable to those who employ them, it certainly ought to be as profitable to the institution, and so far as the mere profit is concerned ought to inure to its benefit, producing an important addition to its receipts, besides the accession of a number of officers, who would not only be serviceable in the work shops, but in many other respects. Those entrusted with the management of the boys in the shops would be selected, not merely with reference to their mechanical skill, but a capactity for imparting instruction, a kindly disposition, and correct moral habits, would be indispensable qualifications.

If a reformatory institution availed itself of the entire profit of the labor of the boys, its receipts would be materially increased; there would be the enforcement of better discipline in the shops, and the opportunity afforded to those constantly with the boys to inculcate wholesome, moral truths connected with their avocations.

Rhode Island.—The labor of the children is let out on the contract principle.

Wisconsin.—All work for the institution under the supervision of our own officers.

Qestion XXXV.

Has the institution a chaplain? If so, how much of his time is given to the inmates?

Answers.

There are but two of these reformatories, which report resident chaplains—those of Ohio and Michigan—and the latter of these was vacant at the time we made our tour of inspection. In one— the Massachusetts State Industrial School for Girls—the superintendent, Rev. Mr. Ames, holds, at the same time, the position of chaplain. In all the others, religious services are conducted either by the superintendents or by clergymen of the place, in rotation.

Question XXXVI.

To what extent are efforts made to cultivate the hearts of the children, and to inculcate the principles of religion and morality ?

Answers.

Connecticut.—By "precept upon precept—here a little and there a little."

Illinois.—Efforts are constantly made to this end.

Maryland.—Morning and evening · devotional exercises, and Sabbath-school, with teachers from the various churches in the city, and regular preaching in the afternoon of each Sabbath by clergymen of the city

Massachusetts.—State Reform School.—As much as can be made by precept and example.

Nautical Branch.—"We do what we can." Girls' Industrial— efforts are made under the present board of officers, to a remarkable extent.

Michigan.—We labor daily, as opportunity offers, while mingling with the boys, to give advice with regard to this life and the next, pointing to the Bible as the chart to be guided by, in connection with our Sabbath-school — and puplic worship every Sabbath.

Missouri.—We aim to secure the services of pious men and women in every department of the institution. The scriptures are read morning and evening, in presence of all, officers and inmates. Christian duties are inculcated both by precept and example, and every possible effort is made to secure the services of employés whose daily lives are in harmony with the spirit of christianity, as exhibited in the New Testament. On the Sabbath, faithful teachers endeavor to impress upon the hearts of our children the words and the spirit of the Bible, or portions which seem to be best adapted to the end in view. "Line upon line and precept upon precept" are given in the firm belief that God will bless his own work in the salvation of the souls committed to our care.

Ohio.—It is a fixed purpose to instil into the minds of the children moral and religious sentiments, and to keep them under these influences as far as possible.

Pennsylvania.—The entire discipline is intended to impress itself upon the hearts of the children and teach them the principles of religion and morality. Special efforts arise from Sabbath-school instruction, chapel exercises, and private conversations.

Wisconsin.—Morning and evening prayers are observed and special, pointed addresses are often made, enforcing particular truths. Great pains are taken to illustrate and enforce the truths of christianity.

Question XXXVII.

How much importance is attached to efforts of this kind ?

Answers.

All respond in substantially the same terms. The following are some of the sentences contained in the replies received:

"It is considered of the highest importance, for unless the heart is reached, nothing is accomplished."

"The greatest importance is attached to the sowing of the truth and impressing it upon the heart in a manner adapted to the capacity and understanding of a child."

"Judicious effort in moral and religious culture cannot be over-estimated."

"We regard it as of the highest importance, believing no reform to be thorough and permanent without this."

"Such efforts, combined with labor, we think the true helps to reform."

"It is our great purpose to reform the children by cultivating their moral and religious sentiments, and urging correct deportment from principle, rather than by exacting it on compulsion."

"The daily administration of the discipline and special efforts to arouse the children to a sense of their duties and obligations as responsible and immortal beings, must afford the only sure hope of their becoming virtuous."

"Great importance is attached to the mental and moral culture of the inmates; it is the groundwork of reformation; we seek to awaken the intellect as the only avenue to the conscience; to subdue vicious propensities by the careful cultivation of virtuous principles."

Question XXXVIII.

When a youth is received into the establishment, are any, and if any, what instructions given him as to his future conduct?

Answers.

Connecticut.—No special instructions are given.

Illinois.—He is told that whatever his former life may have been, it is past; but from the first he will establish his character with us by his behavior each day, and we give him the utmost confidence so long as he proves worthy of it.

Maryland.—He is made to understand, as far as possible, that we are his friends, who are desirous of doing what we can to train him to habits of industry and morality; and, in short, to make him a useful member of the community. He is urged to break away from every evil habit, and make a great effort, for his own good, to improve in every respect.

Massachusetts.—State Ref. School—He is informed of the regulations, and efforts are made to gain his confidence. Girls' Industrial.—That implicit and cheerful obedience will be required.

Michigan.—When a youth is received into the school, we first of all try to make him feel as if the institution was a home, and that he has come to live with friends who will not treat him as a criminal, but as a *mistaken* boy. Many times they come to us in irons, as to a prison, with feelings depressed and hatred toward all. After they become acquainted with us and with the institution, we try to convince them that they have not only broken man's laws, but God's laws, and that to reform, they must begin to acquire such habits as they will want when men.

Missouri.—He is advised to shun the company of those who show themselves to be disobedient and refractory; to be obedient to the instructions of his care-takers, and kind toward his associates. Inmates are brought from the city to the institution—four miles—by officers of the institution, who take these opportunities to converse with children before they are allowed to mingle with the inmates.

Ohio.—When the children are received into the institution, they are informed with regard to their duty and what is expected of them under the rules, and their necessary deportment is clearly defined.

Pennsylvania.—Every one committed here is very kindly told that he has been placed under discipline, that he may become wiser and better—that in his treatment here we shall have no reference to the offence he committed, no matter how grave its nature, but shall look merely to the exhibition of character developed here, and for this only shall he be rewarded or censured. He is then instructed in the general rules that are to regulate his conduct, and encouraged to live up to them.

Rhode Island.—He is carefully and fully instructed as to his duty.

Wisconsin.—All inmates are received upon the same grade. They are informed that the school is not a place for punishment, and their treatment must depend upon their subsequent behavior. The design of the school is often explained to them as opening up before them the only sure avenue to honor and usefulness.

QUESTION XXXIX.

Are the inmates divided into classes according to their conduct; and if so, how many classes are there, and how are the details of the classification arranged?

ANSWERS.

Connecticut.—They are not classsified.

Illinois.—They are graded by to their behavior and have privileges accordingly, the superintendent hearing and deciding upon every case. We are dividing, as rapidly as possible, into families of 30 each, which will be classified in a measure by their character.

Maine.—They are divided into five classes—1st, 2d, 3d and 4th grades, and class of "Truth and Honor." When a boy is received into the school, he is placed in the third grade, and is promoted or degraded according to his deportment.

Maryland.—They are classified. We have five grades known as 4th, 3d, 2d, 1st, and Truth and Honor. When a child is received, he is placed in the third grade. If his conduct is good, he is promoted after a probation of four weeks to the second grade, and in like manner to the 1st and to "Truth and Honor." It usually takes a boy about three weeks to attain the highest grade. We do not regard these grades as a genuine test of character, but simply as a system of discipline, as a shrewd bad boy may make an effort and actually attain the highest grade of the house, merely as a matter of policy, while at heart he may be an unprincipled lad. We keep a daily record of every boy's conduct. The grades are arranged, weekly, from this record, at which time a report is made of each boy's record in presence of the whole school.

Massachusetts.—State Ref. School—The inmates are not divided into classes in the congregate department according to their conduct, but a daily record is kept of each, and the better boys are graded as far as we have room, into places of trust, such as our "Family houses," of which we have three, accommodating 84 boys. Here they work on the farm and garden, eat at the same table and of the same food as their officers and teachers, and have the usual freedom of boys on a farm. From these families, if they do well, they go home on probation, or are indentured to places. If their behaviour is not good, they are returned to the congregate department, and others put in their places. Girls' Industrial.—They are not classified.

Michigan.—Our school is not divided, but we try to keep the older from the younger ones, as will be seen from the report.

Missouri.—We have, in the male department, two play grounds, one for boys 14 to 16 years of age, and the other for boys of 12 years and under. The inmates are all graded or classified according to their behaviour while in the institution. The grades are (beginning with the lowest) 4, 3, 2, 1, and first, second, third and fourth "grades of honor." Every inmate, when received, is placed in grade 3 by giving him 600 merits—the number he must subsequently *earn* by good conduct before he can pass to the next higher grade. If, during the first month, he receives more demerits than the total of 8 merits per day, that is, more than 240 if the month contains 30 days, or 248 if it contains 31 days, he falls from three to four; if, on the contrary, he has a balance in his favor at the end of the month, that balance is carried forward from month to month until he has saved 600 over and above demerits, when he is entitled to grade No, 2. In this way he may go on until he reaches the 4th "grade of honor," which, by a rule adopted by our Board of Managers, entitles him to a discharge. Notice that a balance *against* any boy at the end of the month, *is not carried forward*, but cancelled, so that he has an opportunity of beginning the next month with nothing against him but the fact that he has made *no progress*. The very best deportment for 15 consecutive months will entitle a boy to the 4th " grade of honor," and consequently a discharge. *The demerits for any given misdemeanor, are uniform.* For example: Profanity is *always* 32, disobedience 6, &c. The list of misdemeanors and penalties is the same as that used in the Cincinnati House of Refuge.

Ohio—The boys are separated into 3 divisions and the girls into 2. They are classed by age and character when admitted, or subsequently developed.

Pennsylvania.—White—There are two classes, designated by the letters A and B. Those in division A are *under* 15 years of age; in division B, *over* 15. If we should have an inmate under 15, whose history showed him to be an adept in crime, he would be classed in division B, and if there should be one over 15, whose antecedents were generally of a favorable character, he would be classed in division A.

The association of precocious thieves and burglars, whose habits of vice have been of long continuance, with those younger in years, who, if they have committed crime, have been forced by necessity, or urged on by older and more vicious companions, is eminently unwise and productive of incalculable injury.

No matter how vigilant the supervision of officers may be, opportunities will necessarily occur for the communication of all the details of a corrupt life, with the explanation of technicalities and a practical application of skill, which, in too many instances, render nugatory all the moral and religious advice that may be given. Nor is it strange that such is the case. The natural tendency of the heart being evil, combined with a teaching they occasionally receive, and which best suits their corrupt nature, the efforts of their moral instructors are rendered fruitless.

The protection and salvation of the younger and less hardened class, imperatively demand a separation from the other. And with respect to the more corrupt, there is still the same hope that they may be reclaimed from the error of their ways without the danger of their creating a moral malaria that might poison the more innocent and unsuspecting mind.

We have, then, two classes of children that, for obvious reasons should be kept separate. There is also a third class of children that should not associate with either of them—the vagrant and incorrigible.

The vagrants, whose only misfortune is to be without home or friends, and who are dependent upon the benevolence of the community for support, and the incorrigible whose acts of disobedience have been those of truant-playing, or absenting themselves from home, and who have not been guilty of criminal acts, should constitute the third division.

These divisions should be sub-divided into classes of about forty each. They should be under the care and instruction of judicious, kind and pious teachers, who should impart moral and religious truths to them, and advance them in their scholastic education. They should be constantly with their pupils in the play ground, the work-shop, the dining-room, and convenient to them in their dormitories. They should study their peculiar traits of character and apply such remedies as may cure the moral diseases of each. They should share their joys and sorrows and so identify themselves with them as to be of their number in all their innocent pursuits and pleasures, yet at the same time preceptors whose example must be imitated, and whose precepts kindly received.

With so small a number in each class, and competent persons to mould their youthful characters, much greater good would be accomplished than by the system of assigning to one instructor a hundred or more boys, with only occasional opportunities of contributing to their moral and intellectual advancement.

Colored.—The inmates are classified according to conduct. There are eleven classes. A record of each inmate's offences each month is kept, and promotion to a higher grade, suspension, or degradation awarded at the end of the month.

Rhode Island.—The system consists of four grades and four classes—the lowest grade is the fourth; the highest class is the fourth. Each grade above the third, (this being the one where children are placed as admitted) has its privileges; till, on reaching the second and third classes they are often permitted to visit their friends and to go from the institution unattended. On reaching the fourth class, boys are discharged as reformed, and girls placed on trial with friends, where they have suitable friends to take charge of them. When they have not, care is taken to provide suitable places before they reach this class.

Wisconsin.—There are six classes or grades, which are reviewed every month, and promotions are made from the record of behavior. All serious offences and punishments are recorded.

QUESTION XL.

How far are the antecedents of the inmates recorded?

ANSWERS.

Connecticut.—Their parentage, employment, knowledge of books, crimes, &c., are recorded.

Illinois.—All their history is recorded that can be obtained.

Maine.—Employment, habits, character of parents, and such other facts of interest as can be obtained from the boys themselves, or from the officer committing them.

Maryland.—We record everything of interest concerning each child, including habits, character of parents, &c., &c.

Massachusetts.—State Ref. School.—As far as they can be ascer-

tained, we record the general facts of their early history. Girls'
Industrial—We record their birthplace, parentage and age if they
can be ascertained, previous circumstances and opportunities, so
far as they can be ascertained, and causes of committal.

Michigan.—All important facts that can be ascertained.

Missouri.—We ask and obtain, as far as possible, answers to the
following questions, to wit : How old are you ? Your birthplace ?
Your parents' birthplace ? Where do your parents reside ? Their
occupation ? What has been *your* occupation ? How long have
you attended school ? How frequently have you attended Sunday
school ? Church ? Have you been often to the theatre ? Have
you been drunk ? Used profane language ? Have you slept at
night in sheds, or in other places not suitable for boys at night,
who are not driven by necessity from their beds ? Have you
kept the company of men or boys who steal ? How many times,
previously, have you been arrested ? Have any of your relatives
been imprisoned for crime ? Do your parents ever get drunk ?
Do they quarrel ? Have you a step-father, or step-mother ?
What caused you to come to the house of refuge ? Do your
parents use profane language ?

Ohio.—A brief history of the child is recorded, embracing, as
far as practicable, all important facts in regard to the child and his
parentage, his social relations and moral habits.

Pennsylvania—White.—The entire history of the inmates is
taken, up to the time of their admission into the institution. This
embraces their moral, intellectual and industrial training, together
with such knowledge as may be obtained concerning parents,
guardians, &c. Colored.—So far as to enable us to form an opinion of the general character and disposition of the subject.

Rhode Island.—As far as can be gathered from the children,
and by other reference, where the children are unable to tell much
of themselves or of their families.

Wisconsin.—The history of the family, as well as that of the
inmate, is obtained and recorded, as far as practicable, at the time
of admission.

QUESTION XLI.

How far is their history, while connected with the institution,
made matter of record ?

ANSWERS.

Connecticut.—An occasional record is made of their conduct
and improvement.

Illinois.—Every misdemeanor, however slight, is recorded in full
on a page appropriated to each inmate, every year, for that purpose. The foundations, also, for good conduct are noted in the
same way, thus presenting a complete daily history of the boy's
conduct while in the institution.

Maine.—No record is kept.

Maryland.—Their general history while connected with the institution is recorded in their "grade book," or "daily record," as we term it.

Massachusetts.—State Ref. School—Everything of importance is recorded. Girls' Industrial.—Whatever is of a marked character is recorded.

Michigan.—We keep a "grade list," in which we record the offences committed in the school each month, and these are entered in a book kept in the office of the institution.

Missouri.—The "grade book" shows, from day to day, what the conduct of each inmate is, as measured by our standard.. No other history of inmates, while in the institution, is kept.

Ohio.—A record is kept from the time of their admission till their discharge, and, in the case of such as are indentured, it is continued.

Pennsylvania.—Their history is still continued whilst inmates, but is confined more particularly to the condition of the children, as affected by the discipline of the institution.

Rhode Island.—The books of histories are often written up, though more particularly when the child leaves the institution.

Wisconsin.—Their behavior while in the institution is recorded.

QUESTION XLII.

To what extent and by what means is a knowledge of them kept up after they are indentured or discharged?

ANSWERS.

Connecticut.—No special efforts are made to keep up a correspondence, yet more letters are received from the boys than can be well answered. And the boys frequently visit the institution.

Illinois.—By correspondence, as far as possible. Boys also report in reference to each other.

Maine—Persons to whom boys are indentured are required to report once a year relative to the character and well being of their apprentices. There is no arrangement by which is maintained a knowledge of the character and deportment of discharged boys.

Maryland.—By correspondence and personal investigations as far as possible. All important facts are recorded in the book of histories of each child.

Massachusetts.—State Reform School—By correspondence and visits or any reliable information. Masters are required to write us twice a year, in January and July, of the condition and progress of the boy. Nautical Branch—All intelligence of them is recorded. Girls' Industrial—We keep up a knowledge of those who are under *indenture*, as far as possible, by correspondence and occasional visits by some of the officers. Of those who are discharged, mainly by their voluntary correspondence with their matrons.

Michigan.—Not to a very great extent, and only by letters from the boys themselves, except in case of those released upon leave of absence, who are required to write every three months, or are liable to be returned.

Wisconsin.—Persons who receive inmates under indenture are required to report to the superintendent every year the physical, moral and mental condition of said apprentices. We necessarily lose sight of a large proportion of those who are unconditionally discharged. I am of opinion that children, when returned to parents, should be given up only *conditionally;* in other words, that the board of managers should reserve the right to take any child back to the institution whose parents will not report the condition of said child to the superintendent *twice* every year.

Ohio.—By visiting and corresponding with them and their masters.

Pennsylvania—White and Colored—Printed circulars, containing a number of questions relative to the character of the apprentice, are sent yearly to the masters. These are returned to the institution with the answers. The agent visits each indentured child once a year, and by a personal interview satisfies himself as to the treatment of the apprentice, &c.

Rhode Island.—Children are placed out with the understanding that a written communication be made *once* in each year at least.

Wisconsin.—Their conduct subsequent to their leaving, as far as known, is recorded.

Question XLIII.

What proportion are reformed and turn out well in after life?

Answers.

Connecticut.—More than three-fourths are doing well.

Illinois.—Of those honorably discharged during past six years, I think full seven-eighths are doing well. (Those who have been discharged by courts, or have escaped, or have been returned because improperly committed, are not included in this statement.)

Maine.—It is claimed that 75 per cent are reformed.

Maryland.—From 70 to 80 per cent are reformed.

Massachusetts.—Nautical Branch—More than three-fourths, so far as heard from. Girls' Industrial—Our institution has been in operation for so short a time, that we are unable to give any statistics on this point. We know of many who are now doing well, bravely struggling against temptation, while some are a source of grief to us.

Missouri.—About three-fourths, judging from the necessarily very imperfect data we have.

Ohio.—A large proportion of those discharged; but a history of each after leaving the institution is too extensive an undertaking to be answered definitely.

Pennsylvania—White.—We feel satisfied, from information obtained of the subsequent histories of the children after leaving here, that at least two-thirds of them become respectable members of society. Colored.—Twenty per cent.

Rhode Island.—A question not easily answered. Most of them are improved. Many do very well. Some take a high rank in the standing of good citizens, and some do very badly—others badly enough.

Wisconsin.—The institution has been in operation only five years. It may be safely stated that 85 per cent of those discharged have been permanently reformed.

QUESTION XLIV.

What proportion of those received are orphans, by the loss of both parents?

ANSWERS.

Connecticut.—One-twelfth part have lost both parents.
Illinois.—One-sixth part.
Maine.—Unable to determine.
Maryland.—About one-sixth.
Massachusetts—State Reform School.—Four per cent. Nautical Branch.—About one-eighth. Girls' Industrial.—About one-fifth.
Missouri.—Less than 10 per cent.
Ohio.—One-fourth.
Pennsylvania—White.—Our statistics for 1864 show that of the number received in that year, 45 were orphans by the loss of both parents, and 218 were half orphans. Colored.—Ten per cent.
Rhode Island.—Nearly one-fifth.
Wisconsin.—About one-quarter.

QUESTION XLV.

What proportion are half-orphans?

ANSWERS.

Connecticut.—Nearly half.
Illinois.—About one-half.
Maine.—One-fifth.
Maryland.—About one-half.
Massachusetts—State Reform School.—33 per cent. Nautical Branch.—About one-half. Girls' Industrial.—Nearly one-half.
Missouri.—About one-half.
Ohio.—One-third.
Pennsylvania—White.—No other answer than to last question. Colored.—Ninety per cent.
Rhode Island.—Nearly one-fifth.
Wisconsin.—About one-quarter.

QUESTION XLVI.

What proportion have idle or vicious parents by whose example they have been led on to crime?

ANSWERS.

Connecticut.—Perhaps one-third.

Illinois.—Our statistics do not fully show this—should think one-half.

Maine.—Unable to determine.

Maryland.—About three-fifths.

Massachusetts—State Reform School.—Nearly all. Nautical Branch.—Nearly one-half. Girls' Industrial.—More than half.

Michigan.—About two-thirds.

Missouri.—About thirty-five per cent.

Pennsylvania—White.—About one-fourth have parents whose example and neglect have been the chief causes of their children's going astray. Colored—Fifty per cent.

Rhode Island.—One-half or more.

Wisconsin.—Nearly one-half.

QUESTION XLVII.

What are the recreations of the children?

ANSWERS.

Connecticut.—Plays of all kinds in the yard.

Illinois.—All proper amusements common with children.

Maine.—They have three hours per day for recreation in the winter months, and between four and five in the warm months. In hours of recreation they are allowed the fullest liberty to indulge in all plays that are proper for any boys to engage in.

Maryland.—About the same as those of an ordinary school. .

Massachusetts.—State Reform School—The gymnasium, foot ball, base ball, marbles, &c., &c. Nautical Branch—Such plays as they may choose. Girls' Industrial—Walks, nutting, berrying, skating, and various in-door and out-door games as in other families.

Michigan.—Ball, marbles, skating, swimming, and games usual in common schools, besides a gymnasium in the yard.

Missouri.—Those amusements usually allowed to the pupils of the public schools. Games having a tendency to do mischief excluded. Marbles are allowed, but taken away as soon as a disposition to quarrel is manifested, in consequence of "playing for keeps," as the boys call it.

Ohio.—They are upon the play grounds about two hours and a half each day, when they are allowed to indulge in such exercise and games as may please them, only being restrained from excess.

Pennsylvania.—White and Colored—The various plays and

games peculiar to children, except such as have a tendency to gambling.

Rhode Island.—Such as are common to children of their age.

Wisconsin.—Common amusements in the yard, except games of chance. No playing of marbles is allowed.

QUESTION XLVIII.

Are they under supervision while at play?

ANSWERS.

All respond in the affirmative; and Mr. Allen, of the Massachusetts State Reform School, adds: "The play ground, we think, is one of the best places to influence boys for good."

QUESTION XLIX.

Do the persons who have charge of the children, at such times, ever take part in their games?

ANSWERS.

Connecticut.—Occasionally they do take part in their games.

Illinois.—Sometimes they do.

Maine.—They frequently do.

Maryland.—They do.

Massachusetts.—State Reformed School—They do. Nautical Branch—They do. Girls' Industrial—Yes.

Michigan.—Sometimes they do.

Missouri.—They do frequently, when they have sufficient dignity to secure the respect of the children. Persons inexperienced in the management of the young, and with little tact, are usually in constant fear of losing their influence over them by freely mingling with them in their sports.

Ohio.—They do not take part in their games.

Pennsylvania—White.—Sometimes the officers in charge take part in their plays. Colored.—Frequently, the superintendent sometimes joining them.

Rhode Island.—They do.

Wisconsin.—Frequently they do.

QUESTION L.

What is the dietary?

ANSWERS.

Connecticut.—Meat once a day, coffee and wheat bread for breakfast, milk and bread, or mush and milk or molasses for supper.

Illinois.—Breakfast—Bread and molasses and coffee every morning. Dinner—Corned beef and vegetables, fresh beef, with soup and vegetables, and pork and beans alternately. Supper— hominy, rice, mush and bread alternately.

Maine.—Monday, Breakfast—White bread and coffee boiled with milk. Dinner—Corned beef, beats, cabbage and brown bread. Supper—The same as breakfast. Tuesday, Breakfast— Same as Monday. Dinner—Fresh meat, soup and brown bread. Supper—Mush and molasses. Wednesday, Breakfast—Same as Monday. Dinner—Baked beans and brown bread. Supper— Same as breakfast. Thursday, Breakfast—Same as Monday. Dinner—Same as Tuesday. Supper—Mush and molasses. Friday—Breakfast same as Monday. Dinner—Salt fish, potatoes and bread. Supper—Same as breakfast. Saturday, Breakfast— Same as Monday, Dinner—Same as Tuesday. Supper—Same as breakfast. Sunday, Breakfast—Same as Monday. Dinner— Mush and molasses. Supper—White bread, gingerbread and coffee.

Maryland.—Meat once a day, either in soup or baked, with vegetables. bread, coffee and tea, with more or less fruit in the season. From the farm we are able to give them quite a variety of vegetables.

Massachusetts—State Reform School.—Plain, garden vegetables in abundance; meat once a day, brown bread and white bread. Nautical Branch.—Breakfast and Supper—Coffee and hard bread. Dinner—Sunday, fresh beef and soup; Monday, corned beef and bread pudding; Tuesday, pork and beans; Wednesday, fresh beef and soup; Thursday, corn beef and duff; Friday, pork and beans; Saturday, salt fish and potatoes, fresh fish occasionally. Girls' Industrial.—Breakfast, bread and milk; Dinner, beans, mush, corned beef and vegetables, rice, fish and soup and on Sunday gingerbread; Supper, bread and butter, or bread and syrup.

Michigan.—Breakfast, wheat bread and barley coffee, and sometimes potatoes and butter; Dinner, fresh beef, bread and vegetables; Supper, bread and butter, or molasses. Sometimes they have soup, at other times beans.

Missouri.—In summer we give them a good variety of vegetables in their season, good fresh beef and mutton once a day, and first rate bread at every meal. In winter, fresh meat (mutton or beef) once and sometimes twice a day. If twice, it is boiled for dinner, and the remaining portion sliced and eaten cold for supper. Hash is served for breakfast. The bill of fare for the winter is as follows:

Sunday—Breakfast, bread and coffee; class of honor, fish or meat hash; Dinner, meat hash and pickle, bread and water; class of honor, desert, pie or pudding; Supper, bread and sorghum, with water; when very cold, weak coffee.

Monday—Breakfast, corn bread and coffee; Dinner, stewed beef, with onions and potatoes; Supper, bread and coffee.

Tuesday—Breakfast, cold sliced beef and bread, with coffee; class of honor, stewed meat and potatoes, bread and coffee; Dinner, boiled beef, beans, soup and bread; class of honor, desert, boiled rice or hominy and sorghum; Supper mush and molasses.

Wednesday—Breakfast, meat hash, bread and coffee; Dinner, boiled beef, hominy or vegetable soup and bread, and baked bread pudding; Supper, corn bread and coffee.

Thursday—Breakfast, corn bread and coffee; dinner, boiled beef and beans, soup with bread; class of honor, desert, rice pudding; Supper, bread and coffee.

Friday—Breakfast, meat hash, bread and coffee; dinner, codfish and potatoes, or cold meat and suet pudding; Supper, mush and molasses.

Saturday—Breakfast, cold sliced meat, bread and coffee; Dinner boiled beef and bean soup, or baked beans; class of honor, desert, bread and sorghum; Supper, bread and coffee.

Ohio.—For dinner, Sunday, corned beef, bread and butter; Monday, fresh beef and vegetables; Tuesday, pork and beans and soup; Wednesday, corned beef and bean soup; Thursday, fresh beef and potatoes; Friday, fresh beef and potatoes; Saturday, fresh beef and vegetables. Coffee for breakfast during cold weather. Holidays, extras.

Pennsylvania.—White—Breakfast, bread and coffee: Dinner, meat soup, potatoes, and other vegetables, with bread; Supper, mush and molasses three times, and bread and molasses four times. Colored—plain but wholesome food, an abundance of which is furnished, except when in the administration of severe discipline a deprivation becomes necessary.

Rhode Island.—Food always provided with direct reference to the season of the year and the condition of the children, without any set rules, except to have it fully sufficient in quantity, wholesome and palatable in quality, and thoroughly cooked.

Wisconsin.—Breakfast, wheat bread, potatoes, with butter or meat gravy, no coffee or tea is given; Dinner, soup, beans, meat, codfish and mush, changing daily; Supper, white bread and butter or syrup.

Question LI.

Are the inmates allowed any food or luxuries beyond what is provided by the institution?

Answers.

Illinois.—They are allowed any proper thing that may be brought them by their parents or friends.

Maine.—Parents and friends of the boys are permitted to furnish them with any luxuries that are not thought to be injurious to their health.

Maryland.—They are.

Massachusetts.—Parents send boxes of eatables, as in other schools.

Michigan.—They are.

Missouri.—Yes ; cakes, pies, fruits, &c., are often brought by parents and friends of inmates, and under proper restrictions are always allowed.

Ohio.—They are not, except by special permission.

Pennyslvania.—White—Parents and friends are permitted occasionally to furnish them with such articles of food as are not provided for in our dietary, if the conduct of the children has been such as to deserve them. Colored—They are allowed to receive some delicacies from their relatives, only as rewards for good conduct.

Rhode Island.—They may receive food.

Wisconsin.—Sometimes, by friends when visiting them.

QUESTION LII.

What attention is given to enforcing cleanliness ?

ANSWERS.

Connecticut.—They are required to wash daily and bathe once a week.

Illinois.—They are required to wash five times each day, and in every department are required to present a neat and tidy appearance. In winter, they bathe the whole person once a week; in summer, they go to the lake to bathe every other evening.

Maine.—They are required to wash themselves three times a day at least, and bathe the whole person once in two weeks.

Maryland.—Constant supervision by the officers in charge. In summer they bathe the person once a week; in winter not so often.

Massachusetts.—State Reform School: Regular attention. Washing three times a day. Nautical Branch: Very particular. Girls' industrial: Constant attention. Very frequent bathing of the whole person is required in all.

Michigan.—There is an officer in charge when they wash for meals, and each chief is held responsible for the cleanliness of the boys under his charge. They bathe the whole person once a week.

Missouri.—Every inmate is compelled to bathe his entire person every Saturday, and to wash his hands and face before breakfast, dinner and supper.

Ohio.—Much attention is given to cleanliness, which is strictly enforced. They bathe twice a week in summer and once in winter.

Pennsylvania.—Cleanliness, being considered next to godliness, receives its appropriate share of attention. In summer they bathe in pools once a day.

Rhode Island.—The strictest attention is given. Bathing the whole person once a week always, at times oftener.

Wisconsin.—Daily washing before meals. In the summer, frequent bathing in the river. In the winter, weekly washing and bathing the whole person.

QUESTION LIII.

How as to the health of the inmates?

ANSWERS.

The replies are uniform here as to the great and ever remarkable healthfulness of the inmates.

QUESTION LIV.

What percentage, on an average, are on the sick list?

ANSWERS.

The response to this question, in general, is one-fourth or one-half of one per cent. Some reply one or two per cent.; and the colored department at Philadelphia four per cent.

QUESTION LV.

What per centage die annually?

ANSWERS.

Connecticut..—Less than one a year.
Illinois.—16 out of 836 in ten years.
Maine—One and one-ninth per cent.
Maryland—Of the whole number since the opening of the institution, a little less than one and a half per cent.
Massachusetts.—State Ref. School—Less than two per cent since the opening of the school. Statistics of the number of deaths do not, as a general thing, indicate the facts exactly, as it is customary, when boys are declining in health, to allow their parents to take them home and take care of them. If such boys die, their names would not appear as dying at the institution, and the average number of such would also be reduced. Nautical Branch—One-sixth of one per cent. Girls Industrial—Of the 470 who have been inmates, but two have died in the institution.
Michigan.—Two per cent.
Missouri.—Less than three-fourths of one per cent.
Ohio.—During the last eighteen months but one death has occurred in the Institution.
Pennsylvania.—Colored—Two per cent.
Rhode Island.—No death has occurred since 1861, and for previous years less than one-tenth of one per cent, except one year when three deaths occurred.
Wisconsin.—No death has occurred in the school since it was opened, five years ago, out of 353 inmates.

QUESTION LVI.

What are the diseases most prevalent?

ANSWERS.

Connecticut.—No prevailing disease.

Illinois—Do not know.

Maine.—Fevers.

Maryland.—No particular form of disease.

Massachusetts.—State Ref. School—None in particular. Nautical Branch—*Inflammation of the eyes.* Girls Industrial—*Hereditary diseases, syphilitic and scrofulous.*

Michigan.—*Fever and ague* and *measles.*

Missouri.—*Scrofulous opthalmia* is the prevailing disease. We have no running water, but draw all the water we use from cisterns and wells. We have been compelled to use hard water for all purposes several weeks at a time.

Ohio.—*Chills and fever.*

Pennsylvania.—White—Have had so little sickness that we cannot refer to any "prevalent disease." Colored—*Tubercular.*

Rhode Island.—None that can be called prevailing.

QUESTION LVII.

How often does the physician attend?

ANSWERS.

Connecticut.—The superintendent is a physician.

Illinois.—Whenever required.

Maine.—When summoned.

Maryland.—Usually three times a week, oftener when necessary.

Massachusetts.—State Ref. School—Once a week and oftener if needed. Nautical Branch—About fifteen or twenty times a year. Girls' School—Once a week and oftener if necessary.

Michigan.—Once in two weeks, and oftener if desired.

Missouri.—When notified that his *professional services* are required.

Ohio.—Usually but twice each week.

Pennsylvania.—White and Colored—The physician attends twice a week to examine all new inmates, and prescribe for the sick, if there should be any. If his services should be required oftener, it would be his duty to attend.

Rhode Island.—Twice a week.

Wisconsin.—The superintendent is physician.

QUESTION LVIII.

What hospital accommodations are there?

ANSWERS.

Connecticut.—All that is needed.

Illinois.—Have a room on purpose—small, but comfortable.

Maine.—Rooms for hospital use scantily furnished.

Maryland.—A large room in a quiet part of the house.

Massachusetts.—State Reform School—Good accommodation in a building specially adapted. Nautical Branch—We send to Rainsford Island—state hospital. Girls' School—A hospital room in each house is contemplated.

Michigan.—A room in one corner of the building, 16 by 20 feet. Shall have better when we build, as we hope to in the spring.

Missouri.—In the male department none in reality. We have one small room, say, 8 by 12 by 10, with no convenience for warming in the winter, where one or two boys are occasionally placed when unable to leave their beds. This room is the only accommodation we have for such boys, who need to be kept apart from the well. In the female department a hospital room of sufficient size to accommodate six persons is provided.

Ohio.—The various hospitals will accommodate about thirty patients, with bathing rooms and water closets complete.

Pennsylvania.—White—Spacious well ventilated rooms in each department for the sick of either sex. Colored—A boys' infirmary, containing eight beds; a girls' infirmary, containing six beds, with all necessary furniture, &c.

Rhode Island.—Four small rooms, bath room, water closet and sink room.

Wisconsin.—Two large rooms furnished.

QUESTION LIX.

What have been the aggregate annual earnings of the inmates for the last ten years?

ANSWERS.

Connecticut.—About $4,000 per year for work done for parties outside the institution.

Illinois.—Can not give the amount for ten years. Last year their earnings amounted to $10,000. This year I think they will be more.

Maine.—The aggregate annual earnings are as follows:

1856	$2,696 91
1857	1,233 96
1858	718 58

[Assem. No. 35.]   29

1859	$1,025 12
1860	2,529 59
1861	3,307 53
1862	1,183 57
1863	4,327 77
1864	4,155 69
1865	4,745 13

These amounts do not include the value of the boys' labor upon the farm, which would add materially to the gross amount.

Maryland.—The institution has been opened but about ten years. During the first six years little success attended the efforts of those in charge, in remunerating employments. The annual amount received for the last years, from employments, has been about $9,000.

Massachusetts.—State Reform School—Cannot answer, as a large number work on the land in summer, for which we receive nothing in cash. Nautical Branch—No income. Girls' School—We cannot tell. Most of the time is spent in instructing them in household labor and sewing for the family. The present superintendent has been here four years, during which time the girls have earned, by knitting and braiding, $2,000

Michigan.—We have no means of ascertaining the amount previously earned.

Missouri.—Have not the necessary time to answer correctly.

Ohio.—$30,371.15 for the last ten years.

Pennsylvania.—White—For the last ten years the aggregate earnings of the inmates have been $51,543.26. Colored—$23,025.14.

QUESTION LX.

What are the annual aggregate expenses for the same period?

ANSWERS.

Connecticut.—$20,000.

Illinois.—Our total expenditure for five and a half years, including building improvements and all, $151,000.

Maine.—The aggregate annual expenses, are as follows:

1856	$30,627 85
1857	32,696 20
1858	25,783 37
1859	19,452 88
1860	20,027 45
1861	19,799 95
1862	16,553 15
1863	14,636 55
1864	26,536 07
1865	27,772 11

APPENDIX. **451**

Maryland.—The aggregate annual expenses for the last nine years, is $256,373.30.

Massachusetts.—State Reform School—$42,404.48 annually to the state. Nautical Branch—About $24,000 per annum. Girls' School—The institution has been in operation but nine years. Aggregate expenses for that time have been nearly $134,000.

Missouri.—Total expenditures for ten years, ending April 1, 1865, are $191,240.11.

Ohio.—$402,357.18 for the ten years.

Pennsylvania.—White—The aggregate annual expenses for the last 10 years have been $298,284.29. Colored—$126,784.15.

QUESTION LXI.

What has been the average annual cost of each inmate, including all expenses other than the interest on the real estate belonging to the institution?

ANSWERS.

Illinois.—Average cost per year of providing for each inmate for past 5½ years, including buildings and all, after deducting earnings of boys, is $104. This average is lessened considerably by a portion of our inmates being out on ticket-of-leave all the time.

Maine.—$118.

Maryland.—Average annual expense per capita for nine years, $92.92.

Massachusetts.—State Reformed School—$112.63. Nautical Branch—$154. Girls' School—$119.08.

Missouri.—About $130.

Ohio.—$157.90.

Pennsylvania.—White—The average annual cost of each inmate for 1864, including all expenses, was $92.76. Colored—For 1855, the cost per capita was $70.77 (exclusive of earnings); 1856, $66.70; 1857, $74.65; 1858, $74.77; 1859, $77.21; 1860, $77.88; 1861, $75.63; 1862, $70.98; 1863, $84.84; 1864, $110.60.

Wisconsin.—From $180 to $200.

QUESTION LXII.

What is the average period during which children are retained in the institution?

ANSWERS.

Connecticut.—The average stay of inmates is two years and a half.

Illinois.—Should think about two years.

Maine.—Twenty-eight months.

Maryland.—Twenty and a half months.

Massachusetts.—State Reform School—Between two and three years. Last year, two years, two months and 27 days. Nautical Branch—Nine and two-third months. Girls' School—About three years.

Michigan.—About two and a half years.

Missouri.—Hitherto it has not exceeded seven months.

Ohio.—Two years, five months and four days.

Pennsylvania.—White—The rule of the institution obliges them to remain under its discipline one year, in order that they may pass through all the classes denoting moral improvement, and then, if this be the case, they are considered fit for discharge, by indenture or otherwise. As they are not always discharged at the expiration of the year, the average time is something more. Colored—18 months.

Wisconsin.—Two years.

QUESTION LXIII.

What is the average age at which they are received?

ANSWERS.

Connecticut.—The average age is twelve years and a half.

Illinois.—About twelve and a half years of age.

Maine.—Twelve $\frac{9}{10}$ years is the average age at which they are received.

Maryland.—The average age is twelve years.

Massachusetts. — State Reform School — Last year, eleven years, seven months and six days. Nautical Branch—Fifteen years is the average. Girls' School—About thirteen years is the average.

Michigan.—About thirteen years.

Missouri.—The average of the boys is eleven years, one and a half months; girls, seven years and eleven months.

Ohio.—Twelve years, five months and twenty seven days.

Pennsylvania.—White.—The average age of boys received in 1864, was $12\frac{5}{6}$ years, and girls $14\frac{3}{8}$ years. Colored.—Boys 12 years—Girls 14 years.

Wisconsin.—The average age is twelve years.

QUESTION LXIV.

What is the average age at which they are discharged?

ANSWERS.

Connecticut.—Fourteen years.

Illinois.—Between fourteen and fifteen years.

Maine.—Fifteen years two-tenths is the average.

Maryland.—Average age at time of discharge fourteen years.

Massachusetts.—State Reform School.—About fourteen years. Nautical Branch—Fifteen and two-thirds years. Girls' School—

They are not discharged until eighteen, unless for ill health, or occasionally for some other sufficient cause.

Michigan.—About fifteen and a half years.

Missouri.—Boys eleven years and eight and a half months ; girls eight years and six months.

Ohio.—Fourteen years and eleven months is the average age.

Pennsylvania.—White.—Boys about fourteen and girls fifteen and a half. Colored—Boys thirteen and a half, girls fifteen and a half.

Wisconsin.—Fifteen years of age is the average.

QUESTION LXV.

What punishments are employed ?

ANSWERS.

Connecticut.—We hold to *Solomon's* advice, after all other remedies have failed. No strange, cruel, or degrading punishments are allowed.

Illinois.—Change of grades—standing up for reflection—bread and water, and, very rarely, whipping.

Maine.—Solitary confinement, deprivation of play, and corporal punishment.

Maryland.—We rely mainly on our grades ; but as auxiliaries, we use deprivation of play, loss of evening meal, placing in rooms, and, as a last resort, corporal punishment is inflicted.

Massachusetts.—State Reform School.—Deprivation of privileges, simple diet, isolation, and returning from the " families " to the congregate department. Flogging and such cheap punishments, so easily inflicted and so readily resorted to by the passionate and unskillful or inexperienced, we have but little faith in as a means of reformation. *Fear* may restrain, but *love* only can reform. Nautical Branch—Mild corporal punishment. Girls' School—Deprivation of privileges (diet and correspondence with friends), and solitude.

Michigan.—Deprived of play, deprivation of food for one meal, separate confinement, and corporal punishment when necessary.

Missouri.—Demerit marks chiefly, in addition to which are exclusion from the privileges of the play ground, confinement in a light cell, loss of one or more meals, and corporal inflictions.

Ohio.—1st. Privation of play and exercise ; 2d. Sending to bed at sunset ; 3d. Bread and water for breakfast, dinner and supper ; 4th. Confinement in solitary rooms and cells ; and 5th. Corporal punishment.

Pennsylvania.—White and colored—Deprivation of a part of a meal or of play ; confinement, if necessary, upon a diet of bread and water, and corporal punishment in extreme cases, with loss of rank.

Question LXVI.

What rewards, if any, are offered as a stimulus to good conduct?

Answers.

Connecticut.—No general rewards are offered. Presents for good conduct are frequently given.

Illinois.—Promotions in grades ; extra privileges ; visits to the city, &c., &c.—a sufficient variety to keep up constant striving for good behavior.

Maine.—Extra privileges, such as going outside to play ball, skate, &c.

Maryland.—Rewards are gained through their grades, consisting of walks about the neighborhood, either with or without an officer ; liberty of visiting their friends ; choice of clothing and occasional invitations to dine with the superintendent, and many other privileges of like character.

Massachusetts.—State Reform School—The natural rewards of good conduct, which always inspires confidence and regard, and secures privileges. The better boys are always given the places of trust and positions in " family houses." Nautical Branch—Boys are *discharged* for good conduct. Girls' School—We have no *system* of rewards, but each matron offers such as her own judgment may suggest.

Michigan.—Skating, swimming, frequent visits to the city to make purchases with money received from friends, and, the greatest of all, the hope of early returning to their homes and friends.

Missouri.—The privilege of visiting parents or friends occasionally, small sums of money, or its equivalent in such articles as may be selected for food, clothing or innocent amusement, and the right of discharge after having reached the fourth grade of honor.

Ohio.—Merit marks, which hasten the time of discharge, and additional time for play.

Pennsylvania.—White—Promotions in the classes is the general stimulus to good conduct. Colored—Rewards are bestowed on all who reach the " class of honor," our highest class. The late Thomas J. Cope, a president of the board, in his will made provisions for such rewards.

Question LXVII.

Is it customary to present a Bible to each inmate on leaving ?

Answers.

In almost all, either bibles or testaments are given, commonly the former.

Question LXVIII.

If so, is the gift accompanied with counsels, written or oral, as to his future conduct?

ANSWERS.

Connecticut.—It is. He is told that if he follows the teachings of the Bible, he will be safe.

Illinois.—Our boys are kept in monthly correspondence or communication with the school until well settled.

Maryland.—The gift is accompanied with advice.

Massachusetts.—The answer in all three, is yes. In the Girls' School it is accompanied with both oral and written counsels.

Michigan.—Oral counsel is given.

Missouri.—No written counsels are given to inmates upon leaving.

Ohio.—The gift is accompanied by counsels, both written and oral.

Pennsylvania.—White—a private letter of wholesome advice is presented to each inmate. Colored—it is accompanied by both written and oral advice.

Rhode Island.—Oral advice is always given, written sometimes.

QUESTION LXIX.

What classes of boys are found most difficult of reformation ? what, of girls?

ANSWERS.

Connecticut.—The *lowest* class, found in our cities, of both sexes.

Illinois.—Those over fourteen years of age—both sexes.

Maryland.—If there is any particular class more difficult than another, I should say that class of boys who have acquired that roaming, restless disposition that renders it difficult to instil into them any fixed habits.

Massachusetts.—Reform School: Those that come from the lowest grades of society and inherit their vicious propensities, and not those of respectable parentage, who form bad habits from evil associations. Girls' School: Girls from the city, of fifteen and sixteen years of age, who have been exposed to the influences of the street.

Michigan.—Those from our largest cities are most difficult of reformation.

Missouri.—Boys between the ages of fourteen and sixteen years, who have been previously arrested several times, and confined for short periods of time in the city *calaboose* or in the county jail ; and girls who have lost that purity of character which is woman's shield.

Ohio.—Those admitted for incorrigibility.

Pennsylvania.—White: The boys most difficult to reform are those who are advanced in years, and whose vicious habits have been of long continuance, and it is especially the case with some whose greatest propensity has been to disregard the eighth commandment. Of the prevailing faults of both sexes, whilst in the institution, the most difficult to eradicate is a disposition to tell falsehoods.   The girls most difficult to reform are those who have been addicted to lewdness.

Rhode Island.—Those who have been immoral and vile in their associations, both boys and girls.

Question LXX.

Does the institution reserve the right of a guardian over those who have been indentured?

The answer is "yes," from all the reformatories.

Question LXXI.

If an indentured youth leave his master, must he again be brought back to the institution?

Answers.

Connecticut.—He must be brought back, *if he can be found.*

Maine.—He must be brought back.

Maryland.—It would depend somewhat on his age and character; but the usual custom is to cause all such to be returned who are not too old for such an institution.

Massachusetts.—Yes, in all three institutions.

Michigan.—It depends upon the condition of his indenture.

Missouri.—Yes, if he can be found.

Ohio.—Not necessarily, but may be with consent of directors, without a new commitment.

Pennsylvania.—White and colored: If a lad absconds from his master, he can be returned to the institution.   This is done in some cases, but if it should be discovered that he is doing well; he is not intefered with.   When not satisfied with their places, they frequently return of their own accord to the institution.

Rhode Island.—He must.

Questions LXXII.

If this power over the indentured belongs to the institution, does a like power over those who have gone out in other ways belong to it also?

Answers.

Connecticut.—It does in respect to all who leave on their parole of honor.

Illinois.—We hold the power of guardianship over those out on "tickets-of-leave."

Maine.—It does, except in cases of unconditional discharge.

Maryland.—It does not belong to the institution.

Massachusetts.—State Reform School: If the boy is released on probation, it does. Nautical Branch: Not over those who go to sea. Girls' School: The institution does not possess this power.

Michigan.—The board of control reserve the right of control over those who are granted "leave of absence."

Missouri.—In practice, in our institution, the guardianship of the board of managers ceases when the child is delivered into the custody of its parent, or other guardian. It is a legal question whether the board have any further authority over a child who has been conditionally released from the house of refuge. I am of the opinion that every discharge should be conditional; in other words, that every inmate of the house of refuge should be let out when the proper time arrives under indenture. Boys from 18 to 20 years of age may properly form an exception to the rule, when discharged as reformed.

Ohio.—It does not possess this power. Their release makes a new commitment necessary, if returned.

Pennsylvania.—White and colored: Those given up to their friends are absolutely discharged, and the institution has no further claim upon them.

Rhode Island.—Yes, except in respect to those discharged as reformed, or upon expiration of sentence.

V. ADMINISTRATION OF CRIMINAL JUSTICE.

QUESTION I.

What is the *judicial system* of your state? What are the several classes of courts, their jurisdiction and powers?

ANSWERS.

Massachusetts:

GEORGE W. SEARLE, ESQ.—The criminal judicial system of Massachusetts consists primarily of police courts, trial justices and justices of the peace; next of the superior court; and lastly the "supreme judicial court."

There are fourteen counties in the state. Both the supreme and superior are state courts, with terms for the different counties. Some of the larger cities have police courts; while the smaller cities and the towns have trial justices, having final jurisdiction in smaller cases and preliminary jurisdiction in cases of larger magnitude. The superior court has jurisdiction of all criminal cases, except capital ones, beyond the jurisdiction of trial justices. The juries in the superior and supreme court pass only upon the question of guilt or innocence, sentence by the court follows conviction by the jury. Most of the sentences are fixed by statutes, with a large range between the *minimum* and the *maximum* of punishments. An appeal to the superior court in all cases lies from a final conviction by a trial justice. All law questions ruled against a prisoner in the superior court can go to the "supreme court for the commonwealth" on a bill of exceptions. This last named court is the supreme judicial court sitting in full bench for hearing law questions only.

All capital cases are tried before the supreme court with a jury. The indictments in capital cases are found by the grand jury for the respective counties, and are in the first instance returned into the superior court, and by that court certified to the supreme judicial court. In Suffolk county there is a branch of the superior court, known as the superior court for criminal business, devoted exclusively to criminal business, and presided over by judges of the superior court in rotation. In all other counties there are either criminal terms, or else the civil and criminal business is disposed of at different periods in the same term.

New Hampshire :

Hon. S. D. BELL.—The courts of criminal jurisdiction in New Hampshire are the supreme judicial court, consisting of a chief justice and five associate justices; police courts in the cities and a few larger towns, held by one justice; and justices of the peace. These tribunals are also the only courts of civil jurisdiction, except the courts of probate.

Trial terms of the supreme judicial court are held, generally twice a year in each county, by one of the justices; except in capital cases, when two are required to be present.

Exceptions may be taken to any rulings of the presiding judge at a trial term, and transferred for decision to the law terms, which are held twice a year in each of the four districts into which the state is divided. The decisions there upon the exceptions are final, but new trials are awarded in any case of mis-trial.

The jurisdiction of the supreme judicial court extends to all criminal cases, above the jurisdiction of a justice of the peace, to try and determine.

Police courts and justices of the peace have authority to try and decide in cases of petty larceny, assault and battery, and in cases known as police offences, without a jury; but subject in all cases to an appeal to the supreme judicial court, where the cases may be tried by a jury.

Connecticut :

WALTER PITKIN, Esq.—The judicial power of the state of Connecticut, except in cases of impeachment, is vested by the constitution in a Supreme Court of Errors, a Superior Court, Justices of the Peace, "and such inferior courts as the general assembly shall, from time to time, ordain and establish." Of the latter class there have been established Courts of Probate, a City and a Police Court, in each of the cities of Hartford, New Haven, New London, Norwich and Bridgeport, and a city court in the cities of Waterbury and Middletown.

The constitution, powers and jurisdiction of these tribunals, as defined by law, are respectively as follows :

The Supreme Court of Errors consists of one chief judge and four associate judges, who are also judges of the superior court. It has "final and conclusive jurisdiction of all matters brought by way of error or complaint from judgments or decrees of the superior court in matters of law or equity, wherein the rules of law or principles of equity appear from the files, records, or exhibits of said court to have been mistakenly or erroneously adjudged or determined."

The Superior Court consists of nine judges, including the judges of the supreme court. Three terms are holden annually in each county, but the same judge may not preside at two successive terms in the same county. It has

(a.) Civil jurisdiction : 1. Original, of all suits for relief in equity ; of all suits at law in which the matter in demand exceeds the sum of $50, or which are to determine the title to land. 2.

Appellate, of judgments or decrees of probate and city courts, and of justices of the peace, except in cases of summary process.

(b.) Criminal jurisdiction: 1. Original, of all criminal causes (and *exclusively* of those of which the penalty exceeds a fine of $7, or imprisonment for thirty (30) days), except in the cities where police courts have been established (see *infra* " Police Courts"). 2. Appellate, of judgments of justices of the peace and police courts, except for the crimes of drunkenness and profane swearing, and Sabbath breaking.

In trials for offences punishable by death, the judge holding court is required to call in one of the judges of the supreme court, who shall preside at the trial and have a casting vote on all questions to be decided by the court.

Justices of the Peace have exclusive cognizance of all civil suits in which the debt, trespass, damage, or matter in demand does not exceed the sum of $50 (except in the cities where police courts have been established, see *infra* police courts), except actions of disseisin concurrently with the superior court. They have original jurisdiction of all offences and crimes punishable by fine not exceeding $7, or imprisonment in a common jail not exceeding thirty days, or by such fine or imprisonment both (except in the cities where police courts have been established, see *infra* " police courts.")

This is the extent of a justice's *final* jurisdiction in criminal matters, but he may entertain complaints for crimes of which the penalty may exceed and may fall within these limits, binding the accused to answer over to the superior court if his offence requires a greater punishment, otherwise proceeding to judgment.

The duties of Probate Courts are too obvious to need enumeration.

City Courts are composed of three judges, of whom the chief judge is called " recorder." They have a civil jurisdiction extending, generally, to all causes of action arising within the city limits, and where at least one of the parties must reside. In some particulars the powers of these courts vary in the different cities, but these details are believed to be unimportant for the purposes of this statement.

The powers of these courts are not exclusive, so that justices·and the superior court retain their respective jurisdictions in civil matters as well in the cities as elsewhere.

An appeal lies from the judgments of these courts to the superior court.

The Police Courts have, in addition to the ordinary criminal jurisdiction of justices of the peace, the *exclusive* power to hear and to determine charges for crimes and misdemeanors arising within the limits of their respective cities, the punishment of which as prescribed by law does not exceed a fine of $200, or six months' imprisonment in jail or workhouse, or such fine and imprisonment both. An appeal lies from all judgments (except for drunkenness, profane swearing, and Sabbath-breaking), to the superior court.

New Jersey:

CORTLANDT PARKER, Esq.—The state of New Jersey has departed less from the common law in her judicial system, criminal law, civil practice, and, in fact, throughout her whole system of municipal law, than probably any other state, certainly than any state among those known as northern. And those among her citizens, engaged in the administration of justice and pursuits ancillary thereto, consider this fact as the cause of what they regard as her great superiority over most others in the thoroughness, certainty, integrity and promptness with which justice is here administered.

There are, in New Jersey the following courts : I shall mention first those of civil jurisdiction, then those which regulate the estates of deceased persons, lastly those whose duties regard the punishment of crime. And I shall begin with the humblest, and review them in order of authority.

First.—Courts of civil jurisdiction are the following:

I. Courts of small causes held before justices of the peace, having jurisdiction over personal actions, not including slander and assault, involving no more than one hundred dollars.

II. The common pleas, in each county composed of five judges, and of which, when he is present, a justice of the supreme court is president. This court has jurisdiction of all civil controversies not involving the title to land, and has besides an appellate jurisdiction over courts of small causes.

The county circuit courts, held by justices of the supreme court, having original jurisdiction for the county of all civil controversies, and the power to review by certiorari and writ of error, all legal errors in judgments rendered by either of courts before mentioned.

IV. The supreme court, composed of seven judges, having the same jurisdiction, both civil and criminal, possessed by the king's bench in England, both original and appellate; exercising their original jurisdiction by trying causes either at bar or in the various counties where each judge goes on circuit, and their appellate by any for that purpose known to the common law, superintending all inferior courts and official persons.

V. The court of chancery held by the chancellor, having complete equity jurisdiction.

VI. The court of errors and appeals, composed of the chancellor, the seven judges of the supreme court, and six associate judges, and having jurisdiction, appellate only, in all causes both at law and in equity.

Second.—Courts for the regulation of estates of deceased persons, guardianship, &c., are:

I. The surrogate in each county.

II. Orphans' courts, composed of the judges of the common pleas in each county.

III. The prerogation court, held by the chancellor, sitting as ordinary.

Third.—Courts whose duties involve the punishment of crime, are:

I. Justices of the peace, who receive complaints, and arrest and secure offenders by taking bail or commitment.

II. Courts of two justices, for the trial of larceny of goods under the value of $20.

III. The quarter sessions, composed of the judges of the common pleas, having jurisdiction over crimes less than felony at common law.

IV. Oyer and terminer, composed of one or more justices of the supreme court, and at least one judge of the common pleas, having jurisdiction of all crimes whatever.

V. The supreme court, into which criminal causes may be removed and by whose judges as such they may be tried, which likewise possesses jurisdiction to review judgments against criminals by writ of error : and lastly,

VI. The court of errors and appeals, where *all* judgments and decrees may be reviewed.

JOHN F. HEGEMAN, ESQ.—The judicial system of this state is based upon the common law, and retains more of that character than any other state in the union, perhaps. We have the common law courts, and but few that may be regarded purely as the creatures of the statute. As their jurisdiction and powers are so pre-eminently common law, it is useless to define them here.

Pennsylvania:

J. J. BARCLAY, ESQ.—The administration of criminal law in Pennsylvania is vested in the several courts of common pleas of the several counties of the state, whose judges are justices of the court of oyer and terminer and quarter sessions. The jurisdiction of these courts is co-extensive with the respective judicial districts, which may or may not include more than one county, according to legislative enactment. Their powers are most ample, for these courts may try all classes of criminals and every grade of crime. The judges of the supreme court may, in any judicial district of the state, hold a court of oyer and terminer, but in practice this power is seldom exercised.

In all cases, except murder in the first and second degree, and manslaughter, the decisions of the lower courts are final. In the excepted cases, writs of error are allowed, but only on special leave granted by one of the justices of the supreme court, upon motion and cause shown ; and then the cause is removed to the supreme court for final adjudication, upon questions of law and fact, in the usual method. Writs of *certiorari* may be sued out in all criminal cases, but of course the record alone is removed to the court of last resort and alone is the subject of consideration.

Maryland :

A. STERLING, JR., Esq.—The state is divided into circuits presided over by one judge each, except in Baltimore, where there are four courts with one judge each. There is a court of appeals with five judges. The circuit courts possess general, common law and chancery jurisdiction, the chancery side of the court being separate from the common law side, though in the same judge.

The jurisdiction of the courts in Baltimore is regulated chiefly by the amount of money sued for, as over or under $1,000, but there is one court entirely a chancery court, and one court entirely a criminal court.

Justices of the peace have civil jurisdiction to the amount of $100, and the usual jurisdiction of the peace, arrest and holding to bail. Their civil jurisdiction is subject to appeal to the circuit court, and to the court of common pleas in Baltimore. They have the power to try and fine, in some statutory cases, for misdemeanors, as breach of municipal ordinances, and some other cases.

There is in each county and the city of Baltimore, a court of three judges, who may be laymen, which exercises the probate and testamentary jurisdiction. The fourth article of the state constitution of 1864, will explain this more fully.

Kentucky :

E. L. VAN WINKLE, Esq.—Our judicial system is that which prevailed in the mother country—the common law as administered by common law judges, and the civil law as modified and administered by courts of equity ; the only material difference is the union of both jurisdictions in the same officer.

The jury system and forms of procedure known to the common law are, in the main, preserved in the trial of all cases of common law jurisdiction. We have a code regulating proceedings in civil and criminal cases, much resembling that of the state of New York, in its main features, and preserving the right to a jury in all cases where that right existed at the common law.

Our courts consist of those of limited and general jurisdiction. First, justices of the peace are elected in each election precinct of the various counties of the state ; these justices hold quarterly terms within their respective districts, and have jurisdiction of civil controversies when the amount in contest does not exceed fifty dollars, and when the title to real estate is not involved. They also have jurisdiction in penal cases where the punishment is a fine not exceeding sixteen dollars.

County judges are elected by the county, and besides having charge of the fiscal affairs of the county, they have the supervision of roads and the appointment of guardians and administrators, together with the management of estates. They hold quarterly terms, in which all matters of a civil nature, where the amount in controversy does not exceed one hundred dollars, may be adjudicated. These courts also have appellate jurisdiction over the judgments of the justices of the peace They also have jurisdiction of all penal offences where the punishment is a fine not exceeding one hundred dollars.

In all cases of common law jurisdiction which arise in these courts of limited jurisdiction, either party is entitled to a jury, when the matter in controversy exceeds sixteen dollars in value.

The county judge or justices may, at any time, sit as a preliminary court to bind persons accused of crime for their appearance before the circuit court for final trial, and in default of bail may commit.

The circuit courts are held by circuit judges, elected by their respective districts, of which we have fifteen in the state. These courts have general jurisdiction of all subjects of judicial cognizance, both civil and criminal, as well as appellate jurisdiction of the judgments of the quarterly courts held by the county judges.

Over all, we have an appellate court consisting of four judges, elected by the people of the state, whose revisory power extends to all judgments of the circuit courts, civil and criminal. This revisory power is confined, in the main, to errors of law, and in criminal cases, is somewhat restricted.

Indiana:

Hon. CONRAD BAKER.—The judicial system of Indiana comprises the following courts, viz:

First, a supreme court, consisting of four judges elected by the people for six years, and having appellate jurisdiction in civil and criminal cases throughout the state.

The constitution provides that the judicial power of the state shall be vested in a supreme court, in circuit courts, and in such inferior courts as the general assembly may establish.

The legislature has divided the ninety-one counties of the state into fifteen circuits. Each circuit has one judge, who is elected by the people for six years, and a circuit court is held in each county twice in every year.

The legislature has also established courts of common pleas, and for this purpose has divided the state into twenty-one districts. A judge is elected by the people for each district for the term of four years, and he holds three terms each year in each county of his district.

The circuit court has jurisdiction of felonies, but not of misdemeanors. Prosecutions in the circuit court are by indictment. The circuit court has also jurisdiction of all civil actions. The courts of common pleas have jurisdiction of misdemeanors, which are prosecuted by information, filed by the prosecuting attorney, and based on an affidavit charging the offence.

This court has concurrent jurisdiction with the circuit court of felonies, not punishable with death, where the accused is in custody on charge of felony, and no indictment has been found in the circuit court, or where the person charged is on bail, no indictment having been found, and voluntarily, in writing, submits to the jurisdiction of the court.

The court of common pleas has also probate jurisdiction, and has concurrent jurisdiction with the circuit court in nearly all civil actions.

Michigan:

Hovey K. Clarke, Esq.—The judicial system in the state of Michigan is substantially that of the common law of Great Britain. The courts in which jurisdiction of criminal cases is vested are: 1. A circuit court in each county, having general civil and criminal jurisdiction, held by a single "circuit judge." 2. The recorder's court for the city of Detroit, and three courts held by justices of the peace.

The jurisdiction of the circuit courts embraces all cases within the county, except those within the city of Detroit, and those cognizable by justices of the peace. The jurisdiction of the recorder's court for the city of Detroit embraces all cases arising within the city, with a like exception; and the jurisdiction of justices of the peace extends to the following cases: 1. Larceny not charged as a second offence, and when the value of the property does not exceed twenty-five dollars. 2. Assault and battery not committed riotously, nor upon a public officer, nor with intent to commit any other offence. 3. Charges of willfully destroying or injuring mile boards or guide posts. 4. Charges of maliciously injuring the cattle of another, or destroying the personal property of another, when the injury does not exceed twenty-five dollars. 5. Charges of maliciously injuring or removing monuments of boundaries, or defacing buildings, or extinguishing lamps, injuring lamp posts or railings, or any bridge, street or passage. 6. Charges for malicious trespassing on land, or any wharf or• landing place, and carrying away goods to the value of five dollars. 7. Charges of malicious trespasses in gardens, orchards, &c.; and 8. All other offences punishable by fine not exceeding one hundred dollars, or by imprisonment in the county jail not exceeding three months, or both.

Question II.

Are the judges appointed or elected? If elected, how long has this system prevailed? What is found to be its operation—favorable or unfavorable to the integrity and independence of the judiciary?

Massachusetts:

GEORGE W. SEARLE, Esq.—The judges of the supreme court and
superior court are appointed to hold office during good behavior on
the nomination of the executive, which nomination is confirmed by
the excutive council. Trial justices and police justices are also
appointed by the governor during good behavior. This unlimited
term of judicial office has, on the one hand, worked evil results in
keeping upon the bench men who have outlived their usefulness
to the public and their acceptibility to the bar; and this life tenure
has occasionally made them arbitrary in their conduct and rude
in their manners. On the other hand, it has furnished men of
ability and integrity, and generally it has kept them quite too free
from popular impulses. There is, however, I believe, little or no
disposition to attempt the experiment of an elective judiciary. A
limited tenure, of from five to ten years, was favored by some in
the constitutional convention of 1853, but the vast majority were
in favor of the life tenure. This life system is thought by the bulk
of our people to favor judicial integrity and independence. There
is undoubtedly some foundation for these opinions, but less than
is claimed for them. Judicial offices are sought in the first instance
by interested parties, and they are sometimes conferred as rewards
for party services, or are influenced by personal friendships, as
well as for high professional character and standing.

The old " common pleas " court was abolished in 1857, for the
sake of ridding the bar and the people of unpopular and incompetent judges. Had it been thought that there was constitutional
power to do so, there is some ground for supposing that the
supreme judicial court would have shared the same fate, not, however, so much from its incompetency as from desire of change in
its judges and a dissatisfaction with the intolerable delays of the
court. Dilatoriness is a defect in all the criminal courts. My
opinion is that the limited tenures of the judicial office will yet be
established in this state.

New Hampshire:

Hon. S. D. BELL.—The judges of the supreme judicial court
and of the police courts, are appointed by the governor and council, and hold their offices *nominally* during good behavior. In
1850, a constitutional convention adopted an amendment of the
constitution, making judges eligible by popular vote for limited
terms, but it was rejected by the people.

Connecticut:

WALTER PITKIN, Esq.—The judges of the supreme and superior courts are appointed by a concurrent vote of the two branches
of the Legislature, each for a term of eight years. This *mode* of

appointment has prevailed since the adoption of the present constitution (1818); but until the year 1856, when the above limitation was established, the tenure of office was during good behavior, or until the incumbent reached the age of seventy years. The judiciary of Connecticut has rarely been suspected of a want of "integrity" or "independence," and its earlier annals especially contain the names of men of pre-eminent character and talent. While, therefore, experience would impute no necessary disadvantage in these respects to our *method* of selecting judges by popular election rather than by executive appointment (though the latter is unquestionably the more prudent system), it cannot be denied that the substitution of a *short term of office* for a tenure virtually for life, is regarded by our wisest men as an unfortunate innovation. It is believed that the opinion of the profession generally, certainly the weight of its opinion, was originally, and still is, adverse to such a change, as unwise and of pernicious tendency.

New Jersey:

CORTLANDT PARKER, ESQ.—The judges are variously appointed. Justices of the peace are elected, each for five years, not more than five in each township. Judges of the common pleas are appointed by the Legislature in joint meeting, each for five years, one being elected each year. Justices of the supreme court, the chancellor and the judges of the court of errors and appeals are appointed, the last named each for six years, but so that one new judge takes his seat each year; the chancellor and justices of the supreme court each for seven years—all by the governor, with the advice and consent of the senate.

The elective system, strongly advocated in the constitutional convention of 1844, was rejected, except as regards justices of the peace. While their restricted jurisdiction prevents its doing much harm, the operation of the system has been, I think, sufficiently unfavorable to satisfy the public mind that it would be unwise to adopt this mode of appointment for any other judges.

Surrogates, whose duties are mainly ministerial and ex-parte in their character, are likewise elected, one for each county, and hold office five years. All testamentary causes and other litigation in this department come before the orphan's court, and go thence by appeal to the ordinary.

JOHN F. HEGEMAN, ESQ.—The *judges are appointed; justices of the peace* alone are *elected*. The election of justices seems to work well.

Pennsylvania:

J. J. BARCLAY, ESQ.—The judges of the supreme court are elected for terms of fifteen years, the president and law judges of the common pleas for ten years, and the associate judges, not learned in the law, for five years.

The system has thus far worked well, and will probably continue so to do as long as the question of the re-election is not made a political one.

Maryland:

A. STERLING, JR., ESQ.—Judges are elected. This has been the mode since 1850. The term of service is fifteen years. I think the opinion of the profession is adverse to the elective system, but with the present term of service the evils are modified, justice is made less tedious than of old, and the bench is free from special complaint, but the certainty of the law is diminished, as it has been all over the country, by the change of system. The relative ability of the judges is, I think, about the same as ever. In the court of appeals and in Baltimore, the salary is too small to induce persons of large practice to take the places, and, while our judges are good, we are indebted much to special good fortune and the fact that two out of the four are young men, that we are as well off as we are. No salary is over $3,000.

Kentucky:

E. L. VAN WINKLE, ESQ.—As already stated, our judiciary is elective, which practice has prevailed for fifteen years.

I cannot say that the elective system has proven favorable to the integrity and independence of the judiciary; nor, on the other hand, have any marked evils resulted from the elective system, except the tendency of parties in making political services and usefulness, rather than fitness and qualifications, the governing considerations in selecting judicial officers.

Indiana:

HON. CONRAD BAKER.—The judges are elected by the people, and have been since 1852. I do not think that the election of judges has proved unfavorable to the integrity and independence of the judiciary.

Michigan:

H. K. CLARKE, ESQ.—All judges are elected by the people, except when appointed to fill vacancies. This system has prevailed since the year 1851. Its operation has not been found as satisfactory as was expected. The first years of the experiment seemed to indicate that the change in the mode of selecting judges would be found safe, if not positively advantageous; but as the selection of candidates became more and more subject to partisan influences, the system has been regarded with much less favor.

QUESTION III.

What are the punishments annexed to the several crimes forbidden by the law? Please make your answer to this interrogatory full and complete, embracing *all* the violations of law recognized as crimes.

ANSWERS.

Massachusetts:

GEO. W. SEARLE, ESQ.—The punishments are fixed by legislation and imposed by the presiding judge, the jury having nothing to do with it. The penalties annexed to the leading crimes are given in the general statutes of 1860, part IX, and in the annual laws for the subsequent years. As these are in the library of the Association, I omit any enumeration of them.

New Hampshire:

HON. S. D. BELL.—The punishments imposed by statute for offences are as follows:

Note.—S. I., denotes solitary imprisonment.
H. L., denotes hard labor in the state prison.
Y., denotes years.
N. L., denotes not less than.
N. E., denotes not exceeding.
$, denotes —— dollars fine.
C. J., denotes imprisonment in the county jail.
Treason, s. i. 3 y., h. l. for life.
Misprision of treason, h. l. 7 y. or $2,000.
Fraudulent misapplication of public money by any public officer being a receiver by law, h. l. n. e. 2 y., c. j. n. e. 1 y. and n. e. $2,000.
Murder of first degree, death.
Murder of second degree, s. i. 3 y., h. l. n. l. 7 y., and n. e. 30 y.
Manslaughter, n. e. $1,000, or fine n. l. $500 and c. j. n. e. 1 y. or s. i. n. e. 6 mo., and h. l. n. l. 7 y., n. e. 25 y.
Rape and violation of children, s. i. n. e. 6 mo., and h. l. n. l. 7 y. and n. e. 30 y.
Mayhem and malicious disfiguring, s. i. n. e. 1 y., and h. l. n. l. 1 y., n. e., 20 y.
Robbery, s. i. n. e. 6. m., and h. l. n. l. 7 y., n. e. 30 y.
Assault with intent to commit any crime punishable by death or hard labor for life, s. i. n. e. 6 mo., and h. l. n. l. 1 y., n. e. 10 y.
Concealment of birth of a bastard, s. i. n. e. 6 mo., h. l. 1 to 10 y.
Attempt to procure abortion, c. j. n. e. 1 y., or n. e. $1,000, or both.
Attempt to procure, if quick child, n. e. $1,000 or h. l. n. l. 1 y., n. e. 10 y.
Attempt to procure, if death result, murder in 2d degree, s. i. n. l. 3 y., and h. l. n. l. 7 y., n. e, 30. y.

Women voluntarily submitting to such attempt, c. j. n. e. 1 y. n. e. $1,000, or both.

Kidnapping, h. l. n. e. 10 y.

Druggist selling poison without making a record of it, $100.

Arson, s. i. n. e. 6 mo., h. l. n. l. 7 y., n. e. 30 y.

Malicious burning of vessels, bridges or other buildings, s. i. n. e. 6 mo., h. l. n. l. 2 y., n. e. 20 y.

Obstructing railroad tracks where life is endangered, s. i. n. e. 6 mo., h. l. n. l. 2 y. or for life.

Malicious burning stacks of grain, hay, &c., fences, piles of boards, wood, &c., trees or underwood, h. l. n. e. 1 y., n. e. 3 y., or 1,000 and c. j. n. e. 1 y.

Burglary, with intent to commit a crime, the punishment of which may be death or imprisonment for life, s. i. n. e. 6 mo., h. l. n. l. 5 y. or life.

Burglary with intent to commit other crime punishable by hard labor or to commit larceny, s. i. n. c. 60. d., and h. l. n. l. 3 y., n. e. 10 y.

Breaking and entering in the night any office, bank, store, &c., or vessel, &c., with intent to commit any crime, punishable by hard labor, or to commit larceny, h. l. n. l. 3 y., n. e. 6 y.

Breaking or entering in the night or in the day time, breaking and entering any building or vessel with intent to commit any crime punishable by hard labor, h. l. n. l. 1 y., n. e. 7 y.

Breaking or entering in night, or in day breaking and entering dwelling house, office, bank, shop, store, warehouse, barn, granary or mill, meeting-house, court-house, town-house, college, academy, school-house, or vessel, railroad depot, engine-house, repair shop, &c., or freight or passenger cars, and committing any larceny therein, h. l. n. e. 5 y.

Maliciously killing, maiming, wounding, poisoning or disfiguring any horse, cattle, sheep or swine, with intent to injure the owner, h. l. n. l. 1 y., n. e. 3 y., or n. e. $1,000 and c. j. n. e. 1 y.

Larceny from the person of another, h. l. n. l. 1 y., n. e. 7 y.

Stealing any horse, mule, cattle, sheep or swine, h. l. n. l. 3 y., n. e. 7 y.

Stealing any money, bankbills, goods or chattels, or any writing containing evidence of debt contract, liability, promise or ownership of property of the value of $20, or of the receipt, payment or discharge of the like amount, or writings of like kind containing together evidence of like amount, h. l. n. l. 2 y., n. e. 5 y.

Stealing same things as above of less value than 20 dollars, c. j. n. e. 1 y. and $100 and to pay owner treble value, deducting what is returned.

Stealing any deed, will, policy of insurance, bill of sale of a vessel, letter of attorney, any writ, process or record of any court, any public or corporate record, h. l. n. e. 2 y., n. l. 5 y.

Receiving or concealing stolen property, knowing, &c., h. l. n. l. 2 y., n. e. 5 y.

Malicious injury to any tree placed or growing for ornament or use in any garden, yard, street, square, &c., or maliciously doing any act whereby the real or personal estate of another shall be injured, c. j. n. l. 30 d., n. e. 1 y. or n. e. $100 or both.

Fraudulent mortgage, pledge, sale, or conveyance of real or personal estate of $100 value, fraudulent concealment of personal estate of that value to prevent attachment on seizure, on execution, c. j. n. l. 30 d., n. e. 1 y., fine n. e. double value of property or both.

Fraudulent receiving such mortgage, &c., or debtor's property, &c., same as above.

Same acts, value less than $100, c. j. n. l. 10 d., n. e. 6 mo., fine not exceeding double value, or both.

Cheating or defrauding by falsly personating or by false pretences, &c., n. e. $500 or c. j. n. e. 1 y., or h. l. n. e. 7 y.

Fraudulent disposition or conversion, or secretion of money, goods, &c. delivered or entrusted for keeping, carriage, inn, manufacture or work thereon, as for larceny of like value.

Stealing, &c., *as before*, of less value than $10, c. j. n. e. 90 d., or n. e. $10 and treble value, to be imposed by justice, if no appeal.

Malicious trespass, entering into gardens, orchards, &c., or woodlands, with intent to cut, take, carry away, &c., any trees, fruit or vegetables, c. j. n. e. 90 d. or n. e. $10 or both, and treble value to owner.

If value exceed $20, h. l. n. l. 1 y., n. e. 5 y.

Malicious prostrating fences and exposing fields to cattle, &c., n. e. $10 and c. j. n. e. 1 y.

Catching fish in artificial fish ponds, $5.

False marking or counterfeiting or fraudulently altering any public record, writ, process, or proceeding of any court, certificate of any public officer, charter, will, deed, bond, letter of attorney, policy, certificate of state, bill, note, order for moneys, &c., or any writing, purporting to contain evidence of the existence or discharge of any debt, &c., with intent that any person should be defrauded, s. i. n. e. 6 mo. and h. l. n. l. 3y. n. e. 7 y.

Knowingly passing such writing, same.

Falsly making or counterfeiting any other writing, or knowingly using with intent, &c., h. l. n. e. 3 y.

Counterfeiting bank bills or notes with intent, &c., s. i. n. e. 6 mo., h. l. n. l. 2 y. n. e. 5 y.

Offering to pass such, knowing, &c., with intent, &c., s. i. n. e. 4 mo. and h. l. n. l. 2 y., n. e. 5. y.

Making, &c., plates, &c., for counterfeiting, or having such in possion, knowing, &c., with intent they should be used, &c., s. i. n. e. 4 mo. and h. l. n. l. 2 y., n. e. 5 y.

Making false coin, s. i. n. e. 6 mo. and h. l. n. l. 2 y., n. e. 5 y.

Making, &c., dies, &c., or having in possession with intent, &c., s. i. n. e. 4 mo. and h. l. n. l. 2 y., n. e. 5 y.

Perjury, s. i. n. e. 4 mo. and h. l. n. l. 2 y., n. e. 5 y.

Willful false swearing in regard to anything wherein he is required by law to make an oath or affirmation, is perjury.

Subornation of perjury, same punishment.

Willfully assaulting or obstructing any officer in service of lawful process in any civil case, or in any criminal case punishable by imprisonment or fine, or both, c. j. n. e. 1 y and n. l. $300.

Rescue in such case, same.

Willfully assaulting, &c., in criminal case punishable by hard labor, or rescue in such case, h. l. half term of party accused, or c. j. n. e. 2 y. or n. e $500, or both last.

Willfully assaulting, &c., in a criminal case punishable with death or h. l. for life, or rescue in such case, h. l. n. e. 10 y. or c. j. n. l. 2 y., and n. e. $500 ; in any other case, c. j. n. e. 6 mo. or n. e. $500.

Conveying tools into any prison, or aiding escape therefrom without escape, c. j. n. e. 1 y. and n. e. $500; if prisoner convicted of offense punishable with death or hard labor, s. i. n. e. 6 mo. and h. l. n. e. 10 y., or n. e. $500.

Aiding escape of person committed for debt, pay debt and c. j. n. e. 1 y.

Aiding escape of prisoner committed for capital offense, h. l. for life or any term of years.

Aiding escape of prisoner for offense not capital, same punishment as prisoner, or c. j. n. l. 1 y. and n. e. $2,000.

Party having custody permiting escape, same as for aiding.

Party having custody negligently suffering an escape, n. e. $500.

False pretending to be an officer, sheriff, or deputy sheriff, whose duty it is to keep the peace, or apprehend offenders, or require others to aid him as such, n. e. $300.

Clerk of any town or place, willfully and corruptly making false record of vote, or false copy of such record, or false certificate or return of votes, s. i. n. e. 6 mo., h. l. n. l. 2 y., n. e. 5 y.

Assault and battery on conviction before a justice, n. e. $10 or i. j. n. e. 30 d., and surety of peace and good behavior; if of an aggravated nature, n. e. $200 and c. j. n. e. 6 mo., or either.

Rioters remaining after proclamation, or obstructing or assaulting officer known or declared to be such in making proclamation, n. e. $1,000 or c. j. n. e. 1 y.

Breaking or entering a dwelling in the night time, or breaking and entering in the day, and therein committing assault and battery on any inmate of such house, n. e. $1,000, c. j. n. e. 1 y. or h. l. n. e. 7 y.

Assaulting any city, town or ward officer in the discharge of any duty of his office, at the annual or other election, or taking away or destroying the ballot box or check list when in use at such election, n. e. $300, or h. l. n. e. 3 y.

Any person who shall by previous appointment meet another and engage in a fight, h. l. n. e. 1 y. or n. e. $1,000.

Every one present at such fight as aid, second or surgeon, or who shall advise, &c., h. l. n. e. 1 y. or c. j. n. e. 1 y., or n. e. $1,000.

Every inhabitant who shall by previous appointment leave the state and engage in a fight elsewere, h. l. n. e. 1 y., or n. e. $1,000.

Adultery or incest, c. j. n. e. 1 y. and n. e. $500, or h. l. n. l. 1 y. n. e. 3 y.

Gross lewdness, c. j. n. e. 6 mo. and n. e. $200, and sureties of good behavior.

Marrying or cohabiting with another having a wife or husband alive, unless absent, not heard of for three years, or reported and generally believed dead, or where former marriage within the age of consent, as adultery.

Blasphemy, n. e. $200, and may be held to find sureties of good behavior.

Profane swearing, $1 first offence, double for second, and not paid, house of correction n. e. 10 d.

Digging up or removing dead body without authority, h. l. n. e. 1 y., or n. e. $2,000 and c. j. n. e. 1 y.

Defacing, &c., monuments, &c., destroying, &c., fences, trees in places of burial, c. j. n. e. 6 mo., or n. e. $500, or both.

Maliciously maiming, &c., horses, &c., n. e. $100, c. j. n. e. 90 d., or both.

Setting up lottery or disposing of property by lottery, n. e. $500, n. l. $50.

Selling tickets in lottery, printing amounts of lotteries or places where tickets are kept for sale, n. l. $25, n. e. $100.

Keeping gaming house or suffering play for money n. l. $10, n. e. $200, or c. j. n. e. 1 y.

Winning at one sitting $5, double the amount; less than $5, n. l. $2, n. e. $10.

Exposing active poison for destruction of animals on others' lands or in highways &c., n. l. $10 n. e. $100.

Sellng unwholesome provisions without notice, c. j. n. e. 6 mo., or n. e. $200.

Kindling fires on other's land, n. e. $10.

Kindling fires if fire spreads and does damage to other's property, n. l. $10 n. e. $1,000, or c. j. n, l. 1. mo., n. e. 3. y.

Kindling fires carelessly on his own land, and thereby destroying other's property, n. l. $10, n. e. $1,000.

Kindling fires on his own or other's land with intent to injure another whereby the property of another is injured or destroyed, n. l. $30 n. e. $2,000, c. j. n. l. 6 mo. n. e. 3 y.

Accessories before or after the fact and persons who aid in counsel, hire or procure the offence, same punishment as principal offender.

Attempts to commit offences punishable by hard labor for life, s. i. n. l. 6. m. h. l. n. e. 10 y. n. l. 1. y.

Attempts to commit any other offence, n. e. half punishment for com. of offence.

Attempts to commit by counsel, hiring, or procurement of others, same punishment as making attempt.

Accessories to offences committed out of the state before or after the fact, same as if offence committed here.

Besides, there are a large number of lesser offences punishable with small fines, which I have thought unprofitable to attempt to enumerate. If exact information is sought no abstract should be relied upon, but reference should be made to the statute book. For general views, the loose abstract above may be sufficient.

Connecticut:

WALTER PITKIN, ESQ.—The following is believed to be a complete catalogue of the crimes and misdemeanors for which a penalty is provided by the statute law of this state:

(A.) *Offences punishable by death.*

Treason, murder in the first degree, arson or burning of any building causing death.

(B.) *Offences punishable by imprisonment only.*

Murder in the second degree, arson endangering life, perjury with intent to take life, cutting out the tongue or putting out the eye of another by laying in wait, rape, sodomy (if one party is forced or under 15, he is not punished), bestiality—state prison for life.

Assault (including poisoning) with intent to kill—state prison for life or not less than 10 years.

Maiming with intent to disfigure, robbery with personal abuse, burglary with personal abuse, carnal knowledge of female child under ten years, destroying public stores, burning public buildings, arson, burning building endangering a dwelling house, burning a building or vessel with intent to defraud insurers, removing or altering public records, counterfeiting public seal—state prison not less than seven or more than ten years.

Assault with intent to commit rape—state prison not less than three or more than ten years.

Placing obstructions on railroads—state prison not more than ten years.

Embezzlement of funds of banks, railroads, &c., and making false entries in books of same, disinterment of deceased persons, burning buildings containing horses or neat cattle—state prison not less than two or more than ten years.

Robbery—state prison not less than four or more than ten years.

Aiding an escape from state prison, breaking or assisting in breaking jail, perjury and subornation of perjury, assault with intent to. rob, carrying or enticing away a child under twelve years of age, attempting to destroy public stores, attempting to destroy public buildings, forgery (and double damages to party injured), counterfeiting coin, possessing counterfeit coin with intent to pass, possessing counterfeit bills with intent to pass, possessing bank bills with intent to fill up and to pass, selling counterfeit bills with intent to have them passed, forging public securities, making plates for counterfeit bills, possessing plate for forging bank bills, adultery, incest, bigamy, burning vessel or building other than a dwelling house, horse stealing, stealing from the person—state prison not less than two years or more than 5 years.

Burglary, theft of a sum exceeding $50, acting as principal or second in a prize fight—state prison not more than five years.

Breaking and entering a store with intent to rob, breaking and entering a dwelling in day season—state prison not more than four years.

Uttering and passing as money any false token in the similitude of bill or checks of banks, &c.—state prison not less than one year or more than three years.

Attempting to break and enter a building with intent to steal or commit other crime, abetting prize fight—state prison not more than two years.

Obstructing the apprehension of a person complained of—state prison one year.

Embezzlement by bailee of goods to be manufactured—common jail not more than six months.

Keeping or frequenting a house reputed to be of ill fame—workhouse not more than thirty days.

(C.) Offences punishable by fine only.

Challenging another to fight a duel, carrying or delivering such challenge—fine $3,000. (If the challenger is unable to pay the fine, he is punishable by imprisonment in jail for a year, and in either case is disqualified to hold any office of trust or honor.)

Unlawful dissections—not more than $2,000 or less than $500.

Emitting bills of credit, or making or issuing any writing or note payable in goods, or other valuable thing to be used for purposes of general currency—fine not exceeding $600 or less than $100.

Encouraging attempts to produce miscarriage—fine not more than $500.

Importing foreign convicts (each offence)—fine of $334.

Unlicensed exhibition of tumblers, mountebanks, rope walking, &c., unlicensed exhibition of feats of horses, allowing land or buildings to be used for the above purposes, keeping unlicensed billiard tables—not more than $200.

Passing bills of credit, &c., issued with intent to be used as general currency, having an interest in any fund used for gaming, betting on an election or holding stakes, losing or winning money, &c., by playing or betting on games of hazard, and suffering them to be played in one's house or building—not more than $100 or less than $20.

Conversation by or with juror concerning cause on trial—not more than $100.

Secretly assaulting and maiming another—not more than $67.

Giving unlicensed theatrical exhibitions with a view to gain—fine of $50.

Betting on a horse race, or making up a purse for the same—not more than $50 or less than $10.

(If the offender is owner of the horse, it is forfeited.)

Keeping an unlicensed nine-pin alley—not more than $50 or less than $7.

Injuring trees on a public square—not more than $50.

Removal of stone on a common shore—not more than $35.

Disturbance of religious meetings—not more than $34.

Advertising a horse race, or driving or holding stakes at the same—not more than $30 or less than $8.

Barratry—fine of $17.

Public keeping of implements for gaming, allowing building to be used for unlicensed exhibitions of mountebanks, &c., purchasing and distributing obscene books, &c., selling spirituous liquors within two miles of a camp meeting—fine of $7.

Injuring bridges, catching shell-fish growing on bridges, tearing down trees on a public square, theft of an amount not exceeding $15, taking fish from private ponds, being present at a fight between animals—not more than $7.

Using fire crackers, except on 4th July—fine $5.

Gaming for money, head of family allowing games at cards or billiards in his house—fine of $4.

Profane swearing—fine of $1.

(*D.*) *Offences punishable by fine and imprisonment.*

Manslaughter—state prison or jail not more than 10 years, and fine not exceeding $1,000.

Misprison of treason—state prison not more than 7 or less than 3 years, and fine not exceeding $1,000.

Falsely representing a free person to be a slave, seizing a free person with intent to enslave, falsely testifying that any person is a slave—state prison 5 years and a fine of $5,000.

Bribery—state prison not more than 5 or less than 2 years, and fine not exceeding $1,000.

Kidnapping free person—same imprisonment as above, and fine not exceeding $5.

Exposing child under 6 years of age with intent to abandon—same imprisonment as above, and fine not exceeding $400.

Seduction (1st offence)—state prison not more thon 3 years, fine not exceeding $2,000.

Seduction (2d offence)—state prison not more than one year, and fine not exceeding $1,000.

Emitting bills of credit, &c., to be used as general currency—state prison n. e. 1 y., n. l. 3 mos., and fine n. e. $600 n. l. $100.

Concealing death of bastard child, blasphemy—state prison not more than 1 year, and fine n. e. $100.

Theft of an amount between $15 and $50—common jail n. e. 6 mos., and n. l. $100.

Tearing down turnpike gate or toll-house in night season—common jail n. e. 6 n. l. 2 mos., and fine not less than $20.

Unlawful killing of game—common jail n. e. 10 d., fine n. e. $5.

(E.) Offences punishable by fine or imprisonment.

Sale of foreign lottery tickets—common jail not more than 1 year or less than 2 mos., cr fine n. e. $300 or n. l. $50.

Publication of obscene books, &c.—common jail not more than 1 year or less than 2 mos., or fine n. e. $300 or less than $50.

Malicious prosecution—same imprisonment as above or fine n. e. $1,000 or n. l. $20.

Sale of property by lotteries or hazard of any kind—same punishment as above.

Leasing buildings to be used for purposes of prostitution—jail not more than 6 mos., or fine not exceeding $500.

Contempt of court (except justices')—jail not more than 6 mos. or fine not exceeding $100.

Selling diseased flesh or fowl—jail not more than 6 months, or fine not exceeding $100.

Secret delivery of bastard child—jail not more than 3 months, or fine not exceeding $150.

Cruelty to animals—jail not more than 30 days, or fine n. e. $25.

Fornication—jail not more than 30 days, or fine $7.

(f) Offences punishable by fine or imprisonment or both.

Aiding or corresponding with rebels or public enemies—state prison not more. than 7 or less than three years, or fine n. e. $1000 or both.

Attempt to produce miscarriage, accessories to above crime—state prison not more than 5 years, or fine n. e. $1,000 for principal, or $500 for accessory, or both.

Obtaining goods &c., by false pretences—state prison not more than 5 years, or fine n. e. $500, or both.

Embezzlement, fraud or making false entries by officers or agents of corporations—state prison n. e. 5 years, or fine n. e. $100, or both.

Attempt by a woman to produce miscarriage on herself—state prison not more than 2 years, or fine n. e. $500, or both.

Obstructing navigation of canals, or injuring gate locks &c.—jail not more than 1 year or less than 2 months, or fine n. e. $500 or less than $30, or both.

Using indecent or abusive language—jail not more than 1 year, or fine n. e. $500, or both.

Injuring telegraph poles—same imprisonment as above, or fine n. e. $200, or both.

Injuring engines or displacing switch on railroads—same imprisonment as above, or fine n. e. $150, or both.

Poisoning fish ponds—same imprisonment as above, or fine n. e, $100, or both.

Embezzlement and false entries by clerks—jail not more than 1 year, or fine n. e. $100, or both.

Malicious injury to trees, vegetables or fences—jail not more than 1 year, or fine n. e. $100, or both.

Fraudulent procuring naval or military bounty due another—jail n. e. 6 months, or fine n. e. $300, or both.

Wilfully burning woods, grain, &c., or injuring bridges, mill dams, machinery, animals, or cloth in process of manufacture—jail not more than 6 or less than 2 months, or fine n. e. $200 or less than $20, or both.

Keeping or frequenting dance-house, reputed to be a place of assignation—jail not more than six months or less than 30 days, or fine n. e. $100, or both.

Injuring derrick, injuring gas works, painting or printing on the property of another, breaking windows in a dwelling house, injuring signs, vehicles, aqueducts or boundary-marks loosing a horse fastened in a public place, forging or counterfeiting stamps or labels, selling goods having counterfeit stamp—jail not more than 6 months, or fine n. e. $100, or both.

Breach of the peace by threatening &c., using threats &c., to cause workmen to leave their employers, keeping house of ill-fame, acting as bar tender or servant in house of ill-fame—jail not more than 6 months, or fine n. e. $100 or both.

Riotously assembling and not dispersing after proclamation, obstructing proclamation to rioters—jail 6 months, or fine n. e. $67, or both.

Injuring buildings or clothing by putting thereon any noxious substance—jail not more than 4 months, or fine n. e. $100, or both.

"Gift sales," drawing of lotteries, sale of lottery tickets—jail n. e. 3 months, or fine n. e. $17, or both.

Keeping disorderly house—jail n. e. 3 months, or fine n. e. $100, or both.

Exposing person—jail not more than 3 months, or fine n. e. $50, or both.

Using horse or boat without permission of owner—same punishment as above.

Injuring ponds used for breeding fish—jail not more than 3 months, or fine n. e. $25, or both.

Injuring public buildings or furniture, cutting timber trees on the land of another,—jail not more than 3 months, or fine n. e., $17, or both.

Resisting a public officer—jail not more than 2 months, or fine n. e., $34, or both.

Public exhibition of rebel flags or devices—jail n. e. 30 days, or fine, n. e., $100, or both.

Using gas without metre, altering metre, fraud of agent of gas company,—jail not more than 30 days, or fine n. e. $50, or both.

Improper burials—jail n. e. 30 days, or fine n. e. $50, or both.

Interrupting 'or disturbing schools,—jail n. e. 30 days, or fine n. e. $7, or n. l. $100, or both.

Loosing cattle for the purpose of having them impounded, cutting trees on lands of Indians, taking or destroying fish in private ponds, false statements by driver of livery team, breaking windows in a public building in the night season, stealing fruit &c., in the night, or destroying fruit or shrubbery, trespass on cultivated lands, stealing growing cranberries, throwing dead animals into ponds used for domestic purposes, driving on a bridge at a gate faster than a walk, furnishing prisoners with liquor, contempt of court (justices'), lascivious carriage, keeping a place for fighting cocks or animals,—jail not more than 30 days, or fine n. e. $7, or both.

Stealing poultry—jail n. e. 6 months, or fine n. e. $50, or both

New Jersey:

CORTLANDT PARKER, ESQ.—The punishments of crime are as follows:

Treason: death.

Misprision of treason: state prison, 7 years and $1,000 fine.

Murder 1st degree (no discretion): death.

Murder 2d degree: state prison 20 years.

Manslaughter: state prison 10 years and $1,000 fine.

Sodomy: state prison 21 years and $1,000 fine.

Rape: state prison 15 years and $1,000 fine.

Abduction (forcible): state prison 12 years and $1,000 fine

Abduction, with consent of infant under 15: state prison 2 years and $400 fine.

Abduction with consent and deflowering: state prison 5 years and $1,000 fine.

Polygamy: state prison 10 years and $1,000 fine.

Concealment of bastardy: state prison 1 year and $200 fine.

Incest: state prison $1\frac{1}{2}$ years and $500 fine.

Adultery: state prison $1\frac{1}{2}$ years and $100 fine.

Fornication: state prison, fine $14.

Open lewdness: state prison 1 year and $100 fine.

Pretence of supernatural powers: county gaol 3 months and $50 fine.

Impostures in religion: county gaol 6 months and $100 fine.

Blasphemy: state prison 1 year and $200 fine.

Perjury or subornation: disfranchisement and state prison 7 years and $800 fine.

Bribery and accepting bribes: state prison 5 years and $800 fine.

Taking unlawful fees: state prison 2 years and $400 fine.

Embracing and taking bribe as juryman: state prison 2 years and $600 fine.

Arson: state prison 15 years and $2,000 fine.

Burning buildings not parcel of dwelling: state prison 10 years and $1,000 fine.

Attempt at burning: state prison 5 years and $500 fine.

Burglary: state prison 10 years and $500 fine.

Breaking and entering by day: state prison 10 years and $500 fine.

Larceny of or over $20: state prison 10 years and $500 fine; under $20, county jail 3 months and $100 fine; petty, repeated, state prison 7 years and $500 fine.

Robbery: state prison 15 years and $1,000 fine.

Attempt at robbery: state prison 10 years and $500 fine.

Assault with intent to commit murder, rape, burglary, robbery and sodomy: state prison 10 years and $1,000 fine.

Wounding or maiming: state prison 10 years and $1,000 fine..

Entering without breaking with intent to commit above crimes: state prison 5 years and $300 fine.

Poisoning not producing death: state prison 15 years and $1,000 fine.

Embezzlement: state prison 2 years and $100 fine.

Stealing or falsifying records: state prison 7 years and $7,000 fine.

Forgery: state prison 10 years and $3,000 fine.

Uttering: state prison 10 years and $3,000 fine.

False personation in legal matters: state prison 7 years and $3,000 fine.

Embezzlement by public officers: state prison 5 years and $5,000 fine.

Obtaining goods, &c., by false pretences: state prison 3 years and $1,000 fine.

Obstructing officers: state prison 2 years and $800 fine.

Rescues and voluntary permission of escape, if of those guilty of murder or treason: death; of other convicts or accused: state prison 3 years, fine $1,000.

Negligent escapes: state prison 3 years and $1,000 fine.

Breaking prison: state prison 3 years and $1,000 fine.

Aiding in breaking prison: state prison 2 years and $500 fine.

Composition of felony: state prison 1 year and $300 fine.

Conspiracy: state prison 2 years and $500 fine.

Kidnapping, &c.: state prison 5 years and $1,000 fine.

Mayhem: state prison 7 years and $1,000 fine.

Dueling, aiding and abetting, though no death ensue nor duel happen: state prison 2 years and $500 fine.

Fighting or being second in duel: state prison 4 years and $1,000 fine.

Sending threatening letters: state prison 9 months and $300 fine.

Stealing fixtures or growing grain: state prison 9 months and $50 fine.

Destroying papers of pecuniary value with fraudulent intent: state prison 10 months and $800 fine.

Malicious mischief: state prison 2 months and $150 fine.

Injuring railroads: state prison 3 months and $300 fine.

Receiving stolen goods knowing, &c.: state prison 3 months and $300 fine.

Concealing knowledge of felony: state prison 3 months and $500 fine.

Selling diseased and unwholesome articles: county jail 3 months and $50 fine.

Resurrectionizing: state prison 5 years and $2,000 fine.

Prize fighting: state prison 2 years, fine $1,000.

Bringing prize fighters or their abettors here: state prison 2 years and $500 fine.

Citizens of other states coming to witness prize fight: state prison 1 year and $300 fine.

Obstructing firemen on duty: state prison 2 years and $1,000 fine.

Assaults, false imprisonment, riots, nuisances, and all offences at common law not specially provided for: state prison 2 years and fine $500.

Selling coal or other merchandize by persons transporting same: county jail 1 year and fine $500.

Abortion and attempting same, if woman die: state prison 15 years and $1,000 fine; if not: state prison 7 years and $500 fine.

Selling ardent spirits without license: $20 fine.

Selling intoxicating liquor Sunday: $20 fine.

Selling lottery tickets or policies: state prison 1 year and $100 fine.

Gaming: state prison 2 years and $500 fine.

Horse racing and betting on: county jail 6 months and $100 fine.

In making this table, the limits of the discretion of the court are given. No sentence is imperative but that of death, which can only be commuted by the pardoning power. All crimes, whatever their degree at common law, save murder and treason, are statutory misdemeanors, some termed high misdemeanors. Whether the distinction of felony and misdemeanor is abolished otherwise than in pleading is not fully settled.

The punishments annexed by law to crimes and misdemeanors are fines and imprisonments ; sometimes either, sometimes both ; imprisonment to hard labor in state prison or imprisonment in jail. In cases of treason and murder in the first degree, capital punishment by hanging.

Pennsylvania :

J. J. BARCLAY, Esq.—See the penal code: " Act to consolidate, revise and amend the penal laws of this commonwealth, March 31, 1860." Pamp. Laws, 382.

Maryland :

A. STERLING, Jr., Esq.—The common law is in force here, except as specially modified by statute law. The statutes have fixed punishments for many common law offences, and made some statutory offences, but not many except those growing out of slavery, which have nearly all been abolished. They are mainly punishing vagrancy, preventing the sale of liquor, and on Sunday against gambling. The state has made little change in the common law crimes, except as to the punishment.

Kentucky :

E. L. VAN WINKLE, Esq.—The punishment for murder is death.
Manslaughter: 2 to 10 years in penitentiary.
Burglary: confinement in the penitentiary.
Arson: confinement in the penitentiary.
Rape: confinement in the penitentiary, 10 years to 20 years.
Grand larceny: confinement in the penitentiary 2 to 4 years.
Forgery: confinement in the penitentiary.
Rape upon the body of an infant under the age of 12 years: death.
Malicious shooting or stabbing where death ensues within six months: penitentiary for not less than 1 nor more than 6 years.
Carnal knowledge of a white girl under 10 years of age, or of an idiot: penitentiary from 10 to 20 years.
Abduction of a white girl, under 14 years of age, from the possession of parents or person having charge: penitentiary from 1 to 2 years, or fined from $100 to $500.
Decoying child under 10 years, or concealing same, knowing it to have been enticed from its parents or guardians: penitentiary from 1 to 2 years.
Detention of white woman against her will with intention to marry or have her married to another, or with intent to have carnal knowledge—penitentiary 2 to 7 years.
Bigamy—penitentiary 2 to 9 years.
Robbery and burglary—3 to 10 years.
Assault with intent to rob—1 to 2 years.
Feloniously taking property from dwelling, church, school-house, booth, tent or market, or public building—1 to 2 years.
Maiming—1 to 5 years.

Malicious shooting or stabbing and wounding, or poisoning without death—1 to 5 years.

Threatening letters with the intent to extort—1 to 10 years.

Felonious breaking into store-houses, &c.—1 to 7 years.

Willful burning out-houses, stacks of grain, or attempting same—1 to 6 years; for attempt—3 months to 6 years.

Perjury—2 to 6 years.

Subornation—2 to 6 years, besides being ever after disqualified ' from giving evidence.

Bribing a juror—1 to 6 years.

Counterfeiting coin or bank notes—5 to 15 years.

Counterfeiting checks, certificates and other instruments—2 to 6 years.

Deeds, wills, bonds, patents, &c.—2 to 10 years.

Forging seal of state, United States, or of any court or officer, and uttering, publishing or using same—5 to 15 years.

Forgery of any other paper to obtain possession of property of another—2 to 10 years.

Having in possession, with intent to pass, counterfeit bank notes—2 to 10 years.

Plate in possession with intent—same.

Selling or stealing free person—5 to 10 years.

Horse stealing—4 to 8 years.

Hog stealing—2 to 4 years.

Receiving stolen goods—1 to 6 years.

Embezzlement—1 to 10 years.

Obtaining money or property under false pretences—1 to 5 years.

False personation to marry another, to become bail to confess judgment, to do any other act in the course of any suit—1 to 5 years.

Destruction of public works, corner trees, fraudulently: 2 to 4 years.

Escape from penitentiary: 2 to 6 years.

Escape and rescue of prisoners: same term for which the prisoner would have been convicted.

Shooting and stabbing in sudden affray without malice, where death does not ensue: fine $50 to $500 and confinement in county jail 6 to 12 months.

Shooting at with intent to kill or wound, without inflicting wound: fine not exceeding $500 and imprisonment in county jail 6 to 12 months, or either.

Disturbance of religious worship: $10 to $50, or 10 to 20 days, or both.

Duelling or challenging: fine $300 to $500, and forfeiture of office, disqualified for office and loss of suffrage for 7 years.

Lottery ticket selling: $100 to $10,000, &c.

Indiana :

Hon. CONRAD BAKER.—Treason and murder in the first degree are punishable with death or imprisonment for life. Murder in second degree punishable by imprisonment for life.

Manslaughter: imprisonment for not less than 2 nor more than 21 years.

Assault or assault and battery with intent to commit a felony: not less than 2 or more than 14 years imprisonment, and a fine not exceeding $1,000.

Administering poison with intent to kill, when death does not ensue: imprisonment for not less than three years.

Mingling poison with food, drink or medicine, with intent to injure any human being: imprisonment not less than 2 nor more than 14 years.

Malicious mayhem: not less than 2 nor more than 14 years and fine not exceeding $1,000.

Kidnapping: fine not less than $100 nor more than $5,000, and imprisonment not less than 2 nor more than 14 years.

Rape—imprisonment for not less than 2 nor more than 21 years.

Seduction of a female of good moral character, under the age of 21 years, under promise of marriage—imprisonment in penitentiary not less than 1 nor more than 3 years, and fine not exceeding $500, or imprisonment in county jail not exceeding 6 months.

Abducting of a female for purposes of prostitution—imprisonment in penitentiary not less than 2 nor more than 5 years, or imprisonment in county jail not exceeding 1 year and fine not exceeding $500.

Burglary—imprisonment in penitentiary for not less than 2 nor more than 14 years, and fine not exceeding $1,000.

Robbery—imprisonment in penitentiary for not less than 2 nor more than 14 years, and fine not exceeding $1,000.

Grand larceny—imprisonment in state prison for not less than 2 nor more than 14 years, and disfranchisement for any determined period.

Petit larceny—fine not exceeding $500 and imprisonment in state prison not less than 1 or more than three years, with disfranchisement for any determinate period, or fine and disfranchisement as aforesaid, and imprisonment in county jail not exceeding 1 year.

Receiving stolen goods—same as larceny.

Altering marks and brands of cattle with intent to steal—same as grand larceny.

Falsely personating another and receiving property—same as petit or grand larceny according to amount.

Obtaining goods by false pretences—imprisonment in penitentiary for not less than 2 nor more than 7 years, and fine not exceeding double the value of the property so obtained.

Arson—imprisonment in the state prison for not less than 2 nor more than 10 years, and fine not less than double the value of the property destroyed and, should the life of any person be lost thereby, the offender shall be deemed guilty of murder and shall suffer death or imprisonment for life accordingly.

Willfully and maliciously obstructing a railroad track—imprisonment for not less than 1 or more than 7 years, and if death ensue the offence is murder in the second degree and is punished accordingly.

Forgery and counterfeiting—imprisonment in state prison for not less than 2 nor more than 14 years, and fine not exceeding $1,000.

Knowingly having possession of apparatus made use of in forging and counterfeiting—imprisonment in state prison for not less than 2 nor more than 5 years, and fine n. e. $1,000.

Professional gambling—imprisonment for not less than 5 years and disfranchisement for any determined period, or imprisonment in county jail not less than three nor more than 6 months, and disfranchisement as aforesaid.

Bribery—fine not exceeding twice the amount offered or received, and imprisonment in state prison for not less than 2 nor more than 10 years.

Perjury and subornation of perjury—imprisonment in penitentiary for not less than two nor more than 21 years, and fine not exceeding $1,000.

Simple mayhem—fine not less than $5 and not exceeding $2,000, to which may be added imprisonment in county jail not less than 20 days, nor more than six months.

Riot—fine not exceeding $500, to which may be added imprisonment in county jail not exceeding three months.

Rout—fine not more than $1,000, or imprisonment in county jail not more than 60 days.

Affray—fine not exceeding $20, or imprisonment in county jail not exceeding five days.

Assault and battery—fine not exceeding $1,000, to which may be added imprisonment in county jail not exceeding six months.

Nuisance—fine not exceeding $1,000.

All places where intoxicating liquors are sold, if kept in a disorderly manner, are declared to be nuisances, and the keeper is liable to a fine of not less than $20, nor more than $100 for any day the same is kept.

Selling unwholesome provisions—fine not exceeding $100.

Forcible entry or detainer—fine not exceeding $1,000.

Malicious trespass—fine not exceeding two-fold the value of the damage done, to which may be added imprisonment not exceeding one year.

Trespass on lands—fine of five times the value of the injury, to which may be added imprisonment not exceeding one year.

Obstructing navigable streams—fine not less than three nor

more than five hundred dollars for each week the obstruction is continued.

Attempting to influence a jury by bribes, &c.—fine not exceeding $500, and imprisonment not exceeding six months.

Malicious prosecution—fine not exceeding $1,000, to which may be added imprisonment not exceeding six months.

Common barratry—fine not exceeding $500, and imprisonment not exceeding six months.

Usurpation of an office—fine not exceeding $500.

Living in open and notorious fornication or adultery—fine not exceeding $300, and imprisonment not exceeding three months.

Public indecency—fine not exceeding $100 and imprisonment.

Incest—imprisonment in state prison for not less than 2 nor more than 10 years, or in county jail not less than 6 nor more than 12 months.

Bigamy—imprisonment in state prison for not less than 2 nor more than 5 years, or fine not exceeding $1,000, and imprisonment in county jail for not less than 3 nor more than 6 months.

Marriage between a white person and one having one-eighth part or more of negro blood—imprisonment for not less than 1 nor more than 10 years, and a fine not less than one nor more than five thousand dollars.

Maliciously injuring telegraph pole or wire—imprisonment in state prison for not more than two years, or fine not exceeding $500, or imprisonment in county jail not less than 3 nor more than 6 months.

Officer voluntarily permitting prisoners to escape charged with or convicted of a crime the penalty of which is death—imprisonment in penitentiary for not less than 10 nor more than 21 years. In all other cases of voluntary escape, the officer permitting the escape shall suffer the same punishment incident to the crime with which the prisoner escaping shall have been charged or convicted.

Aiding an escape of a person, charged or convicted of crime, by a person not an officer—imprisonment for not less than 2 nor more than 21 years in the state prison.

Every criminal who shall escape, being confined in the state prison, shall, for such escape, be imprisoned not exceeding double the time for which he was originally sentenced, to commence at the end of the original term.

On conviction of a female of any one of the crimes before mentioned, the punishment of which is confinement in the state prison, she may, instead of such imprisonment, be imprisoned in the county jail at hard labor under the direction of the jailor.

When the convict is under the age of 21 years, and the punishment is imprisonment in the state prison, imprisonment in the county jail for any determinate period may be substituted.

Whenever any person is imprisoned in the state prison, he or she shall be kept at hard labor during such imprisonment.

Having carnal knowledge of an insane woman—imprisonment in state prison not less than 2 or more than 10 years.

Misdemeanors:

Duelling in all its phases when death does not ensue—fine not less than $100, and imprisonment in county jail not exceeding 1 year, and the party after conviction shall be ineligible to any office of profit or trust not more than 3 months.

Charging unlawful toll or ferriage—fine not exceeding $100, or imprisonment not exceeding 1 month.

Unlicensed ferry—fine not exceeding $50.

Violating license law—fine not exceeding $200.

Selling liquors to minors or persons intoxicated—fine not less than $5 or more than $15.

Adulterating liquors—fine in any sum not less than $5 or more than $50.

Gaming—fine not exceeding $50.

Keeping gaming house—fine not less than $50 nor more than $500.

Horse racing upon highways—fine not less than $5 nor more than $50.

Lottery not authorized by law—fine not exceeding $500.

Removing monument on boundary of land with intent to destroy such work—fine not exceeding $200, or imprisonment in county jail not exceeding six months.

Setting grounds on fire with intent to injure another person—fine not exceeding $50.

Bringing paupers into the state—fine $500.

Attempting to procure abortion—fine not more than $500 and imprisonment in jail not exceeding 12 months.

Disturbing religious meeting—fine not less than $5 nor more than $50, and imprisonment in county jail, not exceeding thirty days, may be added.

Removing dead bodies from place of interment without proper authority—fine not exceeding $1,000.

Counseling marriage between colored and white persons—fine not less than $100 nor more than $1,000.

Sale and conveyance to defraud creditor or purchaser—fine not exceeding $200 and imprisonment in county jail not exceeding 12 months.

Obstructing process, freeing a person arrested—fine not exceeding $1,000, or imprisonment not exceeding six months.

Negligently suffering prisoner to escape—fine not exceeding $1,000.

Aiding prisoner to escape—fine not exceeding $500, or imprisonment not exceeding 12 months, or both.

Failing to assist in service of process when required—fine in any sum not more than $100.

Returning to after removal from lands mortgaged to the state—fine not more than $100 and imprisonment not exceeding thirty days.

Obstructing habeas corpus—fine not exceeding $1,000, to which may be added imprisonment not exceeding 90 days.

Violation of estray laws—fine not exceeding $100, or imprisonment not exceeding 6 mos.

Uttering obscene books—fine not exceeding $500, and if the exhibition be made to a female, imprisonment may be added not exceeding 3 mos.

Failing to return marriage certificate and license—fine not less than $5, nor more than $100.

Furnishing false tickets to any elector who cannot read the English language—fine not less than two, nor more than one hundred dollars.

Fraudulently causing false vote—fine not less than ten nor more than 100 dollars.

Attempting to vote twice—fine of $50 and disfranchisement for two years.

Judge of an election attempting to influence an elector—fine not exceeding $100.

Illegal voting—fine not less than $5 or more than $100.

Officer of election opening ticket—fine in any sum not exceeding $100.

Offering threat or reward to procure election—fine not exceeding $500, and disfranchisement for 2 yrs.

Performing duties of office before qualifying—fine not exceeding $1,000.

Officer claiming what is not due or failing in duty—fine not exceeding $1,000, and imprisonment may be added not exceeding 6 months.

Auditor, recorder, or clerk, keeping their office in any other building than that provided by board of commissioners—fine not exceeding $100.

County officers purchasing demands against the county for less than the face thereof—fine not exceeding $500.

Obstructing highways—fine not exceeding $500, or imprisonment not exceeding 3 months.

Shutting culvert, water gate, interfering with, &c.—fine not exceeding $500, or imprisonment not exceeding 3 months.

Leading animals upon and obstructing tow-path — fine not exceeding $50.

Supervisor failing in keeping highways and bridges in his district in good repair—fine not less than $5, nor more than $100.

Signing or delivery false bill of lading—fine not exceeding $500.

Desecrating cemetery—fine not exceeding $500, or imprisonment not exceeding 6 months

Disclosing telegraphic dispatch—fine not exceeding $500.

Changing inspectors—fine not exceeding $100.

Keeping gaming tables—fine not exceeding $1,000, to which may be added imprisonment not exceeding 6 months.

Recording deed without indorsement of auditor—fine $5.

Carrying off products of the soil of another without authority—fine not exceeding $50, and imprisonment not exceeding 6 mos.

Failing to give sworn list of taxable property—fine not exceeding $500.

Obstructing ingress of fish into any river or creek emptying into the Ohio, by stretching any net across such river or creek within one mile of its mouth—fine not less than $5, nor more than $20 for every day so obstructed.

Poisoning fish—fine not less than $5, nor more than $20.

Permitting horses witn glanders to run at large—fine not exceeding $50.

Michigan:

H. K. CLARKE, Esq.—The punishments annexed to the several offenses forbidden by law, appear in a schedule annexed hereto. In answering this interrogatory, it is assumed that it is intended to include all offenses, whether denominated "crimes" or "misdemeanors," and all offenses punishable by the general police laws of the state, and to exclude offenses against municipal ordinances and enactments providing for the enforcement of sanitary and inspection laws.

Schedule.

Of punishments prescribed by the laws of Michigan, and for the offenses respectively specified:

Death:

*5,708. Treason against the state.

State prison for life:

5,711. Murder in first degree.

5,723. Attempt to murder by poisoning, &c.

5,745. Burning dwelling house at night.

5,754. Burglary in the night, armed.

State prison for life, or any term of years less than seven:

5,949. Third conviction for felony, in addition to punishment prescribed for such third offense.

State prison for life or any term of years:

5,712. Murder in the second degree.

5,724. Assault with intent to murder.

5,725. Assault and robbery, being armed.

5,730. Rape.

5,732. Abduction to compel marriage.

5,737. Poisoning food or drink.

5,746. Arson of dwelling house in day time.

* The figures refer to sections in the Compiled Laws.

5,816, Counterfeiting coin.

5,820. Perjury in capital case or in cases where the punishment in state prison for life or any term of years.

State prison for any term of years:

5,745. Arson of dwelling house at night by person lawfully in the house.

5,747. Arson of church or other public building at night.

State prison not exceeding 15 years:

5,726. Assault with intent to rob or murder, being armed.

5,727. Robbery, not being armed.

5,755. Burglary, not being armed.

5,756. Burglary in office, &c., at night.

5,763. Larceny, second conviction.

5,785. Destroying vessels.

5,818. Counterfeiting, second conviction.

5,820. Perjury, in other than cases enumerated in first part of this section.

5,822. Subornation of perjury.

5,871. Crime against nature.

State prison not exceeding 15 years or fine not exceeding $1,000, or both:

5,720. Manslaughter.

5,743. Attempt to destroy an unborn child.

State prison not exceeding 15 years, or fine not exceeding $5,000, and county jail not exceeding one year:

5,756. Fitting out vessel with intent that she shall be cast away.

State prison not exceeding 15 years, or fine not exceeding $1,000, and county jail not exceeding 1 year:

5,750. Attempt to commit arson.

State prison not exceeding fifteen years, or county jail not exceeding one year:

5,870. Incest.

State prison not exceeding 14 years, or fine not exceeding $2,000, or county jail not exceeding two years:

5,771. Embezzlement in any state office.

State prison not exceeding 14 years, or county jail not exceeding one year:

5,802. Forgery.

5,803. Uttering forged instruments.

State prison not exceeding 10 years nor less than one year:

5,908. Issuing fraudulent stock.

5,909. Knowingly selling fraudulent stock.

State prison not exceeding 10 years:

5,728, Assault with intent to rob, not being armed.

5,733. Taking a woman with intent to compel marriage.

5,741. Exposing child with intent to abandon.

5,748. Arson of church or public building in day time.

5,749. Arson of store, vessel, &c.

5,753. Burning insured property with intent to injure insurer.

5,759. Entering building at night without breaking, or breaking and entering in the day time, with felonious intent.

5,766. Second conviction for receiving stolen goods, or conviction at same term of court of three acts of receiving, &c.

5,808. Second conviction for counterfeiting, or conviction at same term of court on three charges of said offense.

5,907. Taking from state treasury or defacing bonds deposited by banks.

5,947. Attempt to commit crime punishable by death.

State prison not exceeding 10 years, or a fine not exceeding $1,000, or both.

5,721. Maiming, disfiguring or aiding therein.

5,735. Kidnapping.

State prison not exceeding 10 years, or fine not exceeding $5,000, and county jail not exceeding one year:

5,775. Bankers issuing bills illegally.

5,776. Issuing or circulating spurious notes.

5,788. Making false protest.

State prison not exceeding 10 years, or fine not exceeding $1,000, and county jail not exceeding one year, and incapable of holding any offices in this state:

5,917. Engaging in a duel; challenging to fight or sending or delivering message to fight a duel.

State prison not exceeding 10 years, or county jail not exceeding one year and fine not exceeding $1,000:

5,770. Embezzlement by officers or servant of a corporation.

5,810. Making tools or paper for counterfeiting bank notes.

State prison not exceeding 10 years or fine not exceeding $5,000, and county jail not exceeding one year.

5,783. Obtaining property by false pretences.

State prison not exceeding 10 years, or fine not exceeding $500, or county jail not exceeding one year, or fine not exceeding $1,000:

5,740. Enticing away a child under 12 years of age.

State prison not exceeding 10 years, or fine not exceeding $500, or county jail not exceeding one year:

5,784. Cheat at common law.

State prison not exceeding 10 years, or fine not exceeding $1,000:

5,731. Assault with intent to commit rape.

5,917. Violating seals of ballot box, destroying ballots, or forcibly adding or diminishing the number of ballots legally deposited.

State prison not exceeding seven years:

5,948. Second conviction for a state prison offence, in addition to the punishment for such second offence.

State prison not exceeding seven years, or county jail not exceeding one year:

5,804. Forgery of any instrument issued by a state officer.

5,805. Forgery of any bank note.

5,806. Having ten or more counterfeit notes in possession with intent to utter.

State prison not exceeding ten years, or county jail not exceeding one year, or fine not exceeding $1,000:

5,940. Harboring or assisting felon to escape with intent to avoid detection, arrest, trial or punishment.

State prison not exceeding five years nor less than one, or fine not exceeding $2,000 nor less than $100, and state prison not less than than three nor more than twelve months:

5,927. Trespass on public lands.

State prison not exceeding five years, or fine not less than $100 nor more than $2,000, and state prison not less than three nor more than 12 months:

5,828. Converting tree, timber or lumber from the public lands.

State prison not exceeding five years, or county jail not exceeding two years, and fine not exceeding $1,000:

5,777. Disposing by bank officer of insolvent bank of its property, with intent to defraud creditors.

State prison not exceeding five years, or fine not exceeding $500, or county jail not exceeding two years:

5,738. Assault with intent to commit a felony.

State prison not exceeding five years, or fine not exceeding $5,000, and county jail not exceeding one year:

5,787. Making false bills of lading or invoice, with intent to defraud.

State prison not exceeding five years, or fine not exceeding $3,000, or county jail not exceeding one year:

5,826. Bribing public officer.

State prison not exceeding five years, or county jail not exceeding two years, or fine not exceeding $1,000:

5,709. Misprision of treason.

State prison not exceeding five years, or fine not exceeding $1,000, and county jail not exceeding one year:

5,789. Maliciously killing or maiming beasts, by means not particularly mentioned in this chapter.

QUESTION IV.

When there is a considerable range in the punishments allowed, is there found to be, in practice, a wide diversity in the administration of the law by different judges? Is there or not, in your judgment, too wide a range in the discretion allowed to judges?

ANSWERS.

Massachusetts:

GEORGE W. SEARLE, Esq.—There is a very wide diversity and no uniformity whatever. In my judgment, there should be no range at all by legislature, but the judge should be left free to temper the sentence exactly to the precise merits of each case; or, better still, the jury should pass upon the sentence at the same time, as upon the guilt of the accused. If there is to be a range by legislative enactment, the larger it is the better.

New Hampshire:

Hon. S. D. BELL.—There is said to be some diversity in the apportionment of punishments in cases where a wide discretion is given; this is unavoidable. The law must fix a narrow range of punishment for offences which may have great differences of character, or it must give a broader discretion, which may lead to inequalities of punishment arising from difference of character in judges. Errors may be committed by judges. The law must often do great wrong where little discretion is allowed.

Connecticut:

WALTER PITKIN, Esq.—The quality of an offence is so largely affected by the circumstances attending its commission, or out of which it arises in each particular case, that it is difficult to determine what is a safe and reasonable limit to the range of punishment. It is apparent that these circumstances of mitigation must be fewer and less in degree in certain classes of cases than in others; but with this exception, we must be guided by experience rather than by any definite and general principle. It is believed that the penalties of our law are for the most part judiciously distributed, and that in the same classes of cases they are administered by different judges with reasonable uniformity.

New Jersey:

CORTLANDT PARKER, Esq.—Notwithstanding the great range to these punishments, there is not found in practice any great diversity in the administration of the law by different judges; nor do I think there is too wide a range in the discretion permitted. The supreme court judges are seldom overruled. Their tone is apt to govern the justices of the sessions, who participate in deciding upon sentences; and their constant association with each other in the supreme court, tends to harmonize their ideas on this as well as on other subjects. It might, perhaps, be an improvement if no sentences could be determined on without the supreme court judge concurred. That is the only change I could venture to suggest.

JOHN F. HEGEMAN, Esq.—I do *not* think there is *too wide a range* in punishment, allowed in the discretion of the judges. It is pretty wide, but it is not considered abused in our state.

Pennsylvania:

J. J. BARCLAY, Esq.—As the state is divided into numerous districts, there is a wide diversity in the administration of the law, but the range is not too wide when the number and variety of cases is taken into consideration.

Maryland:

A. STERLING JR., ESQ.—There is a good deal of range in the punishment. Rape and arson are, in the discretion of the court, punished either with death or imprisonment, the longest term of penitentiary confinement, except by an executive commutation of death penalty, is eighteen years, the minimum range from one day to eighteen months; ten is the maximum in most penitentiary cases. Fine, or fine and imprisonment in jail, imprisonment in penitentiary and death are the punishments fixed for offences. There is a law on the statute books, the constitutionality of which is somewhat doubted, now that colored persons, for felony may be sold for a term of years, but it is practically obsolete, and I think cannot work harshly now, if executed. The law allowing colored persons to be flogged for larceny, is also unrepealed, but seldom carried out.

Kentucky:

E. L. VAN WINKLE, ESQ.—There is no range in punishments allowed to the judges; the range is given to the juries, and is usually exercised on the side of mercy, except in those cases where the crime is attended by aggravating circumstances.

Indiana:

Hon. CONRAD BAKER.—Under our system the judges do not assess the punishment. The jury not only finds as to the question of "guilty" or "not guilty," but where there is a verdict of "guilty,, the jury in that verdict assess or declare the punishment to be inflicted, and unless the judgment is arrested or a new trial granted, judgment is rendered by the court according to the verdict.

This practice, if not peculiar to Indiana, certainly does not prevail in many of the states. The writer of this report was educated, and practised for a few years, in a state where the jury cnuld only find "guilty" or "not guilty," leaving 'he assessment of the punishment to the court, and when he came to Indiana was much prejudiced against the practice which he found prevailing here.

Twenty-five years subsequent experience in this state has, however, entirely changed his opinion on this subject, and he now believes that permitting the jury to fix the punishment is a great improvement on the old system.

Under this practice, juries frequently convict, where they would fail to agree, or acquit, if the question of the amount of punishment were submitted to the court.

Of course, there is great diversity in the amount of punishment assessed by different juries for crimes nominally the same; but this diversity is, it is believed, no greater than the degrees of guilt of different persons accused of the same offence.

In my opinion, the best practice is to authorize a wide range in the punishment allowed, and then permit the jury to fix the punishment in each case where they find the defendant guilty.

Michigan:

H. K. CLARKE, ESQ.—A wide diversity does exist in the administration of the law by different judges, some inclining to the maximum limitations of punishments to be inflicted, and others to the minimum. In one year in this state, a prisoner charged with murder, but convicted of manslaughter, was punished by a fine of twenty-five dollars, while a prisoner in an adjoining circuit, convicted of an assault with intent to commit murder, was sentenced to the state prison for fifteen years. Yet the circumstances of these cases may have justified the leniency in the one case and the severity in the other. No one could judge of the circumstances better than the judge before whom the cases were tried; and though the wide diversity in the sentences may be attributable to the mental or moral characteristics of the judge, it is difficult to see how any general concurrence of action in such cases can be attained, without opportunities, which our system does not afford.

HENRY A. MORROW, Esq.—There is a wide diversity in the administration of the law by different judges. I cannot say that in my judgment too wide a range is allowed to the discretion of judges under the present system of criminal procedure. The heinousness of offences is determined by the facts and circumstances by which they are surrounded; so that it often happens that a particular offence coming within the definition of a certain crime, is, by the facts and circumstances surrounding it, robbed of nearly all its turpitude; while another offence, within the same definition of crime, is, by facts and circumstances, of a most aggravated nature. From this I argue that great discretion is to be allowed the judges in the inflicting of punishments, until a more minute classification of crimes has been hit upon by our law makers.

QUESTION V.

Are sheriffs appointed or elected, and for what term of office? Which, in your opinion, is the best system? Is there any limit to their re-eligibility, or may they be re-elected as often as their constituents choose?

ANSWERS.

Massachusetts:

GEO. W. SEARLE, Esq.—Sheriffs are elected by the people for five years. There is no limit to their re-election. In my opinion, no legal executive officer should be elected by the people. The temptations to bend to popular feeling and cater to the lowest interests of the criminal classes, during the tenure of office, and, especially, just before a re-election, is too great to hope for constant resistance from the men who seek such offices. By this it is not intended to intimate that they are not men of character, but simply that they are mostly men of small political and party services, men used to political management. Many here think that neither district attorney nor sheriff should be elective.

New Hampshire :

Hon. S. D. BELL.—Sheriffs are appointed by the governor and council for the term of five years. They may be re-appointed indefinitely, but re-appointments are rare. I have no means of comparing this with any other system. The office has lost its consequence, and is chiefly sought by the deputy sheriffs, who often resume their places as deputies after serving a term as sheriff.

Connecticut :

WALTER PITKIN, Esq.—It is provided by an amendment of the constitution, that sheriffs shall be appointed by the electors of the several counties. They had previously been appointed by the general assembly. Their term of office is three years and there is no limit to their re-eligibility.

New Jersey :

CORTLANDT PARKER, Esq.—Sheriffs are elected yearly. They are only eligible three times in succession, and, by custom, they are, with rare exceptions, elected three times as a matter of course. I do not like the system. Sheriffs would be more independent in their action, if there was no need of cultivating popularity. It would be better to have them elected at once for three years and not re-eligible. In populous cities and counties, the present system of electing sheriffs produces grave evils in the administration of justice ; at least, so it seems. Partisans have to be chosen. Generally the candidates selected are those most popular with the most ignorant and careless classes of society, and they find it necessary to propitiate them. Hence, a worse selection of grand and petit jurors. So that it becomes soon to be true that, as the moral tone of the sheriff, so that of the county itself, as expressed by the action of its courts.

JOHN F. HEGEMAN, Esq.—Sheriffs are elected for one year, re-eligible for three years only. I am of opinion that this system is as good as the other, and yet the office has run down to an inferior class of men, in many, too many, instances; but politics would perhaps make the appointments worse, unless done by the governor, or some other body than joint meeting of the legislature.

Pennsylvania :

J. J. BARCLAY, Esq.—Sheriffs are elected for a period of three years ; no serious objection appears to exist to the method by which these officers are elevated to office. A sheriff cannot be re-elected on the expiration of his term of office, but may be thereafter.

Maryland:

A. STERLING, Esq.—Sheriffs are elected for two years, and are ineligible for re-election. This has been the law for twenty years and more. I think there is no material difference between this and the appointive system. The sheriffs do very well, though not quite as careful as they ought to be in selecting jurors. In Baltimore city, and in one or two counties, the juries are drawn by lot.

Kentucky:

E. L. VAN WINKLE, Esq.—Sheriffs are elected for the term of two years, and are re-eligible for the second term, then one term must intervene before re-eligible. The system is bad, at least it has so proven in Kentucky. The appointing system, to which we had been accustomed, proved far more efficient and satisfactory.

Indiana:

Hon. CONRAD BAKER.—Sheriffs are elected for two years. I prefer elections to appointments. No person is eligible to the office of sheriff for more than four years in any period of six years.

Michigan:

H. K. CLARKE, Esq.—Sheriffs are elected by the people for two years, and are ineligible for a longer period than four years out of any six. I think election, with this restriction upon their re-election, the best mode of selection.

QUESTION VI.

How many justices of the peace are there in each township? How are they chosen, and for how long a term?

ANSWERS.

Massachusetts:

GEO. W. SEARLE, Esq.—See " index of general statutes, titles ;" "trial justices ;" "justices of the peace."

New Hampshire:

Hon. S. D. BELL.—Justices of the peace are appointed by the governor and council for the term of five years. They may be and usually are re-appointed. There is no limit to the number in any town or county. They are thought to be too numerous. There are in this place, with a population not exceeding 20,000, 120 justices. The business, civil and criminal, is confined in the cities to the police courts, but not so in the towns generally.

[Assem. No. 35.]   32

Connecticut :

WALTER PITKIN, Esq.—Justices of the peace are chosen once in two years, by the electors of the several towns, the number for each being equal to the number of jurymen prescribed by law for such town. The inhabitants of any town may, at a meeting specially called for that purpose, reduce the number of justices to be thereafter chosen.

New Jersey ;

CORTLANDT PARKER, Esq.—Justices of the peace are elected each for five years, not more than five in each township.

JOHN F. HEGEMAN, Esq.—Not less than two nor more than *five justices* in *each township*, but where there are more than 7,000 inhabitants, one more for every 3,000 inhabitants are chosen for *five years* by the people.

Pennsylvania :

J. J. BARCLAY, Esq.—This question cannot be answered without reference to special acts of assembly. They are elected for terms of five years.

Maryland :

A. STERLING, jr., Esq.—Justices of the peace are appointed by the governor for two years. From 1850 to 1864 they were elected.

Kentucky :

E. L. VAN WINKLE, Esq.—We have two justices in each township or election precinct, who are elected by the people for a term of four years.

Indiana :

Hon. CONRAD BAKER.—Justices of the peace are elected by the people for four years. The number of justices for each township is regulated by the board of commissioners of the county ; but the number shall not exceed three for each township, and one additional one for each incorporated town therein.

Michigan :

H. K. CLARK, Esq.—Four in each township ; chosen by the people, one annually to serve for four years.

QUESTION VII.

What proportion of persons indicted is, on the average, brought to trial ?

ANSWERS.

Massachusetts :

GEO. W. SEARLE, Esq.—For answer to this question .see 3 vols. of annual reports of the attorney general, in library of the Association.

New Hampshire :

Hon. S. D. BELL.—No statistics are within my reach from which I would be able to say what proportion of those indicted are tried.

Connecticut:

WALTER PITKEN, Esq.—Of persons indicted, an average of three-fourths are brought to trial. This estimate includes those who plead guilty on arraignment.

New Jersey:

CORTLANDT PARKER, Esq.—I reply to the interrogatories VII to XVII, inclusive. They involve the practical merits of our criminal code and our administration of justice in criminal cases. In the rural counties, very few persons are indicted, but, with occasional exceptions, all indicted are brought to trial. No average can be stated. I verily believe that few who ought to be convicted escape. Disagreeing juries are very rare. At least half of those arraigned plead guilty, first or last. A practice of taking pleas to offences of a lower grade than those charged, to which allusion is made in query No. 10. does not exist. No suspicion has ever been suggested, to my knowledge, that any prosecuting officer in New Jersey failed in his duty in this respect. Very few persons charged with homicide are not convicted. Murder, in the first degree, seldom happens. When it does—when the killing is *actually* willful, premeditated, and deliberate, the culprit is almost always convicted; and, if convicted, executed. There are cases coming within the legal definition of "willful, deliberate and premeditated killing," which do not satisfy the popular idea of those words. They are cases where the intent to kill was suddenly formed and instantly executed, or where great provocation or extenuation existed. In such cases, verdicts have mostly been "murder in the second degree." And that verdict has once been rendered in a case where a young *woman* was guilty of poisoning—while the verdict "not guilty, by reason of insanity," has been rendered where a sort of "wild justice" has characterized the case, as in Mercer's case for shooting Heberton; Spencer's for killing his wife; and (it has been thought by some) the case of Margaret Garrity for destroying her seducer. In all these cases, I should observe, especially the last, the accused seemed rather an executioner of what ought to be the law, than the prey of an evil heart. Nor are convictions or executions, after convictions are had, long or improperly delayed. Writs of error, in capital cases are duly granted for evidently good, that is fairly debatable cause. Technical difficulties are seldom allowed to delay punishment. It is not customary to send cases back and forth between criminal courts of different grades. Causes may be removed immediately after indictment to the supreme court. But good reason must exist then, and the time gained is trivial. It is a consequence of this promptness and all but certainty of conviction and punishment, that the law with us is, indeed, a "terror to evil doers." I make no vain boast when I claim for my native state that nowhere else in the civilized world are the rights of citizens, better protected, and their wrongs more promptly and certainly avenged. Our locality, posted as we are between and contiguous to the two largest cities of the continent, exposes us to be resorted to by many vicious strangers. And there is no denying that what has been said can, with less propriety, be asserted of the border counties, Hudson and Camden. Their population is necessarily, suburban in character, habits and sentiments. Yet even there what has been said is mainly correct, and, I think, growing more so.

Our people, for the most part, believe in the propriety of capital punishment for willful murder, and have no qualms respecting circumstantial evidence. And I am very much mistaken, if the belief that with us, criminal justice is sternly administered, does not deter many citizens of other states from venturing to commit crime within our bounds. During the last nine years, only nine indictments for murder have been found in the populous manufacturing county of Essex, which contains about 120,000 people. One was abandoned, because the party accused was evidently a lunatic; a mother who nearly cut off her child's head to keep it from imaginary poverty. Three resulted in convictions of murder in the first degree, and the speedy execution of the culprits. All the others are cases in which the killing did not appear to be deliberate in the ordinary sense of that word, and resulted in convictions for murder in the second degree or manslaughter, except that one man indicted as accessory before the fact was not wrongfully acquitted, and one woman was acquitted of infanticide.

In the populous counties of the State, such as Essex, in which is Newark and Hudson which contain Jersey City and Hoboken, many persons indicted are not found. Judging from my own experience, about one-fifth of the indictments found, are not brought to trial for this reason. Of those tried, perhaps the same proportion escape conviction. About three-fifths of those arraigned, plead guilty either at once, or when about to be tried.

JOHN F. HEGEMAN, ESQ.—I should estimate that in Mercer county, eight in ten of persons indicted are brought to trial on an average.

Pennsylvania:

J. J. BARCLAY, Esq.—It is impossible to answer this question without an extensive examination into the criminal statistics of the state. In Philadelphia county, more than half.

Maryland:

A. STERLING, JR., Esq.—Those indicted are generally brought to trial. Some escape by forfeiting bail, but I think not many. Generally, if escapes take place, it occurs between the action of the justice of the peace and the action of the grand jury. The justices not being as careful in taking bail as the court is, and the private interests of prosecutors and of detective officers saving many from being indicted.

Kentucky:

E. L. VAN WINKLE, Esq.—About two-thirds of those indicted are brought to trial. The proportion varies and is frequently anything but proportionate in different districts.

Indiana:

Hon. CONRAD BAKER.—A large proportion of the persons indicted are brought to trial, but the exact proportion I cannot state.

Michigan:

H. R. CLARKE, Esq.—My professional employments for the last ten or twelve years have not been such as to enable me to answer this interrogatory. (See Gen. Morrow's answer, below.)

HENRY A. MORROW, Esq.—A very large proportion of the persons *informed* against are brought to trial. Under the old system of grand juries, the docket of every term of court showed that a large number of those indicted were not brought to trial, but under the *information* system, there are very few persons informed against, who are not brought to trial.

QUESTION VIII.

Of the tried, what proportion is convicted and what acquitted? In what percentage of cases are juries unable to agree?

ANSWERS.

Massachusetts:

GEO. W. SEARLE, Esq.—See attorney general's reports.

New Hampshire:

Hon. S. D. BELL.—Unable to say what proportion are acquitted.

Connecticut :

WALTER PITKIN.—Of criminals brought to trial, about one in six is acquitted. Juries fail to agree in about one (criminal) case in twenty.

New Jersey :

For Mr. Parker's answer, see answers to question VII, New Jersey, *supra.*

JOHN F. HEGEMAN, Esq.—Of those tried, including those who plead guilty, three-fourths are convicted ; not one in a hundred cases are juries unable ultimately to agree. Upon the *first* trial perhaps 2 in 20 would not agree.

Pennsylvania :

J. J. BARCLAY, Esq.—The same answer as above. In Philadelphia county not more than a third.

Maryland :

A. STERLING, Jr., Esq.—I cannot give an accurate answer to this question as to the proportion convicted. I think a majority of those indicted are convicted, perhaps two-thirds. The disagreement of juries is not common here, perhaps not noticed so much, as a large part of our criminal cases are tried before the court ; the *prisoner* having the right to try his case before the judge at his election, no matter what the offence, and in fact a large part are tried before the court, which of course leaves a smaller part for juries to disagree about. The disagreements of juries are due mainly to the custom of letting cases drag along for days, so that each man's mind becomes fixed; and as juries are generally allowed to separate at the adjournment, they get fixed in their opinions without conferences, and are besides subject to be tampered with; and after they have been kept together for a long time before the trial has ended, the judges do not like to keep them shut up long, and the hope of an early discharge is an inducement not to agree. I think, in civil cases, two-thirds of a jury ought to be competent to a verdict, or we must go back to the old practice of locking them up all the time, trying a case rapidly, and refusing to discharge for a long while. The disagreements have happened mainly in civil cases, and the reasons are, I think, as I have given them.

Kentucky :

E. L. VAN WINKLE, Esq.—The proportion convicted varies in different districts, and often in the same district. In cities where crime abounds, the proportion of convictions is much larger than in the rural districts. Near two-thirds are convicted in the former, and not half in the latter, except at periods when such communities exhibit an abnormal condition from crime.

On an average I would think that juries are unable to agree once in four or five times.

Indiana :

Hon. CONRAD BAKER.—I cannot, for want of satisfactory statistical returns, give the proportion convicted and the proportion acquitted, nor can I give the percentage of cases in which juries are unable to agree.

So far as my knowledge extends, the disagreement of juries has not been so frequent as to attract much attention, or to constitute a serious impediment in the administration of the criminal laws.

New Jersey :

For Mr. Parker's answer, see answer to question VII, New Jersey, *supra.*

Michigan :

HENRY A. MORROW, Esq.—A large proportion of those *informed* against are convicted. But this depends upon the honesty and intelligence of the examining magistrate, who discharges or holds the party over to the circuit court. If he is intelligent and honest, he will only hold over to appear at the circuit court such persons as on the testimony before him would be convicted of the crime charged. Juries disagree in comparatively few cases, and rarely, except in cases where the testimony is of a conflicting character, or in cases where eminent counsel are employed and great public interest has been elicited. I have sometimes thought that many disagreements of juries were caused by the persons being influenced by the argument of counsel or otherwise, rather than by any real doubt they have as to the weight of evidence. In other words, they cease to be *judges* of the facts, and become *advocates* of one side or the other.

QUESTION IX.

Of persons arraigned, what proportion plead guilty, and are convicted on confession?

ANSWERS.

Massachusetts:

GEORGE W. SEARLE, Esq.—See Attorney-General's reports.

New Hampshire:

Hon. S. D. BELL.—I am unable to say what proportion of the accused plead guilty, or do not contend.

Connecticut:

WALTER PITKEN, Esq.—More than one-half of those arraigned plead guilty and are convicted without trial.

New Jersey:

For Mr. Parker's answer, see Question VII, New Jersey, *supra*.

JOHN F. HEGEMAN, Esq.—Of those arraigned, about one-fourth only plead guilty, and are convicted on their own confession.

Pennsylvania:

J. J. BARCLAY, Esq.—The same answer as above. In Philadelphia county, a very small proportion.

Maryland:

A. STERLING, JR.—Of persons arraigned for felony, a small proportion plead guilty. In offenses punished by fine, the large majority plead guilty.

Kentucky:

E. L. VAN WINKLE, Esq.—The proportion that plead guilty is small—say one in twenty.

Indiana:

Hon. CONRAD BAKER.—A large proportion of those convicted plead "not guilty," but the proportion I cannot state.

Michigan:

HENRY A. MORROW, Esq.—The percentage of those arraigned who plead guilty is small. The chances for escape are so many that great criminals never and lesser ones seldom plead guilty. It is in cases where the parties are indifferent as to their fate, or where the influence of friends is exerted in that direction that this plea is entered. Under the laws of Michigan, counsel are assigned to poor criminals, to be paid by the county. There are always lawyers anxious for such cases. The facility with which counsel is procured deter many from pleading guilty who would otherwise do so.

QUESTION X.

Do those who plead guilty generally plead to the offenses with which they stand charged, or to others of a lower grade? If of a lower grade, can you suggest any reason, connected with the prosecution of the charge?

ANSWERS.

Massachusetts:

GEORGE W. SEARLE, Esq.—See Attorney-General's reports.

New Hampshire.

Hon. S. D. BELL.—Prisoners who plead guilty generally limit their plea to the lowest grade of offense charged, where the prosecutor can be induced to accept such plea. Various reasons may lead to the acceptance of such a plea. Perhaps the most usual and forcible is a doubt of the prosecuting officer whether his evidence is such that he can obtain a conviction. In some cases probably a satisfactory adjustment with the prosecutor, as the restoring of stolen property, may lead to the acceptance of such a plea, and not rarely the anxiety of parties and witnesses to avoid the trouble and expense of attending court.

Connecticut:

WALTER PITKIN, Esq.—Criminals plead guilty generally of the offenses with which they stand charged. It is a matter of discretion with the judge to receive a plea to an inferior offense, and the reasons which influence the exercise of their discretion are various, but have relation usually rather to the circumstances of the prisoner than to "the prosecution of the charge."

New Jersey:

JOHN F. HEGEMAN, Esq.—Those that plead guilty, of course, generally plead guilty to the count containing a lower grade of crime, when there are more counts than one, or where the nature of the indictment allows a plea to a lower grade of crime involved in the main charge. The reason, of course, is to escape the higher penalty for the higher offense. It is a kind of compromise between the state and the defendant, and where a conviction is doubtful, it is often advisable to take such a plea on the part of the state.

Pennsylvania:

J. J. BARCLAY, Esq.—Generally, pleas of guilty are pleaded to the offense with which the prisoner stands charged. In cases of murder, of course, the prisoner will not plead guilty to the highest grade of crime.

Maryland:

A. STERLING, Esq.—The reason is, I think, that the lighter the punishment the more the inducement to plead guilty. It is done mainly to diminish exposure, save costs, and get lighter punishment; and in some classes of misdemeanors, such as bawdy house, selling liquors on Sunday, &c., these facts are generally so clear that the party has no object in standing trial.

Kentucky:

E. S. VAN WINKLE, Esq.—When they plead guilty, it is generally with the view of inducing the jury to fix the shortest period of confinement, or with the hope of indemnity against other charges then pending.

Indiana:

Hon. CONRAD BAKER.—Those who plead "guilty," generally plead to the offense with which they stand charged, and not others of a lower grade.

Michigan:

H. A. MORROW, Esq.—It cannot be said that there is any rule on this subject. The discretion lodged in the hands of the judges makes it immaterial, as a general thing, whether he pleads guilty to a higher or lesser offense, so far as punishment is concerned; and I have never discovered, except in occasional cases, where the party was a novice in crime, that the magnitude or grade of the crime had much influence on the *mind* of the criminal. In nine cases out of ten, the punishment alone influences the mind of the criminal, and he is utterly indifferent to the fact whether he is charged with a higher or léssre offense.

QUESTION XI.

Of persons charged with homicide, what proportion is convicted? What proportion executed?

ANSWERS.

Massachusetts:

GEO. W. SEARLE, Esq.—See attorney general's report.

New Hampshire:

S. D. BELL.—No data are within reach to enable one to state what proportion of persons charged with homicide are convicted, or what proportion are executed. In general, it may be said that trials of this kind are not frequent. Many persons drawn as jurors have concientious scruples in relation to capital punishment. Many others assent to verdicts of guilty with great hesitation. Convictions of manslaughter and murder in the second degree, are usual where any pretence for them is found. Executions are rare; they cannot take place within a year after sentence, which gives large opportunity for applications for some modification of the sentence.

Connecticut:

WALTER PITKIN, Esq.—In the majority of capital cases, the convictions are of murder in the second degree, for which the penalty is imprisonment for life. In a small proportion of the cases of conviction of murder in the first degree the extreme penalty has been commuted to imprisonment for life.

New Jersey:

JOHN F. HEGEMAN, Esq.—Of persons charged with homicide, four in six are convicted. Of those convicted of murder in the first degree, three in four are hung. Of those convicted of man·slaughter, 14 in 15 at least, are imprisoned, perhaps more.

Pennsylvania:

J. J. BARCLAY, Esq.—In Philadelphia county, almost all the persons charged with murder, are convicted of murder in the second degree, or manslaughter. Capital convictions are not numerous, though in the last two years several have been thus convicted; but in nearly every case no execution has taken place, sometimes, because of a doubt as to the guilt of the prisoner; sometimes because of a doubt as to the grade of the crime; and often because of the interference of persons whose judgment is paralyzed by a mistaken view of the object of punishment.

Maryland:
No answer.

Kentucky:

E. L. VAN WINKLE.—The proportion convicted of murder is small, say one in ten, or hardly that proportion. If the circumstances allow of a conviction of manslaughter—the punishment for which is confinement in the penitentiary—the juries are much more inclined to convict of the latter offence.

Three-fourths of those convicted of murder are executed—perhaps a greater proportion than that. Unless reversed by the appellate court, the judgment is executed, except in rare instances.

Indiana:

Hon. CONRAD BAKER.—I cannot state what proportion of persons charged with homicide are convicted. So far as my knowledge extends, improper acquittals are not of very frequent occurrence, although they sometimes occur. Murder in the first degree being the only homicide in which the death penalty can be inflicted, and the jury having in this a discretion to inflict that penalty or imprison in the penitentiary for life. Of course, the proportion of cases in which there are executions is small. I cannot state what the proportion is, but can only say that there have been a number of executions in this state since 1846, at which time the discretion above mentioned in cases of murder in the first degree was given to juries.

Michigan:

H. A. MORROW, Esq.—The proportion of convictions depends upon the grade of the crime. The laws of Michigan divide homicide into murder in the first degree, murder in the second degree, and manslaughter. The punishment for the first is solitary confinement for life. Comparatively few convictions for murder in the first degree take place in Michigan, arising, no doubt, from the awful character of the punishment, and from the fact that the killing must be found by the jury to have been " willful, deliberate and premeditated" to warrant a conviction. Sentence in this grade of crime usually follows conviction.

QUESTION XII.

In what classes of offences is the disproportion between the arrested and the convicted apt to be greatest—those of a higher or lower grade ?

ANSWERS.

Massachusetts:

GEO. W. SEARLE, Esq.—See attorney general's report.

New Hampshire:

Hon. S. D. BELL.—No data for an answer to the twelfth questions are within reach.

Connecticut:

WALTER PITKIN, Esq.—The disproportion between the arrested and convicted is greatest in offences of a lower grade, by a ratio of ten to one. Informations in these classes of cases are sometimes procured through malice or accidental misrepresentation, and the circumstances not being generally so well defined as in more atrocious crimes, there is more danger of mistaking the exact nature of the offence.

New Jersey:

For Mr. Parker's answer see Question VII, New Jersey, *supra*.

JOHN F. HEGEMAN, Esq.—In my experience, strange to say, the disproportion between the arrested and the convicted is generally greatest in the lower grade of crime.

Pennsylvania:

J. J. BARCLAY, Esq.—Those of the higher grade.

Maryland:

A. STERLING, Esq.—The larger proportion of convictions is in larceny. Fewer of those indicted for this are acquitted on trial than of any other. I think the proportion of acquittals is larger in the smaller offences, partly because the worst cases of those plead guilty.

Kentucky:

E. L. VAN WINKLE, Esq.—The proportion of convictions is

greatest in crimes of the lower grade. Convictions for murder and perjury are rare.

Indiana:
Hon. CONRAD BAKER.—To the twelfth question I can give no satisfactory answer.

Michigan:
No answer.

QUESTION XIII.

What is about the average length of imprisonment previous to trial ?

ANSWERS.

Massachusetts:
GEO. W. SEARLE, Esq.—See attorney general's report.

New Hampshire:
Hon. S. D. BELL.—No data for an answer to the thirteenth question are within reach.

Connecticut:
WALTER PITKIN, Esq.—Four sessions of the superior court are holden annually in each county, and criminal causes (which have precedence of all others) are generally tried at the first term after arrest or information. Probably the average length of imprisonment, previous to trial, is from four to six weeks.

New Jersey:
For Mr. Parker's answer see Question VII, New Jersey, *supra.*

J. F. HEGEMAN, Esq,—Length of imprisonment previous to trial, averages in Mercer county two months.

Pennsylvania:
J. J. BARCLAY, Esq.—This question cannot be satisfactorily answered, but in Philadelphia county, because of the length of time between the terms of court, it is about, on the average, a month.

Maryland:
A. STERLING, Jr., Esq.—In the counties the imprisonment before trial depends on the time of the arrest, with reference to its nearness to the term of court. After the court meets, the cases are severally all tried in from a week to a month. In some small counties where they have few cases, there are only two terms of

court a year; but in most there are three and four, lasting from two weeks to two months. In Baltimore the imprisonment is not long, a month or six weeks would be the extreme, I think; generally, a week or ten days, except in assaults and batteries, which are tried every Saturday, and the range there is from one day to one week, unless the party by demanding a jury should require further delay, and the regular course by indictment.

Kentucky:

E. L. VAN WINKLE, Esq.—The average length of imprisonment previous to conviction depends upon the frequency of courts. In cities, the imprisonment is short, say three months or less. In the country, where the courts are held only twice a year, the confinement will average nine months.

Indiana:

HON. CONRAD BAKER.—The average length of imprisonment previous to trial is not long. This is about as definite as I can make my answer.

Michigan:

H. A. MORROW, ESQ.—A few weeks at longest in Detroit, and if the public prosecutor does his duty, the term of imprisonment need not exceed ten or fifteen days. The criminal court in Detroit holds monthly sessions. In the country, the period of imprisonment is at longest a few weeks in ordinary cases.

QUESTION XIV.

Is it found that in offences of a higher grade, convictions, when obtained, are frequently so long after the commission of the offence that their moral effect is in great measure nullified ?

ANSWERS.

Massachusetts:

GEORGE W. SEARLE, Esq.—Yes; the delays are occasioned in part by dilatoriness in prosecuting officers, but more by the necessary delays of our legal system. The superior court in Suffolk holds a term once a month, but in the country not oftener than once a quarter: and when a cause goes to the supreme court on exceptions, it is much delayed ; if any exception is sustained, there is a new trial, with indefinite liability to new bills of exceptions.

New Hampshire:

HON. S. D. BELL.—Convictions for the higher grade of offences are often strenuously resisted and long delayed. This may probably diminish the moral effect of the punishment.

Connecticut:

WALTER PITKIN, ESQ.—The answer to this question must be inferred from the preceding.

New Jersey:

For Mr. Parker's answer, see Question VII, New Jersey *supra*.

JOHN F. HEGEMAN, ESQ.—I cannot say that the convictions are so long after the commission of the offences that the moral effect is in great measure nullified in higher grades of offence. It is so in some measure, but not in great measure. We do not have a long delay as a general thing.

Pennsylvania:

J. J. BARCLAY, ESQ.—Yes.

Maryland:

No answer.

Kentucky:

E. L. VAN WINKLE, ESQ.—When the crime is of a startling nature, and the circumstances pregnant with guilt, the prisoner usually resorts to all the shifts that can be devised for delay, and often escapes from punishment by *outliving the charge*. The death of witnesses, the slackened energy of the prosecution, and finally the loss of public interest in the prosecution, tends strongly in favor of an acquittal. Nevertheless, when a conviction does occur, and the death penalty is inflicted, its full effect is felt, and the long confinement and presence of the criminal at the bar, together with his tragic end, heightens rather than diminishes the effect upon the public mind. It is the uncertainty of the punishment for these high crimes that fosters their commission.

Indiana:

HON. CONRAD BAKER.—In offences of a higher grade it does sometimes happen that the convictions, when obtained, are so long after the offence as to, in a great measure, nullify their moral effect. I do not, however, think this is a very frequent occurrence.

Michigan:

H. A. MORROW, ESQ.—It often happens that convictions take place so long after the commission of the crime, that the moral effect is entirely destroyed. My own observation has taught me that speedy and certain punishment is far more efficacious in preventing the commission of crime than are slow and severe punishments.

Question XV.

If such delays occur, what are conceived to be the causes? Is it customary to send causes back and forth between criminal courts of different grades, as, for example, the general sessions and the oyer and terminer?

Answers.

Massachusetts:

George W. Searle, Esq.—For answer, see Question XIV.

New Hampshire:

Hon. S. D. Bell.—The great motives for delay in criminal cases where a conviction is resisted, is the hope of advantage from mere lapse of time; the subsiding of public feeling; the forgetfulness of witnesses as to details; the loose talk of others exposing them to contradiction; the increased opportunity to prepare a defence; the finding of evidence often kept back at first, &c.

In obstinately contested cases, it is not unusual that many exceptions to evidence are taken and transferred to the law terms for decision, which may produce a delay of several months.

Connecticut:

Walter Pitkin, Esq.—The only criminal tribunals are justices' (in cities, "police") courts and the superior court; causes originating in the latter, or brought there by appeal from the former (and there is no other appellate court), are in all cases concluded.

New Jersey:

John F. Hegeman, Esq.—There is no delay by postponing causes over to another term, except in rare cases. Sometimes when cases are appealed by writ of error, there is necessarily a delay and the moral effect of ultimate punishment is neutralized to a great degree, but the higher the offence the less the delay, owing to the rule and disposition of courts to give prompt attention and preference to criminal cases.

Pennsylvania:

J. J. Barclay, Esq.—Ingenuity of counsel, and the time which in practice must be taken to dispose of motions for new trial and in arrest of the judgments.

It is not customary in Pennsylvania, to send causes back and forth in the criminal courts, but this remark does not apply to the cases sent to the supreme court, which, in any event, and because of the system described in the answer to question No. 1, are very few.

Maryland:

A. Sterling, Esq.—We have no criminal courts of different grades, nor is there any appeal in criminal cases, except the common law right of a writ of error to take up the record, which only extends to the sufficiency in law of the indictment and the actual record proceeding, including the legality of the sentence, but no rulings of the judge are reversable. We have no "bills of exception," in criminal cases.

Parties indicted have the right to remove their cases to some adjoining county for trial, on their affidavit that they believe they cannot have an impartial trial in the county where the facts arose. While a valuable barrier against injustice and popular vengeance, it is abused somewhat to delay and defeat justice.

Kentucky:

E. L. Van. Winkle, Esq.—The delays that occur in the trial of the crime of murder are attributable in part to the lenity of the courts, produced by the powerful inclination to extend every possible legal advantage in favor of life.

The noticeable failures of courts to convict of the higher order of crimes arise chiefly in those cases where the death penalty is attached, without any choice being left to the juries to graduate the punishment.

I am satisfied from an experience of fifteen years active professional life, during which time I discharged the duties of commonwealth's attorney for six years, that the loose practice of permitting prisoners to give insufficient bail, and thus enable them to escape punishment or loss, has contributed more to the impunity of crime, than all unwise legislation in graduating punishments.

Indiana:

Hon. Conrad Baker.—It is not customary to send causes back and forth between criminal courts of different grades. Changes of venue sometimes occur, but as the granting of an application for a change is in the discretion of the court, they are not granted often enough to constitute an abuse.

Michigan:

H. A. Morrow, Esq.—Under our system delays are produced as a general rule by the action of the criminal himself. Delays are generally beneficial to the accused, and shrewd counsel always delay the trial. No opportunity occurs in this state for sending cases from one court to another.

Question XVI.

Do the courts, or not, fail *very often* to convict, in cases where prisoners are on trial for crimes of a higher order?

ANSWERS.

Massachusetts:

GEORGE W. SEARLE, Esq.—The courts do not very often fail to convict in such cases, unless the prisoners are defended by especially successful counsel, such as the late Mr. Choate, or there is a diversity of popular and court opinion as to the guilt of the prisoner. The present chief justice usually presides with two or more of his associates on such trials. He acts upon the principle, that it is the duty of the judge, as well as the prosecuting officer, to see that the guilty are convicted, when it does not require a too bold assumption by the court of the office of the advocate. By this answer, it is not intended to reflect upon the judicial impartiality of the very able chief justice, but only to state the executive character which belongs to his administration of justice.

New Hampshire:

Hon. S. D. BELL.—No data exist for the comparison implied in the words *very often.* Perhaps convictions are less frequent where the penalty is very severe, because the motive for obstinate resistance is much the highest in that class.

Connecticut:

WALTER PITKIN, Esq.—Our courts rarely fail to convict in cases where prisoners are on trial for crimes of a high order. (See answer to 12th question).

New Jersey:

JOHN F. HEGEMAN, Esq.—*Not very often* do the courts fail to convict for crimes of a higher order. Such is the case *occasionally* rather than *very often.*

Pennsylvania:

J. J. BARCLAY, Esq.—The judges do their duty, but human nature is the same everywhere, and juries sometimes, but not recently, fail to do their duty.

Maryland:

A. STERLING, Esq.—The court do not very often fail to convict in high grades of offence; there is a tendency in juries somewhat against capital punishment, and a disposition to find a lower degree of homicide. I think the escape of criminals is mainly due here, as elsewhere, to the department which arrests, especially to the independent, private detectives, who are very useful to enable private individuals to make good their losses, but who allow often the thieves to escape on surrendering their booty.

Our police here is very good, but the detective department, as elsewhere, I think, liable to this trouble. The point where the fingers of justice actually come in contact with crime and criminals, is where the contact soils, and where the rogue slips through.

Strict care of the police system and rigid discipline is the cure, but our changes of "personnel" are difficulties. We are becoming more stable. Our police is a copy in form of the Metropolitan, and much more stable than before. Our policemen must be permanent and rigidly controlled to make the system safe.

Kentucky:

E. L. VAN WINKLE, Esq.—Courts do *often fail* to convict in cases where prisoners are on trial for crimes of a higher order, and such escapes from punishment necessarily have a tendency to encourage those who make their living by unlawful means.

Indiana:

HON. CONRAD BAKER, Esq.—Courts do not *very often* fail to convict in cases where prisoners are on trial for crimes of a higher order.

Michigan:

H. A. MORROW, Esq.—Courts and juries do very often fail to convict in the higher grades of crimes.

QUESTION XVII.

If yes, what is the effect of such failure on the criminal population; that is, those who follow crime as a means of obtaining a livelihood? Are the terrors of the law found to have much of a deterrent effect upon this class of persons, or not?

ANSWERS.

Massachusetts:

GEORGE W. SEARLE, Esq.—These delays tend to embolden the criminal population, and convince them that the law is lacking in its executive power, and in the certainty and dispatch of its decrees.

New Hampshire:

HON. S. D. BELL.—No data are known on which an answer to to this question can be founded. Generally everything which diminishes the certainty of punishment, is supposed to lessen the effect of the criminal law. The law is not supposed to deter confirmed rogues from offending but in a very slight degree. Its effect is mainly on those who have not yielded to temptation.

Connecticut:

No answer is given to this question by Mr. Pitkin.

New Jersey:

For Mr. Parker's answer, see Question VII, New Jersey, *supra*. JOHN F. HEGEMAN, Esq.—Answered above.

Pennsylvania :

J. J. BARCLAY, Esq.—The effect is of course bad whenever there is a clear failure of justice. The terrors of the law have their effect in driving the criminals *out of the jurisdiction of a court* whose judges act with firmness, and without "fear, favor or affection."

Maryland :

No answer is given by Mr. Sterling.

Kentucky :

For answer see question XVI, Kentucky, *supra*.

Indiana :

Hon. CONRAD BAKER.—In my opinion, the fear of the penitentiary prevents many from committing crime, who are restrained by no higher considerations.

Michigan :

H. A. MORROW, Esq.—Failure to convict in cases free from doubt or complicacy give encouragement to criminals. The superior courts often find themselves obliged to set aside sentences for errors and to order new trials, and where this occurs in many cases, criminals are encouraged by the hope that as a last resort the superior court may relieve them.

Punishment, to have the effect to deter others from the commission of similar offences, must be certain and speedy. Where justice is delayed or uncertain, the law has no terror for criminals.

QUESTION XVIII.

Are prosecuting attorneys appointed or elected ?

ANSWERS.

Massachusetts :

GEO. W. SEARLE, Esq.—The prosecuting officers consist of an attorney general, who tries the capital cases in the supreme court, generally in conjunction with the local prosecuting officers of the county in which the case is tried. In each county there is a district attorney. Both the attorney general and district attorney are elected. In Suffolk there is an assistant district attorney, who is appointed by the executive.

New Hampshire :

Hon. S. D. BELL.—The prosecuting attorneys, the attorney general for the state, and solicitors for the counties, are appointed by the governor and council for five years.

Connecticut₁:

WALTER PITKIN, Esq.—Prosecuting attorneys are appointed, one for each county, by the judges of the superior court, and hold office for two years.

New Jersey :

CORTLANDT PARKER, Esq.—Prosecuting attorneys are appointed by the governor, with the advice and consent of the senate, and hold office five years. Their compensation is entirely by fees. For every indictment, to which there is a plea of guilty, they receive ten dollars; for every indictment to which, after not guilty pleaded, defendant retracts and pleads guilty, twelve dollars ; for every verdict of guilty, after trial, fifteen dollars. The taxable costs of other officers are recoverable likewise only on conviction obtained. This system of payment seems theoretically wrong. Practically, it works well. It is a great stimulus to vigilance in minor matters. Men indicted are brought to trial. Few errors occur in drawing indictments. Causes are well prepared. But the character of the bar 'of New Jersey is such, and the fees themselves so small. that it is not believed that the necessity of success to emolument leads any men to improper exertion. Indeed, the possibility of such a thing protects the innocent from undue prosecution. Too great zeal defeats itself.

Pennsylvania :

J. J. BARCLAY, Esq.—They are elected.

Maryland :

A. STERLING, Esq.—Prosecuting attorneys are elected for four years.

Kentucky :

E. L. VAN WINKLE, Esq.—Prosecuting attorneys are elected. Compensation in part by salary, and in part by fees.

Indiana :

Hon. CONRAD BAKER.—Prosecuting attorneys are elected.

Michigan :

H. R. CLARKE, Esq.—Prosecuting attorneys are elected by the people for two years.

QUESTION XIX.

Is their compensation by salaries or fees?

ANSWERS.

Massachusetts :

GEO. W. SEARLE, Esq.—All these are remunerated by fixed salaries, and have no fees beyond them.

New Hampshire :

Hon. S. D. BELL.—They are paid by salaries.

Connecticut :

W. PITKIN, Esq.—Their compensation is by fees.

New Jersey :

For Mr. Parker's answer see Question XVIII, New Jersey, *supra.*

JOHN F. HEGEMAN, Esq.—Their compensation is by fees upon conviction—nothing in cases of acquittal.

Pennsylvania :

J. J. BARCLAY, Esq.—Fees.

Maryland :

A. STERLING, jr., Esq.—They are paid by fines. Maximum allowed, $3,000.

Kentucky :

E. L. VAN WINKLE, Esq.—They receive fixed salaries, and a percentage on all judgments of conviction, where such judgments are assessed by way of fine.

Indiana :

Hon. CONRAD BAKER.—The compensation is of a mixed nature, a part of it being by way of salary, and the residue as fees.

Michigan :

H. K. CLARK. Esq.—The compensation is fixed by the board of supervisors, (composed of one from each township) and generally by the allowance of an annual salary.

QUESTION XX.

If by salaries, what effect, if any, is this found to have upon their fidelity?

ANSWERS.

Massachusetts :

GEO. W. SEARLE, Esq.—The effect upon their fidelity is favorable.

New Hampshire :

Hon. S. D. BELL. It is not suggested that their fidelity is affected by this mode of compensation, so far as I have heard.

Connecticut :
No answer.

New Jersey :

For Mr. Parker's answer see Question XVIII, New Jersey, *supra.*

JOHN F. HEGEMAN, Esq.—This system of compensation by fees is bad, tempting to undue exertion to convict, and tempting to receive rewards from the defendants to favor them.

Pennsylvania :

J. J. BARCLAY, Esq.—The system of salaries has not been tried in Pennsylvania.

Maryland :
No answer.

Kentucky :

E. L. VAN WINKLE, Esq.—As a general thing, our prosecuting attorneys are sufficiently vigilant, and, inasmuch as they get thirty per cent of all judgments upon forfeited bail bonds and recognizances, it is not often that such judgments are not collected, except where the parties are insolvent.

Indiana :

Hon. CONRAD BAKER.—I do not think, as a general rule, that allowing a salary injuriously affects their fidelity.

Michigan :

H. K. CLARKE, Esq.—Salaries may, and in some instances, doubtless, do, lead to the neglect of cases that ought to be prosecuted ; but, in my judgment, making the compensation to depend *entirely* upon the amount of business done would lead to other and much greater evils in the opposite direction. An upright and competent prosecutor ought to have a liberal salary. For the unworthy and incompetent no method of compensation can be devised with any confidence that it will not prove excessive.

H. A. MORROW, Esq.—The system of paying salaries to public prosecutors is altogether preferable to that of paying fees. The latter system has a most pernicious effect on the officer. It is a strong inducement to multiply cases, and is injurious to the public in a variety of ways.

QUESTION XXI.

To what extent in general are forfeited recognizances enforced, and bail money collected?

ANSWERS.

Massachusetts:

GEO. W. SEARLE, Esq.—There is, I suspect, much and unnecessary neglect in this respect; I am not able to make more specific answer.

New Hampshire:

S. D. BELL.—No data are known for an answer.

Connecticut:

WALTER PITKIN, Esq.—Forfeited recognizances are enforced and bail money collected almost invariably.

New Jersey:

CORTLANDT PARKER, Esq.—There is great want of system and thoroughness in enforcing forfeited recognizances and collecting justices' fines. No special direction is given by law to these moneys. Bail money goes to the state; fines to the county. The law in regard to both of them will soon need revision, if it does not now. The subject grows daily in importance.

JOHN HEGEMAN, Esq.—Forfeited recognizances in this (Mercer) county are generally enforced, and the bail money collected, when the recognizance is duly taken and the bail responsible—which is not always the case.

Maryland:

A. STERLING, Esq.—Recognizances are not rigidly enforced. In Baltimore, the bail is liable to an attachment against his person on the failure of the party to perform, and this has a good effect in securing the appearance of parties bailed. Practically, since Judge Bond has been on the bench, the effect has been good. The bail system is not rigid anywhere, and can scarcely be made so. If the bail is innocent of aiding an escape, and is poor and cannot find the party, equitable considerations and kind feelings will keep the officers of the law from being rigid, and it is difficult to provide a remedy. If the bail is able to produce the party, he is generally made to do so here, or to pay the money.

Pennsylvania:

J. J. BARCLAY, ESQ.—To a very limited extent.

Kentucky:

See Question **XX.**, Kentucky, *supra.*

Indiana:

HON. CONRAD BAKER.—I cannot answer this question. The number of remissions of forfeitures by the governor is not large, and I have heard no general complaint of want of fidelity in enforcing the collection of forfeited recognizances.

Michigan:

H. A. MORROW, ESQ.—Very seldom indeed is a forfeited recognizance enforced by the collection of the money. A system for entering immediate judgment on forfeited recognizances should be devised; an action on the bond is usually unsuccessful. Immediate judgments are entered on forfeited bonds in the recorder's court of the city of Detroit, and it is found to work admirably. During the five years of my administration in that court, there were not over a half dozen recognizances forfeited. The party seldom failed to appear when it was known that immediate judgment would be entered on his bond.

QUESTION XXII.

How as to justice's fines—is there a rigid system of accountability here, or are matters in this department left at loose ends? If the former, what *is* the system? If the latter, what remedy can you suggest?

ANSWERS.

Massachusetts:

GEO. W. SEARLE, ESQ.—This question I am unable to answer from personal information, but I think the general laws, the reports of the attorney-general, and other reports of this state in the possession of the association, will afford the desired information.

New Hampshire:

Hon. S. D. Bell.—No data are known for an answer to this question. The law requires all public officers who receive money as fines, costs or forfeitures, to settle an account annually. I have the impression that little money is paid by justices into the public treasury, and that the system of accountability is practically ineffective. Perhaps the first step to remedy this, would be to reduce the number of those magistrates.

Connecticut:

W. Pitkin, Esq.—Fines collected by justices, unless otherwise specially disposed of, belong to the treasury of the towns where the offences are committed. I am unable to find that our law provides any system of accountability in this matter. It would seem proper in this, as in other cases, to require from the custodians of public funds at least an annual sworn statement of the condition of such funds.

New Jersey:

For Mr. Parker's answer see Question XXI, New Jersey, *supra*.

John F. Hegeman, Esq.—It is very rare that fines are imposed by a justice, except as penalties, and then they are almost invariably paid over as the statute directs. It is so seldom the case, that there is no *system* about it in this county.

Pennsylvania:

J. J. Barclay, Esq.—There is a system in Philadelphia Co., but it is left "at loose ends." The only remedy which can at present be suggested is the enactment of a law, obliging every justice to make a return of each case with the *names of the parties* monthly, said return to be published in a daily newspaper under a severe penalty.

Maryland:

A. Sterling, Jr., Esq.—Justices of the peace are required to account to the county clerks for all fines collected by them which are by law payable into the state treasury, and to the county and municipal authorities for all fines which by law are payable to the county treasury. They report regularly, though there have been failures to be exact, mainly due to the election of justices for short terms which formerly prevailed.

Kentucky:

E. L. Van Winkle, Esq.—Justices' fines are collected and paid to the trustees of the jury fund—they report twice a year on oath to the trustees, and the latter report to the state auditor. Constables do the collecting and are sufficiently rigid.

[Assuming that the object of this question is to ascertain whether petty offenses are sufficiently punished by justices' fines] I take it that petty offenses are sufficiently punished by the present system.

I am thoroughly impressed with the conviction that legal enactments in many of the minor offenses are without any beneficial effects so far as the punishment is concerned, as the justices are not appealed to once in ten cases, except in that class involving personal injury, which prompts the enforcement of the penalty.

Indiana.

Hon. CONRAD BAKER.—I think, as a general rule, fines by justices of the peace are collected and accounted for.

Justices are required, at stated periods, to make reports under oath to the clerk of the circuit, showing the fines assessed and collected by them and the disposition made thereof. For any failure of duty in this respect they are punishable, and also they and their sureties are liable on their official bonds.

Michigan:

H. K. CLARKE, Esq.—There is a rigid system of accountability in the collection of fines imposed by justices of the peace or by the higher courts. I know of no better remedy for this evil than to devote by law all fines to the maintenance of some fund which the people have an interest in increasing, and providing for a liberal compensation to some officer to collect them, to be paid by commissioners out of the sums collected. The collecting officer should be appointed by the custodians of the fund, or those who have in charge the object which the fund is designed to promote.

QUESTION XXIII.

Is any special direction given to moneys collected in this way, looking to some public object (as, for example, the increase of school libraries), or do they go into the treasury of the county for general purposes?

ANSWERS.

Massachusetts:

GEORGE W. SEARLE, Esq.—They go into the treasury of the state for general purposes.

New Hampshire:

Hon. S. D. BELL.—Fines and forfeitures are generally payable to the counties in aid of their general funds. In some cases they are paid to towns for like purposes. They are rarely devoted to such objects as school libraries. In some cases they go to the support of the poor. Forfeitures are applied, in some cases, to indemnify prosecutors.

Connecticut:

See answer to Question **XXII**, Connecticut, *supra*.

New Jersey:

See Question **XXI**, New Jersey, *supra*, for Mr. Parker's answer.

JOHN F. HEGEMAN, Esq.—Such moneys almost universally go to some public object, as the poor, or the state or county.

Pennsylvania:

J. J. BARCLAY, Esq.—In Philadelphia into the city treasury.

Kentucky:

No answer.

Maryland:

A. STERLING, Esq.—Fines imposed by statute, except for violation of the license laws, go to the counties, common law fines to the state. In Baltimore, one-half of all fines go to the municipal corporation, except those for bawdy houses, which go by statute to the support of the dispensatories or free apothecary shops, of which there are three, with a corps of physicians attached, and which are supplied from this source and by private contribution.

Indiana:

Hon. CONRAD BAKER.—By the constitution of the state, all fines and forfeitures belong to the common school fund.

Michigan:

H. K. CLARKE.—The constitution of the state provides that all fines for any breach of the penal laws shall be exclusively applied to the support of township libraries.

QUESTION XXIV.

Are policemen and constables found to be guilty, to any considerable extent, of corruption in the administration of their offices?

ANSWERS.

Massachusetts:

GEO. W. SEARLE, Esq.—My opinion is that the vast majority of policemen in all our large cities are guilty of corruption to a very considerable extent in the administration of their offices, especially in regard to drunkenness, tippling shops, bawdy houses, and gambling hells. The poor inebriate is abused, and on the least pretence of disrespect to the policeman's authority hurried to the lock up and the police courts, and there tried in the most hurried and indecorous manner, and upon the *ex parte* statement of the policeman, backed by his associates, ready to swear to anything the arresting officer may find needful to justify his too frequently unlawful arrest. The prisoner's only chance for justice is generally an appeal. This is expensive, dilatory, and, if friendless, involving an imprisonment in jail for want of bail, quite as long as the ordinary sentence would be. But the dram shop, the brothel, and the gambling rooms too often find a friendly ally, if not a patron, in the policeman. It has been reported that they draw a regular stipend for reticence from such establishments on their beats, and the fact of their notorious hostility to the officers of the state constabulary in their prosecutions, lends countenance to this theory. The remedies for these evils will be found in the causes which produce them. A higher tone of character must be sought for in the policeman; he must be a just, humane, and incorruptible man. For such men, higher prices must be paid than are now paid policemen. With the present salary an inferior order of cheap men are employed, and the need of increasing their revenues by contributions from such sources, is almost irresistible. It may be questioned, too, whether the chiefs of police are always the men they should be.

The printed code in Boston, for the secret government of the police force may also need reforming. Of course, it may be argued that the rough qualities which are engendered of such contact may fit the policeman for the coarser duties of his office in the detection of notorious criminals; but it is a false social justice which would set a rogue to catch a rogue; whether such officers are accustomed to accept bribes from criminals to keep still or let them slip, I question; but indirectly, such men are in the pay of an enterprising criminal lawyer to whom they, for a consideration, recommend the prisoners, and at the trial, the government's case *may, or may not, break down according to circumstances.*

If this question in the use of the phrase " found to be guilty," is intended to relate to prosecutions and convictions of policemen and constables in the courts or to their dismissal, the answer must be, that there is seldom such an occurrence, but the occasion of this is believed to be, not the absence of just cause, but from the want of an efficient, summary and regular system of accountability before some board especially charged with the hearing and investigation of all old complaints.

New Hampshire :

Hon. S. D. BELL.—No data are known on this question. We hear of such charges against the police of great cities. Little is said or known on the subject among our scattered population.

Connecticut:

WALTER PITKIN, Esq.—It is believed that our constables and policemen administer their respective offices with general fairness and honesty.

New Jersey:

CORTLANDT PARKER, Esq.—I do not think that policemen and constables are found to be guilty to any considerable extent of corruption. Much is suspected; but there is little warrant for suspicion in any known facts.

J. F. HEGEMAN, Esq.—Policemen and constables are often corrupt, to a considerable extent, in the administration of their office (in the cities). This is the greatest obstacle to the faithful administration of criminal law in this county.

Pennsylvania:

J. J. BARCLAY, Esq.—Cases of this kind have not been established by legal proof, except in one or two instances.

Maryland:

A. STERLING, Esq.—I think our police may be regarded as very reasonably free from corruption. The complaints are few.

Kentucky:

No answer.

Indiana:

Hon. CONRAD BAKER.—I think not; but in the cities and larger towns this evil is believed to exist, to a limited extent, and to be on the increase.

Michigan:

H. K. CLARKE, Esq.—I do not know.

QUESTION XXV.

Are witnesses, who are imprisoned to secure their testimony confined with persons arrested for crime? Do they receive any compensation for their loss of time while thus imprisoned?

ANSWERS.

Massachusetts:

GEORGE W. SEARLE, Esq.—Witnesses are imprisoned in the debtor's apartment, and not with the prisoners arrested for crime. The courts have discretionary power to allow them compensation for loss of time, and the allowance made is generally what they would have earned otherwise.

New Hampshire:

HON. S. D. BELL.—Cases of the kind referred to are very rare. The witness who cannot or will not recognize, is confined in the common jail, with those who happen to be there; and they are not ordinarily compensated for loss of time.

Connecticut:

WALTER PITKIN, Esq.—There is no law in our state for the imprisonment of witnesses.

New Jersey:

CORTLANDT PARKER, Esq.—It is a blot upon our system of criminal proceedings that witnesses, who are imprisoned to secure their testimony, are confined in the goals appropriated to criminals. In the county of Essex, they are in separate apartments, those inhabited by fraudulent debtors. Effort is made, and it is believed generally with success, to separate them from criminals in most other counties. But it is a shame that no more is done. They should have pleasant apartments, and all liberty consistent with securing their testimony. In Essex county, the· practice is to give them witness fees in the cause or causes in which they finally testify for all the time they are detained. I believe this practice obtains generally. But it is shameful that so little attention is paid to this subject. I have known sad instances of grievous suffering by persons whose only offence was, that they had witnessed the commission of a crime, and were, therefore, necessary to the safety of the community.

JOHN F. HEGEMAN, Esq.—Witnesses are extremely seldom confined in jail to secure their testimony. When so, they are not wholly excluded from persons committed for crime. There is no provision made for their compensation for loss of time while confined. They would not be so confined, except for very high crime, and there are not many of such in this (Mercer) county.

Pennsylvania:

J. J. BARCLAY, Esq.—In Philadelphia they are not so imprisoned, but are kept in the "debtor's apartment." They are paid a small compensation.

Maryland:

A. STERLING, jr., Esq.—In our county jails, there is little or no separation of witnesses from persons charged with crimes. In Baltimore, the jail is a very superior building,·and very comfortable, and the rooms allotted to witnesses are as good as could be allotted to witnesses in any system, but they are not systematically separated, though partial efforts have been made to do so. An entire separation is greatly to be desired. Witnesses in jail are paid a per diem of $1.

Kentucky:
No answer.

Indiana:

HON. CONRAD BAKER.—It is a very rare occurrence in this state that witnesses are imprisoned to secure their testimony. There is no provision for compensating them for loss of time.

Michigan:

H. K. CLARKE, Esq.—Sometimes they are, but not always. Their compensation, like that of all other witnesses in criminal cases, is entirely at the discretion of the board of supervisors, except in cases where a satisfactory showing is made to the court, that a witness is poor; in which case the court has power to direct the payment of an allowance out of the county treasury.

QUESTION XXVI.

Has the death penalty been abolished? If not, for what offenses is it inflicted? If it has been abolished, for how long a period has the new system been in force, and what effect, if any, has it had in increasing or diminishing the crimes for which it was formerly inflicted.

ANSWERS.

Massachusetts:

GEORGE W. SEARLE, Esq.—The death penalty has not been abolished; it is enforced only for murder in the first degree.

New Hampshire:

HON. S. D. BELL.—The death penalty has not been abolished, but it is limited to the single case of murder in the first degree. Opinions differ as to the effect of its disuse, in many cases where the law formerly would have inflicted it. No means exist to determine the question.

Connecticut:

WALTER PITKIN, ESQ.—The death penalty is inflicted for treason, murder in the first degree, and arson causing death.

New Jersey:

CORTLANDT PARKER, ESQ.—The death penalty has not been abolished for murder and treason, nor do I think it ever will be in New Jersey. There are few who desire it—none who openly advocate it. No attempt in that direction has been made. It is felt to be the only check upon those whose passions impel them to extreme violence. Its existence does not increase the difficulty of obtaining verdicts, not even. in circumstantial cases. The solemnity of the issue in murder trials makes jurors careful, but not captious. Whenever the death of a fellow creature is deliberately compassed, and the case is really proven, there is no escape.

On several occasions, where men have been on trial for life in New Jersey, the jurors established regular morning and evening prayer during their confinement together, and immediately on retiring for final deliberation, knelt together while one implored wisdom from above. Such jurors do their duty.

JOHN F. HEGEMAN, ESQ.—The death penalty has not been abolished. It is inflicted for treason and murder in the first degree.

Pennsylvania:

J. J. BARCLAY, ESQ.—It has not; but it is inflicted for murder of the first degree alone.

Maryland:

A. STERLING, JR., ESQ.—The death penalty exists for murder with premeditation, for rape and arson; in the two latter cases discretionary with the judge.

Kentucky:

E. L. VAN WINKLE, ESQ.—The death penalty, as before stated, has not been abolished.

I believe that a change in our criminal law abolishing the death penalty, except in case of *express* malice, such as antecedent threats, lying in wait, or where the crime of murder is committed in robbery or burglary or poisoning, or an attempt at either would relieve the subject of much difficulty by insuring punishment in the great majority of cases where improper acquittals now obtain-

Our law as to murder is the common law without any statutory changes.

Indiana:

HON. CONRAD BAKER, ESQ.—The death penalty has not been abolished. It or imprisonment for life may, in the discretion of the jury, be inflicted for treason and murder in the first degree.

This discretion has existed since 1841, and is believed to be an improvement on the previous legislation, which made death the penalty in all cases of treason and murder in the first degree.

Michigan:

H. R. CLARK, ESQ.—The *principle* of the death penalty has been retained, that being the punishment which is prescribed for treason against the state; but it has been *practically* abolished, as it is allowed in no other case, since the general revision of the statutes in 1846, which took effect in March, 1847. What effect this change has had upon the commission of the crime, it is not very easy to say. I know that the opinion has been expressed by gentlemen whose official position would entitle their opinions to much consideration, that the effect has not been to increase the commission of the crime. There are no statistics published, that I am aware of, which afford any reliable data for such comparisons as might lead to well founded conclusions. The nearest approach we have to any such statistics are the annual reports by the prosecuting attorneys to the attorney general. These are usually published with the attorney general's report and such facts as they exhibit from 1840 to 1864 inclusive, except for the years 1851 and 1855, which are not just now accessible to me, may be found in the following schedule:

POPULATION.	YEAR.	Whole No. of counties.	Counties reporting.	Murders reported.	
212,267	1840	31	9	2	
	1841	31	24	4	
	1842	31	18	1	
	1843	31	22	5	
	1844	31	20	2	93 : 14 : : 155 : 23
		155	93	2	
302,553	1845	31	20	1	
	1846	31	17	5	
	1847	31	22	1	
	1848	31	22	8	
	1849	31	25	5	
		155	196	20	
397,654	1850	31	20	7	
212 : 23 :: 397 : 43	1851	......	......	......	
	1852	34	27	4	
	1853	34	27	4	
	1854	36	26	8	100 : 22 : : 135 : 30
		135	100	22	
511,720	1855	......	......	......	
212 : 23 :: 511 : 56	1856	41	28	16	
	1857	46	22	9	
	1858	49	29	25	
	1859	53	31	19	110 : 69 : : 189 : 118
		189	110	69	
749,113	1860	54	22	4	
212 : 23 :: 749 : 81	1861	54	42	14	
	1862	54	39	10	
	1863	56	42	11	
	1864	59	44	18	189 : 57 : : 277 : 83
		277	189	57	

But it will be observed that not much more than two-thirds of the prosecuting attorneys make any report, in some years, not one-half. To estimate the whole from data furnished by a part may approximate a correct result; but of course they cannot be relied upon with sufficient confidence to justify any very positive conclusions as to the effect of the abolition of the death penalty for murder upon the commission of that offence. The great increase of population during the twenty five years referred to makes another element in the calculation, which increases the difficulty of coming with any certainty to a reasonably just conclusion.

By referring to the schedule it will be seen that during the period of the first five years, all of which was before the death penalty was abolished, *fourteen* murders are reported by the prosecuting attorneys to have been committed. There are, however, but ninety-three of these reports, when the whole number should have been one hundred and fifty-five. Assuming, then, that if all had reported, the number of murders would have been found to be in the same proportion, the whole number would be twenty-three in five years, among a population, which at the beginning of the period, numbered 212,267.

Passing over the next period of five years; that being the one during which the change in the law takes place, and estimating the probable number of murders committed from 1850 to 1864 included, by the actual reports in the same manner as before, a total of thirty—an increase of seven. But the population had increased from 212,267 at the beginning of the first period (1840) of five years, to 397,654 at the beginning of the third, (1850); and if crime had increased with the population, then the actual number of murders committed should have been forty.three ; and thus, though an actual increase of about twenty-five per cent is shown, there is a decrease relatively to the population of about the same percentage.

The fourth period, however, (from 1855 to 1859), shows a large increase. Ascertained in the same manner as before, the number of murders committed are now one hundred and eighteen, while the number, if no greater in proportion to the increased population than from 1840 to 1844, would have been only fifty-six ; an increase of only fifty-six per cent. To what shall we attribute this great increase ? To the now well understood fact which has reached all classes of the community, so that it may be reasonably supposed to influence the conduct of men—that murder is only a state prison offence ; and that its real turpitude has diminished in the popular apprehension in the ratio of punishment ? Perhaps so. But then, what shall we do with the facts as exhibited during the next five years, from 1860 to 1864 ? The actual and estimated number of murders during this period amounts to eighty-three ; but no more than the proportion at the commencement of the period, by the same method of computation, would require scarcely eighty-one. Shall we attribute the relative diminution to the war which had drawn off to other scenes the more turbulent spirits, who, if not thus employed would have greatly increased the aggregate of crime? This is certainly a reasonable hypothesis. But it is evident that the data are, as yet, too few and too uncertain to base *on them* any satisfactory conclusions as to the effect which the abolition of this state of the death penalty has had on increasing or diminshing the crimes for which it was formerly inflicted. They certainly do not prove a diminution of crime; whether there be really an increase, and whether that increase be attributable to this cause, are questions which must depend, for their solution, upon a much more accurate analysis of facts than I have been able to make, and, pehaps, upon the consideration of a much wider range of operating and influencing causes.

H. A. MORROW, Esq.—Yes, since 1846. It has *not* had the effect to increase the crime of murder.

QUESTION XXVII.

Has the method of indictment by a grand jury been abolished in your state, and if so, what system has been substituted in its place, and what has been found to be the operation of the new system? Please state your opinion on this point, and the grounds of it. If not abolished, has any attempt in that direction been made?

ANSWERS.

Massachusetts :

GEO. W. SEARLE, Esq.—Indictment by a grand jury is still retained, and no effort at the abolition of the grand jury system has been attempted. I think all *ex parte* hearings objectionable, and that the grand jury system will yet be abolished.

New Hampshire :

Hon. S. D. BELL.—Indictments are not abolished. By our constitution no person can be convicted of a capital or infamous crime, except on indictment. In misdemeanors, informations by the attorney general or solicitor are sustained, and are occasionally filed. Prosecutions before justices of the peace are commenced by complaint, and are tried, even on appeal, on such complaint. Justices have the usual power to bind over to a higher court for trial for offences beyond their own jurisdiction, but in such cases indictments or informations are required. No attempt has been made to change the system. It is regarded as one of the most important safeguards of the public liberty.

Connecticut :

W. PITKIN, Esq.—It is not necessary in Connecticut that an indictment be found by a grand jury, except for offences punishable by death, and in our practice it is confined to such cases.

New Jersey :

CORTLANDT PARKER, Esq.—We adhere to the common law system of indictments. No man is tried, except he waive his privilege, without indictment. And the constitution guarantees this and trial by jury. It might be better perhaps, in minor offences, to dispense with or modify these provisions.

J. F. HEGEMAN, Esq.—The method of presenting crime by indictment by grand jury has not been abolished; hardly even suggested to abolish it.

Pennsylvania :

J. J. BARCLAY, Esq.—It has not been abolished, and it is hoped it never will be. Some modification might be made, whereby the prisoner or defendant in *misdemeanors* might *waive* the action of the grand jury upon a bill prepared by the district attorney. Some general effort has been made in this direction, but it has assumed no definite shape.

Maryland :

A. STERLING, Jr., Esq.—The method of indictment by grand jury remains as at common law.

Kentucky :

E. L. VAN WINKLE, Esq.—The grand jury has not been abolished, nor has any attempt been made in that direction.

Indiana :

Hon. CONRAD BAKER.—It has been abolished as to misdemeanors, but not as to felonies. The substitute in case of misdemeanors is an information by the prosecuting attorney, based on the affidavit of some witness or person. This system has been in force since 1852, and its effect has been to increase crime by failing to punish the minor offences. It is found by experience that men will not, unless it is made their own duty, inform upon their neighbors for minor offences. The result is, these minor offences go unpunished, and this begets a disregard of law, and increases crime.

Michigan :

H. K. CLARKE, Esq.—The method of indictment by a grand jury has not been abolished ; but a proceeding by *information* presented by the prosecuting attorney, is now permitted, which has superseded almost entirely the method of proceeding by indictment. Grand juries are occasionally summoned when, in the opinion of the court, usually upon the suggestion of the prosecuting attorney, any useful purpose will be served by such an order. After about a year's experience of the practical effect of the method of prosecuting accusations by " information," the Hon. Jacob M.

Howard, then attorney general of the state (now one of the sena-tors representing this state in congress), a gentleman of great ex-perience and ability, and thoroughly competent to express an opinion on the question, expresses that opinion in his annual report to the governor in the following terms :

" It affords me pleasure to be able to report that the act of last session ' To provide for the trial of offenses by information,' has been found to work well in practice. Very few grand juries have been called since it went into operation, and a very great saving of expense to the counties has thus been secured. I have thus far heard of no instance in which complaint has arisen of any oppres-sive use being made of the powers given to the prosecuting attor-ney under the act, and I cannot doubt that with such trifling modifications as time and experience may suggest, the mode now adopted will not only continue to be the policy of the state, but will be imitated by many of our sister states." Joint documents of 1859, No. 8, page 34.

I have reason to believe that experience and observation since that time have very generally confirmed these views.

H. A. MORROW, Esq.—The system of indictment has been abol-ished in Michigan, and that by information substituted in its stead. The new system has fully satisfied the anticipations of its friends. Under it there are fewer arraignments and more convictions; and the saving in expense to the public is about half. Its advantages are so many and so obvious over the grand jury system, that there is no one in Michigan who would return to the latter.

QUESTION XXVIII.

Is there, or is there not, found to be any considerable variety in the instructions given to juries, by different judges, when the question of insanity is at issue?

ANSWERS.

Massachusetts:

GEO. W. SEARLE, Esq.—The instructions given are generally, in substance, the same as the late Chief Justice Shaw gave in the case of the Commonwealth *vs.* Abner Rogers (see the report of that trial). The need of a more comprehensive formula for crimi-nal lunacy, and a more philosophical analysis of the mind's dis-ease, with a tribunal of experts fully learned in all the scientific relations of insanity to crime, both in its medical and legal rami-fications, and fully experiened in all the practical branches of the subject, is felt every time the defense of insanity is, in good faith, interposed in behalf of a criminal.

New Hampshire:

Hon. S. D. Bell.—There may be, and probably is, much differ-ence in the instructions given to juries by different judges, upon the subject of insanity. It is a very difficult subject. Few of the judges are, or feel themselves to be, experts. They do as their predecessors have done, that is, endeavor to express themselves as nearly as they can in the language of the highest authorities on the subject.

Connecticut:

W. Pitkin, Esq.—There has been little diversity in the in-structions of our different judges upon the subject of insanity.

New Jersey:

Cortlandt Parker, Esq.—Nor are our juries often astray on the question of insanity. When homicide has been committed by those smarting under injury to the domestic affections, for which the ordinary remedies of law are insufficient, as where a relative or a victim slays a seducer, they have, perhaps, gone wrong. But research will prove that neither in Great Baitain or the United States, was there ever a well contested case where such error failed to occur. It seems to be common law in the sense of the established rules for the action of the common people, that homi-cide in such cases serves the guilty right.

In instances other than this exceptional class of cases, however, Jersey juries are no friends of the plea of insanity. The law on the subject is well settled in New Jersey, and the instruction of judges to juries are identical. Chief Justice Hornblower's opin-ion, in the case of Spencer, has been adopted by our highest tri-bunals, and has been put in full uniformity. If a prisoner can prove clearly that through mental disease he did not know the homicide he committed was wrong, he will be acquitted. If he cannot, if his notion was revenge, and he knew that he did what God and man forbid, no comparative feebleness of mind, or eccen-tric hallucination will save him.

The rule established in New Jersey on the subject of challenges to jurors is, and has been, of great practical utility and importance. In New York and elsewhere, if a man has formed or expressed an opinion as to the guilt or innocence of the prisoner, he is set aside. Consequently, men who desire not to be empanelled—a very large class in capital cases—have only to read, or hear, and form an opinion. And the number and enterprise of newspapers practi-cally excludes all intelligent men, for who does not read and does not make up his mind, so far as informed? In New Jersey the old common law rule prevails. The juror is to be sworn to give his verdict upon the evidence. If he has a malicious bias against either side, so that in consequence, if what he has heard, he is not likely to keep his oath, then, but only then, is he excluded. Such a bias seldom occurs. It must be found to exist by triers. And hence, a better class of men for jurers.

J. F. HEGEMAN, Esq.—There is a great unity in the views and charges of our judges touching the insanity of defendants. The law on that subject is well defined, and there is but little variance in the instructions to juries on the subject.

Pennsylvania :

J. J. BARCLAY, Esq.—There have been differences of opinion, but not to any considerable extent. Chief Justice Gibson, in Commonwealth vs. Moster, 4 Barr, stated the law upon the subject of insanity, and it has remained unchanged.

Maryland :

A. STERLING, Esq.—The jury are the judges of fact and law with us, in criminal cases, that is, by our constitution. The judge of course decides all questions arising during the trial. It has never been the practice to charge the jury on the evidence in criminal cases, nor on the law, unless specifically asked for by counsel. If counsel ask instructions on law, the courts sometimes refuse to let them argue the contrary to the jury, but practice differs a little. The law is generally argued to the jury without any instruction from the court. The jury may, of course, ask the advice of the court, and, in purely legal points, unmixed by fact, frequently do so where there is difficulty.

Kentucky :

E. L. VAN WINKLE, Esq.—Much contrariety exists in this state in the law of insanity, as expounded by our circuit judges ; especially is this the case, where the defence relies upon moral insanity and intellectual monomania. The recent expositions of the law governing, questions of this character, by our appellate court, will doubtless cure this evil at an early day.

Indiana :

Hon. CONRAD BAKER.—I think not. This is not a fashionable defence in Indiana.

Michigan :

H. K. CLARKE, Esq.—I am not able to answer.

H. A. MORROW, Esq.—There is a considerable variety of instructions given to juries in this class of cases.

QUESTION XXIX.

Does the exercise of the pardoning power unfavorably affect the administration of justice ? Is this power so often exercised as; in your judgment, to constitute an abuse thereof ? Would it be expedient to have this power in any way restricted by law, and if so, what limitations would, in your opinion, be likely to prove wise and effective ?

ANSWERS.

Massachusetts:

GEORGE W. SEARLE, Esq.—In my opinion a too free exercise of the pardoning power has of late years unfavorably affected the administration of justice in various ways. A very long sentence is considered by an expert criminal as the most favorable one he can receive, greatly advancing his prospects of release by a pardon at an early day. Many criminals and their friends neglect to make a strong defence where one really may exist, relying upon subsequent executive clemency. Young people frequently receive such clemency at the expense of all security of the public, and with the jeopardy of the entire criminal fabric as a system of rigorous judgment.

New Hampshire:

Hon. S. D. BELL.—I think judges generally regard the pardoning power as operating unfavorably upon the administration of justice. Cases occasionally occur of pardons which astonish the courts before which the trials were had ; but the courts are almost never consulted on the subject, and the grounds of pardons are never communicated to them. I have never known them to sit in judgment on the action of the executive. I have no opinion whether or in what way the pardoning power could be wisely or usefully limited.

Connecticut:

WALTER PITKIN, Esq.—The pardoning power in this state is vested in the legislature. It is believed by those most conversant with criminal affairs, that it is in many cases improperly exercised. Wherever this power resides, its exercise is necessarily a matter of discretion, and it would be difficult, if not impracticable, to define by law the cases or manner in which it must be exercised. All that can be done is to locate their discretion where it is most likely to be exercised intelligently, and " without fear, favor or hope of reward."

New Jersey:

CORTLANDT PARKER, Esq.—The pardoning power of New Jersey is lodged in a court of pardons, so popularly called, composed of the governor, the chancellor, and the six associate judges of the court of appeals—those, namely, who are *not* justices of the supreme court. The governor must concur in all pardons. The plan is not without its merits. It would have been better had the justices of the supreme court been among its members, instead of or besides the other judges of the court of appeals. The "court" acts without publicity, and therefore it frequently errs. I think it *does* "unfavorably affect the administration of justice." Yet its errors are unintentional and not numerous. If it were required that the application for pardon in all cases should be reported upon by the judge and district attorney under whom the applicant was convicted, it would not pardon so often or so wrongfully.

J. F. HEGEMAN, Esq.—I cannot say that the exercise of the pardoning power is abused in this state and operates against justice. It is judiciously exercised upon the whole. In rare cases there may be error, but as a whole there is no ground to interfere with it or restrict it. A complaint against this power, or the abuse of its exercise, is scarcely ever heard.

Pennsylvania:

J. J. BARCLAY, Esq.—There has been in time past an abuse of this power, but for several years the executive of this commonwealth, aided by the eminent attorney-general of the state, has adopted a series of rules upon the subject, which have had an excellent effect.

This power ought to be placed in the hands of a "court of pardons," to consist of the governor, the judges of the supreme court, and the president of the common pleas, or law associates; the court to be composed of a given number (say five members), and the judges to rotate from year to year, say one or two judges of the supreme court, with two of the common pleas.

Maryland:

J. A. STERLING, JR., Esq.—The pardoning power is restricted in Maryland so far as to require the governor to give public notice of all applications, to call on all persons who choose to show cause why a pardon should not be granted, and to report all pardons to the legislature. This has had a good effect, though still there has been some injury done to justice, little by our late executive, Governor Bradford, who has been very careful. His successor has only been in office a few days, and has not had a chance to show his practice.

The pardoning power, it seems, must rest somewhere, and it cannot be absolutely guarded against abuse.

Kentucky:

E. L. VAN WINKLE, Esq.—The pardoning power does often unfavorably affect the administration of justice, and when so, is certainly an abuse of the power. I would, however, be disinclined to limit its exercise until all other remedies were exhausted. If the executive was required to report each case of its exercise, with *the list* of the *names* of petitioners applying for the pardon, much good would result. That is, if the law required the governor to publish a list of the names of petitioners in an annual report to the legislature *merely*, without any ulterior object except to give publicity to the action of those procuring the pardon, such legislation would impose a proper restraint upon those who recklessly sign all manner of petitions without regard to the merits of any given case, and thus impose upon the executive blame which should properly attach to others.

Indiana:

Hon. CONRAD BAKER.—I do not think the exercise of the pardoning power does unfavorably affect the administration of justice. It is sparingly and discreetly exercised. I have no suggestion to make as to its restriction.

Michigan:

H. K. CLARKE, Esq.—I have no doubt that the frequent exercise of the pardoning power does unfavorably affect the administration of justice. The procuring of pardons has become an important practice in criminal cases. I have heard that it is not unusual to include in the counsel fee for a criminal defence, services to be rendered in procuring a pardon in case of conviction. Yet I do not see where the power to pardon offences can be more safely and appropriately lodged than with the chief magistrate of a state.

H. A. MORROW, Esq.—The exercise of the pardoning power affects most injuriously the administration of criminal justice in this state. It is exercised too often with too little regard to the crimes committed. It should be restricted by positive law, and the limitation should be this: No pardon should be granted except on the recommendation of the judge who sentenced, and only in cases where new evidence had come to light since the conviction which would, if produced on the trial, have altered or modified the sentence.

QUESTION XXX.

Are persons sentenced for life more frequently pardoned than those imprisoned for a term of years? If yes, what is believed to be the cause of the difference?

ANSWERS.

Massachusetts:

GEORGE W. SEARLE, Esq.—My impression is that persons sentenced for life are not more frequently pardoned than those imprisoned for a term of years. The reason doubtless is that there are but few original sentences for life, and those prisoners who are there for life have had capital sentences commuted to a life imprisonment; and it would probably be a rare case of that kind which would meet with executive pardon.

New Hampshire:

Hon. S. D. BELL.—No data are known for an opinion on this question.

Connecticut:

W. PITKIN, Esq.—Persons imprisoned for life are less frequently pardoned than those imprisoned only for a term of years.

New Jersey:

C. PARKER, Esq.—I am not able to answer this question. We have no imprisonment for life.

J. F. HEGEMAN, Esq.—I cannot answer this question. I don't think there is any difference caused by the term of the imprisonment. The grounds of pardon are generally health, repentance, doubt as to the evidence which convicted, new evidence, and general considerations of public policy.

Pennsylvania:

J. J. BARCLAY, Esq.—This question cannot be answered, as we believe imprisonment for life is not a penalty inflicted in Pennsylvania by the code.

Maryland:

A. STERLING, JR., Esq.—We have no life sentences except by the force of a commutation of death.

There are, I think, more pardons in short than long terms. In the very long ones the party becomes forgotten somewhat, while the shorter ones are more restless and their friends more active. Again, the shorter ones generally have some element of alleviation in their cases. It is somewhat the custom, too, to pardon convicts on good behavior a short time before the expiration of their sentence.

Kentucky:

No answer.

Indiana:

Hon. CONRAD BAKER.—I do not believe persons sentenced for life are more frequently pardoned than those imprisoned for a term of years, but my information is not full on this point.

Michigan:

H. K. CLARKE, Esq.—I do not know that this is so.

Question XXXI.

Is there in your state a system of annual returns of criminal statistics? If so, what are the items of information embraced in it, and to what officer are the returns made?

Answers.

Massachusetts:

George W. Searle, Esq.—There are somewhat extensive returns of criminal statistics, but there is no unit system. See reports of Attorney-General and the various reports of the prisons in Massachusetts, in the library of the New York Prison Association, for the answer to the remainder of this question.

New Hampshire:

Hon. S, D. Bell.—There is no system of returns of criminal statistics.

Connecticut:

Walter Pitkin, Esq.—There is in this state no system, strictly speaking, of returns of criminal statistics. An annual report is, however, made to the legislature by the superintendent of the state prison and the jailors of the several counties, of all facts and transactions within their respective departments, with many important classifications.

New Jersey:

C. Parker, Esq.—There is no system of annual returns of criminal statistics.

J. F. Hegeman.—I have seen state prison returns setting forth the number of prisoners, their ages, sexes, color, crimes, nationality, whether able to read and write, &c., but I cannot now lay my hand upon any statute requiring this to be done.

Note.—I find the statute requiring the State Prison Inspectors to report such returns yearly to the Legislature. *Nixon's Digest, page* 812.

Pennsylvania:

J. J. Barclay, Esq.—Inspectors of prisons report to the legislature at each annual session; the items are those usually embraced in such reports, and reference can be made to these reports.

Maryland:

A. Sterling, jr., Esq.—The board of police in Baltimore, make a report to the legislature, of arrests and their causes and of the disposition made of the parties. The managers of the house of refuge report to the legislature, also the directors of the penitentiary. The grand jury of the city make a report to the criminal court, of the condition of the jail and penitentiary, the number of prisoners and their alleged offences, the age, sex and color are severally specified, but these reports are not digested, nor made into any general system.

Kentucky:

E. S. VAN WINKLE, ESQ.—We have no system of annual returns of criminal statistics, except that shown by the keeper of the penitentiary, which simply contains the names of convicts, the crime for which they were convicted, the county where done and the term of confinement.

Indiana:

HON. CONRAD BAKER,—There is no such system of returns.

Michigan:

H. K. CLARKE, ESQ.—The only system of annual returns of criminal statistics, provided for in this state, is that which is contemplated by the law, requiring prosecuting attorneys to make annual reports to the attorney general. The neglect of this duty renders the officer liable to a penalty of fifty dollars. The violations of the obligation are numerous, but prosecutions for the penalty, I believe, are unknown.

The annual reports of the inspectors of state prison, are published in the annual volume of "Joint Documents," and certain items that may be regarded as of a statistical character.

QUESTION XXXII.

Has any code of criminal procedure been adopted, or does the common law practice in the main prevail.

ANSWERS.

Massachusetts:

GEO. W. SEARLE, ESQ.—There is no code of criminal procedure; one is much needed.

New Hampshire:

HON. S. D. BEEL,—No code of criminal procedure has been adopted. The common law practice prevails, as modified by early usage and numerous statutes.

Connecticut:

W. PITKIN, ESQ.—Our criminal practice is substantially that of the common law.

New Jersey:

C. PARKER, ESQ.—No code of criminal procedure has been adopted; the common law practice in the main prevails.

Pennsylvania:

J. J. BARCLAY, ESQ.—Yes, the present criminal code, already referred to, was adopted in 1860.

Maryland:

A. STERLING JR., ESQ.—We have no codification of criminal law. Our code is a mere digest of statute law.

Kentucky:

E. S. VAN WINKLE, ESQ.—We have an entire new system of criminal procedure, known as the criminal code; nevertheless, we preserve the *substance* of the old in all its essential features, without its useless formalities.

Indiana:

HON. CONRAD BAKER,—We have a practice act, but the common law in the main prevails.

Michigan:

H. K. CLARKE, ESQ.—The common law practice remains in full force, with but two exceptions, as I now remember, viz., the accusation by information instead of by indictment, as specified in answer to interrogatory No. 27, and the change which permits a prisoner to make an unsworn statement of facts, which the jury are allowed to consider in making up their verdict.

QUESTION XXXIII.

What, in your judgment, if any, are the defects in the existing system of criminal procedure, and what suggestions can you offer on the subject of improvements to be made therein?

ANSWERS.

Massachusetts:

GEO. W. SEARLE, Esq.—For my ideas on the defects of our system of criminal procedure, and for some suggestions on the subject of improvements to be made, see my article on the *Penal System of Massachusetts*, in the annual report of the Prison Association for 1864.

New Hampshire:

Hon. S. D. BELL.—I am not prepared to suggest defects or improvements in our system.

Connecticut:

WALTER PITKIN, Esq.—A proper answer to this question would require a more elaborate examination of our entire system (and indeed of the systems in the other states, by way of comparison), than I have been able to give it.

New Jersey:

C. PARKER, Esq.—This last question I hardly venture to answer. Undoubtedly there are defects in the criminal law of New Jersey. No law can be perfect. The merit of our state is, that her legislators have reverenced the common law, and been very careful to avoid making many changes of its provisions. One great excellence of the common law is its expansive power. No changes in society can affect its force. It strives to punish all moral crime which is injurious to the community. New Jersey, guided here by the calm and judicious mind of Judge Paterson, one of the most profound jurists and excellent men the country has produced, first re-enacted the criminal code of England, as found on her statute book, and then provided that all offences against the common law should be properly punished.

The defects of the system of New Jersey are, therefore, for the most part, those of the common law; and one is the system of pleading. It is altogether too precise and rigorous. Ancient law was too severe. The penalty for almost everything was *death*. Hence judges set themselves to work to find ways of escape for the poor creatures accused of minor crimes. The result was the escape of many flagrant offenders, through the rigor of the rules adopted by ancient judges. Were I a legislator, I would enact here the code for pleading, established a few years ago in England, remarkable, above all others, for its simplicity and comprehensiveness; and I would, besides, authorize any amendment at or before trial, which appeared necessary and fair.

Another serious defect is the absence of any officer whose duty it is to see to the prevention and detection of crime. We have no district attorneys; we have only prosecutors of the pleas—that is, officers whose duty it is to *prosecute* what grand juries indict, not to see to it that all offences are indicted. Keeping the mode of emolument as it is, dependent on success, and giving prosecutors the task of prevention and detection, it is easy to see how diligent they might be found. Crime mostly springs from intemperance. As the law now stands, the prosecutor who aims at checking this, by indicting rum sellers, is a simple volunteer—his motive gain. Make it his duty and retain the motive, and he would be likely, generally, to show much, though it is hoped not too much, diligence.

Another serious defect is the mode of selecting grand and petit juries. The sheriff selects grand juries. He is elected by the people. They then, mediately, select the grand jury. If they choose a good sheriff, a man of duty, depend upon it the standard of morals is high; and so if otherwise. As the sheriff, so the morals of the county. Yet that officer, being eligible each year three times, is tempted to pander to the powerful class of citizens, whose business is serving drink to other people. He should be elected for three years, and not be re-eligible; and grand juries should be selected, in part, by the supreme court judge of the circuit. The petit juries, too, should be selected more carefully than they are.

But after all, these are but small matters, comparatively. It is the happiness of Jerseymen to live in a state where law is carefully and, for the most part, justly administered; where the rights of life, liberty and property are thoroughly protected; where honest men thrive, and the dishonest and criminal very rarely escape punishment.

JOHN F. HEGEMAN, Esq.—The mode of procedure is not much defective; it would be hard to suggest material improvements. A multitude of small offences—misdemeanors, arising out of the liquor laws, Sunday laws and petit larcenies, common assaults, &c.,—in the cities, ought to be punished more promptly, more certainly and less expensively, by municipal police courts. By depending on a county grand jury, a large number are passed by without any notice and punishment whatever—I speak of this county, and Trenton as the city.

Another improvement would be in increasing the number of peremptory challenges on the part of the state. We now have only *four*. There are more than this number of jurors on a panel of forty-eight who sympathize with every criminal defendant, and will, if possible, acquit either for reward or sympathy.

The costs on an indictment in case of conviction are too *high*. Jurors are reluctant to convict in many cases of lesser crimes where the defendant is poor, and where the costs will fall on the state or county ultimately in case of conviction.

The mode of procedure is not defective, but the want of integrity and impartiality in the jurors and in the officers who aid in administering the law, is the great want. Intelligent and conscientious men could do all that is required or desirable under the present mode of procedure. A pure public morality, a gospel regeneration, a wide pervading religious sentiment—these are what we need to insure a faithful administration of criminal law. We have more of these than some localities have, but our hope is just here.

Pennsylvania:

J. J. BARCLAY, Esq.—There are defects, of course, in the present system, but in practice these defects are to be observed in the working of the system in large cities rather than in the country districts.

In the country, where the population is small, the courts have abundant time to dispose of all cases, and the delays are not lengthy, but in a city like Philadelphia, the population being large, cases are very numerous, and various causes contribute to produce unfortunate results, for—

1st. The committing magistrates are elected, and men are generally chosen who have no knowledge of law, and who, in many cases, being paid *by fees*, endeavor to increase their own gains, having no regard to the welfare of the public; in many instances, cases are sealed by the discharge of the party arrested, or insufficient bail is taken, and the prisoner thus escapes. It is unnecessary to enlarge upon the defects of this system, as it can at once be understood by any person familiar with the administration of criminal justice. This is the chief defect in our system.

2d. After cases are returned to court, they are so numerous that it is almost impossible to try them, and hence many delays take place, but this defect, it is believed, will be remedied by increasing the judicial force.

In the criminal code, a large discretion is vested in the courts, and as long as the judges bring to the performance of their duties honest hearts, a reasonable amount of legal learning and common sense, the system will be found to be an admirable one, and it is hoped that the day will not soon arrive when the judges will be selected without reference to individual merit. At present the system works very well, reference being had to the powers of the judge alone.

Maryland:

A. Sterling, jr., Esq.—I am in favor of allowing parties charged with crime to testify in their own behalf, believing that it will protect innocence and punish guilt. I think that many of the technicalities of criminal law might safely be removed, keeping the substantial barriers of clearness and definiteness of charges of crime. This has been somewhat done here by allowing limited amendments of indictments. The criminal procedure, though, is generally the most scientific and best defined branch of the law. Reformatory institutions are the most important. Specially essential are the reformation and punishment of the criminal classes of children. The criminals who perpetrate crimes in cold blood generally begin young, and seldom reform after 20 years of age. If they can be taken before 16 or 18, they may be reformed, and everything ought to be done to take these children and change their habits and character by removing them from the circumstances among which they are growing up. I think, good as the houses of refuge are, the children are too much together there. They ought to be more diffused and separated. We have had a manual labor school, a house of refuge, a home for female vagrant children, an aid society which takes children not charged with crime, but of the vagrant class, and sends them to the country; but in all our cities we want more means of this sort.

Kentucky:

E. L. VAN WINKLE, Esq.—I have no suggestions in regard to the improvement of our criminal system of procedure, except adding more stringent rules for courts in determining the sufficiency of bail, and the grounds for postponement of trials, for herein lies the principal source of escape from punishment in the administration of criminal law in Kentucky, &c.

Indiana:

HON. C. BAKER.—The prominent defects in the existing system of criminal procedure are, in my judgment, two, and both have their origin in the innovations made in 1852.

The *first* consists in taking from the grand juries their jurisdiction over misdemeanors; the *second*, in giving to the defendants' attorney in all prosecutions, the right to make the closing argument to the jury.

A return to the ancient landmarks on these two points, with an increased rate of compensation to the prosecuting attorneys, such as would induce men of a higher order of talent to accept these positions, would add greatly to the efficiency of our system.

As it is, my belief is that it will compare favorably, so far as results are concerned, with the systems of other states of the union.

Michigan:

H. K. CLARKE, Esq.—I have nothing to offer in reply to this question.